Forecasting economic time series

This book provides a formal analysis of the models, procedures and measures of economic forecasting with a view to improving forecasting practice. Clements and Hendry base the analyses on assumptions pertinent to the economies to be forecast, viz. a non-constant, evolving economic system, whose form and structure is unknown a priori. Clements and Hendry find that conclusions which can be established for constant-parameter stationary processes and correctly specified models do not hold when these unrealistic assumptions are relaxed. Despite the difficulty of proceeding formally when models are mis-specified in unknown ways for non-stationary processes that are subject to structural breaks, Clements and Hendry show that significant insights can be gleaned. For example, a formal taxonomy of forecasting errors can be developed, the role of causal information clarified, intercept corrections re-established as a method for achieving robustness against forms of structural change and measures of forecast accuracy re-interpreted.

Michael P. Clements is Research Fellow in Economics, Department of Economics, University of Warwick.

David F. Hendry is Leverhulme Personal Research Professor of Economics, and Fellow of Nuffied College, Oxford University.

Forecasting economic time series

MICHAEL P. CLEMENTS

and

DAVID F. HENDRY

CAMBRIDGE
UNIVERSITY PRESS

PUBLISHED BY THE PRESS SYNDICATE OF THE UNIVERSITY OF CAMBRIDGE
The Pitt Building, Trumpington Street, Cambridge CB2 1RP, United Kingdom

CAMBRIDGE UNIVERSITY PRESS
The Edinburgh Building, Cambridge CB2 2RU, UK http://www.cup.cam.ac.uk
40 West 20th Street, New York, NY 10011-4211, USA http://www.cup.org
10 Stamford Road, Oakleigh, Melbourne 3166, Australia

First published 1998

Printed in the United Kingdom at the University Press, Cambridge

Typeset in Times 9/11 [Au]

A catalogue record for this book is available from the British Library

Library of Congress Cataloguing in Publication data

Clements, Michael P.
The Marshall lectures on economic forecasting /
Michael P. Clements and David F. Hendry.
p. cm. – (Forecasting economic time series)
Includes bibliographical references and index.
ISBN 0-521-63242-0
1. Economic forecasting–Econometric models. 2. Econometrics.
3. Microeconomics. I. Hendry, David. F. II. Title. III. Series.
HB 3730.C555 1998
330'.01'12–dc21 97-52674 CIP

ISBN 0 521 632420 hardback
ISBN 0 521 634806 paperback

To
Carolyn, Anna and William
and
Evelyn and Vivien

All these clever men were prophesying with every variety of ingenuity what would happen soon, and they all did it in the same way, by taking something they saw 'going strong', as the saying is, and carrying it as far as ever their imagination could stretch. This, they said, was the true and simple way of anticipating the future. 'Just as,' said Dr Pellkins, in a fine passage – 'just as when we see a pig in a litter a little larger than the other pigs, we know that by an unalterable law of the Inscrutable it will some day be larger than an elephant – just as we know when we see weeds and dandelions growing more and more thickly in a garden, that they must, in spite of all our efforts, grow taller than the chimney-pots and swallow the house from sight, so we know and reverently acknowledge, that when any power in human politics has shown for any period of time any considerable activity, it will go on until it reaches the sky.'

G. K. Chesterton, The Napoleon of Notting Hill.

Contents

Figures

Tables

Preface

This book is the first of two volumes on macroeconomic forecasting. Its objective is to provide a formal analysis of the models, procedures and measures of economic forecasting with a view to improving forecasting practice. The first volume sets the scene, focusing on forecasting when the underlying process can be described by a stationary representation, perhaps after differencing the data. Our companion volume, entitled *The Zeuthen Lectures on Economic Forecasting*, will discuss forecasting in the presence of deterministic non-stationarities. Both volumes are the outcomes of Lecture Invitations, the first – the Marshall Lectures – at Cambridge University; the second at Copenhagen University. Of course, the choice of topics for these lecture series was conditioned by our on-going research interests. Our focus on forecasting began in 1991 when David Hendry was invited to act as a Special Adviser to the House of Commons Select Committee on the Enquiry into Official Economic Forecasting, and found a dearth of theory to explain the systematic mis-forecasting that had occurred in the mid and late 1980s. The literature on statistical forecasting also argued that there was a marked discrepancy between theory and practice: see, for example, Fildes and Makridakis (1995) and Makridakis (1982), among others. Thus, we were delighted to take up the implicit challenge of developing a theory of economic forecasting with practical implications.

The two volumes seek to address the key problems facing a theory of forecasting in macroeconomics based on empirical econometric models. To deliver relevant conclusions about macroeconomic forecasting, analyses must be based on assumptions pertinent to the economies to be forecast. This forces the analysis to contend with non-constant, evolving processes for which estimated econometric models are far from being facsimiles. It transpires that conclusions which can be established formally for constant-parameter stationary processes and correctly specified models often do not hold when those unrealistic assumptions are relaxed. Despite the difficulty of proceeding formally when models are mis-specified in unknown ways for non-stationary processes that are subject to structural breaks, we believe significant insights can be gleaned. For example, a formal taxonomy of forecasting errors can be developed; the role of causal information clarified; intercept corrections re-established as a method for achieving robustness against some forms of structural change; and measures of forecast accuracy reinterpreted.

Although in part critical of some current practices, we do not intend to embark on a nihilistic attack on economic forecasting, claiming its futility in the face of the whims and vagaries of human conduct. Certainly, we worry about the low-quality of some of the data presently available, and the constant stream of revisions to which it is often subject (witness the recent major changes to estimates of UK savings behaviour in the 1970s and 1980s: see Hendry, 1994), and about the inconsistency of governmental policy which induces large, intermittent regime switches affecting much of economic life. The macroeconomy is frighteningly complicated, and there are many difficult problems in modelling it, let alone forecasting future outcomes, or calculating confidence intervals around them. But if there is a central criticism or complaint, it is the dearth of previous formal research into the nature of macroeconomic forecasting. There are many excellent previous studies, referenced throughout our book, and important advances have been achieved on which we seek to build. However, in some instances, there has been little attempt to rationalize or explain certain forecasting practices (such as intercept corrections) before condemning them: we do not exempt ourselves, but are now seeking to remedy that lacuna by analysing what macroeconomic forecasters do. While we are surprised at the high percentage of the resulting book that is algebra, we make no apology: rather the main caveat must be our inability to develop general formulations – which perforce would be more complex still. Even so, there are a number of positive findings to offer, and many of the conclusions entail positive prescriptions for action. Many are surprising and at first sight counter-intuitive (but then intuition is often just the legacy of previously unquestioned beliefs), and several earlier criticisms have clear remedies. In particular, since we have only just begun to explore the implications for forecasting when the model is an incomplete and incorrect maquette, estimated from small samples of heterogeneous data generated by a high-dimensional, dynamic and non-constant process, many more surprising findings undoubtedly await future researchers.

We draw extensively on our published papers, many of which were written to resolve problems encountered while writing this volume: chapter 1 draws on Hendry and Morgan (1995); chapter 2 on Hendry (1997); chapter 3 on Clements and Hendry (1993a, 1993b) and Clements (1995); chapter 6 on Clements and Hendry (1995a); chapter 7 on Clements and Hendry (1994, 1996a); chapter 8 on Hendry and Clements (1994b) and Clements and Hendry (1996b); chapter 9 on Emerson and Hendry (1996); chapter 11 on Clements and Hendry (1996c); chapter 12 on Hendry and Clements (1993) and Hendry (1997); and chapter 13 on Chong and Hendry (1986) and Hendry (1986).

We are grateful to the following publishers for permission to draw on the material listed below.

Clements and Hendry (1993a, 1993b) 'On the Limitations of Comparing Mean Squared Forecast Errors' and 'A Reply', *Journal of Forecasting*, 12, 617–37 and 669–76, Emerson and Hendry (1996) 'An Evaluation of Forecasting using Leading Indicators', *Journal of Forecasting*, 15, 271–91, Clements and Hendry (1995a) 'Forecasting in Cointegrated Systems', *Journal of Applied Econometrics*, 10, 127–46, and Clements and Hendry (1996b) 'Intercept Corrections and Structural Change', *Journal of Applied*

Econometrics, 11, 475–94, are used with permission of John Wiley and Sons. Permission to reproduce parts of Clements and Hendry (1996c) 'Multi-step Estimation for Forecasting', *Oxford Bulletin of Economics and Statistics*, 58, 657–84, Clements (1995) 'Rationality and the role of judgement in macroeconomic forecasting', *Economic Journal*, 105, 410–20, and Clements and Hendry (1995b) 'Macroeconomic forecasting and modelling', *Economic Journal*, 105, 1001–13 was granted by Blackwell Publishers. Permission to reproduce parts of Hendry and Clements (1994b) 'On a Theory of Intercept Corrections in Macro-Economic Forecasting' in S. Holly (ed.) *Money, Inflation and Employment: Essays in Honour of James Ball*, 160–82, was granted by Edward Elgar Publishing. The material in Clements and Hendry (1994) 'Towards a Theory of Economic Forecasting', in C. P. Hargreaves (ed.) *Nonstationary Time Series analysis and Cointegration*, 9–52, is used by permission of Oxford University Press.

We are indebted to many colleagues and friends for their comments, discussions and criticisms of our ideas and the various drafts of this book. In particular, we wish to thank: Manuel Arellano, Anindya Banerjee, Olympia Bover, Gunnar Bårdsen, Julia Campos, Jurgen Doornik, Rob Engle, Rebecca Emerson, Neil Ericsson, Tony Espasa, Clive Granger, Eilev Jansen, Søren Johansen, Katarina Juselius, Hans-Martin Krolzig, John Muellbauer, Grayham Mizon, Bent Nielsen, Jean-François Richard, Marianne Sensier, Neil Shephard and Timo Teräsvirta. We are very grateful to Jurgen Doornik for his immense help in organizing the styles and computing background for the camera-ready production, especially the use of his excellent OxEdit program. Rebecca Emerson kindly allowed us to draw extensively from Emerson and Hendry (1996).

The research reported was generously financed by the United Kingdom Economic and Social Research Council, and we are delighted to record our gratitude for their sustained level of support over the last seven years. DFH is also indebted to the Leverhulme Trustees for the award of a Personal Research Professorship that enabled him to develop many of the fundamental ideas in his part of the project. We are also grateful to Cambridge and Copenhagen Universities for their stimulus to integrate the research into monographs.

All the computations reported in this paper were performed in the PcGive suite of programs (see Hendry and Doornik, 1996a, Doornik and Hendry, 1997 and Hendry and Doornik, 1996b) or using the Gauss Programming Language 3.2., Aptech Systems, Washington. A demonstration version of GiveWin and PcGive can be found on the Web page:

http://www.nuff.ox.ac.uk/users/hendry/

Information on corrections will also be placed there.

Scientific Word (TCI Software Research, New Mexico) in combination with emTeX, MikTeXand DVIPS eased the writing of the book in LaTeX.

Michael P. Clements and David F. Hendry, July, 1997

Common acronyms

AIC	Akaike information criterion
AR	autoregressive process
ARCH	autoregressive conditional heteroscedasticity
ARIMA	autoregressive integrated moving average
ARMA	autoregressive-moving average
BVAR	Bayesian vector autoregression
CE	conditional efficiency
CLI	composite leading indicator
DE	dynamic estimator (multi-step criterion minimization)
DF	Dickey–Fuller (distribution or statistic)
DGP	data-generation process
DS	difference stationary
DV	vector autoregression in first differences
DW	Durbin–Watson statistic
EqCM	equilibrium-correction mechanism
EWMA	exponentially weighted moving average
FPE	final prediction error
FIML	full-information maximum likelihood
GARCH	generalized ARCH
GFESM	generalized forecast-error second-moment criterion
GNP	gross national product
IGARCH	integrated GARCH
IID	independent, identically distributed
IMA	integrated moving average
IV	instrumental variables
IVDE	instrumental variables dynamic estimator
LEI	leading economic indicator
LLI	longer leading indicator
MA	moving-average process
MAE	mean absolute error
MCSD	Monte Carlo standard deviation
MCSE	Monte Carlo standard error
MDS	martingale difference sequence
ML	maximum likelihood
MSE	mean-square error
MMSFE	minimum mean-square forecast error
MSFE	mean-square forecast error
MSFEM	mean-square forecast-error matrix
RMSFE	root mean-square forecast error
OLS	ordinary least squares
SC	Schwarz criterion
SLI	shorter leading indicator
TMSFE	trace mean-square forecast error
TS	trend stationary
URF	unrestricted reduced form
VAR	vector autoregressive representation
VARMA	vector autoregressive moving-average representation
VMA	vector moving-average representation
VEqCM	vector EqCM
WN	white noise

Chapter 1

An introduction to forecasting

Our objective is to develop an econometric theory applicable to macroeconomic forecasting. Such a theory must, therefore, allow for non-stationary processes which are subject to intermittent structural breaks, using models that may differ from the mechanism which generated the data, and that are selected from data evidence. In this volume, we primarily focus on the more tractable case without structural breaks, but note any important differences which result when there are breaks. We begin by setting the scene, and then we review the checkered history of our subject. We develop a framework within which to analyse economic forecasting, then consider alternative forecasting methods. The final section examines forecasting in an artificial (computer-generated) process as a precursor to the remaining analysis.

1.1 Background

This book addresses the key problems facing a theory of macroeconomic forecasting based on empirical econometric models. Many treatments sidestep important facets of the real world, thereby limiting the practical relevance of their conclusions. Properties of forecasting models are often derived assuming that the model is correctly specified, in that it coincides with the mechanism which generated the observed data. Econometric theory comprises a body of tools and techniques for analysing the properties of prospective methods under hypothetical states of nature. In order to deliver relevant conclusions about particular approaches, those 'hypothetical' states must adequately capture appropriate aspects of the real world. This statement applies forcibly to the analysis of forecasting. Nevertheless, many analyses of economic forecasting have been based on the assumptions of a constant, time-invariant, data generating process (DGP), that is stationary (non-integrated), and coincides with the econometric model used.

The first assumption – that of a constant, time-invariant DGP – rules out evolution of the economy brought about by intermittent structural changes and regime shifts. Such shifts call into question the standard results on optimal forecasting. A simple example is that when the process has undergone a regime shift, forecasts based on past information need not be unbiased despite being the previous conditional expectation. Forecasting in the presence of deterministic non-stationarities is a topic of current ongoing research, and while some results are presented in this book, a more complete treatment follows in the companion volume. In the present book, a preliminary analysis of the implications for forecasting is given in sections 2.9, 7.4, 8.6 and 12.6. Section 2.9 reconsiders the value of causal information when the model is mis-specified for the DGP and there are structural breaks, and finds a surprising role for non-causal factors in such a state of nature. In section 7.4, we present structural change as one source of forecast error in a general taxonomy of sources of forecast error and forecast-error uncertainty; and in section 8.6, the merits of a potential partial remedy are discussed, that is, the often-maligned practice of intercept correcting the equations of the macroeconometric model. It is shown that intercept corrections can improve forecast accuracy against a class of structural breaks, even though the model proprietor does not know the timing, the size, the sign or the form of the break. In effect, 'add-factors' can robustify forecasts against some forms of structural change. Finally, section 12.6 shows that collinearity between regressors in forecasting equations has little impact on forecast accuracy in stationary processes, but can be important when there are structural breaks.

Secondly, we investigate the consequences for forecasting of the DGP being an integrated-cointegrated system rather than a stationary vector process. The properties of forecast-error variances for integrated series can differ notably from those of stationary variables, so the behaviour of forecast-error variances depends on the choice of data transform examined, namely integrated levels, stationary differences or cointegrating combinations. The analysis of this problem begins in chapter 4, where we review the theory of prediction for univariate processes as a precursor to the systems analysis in chapter 6. In chapter 4, we contrast forecasting in processes that are difference stationary with those which are trend stationary, assuming at this stage that the model coincides with the DGP. We also discuss forecasting in non-linear models, noting the impact of autoregressive conditional heteroscedasticity (ARCH) on prediction intervals. The importance of the time-series properties of the data is a recurring theme throughout the book. The impact on forecast uncertainty of the data process being integrated is discussed in chapter 6 when there are cointegration relationships, and the effects of parameter uncertainty are studied in a simulation analysis. Also, in chapter 11, we derive expressions for multi-step parameter estimation uncertainty in integrated processes, for a number of estimators, including methods based on multi-step criteria.

Dropping the third assumption – the coincidence of the model with the DGP – leads to a discussion of the nature of empirical econometric models in section 7.2, and of possible tensions between choosing models for forecasting, as against goodness of fit, or policy analysis (see chapter 12). Chapter 7 considers the problems that arise more generally in using large-scale macroeconometric models for forecasting. A taxonomy of sources of forecast error is developed to enable a systematic treatment, extending the sources of error covered in chapters 4 and 6. The taxonomy comprises five categories, namely parameter non-constancy, model mis-specification, sampling variability, data mis-measurement and error uncertainty: it also suggests partial remedies.

First, chapter 2 considers the concepts of unpredictability and forecastability, and investigates the potential role of causal information in forecasting models. There are many steps between predictability and actually being able to forecast accurately, and that one cannot in general establish the value of causal information once the model is mis-specified in unknown ways for a non-stationary DGP that is subject to breaks. It is possible to develop many useful aspects of forecasting theory despite the fact that the model is allowed to be mis-specified and the DGP non-stationary. Indeed, the features of the real-world forecasting venture that give rise to the sources of forecast error outlined in the taxonomy in section 7.3 induce a fairly radical departure from the literature on 'optimal' forecasting (under appropriate hypothetical states of nature) and at the same time help to explain why some apparently *ad hoc* procedures work in practice. Actual economic forecasts are rarely purely model-based or mechanistic, and other methods of forecasting usually come into play, often via the specification of non-zero intercept corrections in the model's equations over the forecast period. A fuller discussion of the role of judgement in macroeconometric forecasting is the subject matter of chapter 8, where we seek to develop a general theory of intercept corrections. The theory of intercept corrections offered is wide ranging, and subsumes the justifications usually given in the literature as special cases. It shows that the efficacy of the habitual practices of forecasters can be understood given the environment in which they operate.

We also critically appraise the traditional uses of econometric tools and techniques in the generation and evaluation of forecasts. For example, in chapter 7, we discuss the inadequacies of some of the techniques traditionally used to evaluate large-scale macroeconometric model-based forecasts. In chapter 10, the merits of a newer method, that of forecast encompassing, are explored. We re-examine the properties of various criteria traditionally used for assessing forecast accuracy. In certain circumstances, the lack of invariance of these measures can seriously limit their usefulness, and again we suggest an alternative. For instance, investigators may reasonably choose to assess forecast accuracy in terms of any one of a number of transformations of the data such as future values of the levels of the data, growth rates or financial returns. The choice of transformation may be central to the outcomes of forecast comparisons when based on the widely used mean square forecast error (MSFE) criterion. MSFEs are criticized as a basis for model selection due to their non-invariance to linear transforms for a model class that is invariant. A generalized forecast-error second-moment (GFESM) measure that is invariant is proposed.

1.2 Structure of the book

The structure of the book is as follows. This chapter reviews the history of economic forecasting and the framework we adopt, then illustrates many of the main issues using a computer-generated data set. Chapter 2 discusses the principles and concepts that underpin the later developments. The main results concern the distinction between predictability (a property of a random variable in relation to available information) and forecastability (the result of an action by a human), and that causal variables need not dominate non-causal variables when processes are subject to structural breaks. Since forecasts can be evaluated in many ways and from different perspectives, there is a large literature on this topic which we review in chapter 3, and which sets the scene for our criticisms of the lack of invariance in section 3.5, leading to the invariant measure proposed in section 3.6. We also review the evaluation of fixed-event, as opposed to rolling-event, forecasts in section 3.2.3.

Chapter 4 examines forecasting in univariate processes to establish notation, tools and techniques, as well as model classes of relevance. Many settings unfortunately lead to analytically intractable derivations, so chapter 5 sketches the central Monte Carlo simulation techniques used in the remainder of the text. From this platform, we explore forecasting in integrated-cointegrated processes in chapter 6, which also illustrates the power of Monte Carlo in assessing finite-sample behaviour. Chapter 7 then considers forecasting from large-scale macroeconometric models, and develops a taxonomy of forecast errors. This suggests ways of improving the reliability of such forecasts, so chapter 8 examines the value of intercept corrections.

Chapter 9 is partly digressionary, as it evaluates the role of leading indicators in economic forecasting, both on their own and as adjuncts to econometric models. The analysis concludes that leading indicators suffer from many of the same problems as econometric models, but, by lacking the economic theory underpinning, offer less prospect for progress, especially if the indicators are not causally related to the targets.

In chapter 10, we critically review the literature on the combination of forecasts. We draw a distinction between the combination of different sources of information in forecasting, and the combination of forecasts from two or more rival models. In brief, we argue that any need to pool forecasts from distinct models can be taken as evidence of model mis-specification. Each model has available to it the same information set as its rivals, so that if a rival model explains an additional feature, the model under scrutiny could be amended to do so. Whether or not the forecasts of one model can explain the forecast errors made by another gives rise to the concept of forecast encompassing, so pooling will not necessarily yield gains. However, pooling between complementary sources may yield gains, since the previous strictures are not applicable to different types of information. For example, survey data can be a useful adjunct within models (rather than a substitute for econometric systems): the importance for forecast accuracy of the reliability of the forecast origin is dealt with in chapter 8, and survey information may provide an alternative reading on the current state of the economy. As ever, we find that when structural breaks are introduced the basic results can be overturned. Different models can vary greatly in their susceptibility or robustness to breaks, so there may exist ways of exploiting those differences by pooling.

Chapter 11 evaluates the role of an alternative estimation strategy, namely optimizing multi-period forecast-error criteria, rather than the usual 1-step criterion. We show that there will be little gain in stationary processes, unless they are near non-stationary, but potential gains in integrated processes when the model is seriously mis-specified for the DGP. However, other solutions than multi-step estimation exist to that problem, and may be preferable.

In chapter 12, we continue the theme of the impact of parameter uncertainty by considering *a priori* restrictions on parameter values, and demonstrate that even false restrictions may lead to improvements in forecast performance. The advantages of imposing parsimony may depend on the forecast horizon. In cointegrated processes that can be reduced to stationarity, collinearity is not a sufficient justification for parsimony *per se*. However, parsimony may be advantageous when the system is subject to breaks.

Chapter 13 draws together and consolidates the implications of our analysis for testing forecast accuracy. Tests of forecast accuracy are invariant to linear transformations of the variables, and the parameter-constancy variety of forecast tests depends only on the 1-step ahead forecast errors.

Finally, chapter 14 concludes and records recommendations for forecasting practice, as well as setting the scene for the second volume.

It is equally important to be aware of the issues that we do not address. Issues of model size and aggregation are not investigated as we have no useful points to make. Intuition suggests that for a restricted budget allocation, the larger the model beyond the minimum size needed to forecast the main aggregates of interest, the poorer its equations, and hence the poorer the forecasts. Also, seasonality is not considered in detail. Fisher and Wallis (1992) discuss seasonality in large-scale macroeconometric models: see, *inter alia*, Hylleberg, Engle, Granger and Yoo (1990), Hylleberg (1992, 1994), Ericsson, Hendry and Tran (1994) and Franses (1996) for references to the recent literature. Our focus is on forecasting outcomes, so we do not investigate probability forecasts (e.g., 'what is the probability of a devaluation next month?': see, *inter alia*, Murphy and Winkler, 1992). Finally, we do not address forecasting from 'structural' time-series models or the Kalman filter because these have been well explained in the literature (see, *inter alia*, Kalman, 1960, Harvey, 1981b, 1992, and Harvey and Shephard, 1992).

The remainder of this introductory chapter consists of the following. Section 1.3 begins with a summary of some of the salient developments in the history of economic forecasting theory, and of the roles played by models in particular, to set the scene. This brief history gives a longer perspective to some of the themes in the book, and suggests that the current lack of confidence in economic forecasting is not without precedent. Economic forecasting has had a checkered history, ranging from a denial of the possibility of economic forecasting in principle (see Morgenstern, 1928), through a period of increasing optimism in the value of model-based forecasting in the late 1960s and early 1970s (see, e.g., Klein, 1971, and Burns, 1986), to the current, rather downbeat assessment of the value of such models. Section 1.4 sets out a framework for economic forecasting, followed by a critical description of some of the main forecasting methods (section 1.5). This chapter ends with an illustration of some of the basic notions and concepts of forecasting based on an artificial (computer generated) data set and associated models (section 1.6). In particular, the concept of the horizon over which forecasts are informative, and the corresponding need to report forecast confidence intervals, are discussed, with a more detailed treatment delayed to subsequent chapters. The econometric theory background assumes a level such as that in Hendry (1995a), although we have tried to make the treatment as self-contained as feasible.

1.3 A history of the theory of economic forecasting

There are comments about forecasting and forecasting methods throughout the statistics and economics literature in the first quarter of the twentieth century (see, e.g., Morgan, 1990). Much of the early work is concerned with developing 'business barometers', especially that of Persons (1924) (we postpone the discussion of leading indicators to section 1.5.3 and chapter 9). However, the first comprehensive treatise seems to be that in Morgenstern (1928), who analysed the methodology of economic forecasting. We know of no translation into English, but the book was extensively reviewed by Marget (1929) as discussed in Hendry and Morgan (1995), and we draw on those sources for our analysis.

Morgenstern argued against the possibility of economic and business forecasting in principle. His first argument adopted the (then widely held) belief that economic forecasting could not rely on probability reasoning because economic data are neither homogeneous nor independently distributed 'as required by statistical theory'. Samples of the size which satisfied the assumptions would be too small to be usable (see Krüger, Gigerenzer and Morgan, 1987, on the probability revolution in the sciences). Other eminent econometricians of the day, such as Persons (1925), held a similar view. Despite the almost universal distrust of the probability approach prior to Haavelmo (1944) (as documented by Morgan, 1990), economists at the time had been making increasing use of statistical methods and statistical inference to 'test' economic theories against the data. Standard errors and multiple correlation coefficients were sometimes given as a gauge of the validity of the relationship. Haavelmo argued forcibly that the use of such tools alongside the eschewal of formal probability models was insupportable: 'For *no tool developed in the theory of statistics has any meaning* – except, perhaps, for descriptive purposes – *without being referred to some stochastic scheme*' (Haavelmo, 1944, from the Preface, original italics).

Secondly, Morgenstern raised the problem that forecasts would be invalidated by agents' reactions to them. This is an early variant of the now named 'Lucas critique' (Lucas, 1976) in the form of self-fulfilling expectations, and was an issue which concerned many business-cycle analysts of the period. We discuss the implications of this critique in section 7.4.4. Because of the inherent impossibility of economic forecasting, and the adverse impact it could have on agents' decisions, Morgenstern foresaw dangers in the use of forecasting for stabilization and social control. Thus, he made an all-out assault on economic forecasting and its applications.

Confirming the contemporary view of probability reasoning in the social sciences, Marget agreed with Morgenstern's first point, but not his conclusion, since most economic forecasting from statistical data depended on extrapolating previous patterns, rather than on probability-based forecasting techniques. However, to the extent that statistical tools help identify the 'patterns' to be extrapolated, Marget's defence of forecasting is suspect. Further, Marget argued that if a causal explanation were possible, even if not exact or entirely regular, forecasting should be feasible. This presupposes that causation implies predictability, which is not obviously the case: a potential counterexample is the theory of evolution. Section 2.9 shows that causal links need not be a reliable basis for economic forecasting, but equally, the absence of causality does not preclude forecasting, and section 4.3.2 discusses when forecasts are informative.

On a more mundane level, Marget's counter to Morgenstern requires regularity between causes and their effects. As noted below in discussing Haavelmo's views on prediction, this was explicitly recognized as a necessary ingredient for success. Nihilistic critiques, such as that of Robbins (1932), denied there were good reasons to believe that this would be the case: on the claim that average elasticities calculated for certain epochs could be described as 'laws', he wrote: 'there is no reason to suppose that their having been so in the past is the result of the operation of homogeneous causes, nor that their changes in the future will be due to the causes which have operated in the past' (Robbins, 1932, p.101).

Morgenstern was one of the first to raise explicitly the problem of 'bandwagon feedback effects', but Marget denied that the problem was either specific to economics or that it precluded accurate forecasting. He constructed a counter-example based on continuous responses such that a 'fixed-point' forecast existed which would equal the outcome despite the latter responding to the announced forecast. Finally, Marget argued for using forecasting to test economic theories. This seems to have been a new proposal, and by the middle 1930s, economists had begun to use economic forecasting for testing their models: Tinbergen (1939) was one of those responsible for developing forecasting tests of econometric models, partly in response to the criticisms of Keynes (1939) and Frisch (1938) (see also Friedman, 1940). At the conclusion of the debate between Marget and Morgenstern, some of the limitations to, and possibilities for, economic forecasting had been clarified, but no formal theory was established – nor had the practice been abandoned.

Haavelmo (1944) treated forecasting as a straightforward application of his general methodology, namely a probability statement about the location of a sample point not yet observed. Given the joint data density function, there were no additional problems specifically associated with prediction. Since Haavelmo's treatment of forecasting (or prediction, in his terminology) in a probabilistic framework was in many ways the progenitor of the textbook approach to economic forecasting, we now sketch his analysis.

Suppose there are T observable values $(x_1, \ldots, x_T)$ on the random variable X, from which to predict the H future values $(x_{T+1}, \ldots, x_{T+H})$. Let the joint probability of the observed and future xs be denoted by $\mathsf{D}_{\mathsf{X}}(\cdot)$, which is assumed known. Denote the probability distribution of the future xs conditional on past xs by:

$$\mathsf{D}_{\mathsf{X}_2|\mathsf{X}_1}(x_{T+1}, \ldots, x_{T+H}|x_1, \ldots, x_T),$$

and the probability distribution of the observed xs as $\mathsf{D}_{\mathsf{X}_1}(\cdot)$, then, factorizing into conditional and marginal probabilities:

$$\mathsf{D}_{\mathsf{X}}(x_1, \ldots, x_{T+H}) = \mathsf{D}_{\mathsf{X}_2|\mathsf{X}_1}(x_{T+1}, \ldots, x_{T+H} \mid x_1, \ldots, x_T) \times \mathsf{D}_{\mathsf{X}_1}(x_1, \ldots, x_T).$$

Thus, for a realization of the observed xs, denoted by the vector $\mathbf{x}_T^1 \in \mathbb{R}^T$, we can calculate from $\mathsf{D}_{\mathsf{X}_2|\mathsf{X}_1}(\cdot)$ the probability that the future xs will lie in any set $E_2 \subseteq \mathbb{R}^H$. Conversely, for a given probability we can calculate 'regions of prediction'. Thus, 'the problem of prediction... (is) ...merely...a problem of probability calculus' (p.107).

In practice $\mathsf{D}_{\mathsf{X}_2|\mathsf{X}_1}(\cdot)$ is not known and must be estimated on the basis of the realization $\mathbf{x}_T^1$, which requires the 'basic assumption' that: 'The probability law $\mathsf{D}_{\mathsf{X}}(\cdot)$ of the $T + H$ variables $(x_1, \ldots, x_{T+H})$ is of such a type that the specification of $\mathsf{D}_{\mathsf{X}_1}(\cdot)$ implies the complete specification of $\mathsf{D}_{\mathsf{X}}(\cdot)$ and, therefore, of $\mathsf{D}_{\mathsf{X}_2|\mathsf{X}_1}(\cdot)$' (p.107: our notation). Loosely, this requires the sort of regularity denied by Robbins, or again quoting from Haavelmo, 'a certain persistence in the type of mechanism that produces the series to be predicted' (p.107). We will consider the extent to which the failure of this type of persistence (e.g., structural breaks) can be countered by alternative forecasting technique (see sections 7.4.1 and 8.6).

Prior to Haavelmo's 1944 paper, the first macroeconomic model had been built by Tinbergen at the Central Planning Bureau of the Netherlands in the 1930s. The pioneering work of Tinbergen on model construction and policy analysis received prominence in two reports commissioned by the League of Nations. Morgan (1990, chapter 4) details these developments and the critical reaction from Keynes (1939) and others. Crudely, Keynes' position was that if the data analysis failed to confirm the theory, then blame the data and statistical methods employed. On the contrary, 'For Tinbergen, econometrics was concerned both with discovery and criticism' (Morgan, 1990, p.124).[1] The influence of Tinbergen ensured that official Dutch economic forecasting was more model-orientated than anywhere else in the world, and the role of econometric modelling and forecasting was further strengthened by Theil (1961, 1966). For example, Marris (1954) compares the Dutch and British approaches to forecasting, and concludes that the British makes use of 'informal models' (what Theil, 1961, p.51, describes as a 'trial and error' method) where, as already mentioned, the Dutch approach

[1] The elements of this debate survive to the present day: see Hendry (1993a).

is based on a formal model. Although Marris sides with the Dutch approach, he has some reservations which include 'the danger of its operators becoming wedded to belief in the stability of relationships (parameters) which are not in fact stable' (Marris, 1954, p.772). In other words, Marris fears the 'mechanistic' adherence to models in the generation of forecasts when the economic system changes. More generally, a recognition of the scope for, and importance of, adjusting purely model-based forecasts has a long lineage: see, *inter alia*, Theil (1961, p.57), Klein (1971), Klein, Howrey and MacCarthy (1974); the sequence of reviews by the UK ESRC Macroeconomic Modelling Bureau in Wallis, Andrews, Bell, Fisher and Whitley (1984), Wallis, Andrews, Bell, Fisher and Whitley (1985), Wallis, Andrews, Fisher, Longbottom and Whitley (1986), Turner (1990) and Wallis and Whitley (1991). In recent work (reviewed in chapter 8), we have attempted to establish a general framework for the analysis of adjustments to model-based forecasts. It is based on the relationships between the DGP, the estimated econometric model, the mechanics of the forecasting technique, data accuracy, and any information about future events held at the beginning of the forecast period. The key motivating factors are the recognition that typically the DGP will not be constant over time and that, in practice, the econometric model and the DGP will not coincide.

Haavelmo's probability approach appears to have been generally accepted by the end of the 1940s, especially in the US, where it underlay the macroeconometric model built for the Cowles Commission by Klein, who was one of the prime movers. Klein (1950) explicitly recognizes that, when the goal is forecasting, econometric modelling practice may differ from when explanation or description are the aim. Klein describes a mathematical model consisting of the structural relationships in the economy (production functions, demand equations, etc.) and argues that for forecasting it may not be necessary to uncover the structural parameters but that attention can usefully focus on the reduced form. However, Klein believes that this will result in worse forecasts unless the system is exactly identified, since otherwise there will be a loss of information. Some of our recent results suggest such fears may be exaggerated. However, we show that it may be possible to improve forecast accuracy by imposing restrictions even when the restrictions are false, once proper account is taken of the forecast error variance due to parameter estimation uncertainty (see chapter 12).

Apart from Klein (1950), Brown (1954) (who derived standard errors for forecasts from systems) and Theil (1961, 1966), time-series analysts played the dominant role in developing theoretical methods for forecasting in the postwar period (see, among many others, Wiener, 1949, Kalman, 1960, Box and Jenkins, 1976 and Harvey, 1981a, 1981c; Whittle, 1963, provides an elegant summary of least-squares methods). Recently, numerous texts and specialist journals have appeared; empirical macroeconometric forecasting models abound, and forecast evaluation is standard (for a partial survey, see Fair, 1986). The sequence of appraisals of UK macro-models by Wallis *et al.* (1984) and Wallis *et al.* (1986) provides detailed analyses of forecasting performance and the sources of forecast errors. Both Klein and Burmeister (1976) and Klein (1991) provide similar analyses of the US industry of macro-forecasting. Wallis (1989) references some of the important contributions of the 1970s and 1980s.

However, there remain difficulties with existing approaches. The survey of forecast evaluation criteria in Granger and Newbold (1973) reveals a number of *ad hoc* methods which they find to be either inadequate or misleading. Chong and Hendry (1986) argue that three commonly used procedures for assessing overall model adequacy are problematical: namely, dynamic simulation performance, the historical record of genuine forecast outcomes and the economic plausibility of the estimated system. Some of the points they raise are reviewed in section 7.5. Chong and Hendry propose a test of forecast encompassing to evaluate the forecasts from large-scale macroeconomic models when data limitations render standard tests infeasible (see also Hendry, 1986, and section 10.3 for a review and some extensions). We argue that as an application of the encompassing principle, forecast encompassing is more soundly based than some of the criteria criticized by Granger and Newbold (1973), and discussed in section 3.2: also see Lu and Mizon (1991). Ericsson (1992) considers the traditional use of MSFEs in forecast evaluation and the relationship between a model having the minimum MSFE, in a certain class, and the notion of constancy. These ideas are discussed in section 3.4 and section 3.5 along with a critique of MSFEs in terms of their lack of invariance to linear transformations for a model class that is itself invariant.

Notwithstanding these criticisms, the theory of economic forecasting when the econometric model and the mechanism generating the data coincide in an unchanging world is reasonably well developed and exposited in a number of texts, such as Granger and Newbold (1977). We focus on the wider implications of forecasting in an evolutionary world where the model and mechanism differ.

1.4 A framework for forecasting

There are many attributes of the system to be forecast that impinge on the choice of method by which to forecast and on the likelihood of obtaining reasonably accurate forecasts. Here we distinguish six different facets: *(A)* the nature of the DGP; *(B)* the knowledge level about that DGP; *(C)* the dimensionality of the system under investigation; *(D)* the form of the analysis; *(E)* the forecast horizon; and *(F)* the linearity or otherwise of the system.

In more detail, using $\boldsymbol{\theta} \in \boldsymbol{\Theta} \subseteq \mathbb{R}^k$ as a shorthand for the DGP parameter vector, and $\mathbf{x}_t$ as the vector of outcomes at time t, with the entire sample from $t = 1$ to $t = T + H$ being denoted by $\mathbf{X}^1_{T+H} = (\mathbf{X}^1_{t-1}, \mathbf{x}_t, \mathbf{X}^{t+1}_T, \mathbf{X}^{T+1}_{T+H})$, the DGP for the outcome at time t is written as $\mathsf{D}_{\mathbf{x}_t}(\mathbf{x}_t|\mathbf{X}^1_{t-1}, \mathbf{X}_0, \boldsymbol{\theta})$, where $\mathbf{X}_0$ denotes the initial (pre-sample) conditions (we reserve the phrase 'forecast origin' to denote the start of the forecast period). A forecast is a function of past information, and for period $t + h$ is given by $\widehat{\mathbf{x}}_{t+h} = \mathbf{f}_h(\mathbf{X}_{t-1})$ where $\mathbf{f}_h(\cdot)$ may depend on a prior estimate of $\boldsymbol{\theta}$. Table 1.1 sketches a framework for considering issues that relate to forecasting.

Table 1.1 Forecasting framework

(A)	**Nature of the DGP**
(i)	Stationary DGP
(ii)	Co-integrated stationary DGP
(iii)	Evolutionary, non-stationary DGP
(B)	**Knowledge level**
(i)	Known DGP, known $\boldsymbol{\theta}$
(ii)	Known DGP, unknown $\boldsymbol{\theta}$
(iii)	Unknown DGP, unknown $\boldsymbol{\theta}$
(C)	**Dimensionality of the system**
(i)	Scalar process
(ii)	Closed vector process
(iii)	Open vector process
(D)	**Form of analysis**
(i)	Asymptotic analysis
(ii)	Finite sample results
(E)	**Forecast horizon**
(i)	1-step;
(ii)	Multi-step
(F)	**Linearity of the system**
(i)	Linear
(ii)	Non-linear

An exhaustive analysis under this taxonomy would generate 216 cases. In what follows, we will consider a number of the examples in detail. If we denote a state by a selection from $\{A, B, C, D, E, F\}$, then it is apparent that the state $\{i,\ i,\ i,\ i,\ i,\ i\}$ is the simplest that can be considered and is far from realistic, but nevertheless will serve to establish concepts, notation and technique. It can also be used to illustrate results that can be proved in more general settings, but only with complicated analyses. More realism at the cost of greater complexity ensues as we move to $\{i,\ iii,\ i,\ i,\ i,\ i\}$ (unknown model specification with parameter estimation uncertainty), or to $\{ii,\ i,\ i,\ i,\ i,\ i\}$ (non-stationary world), then up to $\{ii,\ iii,\ iii,\ ii,\ ii\}$, and finally to $\{iii,\ iii,\ iii,\ ii,\ ii,\ ii\}$ (the most realistic). The later cases suggest practical ideas and approaches, which we shall discuss in what follows. Our primary focus will be on linear models, but in chapter 4, we discuss forecasting with non-linear univariate models. See Salmon and Wallis (1982) and Mariano and Brown (1991) for references to the forecasting literature on non-linear models, and Granger and Teräsvirta (1993) for references to, and a discussion of, modelling non-linearities in long-run relationships between variables.

Following Haavelmo (1944), we assume that the DGP is inherently stochastic. There has been considerable recent interest in deterministic non-linear dynamic (chaotic) processes, which at first sight seem to lie outside our framework. However, most computer random-number generators are based on congruential-modulo methods, which are non-linear deterministic algorithms, yet these are the mainstay for simulating stochastic processes. They are widely used below in our Monte Carlo studies, so the extent to which the paradigms are fundamentally different is unclear. Nevertheless, we do not explicitly consider such DGPs, nor will we devote a great deal of attention to non-linearity here (several popular non-linear models are investigated in our *Zeuthen Lectures*).

1.5 Alternative forecasting methods

There are many ways of making forecasts, and the present focus is on how well any proposed methods are likely to fare as forecasting devices. Irrespective of the method selected, a number of ingredients would appear to be required for success:

(i) that there are regularities to capture;
(ii) that such regularities are informative about the future;
(iii) they are encapsulated in the selected forecasting method; and
(iv) non-regularities are excluded.

The first two are properties (or otherwise) of the economic system common to all forecasting methods, whereas the third and fourth depend specifically on the method proposed. Economies appear to exhibit some constant features which can be embodied in appropriate methods; but not all features are constant, and care must be taken not to extrapolate transient characteristics of the data (for example, outlier observations). We now review the main alternatives.

1.5.1 Guessing

This approach relies on luck, and can be ruled out as a generally useful method, even if at any point in time, some 'oracle' manages to forecast accurately. The usual flaw of this method is that one cannot predict which oracle will be successful. However, 'expert systems' are not oracles, but extensions of formal procedures to flexibly incorporate expert knowledge that the associated model (such as an econometric system) might not otherwise be able to exploit (see, e.g., Artis, Moss and Ormerod, 1992). To the extent that a given expert modifies a model's forecast on a particular occasion, then he/she is acting as an oracle, albeit that there may be a substantive basis for the modification.

1.5.2 Extrapolation

This method is fine so long as the perceived tendencies do indeed persist, but the likelihood of that is itself in doubt. Here the telling feature is that different extrapolators are used at different points in time. Moreover, forecasts are most useful when they predict changes in tendencies, and extrapolative methods cannot do so. Conversely, the next forecasting technique aims to do exactly this.

1.5.3 Leading indicators

Forecasting based on current, leading, and lagging indicators has a long history, as noted in section 1.3. The composite leading economic indicator (CLI) approach to business and economic forecasting was developed over 50 years ago at the National Bureau of Economic Research, has been continually in use since that time, and is now used extensively throughout the world. To paraphrase the introduction in Lahiri and Moore (1991), the philosophy behind the CLI approach is that market economies are characterized by business cycles which are sequences of expansions and contractions in economic activity. The aim is to identify the cycles by their turning points, to relate the cycles to economic indicators which lead their emerging stages, and to use the indicators to predict future turning points. Compared to the traditional macroeconometric models which they pre-date, CLIs emphasize identifying business cycles and the recession and expansion stages of the cycle. Again compared to macroeconometric models, CLIs are a relatively cheap and easy to use forecasting tool, and are described in De Leeuw (1991, p.15), as 'perhaps the least theoretical of forecasting tools'. Proponents of CLIs take their success as forecasting tools largely for granted, pointing to their continued use over the last half century, so much so that De Leeuw feels it necessary to defend his attempt to supply a theoretical basis for CLIs against the possible retort, 'Why bother?'

Unfortunately, such methods are unreliable unless the reasons for the apparent link of the past to the future are clear, as with (say) orders preceding production. De Leeuw suggests production time may be one rationale for leading indicators, so that new orders are viewed as an early stage of the production process. Even so, the delay period is uncertain and may depend on many uncontrolled factors. De Leeuw notes that this connection will be lost if producers attempt to anticipate orders rather than waiting for the orders to come through, in which case the lag from orders to production taking place may turn into a lead. Advocates of CLIs do not appear to be unduly concerned that regular changes in the composition of the indices are required over time in order for them to continue to forecast. The 'meta-forecasting' problem within this framework – of how to predict in advance when to change the indices – appears to be ignored, so that changes are only made after the event.

The specific focus on the business cycle as the phenomenon of interest would appear to make the forecasting venture all the more difficult. There are two basic problems of identification. The first concerns the identification of the business cycle from the raw macro-aggregates on GDP, unemployment, etc. McNees (1991) shows that changes in real GNP, for example, are not closely correlated with the NBER business cycle chronology. Nor do rules of thumb, such as two consecutive quarterly declines in real GNP, perform much better. The official chronology is based on monthly movements in variables and is essentially judgemental: at the very least, rules of thumb should have to take into account the magnitudes of the changes in GNP. One may even question the relevance of studying the business cycle. For example, Layard, Nickell and Jackman (1991) show that 'Conventional business cycles account for relatively little of the history of unemployment' (p.2). Nelson (1972) suggests that we should be concerned about predicting '*any* large disturbance' (p.909) and not just those which result in turning points, given that producing accurate forecasts would appear to be a sensible overall aim. The second problem is of translating movements in the CLIs into predictions about turning points (see, e.g., Stekler, 1991).

Examples which illustrate the potential problems of CLIs are the Harvard Barometer $A - B - C$ curves (see Persons, 1924 and Samuelson, 1987), and models which try to predict from data-based relationships which are actually chance correlations, and not substantive (see Coen, Gomme and Kendall, 1969). Despite such difficulties, forecasting based on leading indicators is undergoing a revival of interest: see Stock and Watson (1989, 1992) and the collection of papers edited by Lahiri and Moore (1991). Given the historical record, it would seem unwise to rely on CLIs as the primary forecasting tool, and we recognize that they have usually been proposed for more limited objectives, such as predicting phases of the business cycle (peaks, troughs), or very short-term horizons when updated measures of other variables may not be available, as with weekly data. Most economic time series are highly autocorrelated and intercorrelated, so it is hard to tell chance correlations from ones which capture persistent regularities. The attempt to do so by blending economic theory with careful data analysis is precisely what distinguishes econometric modelling efforts. In so far as econometric models can forecast the future, they do so on the basis of available past and present information, and hence can be viewed as (complex) formalized and tested leading-indicator systems. However, since CLIs are an inexpensive source of information, they may fulfill a useful role alongside mainstream macroeconometric models. The timeliness of the series on which they are based could provide an up-to-date reading of the actual state of the economy to be used as an input into the model-based forecasting procedures. We examine their formal basis in chapter 9, and suggest some grounds for doubt about the potential of CLIs, as well as questioning the wisdom of using CLIs as additional regressors in econometric systems.

1.5.4 Surveys

Sample surveys of plans, expectations, and anticipations by consumers and businesses can be informative about future events. However, before using survey information directly for forecasting, more research is needed on the extent to which plans are realized in practice, and if not, what explains their departures from outcomes (see Nerlove, 1983). Although pooling from distinct information sources has advantages (see chapter10), there remains an issue as to how to incorporate the relevant information into the forecasting procedure. Thus, while survey information can be a useful adjunct within formal models, it is best viewed as such rather than as a substitute for econometric systems. As with CLIs, we do not think survey variables should simply be added to existing models except as formal measures of latent variables: for example, anticipated orders or expected output can proxy otherwise unobserved expectational variables in econometric systems. Again, persistent links are needed, so greater research on this topic is merited.

An alternative avenue is to treat survey information as an additional reading on the state of the economy. Since forecast origins play an important role in forecasting, and surveys can help determine the point of departure for forecasts, the form of pooling we have in mind is to estimate the pre-forecast state using survey data, past forecasts, indicators, and preliminary measurements, treating the problem as one of signal extraction: see chapter 8 for details.

1.5.5 Time-series models

Scalar versions of time-series models usually take the form proposed by Kalman (1960) or Box and Jenkins (1976). There are good reasons why integrated autoregressive moving-average models (ARIMAs) might be regarded as the dominant class of scalar time-series models. The Wold decomposition theorem (see Wold, 1938: section 4.2 provides a brief discussion) states that any purely indeterministic stationary time series has an infinite moving-average (MA) representation (see Cox and Miller, 1965, pp.286–8, for a lucid discussion). Moreover, any infinite MA can be approximated to any required degree of accuracy by an ARMA model. Typically the order of the AR and MA polynomials (p and q) required to adequately fit the series may be relatively low. Many economic time series may be non-stationary, but provided they can be made stationary by differencing, then they are amenable to analysis within the Box–Jenkins framework, in which case we obtain ARIMA rather than ARMA models (where the order of the integrated component is d, the minimum number of times the series has to be differenced to be stationary). Similarly, at least in principle, deterministic components such as linear functions of time can be readily handled by a prior regression with the Box–Jenkins' approach applied to the remainder. d^{th}-order differencing will also eliminate a deterministic polynomial in time of degree $(d - 1)$.

Harvey (1989), pp.80–1, notes some problems with ARIMA modelling, although historically this approach has been claimed to perform well relative to econometric methods: see, *inter alia*, Cooper (1972), Naylor, Seaks and Wichern (1972) and Nelson (1972). Some of this success is probably due to dynamic mis-specification in econometric models, and the failure to adequately account for the data being integrated, although such a source of error was greatly reduced during the 1980s as modern methods were adopted (see, e.g., Harvey, 1993).

Harvey (1989) has proposed a class of models known as 'structural' time-series models. The series is modelled as the sum of a number of unobserved components which nevertheless have a direct interpretation as trend, seasonal and irregular components. Typically such models contain a number of disturbance terms. From the structural time-series models, we can derive reduced forms with a single disturbance term. These reduced forms are particular Box–Jenkins ARIMA models, although the derivation from a structural model implies certain restrictions on the parameters of the ARIMA model. Harvey (1989, pp.68–70) derives the ARIMA models implied by the principal structural models.

The multivariate successor to Box–Jenkins is the vector autoregressive representation (VAR: see, e.g., Doan, Litterman and Sims, 1984; Lütkepohl, 1991, discusses VAR models with vector moving-average errors), and in the USA this approach has claimed success. There is a role for unrestricted VARs in model evaluation (see Hendry and Mizon, 1993 and Clements and Mizon, 1991), but it should be possible for econometric systems to outperform them as forecasting devices. Because economic data are integrated, VARs are often expressed in changes and hence omit equilibrium-correction feedbacks. Conversely, VARs in levels often retain integrated components of variables and so could predict poorly. The outcome of a Monte Carlo study investigating the issue in a bivariate system, which should favour unrestricted systems relative to multi-variate formulations, is reported in sections 6.7 and 6.8.

1.5.6 Econometric systems

Formal econometric systems of national economies fulfill many useful roles other than just being devices for generating forecasts; for example, such models consolidate existing empirical and theoretical knowledge of how economies function, provide a framework for a progressive research strategy, and help explain their own failures. They are open to adversarial scrutiny, are replicable, and hence offer a scientific basis for research: compare, in particular, guessing, extrapolation, and the use of informal models.

Perhaps at least as importantly, time-series and econometric methods are based on statistical models, and therefore allow derivations of measures of forecast uncertainty, and associated tests of forecast adequacy.[2] It is unclear how to interpret point forecasts in the absence of any guidance as to their accuracy, and we contend that this factor alone constitutes a major way in which econometrics can improve the value of economic forecasts. In a review article, Chatfield (1993) argues strongly in favour of interval forecasts, and assesses the ways in which these can be calculated. A prediction interval is a range within which predictions will fall with a certain probability (commonly taken as 95 percent). In chapter 4, we illustrate the calculation of prediction intervals for simple univariate processes, both when the parameters of the model are assumed known and

[2] Harvey (1989), for example, terms forecasting methods not based on statistical models *ad hoc*. This description might be thought to apply to many popular techniques, such as exponentially weighted moving averages (EWMA) and the schemes of Holt (1957) and Winters (1960), which effectively fit linear functions of time to the series but place greater weight on the more recent observations. The intuitive appeal of such schemes stems from the belief that the future is more likely to resemble the recent, rather than the remote, past. Harvey (1989) shows that such procedures can be given a sound statistical basis since they are derivable from the class of structural time-series models.

when they are estimated. The calculations are relatively straightforward for scalar or vector representations of stationary processes in the absence of parameter uncertainty, but otherwise require recourse to the formulae in Schmidt (1974, 1977) and Calzolari (1981) for estimated parameters, and a rather different approach, developed in chapters 6 and 11, for non-stationary processes. However, forecast-error variances are more difficult to calculate for large, non-linear macroeconometric models, so analogous expressions for prediction intervals are not available, although various simulation methods could be employed (see for example Fair, 1980, 1982 and Bianchi and Calzolari, 1982). Non-modelled variables can in principle be handled, but their treatment in practice may have a significant influence on the results: treating variables which are hard to model as 'exogenous', then supposing that such variables are known with certainty, may seriously understate the uncertainty of the forecasts, as it may prove difficult to forecast such variables. Furthermore, it is not clear what the impact of forecasters' judgements, or intercept corrections, will be on prediction intervals.

Nevertheless, we regard economic forecasting from econometric models as the primary method used in the rest of the book, although other methods may well have a useful contributory role to play. Although conceptually distinct, the various methods of forecasting draw on each other to a greater extent than is usually acknowledged. Most macroeconometric model-based forecasts make use of several methods, according them complementary rather than adversarial roles. In using intercept corrections, for example, the forecaster is engaged in many of these methods of forecasting.

It is impossible to formulate necessary conditions for forecast accuracy: as noted above, guessing could work, or several errors could cancel each other. Sufficient conditions for a macroeconometric model to capture the constant features of the economic system, and to forecast reasonably accurately and more reliably than the alternatives are given by the following criteria:

(i) it is well specified, which requires its congruence, so that the model fully embodies the available data information;
(ii) it dominates alternatives, which is its encompassing ability, namely how well it accounts for the results obtained by rival explanations;
(iii) it remains constant even if economic policies change, which is its invariance to regime shifts and structural change;
(iv) it is accurately and precisely estimated, to minimize the impact of estimation uncertainty.

There are necessary conditions for these in turn, and the importance of these requirements will become apparent in what follows. Chapter 2 examines this aspect in more detail.

1.6 An artificial-data example

To illustrate a number of the main ideas and concepts, we now formulate an artificial data model. This section can be read as a general overview: in subsequent chapters we fill in many of the details. The example provides a cautionary tale as to the degree of accuracy that we hope to attain in our forecasts.

1.6.1 The DGP

A set of data was generated to mimic some of the time-series properties typical of macroeconomics data. The mechanism by which the data were created is, therefore, known to the authors. The data are named 'consumption', 'income' and 'saving' (denoted by C, Y and S respectively) to provide a concrete analog, but have no direct relationship to actual series with these names. The system used to generate the data comprised the following three equations:

$$\Delta C_t = 0.02 + 0.5\Delta Y_t + 0.2S_{t-1} + \epsilon_{1t} \tag{1.1}$$

$$\Delta Y_t = 0.05 + 0.5\Delta Y_{t-1} + \epsilon_{2t} \tag{1.2}$$

$$S_t \equiv Y_t - C_t, \tag{1.3}$$

where $\epsilon_{it} \sim \mathsf{IN}[0, \sigma_{ii}]$ with $\mathsf{E}[\epsilon_{1t}\epsilon_{2s}] = 0\ \forall t, s$, and $\sigma_{11} = (0.05)^2$ and $\sigma_{22} = (0.1)^2$. The notation $\mathsf{IN}[\mu, \sigma_{ii}]$ denotes an independently sampled, normal random variable with expectation (denoted $\mathsf{E}[\cdot]$) of μ and variance of σ_{ii}. Initially, we generated time series for C, Y and S consisting of 238 observation, assuming that the vector process started with initial values of zero, replacing $\{\epsilon_{1t}\}$ and $\{\epsilon_{2t}\}$ by suitably scaled numbers from a random number generator. (The random number generator used was that in PcNaive: see Hendry, Neale and Ericsson, 1991). To counter the dependence on the non-stochastic start-up conditions, we discarded the first 50 observations: the resulting time series were of length 188, corresponding to quarterly data from 1950:1 to 1996:4, say. All subsequent calculations and graphing of the data are performed using PcGive (see Hendry and Doornik, 1996b) and PcFiml (see Doornik and Hendry, 1997).

The units and form of the model actually correspond best to a logarithmic formulation on annual data, so that S_t denotes the annual (log) savings ratio rather than the level of saving. However, we will continue to express the data as quarterly. Thus, (1.1) matches a simplified version of the model in Davidson, Hendry, Srba and Yeo (1978), and (1.3) defines their equilibrium-correction mechanism (EqCM). The equation standard errors are a constant proportion of the levels of the variables. Immediate consequences of the system as formulated in (1.1)–(1.3) are that the data are integrated of first order (denoted $\mathsf{I}(1)$) and C_t and Y_t are cointegrated (see Engle and Granger, 1987; Banerjee, Dolado, Galbraith and Hendry, 1993, provide an exposition). Cointegrating relationships are those that hold in the long run: despite levels of variables changing without bound, combinations of variables move together, such that departures from the linear relation are stationary. Thus, the main points of interest are that the growth of the income series satisfies an autoregressive model; that consumption is determined by income and lagged saving, such that consumption and income are cointegrated; and that saving is stationary.

Solving (1.1) and (1.2) for the reduced-form consumption equation yields:

$$\Delta C_t = 0.045 + 0.25\Delta Y_{t-1} + 0.2S_{t-1} + \epsilon_{1t} + 0.5\epsilon_{2t}, \quad (1.4)$$

so that the EqCM equation is:

$$S_t = 0.005 + 0.25\Delta Y_{t-1} + 0.8S_{t-1} - \epsilon_{1t} + 0.5\epsilon_{2t}. \quad (1.5)$$

Since $\mathsf{E}[\Delta Y_t] = 0.1$, then (1.5) yields a long-run savings ratio $\mathsf{E}[S_t]$ of 15 percent.

Equations (1.2) and (1.5) define the 2-equation model in stationary or $\mathsf{I}(0)$ space. We can write this in vector notation as:

$$\mathbf{f}_t = \boldsymbol{\mu} + \boldsymbol{\Pi}\mathbf{f}_{t-1} + \mathbf{v}_t, \quad (1.6)$$

where $\mathbf{f}_t = (S_t, \ \Delta Y_t)'$. In terms of the $\boldsymbol{\mu}$ vector and $\boldsymbol{\Pi}$ matrix, the coefficients are:

$$\mathbf{f}_t = \begin{pmatrix} 0.005 \\ 0.05 \end{pmatrix} + \begin{pmatrix} 0.8 & 0.25 \\ 0.0 & 0.50 \end{pmatrix} \mathbf{f}_{t-1} + \mathbf{v}_t. \quad (1.7)$$

This representation retains the correct number of differenced variables and cointegrating combinations: values of other linear combinations can be obtained from the identities.

If the model is reduced to contain only first differences of the variables (or growth rates), to ensure that only $\mathsf{I}(0)$ variables are used, as generally occurs with VAR models in the USA (see Todd, 1990), the two equations become:

$$\Delta C_t = \alpha_{10} + \alpha_{11}\Delta Y_{t-1} + \xi_{1t}, \quad (1.8)$$

$$\Delta Y_t = \alpha_{20} + \alpha_{21}\Delta Y_{t-1} + \xi_{2t}, \quad (1.9)$$

where ξ_{1t} contains S_{t-1} (compare to (1.4)),[3] and the income equation is unchanged relative to (1.2). Further lags of ΔC_t, ΔY_t may remove the resulting autocorrelation in ξ_{1t}. However, there will be a cost in terms of forecast efficiency, and possibly poor policy advice, when past disequilibria are important in determining future behaviour. Conversely, if either the level of C_t or Y_t (or any linear combination other than S_t) were retained, the resulting links must be spurious as they are $\mathsf{I}(1)$ functions, which may have a detrimental effect on forecasting (see chapter 6 for analytical and simulation evidence).

[3] Strictly, the orthogonal component of S_{t-1} relative to $(1, \Delta Y_{t-1})$.

When the model is expressed in levels, it can be written as:

$$C_t = 0.045 + 0.45Y_{t-1} - 0.25Y_{t-2} + 0.8C_{t-1} + \epsilon_{1t} + 0.5\epsilon_{2t} \quad (1.10)$$

$$Y_t = 0.05 + 1.5Y_{t-1} - 0.5Y_{t-2} + \epsilon_{2t}. \quad (1.11)$$

Both variables in (1.10) and (1.11) are $\mathsf{I}(1)$ and have trending means and variances, so inference is suspect unless appropriate critical values are used for tests: these values differ according to whether the test involves I(0) or I(1) combinations (see Sims, Stock and Watson, 1990). In $\mathsf{I}(1)$ processes, some statistics have non-standard distributions with larger critical values than conventionally used.

1.6.2 The data

Figure 1.1 shows a block of four time-series graphs for the levels of consumption and income, their first and four quarterly (or annual) differences, and saving. The first graph shows the strong trends due to the non-zero intercepts in the difference formulation and the relative 'smoothness' or persistence in the series characteristic of the unit root in the dynamics. The second and fourth graphs for the quarterly differences of consumption and income, and the level of savings, respectively, both portray I(0) series. Notice that the levels of consumption and income have a unit root at the zero frequency (by construction), so that the first differences of the series are I(0). Fourth differencing (as in the third graph of the set) will not only eliminate unit roots at the zero frequency but will 'over-difference' at the seasonal frequencies (given that the DGP does not contain seasonal unit roots). See Hylleberg *et al.* (1990) for a discussion of unit roots at frequencies other than zero. Nonetheless, the quarterly changes in the series for consumption and income, although irregular, are closely matched.

The fitted values and residuals derived from a second-order levels VAR for C_t and S_t, corresponding to single equation estimation of C_t and S_t respectively on the regressors $\{C_{t-1}, C_{t-2}, Y_{t-1}, Y_{t-2}\}$, are shown in figures 1.2 and 1.3.[4] Each figure also shows the correlogram and histogram, with non-parametrically estimated density, of the scaled residuals. Figure 1.4 reveals a similarly good fit for Y_t on the same regressor set, with both the trend and the cycle being accurately tracked.

Figure 1.5 transposes the same information to a graph of the changes in income derived by regressing ΔY_t on the same regressor set: clear departures between the fitted and actual values are now apparent, and, although the track remains good, the correlation between fitted values and outcomes is much lower (0.501 compared to 0.998 for the levels). Despite the apparent change in goodness of fit, this linear model is invariant to such transformations, as we establish formally in section 6.3.

Overall, the VAR is well fitting on almost any measure, is constant and is correctly specified, so should represent something close to an upper bound for how well we can expect to forecast.

[4] Since $S_t \equiv Y_t - C_t$, this is equivalent to regression on $\{C_{t-1}, C_{t-2}, S_{t-1}, S_{t-2}\}$.

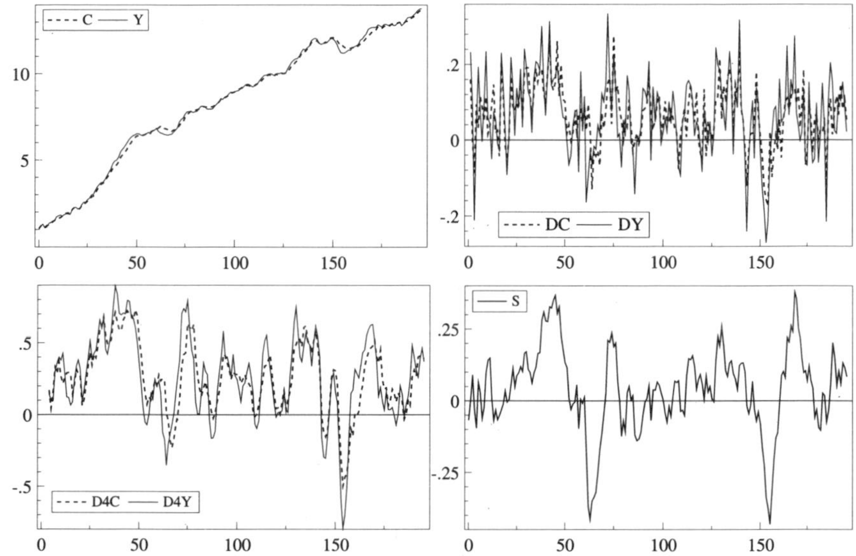

Figure 1.1 Time-series graphs of artificial data

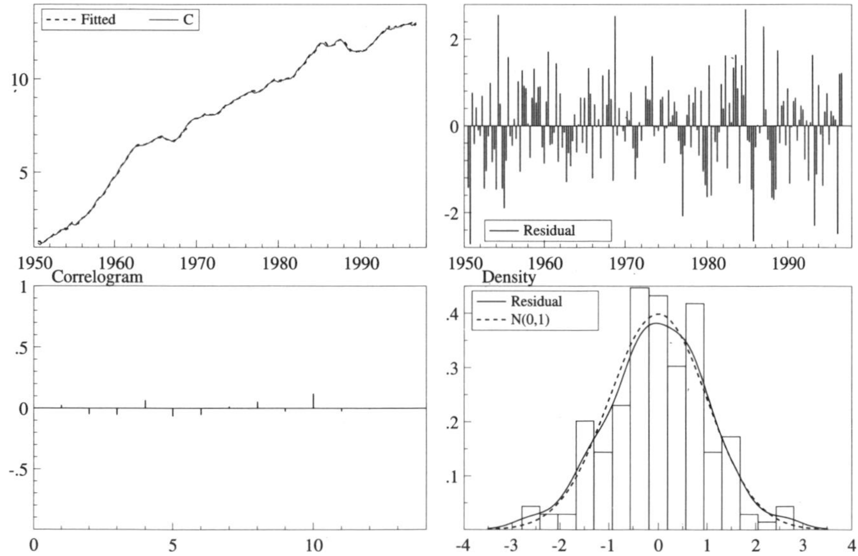

Figure 1.2 Actual and fitted, residuals and graphical statistics for consumption

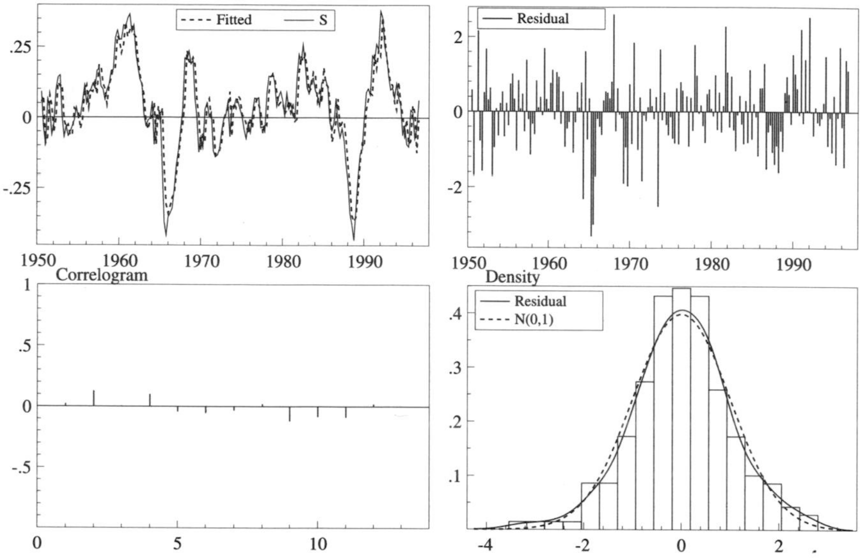

Figure 1.3 Actual and fitted, residuals and graphical statistics for saving

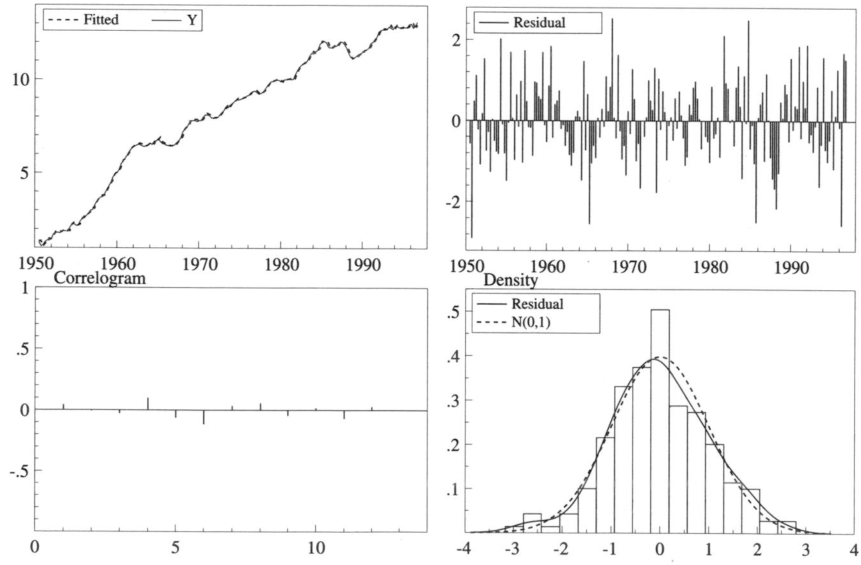

Figure 1.4 Actual and fitted, residuals and graphical statistics for income

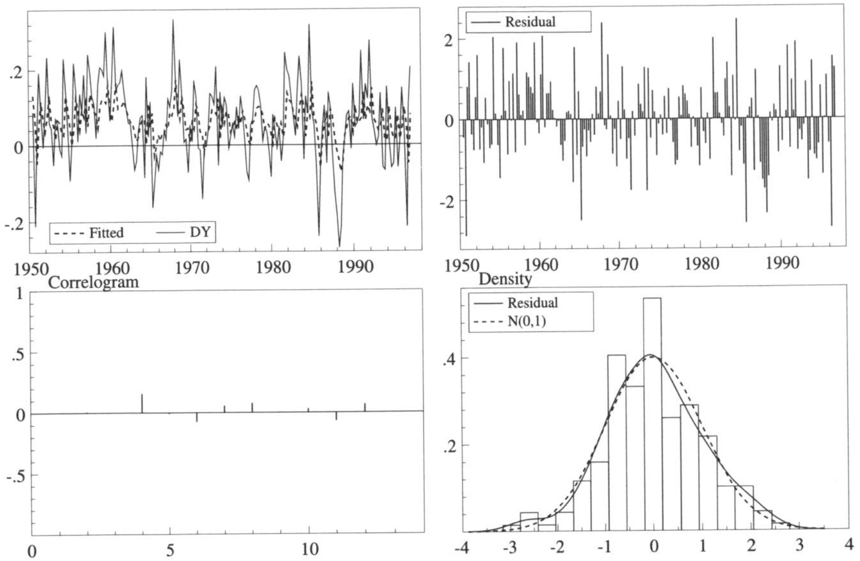

Figure 1.5 Actual and fitted, residuals and graphical statistics for growth in income

So far we have only considered the system or the unrestricted reduced form (URF) for the model given in (1.1).[5] We can also consider models which are over-identified reductions of the system, and since we are in a unique position (relative to applied research) of actually knowing the DGP, we can also consider forecasting when the role of economic modelling is simply to calibrate the values of the parameters of the known specification (corresponding to modelling at knowledge level (ii) in table 1.1).

1.6.3 System estimation

Before doing that, we will report the results of a systems cointegration analysis carried out on a second-order VAR. The technique we employ is the maximum likelihood procedure of Johansen (1988a). The results are summarized in tables 1.2, 1.3 and 1.4.

The procedure is now well known (see Johansen, 1988a, Johansen and Juselius, 1990, Banerjee *et al.*, 1993 and Johansen, 1995, for expositions) so a brief discussion should suffice. In this instance, the estimated system is given by:

$$\Delta \mathbf{x}_t = \boldsymbol{\Gamma} \Delta \mathbf{x}_{t-1} + \boldsymbol{\pi} \mathbf{x}_{t-1} + \boldsymbol{\mu} + \boldsymbol{\epsilon}_t,$$

where it is assumed that $\boldsymbol{\epsilon}_t \sim \mathsf{IN}_2[\mathbf{0}, \boldsymbol{\Omega}]$, $\mathbf{x}_t = [C_t, Y_t]'$, and $\boldsymbol{\pi}$, the long-run, or cointegrating, matrix is factored as $\boldsymbol{\alpha}\boldsymbol{\beta}'$, and will be estimated as a reduced-rank matrix

[5] The conventional textbook approach begins with the structural model and then derives the URF. In Hendry and Mizon (1993), and as exemplified in the econometric systems modelling package PcFiml (Doornik and Hendry, 1997), the relative primacy of the two is inverted.

whenever the column dimension of $\boldsymbol{\alpha}$ and $\boldsymbol{\beta}$ is less than the number of variables in the system. Table 1.2 reports trace and maximum eigenvalue tests for the rank of $\boldsymbol{\pi}$, along with the 95 percent critical values (given automatically by PcFiml). We (correctly) infer that the cointegrating rank is 1, so that there is one stationary or I(0) linear combination of the variables. Finding two linearly independent I(0) combinations would have been at odds with C_t and Y_t being individually I(1).

Table 1.2 Tests of the cointegrating rank

λ_i	$-(T-k)\ln(1-\lambda_i)$	95%	$-(T-k)\ln\sum(1-\lambda_i)$	95%
0.328	75.53	14.1	77.13	15.4
0.008	1.60	3.8	1.60	3.8

The stationary combination is given by the first column of $\boldsymbol{\beta} = [\boldsymbol{\beta}_1 : \boldsymbol{\beta}_2]$, which is the eigenvector corresponding to the largest eigenvalue in table 1.2, shown as the first row of table 1.3. This is numerically close to the population vector of $[1 : -1]$, and its equivalence can be formally established using the tests outlined in Johansen and Juselius (1990). Moreover, the only element of $\boldsymbol{\alpha}$ significantly different from zero (again, this can be established formally) is the weighting on the first eigenvector in the equation for consumption: at -0.26 (see table 1.4) this is close to the population value of -0.2.

Table 1.3 The standardized eigenvectors

	C_t	Y_t
$\boldsymbol{\beta}_1'$	1	-0.992
$\boldsymbol{\beta}_2'$	-0.789	1

Table 1.4 The standardized loadings

	C_t	Y_t
α_1'	-0.258	-0.006
α_2'	-0.030	-0.011

Figure 1.6 plots the two levels combinations given by $\boldsymbol{\beta}_1'\mathbf{x}_t$ and $\boldsymbol{\beta}_2'\mathbf{x}_t$, and provides visual support for the proposition that the former is I(0) while the latter is I(1). Moreover CI1 is just $-S_t$.

Having established that the variables cointegrate, we then estimate the dynamic system given by treating ΔC_t and ΔY_t as endogenous, and ΔY_{t-1}, S_{t-1} and a constant as regressors, which we write as:

$$\mathsf{URF}_1 = \{\Delta C_t, \Delta Y_t : \Delta Y_{t-1}, S_{t-1}, 1\}.$$

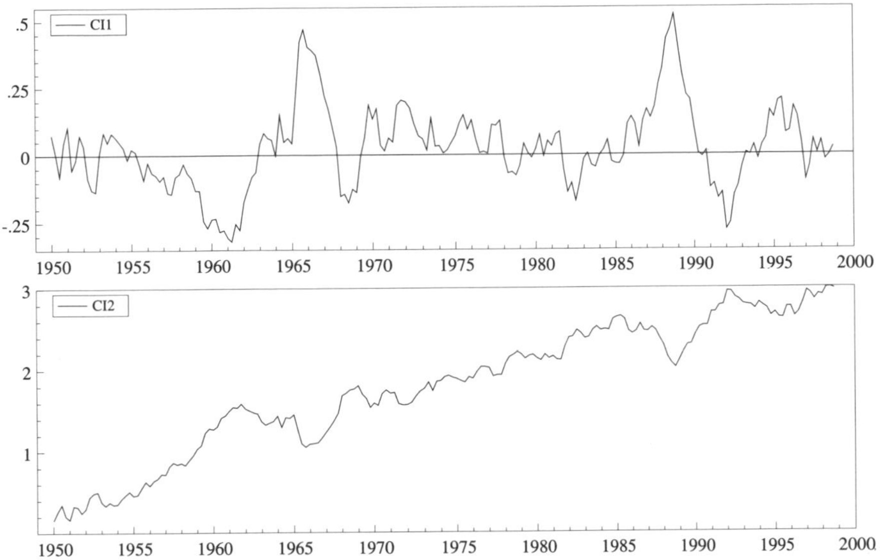

Figure 1.6 Cointegrating vector and non-stationary combination

This parameterization is a restricted version of the second-order VAR. One may contend that it follows naturally from the levels VAR parameter estimates, as given in table 1.5, assuming ignorance of (1.1), but that is peripheral to the aim of this example.

The model given by (1.1)–(1.2), denoted by M_1 (which in this case is also the DGP), is then over-identified relative to URF_1, with three over-identifying restrictions. Estimation of M_1 by full information maximum likelihood (FIML) yielded the parameter estimates in table 1.6.

The parameter estimates are close to their population values, and the likelihood-ratio test of over-identifying restrictions is not significant assuming the test has its standard distribution, but see Sims *et al.* (1990). This test can be interpreted as a test of whether the structural model encompasses the VAR (see Hendry and Mizon, 1993 and Clements and Mizon, 1991).

Recursive estimation of this model indicates that the parameters are constant over time, confirming that the model is well specified. The first two graphs in figure 1.7 show the recursively calculated 1-step residuals $\pm$ two standard errors for the two equations. The remaining two depict Chow (1960) F-tests scaled by their 2.5 percent significance levels at each observation, so values greater than unity indicate rejections. The Chow tests are the 1-step and the N-step relative to the end point of the sample (break-point test). Full details are provided in Doornik and Hendry (1997).

Alternatively, we could transform the URF of (1.1), URF_1, to obtain a parameterization in terms of the growth in consumption and savings. Here, we write the model

Table 1.5 Second-order VAR parameter estimates

Variable	Coefficient	Std. Error	t-value	t-prob.
Equation for C_t				
C_{t-1}	0.92	0.11	8.30	0
C_{t-2}	-0.17	0.09	-1.84	0.07
Y_{t-1}	0.25	0.07	3.51	0
Y_{t-2}	0.00	0.07	0.05	0.96
1	0.07	0.01	5.40	0
	$\sqrt{\widehat{\omega}_{11}} = 0.064$			
Equation for Y_t				
C_{t-1}	0.28	0.17	1.70	0.09
C_{t-2}	-0.31	0.14	-2.17	0.03
Y_{t-1}	1.22	0.11	11.47	0
Y_{t-2}	-0.20	0.10	-1.89	0.06
1	0.05	0.02	2.70	0.01
	$\sqrt{\widehat{\omega}_{22}} = 0.097$			

(which is already in reduced form) as:

$$\mathsf{M}_2 = \{\Delta C_t, \Delta S_t : \Delta Y_{t-1}, S_{t-1}, 1\},$$

again an invariant linear transformation of URF_1 (with an identical likelihood). Invariant linear transformations in this context are discussed in detail in section 6.3, but the parameterization of the endogenous variables in M_2 can be derived from that in URF_1 by pre-multiplying $[\Delta C_t : \Delta Y_t]'$ by:

$$\mathbf{M} = \begin{pmatrix} 1 & 0 \\ -1 & 1 \end{pmatrix}$$

to give $[\Delta C_t : \Delta S_t]'$, which is equivalent to $[\Delta C_t : S_t]'$ since S_{t-1} is in the list of regressors.

We now examine how well we can forecast when the model is the DGP, although the parameters are not known and are replaced by sample estimates. Figure 1.8 shows the sequence of 1-step forecasts for ΔC_t and S_t respectively over the last 20 data points 1988(1)–1992(4) (but artificial dating). We have also graphed the implied 1-step ahead forecasts for the level of consumption, C_t and the change in income ΔY_t. The forecast confidence intervals at a 95 percent level are shown by the error bands, centered on the forecasts. These measures correctly reflect the uncertainty due to the equations' innovation errors, but not the fact that the parameter values have been estimated. Almost all of the realized outcomes lie within their associated confidence interval, and there is no change in the size of the bands as the forecast period advances.

Table 1.6 Structural model (M_1)

Variable	Coefficient	Std. Error	t-value	t-prob.
Equation for ΔC_t				
ΔY_t	0.30	0.09	3.31	0
S_{t-1}	0.24	0.03	9.70	0
1	0.04	0.01	5.47	0
		$\sqrt{\widehat{\sigma}_{11}} = 0.046$		
Equation for ΔY_t				
ΔY_{t-1}	0.40	0.07	6.13	0
1	0.04	0.01	4.64	0
		$\sqrt{\widehat{\sigma}_{22}} = 0.098$		

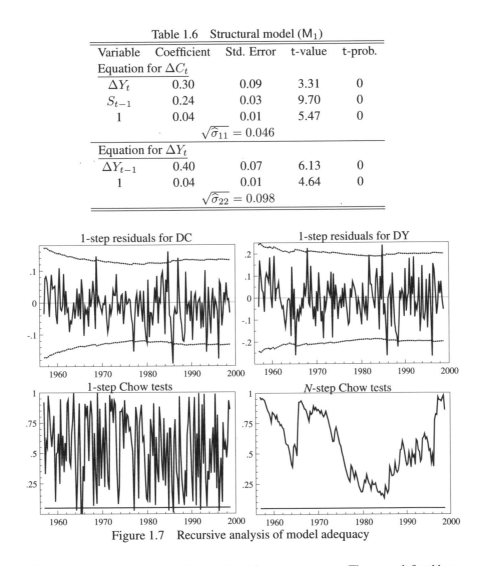

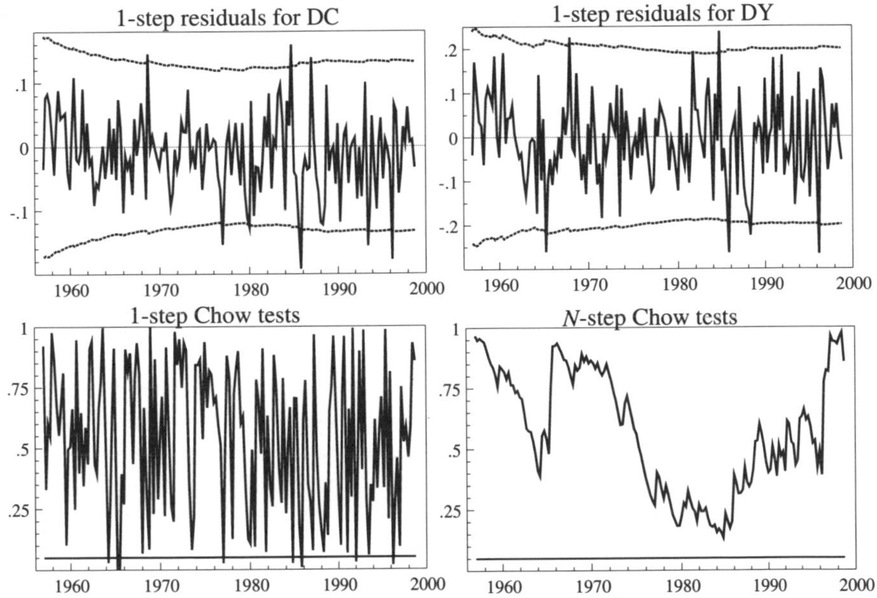

Figure 1.7 Recursive analysis of model adequacy

PcFiml provides various tests of 1-step ahead forecast accuracy. Three are defined by:

$$
\begin{aligned}
\xi_1 &= \sum_{i=1}^{h} \mathbf{e}'_{T+i} \widehat{\boldsymbol{\Omega}}^{-1} \mathbf{e}_{T+i} &\underset{a}{\sim}\ & \chi^2(nh) \\
\xi_2 &= \sum_{i=1}^{h} \mathbf{e}'_{T+i} \widehat{\boldsymbol{\Psi}}_{T+i}^{-1} \mathbf{e}_{T+i} &\underset{a}{\sim}\ & \chi^2(nh) \\
\xi_3 &= \xi_2 \tfrac{T-k}{nhT} &\underset{a}{\sim}\ & \mathsf{F}^{nh}_{T-k}(0)
\end{aligned}
\tag{1.12}
$$

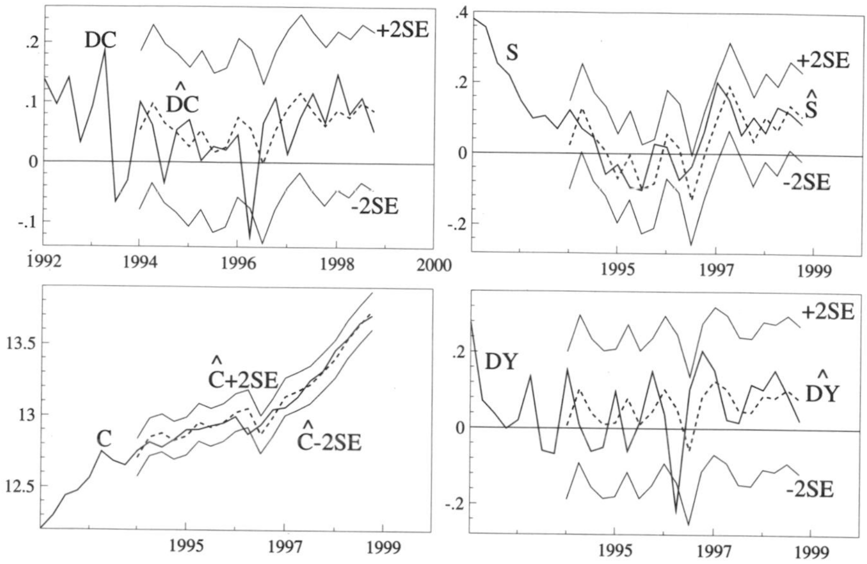

Figure 1.8 1-step ahead forecasts and confidence bands

(see section 13.5). In (1.12), $\mathbf{e}_{T+i}$ is the vector of 1-step forecast errors in predicting the dependent variables in period $T+i$, $\widehat{\mathbf{\Omega}}$ is a sample estimate of the restricted reduced-form covariance matrix of the residuals (scaled by $T-k$ for k estimated parameters), and $\widehat{\mathbf{\Psi}}_{T+i}$ is the covariance matrix of the 1-step forecast errors, $\mathbf{e}_{T+i}$, in period $T+i$. Thus ξ_2 incorporates parameter estimation uncertainty, unlike ξ_1. In the present example, $n=2$ (the number of endogenous variables), $h=20$ (the number of 1-step ahead forecast errors), and $k=3$ (the number of regressors in the system). ξ_3 is the F-test equivalent of ξ_2 and might be expected to have better small-sample properties (see, e.g., Kiviet, 1986). These tests ignore covariances between forecast errors across time periods. Full details are provided in Doornik and Hendry (1997), from which (1.12) is taken. Chapter 13 motivates this type of test of forecast accuracy.

The test outcomes for ΔC_t and S_t over the last 20 data points are given in table 1.6.

Table 1.7 1-step ahead forecast tests for M_2 ($\equiv \mathsf{URF}_1$)

Test statistic	Value	p-value
ξ_1	38.2	0.55
ξ_2	37.7	0.57
ξ_3	0.94	0.57

While the 1-step forecast tests tell us a great deal about parameter constancy (a necessary condition for a valid model), they are relatively uninformative about the ability to predict at longer horizons. Concerning the predictability of the future from economic models, return to equation (1.6) above, now applied to forecasting. For time $T+j,\ j>0$, we have:

$$\mathbf{f}_{T+j} = \boldsymbol{\mu} + \boldsymbol{\Pi}\mathbf{f}_{T+j-1} + \mathbf{v}_{T+j},$$

so that by successive substitution, conditional on the outcome at time T, we obtain:

$$\begin{aligned}\mathbf{f}_{T+j} &= (\mathbf{I}_n + \boldsymbol{\Pi})\,\boldsymbol{\mu} + \boldsymbol{\Pi}^2\mathbf{f}_{T+j-2} + \mathbf{v}_{T+j} + \boldsymbol{\Pi}\mathbf{v}_{T+j-1} \\ &\ \vdots \\ &= \left(\sum_{k=0}^{j-1}\boldsymbol{\Pi}^k\right)\boldsymbol{\mu} + \boldsymbol{\Pi}^j\mathbf{f}_T + \sum_{k=0}^{j-1}\boldsymbol{\Pi}^k\mathbf{v}_{T+j-k}.\end{aligned}$$

Since $\mathsf{E}[\mathbf{v}_{T+j-k}] = \mathbf{0}$ at all future periods, we compute the forecasts using:

$$\widehat{\mathbf{f}}_{T+j} = \left(\sum_{k=0}^{j-1}\boldsymbol{\Pi}^k\right)\boldsymbol{\mu} + \boldsymbol{\Pi}^j\mathbf{f}_T. \qquad (1.13)$$

For stationary processes, $\boldsymbol{\Pi}^j \to \mathbf{0}$ as j increases, so eventually the forecast $\widehat{\mathbf{f}}_{T+j}$ is simply the limit of:

$$\left(\sum_{k=0}^{j-1}\boldsymbol{\Pi}^k\right)\boldsymbol{\mu} \to (\mathbf{I}_n - \boldsymbol{\Pi})^{-1}\boldsymbol{\mu} \ \text{ as } \ j \to \infty,$$

which is the unconditional mean of the process. Thus, for stationary processes, conditional forecasts approach the unconditional first moment of the process as the horizon increases, and in this sense eventually lack substantive content. The forecasts deviate from the outcomes by the accumulated noise $\sum_{k=0}^{j-1}\boldsymbol{\Pi}^k\mathbf{v}_{T+j-k}$. In our illustrative model, the various powers of $\boldsymbol{\Pi}$ are as follows:

$$\boldsymbol{\Pi}^2 = \begin{pmatrix} 0.64 & 0.325 \\ 0.0 & 0.250 \end{pmatrix} \quad \boldsymbol{\Pi}^3 = \begin{pmatrix} 0.512 & 0.323 \\ 0.0 & 0.125 \end{pmatrix}$$

$$\boldsymbol{\Pi}^4 = \begin{pmatrix} 0.41 & 0.289 \\ 0.0 & 0.063 \end{pmatrix} \quad \boldsymbol{\Pi}^5 = \begin{pmatrix} 0.328 & 0.247 \\ 0.0 & 0.031 \end{pmatrix}$$

All ability to predict ΔY_t even with known parameters has vanished by five periods, and little remains for S_t. For stationary combinations of series, this seems a realistic implication. We call the horizon H at which the forecast error variance is within 100α percent of the unconditional variance, the limit to forecastability, taking α at 0.05 or 0.01: see chapter 2 for details.

In many respects, this is an 'ideal' illustration since the model passes all the tests of the adequacy of its specification, explains most of the variation in the data, and does not suffer from any of the practical difficulties of measurement errors, parameter change or non-modelled variables. Indeed, it coincides in formulation with the DGP. Thus, it seems reasonable to attempt a longer-period forecast as in (1.13), and figure 1.9 shows such projections for ΔC_t, S_t, C_t and ΔY_t. The second last follows the trend due to μ, and the three I(0) transformations of the data converge on their long-run average values. Certainly 20 quarters ahead is a long horizon, but both graphs show that convergence is rapid, so we merely caricature the forecaster's practice. This is the usual reporting mode for a central forecast, namely the central trend without any indices of uncertainty. It may look impressive, but is it?

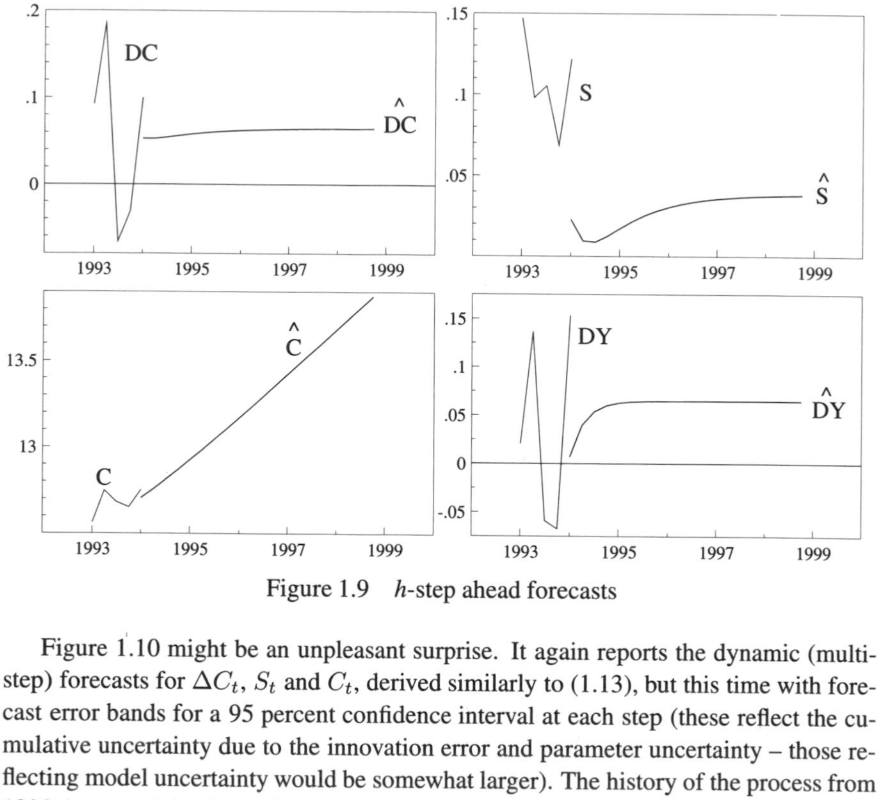

Figure 1.9 *h*-step ahead forecasts

Figure 1.10 might be an unpleasant surprise. It again reports the dynamic (multi-step) forecasts for ΔC_t, S_t and C_t, derived similarly to (1.13), but this time with forecast error bands for a 95 percent confidence interval at each step (these reflect the cumulative uncertainty due to the innovation error and parameter uncertainty – those reflecting model uncertainty would be somewhat larger). The history of the process from 1993:1 onwards is shown for comparison. The large width of the forecast standard errors is obvious: for ΔC_t, S_t they balloon out rapidly before levelling off to span a range similar to that of the previous data observations. For the non-stationary variable, C_t, the mean and variance of the forecast quickly become linear trends, and the forecasts are almost totally uninformative after about eight periods due to the large variances. The 5 percent limit to the forecastability horizon in this system is about six periods, in line with the calculations presented above.

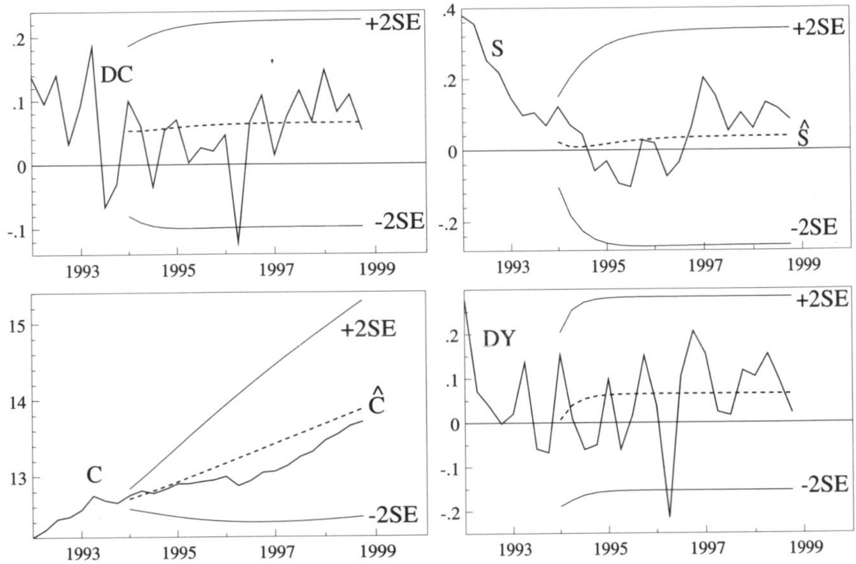

Figure 1.10 *h*-step ahead forecasts and confidence bands

Clearly, either a large recession or a major boom would be compatible with the confidence intervals calculated. Outcomes with markedly different social welfare implications over the medium term are compatible with the model described here. We believe that the onus is on forecasters to move away from point forecasts and to provide a reasonable idea of the uncertainties inherent in their predictions. This would appear to be a necessary precursor to a well-informed judgement on what models can and cannot contribute to debates over government economic policy.[6]

The apparent gap between the last observed outcome and the first forecast is noticeable; we will discuss the effects of its removal in chapter 8.

Finally, as we have stressed, the coincidence of the econometric model and the mechanism that generated the data is simply a pedagogic device that puts the forecast performance of the econometric model in its best possible light. Suppose, for example, that through ignorance we omit the savings term from the consumption equation, so that we end up estimating the equations given by (1.8) and (1.9). In this case, the 1-step ahead forecast tests are given in table 1.8.

There is no evidence of model non-constancy from any of these statistics. However, the plots of the dynamic forecasts in figure 1.11 (compare figure 1.10) indicate the

[6] As positive examples, the UK National Institute for Economic and Social Research now reports confidence bands around the main forecasts from its macroeconometric system, and the Bank of England does so graphically for its inflation forecasts (known in the trade as 'rivers of blood' from the colour coding).

Table 1.8 Forecast tests for model given by (1.8) and (1.9)

Test statistic	Value	p-value
ξ_1	42.14	0.37
ξ_2	40.96	0.43
ξ_3	1.02	0.44

deterioration in forecast performance, particularly for S_t. In chapter 6, we provide a formal analysis of the impact of omitting equilibrium correction terms.

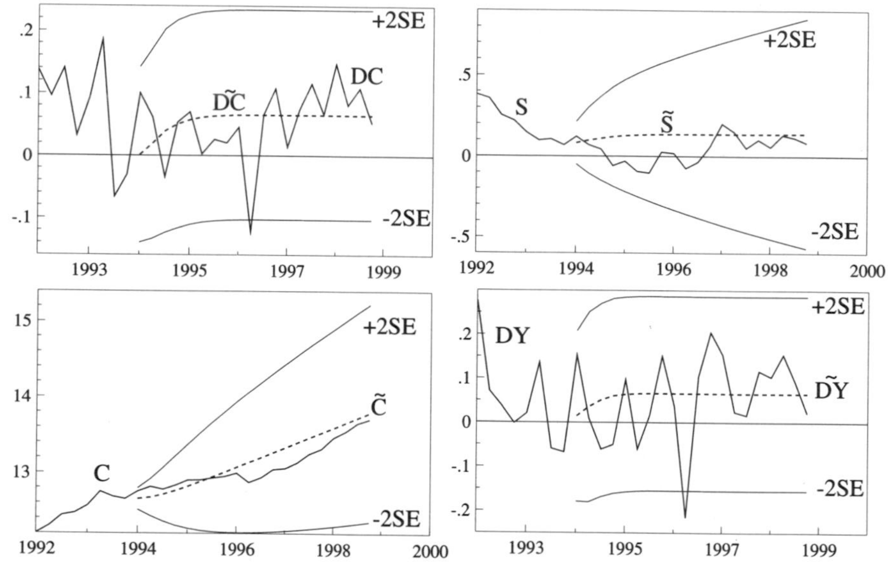

Figure 1.11 *h*-step ahead forecasts and confidence bands for the DVAR

We shall return to many of these issues in the remainder of the book as we investigate the theory of economic forecasting in more detail.

Chapter 2

First principles

This chapter sets the scene for the remainder of the book. The basic concepts of unpredictability and forecastability are defined, and the notions of loss functions and optimal predictors addressed. The mechanics of generating forecasts using time-series ARIMA models are described. The role of causal information in forecasting is investigated under a variety of assumptions about the relationship between the process that generated the observed data and the forecasting model of that process.

2.1 Introduction

As in chapter 1, the variables to be forecast are an n-dimensional discrete-time stochastic process $\{\mathbf{x}_t\}$, where $\mathbf{x}'_t = (x_{1,t} \ldots x_{n,t})$ for $t = 1, \ldots, T + H$. The joint density of $\mathbf{x}_t$ at time t, given the history of the process, is assumed to exist and is $\mathsf{D}_{\mathbf{x}_t}(\mathbf{x}_t|\mathbf{X}_{t-1}, \boldsymbol{\theta})$ where the vector of k parameters $\boldsymbol{\theta} \in \boldsymbol{\Theta} \subseteq \mathbb{R}^k$. Thus, $\mathsf{D}_{\mathbf{x}_t}(\cdot)$ is a function of past information: $\mathbf{X}_{t-1} = (\ldots \mathbf{x}_1 \ldots \mathbf{x}_{t-1})$. We assume the existence of any necessary pre-sample information, $\mathbf{X}_0$, and use the notation $\mathbf{X}_{t-1} = (\mathbf{X}_0, \mathbf{X}^1_{t-1})$ so $\mathbf{X}^1_{t-1} = (\mathbf{x}_1 \ldots \mathbf{x}_{t-1})$.

The period up to T is deemed to have occurred, and that from $T + 1, \ldots, T + H$ is the forecast interval: as real time passes, T increases, and hence the forecast origin is a relative concept. A statistical forecast $\widetilde{\mathbf{x}}_{T+h}$ for period $T + h$, conditional on information up to period T, is given by $\widetilde{\mathbf{x}}_{T+h} = \mathbf{f}_h(\mathbf{X}_T)$, where a prior estimate of $\boldsymbol{\theta}$ may be needed in order to compute the forecast. We do not allow for any known values of $\mathbf{X}^{T+1}_{T+H}$ although there may be deterministic factors (such as intercepts and linear trends) which are known over the forecast horizon. Finally, $\boldsymbol{\theta}$ is assumed to be the same over $t = 1, \ldots, T$, but, although not explicit in the notation, all elements of $\boldsymbol{\theta}$ need not be relevant at all points in time, so transient and changing parameters are not excluded. For illustration, we will usually take $n = 1$, and for notational convenience we will refer to a scalar element of $\mathbf{x}_t$ as y_t.

Perhaps the best-known theorem is that, when the first two moments exist, forecasts calculated as the conditional expectation $\widehat{y}_{T+h} = \mathsf{E}[y_{T+h}|\mathbf{Y}_T]$ are unbiased (where $\mathbf{Y}_T = (\ldots y_1 \ldots y_T)$), and no other predictor conditional on $\mathbf{Y}_T$ alone has a smaller mean-square forecast error (MSFE):

$$\mathsf{M}_h\left[\widehat{y}_{T+h} \mid \mathbf{Y}_T\right] = \mathsf{E}\left[\left(y_{T+h} - \widehat{y}_{T+h}\right)^2 \mid \mathbf{Y}_T\right].$$

We will prove this result when $h = 1$, as its implications need to be understood. Generalizations to $h > 1$ and vector processes are discussed in section 2.7.2.

Consider any other conditional predictor $\widetilde{y}_{T+1} = g(y_{T+1}|\mathbf{Y}_T)$ such that:

$$\mathsf{E}\left[\widetilde{y}_{T+1} \mid \mathbf{Y}_T\right] = \mathsf{E}\left[g\left(y_{T+1} \mid \mathbf{Y}_T\right)\right] = \mathsf{E}\left[y_{T+1} \mid \mathbf{Y}_T\right],$$

so $\widetilde{y}_{T+1}$ is also unbiased conditionally. Then:

$$\begin{aligned}
\mathsf{E}\left[\left(y_{T+1} - \widetilde{y}_{T+1}\right)^2 \mid \mathbf{X}_T\right] &= \mathsf{E}\left[\left(\{y_{T+1} - \widehat{y}_{T+1}\} - \{\widetilde{y}_{T+1} - \widehat{y}_{T+1}\}\right)^2 \mid \mathbf{Y}_T\right] \\
&= \mathsf{E}\left[\left(y_{T+1} - \widehat{y}_{T+1}\right)^2 + \left(\widetilde{y}_{T+1} - \widehat{y}_{T+1}\right)^2 \mid \mathbf{Y}_T\right] \\
&= \mathsf{M}_1\left[\widehat{y}_{T+1} \mid \mathbf{Y}_T\right] + v \\
&\geq \mathsf{M}_1\left[\widehat{y}_{T+1} \mid \mathbf{Y}_T\right], \qquad (2.1)
\end{aligned}$$

as $v \geq 0$, and the cross product:

$$\mathsf{E}\left[\left(y_{T+1} - \widehat{y}_{T+1}\right)\left(\widetilde{y}_{T+1} - \widehat{y}_{T+1}\right) \mid \mathbf{Y}_T\right] = 0$$

by the unbiasedness of $\widehat{y}_{T+1}$ and the fact that both $\widehat{y}_{T+1}$ and $\widetilde{y}_{T+1}$ are conditional on $\mathbf{Y}_T$. Thus, $\widehat{y}_{T+1}$ has desirable properties. It is conditionally unbiased and no other unbiased predictor has a smaller variance. Moreover, these results hold irrespective of the underlying distribution, beyond needing the first two moments to exist, and do not assume that the universe of information comprises only $\mathbf{Y}_T$. For the simple case of an AR(1) process, section 2.7.2 below illustrates the conditional expectation as the minimum mean-square forecast error (MMSFE) predictor.

However, MSFE is not necessarily the most desirable criterion, and under other loss functions, the conditional expectation may not be optimal. For example, one may be concerned with the 'profitability' resulting from a forecast; or the costs of forecast errors may not be symmetric. Granger and Pesaran (1996) discuss a decision-theoretic approach to forecast evaluation which illustrates the former. By specifying the costs and benefits of actions taken in response to the forecast, different forecasts can be compared on the basis of their average realized value to the decision maker. We discuss the second possibility, that of asymmetry, in section 4.9, but the argument is straightforward. If loss is asymmetric, so that there are proportionately greater costs attached to, say, under-prediction than over-prediction, an optimal predictor would on average over-predict.[1]

[1] For example, a trade union bargaining over nominal wages, intent on obtaining a minimum real wage for its members, may attach greater costs to under-predicting inflation than being wrong in the other direction.

This suggests setting the future values of the disturbances to some positive amount. In section 3.4.1 we argue that context-specific loss functions are rarely available to the macroeconomic forecaster. Moreover, while asymmetries are clearly important for individual agents' decisions (compare arriving 5 minutes early for a train with being 5 minutes late) their importance at the macro-level is less obvious.

In this book, the conditional expectation is the workhorse predictor. In terms of the optimal-prediction literature, which begins with the specification of a loss function and then derives the predictor by minimizing expected loss, this suggests that our loss function is squared-error loss. With the exception of asymmetry mentioned above, departures from the conditional expectation arise for reasons other than those associated with the form of loss function. For example, in the above derivation of the conditional expectation as the optimal predictor for squared-error loss, the expectations operator was not dated. However, it needs to be relevant to $\mathsf{D}_{\mathsf{x}_{T+1}}(\mathbf{x}_{T+1}|\mathbf{X}_T, \boldsymbol{\theta})$, whereas the correct distributional form will not be known at the time genuine forecasts are made. Finally, the correct conditional expectation itself is never known in an empirical science, but must be estimated from available information, so estimated approximations to $\mathsf{E}[\mathbf{x}_{T+1}|\mathbf{X}_T]$ must be used in practice. Consequently, despite the power of the result in (2.1), there are many intervening steps to producing useful forecasts, and we proceed to consider some of these in more detail below: we reconsider the choice of forecast-evaluation criterion in chapter 3.

The next section defines the notion of an unpredictable process, and notes some of its implications. Unpredictability is a property of a random variable in relation to an information set, so is well defined. The same cannot be said of the next two concepts, namely informativeness, which is a relationship between information and a pre-existing knowledge state, and forecasting, which is a process of producing statements about future events. It is exceptionally difficult to analyse forecasting generically for the reasons seen in chapter 1, namely that non-statistical methods (such as guessing or extrapolating) exist, and there may be multiple objectives in any forecasting exercise ('closeness' to the target on any of a number of metrics, and then use of the forecast to achieve some further aim). Nevertheless, we will see how far we can advance, before applying the ideas to investigate the role of causal information in forecasting.

2.2 Unpredictability

The definition of unpredictability offered below is equivalent to the statistical independence of an m-dimensional stochastic variable $\boldsymbol{\nu}_t$ (with non-degenerate density $\mathsf{D}_{\nu_t}(\cdot)$) from an information set denoted $\mathcal{I}_{t-1}$. Then, $\boldsymbol{\nu}_t$ is unpredictable with respect to $\mathcal{I}_{t-1}$ if the conditional and unconditional distributions coincide:

$$\mathsf{D}_{\nu_t}(\boldsymbol{\nu}_t \mid \mathcal{I}_{t-1}) = \mathsf{D}_{\nu_t}(\boldsymbol{\nu}_t). \tag{2.2}$$

The concept does not connote so 'erratic' or wild' that nothing useful can be said. Rather, it entails that knowledge of $\mathcal{I}_{t-1}$ does not improve prediction or reduce any aspect of the uncertainty about $\boldsymbol{\nu}_t$. As noted above, this concept describes a property of a random variable relative to information. A simple example is random tossing of an unbiased coin: the next outcome of a head or a tail is unpredictable however many previous trials are observed, but one of these two outcomes is certain (excluding edges).

Unpredictability as defined in (2.2) is invariant under non-singular contemporaneous transforms: e.g., if $\boldsymbol{\nu}_t$ is unpredictable, so is $\mathbf{B}\boldsymbol{\nu}_t$ where $\mathbf{B}$ is $m \times m$ and $|\mathbf{B}| \neq 0$. Conversely, unpredictability is not invariant under intertemporal transforms since if $\mathbf{u}_t = \boldsymbol{\nu}_t + \mathbf{A}\mathbf{f}(\mathcal{I}_{t-1})$ (say), then:

$$\mathsf{D}_{\mathsf{u}_t}(\mathbf{u}_t \mid \mathcal{I}_{t-1}) \neq \mathsf{D}_{\mathsf{u}_t}(\mathbf{u}_t),$$

when $\mathbf{A} \neq \mathbf{0}$, since (for example) $\mathsf{E}[\mathbf{u}_t|\mathcal{I}_{t-1}] = \mathbf{A}\mathbf{f}(\mathcal{I}_{t-1})$. Such a concept helps remove a possible 'paradox': the change in the log of real equity prices seems to be unpredictable in mean (so $\mathsf{E}[\Delta y_t|\mathbf{Y}_{t-1}] = \mathsf{E}[\Delta y_t] = 0$), but the level is predictable ($\mathsf{E}[y_t|\mathbf{Y}_{t-1}] \neq 0$): however, since $y_t = \Delta y_t + y_{t-1}$, the 'prediction' of the current level is merely its immediate past value, $\mathsf{E}[y_t|\mathbf{Y}_{t-1}] = y_{t-1}$. Below, when the time series $\mathbf{x}_t$ is of interest, we assume the information set $\mathcal{I}_{t-1}$ includes at least the history of $\mathbf{x}_t$. Thus, a necessary condition for $\mathbf{x}_t$ to be unpredictable is that it is an innovation, and (weak) white noise (when its variance exists).

Unpredictability is relative to the information set used; when $\mathcal{J}_{t-1} \subset \mathcal{I}_{t-1}$ it is possible that:

$$\mathsf{D}_{\mathsf{u}_t}(\mathbf{u}_t \mid \mathcal{J}_{t-1}) = \mathsf{D}_{\mathsf{u}_t}(\mathbf{u}_t) \;\; \text{yet} \;\; \mathsf{D}_{\mathsf{u}_t}(\mathbf{u}_t \mid \mathcal{I}_{t-1}) \neq \mathsf{D}_{\mathsf{u}_t}(\mathbf{u}_t).$$

An extreme example is when $\mathcal{J}_{t-1}$ does not, but $\mathcal{I}_{t-1}$ does, contain knowledge of the formula for the random number generator producing $\{\mathbf{u}_t\}$. On the other hand, that $\mathcal{J}_{t-1} \subset \mathcal{I}_{t-1}$ does not by itself rule out predictability from the smaller information set.

Unpredictability is also relative to the time period, since we might find:

$$\mathsf{D}_{\mathsf{u}_t}(\mathbf{u}_t \mid \mathcal{I}_{t-1}) \neq \mathsf{D}_{\mathsf{u}_t}(\mathbf{u}_t) \;\; \text{for} \;\; t = 1, \ldots, T \tag{2.3}$$

yet:

$$\mathsf{D}_{\mathsf{u}_t}(\mathbf{u}_t \mid \mathcal{I}_{t-1}) = \mathsf{D}_{\mathsf{u}_t}(\mathbf{u}_t) \;\; \text{for} \;\; t = T+1, \ldots, T+H; \tag{2.4}$$

or even vice versa (perhaps after a move from fixed to floating exchange rates).

Further, unpredictability is relative to the horizon considered in that we could have:

$$\mathsf{D}_{\mathsf{u}_t}(\mathbf{u}_t \mid \mathcal{I}_{t-2}) = \mathsf{D}_{\mathsf{u}_t}(\mathbf{u}_t) \;\; \text{yet} \;\; \mathsf{D}_{\mathsf{u}_t}(\mathbf{u}_t \mid \mathcal{I}_{t-1}) \neq \mathsf{D}_{\mathsf{u}_t}(\mathbf{u}_t).$$

The converse, that :

$$\mathsf{D}_{\mathsf{u}_t}(\mathbf{u}_t \mid \mathcal{I}_{t-1}) = \mathsf{D}_{\mathsf{u}_t}(\mathbf{u}_t) \;\; \text{yet} \;\; \mathsf{D}_{\mathsf{u}_t}(\mathbf{u}_t \mid \mathcal{I}_{t-2}) \neq \mathsf{D}_{\mathsf{u}_t}(\mathbf{u}_t)$$

is impossible as $\mathcal{I}_{t-2} \subseteq \mathcal{I}_{t-1}$ by definition.

Any joint density $\mathsf{D}_{\mathsf{X}}(\mathbf{X}_T^1|\mathbf{X}_0,\boldsymbol{\theta})$ can be sequentially factorized as (see, e.g., Schweppe, 1965 and Hendry, 1995a):

$$\mathsf{D}_{\mathsf{X}}\left(\mathbf{X}_T^1 \mid \mathbf{X}_0,\boldsymbol{\theta}\right) = \prod_{t=1}^{T} \mathsf{D}_{\mathbf{x}_t}\left(\mathbf{x}_t \mid \mathbf{X}_{t-1},\boldsymbol{\theta}\right). \tag{2.5}$$

If we define the 1-step error $\mathbf{e}_t$ as:

$$\mathbf{e}_t = \mathbf{x}_t - \mathsf{E}\left[\mathbf{x}_t \mid \mathbf{X}_{t-1}\right]$$

then:

$$\mathsf{E}\left[\mathbf{e}_t \mid \mathbf{X}_{t-1}\right] = \mathbf{0} = \mathsf{E}\left[\mathbf{e}_t\right] = 0$$

and is unpredictable by construction. Consequently, predictability requires combinations of the unpredictable with $\mathcal{I}$. In an odd sense, we can only predict what has already happened – or, less paradoxically, the 'causes' must already be in train. Such 'causes' need not be direct, and could be very indirect in that the lags of the variables to be predicted may 'capture' the actual causes operating in the past. Further, the conditional variance of $\mathbf{x}_t$ is the same as that of $\mathbf{e}_t$ by construction, $\mathsf{V}[\mathbf{x}_t|\mathbf{X}_{t-1}] = \mathsf{V}[\mathbf{e}_t|\mathbf{X}_{t-1}]$, so that aspect is invariant to intertemporal transforms even though their predictability is not. We briefly discuss measuring predictability in section 3.7.1.

For forecasting, a view has to be taken concerning both the relevant information set, $\mathcal{I}_{t-1}$ (possibly just the history of the variable), and the form of the conditional density that relates the quantity to be forecast to the information set. When forecasting under changed conditions, the latter is unlikely to be known to the forecaster. Thus, a variable may be predictable by (2.2), but not by any human agency lacking omniscience. This problem has important implications for understanding why *ad hoc* methods can work, and we return to it shortly.

2.3 Informativeness

Informativeness is a relative concept, dependent on the pre-existing state of the recipient's information set $\mathcal{J}_{t-1}$. If one knew nothing about a dice-rolling experiment, then it is informative to be told that the only possible outcomes are the integers 1 through 6. Once the equal probability of such outcomes is known, then the forecast that the next outcome has a uniform distribution over [1,6] is uninformative.

If a variable is unpredictable, then forecasts of it would seem to be 'uninformative'. Whether or not that is the case, however, depends on the background information. In practice, simply knowing the form of $\mathsf{D}_{\nu_t}(\boldsymbol{\nu}_t)$ may be highly informative relative to not knowing it. For example, knowing that the FTSE 100 stock-market index has a value of around 4,000 in September 1996 with a daily standard deviation of 1 percent would be very informative to a novice investor previously unaware of such facts (the Nikkei at around 20,000 and the Madrid SE at about 350 illustrates the range). Equity prices seem to be members of the class of non-stationary evolutionary processes (e.g., those with unit roots) so do not have well-behaved unconditional distributions. Hence, the conditional prediction of the next period's level is far more concentrated than the unconditional. However, if the optimal prediction of the change in the log of equity prices is zero, few investors would attach value to the forecast that tomorrow's level will be the same as today's on average, although an extra-terrestrial may do.

One might take one forecast to be more 'informative' than another if its forecast error has a more concentrated probability distribution given $\mathcal{J}$. For example, over a horizon of H periods for two forecasts $\mathbf{f}_{T+h}$ and $\mathbf{g}_{T+h}$, consider an ϵ-neighbourhood $\mathcal{N}_\epsilon(\cdot)$, such that:

$$\mathsf{P}\left(\mathbf{F}_{T+H}^{T+1} \in \mathcal{N}_\epsilon\left(\mathbf{X}_{T+H}^{T+1}\right) \mid \mathcal{J}_T\right) > \mathsf{P}\left(\mathbf{G}_{T+H}^{T+1} \in \mathcal{N}_\epsilon\left(\mathbf{X}_{T+H}^{T+1}\right) \mid \mathcal{J}_T\right),$$

where $\mathbf{F}_{T+H}^{T+1} = (\mathbf{f}_{T+1} \dots \mathbf{f}_{T+H})$, then $\mathbf{f}$ is the more informative. Such a definition is not unproblematic. Consider predicting income, consumption and saving when $I_t \equiv C_t + S_t$. Then, although it is extremely concentrated, the linear combination $\widehat{I}_{T+1} - \widehat{C}_{T+1} - \widehat{S}_{T+1} \equiv 0$ is an uninformative prediction as it is always true, yet the components could be more or less accurately predicted.[2] Thus, informativeness is not an invariant construct (even under contemporaneous linear transforms), nor is uninformativeness by the obverse argument. However, informativeness is invariant if we consider non-singular transforms: if a forecast is informative for $\{I_{T+1}, C_{T+1}, S_{T+1}\}$ then it remains so for $\{I_{T+1} - C_{T+1} - S_{T+1}, C_{T+1}, S_{T+1}\}$. We return to this issue in section 4.3.2.

2.4 Moments

Many forecasting agencies focus on the first and second moments of variables, assuming these exist. Then, $\boldsymbol{\nu}_t$ is unpredictable in mean at t if:

$$\mathsf{E}\left[\boldsymbol{\nu}_t \mid \mathcal{I}_{t-1}\right] = \mathsf{E}\left[\boldsymbol{\nu}_t\right]. \tag{2.6}$$

Similarly $\boldsymbol{\nu}_t$ is unpredictable in variance at t if:

$$\mathsf{V}\left[\boldsymbol{\nu}_t \mid \mathcal{I}_{t-1}\right] = \mathsf{V}\left[\boldsymbol{\nu}_t\right]. \tag{2.7}$$

An unpredictable process is unpredictable in both mean and variance. Examples of predictable variances include autoregressive conditional-heteroscedastic processes (ARCH or GARCH: see Engle, 1982, Bollerslev, Chou and Kroner, 1992 and Bollerslev, Engle and Nelson, 1994), and stochastic volatility schemes (see Shephard, 1996).

[2] Theil (1961, pp.14–15) discusses whether forecasts should obey 'internal consistency', in that they obey the same identities as the outcomes, and suggests that other considerations may contradict this requirement.

An immediate consequence of (2.6) and (2.7) is that unpredictability in mean is not invariant under non-linear transforms since for a (weak) white-noise ARCH process:

$$\mathsf{E}\left[\boldsymbol{\nu}_t \mid \mathcal{I}_{t-1}\right] = \mathsf{E}\left[\boldsymbol{\nu}_t\right] \quad \text{but} \quad \mathsf{E}\left[\boldsymbol{\nu}_t\boldsymbol{\nu}_t' \mid \mathcal{I}_{t-1}\right] \neq \mathsf{E}\left[\boldsymbol{\nu}_t\boldsymbol{\nu}_t'\right].$$

Nevertheless, $\mathsf{E}[\boldsymbol{\nu}_t|\mathcal{I}_{t-1}]$ produces the minimum MSFE. Sections 4.8 and 4.9 briefly discuss forecasting processes with conditional second-moment dependence.

2.5 Forecastability

A forecasting rule is any systematic operational procedure for making statements about future events. As noted above, we will focus on statistical forecasting using formal estimated econometric models. Whereas predictability is a property of a stochastic process in relation to an information set, forecasting is a procedure. We will use these terms in those specific senses hereafter, even though they are often treated as synonyms, or the latter may be restricted to future events. Since forecasting is undertaken for a purpose, and is usually instrumental in decisions rather than an objective in its own right, its evaluation must depend on how well it achieves its aims. Thus, it is extremely difficult to define 'forecastable', or its converse 'unforecastable'. One could perhaps define events as forecastable relative to a loss measure if the relevant procedure produced a lower expected loss than (say) the unconditional mean. This would be consistent with the change in the log of real equity prices being unforecastable, but the level forecastable using a random walk, on the criteria of bias or MSFE. However, MSFE rankings for multivariate, multi-step forecasts depend on the data transformations examined, so can alter in accuracy relative to the historical mean of the transform, rendering even that weak definition ambiguous: see section 3.5.

2.5.1 Horizon

For a weakly stationary, scalar time series, we define the 'limit of forecastability' horizon H to be such that:

$$\mathsf{V}\left[y_{T+H} \mid \mathcal{I}_T\right] > (1-\alpha)\,\mathsf{V}\left[y_{T+H}\right]. \tag{2.8}$$

Here, α may be 0.05, 0.01, etc., so the forecast error variance is within 100α percent of the unconditional variance. The choice of α will depend on the context and objectives of forecasting. The value of H at which the limit is reached will depend on the dynamics of the time series. Chapter 1 provided an illustrative example.

When the time series is non-stationary (integrated of order one, $\mathsf{I}(1)$, say), suitable differencing might reduce it to stationarity so (2.8) could be applied to the differenced series. If the series is inherently positive, one could use instead:

$$\sqrt{\mathsf{V}\left[y_{T+H} \mid \mathcal{I}_T\right]} > \kappa\overline{y}.$$

Here, κ may be 0.25, 0.5, etc.; alternatively, scaling could be relative to y_T. If y_t is in logs, there is no need to scale by the sample mean or initial forecast ($\overline{y}$). Empirically, the horizon may be short due to unmodelled factors.

2.6 Implications

These concepts have a number of important implications applicable to most statistical forecasting methods. First, from (2.2), since the conditional mean of an unpredictable process is its unconditional mean, predictability is necessary for forecastability. However, it is not sufficient, since the relevant information set may be unknown in practice. Further, the impact of the ambiguity in the use of the phrase 'information set' differs in the contexts of predictability and forecasting. $\mathcal{I}_{t-1}$ denotes the conditioning set of the relevant events and events are, or are not, predictable relative to $\mathcal{I}_{t-1}$. But, as an action by humans, forecasting also requires knowledge of how $\mathcal{I}_{t-1}$ enters the conditional density in (2.2). For example, $\boldsymbol{\nu}_{t-1}$ may matter in fact, yet in an awkward non-linear way that eludes empirical modelling.

Secondly, translating 'regularity' as a systematic relation between the entity to be forecast and the available information, then conditions (*i*)–(*iv*) in section 1.5 are sufficient for forecastability. They may not be necessary in principle (e.g., inspired guessing, precognition, etc. may occur), but for statistical forecasting, they seem close to necessary intuitively, as can be seen by considering the removal of any one or more of them (e.g., if no regularities exist to be captured).

Thirdly, if the occurrence of large *ex ante* unpredictable shocks (such as earthquakes, or oil crises) induces their inclusion in later information sets the past will be more explicable than the future is forecastable. Thus, when the 'true' $\mathcal{I}_{t-1}$ is unknown, to prevent the baseline innovation error variance being an underestimate, forecast-accuracy evaluation may require 'unconditioning' from within-sample rare events that have been modelled *post hoc*.

Fourthly, from (2.5) intertemporal transforms affect predictability, so no unique measure of predictability, and hence of forecast accuracy, exists. Linear dynamic econometric systems are invariant under linear transforms in that they retain the same error process, and transformed estimates of the original are usually the direct estimates in the transformed system: such transforms are used regularly in empirical research. But by definition, the predictability of the transformed variables is altered by any transforms that are intertemporal. For example, switching from y_t on y_{t-1} to Δy_t on y_{t-1} reduces a random walk from predictable to unpredictable, and although that transform does not affect 1-step MSFEs, measures such as R^2 are altered. This precludes unique generic rankings of methods, adding to the difficulty of theoretical analysis and practical appraisal.

Next, because new unpredictable components can enter in each period, forecast uncertainty could increase or decrease over increasing horizons from any given T, as a consequence of (2.3) versus (2.4). For integrated processes, $\mathsf{V}[y_{T+h}|\mathcal{I}_T]$ is non-decreasing in h when the innovation distribution is homoscedastic. When the innovation distribution is heteroscedastic, for a given T, forecast uncertainty may increase or decrease in h. However, if we consider a set of sequences of 1- to h-step forecasts, generated by moving the forecast origin forward by 1 period each time, then systematic (i.e., on average over the set) decreases in forecast uncertainty as h increases are highly unlikely (since a time h-steps ahead from T becomes $h-1$ from $T+1$). Further, Chong and Hendry (1986) show that forecast confidence intervals may be non-monotonic in h when parameters are estimated, and we return to that issue below.

Finally, when the 'true' $\mathcal{I}_{t-1}$ is unknown one cannot prove that 'genuinely' relevant (i.e., causal) information is needed to forecast. Rather, one can show in examples that non-causal variables can be the 'best available' forecasting devices on some measures in the absence of omniscience (i.e., when the model is not the DGP). As this issue is central to econometric modelling for forecasting, we analyse it in some detail in section 2.9, after explaining how forecasts are obtained from time-series models.

2.7 The mechanics of forecasting

By way of background material for subsequent developments, we now discuss the mechanics of forecasting from dynamic models. We begin with scalar processes in the Box and Jenkins (1976) tradition, briefly noted in 1.5.5. The extension to the multivariate case is straightforward. In chapter 7, we discuss some of the complicating factors that arise in many practical forecasting exercises based on large-scale macroeconomic models, but the discussion here just aims to illustrate the principles.

2.7.1 Forecasting with ARIMA models

Suppose that the scalar process $\{y_t\}$ we wish to forecast can be written as an ARIMA (p,d,q) model:

$$\phi(L)\,\Delta^d y_t = \mu + \theta(L)\,v_t, \tag{2.9}$$

where $v_t \sim \mathsf{IN}[0,\sigma_v^2]$. $\phi(L)$ and $\theta(L)$ are the AR and MA polynomials, respectively, with orders p and q, so that:

$$\phi(L) = 1 - \phi_1 L - \cdots - \phi_p L^p, \qquad \theta(L) = 1 + \theta_1 L + \cdots + \theta_q L^q,$$

setting $\phi_0 = 1$ and $\theta_0 = 1$. These polynomials are assumed to have no roots in common. We can allow the AR polynomial to contain roots on the unit circle, so that the ARMA($p+d$,q) subsumes an ARIMA(p,d,q), where there are d unit roots (see Box and Jenkins, 1976), in which case we can write the AR polynomial as $\varphi(L) = \phi(L)\Delta^d$. The impact of unit roots on forecasts and measures of predictive accuracy is discussed in detail in chapter 4, but they make little substantive difference to the technique used for obtaining forecasts.

For simplicity we assume that:

(1) the model (2.9) for y_t is the process that actually generated the data, and
(2) the parameters of the model are known.

Neither of these assumptions will hold in practice, and the consequences of relaxing them will be treated in due course. To a first approximation, the second assumption can be relaxed by replacing the parameters $\phi(L)$ and $\theta(L)$ by estimates $\widehat{\phi}(L)$ and $\widehat{\theta}(L)$. The following analysis cannot be so easily adapted to deal with the case when the first assumption fails to hold, as discussed in section 2.9.

Assume we wish to forecast the future values of the process over $t = T+1, \ldots, T+H$ conditional on information up to period T, using $\mathbf{Y}_T = (\ldots, y_{T-1}, y_T)$. A single subscript denotes the forecast lead ($h \in 1, \ldots, H$) and origin (T) when no ambiguity arises. From (2.9), the value of the process in period $T+h$ is:

$$y_{T+h} = \mu + \varphi_1 y_{T+h-1} + \cdots + \varphi_{p+d} y_{T+h-p-d} + v_{T+h} + \theta_1 v_{T+h-1} + \cdots + \theta_q v_{T+h-q}. \tag{2.10}$$

This can be solved recursively. If we consider the AR portion of (2.10) first, then the y_{T+h-j}, for $1 \leq j \leq p+d$, are forecasts for $j < h$, and otherwise are known values. For the MA terms, for v_{T+h-l}, where $0 \leq l \leq q$, then v_{T+h-l} is set to zero for $l < h$. Since the vs are zero-mean and independently distributed, the best forecasts of their future values are all zero. For $l \geq h$, then we need to calculate the vs recursively from the within-sample observations, for example:

$$v_t = \varphi(L) y_t - \mu - \theta^*(L) v_t,$$

where $\theta(L) = 1 + \theta^*(L)$, and $\theta^*(L)$ contains terms in L higher than L^0. The recursion runs from $p+d+1$ to T, with $v_t = 0$ for $t \leq p+d$. The above approach generates the conditional expectation, $\mathsf{E}[y_{T+h}|\mathbf{Y}_T]$, of y_{T+h} given $\mathbf{Y}_T$ and the model (2.9).

The AR(1) model arises as the special case of (2.10) with $\varphi_2 = \cdots = \varphi_{p+d} = 0$ and $\theta_1 = \cdots = \theta_q = 0$:

$$y_{T+h} = \mu + \varphi_1 y_{T+h-1} + v_{T+h}. \tag{2.11}$$

For an ARIMA (p,d,q) process, the eventual forecast function (y_{T+h} as a function of $\mathbf{Y}_T$ as $h \to \infty$) is a polynomial of order d ($d-1$ in the absence of a constant term μ in (2.9): see Harvey, 1993, p.116, for a detailed analysis). When (2.9) contains a constant, the forecast function eventually becomes a polynomial of order d. For example, in the random walk with drift, so that $d = 1$ (which is (2.11) with $\varphi_1 = 1$), the forecast function is (2.12):

$$\widetilde{y}_{T+h} = \mu + \widetilde{y}_{T+h-1} = \mu h + y_T, \tag{2.12}$$

where $\widetilde{y}_{T+h} = \mathsf{E}[y_{T+h}|\mathbf{Y}_T]$, $h \in [1, \ldots, H]$, that is, a first-order polynomial (linear time trend) when $\mu \neq 0$, and otherwise simply a straight line.

Now, suppose we generalize the model to contain an MA component, so it becomes an ARIMA(0,1,1), say, then:

$$\begin{aligned}
\widetilde{y}_{T+1} &= \mu + y_T + \theta_1 v_T \\
\widetilde{y}_{T+2} &= \mu + \widetilde{y}_{T+1} = 2\mu + y_T + \theta_1 v_T \\
\vdots \quad & \vdots \quad \vdots \\
\widetilde{y}_{T+h} &= \mu h + y_T + \theta_1 v_T
\end{aligned}$$

so that the MA component only affects the initial location of the forecast function.

In the presence of AR and MA parameters the MSFE can be derived by first expressing the model as an infinite MA:

$$y_{T+h} = \psi(L) v_{T+h} = \sum_{j=1}^{h} \psi_{h-j} v_{T+j} + \sum_{j=0}^{\infty} \psi_{h+j} v_{T-j}, \tag{2.13}$$

where we assume that the $\psi(L)$ polynomial is absolutely summable. We form the forecast $\widetilde{y}_{T+h}$ by setting $v_{T+j} = 0 \; \forall j > 0$, to give the h-step forecast error as:

$$e_{T+h} = \sum_{j=1}^{h} \psi_{h-j} v_{T+j} \tag{2.14}$$

with MSFE equal to the forecast-error variance in this instance, calculated as:

$$\mathsf{V}[e_{T+h}] = \sum_{j=1}^{h} \psi_{h-j}^2 \mathsf{E}\left[v_{T+j}^2\right] = \sigma_v^2 \sum_{j=1}^{h} \psi_{h-j}^2. \tag{2.15}$$

The second equality in (2.15) holds because as well as being serially uncorrelated the vs are assumed homoscedastic. In section 4.8 we drop this assumption, and in particular consider the effects of allowing for time-dependent conditional heteroscedasticity.

The coefficients $\psi_1, \ldots, \psi_{h-1}$ can be obtained by equating coefficients on powers of L in:

$$\psi(L)\phi(L)\Delta^d = \theta(L).$$

For example, for the AR(1) model, $\theta(L) = 1$, $\Delta^d = 1$ and $\phi(L) = 1 - \phi_1 L$, then:

$$\psi(L) = \frac{1}{1 - \phi_1 L} = 1 + \phi_1 L + \phi_1^2 L^2 + \ldots$$

so that $\psi_0 = 1$, $\psi_1 = \phi_1$, $\psi_2 = \phi_1^2$, etc. Substituting into (2.15):

$$\mathsf{V}[e_{T+h}] = \sigma_v^2 \sum_{j=0}^{h-1} \phi_1^{2j} = \sigma_v^2 \frac{1 - \phi_1^{2h}}{1 - \phi_1^2}.$$

2.7.2 The conditional mean is the minimum MSFE

From (2.11) we have the conditional mean predictor for 1-step ahead predictions defined by:

$$\widetilde{y}_{T+1} = \mathsf{E}\left[y_{T+1} \mid y_T\right] = \mu + \varphi_1 y_T \tag{2.16}$$

with a forecast error:

$$e_{T+1} = y_{T+1} - \widetilde{y}_{T+1} = v_{T+1}. \tag{2.17}$$

We demonstrated in section 2.1 above the proposition that the conditional expectation for 1-step ahead forecasts has the minimum MSFE given all the available information. The generalization to h-step ahead forecasts is straightforward as follows.

Let $\mathcal{I}_T$ denote the information set at time T, and decompose the random variable y_{T+h} as:

$$y_{T+h} = \mathsf{E}\left[y_{T+h} \mid \mathcal{I}_T\right] + u_{T+h} = \vartheta_{T+h} + u_{T+h}. \tag{2.18}$$

Then $\mathsf{E}[u_{T+h}|\mathcal{I}_T] = 0$ and $\mathsf{E}[u_{T+h}\vartheta_{T+h}] = 0$. Let $\mathsf{E}[u^2_{T+h}|\mathcal{I}_T] = \sigma^2_{T+h}$, and let $\mathsf{G}(y_{T+h}|\mathcal{I}_T) = \mu_{T+h}$ denote any other predictor of y_{T+h}. Then setting $\eta_{T+h} = \vartheta_{T+h} - \mu_{T+h}$ and noting that:

$$\mathsf{E}\left[u_{T+h}\eta_{T+h}\right] = \mathsf{E}\left[u_{T+h}\vartheta_{T+h}\right] - \mathsf{E}_{\mathcal{I}}\left[\mathsf{E}\left[u_{T+h}\mu_{T+h} \mid \mathcal{I}_T\right]\right] = 0, \tag{2.19}$$

then:

$$\begin{aligned} \mathsf{E}\left[y_{T+h} - \mathsf{G}\left(y_{T+h} \mid \mathcal{I}_T\right)\right]^2 &= \mathsf{E}\left[\left(y_{T+h} - \vartheta_{T+h}\right) + \left(\vartheta_{T+h} - \mu_{T+h}\right)\right]^2 \\ &= \mathsf{E}\left[u_{T+h} + \eta_{T+h}\right]^2 \\ &= \sigma^2_{T+h} + \mathsf{E}\left[\eta^2_{T+h}\right] \geq \sigma^2_{T+h}. \end{aligned} \tag{2.20}$$

A generalization of (2.20) holds for a vector of variables $\mathbf{x}_{T+1}$, whence $\boldsymbol{\vartheta}_{T+1} \equiv \mathsf{E}[\mathbf{x}_{T+1}|\mathcal{I}_T]$ delivers a MSFE matrix which is less than that of $\boldsymbol{\mu}_{T+1} = \mathsf{G}(\mathbf{x}_{T+1}|\mathcal{I}_T)$ by a positive semi-definite matrix. To see this, let:

$$\overline{\mathbf{e}}_{T+1} = \mathbf{x}_{T+1} - \mathsf{G}(\mathbf{x}_{T+1}|\mathcal{I}_T) = (\mathbf{x}_{T+1} - \boldsymbol{\vartheta}_{T+1}) + (\boldsymbol{\vartheta}_{T+1} - \boldsymbol{\mu}_{T+1}),$$

then $\mathsf{E}\left[\overline{\mathbf{e}}_{T+1}\overline{\mathbf{e}}'_{T+1}\right]$ is:

$$\begin{aligned} &\mathsf{E}\left[\left(\mathbf{x}_{T+1} - \boldsymbol{\vartheta}_{T+1}\right)\left(\mathbf{x}_{T+1} - \boldsymbol{\vartheta}_{T+1}\right)'\right] + \mathsf{E}\left[\left(\boldsymbol{\vartheta}_{T+1} - \boldsymbol{\mu}_{T+1}\right)\left(\boldsymbol{\vartheta}_{T+1} - \boldsymbol{\mu}_{T+1}\right)'\right] \\ = \; &\boldsymbol{\Omega}_{\vartheta} + \boldsymbol{\Omega}_{\vartheta-\mu}, \end{aligned}$$

where the cross-products between $(\mathbf{x}_{T+1} - \boldsymbol{\vartheta}_{T+1})$ and $(\boldsymbol{\vartheta}_{T+1} - \boldsymbol{\mu}_{T+1})$ are zero (as a matrix generalization of (2.19)). Thus, the MSFE matrix for $\boldsymbol{\mu}_{T+1}$ exceeds that of the conditional expectation ($\boldsymbol{\Omega}_{\vartheta}$) by a positive-semi-definite matrix $\boldsymbol{\Omega}_{\vartheta-\mu}$ (since $\boldsymbol{\Omega}_{\vartheta-\mu}$ is a covariance matrix). The MSFE matrices contain all the contemporaneous covariances between the errors in forecasting the variables that constitute $\mathbf{x}_{T+1}$. Finally, instead of considering the MSFE matrix for a vector of variables at 1-step ahead, the same analysis applies to a vector of 1- to h-step ahead forecasts of a scalar (or even a vector, simply by stacking). We can then show that any predictor $\boldsymbol{\mu}_{T+h}$ (which is now of dimension $n \times h$ for a vector of n variables) will have a MSFE matrix that exceeds that of the conditional expectation by a matrix which is positive-semi-definite. The matrices will include not just the contemporaneous covariances between the n variables, but also the temporal covariances for each of the n variables, and the covariances between different variables at different forecast horizons. We show in sections 3.5 and 3.6 that each of these covariances has to be taken into account if we wish to derive invariant measures of forecast accuracy.

The fact that $\mathsf{E}[y_{T+1}|\mathcal{I}_T]$ is the MMSFE predictor for any given $\mathcal{I}_T$ does not entail the converse: in a given set of methods or models, the one with the MMSFE need not be the conditional expectation given all the information available to that set since a model not included in the set may have the overall MMSFE. For example, every model may use only a subset of the information. This is analogous to the problem that variance dominance in a group of fitted models is insufficient to ensure model validity (see Hendry and Richard, 1982). In sections 3.4 and 3.5, we present a critique of mean-square forecast errors.

We now illustrate that the conditional expectation is the MMSFE predictor for a general ARMA process. From (2.13) the conditional expectation is given by $\mathsf{E}[y_{T+h}|\mathcal{I}_T]$ which is:

$$\widetilde{y}_{T+h} = \sum_{j=0}^{\infty} \psi_{h+j} v_{T-j}, \tag{2.21}$$

since $\mathsf{E}[v_{T+j}|\mathcal{I}_T] = 0$ for $j > 0$, with MSFE given by (2.15). Consider any other linear predictor formed by a linear combination of the v_{T-j}, $j \geq 0$, for example:

$$\overline{y}_{T+h} = \sum_{j=0}^{\infty} \rho_{h+j} v_{T-j}. \tag{2.22}$$

Then the ρ_j that minimize:

$$\begin{aligned} \mathsf{E}\left[\left(y_{T+h} - \overline{y}_{T+h}\right)^2\right] &= \mathsf{E}\left[\left(\sum_{j=1}^{h} \psi_{h-j} v_{T+j} + \sum_{j=0}^{\infty} \left(\psi_{h+j} - \rho_{h+j}\right) v_{T-j}\right)^2\right] \\ &= \sigma_v^2 \sum_{j=1}^{h} \psi_{h-j}^2 + \sigma_v^2 \sum_{j=0}^{\infty} \left(\psi_{h+j} - \rho_{h+j}\right)^2 \end{aligned} \tag{2.23}$$

are given by $\psi_{h+j} = \rho_{h+j}$ for all h and j, since $\mathsf{E}[v_s v_t] = 0$, $s \neq t$, so the MMSFE is then (2.15).

2.8 Forecasting in a multivariate framework

A natural generalization of an ARMA model to a multivariate setting is to adopt a vector ARMA (VARMA) model. Such models are however relatively uncommon (but see for example Lütkepohl and Claessen, 1993) and attention has instead focused on vector AR (VAR) models (following Sims, 1980). No new conceptual issues arise in deriving forecasts from such models relative to the scalar models of the previous sections. For example, consider the vector of n variables of interest, denoted by $\mathbf{x}_t$, which follows the first-order VAR:

$$\mathbf{x}_t = \boldsymbol{\tau} + \boldsymbol{\Upsilon}\mathbf{x}_{t-1} + \boldsymbol{\nu}_t, \tag{2.24}$$

where $\boldsymbol{\Upsilon}$ is an $n \times n$ matrix of coefficients, and $\boldsymbol{\tau}$ is an n dimensional vector of constant terms. The error $\boldsymbol{\nu}_t \sim \mathsf{IN}_n[\mathbf{0}, \boldsymbol{\Omega}]$, with expectation $\mathsf{E}[\boldsymbol{\nu}_t] = \mathbf{0}$ and variance matrix $\mathsf{V}[\boldsymbol{\nu}_t] = \boldsymbol{\Omega}$. We again assume that the forecasting model coincides with the DGP, and that parameters are known. The h-step predictor given by the conditional expectation can be obtained by solving recursively:

$$\widetilde{\mathbf{x}}_{T+h} = \boldsymbol{\tau} + \boldsymbol{\Upsilon}\widetilde{\mathbf{x}}_{T+h-1} \tag{2.25}$$

that is:

$$\widetilde{\mathbf{x}}_{T+h} = \sum_{i=0}^{h-1} \boldsymbol{\Upsilon}^i \boldsymbol{\tau} + \boldsymbol{\Upsilon}^h \mathbf{x}_T. \tag{2.26}$$

The resulting forecasts are unbiased:

$$\mathsf{E}\left[\mathbf{x}_{T+h} - \widetilde{\mathbf{x}}_{T+h}\right] = \mathbf{0} \tag{2.27}$$

with forecast-error variance (equal to the matrix MSFE):

$$\mathsf{V}\left[\mathbf{x}_{T+h} - \widetilde{\mathbf{x}}_{T+h}\right] = \sum_{i=0}^{h-1} \boldsymbol{\Upsilon}^i \boldsymbol{\Omega} \boldsymbol{\Upsilon}'^i \tag{2.28}$$

which, as in the scalar case, relies on the disturbances being homoscedastic and serially uncorrelated (as defined following (2.24)).

Later, we shall allow the model to be mis-specified for the DGP. We will often assume that the form of the model coincides with (2.24) as a linear representation of $\mathbf{x}_t$, but allow for mis-specification, so that, for example:

$$\mathbf{x}_t = \boldsymbol{\tau}_p + \boldsymbol{\Upsilon}_p \mathbf{x}_{t-1} + \mathbf{u}_t, \tag{2.29}$$

where the parameter estimates $(\widehat{\boldsymbol{\tau}} : \widehat{\boldsymbol{\Upsilon}} : \widehat{\boldsymbol{\Omega}})$ are possibly inconsistent, with $\boldsymbol{\tau}_p \neq \boldsymbol{\tau}$ and $\boldsymbol{\Upsilon}_p \neq \boldsymbol{\Upsilon}$. The mechanics of deriving forecasts from such models will be unaffected, but the results concerning the properties of forecasts and forecast errors (such as (2.27) and (2.28)) may no longer hold.

Having established notation and technology, we can now evaluate the role of causal information.

2.9 Causal information in economic forecasting

We consider the role of causal information in economic forecasting when:

(1) the mechanism is constant over time,
(2) the mechanism is non-constant over time.

For each assumption concerning the DGP, we can suppose either that the model is correctly specified or mis-specified, so that there are four situations to examine. When the DGP is constant, causal information is always useful, and can produce better forecasts than non-causal, irrespective of whether the model is mis-specified or not. We show via a simple example that adding further causally relevant variables improves forecasts when the model is mis-specified. However, such a result cannot be shown in the second case (non-constant DGP) when the model is mis-specified, and non-causal additional variables can be more useful than causally relevant ones so long as the model remains mis-specified.

We assume all parameters are known: estimation uncertainty would reinforce the central conclusion drawn, though sufficiently poor estimates would weaken the conclusions from the first three cases concerning the beneficial effects of causal information. However, our primary concern is to establish that causally relevant variables cannot be relied upon to produce the 'best' forecasts, so poor estimates would strengthen our finding.

2.9.1 Constant mechanism

To illustrate the analysis, we consider a very simple data generation process defined by a stationary, first-order scalar autoregressive process (AR) in y_t:

$$y_t = \alpha + \rho y_{t-1} + \epsilon_t, \tag{2.30}$$

where $|\rho| < 1$ and $\epsilon_t \sim \mathsf{IN}[0, \sigma^2_\epsilon]$ denotes an independent normal error with expectation $\mathsf{E}[\epsilon_t] = 0$ and variance $\mathsf{V}[\epsilon_t] = \sigma^2_\epsilon$. Equation (2.30) is both the model and the DGP, and we assume the parameters are known. Then (assuming a stationary initial condition), $\mathsf{E}[y_t] = \alpha/(1-\rho)$ and $\mathsf{E}[y_t^2] = \sigma^2_y = \sigma^2_\epsilon/(1-\rho^2)$, with $\mathsf{D}_{y_t}(y_t|y_{t-1}, \boldsymbol{\theta}) = \mathsf{N}[\alpha + \rho y_{t-1}, \sigma^2_\epsilon]$ where $\boldsymbol{\theta}' = (\alpha, \rho, \sigma^2_\epsilon)$.

The conditional expectation of y_t given y_{t-1} is:

$$\mathsf{E}[y_t \mid y_{t-1}] = \alpha + \rho y_{t-1},$$

and $\widehat{y}_{T+1} = \alpha + \rho y_T$ delivers the minimum mean-square forecast error (MMSFE). The resulting forecast error $(y_{T+1} - \widehat{y}_{T+1})$ is a homoscedastic innovation against all further information, since:

$$\mathsf{E}[\epsilon_t \mid y_{t-1}] = 0 \text{ and } \mathsf{V}[\epsilon_t \mid y_{t-1}] = \sigma^2_\epsilon. \tag{2.31}$$

Consequently, adding any additional explanatory variable(s) z_{t-1} to (2.30) will not improve the forecast mean or variance.

The proof of this assertion is immediate:

$$\mathsf{D}_{\mathrm{y}_t}(y_t \mid y_{t-1}, z_{t-1}, \cdot) = \mathsf{D}_{\mathrm{y}_t}(y_t \mid y_{t-1}, \boldsymbol{\theta}).$$

In particular:

$$\mathsf{E}[y_t \mid y_{t-1}, z_{t-1}] = \mathsf{E}[y_t \mid y_{t-1}].$$

Thus, the causal information dominates – non-causal variables cannot be used to improve the forecast.

Conversely, when the model is correctly specified, dropping a variable from the model ensures it will forecast less well than the DGP. Although it will then provide inefficient forecasts, it will forecast as anticipated from the sample fit so long as the DGP is constant. This last implication is based on the analysis in Hendry (1979b), that in stationary processes, predictive failure is unconditionally unlikely, irrespective of how badly the model is specified.

The mis-specification we consider is replacing y_{t-1} by a related variable z_{t-1}. We assume least-squares estimation, albeit in the population. Denote the resulting model by:

$$y_t = \gamma + \lambda z_{t-1} + e_t, \tag{2.32}$$

where:

$$e_t = y_t - \gamma - \lambda z_{t-1} = \alpha + \rho y_{t-1} - \gamma - \lambda z_{t-1} + \epsilon_t. \tag{2.33}$$

When $\rho \neq 0$, e_t will be autocorrelated: this will need to be taken into account when calculating forecast confidence errors. Let the connection between y_t and z_t be given by:

$$y_t = \delta + \phi z_t + w_t, \tag{2.34}$$

where:

$$\mathsf{E}[y_t \mid z_t] = \delta + \phi z_t \text{ and } \mathsf{E}[w_t \mid z_t] = 0,$$

with:

$$\mathsf{V}[w_t \mid z_t] = \omega^2.$$

However, the model in (2.32) must be derived from (2.30) and (2.34):

$$\begin{aligned} y_t &= \alpha + \rho y_{t-1} + \epsilon_t \\ &= \alpha + \rho(\delta + \phi z_{t-1} + w_{t-1}) + \epsilon_t \end{aligned}$$

so $\gamma = \alpha + \rho\delta$ and $\lambda = \rho\phi$. Then, from (2.33):

$$e_t = (\alpha - \gamma + \rho\delta) + (\rho\phi - \lambda) z_{t-1} + \epsilon_t + \rho w_{t-1} = \epsilon_t + \rho w_{t-1}$$

and so has conditional mean:

$$\mathsf{E}[e_t \mid z_{t-1}] = 0 \tag{2.35}$$

and variance:

$$\mathsf{V}\left[e_t \mid z_{t-1}\right] = \sigma_\epsilon^2 + \rho^2\omega^2 \geq \sigma_\epsilon^2. \tag{2.36}$$

The mis-specified model will lead to inefficient forecasts unless there is perfect correlation between y_t and z_t. The forecast $\widetilde{y}_{T+1}$ is:

$$\widetilde{y}_{T+1} = \gamma + \lambda z_T,$$

so the forecast error is:

$$y_{T+1} - \widetilde{y}_{T+1} = (\alpha - \gamma) + \rho y_T - \lambda z_T + \epsilon_{T+1} = e_{T+1}. \tag{2.37}$$

This is the model error at $T+1$, so from (2.35) and (2.36), the forecasts are conditionally unbiased ($\rho\phi = \lambda$), but inefficient relative to the correctly specified model on MSFE (unless $\rho = 0$). Adding y_{t-1} to the model will improve the fit and later forecasts as $\mathsf{E}[e_t|y_{t-1}] = \rho\mathsf{E}[w_{t-1}|y_{t-1}] \neq 0$.

Nevertheless, because the DGP is time invariant, the forecasts will have the same first two moments as the fitted values, and so will not indicate any predictive failure on the basis of tests that compare in-sample fit with out-of-sample performance: see section 13.2.

2.9.2 Non-constant mechanism

The most interesting non-constancy in our simple setting is a change in α in (2.30): changes in ρ are mainly interesting in so far as they change the long-run mean (see Hendry and Doornik, 1997).

Let α change to α^* at time $T+1$, so the DGP in the forecast period becomes:

$$y_{T+1} = \alpha^* + \rho y_T + \epsilon_{T+1}. \tag{2.38}$$

Providing the model also coincides with (2.38), the forecast errors have the same properties as in (2.31): adding variables to the model will not improve the forecasts while omitting variables will worsen them. This can be established formally from a generalization of the argument in section 2.9.1, but is clear intuitively.

However, once the model does not coincide with a non-constant mechanism, we can not prove either that adding causal information will help (provided the model remains mis-specified) or that dropping causal variables will worsen the forecast performance.

The actual forecast based on the causal model, which is also the in-sample DGP is:

$$\widehat{y}_{T+1} = \alpha + \rho y_T \tag{2.39}$$

and hence the forecast error is:

$$e_{T+1} = y_{T+1} - \widehat{y}_{T+1} = (\alpha^* - \alpha) + \epsilon_{T+1},$$

which has mean $\alpha^* - \alpha$.

Consider the mechanical, or extrapolative, forecasting rule:

$$\widetilde{y}_{T+1} = y_T. \tag{2.40}$$

This has a forecast error:

$$u_{T+1} = y_{T+1} - \widetilde{y}_{T+1} = \alpha^* + (\rho - 1)\, y_T + \epsilon_{T+1} \tag{2.41}$$

which on average is also $\alpha^* - \alpha$ (as $\mathsf{E}[y_T] = \alpha/(1-\rho)$). Now envisage what happens one period later (i.e., time $T+2$). (2.39) remains:

$$\widehat{y}_{T+2} = \alpha + \rho y_{T+1},$$

with forecast error:

$$e_{T+2} = y_{T+2} - \widehat{y}_{T+2} = (\alpha^* - \alpha) + \epsilon_{T+2}$$

which still has mean $\alpha^* - \alpha$. However, (2.40) is:

$$\widetilde{y}_{T+2} = y_{T+1} \tag{2.42}$$

with forecast error:

$$\begin{aligned} u_{T+2} &= \alpha^* + \rho y_{T+1} - y_{T+1} + \epsilon_{T+2} \\ &= \alpha^* + \rho y_{T+1} - \alpha^* - \rho y_T + \epsilon_{T+2} - \epsilon_{T+1} \\ &= \rho \Delta y_{T+1} + \Delta \epsilon_{T+2}. \end{aligned}$$

From (2.41), $\Delta y_{T+1} = u_{T+1}$, so the average forecast error of $\widetilde{y}_{T+2}$ is $\rho(\alpha^* - \alpha)$ which is never larger than the average forecast error using $\widehat{y}_{T+2}$. This effect increasingly favours $\widetilde{y}$ as time passes, unless the model is revised. In MSFE terms, $\widetilde{y}$ has twice the variance of $\widehat{y}$ (owing to differencing), so always loses at $T+1$, but at $T+2$:

$$\mathsf{M}_2\left[\widehat{y}_{T+2}\right] = \sigma_\epsilon^2 + (\alpha^* - \alpha)^2 \quad \text{whereas} \quad \mathsf{M}_2\left[\widetilde{y}_{T+2}\right] = 2\sigma_\epsilon^2 + \rho^2 (\alpha^* - \alpha)^2,$$

so the latter will be smaller for a sufficiently large structural break. When y denotes the log-difference of an original series, small values of ρ are likely, so the gain can be large: this effect may be part of the explanation for the success of Box and Jenkins (1976) methods.

The case that illustrates that non-causal information may dominate is precisely when $\rho = 0$, so y_{t-1} is irrelevant, whereas the intercept is relevant. For all breaks larger than one error standard deviation (σ_ϵ), $\widetilde{y}$ has a smaller bias and smaller MSFE than $\widehat{y}$ (for multivariate examples and simulation evidence, see Hendry and Doornik, 1997).

2.10 Overview

In this chapter we introduced a number of basic concepts. In particular, we distinguish between (un)predictability and (un)forecastability, recognizing that the two are commonly used interchangeably. The distinction we make is the following. Predictability is a statistical concept that refers to the relationship between a random variable and an information set – a variable is unpredictable if the conditional distribution (given that information set) is just the unconditional distribution of the variable. Predictability is necessary but not sufficient for forecastability, since we also need to know the form of the conditional density of the variable, i.e., the way in which the information set can be used to generate predictions. This knowledge is akin to knowing the DGP, i.e., the model being correctly specified for the DGP. Under this assumption of omniscience predictability and forecastability become the same thing.

Next, we discussed the mechanics of generating forecasts, and the optimality properties of the conditional expectation.

Finally, we also established that non-causal variables may be more relevant than (previously) causally relevant variables if the model is mis-specified for the DGP and the DGP undergoes a structural break. Unfortunately, this state of affairs (a mis-specified model and a non-constant DGP) is not uncommon in economics, so that forecasting with an empirical model may be fundamentally different from predicting using the DGP.

The main message is that we cannot forecast the unpredictable. This all too obvious statement nevertheless transpires to have profound implications: for example, more aspects of reality may transpire to be unpredictable than just the stochastic error on postulated equations, which is all that forecast-error variance formulae reflect. Indeed, the existence of forecast failure reveals that other unanticipated changes occurred over the forecast horizon. This theme is explored in more detail in section 7.3 below, and in Hendry and Doornik (1997).

Chapter 3

Evaluating forecast accuracy

This chapter considers the evaluation of forecasts. It begins with the evaluation of forecast performance based on the efficient use of information, for both rolling-event and fixed-event forecasts. Notions of efficiency and unbiasedness are viewed as desirable properties for forecasts to possess, but, in practice, comparisons between forecasts produced by rival models would seem to be a preferable alternative to evaluation based on a comparison of individual-model forecasts with outcomes. This requires a metric for assessing forecast accuracy. Although context-specific cost functions defining mappings between forecast errors and the costs of making those errors may exist in some instances, general MSFE-based measures have been the dominant criteria for assessing forecast accuracy in macroeconomic forecasting. However, such measures typically are not invariant to non-singular, scale-preserving linear transforms, even though linear models are. Consequently, different rankings across models or methods can be obtained from various MSFE measures by choosing alternative yet isomorphic representations of a given model. Thus, MSFE rankings can be an artefact of the linear transformation selected. A generalized forecast-error second-moment criterion is proposed with the property of invariance, but interesting problems relating to model choice and the forecast horizon remain.

3.1 Introduction

Various methods have been used in economics for assessing forecast accuracy and evaluating forecasts. Granger and Newbold (1973) provide a critique of many of the practices prevalent at that time, and their main contentions can be put succinctly as:

(i) methods of gauging forecast accuracy cannot usefully be based on comparisons of the time series, or the distributional properties, of the actual (A) and predicted (P) series. It makes more sense to analyse the difference between the two, that is the forecast error (e);

(ii) useful information can result from comparison across predictors; but

(iii) forecast comparisons across rival forecasts should not typically result in one being adopted at the expense of the others. Granger and Newbold claim that it is generally better to combine forecasts since typically the dominated forecasts still contain information that can be utilized to obtain a superior forecast.

We accept their first two contentions, but discuss the third in chapter 10, where we suggest that in some circumstances forecast combination may serve as a useful test of model adequacy (where more traditional tests are for some reason inapplicable). Our view is based on the concept of encompassing (see Hendry, 1995a), with different operational implications for forecast combination as a method of generating forecasts.

We begin in section 3.2 by reviewing measures of forecast performance which are based on the relationship between forecasts and outcomes, and where we are concerned with the rationality of forecasts, and the efficient use of information. We discuss rationality in terms of unbiasedness and various notions of efficiency, which are necessary attributes for forecasts to be useful. In section 3.3, we consider comparing a model's forecasts with those of a rival model as a method of assessing forecast accuracy. In practice the minimum attainable MSFE will not be known, and will differ from variable to variable reflecting the intrinsic degree of variability and unpredictability of that variable. In terms of an AR(1) model of a log transform with non-zero mean, the degree of unpredictability is proportional to the standard deviation of the underlying disturbance term. For a variable in (non-log) levels, however, the error standard deviation can always be scaled to unity. Thus, in the absence of an 'absolute' benchmark, the performance of rival models (or sets of forecasts) may provide an indication of the usefulness of a particular model, or set of forecasts.

For illustrative purposes we generally use squared error loss as the metric for assessing forecast accuracy. However, as we show in subsequent sections, such a measure is questionable in many circumstances. In section 3.4.1, we consider the relevance of general cost functions, versus context-specific or 'real-world' cost functions, where for a particular problem there is a well-defined mapping between forecast errors and the cost of making those errors, which yields a natural measure for assessing forecast quality. We do not rule out the latter as being relevant in many instances, but in macroeconomics, general measures such as MSFEs, or their square roots (RMSFEs), have held sway. For scalar processes and 1-step forecasts, the concept of MSFE is unambiguous. For systems there are a number of measures based on the second-moment matrix of forecast errors that can be used. In practice, the trace of the MSFE matrix (TMSFE) is routinely calculated. There are a number of well-known problems in using MSFEs as a gauge of forecast accuracy. These are discussed in section 3.4.2.

In section 3.5, we present a critique of MSFEs in terms of their lack of invariance to non-singular, scale-preserving linear transforms, for a model class that is itself invariant to such transforms. It follows that mean absolute errors (MAEs: see Burns, 1986) are also not invariant either across isomorphic model representations, and hereafter are subsumed by the results on MSFEs. Such non-invariance implies that rankings across models and/or methods can vary by choosing alternative yet isomorphic representations of a given process. For instance, one approach or model can dominate all others for comparisons in the levels of a set of variables, yet lose to one of the others for differences, to a second for cointegrating vectors, and to a third for other linear combinations of the variables.

Section 3.5 begins with an analysis of the forms of admissible transformations. Two classes of non-singular, scale-preserving transforms are distinguished; $\mathbf{M}$ and $\mathbf{P}$ transforms. The lack of invariance of MSFEs to the $\mathbf{M}$ and $\mathbf{P}$ transforms of section 6.3 is illustrated with two examples in sections 3.5.1 and 3.5.3, one for scalar multi-step forecasts and one for forecasts from systems of equations. In section 3.5.4, a formal statement is given. The practical importance of the invariance failure is illustrated in section 6.8 where we present the results of a Monte Carlo study.

In section 3.6, we outline a generalized forecast-error second-moment (GFESM) criterion that is invariant to non-singular, scale-preserving linear transformations for all forecast horizons. The GFESM is the determinant of the forecast-error second-moment matrix pooled across all horizons. The properties of the GFESM are examined and the reasons for the inadequacy of other MSFE-based measures become apparent. Section 3.7 outlines the related statistical literature on predictive likelihood (see, e.g., Bjørnstad, 1990, for a survey).

3.2 Comparing outcomes and predictions

3.2.1 Cost functions and MSFEs

We begin by discussing cost functions as measures of forecast accuracy, although a more in-depth analysis will be postponed until section 3.4 and later. A generic criterion for measuring *ex post* forecast accuracy defined on the actual values of a series or outcomes (denoted by A_t) and the predicted values (P_t) can be written as:

$$\mathtt{I}\left(P_t, A_t\right). \tag{3.1}$$

The general ideas in this section do not require a precise formulation of the forecast origin and length, and we leave these unspecified. The optimal prediction based on (3.1) would then be that P_t for which $\mathtt{I}(\cdot)$ obtained an extremum. Contention (*i*) of Granger and Newbold (1973) (see section 3.1), suggests that (3.1) could be specialized to:

$$\mathtt{I}\left(P_t, A_t\right) = \mathtt{I}\left(A_t - P_t, A_t\right) = \mathtt{I}\left(e_t, A_t\right) = \mathtt{C}\left(e_t\right), \tag{3.2}$$

where:

$$e_t = A_t - P_t, \tag{3.3}$$

that is, the criterion assumes that costs are only a function of the forecast error e_t, and not of A_t and P_t separately. There are cases where this is inappropriate because $e_t > 0$ is costly when A_t is high, but not when it is low, and vice versa. If we take $\mathtt{C}(\cdot)$ to be a quadratic function, then we have a squared error criterion, so that averaging over a number of (squared) errors leads to the mean square forecast error (MSFE) criterion. The specialization of (3.2) to a quadratic function is largely due to mathematical tractability and reflects the pervasiveness of the least-squares principle in the econometrics literature. One justification for the apparent arbitrariness in the choice of quadratic costs in (3.2) is that large errors are proportionately more serious than small, and that, for many decisions, over- and under-prediction have similar costs. Granted symmetry, the precise functional form of $\mathsf{C}(\cdot)$ may not matter too much as the crucial property is then the monotonicity of $\mathsf{C}(\cdot)$ (see section 3.2.4). However, asymmetry often matters (sometimes inducing the opposite behaviour depending on sign, as in buying or selling equity), and judgements as to how much better one forecast is than another depend on the precise form of the cost function. Nonetheless, as a general criterion, least squares is often used for want of a readily superior alternative.

The minimum mean-square forecast-error (MMSFE) predictor minimizes:

$$\mathsf{E}\left[e_t^2\right] \tag{3.4}$$

with a sample counterpart:

$$\mathsf{MSFE}_h = H^{-1}\sum_{h=1}^{H} e_{T+h}^2 \tag{3.5}$$

where the summation is over forecast errors e_{T+h} from 1 through H steps ahead, commencing at time $T+1$. Alternatively, in a Monte Carlo setting, (3.4) would typically be evaluated by summing over replications. We demonstrated in section 2.7.2 that the conditional expectation, given all the available information, has the minimum MSFE, but noted that the converse will not necessarily hold, if, for example, each model uses only a subset of the relevant available information.

It is useful to consider some of the reasons for making the step from (3.1) to (3.2). Granger and Newbold argue that because A_t and P_t will have different time-series properties, a direct comparison of the two may not be very revealing. From the definition of (3.3):

$$\mathsf{V}\left[A_t\right] = \mathsf{V}\left[P_t\right] + \mathsf{V}\left[e_t\right] \tag{3.6}$$

assuming that the prediction and forecast error are uncorrelated, $\mathsf{E}[P_t e_t] = 0$. This will be the case in models such as:

$$y_t = \kappa + \rho y_{t-1} + v_t, \tag{3.7}$$

where $v_t \sim \mathsf{IN}[0, \sigma_v^2]$ is an innovation against $\mathcal{I}_{t-1}$ $[y_{t-j},\ j > 1]$ and where stationarity is assumed. Then $P_t \equiv \mathsf{E}[y_t|\mathcal{I}_{t-1}]$, that is, the conditional expectation of y_t given its history. In the absence of parameter uncertainty, and for 1-step ahead forecast, $\mathsf{E}[y_t|\mathcal{I}_{t-1}] = \kappa + \rho y_{t-1}$, so that the forecast error is just the underlying innovation disturbance term:

$$e_t = v_t. \tag{3.8}$$

Although these assumptions are overly restrictive, and unlikely to be met in practice, we can usually design models to have the property that $\mathsf{E}[P_t e_t] \simeq 0$. Then, from (3.6), the variance of the predictor will be less than the variance of the series: the relationship between the two depends on the variance of the underlying disturbance term (σ_v^2 in (3.7)). Since σ_v^2 is typically unknown, forecast-accuracy assessments based on the time-series properties of the actual and predicted series are likely to be uninformative in general. Thus, Granger and Newbold favour evaluation techniques based on the time-series properties of the forecast-error series instead.

The story remains essentially the same if we allow for parameter uncertainty, so that $P_{T+1} = \widehat{\kappa} + \widehat{\rho} y_T$, where $\widehat{}$ denotes an estimate based on $\mathcal{I}_T$. In that case, the prediction and the forecast error will no longer be exactly uncorrelated, but related by an effect of order T^{-1}. Taking the zero-mean case for simplicity ($\kappa = 0$, so $\mathsf{E}[y_T] = 0$):

$$\mathsf{E}\left[e_{T+1} P_{T+1}\right] = \mathsf{E}\left[\left(\rho - \widehat{\rho}\right) \widehat{\rho} y_T^2\right] + \mathsf{E}\left[\widehat{\rho} y_T v_{T+1}\right]. \tag{3.9}$$

The last term is zero since v_{T+1} is an innovation with respect to y_T. Neglecting the slight dependence of $\widehat{\rho}$ on y_T, taking expectations conditional on y_T, and approximating $\mathsf{E}[\widehat{\rho}] = \rho - 2\rho/T$ (see White, 1961), the first term is:

$$\begin{aligned} \mathsf{E}\left[\left(\rho - \widehat{\rho}\right) \widehat{\rho} y_T^2 \mid y_T\right] &= \left(\rho \mathsf{E}\left[\widehat{\rho}\right] - \mathsf{E}\left[\widehat{\rho}^2\right]\right) y_T^2 \\ &\simeq \left(\frac{2\rho^2}{T} - \mathsf{V}\left[\widehat{\rho}\right]\right) y_T^2 \\ &\simeq -T^{-1}\left(1 - 3\rho^2\right) y_T^2 \end{aligned} \tag{3.10}$$

which is of order T^{-1}. The forecast-error variance remains a function of the unknown quantity σ_v^2, since:

$$e_{T+1} = \left(\rho - \widehat{\rho}\right) y_T + v_{T+1} \tag{3.11}$$

and so (unconditionally), taking $\mathsf{E}[e_{T+1}] = 0$ (see chapter 5):

$$\begin{aligned} \mathsf{V}\left[e_{T+1}\right] &= \mathsf{V}\left[\widehat{\rho}\right] \mathsf{V}\left[y_T\right] + \mathsf{V}\left[v_{T+1}\right] \\ &\simeq T^{-1}\left(1 - \rho^2\right) \frac{\sigma_v^2}{\left(1 - \rho^2\right)} + \sigma_v^2 \\ &= \sigma_v^2\left(1 + T^{-1}\right), \end{aligned} \tag{3.12}$$

where we have again ignored the slight inter-dependence between $(\rho - \widehat{\rho})$ and y_T. To a first approximation, therefore, the known-parameter situation points up the main issues.

3.2.2 Forecast rationality

There are a number of notions of rationality of forecasts. These include those of unbiasedness and efficiency, and are examples of forecast-evaluation criteria based on the relationship between the predictions and outcomes. 'Weak' rationality is often used to refer to the consistency of forecasts in the sense that forecasters are not systematically mistaken in their forecasts. This property can be tested from the realizations and forecasts of the series in question alone, without recourse to outside information. 'Strong' rationality, or efficiency, requires that the forecast errors are uncorrelated with other series or information available at the time the forecasts were made. There have been many studies of the rationality of macroeconomic forecasts, of survey-based predictions etc., including Mincer and Zarnowitz (1969), Figlewski and Wachtel (1981), Zarnowitz (1985) and Keane and Runkle (1990).

Tests of unbiasedness are often based on a regression equation of the form:

$$A_{T+h} = \alpha + \beta P_{T+h|T} + \epsilon_{T+h} \tag{3.13}$$

where $P_{T+h|T}$ is the h-step ahead forecast of A_{T+h} made at period T. If we consider the case where h is assumed fixed, and T varies, then the notational simplification of replacing $P_{T+h|T}$ by P_{T+h} should not cause any confusion. Suppose that time runs from $T+1-h$ to $T+H-h$, and that a forecast is made at each value of t, giving a sample of dimension H. Notice that for $h > 1$, the forecast horizon will exceed the sampling frequency (assumed to be 1), so that forecasts overlap in the sense that they are made before knowing the error in the previous forecast. Thus, rationality does not rule out serial correlation in the error process ϵ_{T+h} of a moving average of order $h-1$. While the coefficient estimates obtained from ordinary least squares (OLS) on (3.13) will remain unbiased, the estimate of the covariance matrix of the parameter estimates (necessary for tests of the significance of the parameters in (3.13)) will be inconsistent. This is typically dealt with by using the Hansen and Hodrick (1980) correction (see, for example, Brown and Maital, 1981).

The joint null hypothesis $\alpha = 0$ and $\beta = 1$ entails unbiasedness. From (3.13):

$$\mathsf{E}\left[A_{T+h}\right] = \alpha + \beta \mathsf{E}\left[P_{T+h}\right], \tag{3.14}$$

so the requirement for unbiasedness is $\mathsf{E}[A_{T+h} - P_{T+h}] = 0$. As noted recently by Holden and Peel (1990), $\alpha = 0$ and $\beta = 1$ is a sufficient, but not a necessary, condition for unbiasedness, since (3.14) is satisfied more generally by:

$$\alpha = (1-\beta)\,\mathsf{E}\left[P_{T+h}\right]. \tag{3.15}$$

They suggest testing unbiasedness via a test of $\tau = 0$ in the regression:

$$A_{T+h} - P_{T+h} = \tau + \epsilon_{T+h}. \tag{3.16}$$

If unbiasedness is not rejected, then this is typically formulated as part of the maintained hypothesis, and various tests of the forecast error being an innovation (against the past of the process, for example), can be conducted. In addition, we can construct more stringent tests of efficiency by broadening the information set to include any variables that would have been available to the forecaster at period T. The latter are often termed orthogonality tests:

$$A_{T+h} - P_{T+h} = \boldsymbol{\gamma}'\mathbf{z}_T + \epsilon_{T+h}, \tag{3.17}$$

where $\mathbf{z}_T$ is the designated vector of variables known at period T.

Although a test of the joint hypothesis $\alpha = 0$ and $\beta = 1$ is often described as a test of unbiasedness, it can also be viewed as a test of efficiency, in the sense of checking that forecasts and their errors are uncorrelated. If there is a systematic relationship between the two, then this could be exploited to help predict future errors, and could be used to adjust the forecast-generating mechanism accordingly. Mincer and Zarnowitz (1969) used the concept of efficiency in this sense. They define forecast efficiency as the condition that $\beta = 1$ in the OLS regression equation (3.13), so that the residual variance in the regression is equal to the variance of the forecast error. To see this, reparameterize (3.13) as:

$$e_{T+h} = A_{T+h} - P_{T+h} = \alpha + (\beta - 1) P_{T+h} + \epsilon_{T+h}, \tag{3.18}$$

then:

$$\mathsf{V}[e_{T+h}] = (\beta - 1)^2 \mathsf{V}[P_{T+h}] + \mathsf{V}[\epsilon_{T+h}] + 2(\beta - 1)\mathsf{C}[P_{T+h}, \epsilon_{T+h}] \tag{3.19}$$

(where $\mathsf{C}[\cdot, \cdot]$ denotes covariance), so that $\beta = 1$ implies $\mathsf{V}[e_{T+h}] = \mathsf{V}[\epsilon_{T+h}]$ whatever the value of α. If $\alpha = 0$, as well as $\beta = 1$, then:

$$\mathsf{MSFE} = \mathsf{E}\left[e_{T+h}^2\right] = \mathsf{V}[e_{T+h}] = \mathsf{V}[\epsilon_{T+h}].$$

Under these conditions, the forecast error and predictor are uncorrelated:

$$\mathsf{E}[P_{T+h}e_{T+h}] = \alpha\mathsf{E}[P_{T+h}] + (\beta - 1)\mathsf{E}\left[P_{T+h}^2\right] + \mathsf{E}[P_{T+h}\epsilon_{T+h}] = 0.$$

The properties of unbiasedness and efficiency are often presented as minimum requirements for optimal or rational forecasts. However, the identification of the unbiasedness property with optimality requires that the loss function is symmetric, as in the case of quadratic costs (see Zellner, 1986, and the discussion in section 4.9).

When the data are non-stationary, integrated series, then a natural further requirement of the relationship between the actual and predicted series is that they are cointegrated. Otherwise the forecast error would have an unbounded variance. Again, this is only a necessary requirement, since if $A_{T+h} \sim \mathsf{I}(1)$ and is cointegrated with P_{T+h}, $A_{T+h} - P_{T+h} \sim \mathsf{I}(0)$, then so is any predictor $P_{T+h}^* = P_{T+h} + w_{T+h}$ where $w_{T+h} \sim \mathsf{I}(0)$.

Many studies have used tests of this sort to evaluate forecast performance. One of the earliest is Mincer and Zarnowitz (1969), who give the results of regressions of the form of (3.13) for several sets of forecasts of various economic series, for both levels (table 1.1, pp.12 and 13) and changes (table 1.2, pp.16 and 17). In most cases, they report that for the levels the joint hypothesis of ($\alpha = 0$ and $\beta = 1$) is rejected, preponderantly due $\alpha \neq 0$, and that although β is less than one, it is generally close to unity. The modern theory of regressions involving $\mathsf{I}(1)$ processes (see, *inter alia*, Banerjee, Dolado, Galbraith and Hendry, 1993) suggests that such levels regressions should be re-examined to see if there is evidence that the variables are integrated yet the residuals remain $\mathsf{I}(0)$.

A contemporary application of regression analysis of outturns and forecasts is Pain and Britton (1992), who undertake a thorough analysis of forecasts from the NIESR model over the period 1968 to 1991. They test for $\alpha = 0$ and $\beta = 1$ in (3.13), and for $\gamma = \mathbf{0}$ in (3.17) for various sets of variables $\mathbf{z}_T$. For example, they consider previous forecast errors known at the time the forecast was made, such as past values of the process, and 'outside information' – business survey measures and housing and financial market variables. They also run variants of some of these regressions, including dummy variables to allow for the effects of unanticipated exogenous shocks which could not realistically have been foreseen in advance (e.g., strikes, oil-price shocks), and dummy variables to test whether forecast performance has changed over time. Pain and Britton report evidence of significant correlations between successive forecast errors and of correlations between forecast errors and outside information, over the more recent period.

Granger and Newbold (1973) note a problem with the Mincer and Zarnowitz (1969) notion of efficiency, which arises for an integrated series. Suppose, for example, that the DGP is given by (3.7) with $\kappa = 0$ and $\rho = 1$, so that y_t is a random walk. Then, asymptotically at least, all of the forecast series given by $\mathsf{E}[y_t|\mathcal{I}_{t-h}] = y_{t-h}$, for $h > 1$, will satisfy the conditions for forecast efficiency. In the regression corresponding to (3.13), we have:

$$y_{T+h} = \alpha + \beta y_{T+h-j} + \epsilon_{T+h},$$

where:

$$y_{T+h} = y_{T+h-j} + \sum_{s=0}^{j} v_{T+h-s} \cdot$$

so that:

$$y_{T+h-j} = \alpha + \beta y_{T+h-j} + \left(\epsilon_{T+h} - \sum_{s=0}^{j} v_{T+h-s} \right)$$

and despite the autocorrelation in the error term, the orders of integration of the variables ensure that $\widehat{\beta} \to 1$ asymptotically. It is also the case that y_{T+h} and the predictor series y_{T+h-j} are cointegrated for all finite j. Thus, comparisons of outturns and predictions may not identify the MMSFE predictor of y_{T+h} as y_{T+h-1} (i.e., $j = 1$). Comparing MSFEs could indicate a worse performance for some values $j > 1$.

3.2.3 Fixed-event forecasts

So far, we have discussed ways of assessing the rationality of forecasts where h is fixed and T changes. Nordhaus (1987) suggests analysing fixed-event forecasts as an alternative to these rolling-event forecasts, where we consider the properties of forecasts of a given event (say, A_t at $t = \tau$) made at a variety of different times (variable h). Formally, the forecasts are denoted by $P_{\tau|\tau-h}$. Within this framework, Nordhaus defines a notion of efficiency which measures the extent to which information is incorporated into forecasts, and is testable from the forecast revisions. Strong efficiency requires that all available information is incorporated into the forecast, paralleling the strong form of rational expectations, whereby agents are assumed to have access to all the necessary information, including knowledge of the structure of the economy. The more useful notion in practice is that of weak efficiency, which requires that forecasts efficiently incorporate information from past forecasts. To see how this works, notice that we can decompose a fixed-event forecast error into the sum of all the revisions that have been made to the forecasts of that event over time:

$$e_{\tau|\tau-h} = P_{\tau|\tau-h} - A_\tau = v_{\tau|\tau-h+1} + \cdots + v_{\tau|\tau},$$

where $v_{\tau|j}$ defines the forecast revision from period $j-1$ to period j, that is:

$$v_{\tau|j} = P_{\tau|j-1} - P_{\tau|j}, \quad \text{and} \quad P_{\tau|\tau} \equiv A_\tau.$$

Then weak efficiency implies that:

(1) the forecast error at $\tau - h$ is independent of all forecast revisions up to $\tau - h$:

$$\mathsf{E}\left[e_{\tau|\tau-h} \mid v_{\tau|\tau-h}, \ldots, v_{\tau|0}\right] = 0, \quad \text{all } \tau - h;$$

(2) the forecast revision at $\tau - h$ is independent of all revisions up to $\tau - h - 1$:

$$\mathsf{E}\left[v_{\tau|\tau-h} \mid v_{\tau|\tau-h-1}, \ldots, v_{\tau|0}\right] = 0, \quad \text{all } \tau - h.$$

This implies that forecast revisions should be an innovation series, $P_{\tau|j-1} - P_{\tau|j} = -\varepsilon_j$, where $\varepsilon_j \sim \mathsf{ID}(0, \sigma_j^2)$, say. Thus, forecasts should follow a (possibly heteroscedastic) random walk:

$$P_{\tau|j} = \sum_{s=0}^{j} \varepsilon_s.$$

If $P_{\tau|j}$ is a stationary first-order autoregressive process, say, then this implies that forecast revisions are in part predictable from past revisions, and thus are not weakly efficient. One test for weak efficiency is then to calculate the first-order autoregressive coefficient of revisions and test whether it differs significantly from zero. Nordhaus finds evidence of serial correlation in forecast revisions for nearly all the forecasts he examines, which include macroeconomic forecasts. Thus forecasts typically do not have the 'ragged' property of the random walk, but are too smooth. Nordhaus speculates that this could be due to: the bureaucratic nature of forecast agencies that need to achieve a consensus view, so that there is a degree of inertia in revising forecasts; forecasts are more credible and consumers happier if forecasts change only slowly; and 'a tilt toward wishing to hold on to old notions that are relatively familiar rather than to adjust to surprises' (p.673).

Clements (1995) address the question of whether intercept corrections (discussed in detail in chapter 8) are used by macro-forecasters to 'smooth' revisions to purely model-based forecasts for any number of these reasons. Clements (1995) calculates the first-order serial correlation coefficient for series of revisions to both judgemental forecasts (which incorporate 'discretionary' intercept corrections) and mechanical forecasts. The forecasts are monthly forecasts of the rate of inflation (Δp), output (y) and output growth (Δy) made by a forecasting group for three target dates, 1991, 1992 and 1993. Table 3.1 reports t-tests of no first-order autocorrelation in revisions, and p-values of the F-test of the joint insignificance of all the regressors in (3.20) (other than the constant):

$$v_{\tau|j} = \alpha_0 + \alpha_1 j + \sum_{s=1}^{4} \alpha_{s+1} v_{\tau|j-s} + \nu_j, \tag{3.20}$$

which allows for more general forms of serial correlation in revisions. The regression is over j for a given τ. Significance at the 5 percent level and 1 percent levels are denoted by * and **, respectively, where the t-test is two-sided. The mechanical forecasts are denoted by MF4 and MF8 (depending on what is thought to constitute a neutral equation error setting over the future), and the actual, judgemental forecasts by AF.

Table 3.1 Tests of serial correlation in forecast revisions

	Δy_{91}	y_{91}	Δp_{91}	Δy_{92}	y_{92}	Δp_{92}	Δy_{93}	y_{93}	Δp_{93}
					AF				
t	0.15	0.21	-1.02	0.97	0.84	-0.71	-1.53	-0.12	-1.16
F	0.23	0.87	0.72	0.98	0.51	0.84	0.52	0.58	0.16
					MF8				
t	-0.82	-0.16	-3.12**	0.89	0.20	-3.10**	-2.34*	-0.14	-3.52**
F	0.10	0.24	0.01*	0.71	0.42	0.00**	0.25	0.24	0.00**
					MF4				
t	-0.40	-0.17	-1.05	0.90	0.09	-1.99	-2.04	-0.11	-1.64
F	0.01**	0.26	0.03*	0.77	0.30	0.01**	0.40	0.26	0.04*

There is no evidence of significant positive first-order serial correlation in the revisions for either the judgemental or mechanical forecasts. In this example, forecast revisions are not excessively smooth in the Nordhaus sense. However, there is evidence of negative first-order serial correlation in the mechanical forecasts of inflation, particularly for MF8. This is also apparent for MF4, but in that case the serial correlation seems to be of a higher order (judging by the F-tests). In contrast, this correlation is a good deal less marked when the residuals are set judgementally (AF). A possible explanation for negative correlation in series of revisions is given in Clements (1997).

Clements (1997) also considers the scope for pooling fixed-event forecasts across 'events' to deliver more powerful tests of the weak-efficiency hypothesis, as well as exploring the relationship between weak efficiency and rationality when loss functions are asymmetric and prediction error variances are time varying (as in section 4.9). The weak-efficiency and forecast-accuracy tests are distinct. As Nordhaus (1987, p.673) states: 'A baboon could generate a series of weakly efficient forecasts by simply wiring himself to a random-number generator, but such a series of forecasts would be completely useless.'

Finally, is there any reason to suppose that fixed-event forecast tests may be more powerful than rolling-event tests? Nordhaus suggests that under some circumstances the former may be able to detect the smoothing of forecasts following the arrival of new information, but that this would not be apparent from the more traditional approach.

As mentioned in the introduction to this chapter, although there is considerable interest in the efficiency of forecasts, these concepts of rationality may not be particularly useful in practice. Such criteria constitute desirable properties for any forecast to possess (assuming a symmetric loss function), but are typically not sufficient, as the example from Granger and Newbold (1973) illustrates. Notions of rationality are unlikely of themselves to be a good way of determining which forecasts are useful. Faced with a number of forecasts, the decision-maker requires some way of choosing between them (combination is assumed not to be an option for the moment, but is evaluated in chapter 10). The tests for efficiency and unbiasedness discussed above may be too slack in that they are satisfied by more than one predictor, or conversely, too stringent given the typical non-optimality of most forecasts, stemming from the complexity of economic relationships, and the open-ended number of variables that could conceivably affect the variable(s) of interest. Such criteria may, therefore, be of limited value as means of forecast selection leading to a plethora of forecasts, or none at all, if only these criteria are used. Moreover, deliberately smoothed forecasts would always be rejected.

One solution may be to compare the model's forecast performance against how it fared over the past (or estimation sample period). This idea underlies the formal tests of predictive accuracy which compare an estimate of the forecast-error variance obtained from the past residuals with the actual mean-squared error of the forecast (see, *inter alia*, Chow, 1960, Christ, 1966 and Hendry, 1974, 1979b). This literature is reviewed in section 13.2. Salmon and Wallis (1982) make the point that this will not provide an absolute measure of predictive accuracy, but only of how well the model performs in the future relative to the past. Salmon and Wallis argue that the absence of absolute standards of forecast performance suggests evaluating forecasts against those produced by other means, including by other models. If viewed as part of a progressive research strategy that retains the best model at each stage, then we have a resolution to the worry of having too many or too few models. We take up these ideas in section 3.3.

3.2.4 MSFE decompositions and derived measures

Granger and Newbold (1973) use the Theil (1961) inequality coefficient U_1 to demonstrate the dangers involved in using as a means of ranking forecasts any measure that is not a monotonic function of MSFE. The U_1 statistic is defined as:

$$U_1 = \frac{\mathsf{MSFE}^{\frac{1}{2}}}{\left(H^{-1}\sum A_{T+h}^2\right)^{\frac{1}{2}} + \left(H^{-1}\sum P_{T+h}^2\right)^{\frac{1}{2}}}. \tag{3.21}$$

Ash and Smyth (1973, p.25) reference five studies from the 1960s that use U_1. When $e_{T+h} = 0$ for all t, $U_1 = 0$, but it is not monotonic in e_{T+h} due to the term in the predictor series in the denominator. Granger and Newbold show that in the first-order autoregressive process given by (3.7) (with $\kappa = 0$), then the predictor that minimizes (3.21) amongst the class given by:

$$P_{T+h} = \beta y_{T+h-1} \tag{3.22}$$

has $\beta = 1$, and so is not the conditional expectation, $\beta = \rho$. Hence, (3.21) fails to select the optimum predictor. Since $\mathsf{V}[P_{T+h}] = \beta^2\mathsf{V}[y_{T+h-1}]$ is maximized by $\beta = 1$ for $0 \leq \beta \leq 1$, then the criterion (3.21) is satisfied by maximizing the variance of the predictor series. This is perhaps unsurprising given that such a term appears in the denominator of (3.21). Theil was aware that U_1 was not uniquely determined by MSFE, and in later work favoured:

$$U_2 = \frac{\mathsf{MSFE}^{\frac{1}{2}}}{\left(H^{-1}\sum A_{T+h}^2\right)^{\frac{1}{2}}}. \tag{3.23}$$

Ash and Smyth (1973, p.24) again provide a number of references attesting to the popularity of this statistic in the 1960s. U_2 is sometimes known as the standardized root mean-squared error. For ranking alternative forecasts of the same variable, the standardization is unimportant. The idea is to facilitate comparisons between different variables by making some allowance for the underlying variability in the series. Highly variable series will be intrinsically hard to predict relative to those which change little.

We can decompose (3.4) as:

$$\mathsf{MSFE} = \mathsf{E}\left[e_{T+h}^2\right] = \left(\mu_a - \mu_p\right)^2 + \sigma_a^2 + \sigma_p^2 - 2\mathsf{r}\sigma_a\sigma_p \tag{3.24}$$

to bring out the relationship between the MSFE criterion and the correlation between A_{T+h} and P_{T+h}. The notation uses μs to denote means and σs standard deviations. r is the correlation between the actual and predicted (so that $\mathsf{r}\sigma_a\sigma_p$ is the covariance).

Then, the characteristics of the minimum MSFE predictor are given by the solution of the first-order conditions:

$$\frac{\partial \mathsf{MSFE}}{\partial \mu_p} = -2\left(\mu_a - \mu_p\right) = 0, \tag{3.25}$$

$$\frac{\partial \mathsf{MSFE}}{\partial \sigma_p} = 2\left(\sigma_p - \mathsf{r}\sigma_a\right) = 0, \tag{3.26}$$

$$\frac{\partial \mathsf{MSFE}}{\partial \mathsf{r}} = -2\sigma_a\sigma_p = 0. \tag{3.27}$$

The second-order conditions for a minimum are satisfied by the first two conditions, but not by the last. Thus (3.24) will be minimized by $\mu_a = \mu_p$ and $\sigma_p = \mathsf{r}\sigma_a$. Substituting these into (3.24) we obtain:

$$\mathsf{MSFE}_{\rfloor\,\mathrm{min}} = \sigma_p^2\left(\frac{1}{\mathsf{r}^2} - 1\right) \tag{3.28}$$

which is minimized by maximizing r subject to (3.26) holding. Only when the predictor series is perfectly correlated with the actual series ($\mathsf{r} = 1$) should the standard deviations of the two series be equal.

Granger and Newbold's concerns about the sufficiency of a high correlation between predicted and actual as an indicator of forecast adequacy was partly based on the then common practice of presenting graphs depicting the actual and predicted values of the levels of economic time series as a means of establishing forecast accuracy. They were aware that, for random walks, such graphs could be very flattering, and quote Box and Newbold (1971) who showed this in the case of a graph of two independent random walks. They suggest that it would be far more informative to portray actual and predicted changes. As we show in section 3.5, the choice of levels versus differences is not only important in the graphical display of forecast accuracy and in the calculation of correlations between series, but is a problem that affects the usefulness of MSFE-based criteria. Ash and Smyth (1973, p.15) were also aware that the non-stationarity of economic time series could yield misleading indications of forecast accuracy. They argued that growth in series over time would cause forecast errors to be 'swamped by trend factors' (p.15), and analysed series in terms of percentage changes. This prescription is close to the present day practice of taking the first differences of the natural logarithms of economic time series.

Mirroring the decomposition of the population MSFE in (3.24), Theil (1961) proposed two sample counterparts, which he believed had useful interpretations:

$$\mathsf{MSFE} = H^{-1}\sum e_{T+h}^2 = \left(\bar{P} - \bar{A}\right)^2 + \left(S_p - S_a\right)^2 + 2\left(1 - r\right)S_pS_a, \tag{3.29}$$

$$\mathsf{MSFE} = H^{-1}\sum e_{T+h}^2 = \left(\bar{P} - \bar{A}\right)^2 + \left(S_p - rS_a\right)^2 + \left(1 - r^2\right)S_a^2, \tag{3.30}$$

where $^{-}$ denotes a sample mean, S a sample standard deviation and r is the sample correlation coefficient. In each case, both sides of the equation are divided by the left-hand side (MSFE) so that the three components on the right sum to one. The quantities on the right-hand sides of (3.29) and (3.30) have been used in forecast evaluation exercises (for example, Platt, 1971). Granger and Newbold question the usefulness of the first decomposition. For a model such as (3.7) they show that for the optimal predictor (the conditional expectation), the last two terms can take any values depending upon the DGP (here, the value of ρ) subject only to some loose restrictions (see Granger and Newbold, 1973, p.45). Thus, it is difficult to see how these two terms can be amenable to any general interpretation.

The second decomposition is more useful. The main reason is that the formulation of the last two terms implies that the second should now tend to zero (along with the first) for a good forecast, leaving the third term to approach unity after scaling.

3.3 Rival forecasts

Given the problems inherent in adopting an absolutist approach to assessing forecast accuracy, the natural alternative is to take as a benchmark the performance of rival models, assessed in an appropriate metric. In some instances, appropriate rival models may not exist, suggesting a potential role for them specifically as a means of forecast evaluation. In the literature, naive time series models or no-change predictors have been popular candidates for this task. Such rivals may not offer a sufficiently stringent challenge if they are based on restricted information sets and only poorly characterize the process of interest. This sentiment is echoed by Granger and Newbold (1986, p.266), 'the evaluation criteria employed should be as demanding as possible since the object ought to be self-criticism rather than self-congratulation'. The implication in general processes subject to structural breaks is unclear, but in stationary series, autoregressive-distributed lag models or VARs should be preferred over univariate time-series models.

The most naive forecast that has been used for evaluation purposes is the 'no-change rule' of Theil (1966). If the series to be forecast is in changes, then $P_{T+h} = 0$, and the ratio of the MSFE of the model under evaluation to the naive model is given by U_2 in (3.23). Subsequently Dhrymes *et al.* (1972) proposed Box–Jenkins models (see Box and Jenkins, 1976) as the best available univariate extrapolative model.

Mincer and Zarnowitz (1969) suggest defining relative efficiency (RE) as the ratio of the MSFEs of the model under consideration and the rival model. The type of rival model that they favour is a 'benchmark' model, which is basically extrapolative in nature in that it is based on the variable's own past history. They value the simplicity and accessibility of such alternatives. There are two problems with this. First, the RE criterion will indicate which of the two predictors is to be preferred (on the MSFE criterion) but that is all: specifically, it will not indicate whether the inferior predictor contains useful information over and above that contained in the superior one which could be exploited to do better still. Secondly, using a purely extrapolative rival may lead to some (poor) models being rejected, but success will not result in much credence being attached to the model in question. When adequate dynamic specification is a model-building design criterion, such a test may be regarded as not sufficiently stringent. However, when there are structural breaks, such results are thrown into doubt as some extrapolative devices are robust to certain forms of break: see, e.g., Hendry and Doornik (1997).

In section 10.3.2, we will relate the notion of conditional efficiency (CE), proposed by Granger and Newbold, to the idea of forecast encompassing. This can be viewed as a measure of whether there is additional information in a rival model, and is defined by:

$$\mathsf{CE}\left(P_1 \mid P_2\right) = \frac{\mathsf{V}\left[e_{c,T+h}\right]}{\mathsf{V}\left[e_{1,T+h}\right]}, \tag{3.31}$$

where $e_{c,T+h}$ is the forecast error from a predictor formed as a linear combination of two individual predictors, and written as in (3.31) when $\mathsf{V}[e_{1,T+h}] \leq \mathsf{V}[e_{2,T+h}]$. Equation (3.31) is the population measure, with a sample counterpart based on the estimated second moments of the relevant quantities. If $\mathsf{CE} = 1$ then there is no extra information in the pair of models additional to that encapsulated in model 1.

A somewhat different criticism of the use of naive models for evaluating forecasts from econometric models is due to Salmon and Wallis (1982). Rather than not being sufficiently demanding, Salmon and Wallis claim that naive models are not independent tests of econometric models. They show that structural econometric models can generally be approximated by finite-order ARMA models. Although a structural econometric model implies a particular ARMA model, for comparison purposes these restrictions on the ARMA model typically are not applied, and the specification of the ARMA model is data based. Salmon and Wallis view such comparisons as 'a useful diagnostic device during model-building' rather than being 'an independent post-construction check on an econometric model' (p.230). Nerlove (1982) notes in commenting on Salmon and Wallis that a well-specified ARMA model will typically be much more parsimonious in terms of lag structure than that implied by an econometric model, so ARMA models may still serve as a useful check.

3.4 MSFEs

3.4.1 General and context-specific loss functions

In section 3.5, we provide a critique of MSFE-based measures which stresses their lack of invariance to non-singular, scale-preserving linear transformations. A possible counter to that critique is that in specific empirical applications there is a genuine difference between predicting the levels of a series, compared to (say) the changes, so that it does not matter whether the rankings depend on which is considered. If for some reason, an investigator is interested only in predicting future levels of a series, then it is immaterial that a comparison of forecast accuracy for changes may lead to a different ranking, and West (1993) argues persuasively that when there is a natural measure of forecast quality, the fact that other measures give different rankings is irrelevant.

In general, we doubt the availability of such unique natural measures in much macroeconomic forecasting, and this appears to be borne out by empirical practice, where MSFEs hold sway. Granger and Newbold (1973, p.38) remarked that: 'We must admit that the use of the least squares principle is dictated chiefly by convenience. However, in reality there may not exist any clearly superior alternative' due to the difficulties in practice of precisely costing different forecast errors. Such a view is re-affirmed by Granger (1993, p.651): 'real-world cost functions are rarely available'.

If MSFEs have been reported because of the absence of natural measures, specifically defined over errors in predicting levels, for instance, then we surmise that the investigator is ambivalent about which transform to report. It is then surely a matter of concern that different transforms can yield different results. Monte Carlo studies of alternative methods of forecasting, which are unconnected with any specific empirical application, are a case in point. There are many Monte Carlo studies of forecasting, using various transformations (levels, differentials, differences, etc.) but with few caveats about the results being dependent on the specific transform adopted. Any generality that is claimed for the results as a guide to method selection is suspect. Reporting results for a range of potentially interesting loss functions would increase consumption costs by providing a considerable amount of information (which might still not satisfy every potential consumer). Such considerations add up to a strong *prima facie* case for invariant criteria, such as that outlined in section 3.6.

3.4.2 MSFE-based measures

A number of different MSFE-based measures can be derived from the second-moment matrix of forecast errors. In this section, we assume that all the processes under analysis are weakly stationary and have finite unconditional moments of at least second order. Then following from the definition in equation (3.4), we have that the mean-square forecast error from a model of a univariate process $\{y_t\}$ for a time $T+h$ is:

$$\mathsf{E}\left[(y_{T+h} - \widehat{y}_{T+h})^2\right] = \mathsf{E}\left[e^2_{T+h}\right] = \mathsf{MSFE}_h, \tag{3.32}$$

where $\widehat{y}_{T+h}$ is the h-step ahead forecast using information available at time T, and $e_{T+h} = y_{T+h} - \widehat{y}_{T+h}$ is the forecast error. The MSFE combines the squared bias in forecast errors with the forecast-error variance, namely:

$$\begin{aligned}\mathsf{E}\left[e^2_{T+h}\right] &= \left(\mathsf{E}\left[e_{T+h}\right]\right)^2 + \mathsf{E}\left[\left(e_{T+h} - \mathsf{E}\left[e_{T+h}\right]\right)^2\right] && (3.33)\\ &= \left(\mathsf{E}\left[y_{T+h} - \widehat{y}_{T+h}\right]\right)^2 + \mathsf{V}\left[e_{T+h}\right]. && (3.34)\end{aligned}$$

In a multivariate setting, the forecast error is denoted by the vector $\mathbf{e}_{T+h}$, and the MSFE matrix is $\mathsf{E}[\mathbf{e}_{T+h}\mathbf{e}'_{T+h}] = \mathbf{V}_h$ for all h. A commonly used approach is to measure system forecast accuracy using the trace of this matrix. Thus, the h-step ahead trace MSFE is trace$(\mathbf{V}_h)$, denoted TMSFE_h. However, other possibilities arise, such as using the determinant of $\mathbf{V}_h$, or, as in Granger and Newbold (1977, p.228), for example, choosing the method or model for which $\mathbf{d}'\mathbf{V}_h\mathbf{d}$ is the smallest for every non-zero vector $\mathbf{d}$. We denote this last MSFE matrix criterion by MSFEM.

MSFE-based measures have been criticized on a number of grounds. For example, MMSFE is neither necessary nor sufficient for a model to have constant parameters, nor provide accurate forecasts (Ericsson, 1992), both of which one might deem vital concerns for a model to be used in policy. Further, in scalar processes, 1-step MMSFE is not sufficient to ensure forecast encompassing, although it is necessary (see the discussion of forecast encompassing in section 10.3), so that encompassing ensures MMSFE: see Ericsson (1992) and Lu and Mizon (1991) who also discuss the relative merits of, and relations between, forecast-error encompassing test statistics and parameter constancy tests. In the next section, we focus on the non-invariance of MSFE-based measures to linear transformations. In the section after that (section 3.6), we look at a measure that offers a resolution to the non-invariance problem, but note that other problems still remain in ranking models for forecasting. For example, there may be no unambiguous ranking across models:

(1) if either no one model is uniformly better than the others given a single measure;
(2) or one model dominates on one measure, another on a second measure, etc.;
(3) or because dominance may alter with the forecast horizon;
(4) or because dominance may alter with the choice of variable.

We illustrate the impact of the forecast horizon for model choice in section 3.6.

3.5 Lack of invariance of MSFE-based measures

In section 6.3, we formalize the class of isomorphic linear systems and thereby define the class of transformations to which linear models are invariant. Sections 3.5.1 and 3.5.3 provide two examples of the lack of invariance of MSFEs: for a scalar process and in a systems context. The first example allows us to distinguish two distinct ideas concerning the applicability of MSFEs for comparative purposes:

(1) does the measure allow comparisons between different but isomorphic representations of the same system?;
(2) does the outcome of a comparison depend on which representation is selected?

The answers are shown to be 'no' and 'yes', respectively. We then formally state some results concerning the (lack of) invariance of the various MSFE-based measures outlined in section 3.5.4 to the classes of transformation described in section 6.3.

3.5.1 Comparisons using MSFEs for scalar multi-step dynamic forecasts

In the following example, we first show that multi-step MSFEs do not allow comparisons between different but isomorphic representations of the same system, a point which is recognized in the literature (e.g., Granger and Newbold, 1986, p.285). Perhaps more surprisingly, we also show that a common basis for comparison is not sufficient to prevent rank switches.

Consider the stationary first-order autoregression:

$$y_t = \rho y_{t-1} + u_t, \tag{3.35}$$

where $u_t \sim \mathsf{IN}[0, \sigma_u^2]$, $|\rho| < 1$, and $y_0 \sim \mathsf{N}[0, \sigma_u^2/(1-\rho^2)]$. When the parameters are known, $\mathsf{E}[y_{T+1}|y_T] = \widehat{y}_{T+1} = \rho y_T$, so the MSFE for the conditional 1-step forecast is:

$$\mathsf{E}\left[\left(y_{T+1} - \widehat{y}_{T+1}\right)^2 \mid y_T\right] = \mathsf{E}\left[u_{T+1}^2\right] = \sigma_u^2. \tag{3.36}$$

If, instead, the change $\Delta y_t = y_t - y_{t-1}$ is to be forecast using $\widehat{\Delta y}_{T+1} = (\rho - 1)y_T$, then:

$$\mathsf{E}\left[\left(\Delta y_{T+1} - \widehat{\Delta y}_{T+1}\right)^2 \mid y_T\right] = \mathsf{E}\left[u_{T+1}^2\right] = \sigma_u^2 \tag{3.37}$$

so the same MSFE results for conditional 1-step forecasts of levels and changes. However, if a two-period (or more distant) forecast is desired, we have:

$$y_{T+2} = \rho y_{T+1} + u_{T+2} = \rho^2 y_T + u_{T+2} + \rho u_{T+1}. \tag{3.38}$$

Using $\mathsf{E}[y_{T+2}|y_T] = \widehat{y}_{T+2} = \rho^2 y_T$, the MSFE is:

$$\mathsf{E}\left[\left(y_{T+2} - \widehat{y}_{T+2}\right)^2 \mid y_T\right] = \mathsf{E}\left[(u_{T+2} + \rho u_{T+1})^2\right] = \left(1 + \rho^2\right)\sigma_u^2. \tag{3.39}$$

In terms of changes:

$$\Delta y_{T+2} = (\rho - 1)\, y_{T+1} + u_{T+2} = (\rho - 1)\left(\rho y_T + u_{T+1}\right) + u_{T+2} \tag{3.40}$$

and hence using the conditional expectation $\mathsf{E}[\Delta y_{T+2}|y_T] = \widehat{\Delta y}_{T+2} = (\rho - 1)\rho y_T$, the MSFE is:

$$\mathsf{E}\left[\left(\Delta y_{T+2} - \widehat{\Delta y}_{T+2}\right)^2 \mid y_T\right] = \mathsf{E}\left[\left((\rho - 1)\, u_{T+1} + u_{T+2}\right)^2\right] \tag{3.41}$$

$$= \sigma_u^2\left(1 + (\rho - 1)^2\right) \tag{3.42}$$

which is larger (smaller) than (3.39) as $\rho < ½$ ($> ½$). Consequently, no valid comparisons of forecast performance can be made between multi-step MSFEs for the level of a variable and its change: a common choice of variable is essential. Notice that both $\widehat{y}_{T+2}$ and $\widehat{\Delta y}_{T+2}$ are the optimal 2-step ahead predictors of y_{T+2} and Δy_{T+2}, respectively, since they are the conditional expectations and therefore minimum MSFE predictors (as a generalization of section 4.3.1). That they cannot be compared follows because the optimal predictors and associated MSFEs differ (Granger and Newbold, 1977, p.285, stress this point).

When parameter uncertainty is introduced, the ranking of two estimators of (3.35) on MSFE can be reversed by the choice of metric. The 1-step forecast error for estimated parameter values based on a sample up to time t, using $\widehat{y}_{T+1} = \widehat{\rho} y_T$ is:

$$e_{T+1} = y_{T+1} - \widehat{y}_{T+1} = u_{T+1} + (\rho - \widehat{\rho})\, y_T \tag{3.43}$$

with approximate conditional forecast-error variance:

$$\mathsf{V}\left[e_{T+1} \mid y_T\right] = \sigma_u^2 + \mathsf{V}\left[\widehat{\rho}\right] y_T^2.$$

Conditional on information available at the beginning of the forecast period, the 2-step ahead forecast, $\widehat{y}_{T+2}$, is again obtained by backward iteration:

$$\widehat{y}_{T+2} = \widehat{\rho}\widehat{y}_{T+1} = \widehat{\rho}^2 y_T, \tag{3.44}$$

whereas:

$$y_{T+2} = \rho y_{T+1} + u_{T+2} = \rho^2 y_T + \rho u_{T+1} + u_{T+2},$$

so that to a first approximation (neglecting the slight dependence of $\widehat{\rho}$ on y_T):

$$\mathsf{V}\left[e_{T+2} \mid y_T\right] = \mathsf{E}\left[\left(\rho^2 - \widehat{\rho}^2\right)^2\right] y_T^2 + \left(1 + \rho^2\right) \sigma_u^2. \tag{3.45}$$

In terms of changes, (3.43) and (3.44) entail:

$$\Delta y_{T+2} - \widehat{\Delta y}_{T+2} = (\rho - 1)\, \rho y_T + u_{T+2} + (\rho - 1)\, u_{T+1} - (\widehat{\rho} - 1)\, \widehat{\rho} y_T,$$

and hence the MSFE is:

$$\mathsf{E}\left[\left(\Delta y_{T+2} - \widehat{\Delta y}_{T+2}\right)^2 \mid y_T\right] = \mathsf{E}\left[\left(\rho^2 - \widehat{\rho}^2 - (\rho - \widehat{\rho})\right)^2\right] y_T^2 + \sigma_u^2 \left(1 + (\rho - 1)^2\right). \tag{3.46}$$

Since the impact of the estimation error differs between (3.45) and (3.46), it is possible to find two estimators (denoted ^ and ~ respectively) such that:

$$\mathsf{E}\left[\left(\rho^2 - \widehat{\rho}^2\right)^2\right] < \mathsf{E}\left[\left(\rho^2 - \widetilde{\rho}^2\right)^2\right] \tag{3.47}$$

and:

$$\mathsf{E}\left[\left(\rho^2 - \widehat{\rho}^2 - (\rho - \widehat{\rho})\right)^2\right] \geq \mathsf{E}\left[\left(\rho^2 - \widetilde{\rho}^2 - (\rho - \widetilde{\rho})\right)^2\right]. \tag{3.48}$$

For example, $\widehat{\rho} \equiv 1$ and $\widetilde{\rho} \equiv 0$ will satisfy these conditions for ρ near unity, so that a suitably imprecise estimator for the former, and a precise estimator for the latter, can be found which also satisfy (3.48). Consequently, the ranking of two estimators by multi-step TMSFE can be altered by switching the basis of comparison from levels to changes even when a common comparison basis is agreed.

3.5.2 Dynamic systems

Our second example concerns systems of equations. We begin by denoting a linear forecasting system by the succinct notation:

$$\mathbf{\Phi}\mathbf{s}_t = \mathbf{u}_t, \tag{3.49}$$

where $\mathbf{u}_t \sim \mathsf{ID}_n[\mathbf{0}, \mathbf{\Omega}]$, $\mathbf{s}_t' = (\mathbf{x}_t' : \mathbf{z}_t')$, $\mathbf{x}_t$ are the n variables to be forecast and $\mathbf{z}_t$ are k available predetermined variables (perhaps just $\mathbf{x}_{t-1}$ and deterministic terms) with $\mathbf{\Phi} = (\mathbf{I}_n : -\mathbf{B})$ say.[1] The parameters are $(\mathbf{B} : \mathbf{\Omega})$, where $\mathbf{\Omega}$ is symmetric, positive semi-definite. Then the likelihood and generalized variance of the system in (3.49) are invariant under scale-preserving, non-singular transformations of the form:

$$\mathbf{M}\mathbf{\Phi}\mathbf{P}^{-1}\mathbf{P}\mathbf{s}_t = \mathbf{M}\mathbf{u}_t$$

or:

$$\mathbf{\Phi}^*\mathbf{s}_t^* = \mathbf{u}_t^* \quad \text{so} \quad \mathbf{u}_t^* \sim \mathsf{ID}_n\left[\mathbf{0}, \mathbf{M}\mathbf{\Omega}\mathbf{M}'\right]. \tag{3.50}$$

In (3.50), $\mathbf{s}_t^* = \mathbf{P}\mathbf{s}_t$, $\mathbf{M}$ and $\mathbf{P}$ are respectively $n \times n$ and $(k+n) \times (k+n)$ non-singular matrices where $abs(|\mathbf{M}|) = 1$ and $\mathbf{P}$ is upper block-triangular, for example:

$$\mathbf{P} = \begin{pmatrix} \mathbf{I}_n & \mathbf{P}_{12} \\ \mathbf{0} & \mathbf{P}_{22} \end{pmatrix} \quad \text{so that} \quad \mathbf{P}^{-1} = \begin{pmatrix} \mathbf{I}_n & -\mathbf{P}_{12}\mathbf{P}_{22}^{-1} \\ \mathbf{0} & \mathbf{P}_{22}^{-1} \end{pmatrix}.$$

Since we need to be able to calculate $\mathbf{P}^{-1}$, a restriction on $\mathbf{P}$ is that $|\mathbf{P}_{22}| \neq 0$. Then:

$$\mathbf{\Phi}^* = \mathbf{M}\mathbf{\Phi}\mathbf{P}^{-1} = \mathbf{M}\left(\mathbf{I}_n : -(\mathbf{P}_{12} + \mathbf{B})\mathbf{P}_{22}^{-1}\right) = \mathbf{M}\left(\mathbf{I}_n : -\mathbf{B}^*\right).$$

Thus, the transformation from levels to differences for the first-order scalar process in section 3.5.1 is accomplished in this notation by $\mathbf{M} = \mathbf{I}_2$ and:

$$\mathbf{P} = \begin{pmatrix} 1 & -1 \\ 0 & 1 \end{pmatrix}.$$

No restrictions are imposed by these transforms, so the systems (3.49) and (3.50) are isomorphic. Transformations in the class shown in (3.50) are regularly undertaken in applied work, and include as special cases, differences, cointegrating combinations, substitution of identities and differentials *inter alia*. The formalization merely makes explicit the fact that a linear model is defined by its invariance under linear transformations (or affine transforms more generally). Forecasts and forecast confidence intervals made in the original system and transformed after the event to $\mathbf{x}_t^*$ (defined by $\mathbf{s}_t^{*\prime} = (\mathbf{x}_t^{*\prime} : \mathbf{z}_t^{*\prime})$) or made initially from the transformed system will be identical. That is, we will obtain the same results if we consider $\widehat{\mathbf{x}}_t = \widehat{\mathbf{B}}\mathbf{z}_t$ from (3.49) ($\mathbf{z}_t$ known) or $\mathbf{M}\mathbf{x}_t^* \equiv \mathbf{M}\widehat{\mathbf{B}}^*\mathbf{z}_t^*$ from (3.50), where the estimates $\widehat{\mathbf{B}}$ and $\widehat{\mathbf{B}}^*$ of the unknown parameters are obtained by the same estimation method (e.g., maximum likelihood estimation).

[1] For the example in section 3.5.1, $\mathbf{s}_t = (y_t : y_{t-1})'$ and $\mathbf{\Phi} = (1 : -\rho)$.

3.5.3 Non-invariance of the multi-step MSFE matrix in systems

We now show that for multi-step forecasts, the specification of the MSFEM is ambiguous. If $\mathbf{V}_h$ is defined as the MSFE matrix for the h-step ahead forecasts alone, then rank reversals can occur, exactly as the matrix generalization of (3.45) versus (3.46). In terms of levels and changes for known parameters, the MSFEMs are:

$$\mathsf{V}\left[\mathbf{e}_{\mathbf{x}_{T+2}} \mid \mathbf{x}_T\right] = \boldsymbol{\Omega}+\mathbf{B}\boldsymbol{\Omega}\mathbf{B}' \quad \text{and} \quad \mathsf{V}\left[\mathbf{e}_{\Delta\mathbf{x}_{T+2}} \mid \mathbf{x}_T\right] = \boldsymbol{\Omega}+(\mathbf{B}-\mathbf{I}_n)\,\boldsymbol{\Omega}\,(\mathbf{B}-\mathbf{I}_n)'.$$

Assuming a sufficiently large sample that parameter estimation variances are negligible, it is possible to find two models $^\sim$ and $^\wedge$ as above such that:

$$\widehat{\boldsymbol{\Omega}} + \widehat{\mathbf{B}}\widehat{\boldsymbol{\Omega}}\widehat{\mathbf{B}}' - \left(\widetilde{\boldsymbol{\Omega}} + \widetilde{\mathbf{B}}\widetilde{\boldsymbol{\Omega}}\widetilde{\mathbf{B}}'\right) \succ \mathbf{0}$$

and:

$$\widehat{\boldsymbol{\Omega}} + \left(\widehat{\mathbf{B}} - \mathbf{I}_n\right)\widehat{\boldsymbol{\Omega}}\left(\widehat{\mathbf{B}} - \mathbf{I}_n\right)' - \left[\widetilde{\boldsymbol{\Omega}} + \left(\widetilde{\mathbf{B}} - \mathbf{I}_n\right)\widetilde{\boldsymbol{\Omega}}\left(\widetilde{\mathbf{B}} - \mathbf{I}_n\right)'\right] \prec \mathbf{0}. \tag{3.51}$$

For example, for $\widehat{\mathbf{B}} \approx \mathbf{I}_n$ and $\widetilde{\mathbf{B}} \approx \mathbf{0}$ then $2\widehat{\boldsymbol{\Omega}} - \widetilde{\boldsymbol{\Omega}} \succ \mathbf{0}$ but $\widehat{\boldsymbol{\Omega}} - 2\widetilde{\boldsymbol{\Omega}} \prec \mathbf{0}$, which creates such an outcome. Thus, using a comparison basis of levels, the $^\sim$ model appears best on the 2-step ahead MSFEM criterion, whereas the $^\wedge$ model wins if first differences are used. Despite using the 'complete' MSFE matrix, it matters for appraising multi-step forecast accuracy which isomorphic representation of the system is selected: investigators could find one system performing better than a second on levels comparisons, but worse if the same comparisons were conducted for changes. Potential ranking reversals vitiate the use of that criterion to judge forecasting models or methods *per se*.

3.5.4 Invariance of certain MSFE-based measures

We can formulate a general set of results concerning the (in)variance of MSFE measures, which include the two illustrations in sections 3.5.1 and 3.5.3. Consider the transformation in (3.49) and (3.50) from $\mathbf{x}_t$ to $\mathbf{x}_t^*$ where $|\mathbf{M}| = 1$. The h-step ahead forecast errors resulting from $\mathbf{x}_t$ and $\mathbf{x}_t^*$ are denoted by $\mathbf{u}_t$ and $\mathbf{e}_t$ respectively. Then, for transformations using $\mathbf{M}$:

(i) the trace MSFE for $\mathbf{u}_t$ is not in general equivalent to that for $\mathbf{e}_t$:

$$tr(\mathbf{M}\mathbf{V}_h\mathbf{M}') \neq tr(\mathbf{V}_h);$$

(ii) the determinant of the forecast error second-moment matrix is invariant: $|\mathbf{M}\mathbf{V}_h\mathbf{M}'| = |\mathbf{V}_h|$ when $|\mathbf{M}| = 1$;

(iii) the MSFEM is invariant:

$$\mathbf{d}^{*\prime}\mathbf{V}_h\mathbf{d}^* < \mathbf{d}^{*\prime}\mathbf{V}_h^*\mathbf{d} \quad \forall \mathbf{d}^* \neq \mathbf{0}$$

implies that:

$$\mathbf{d}'\mathbf{M}\mathbf{V}_h\mathbf{M}'\mathbf{d} < \mathbf{d}'\mathbf{M}\mathbf{V}_h^*\mathbf{M}'\mathbf{d} \quad \forall \mathbf{d} \neq \mathbf{0}.$$

Therefore a change of contemporaneous transformation of the variables will not induce a switch in the rankings providing a common basis is used.

For transformations using $\mathbf{P}$, as happens with the transformation from $\mathbf{x}_t$ to $\Delta\mathbf{x}_t$, for example, these results continue to hold with the following exceptions:

(i) the trace MSFE is only valid for 1-step forecasts;
(ii) $|\mathbf{V}_h|$ is not invariant except for $h = 1$, when the invariance follows from the conditional nature of the expectations operator as with *(i)*.
(iii) MSFEM is not invariant for $h > 1$, as shown above.

Generally for $h > 1$, the covariances between different step-ahead forecast errors have to be taken into account to obtain an invariant measure.

3.6 An invariant measure of forecast accuracy

The general forecast-error second-moment matrix and its determinant (the GFESM) provide invariant measures. The former is obtained by stacking the forecast errors from all previous step ahead forecasts as in (3.52):

$$\mathbf{\Phi}_h = \mathsf{E}\left[\mathbf{E}\mathbf{E}'\right], \quad \text{where } \mathbf{E}' = \left[\mathbf{e}'_{T+1}, \mathbf{e}'_{T+2}, ..., \mathbf{e}'_{T+h-1}, \mathbf{e}'_{T+h}\right] \tag{3.52}$$

and the latter is just $|\mathbf{\Phi}_h|$.

We can show that transforming the data by $\mathbf{M}$, where $|\mathbf{M}| = 1$ will leave the criterion in (3.52) unaffected. Denote the vector of stacked forecast errors from the transformed model by $\widetilde{\mathbf{E}}'$, so that:

$$\widetilde{\mathbf{E}}' = \left[\mathbf{e}'_{T+1}\mathbf{M}', \mathbf{e}'_{T+2}\mathbf{M}', ..., \mathbf{e}'_{T+h-1}\mathbf{M}', \mathbf{e}'_{T+h}\mathbf{M}'\right]$$

or $\widetilde{\mathbf{E}} = (\mathbf{I}_h \otimes \mathbf{M})\mathbf{E}$, and thus:

$$\begin{aligned}\left|\widetilde{\mathbf{\Phi}}_h\right| &= \left|\mathsf{E}\left[\widetilde{\mathbf{E}}\widetilde{\mathbf{E}}'\right]\right| \\ &= \left|\mathsf{E}\left[(\mathbf{I}_h \otimes \mathbf{M})\,\mathbf{E}\mathbf{E}'\,(\mathbf{I}_h \otimes \mathbf{M})\right]\right| \\ &= \left|\mathsf{E}\left[\mathbf{E}\mathbf{E}'\right]\right| \times \left|\mathbf{I}_h \otimes \mathbf{M}\right|^2 \\ &= \left|\mathsf{E}\left[\mathbf{E}\mathbf{E}'\right]\right|\end{aligned}$$

since:

$$|\mathbf{I}_h \otimes \mathbf{M}| = |\mathbf{I}_h \otimes \mathbf{M}'| = 1^h \times |\mathbf{M}|^h = 1.$$

Transforming by $\mathbf{P}$ leaves the error process $\{\mathbf{u}_{T+i}\}$ unaffected, so (3.52) is invariant to $\mathbf{P}$ transforms.

The MSFEM criterion can be generalized to apply to the pooled or stacked forecast-error second-moment matrix $\mathbf{\Phi}_h$. In that case, the model denoted by $\sim$ dominates $\wedge$ if:

$$\widehat{\mathbf{\Phi}}_h - \widetilde{\mathbf{\Phi}}_h \succ \mathbf{0},$$

that is, if the difference between the two estimates of the stacked matrix is positive definite. It follows that MSFEM dominance on the stacked MSFE matrix is sufficient but not necessary for GFESM dominance, that is:

$$\widehat{\mathbf{\Phi}}_h - \widetilde{\mathbf{\Phi}}_h \succ \mathbf{0} \text{ implies } \left|\widehat{\mathbf{\Phi}}_h\right| > \left|\widetilde{\mathbf{\Phi}}_h\right|,$$

since $\widehat{\mathbf{\Phi}}_h$ and $\widetilde{\mathbf{\Phi}}_h$ are positive definite (see, e.g., Dhrymes, 1984, prop. 66, p.77). Thus, GFESM dominance is a weaker condition than MSFEM applied to the stacked MSFE matrix. It can also be related to the statistical literature on predictive likelihood (see section 3.7).

It is straightforward to show that the 1-step forecast errors determine the complete ranking for the GFESM when there is no parameter uncertainty and the model is correctly specified. We then derive its distribution. Consider for simplicity the VAR(1) process, where with known parameters, we can set the intercept to zero without loss of generality:

$$\mathbf{x}_t = \mathbf{B}\mathbf{x}_{t-1} + \mathbf{u}_t \quad \text{and} \quad \mathsf{E}\left[\mathbf{v}_t\mathbf{v}_t'\right] = \mathbf{\Omega}. \tag{3.53}$$

Hence:

$$\mathbf{x}_{T+h} = \mathbf{B}^h\mathbf{x}_T + \sum_{j=0}^{h-1}\mathbf{B}^j\mathbf{u}_{T+h-j}. \tag{3.54}$$

When $\widehat{\mathbf{x}}_{T+h} = \mathbf{B}^h\mathbf{x}_T$ and $\mathbf{e}_{T+h} = \mathbf{x}_{T+h} - \widehat{\mathbf{x}}_{T+h} = \Sigma_{j=0}^{h-1}\mathbf{B}^j\mathbf{u}_{T+h-j}$:

$$\mathsf{E}\left[\mathbf{e}_{T+h}\mathbf{e}_{T+h}'\right] = \mathbf{V}_h = \sum_{j=0}^{h-1}\mathbf{B}^j\mathbf{\Omega}\mathbf{B}^{j\prime}, \tag{3.55}$$

where (3.55) uses the assumption that the $\mathbf{v}$s are IID. Thus, for a 1-step forecast, the criterion is $|\mathbf{\Phi}_1| = |\mathbf{V}_1| = |\mathbf{\Omega}|$. For a 2-step forecast, the covariance $\mathsf{E}[\mathbf{e}_{T+1}\mathbf{e}_{T+2}'] = \mathbf{\Omega}\mathbf{B}'$, so the complete second-moment matrix is:

$$\begin{aligned} |\mathbf{\Phi}_2| &= \left|\begin{pmatrix} \mathbf{\Omega} & \mathbf{\Omega}\mathbf{B}' \\ \mathbf{B}\mathbf{\Omega} & \mathbf{\Omega} + \mathbf{B}\mathbf{\Omega}\mathbf{B}' \end{pmatrix}\right| \\ &= |\mathbf{\Omega}| \cdot \left|(\mathbf{\Omega} + \mathbf{B}\mathbf{\Omega}\mathbf{B}') - (\mathbf{B}\mathbf{\Omega})\,\mathbf{\Omega}^{-1}(\mathbf{\Omega}\mathbf{B}')\right| \\ &= |\mathbf{\Omega}|^2. \end{aligned} \tag{3.56}$$

By partitioned inversion, the determinant in (3.56) is $|\mathbf{\Omega}|^2$. This recursion continues to any order and so the criterion $|\mathbf{\Phi}_h|$ is just $|\mathbf{\Omega}|^h$ for h-step ahead forecasts. Thus, the generalized second moment of the 1-step forecast error determines the complete ranking when parameters are known and the model is correctly specified.

When parameters are unknown and have to be estimated:

$$\widehat{\mathbf{e}}_{T+h} = \mathbf{e}_{T+h} + (\mathbf{B}^h - \widehat{\mathbf{B}}^h)\mathbf{x}_T,$$

so that:

$$\mathsf{E}\left[\widehat{\mathbf{e}}_{T+h}\widehat{\mathbf{e}}'_{T+h}\right] = \left(\mathbf{I}_n \otimes \mathbf{x}'_T\right)\mathbf{Q}\left(h\right)'\mathsf{V}\left[\widehat{\mathbf{B}}^{v}\right]\mathbf{Q}\left(h\right)\left(\mathbf{I}_n \otimes \mathbf{x}_T\right) + \sum_{j=0}^{h-1}\mathbf{B}^j\boldsymbol{\Omega}\mathbf{B}^{j\prime}, \quad (3.57)$$

where $\mathbf{Q}(h)$ is the derivative of $\left(\mathbf{B}^h\right)^v$ with respect to $\mathbf{B}^v$ when $(\cdot)^v$ denotes vectoring (see, e.g., Schmidt, 1974). The forecast uncertainty is not a monotonically increasing function of the forecast horizon, so rankings can alter as h increases even when the complete generalized second moment of forecast errors is used. We return to multi-step forecasting in chapter 11.

We end this section with an illustration of the impact of the forecast horizon. Independent of the measure of forecast accuracy, one model may dominate at certain horizons and another at other horizons. We address these issues more formally in chapter 12, where we analyse the differential effects as the horizon alters of imposing (incorrect) parameter values versus estimating them. Here we ignore parameter uncertainty.

Baillie (1993) and Newbold (1993) both consider the comparison of forecasts from two mis-specified models of a moving-average process, namely an autoregressive model and a white-noise model, to establish formally that rankings may depend on the forecast horizon, and to warn against focusing exclusively on 1-step ahead forecasts. We sketch their analyses, but in addition demonstrate the effect of analysing differences versus levels of the data, and include GFESM calculations. The DGP and rival models are:

$$\begin{array}{llll} \mathsf{DGP}: & y_t = \epsilon_t + \theta\epsilon_{t-1} & \text{where} & \epsilon_t \sim \mathsf{IN}\left[0, \sigma^2_\epsilon\right] \\ \mathsf{M}_1: & y_t = \rho y_{t-1} + \nu_t & \text{where} & \nu_t \underset{h}{\sim} \mathsf{IN}\left[0, \sigma^2_v\right] \\ \mathsf{M}_2: & y_t = \eta_t & \text{where} & \eta_t \underset{h}{\sim} \mathsf{IN}\left[0, \sigma^2_\eta\right] \end{array}$$

and $\underset{h}{\sim}$ denotes 'is hypothesized to be distributed as'. From the DGP:

$$\mathsf{V}\left[y_t\right] = \sigma^2_\epsilon(1+\theta^2), \quad \mathsf{E}\left[y_t y_{t-1}\right] = \theta\sigma^2_\epsilon \quad \text{and} \quad \mathsf{E}\left[y_t y_{t-j}\right] = 0\;\forall\, j > 1,$$

so that $\rho = \theta/(1+\theta^2)$. The forecasts of $(y_{T+1}, \ldots, y_{T+H})$ from M_1 (denoted by ^) and M_2 (~) for known parameters and a horizon $j > 1$ are given by:

$$\begin{array}{lll} & \text{Levels} & & \text{Differences} \\ \mathsf{M}_1: & \widehat{y}_{T+j} = \rho\widehat{y}_{T+j-1} & \text{and} & \Delta\widehat{y}_{T+j} = \rho^{j-1}\left(\rho-1\right)y_T; \\ \mathsf{M}_2: & \widetilde{y}_{T+j} = 0 & \text{and} & \Delta\widetilde{y}_{T+j} = 0. \end{array}$$

For 1-step, from M_1, $\widehat{y}_{T+1} = \rho y_T$ and $\Delta\widehat{y}_{T+1} = (\rho-1)y_T$; and from M_2, $\widetilde{y}_{T+1} = 0$ and $\Delta\widetilde{y}_{T+1} = -y_T$.

The first point is that for 1-step forecasts using MSFE on levels or differences, M_1 'wins':

$$\mathsf{M}_1: \; \mathsf{V}\left[\widehat{u}_{T+1}\right] = \sigma^2_\epsilon\left(1+\theta^2\right)\left(1-\rho^2\right) \quad \text{whereas} \quad \mathsf{M}_2: \; \mathsf{V}\left[\widetilde{u}_{T+1}\right] = \sigma^2_\epsilon\left(1+\theta^2\right),$$

when u denotes the forecast error. Next, for 2-step forecasts using MSFE for levels:

$$\mathsf{M}_1\colon\ \mathsf{V}\left[\widehat{u}_{T+2}\right] = \sigma_\epsilon^2\left(1+\theta^2\right)\left(1+\rho^4\right) \text{ whereas } \mathsf{M}_2\colon\ \mathsf{V}\left[\widetilde{u}_{T+2}\right] = \sigma_\epsilon^2\left(1+\theta^2\right),$$

so M_2 'wins' (and does so for longer horizon forecasts).

For a combined 1- and 2-step forecast, we have:

$$\mathsf{M}_1\colon\quad \widehat{\mathsf{G}}_2 = \sigma_\epsilon^2\left(1+\theta\right)^2\begin{bmatrix}(1-\rho)^2 & \rho \\ \rho & (1+\rho^4)\end{bmatrix},$$

and:

$$\mathsf{M}_2\colon\quad \widetilde{\mathsf{G}}_2 = \sigma_\epsilon^2\left(1+\theta\right)^2\begin{pmatrix}1 & \rho \\ \rho & 1\end{pmatrix},$$

so the ratio of the GFESM measures is

$$\frac{\left|\widehat{\mathsf{G}}_2\right|}{\left|\widetilde{\mathsf{G}}_2\right|} = \left(1-\rho^2\right) - \frac{\rho^6}{\left(1-\rho^2\right)} < 1.$$

This pattern continues as the forecast horizon increases: M_1 'beats' M_2 on average because of the gain on period 1.

However, for 2-step forecasts using MSFE for differences, a reversal relative to the 2-step ahead ranking in levels occurs since, using w to denote the forecast errors:

$$\mathsf{M}_1\colon\quad \mathsf{V}\left[\widehat{w}_{T+2}\right] = 2\sigma_\epsilon^2\left(1+\theta^2\right)\left(1-\rho\right)\left[1-\frac{1}{2}\rho^2\left(1+\rho\right)\right],$$

whereas:

$$\mathsf{M}_2\colon\quad \mathsf{V}\left[\widetilde{w}_{T+2}\right] = 2\sigma_\epsilon^2\left(1+\theta^2\right)\left(1-\rho\right),$$

hence M_1 now 'wins'. Thus the claim in Baillie (1993) that M_2 wins for more than 2-step ahead forecasts on MSFE is seen to depend on the transformation of the variables for which forecast accuracy is assessed. Such switches of rankings can be ruled out if we use invariant criteria such as GFESM. The GFESM measure implicitly weights the levels and differences forecasts, and highlights that on average, M_1 is the better model. Only if one were certain that levels alone mattered would use of MSFE comparisons of levels predictions be justified – see section 3.4.1.

3.7 Predictive likelihood

In general terms, prediction involves two unknowns: the parameters of the model and the outcomes of the random variables to be predicted.[2] Denote the joint density function of the sample $(\mathbf{X})$ and the variables to be predicted $(\mathbf{p})$ given the parameters of

[2] We are grateful to Neil Shephard for suggesting the approach in this section.

interest, $\boldsymbol{\theta}$ say, by $\mathsf{f}(\mathbf{p}, \mathbf{X}|\boldsymbol{\theta})$. In predicting $\mathbf{p}$, $\boldsymbol{\theta}$ become nuisance parameters and must be eliminated from the prediction rule. The approach adopted above corresponded to eliminating $\boldsymbol{\theta}$ by replacing it by an estimate $\widehat{\boldsymbol{\theta}}$, and when $\widehat{\boldsymbol{\theta}}$ is the maximum likelihood estimator (MLE), this leads to a profile predictive likelihood method, noting that 'profile' in statistics denotes the same as 'concentrated' in econometrics.

For example, from (3.35) using the scalar version of (3.54):

$$y_{T+h} = \rho^h y_T + \sum_{j=0}^{h-1} \rho^j u_{T+h-j}. \tag{3.58}$$

For known parameters $\boldsymbol{\theta}' = (\rho, \sigma^2)$, $\mathbf{p} = (y_{T+1}, ..., y_{T+h})'$, $\mathbf{Y} = (y_1, ..., y_T)'$:

$$\mathbf{p} \mid \mathbf{Y}, \boldsymbol{\theta} \sim \mathsf{N}\left[\mathbf{r}y_T, \boldsymbol{\Phi}_h\right], \tag{3.59}$$

where $\mathbf{r}' = (\rho, \rho^2, ..., \rho^h)$, and $\boldsymbol{\Phi}_h$ is defined in (3.52) and (e.g.) (3.56) for $h = 2$. Thus, the profile predictive log-likelihood is:

$$\mathsf{L}_p\left(\mathbf{p}; \widehat{\rho}, \widehat{\sigma}^2 \mid \mathbf{Y}\right) = K - \tfrac{1}{2} \log\left|\widehat{\boldsymbol{\Phi}}_h\right| - \tfrac{1}{2} \left(\mathbf{p} - \widehat{\mathbf{r}}y_T\right)' \widehat{\boldsymbol{\Phi}}_h^{-1} \left(\mathbf{p} - \widehat{\mathbf{r}}y_T\right). \tag{3.60}$$

Maximizing $\mathsf{L}_p(\mathbf{p}; \widehat{\rho}, \widehat{\sigma}^2|\mathbf{Y})$ with respect to $\mathbf{p}$ yields $\widehat{\mathbf{p}} = \widehat{\mathbf{r}}y_T$, and a further concentrated log-likelihood function which only depends on $\log|\widehat{\boldsymbol{\Phi}}_h|$. This outcome is invariant to transformations with a unit Jacobian, as required of $\mathbf{M}$ above. However, it is well known from the prediction error decomposition that:

$$\mathsf{f}\left(\mathbf{p} \mid \mathbf{Y}, \boldsymbol{\theta}\right) = \prod_{T+1}^{T+h} \mathsf{f}\left(y_j \mid y_1, ..., y_{j-1}; \boldsymbol{\theta}\right), \tag{3.61}$$

so the predictive likelihood measure may be applicable in a wider class of model than the generalized second moment. In particular, $|\widehat{\boldsymbol{\Phi}}|$ assumes the existence of estimator second moments, and the sufficiency of a second-moment measure.

3.7.1 Measuring predictability

This can be done in many ways, but building on chapter 2, we note one measure based on a direct comparison of the conditional and unconditional densities. Reconsider the stationary AR(1) model in section 3.5.1. Then, in an obvious notation:

$$\mathsf{D}_{\mathsf{y}_t|\mathsf{y}_{t-1}}\left(y_t \mid y_{t-1}; \rho, \sigma_u^2\right) = \frac{1}{\sqrt{2\pi\sigma_u^2}} \exp\left(-\frac{\left(y_t - \rho y_{t-1}\right)^2}{2\sigma_u^2}\right),$$

whereas:

$$\mathsf{D}_{\mathsf{y}_t}\left(y_t \mid \rho, \sigma_u^2\right) = \frac{\sqrt{1-\rho^2}}{\sqrt{2\pi\sigma_u^2}} \exp\left(-\frac{\left(1-\rho^2\right) y_t^2}{2\sigma_u^2}\right).$$

Thus, a possible measure is the expected difference between the log densities, essentially the log-likelihood ratio:

$$\mathsf{E}\left[\log \mathsf{D}_{\mathsf{y}_t|\mathsf{y}_{t-1}} - \log \mathsf{D}_{\mathsf{y}_t}\right] = -\ \tfrac{1}{2}\ \log\left(1-\rho^2\right),$$

which is zero when $\rho = 0$, and positive otherwise. Moreover, it equals the log ratio of the respective error variances.

3.8 Overview

In this chapter we have argued that, although it is desirable that forecasts are unbiased and efficient, in practice performance relative to that of rival forecasts will determine the worth of a particular forecasting procedure. This raises the thorny issue of an appropriate metric for assessing forecast accuracy. We suggest that in macroeconomics the situation where there is a well-defined mapping between forecast errors and the costs of making those errors is relatively rare, so that often forecasts will be evaluated according to some general loss function, such as squared error. Further, if there is no compelling reason for choosing the MMSFE predictor of the forecasts of the levels, as opposed to, say, the differences, then there is a case for choosing a measure that leaves rankings between models/forecasts unaltered by this switch.

The generalized forecast-error second-moment GFESM is such a measure. Unlike MSFE-based measures, it is invariant to non-singular, scale-preserving linear transforms. Rankings across models or methods will not alter if a different transform is selected. In chapter 6 we contrast forecast accuracy comparisons between different models made on the basis of TMSFE for a number of linear transformations. We also report the ranking of the models induced by GFESM.

Chapter 4

Forecasting in univariate processes

The class of univariate processes considered in this chapter includes stationary and non-stationary cases, where the latter are either integrated (and so can be made stationary by an appropriate level of differencing) or are stationary around a deterministic polynomial of time. We assume in all cases that the model is the process that generated the data: in subsequent chapters, this assumption is relaxed. We define forecasts, forecast errors, forecast-error variances and prediction intervals, and make explicit the distinction between conditional and unconditional forecasts. The impact of parameter estimation uncertainty is discussed. We reconsider the 'informativeness of forecasts', with an illustration in terms of predicting stock-market prices, and the related notion of 'the limit to forecastability' (the horizon up to which forecasts are informative). We also discuss forecasting in non-linear models, the impact of ARCH on prediction intervals, and point predictions for asymmetric loss functions.

4.1 Introduction

We will mainly restrict our attention to autoregressive models, rather than the more general class of autoregressive-moving average models. In section 2.7.1, we set out the mechanics of forecasting from a general ARIMA(p,d,q), and the calculation of forecast-error variances from the Wold (1938) representation. As special cases, AR models are simpler to deal with. Estimation is by OLS and forecasting is not complicated by backward solution of the MA component. However, we discuss MA components in chapter 11 where it is argued that the neglect of such terms (when they are a feature of the DGP) may provide a rationale for multi-step estimation criteria.

More generally, there are a number of reasons for focusing on AR models. First, a focus of interest is the impact of integratedness on forecastability. Whether a series is integrated or not depends on the roots of the AR polynomial (see below) and can be analysed without recourse to the MA polynomial (assuming invertibility and no redundant roots). For this purpose, there is no loss of generality in considering the model class given by ARIMA(p,d,0), which is just a pth order AR process with d unit roots. Moreover, an ARMA model can be approximated by an AR model, although typically the number of parameters will exceed $p + q$, and there will be problems if the MA is non-invertible (has a root of modulus 1) or has a root close to 1 (see chapter 11). Finally, estimated econometric systems rarely contain MA components, and are more closely related to pure AR processes (not withstanding the importance of explanatory variables), although their final forms will have MA errors. The seminal work on forecasting in univariate ARIMA time-series models is Box and Jenkins (1976). In section 2.7.1, we sketched the calculation of forecasts and prediction intervals for ARIMA models, and explained how the order of integration determines the form of the eventual forecast function (as the forecast horizon goes to infinity).

In section 4.3–4.5, we analyse the implications of the time-series properties of the variables for the behaviour of forecast-error variances and prediction intervals, and in section 4.6, briefly review the class of fractional ARIMA models.

The remaining sections discuss forecasting with non-linear models, and models whose errors exhibit dependence in their conditional second moments. Non-linear models have been the subject of much recent research, see, for example, the review by De Gooijer and Kumar (1992). In section 4.7, we discuss some of the issues involved in calculating multi-step forecasts for such models, and briefly consider two classes of non-linear model that have been used extensively to model economic time series: self-exciting threshold autoregressive (SETAR) models and Markov-switching autoregressive (MS-AR) models. Finally, time-dependent conditional heteroscedasticity (ARCH and related models: see Engle, 1982, Bollerslev, Chou and Kroner, 1992and Bollerslev, Engle and Nelson, 1994) appears to be an important characteristic of many financial variables and some economics data, and the issues raised by these features of the data are discussed in sections 4.8 and 4.9. In section 4.8 we show how ARCH may affect prediction intervals, and in section 4.9, the impact on point predictions under asymmetric loss is discussed.

Even in some of the simple cases considered here, it is not always straightforward to obtain the exact means and variances of the forecast errors when parameters have to be estimated, so these (and usually the distributional form) can only be approximated. The detailed mathematics of the approximations that yield the second moments of powers of the estimated parameters are provided in an appendix. Appendix 4.11 outlines the calculations which allow us to investigate the relationship between parameter estimation uncertainty and the forecast horizon.

4.2 Stationary stochastic processes

Given the different implications for forecasting of whether or not a series is stationary (see below, section 4.3, section 4.4 and section 4.5) we first define this concept. A more detailed treatment can be found in textbook discussions of stochastic processes (e.g., Cox and Miller, 1965 and McCabe and Tremayne, 1993). A process $\{y_t\}$ is said to be strictly stationary if the joint distribution of:

$$y_{t_1}, \ldots, y_{t_2}$$

is exactly the same as that of:

$$y_{t_1+l}, \ldots, y_{t_2+l}$$

for all l, and for every set $t_1, \ldots, t_2$. That is, the process 'looks the same' for arbitrary shifts along the time axis of a given interval: a strictly stationary process has a joint distribution function which is invariant to translations of time.

Alternatively, weak, covariance or second-order stationarity requires that the first two moments of the process exist, and they, rather than the complete distribution, are invariant to arbitrary shifts along the time axis. That is:

(1) the mean of the process $\mathsf{E}[y_{t_1}]$ is constant and finite, for all t_1, so that $\mathsf{E}[y_{t_1}] = \mu$, say;
(2) the autocovariance function depends only on the distance between two points, so that $\mathsf{C}[y_{t_1}, y_{t_1-k}]$ is a function of k alone and not t_1.

Thus, the first two moments of weakly stationary processes do not change over time, so the population mean and variance are well-defined concepts, and can be estimated from a single realization of the process: that is, variability over time can be used to estimate these properties of the series at a single point in time. Notice that strict stationarity is defined in terms of the distribution function, so that there is no presumption that the moments exist. Thus, a series may be strictly stationary but not weakly stationary if, for example, the variance of the process is infinite.[1] However, when the first two moments do exist, strict stationarity implies weak stationarity. Since the normal distribution is completely defined by the first two moments, it follows immediately that for Gaussian processes, strict and weak stationarity are the same.

The following AR(1) process is weakly stationary, for appropriate initial conditions (shown in (4.2) below), when $|\rho| < 1$ (see section 4.3), and when the disturbance term $\{v_t\}$ is taken to be a serially uncorrelated (not necessarily independent) identically distributed random variable with zero mean and constant variance σ_v^2, denoted by $v_t \sim \mathsf{D}_v(0, \sigma_v^2)$:

$$y_t = \mu + \rho y_{t-1} + v_t \quad \forall t. \tag{4.1}$$

The process is strictly stationary when the disturbance term $\{v_t\}$ is IID even without the normality of the disturbances (McCabe and Tremayne, 1993, p.221).

More generally, consider the ARMA model given by:

$$\varphi(L)\, y_t = \theta(L)\, v_t,$$

[1] See, for example, the results of Nelson (1990) and Bougerol and Picard (1992) for GARCH processes.

where v_t is as in (4.1) and $\varphi(L)$ and $\theta(L)$ are the AR and MA polynomials, respectively, with orders p and q. Then a necessary condition for y_t to be stationary is that the roots of $\varphi(L)$ lie outside the unit circle. For (4.1), the root(s) of $\varphi(Z)$ are given by:

$$\varphi(Z) = 1 - \rho_1 Z = 0 \quad \text{which implies that} \quad Z = \frac{1}{\rho_1}$$

so that $|Z| > 1$ if $|\rho_1| < 1$. That the second moment of the process is not time invariant when $|\rho_1| = 1$ is demonstrated for the AR(1) process in section 4.4.

If roots lie inside the unit circle, then the process is explosive ($|\rho_1| > 1$). An important class of non-stationary time series arises when there are no roots inside the unit circle, but there are roots on the unit circle. Such processes are called integrated because they have to be differenced a certain number of times to achieve (weak) stationarity (often written as I(0)). The minimum number of times such series have to be differenced defines the order of integration, which we will typically take to be 1 (see Banerjee, Dolado, Galbraith and Hendry, 1993 and Johansen, 1995, for details). Other types of non-stationarity may be important, including cases when the series contains components which are functions of time, so that the moments depend on time (see section 4.5), or seasonal unit roots. In the following sections, we analyse the implications of these properties for forecastability (eschewing seasonality here).

For simplicity, we expound the basic ideas in the AR(1) model given by (4.1) although nothing crucial depends on setting $p = 1$. To simplify notation, let $\mathbf{x}_t = (1 : y_t)'$ and $\boldsymbol{\theta} = (\mu : \rho)'$. A sample $\mathbf{Y}_T^1$ is available for estimating the parameters of the model, and forecasts are made over the period $T+1$ to $T+H$. The generalization of the 1-step ahead forecast to multi-step ahead forecasts will be denoted by h, $h \in \{1, \ldots, H\}$. Finally, MSFE_h is the second-moment measure of the costs of forecast errors at horizon h, defined for forecasting y_{T+h} by $\widehat{y}_{T+h}$ as:

$$\mathsf{MSFE}_h = \mathsf{E}\left[(y_{T+h} - \widehat{y}_{T+h})^2 \mid y_T\right] = \mathsf{V}\left[e_{T+h}\right] + \left(\mathsf{E}\left[e_{T+h}\right]\right)^2$$

that is, the variance, plus the squared bias of the forecast error, $e_{T+h} = y_{T+h} - \widehat{y}_{T+h}$, where $\mathsf{E}[\cdot]$ and $\mathsf{V}[\cdot]$ denote expectation and variance respectively.

4.3 Stationarity

4.3.1 1-step ahead forecasts

In the stationary case, $-1 < \rho < 1$, the unconditional mean and variance exist:

$$\mathsf{E}\left[y_t\right] = \frac{\mu}{(1-\rho)} \quad \text{and} \quad \mathsf{V}\left[y_t\right] = \frac{\sigma_v^2}{1-\rho^2}. \tag{4.2}$$

Given the information available at time T, for known parameters, the conditional mean is the MMSFE predictor of y in the next period (see section 2.7.2), denoted $\widetilde{y}_{T+1}$:

$$\mathsf{E}\left[y_{T+1} \mid y_T\right] = \widetilde{y}_{T+1} = \mu + \rho y_T \tag{4.3}$$

with forecast error:

$$e_{T+1} = y_{T+1} - \widetilde{y}_{T+1} = v_{T+1}. \tag{4.4}$$

From expressions (4.3) and (4.4), $\mathsf{V}[y_{T+1}|y_T] = \mathsf{V}[e_{T+1}|y_T] = \sigma_v^2$ so the error variance, the conditional forecast-error variance and the conditional variance of the process are all equal.

In (4.3), y_{T+1} is a random variable but $\widetilde{y}_{T+1}$ is not: given information available at period T, it is completely determined. The forecast error e_{T+1} in (4.4) is a random variable because of y_{T+1}. In many statistics texts, upper- and lower-case letters distinguish random variables and their realizations. We do not do so for notational simplicity, and trust that from the context it will be clear which is meant.

In practice, the values of the parameters μ and ρ must be estimated. The forecast error for estimated parameter values $\widehat{\mu}$ and $\widehat{\rho}$ becomes:

$$\widehat{e}_{T+1} = y_{T+1} - \widehat{y}_{T+1} = v_{T+1} + (\mu - \widehat{\mu}) + (\rho - \widehat{\rho})\, y_T = v_{T+1} + \left(\boldsymbol{\theta} - \widehat{\boldsymbol{\theta}}\right)' \mathbf{x}_T. \tag{4.5}$$

The variance of the forecast error is (ignoring a slight dependence of $\widehat{\boldsymbol{\theta}}$ on $\mathbf{x}_T$):

$$\mathsf{V}\left[\widehat{e}_{T+1} \mid y_T\right] = \sigma_v^2 + \mathbf{x}_T' \mathsf{V}\left[\widehat{\boldsymbol{\theta}}\right] \mathbf{x}_T, \tag{4.6}$$

which depends upon the variance σ_v^2 of the innovation process, the variances of the estimated parameters $\mathsf{V}[\widehat{\boldsymbol{\theta}}]$ and the forecast origin. The conditional variance is less than the unconditional variance when the parameters are known (so $\mathsf{V}[\widehat{\boldsymbol{\theta}}] = \mathbf{0}$ in (4.6): compare to (4.2)), but otherwise could be larger or smaller. In (4.6) (ignoring the first observation):

$$\begin{aligned} \mathsf{V}\left[\widehat{\boldsymbol{\theta}}\right] = \mathsf{V}\begin{bmatrix} \widehat{\mu} \\ \widehat{\rho} \end{bmatrix} &= \sigma_v^2 \mathsf{E}\begin{bmatrix} T & \sum_{t=1}^{T} y_{t-1} \\ \sum_{t=1}^{T} y_{t-1} & \sum_{t=1}^{T} y_{t-1}^2 \end{bmatrix}^{-1} \\ &\simeq T^{-1}\begin{bmatrix} \sigma_v^2 + \mu^2 (1+\rho)(1-\rho)^{-1} & -\mu(1+\rho) \\ -\mu(1+\rho) & (1-\rho^2) \end{bmatrix}. \end{aligned} \tag{4.7}$$

The last approximation is valid asymptotically and is used below. When (4.6) uses the asymptotic variance of the estimated model parameters, as in (4.7), it is known as the approximate forecast-error variance (or MSFE, more generally), as distinct from the asymptotic MSFE (no parameter estimation uncertainty).

The forecast errors as defined in (4.5) could be calculated within-sample; for example, if the parameter estimates obtained on a sub-sample up to t, $t \in \{1, \ldots, T\}$, are denoted by $\{\widehat{\mu}_t, \widehat{\rho}_t\}$ then:

$$\widehat{e}_{t+1} = y_{t+1} - \widehat{y}_{t+1} = v_{t+1} + (\mu - \widehat{\mu}_t) + (\rho - \widehat{\rho}_t)\, y_t = v_{t+1} + \left(\boldsymbol{\theta} - \widehat{\boldsymbol{\theta}}_t\right)' \mathbf{x}_t,$$

which will differ from the model residuals (defined as actual less fitted) which use the full-period estimates. Only in the absence of parameter uncertainty will both these types of error coincide with the underlying disturbances (as in (4.4)).

When the forecasts are unbiased, $\mathsf{E}[\widehat{e}_{T+1}] = 0$, then $\mathsf{V}[\widehat{e}_{T+1}|y_T] = \mathsf{E}[(\widehat{e}_{T+1}|y_T)^2]$, indicating that the forecast-error variance corresponds to the MSFE. In section 5.4, we use symmetry arguments to establish conditions under which forecasts are unbiased even when parameters are estimated, even though the OLS estimator of ρ has small-sample bias.

If we set $\mu = 0$ and do not estimate an intercept, then it is apparent that the unconditional expectation of the forecast error will be zero, since we are effectively averaging over the zero-mean forecast origin:

$$\mathsf{E}\left[\mathsf{E}\left[\widehat{e}_{T+1} \mid y_T\right]\right] = \mathsf{E}\left[\mathsf{E}\left[(\rho - \widehat{\rho})\right] y_T \mid y_T\right] = \mathsf{E}\left[(\rho - \widehat{\rho})\right] \mathsf{E}\left[y_T\right] = 0.$$

From (4.7), the correction to MSFEs for parameter estimation uncertainty is of order T^{-1}, which is what is generally found (see Chatfield, 1993 pp.123–4, for a discussion of the impact of parameter uncertainty on forecasts).

4.3.2 When are forecasts informative?

We considered the informativeness of a forecast in chapter 2.3 above. When the data are stationary (as in this section), or when there exist transforms of data such that the unconditional distribution is well defined, a forecast could be defined as informative when the forecast error has a more concentrated probability distribution than the unconditional distribution of the variable being forecast. Consider as an example the stationary first-order autoregressive process in (4.1) with normal errors and $\mu = 0$. The first two moments of the process are given by (4.2), and the unconditional distribution is well defined:

$$y_t \sim \mathsf{N}\left[0, \frac{\sigma_v^2}{1-\rho^2}\right] \qquad \text{for all } t.$$

When ρ is known, the forecast of the value of the process in period $T+1$, conditional on information in period T, yields a 1-step ahead forecast error of $e_{T+1} = y_{T+1} - \widetilde{y}_{T+1} = v_{T+1}$, so that $\mathsf{V}[e_{T+1}|y_T] = \sigma_v^2 < \sigma_y^2 \equiv \mathsf{V}[y_t]$. Thus, 1-step forecasts are informative in the sense that the forecast error is more concentrated than the unconditional variance of the process. We show below that as h increases, $\mathsf{V}[e_{T+h}|y_T] \to \mathsf{V}[y_t]$ (monotonically from below for known parameters) so that informativeness disappears.

From the forecast-error variance, we can define the $100(1-\alpha)$ percent forecast interval as the range that should include that percentage of future realizations, by:

$$\widetilde{y}_{T+1} \pm z_{\alpha/2}\sqrt{\mathsf{V}\left[e_{T+1} \mid y_T\right]}$$

where $z_{\alpha/2}$ denotes the percentage point of the standard normal distribution. The generalization to h-steps ahead follows immediately.

Consider applying this notion of informativeness to predicting the change in the log of real equity prices (y_t in (4.1)), which is believed to be nearly white noise (so that ρ is close to zero):

(a) the log-difference transform assumes a more standardized behaviour of percentage changes compared to absolute changes;
(b) the direction of change from day to day is difficult to predict so the conventional comment that 'real equity price changes are unpredictable' probably refers to this aspect (when $\rho \simeq 0$, then $\sigma_v^2 \simeq \sigma_y^2$ and forecasts are close to being uninformative);
(c) however, to a novice, many helpful features may need highlighting, such as the asymmetry of changes, the high probability of 'outliers' (thick tails), the non-normality of $\mathsf{D}(\cdot)$, etc.;
(d) even so, a stockbroker may be able to make money from a prediction where the forecast error is only a little more concentrated than the outcome; and
(e) a trader in derivatives, such as options, may also make money from predicting the conditional variance more accurately than σ_v^2.

If the prediction of zero for the change in the log of real equity prices is uninformative, is that of the level? Again the issue turns on the state of existing information. Non-stationary, evolutionary processes (such as those with unit roots) do not have well-behaved unconditional distributions, so the conditional prediction of the level next day is much more concentrated than the unconditional. Nevertheless, when the optimal prediction of the change in the log of real equity prices is zero, we doubt that investors would attach any value to the prediction that next day's level will be the same as today's on average.

Whilst we have defined most concepts for 1-step ahead forecasts, the generalizations to h-steps ahead follow directly, as will become apparent below.

4.3.3 h-step ahead forecasts

Conditional on information available at the beginning of the forecast period, for known parameters, the h-step ahead forecast is obtained by backward iteration of $y_{T+h} = \mu + \rho y_{T+h-1}$, so denoting it by $\widetilde{y}_{T+h}$:

$$\widetilde{y}_{T+h} = \mu \frac{(1-\rho^h)}{(1-\rho)} + \rho^h y_T. \tag{4.8}$$

This is the conditional mean of y_{T+h} given y_T. In the stationary case, ρ^h tends to zero as h increases, and the forecast converges to the unconditional mean $\mu/(1-\rho)$. In this sense, stationary processes are well behaved. The actual value of y_{T+h} from (4.1) is:

$$y_{T+h} = \mu \frac{(1-\rho^h)}{(1-\rho)} + \rho^h y_T + \sum_{i=0}^{h-1} \rho^i v_{T+h-i}. \tag{4.9}$$

So $e_{T+h} = y_{T+h} - \widetilde{y}_{T+h}$, and the multi-period forecast-error variance for known parameters is:

$$\mathsf{V}\left[e_{T+h}\right] = \sigma_v^2 \frac{\left(1-\rho^{2h}\right)}{\left(1-\rho^2\right)}. \tag{4.10}$$

Then, $\mathsf{V}[e_{T+h}]$ is also $\mathsf{V}[y_{T+h}|y_T]$, and from (4.10), it increases with h, converging to the unconditional variance of the process. In section 2.5.1, we defined the forecast horizon at which the conditional variance is within α percent of the unconditional variance, the 'horizon of no information'. This establishes the limit to forecastability beyond the unconditional mean, and shows how the informativeness of forecasts falls monotonically in the forecast horizon, in this instance.

When parameters are not known but have to be estimated, (4.8) becomes:

$$\widehat{y}_{T+h} = \widehat{\mu}\frac{\left(1-\widehat{\rho}^h\right)}{\left(1-\widehat{\rho}\right)} + \widehat{\rho}^h y_T, \tag{4.11}$$

and hence:

$$\widehat{e}_{T+h} = \sum_{i=0}^{h-1}\left(\mu\rho^i - \widehat{\mu}\widehat{\rho}^i\right) + \left(\rho^h - \widehat{\rho}^h\right)y_T + \sum_{i=0}^{h-1}\rho^i v_{T+h-i}. \tag{4.12}$$

Thus, assuming that $\mathsf{E}[\widehat{e}_{T+h}]$ is approximately zero,[2] and $\mathsf{E}[e^h_{T+h} - \widehat{e}^h_{T+h}] = 0$:

$$\begin{aligned}\mathsf{V}\left[\widehat{e}_{T+h} \mid y_T\right] &= \sigma_v^2\frac{\left(1-\rho^{2h}\right)}{\left(1-\rho^2\right)} + \mathsf{E}\left[\left\{\sum_{i=0}^{h-1}\left(\mu\rho^i - \widehat{\mu}\widehat{\rho}^i\right)\right\}^2\right] + \mathsf{V}\left[\left(\rho^h - \widehat{\rho}^h\right)\right]y_T^2 \\ &\quad +2\mathsf{E}\left[\left\{\sum_{i=0}^{h-1}\left(\mu\rho^i - \widehat{\mu}\widehat{\rho}^i\right)\right\}\left(\rho^h - \widehat{\rho}^h\right)\right]y_T. \end{aligned} \tag{4.13}$$

The four components correspond to the innovation variance accumulation, the intercept estimation variance, the autoregressive parameter estimation variance, and their covariance, but in awkward combinations of sums of powers. In appendix 4.11, we approximate (4.13) by:

$$\mathsf{V}\left[\widehat{e}_{T+h} \mid y_T\right] = \sigma_v^2\frac{\left(1-\rho^{2h}\right)}{\left(1-\rho^2\right)} + \mathbf{d}'\mathsf{V}\left[\widehat{\boldsymbol{\theta}}\right]\mathbf{d}, \tag{4.14}$$

where:

$$\mathbf{d}' = \left(\frac{\left(1-\rho^h\right)}{\left(1-\rho\right)} : \left\{\mu\frac{\left[1 - h\rho^{h-1}\left(1-\rho\right) - \rho^h\right]}{\left(1-\rho\right)^2} + h\rho^{h-1}y_T\right\}\right).$$

[2] See section 5.4, where we show that for symmetric error distributions, this is a good approximation even though the parameter estimators are biased.

When (4.14) uses the asymptotic variance of the estimated parameters, as in (4.7), it is known as the approximate forecast-error variance (or MSFE, more generally), as distinct from either the asymptotic MSFE (no parameter estimation uncertainty, so that the second term in (4.14) is zero), or the exact MSFE. As Ericsson and Marquez (1996) note, there are four reasons why the approximate MSFE will differ from the exact. The first we have already mentioned: the finite-sample variance of the estimated parameters will differ from the asymptotic (the approximation in (4.7)). Also, the estimated parameters (and powers thereof) are biased in finite samples, but not asymptotically; a first-order Taylor series expansion for $\widehat{\rho}^h$ is used (see section 4.11); and y_T is conditioned on rather than being treated as stochastic. The exact MSFE could be obtained by numerical integration.

In section 6.4 we calculate asymptotic forecast-error variances for models of cointegrated systems, and in sections 6.6–6.8, estimate the exact MSFEs by Monte Carlo.

In section 8.4, we demonstrate that (4.14) may exceed the unconditional variance of y_t, $\mathsf{V}[y_t] = \sigma_v^2(1-\rho^2)^{-1}$ for some forecast horizons, due to the non-monotonicity of the second term in (4.14) (which would also apply to the exact MSFE).

4.4 Stochastic non-stationarity

4.4.1 1-step ahead forecasts

The class of non-stationary processes considered in this section contain stochastic trends, integrated of order one, denoted I(1). Many of the essential points arise when $\rho = 1$ in (4.1):

$$y_t = y_{t-1} + \mu + v_t \qquad \text{so} \qquad \Delta y_t = \mu + v_t, \tag{4.15}$$

where $v_t \sim \mathsf{ID}(0, \sigma_v^2)$. This class of equation is called difference stationary, since its first difference is a stationary process under the stated assumptions.

The difference stationary model is a special case of the basic 'structural time-series' class of models of Harvey (1989). If we ignore cyclical and seasonal components, then we can write the structural time-series model as:

$$y_t = \nu_t + \xi_t \tag{4.16}$$

where:

$$\begin{aligned} \nu_t &= \nu_{t-1} + \mu_{t-1} + \eta_t \\ \mu_t &= \mu_{t-1} + \zeta_t \end{aligned} \tag{4.17}$$

and the disturbance terms η_t, ζ_t and ξ_t are zero mean, uncorrelated white noise, with variances given by σ_η^2, σ_ζ^2 and σ_ξ^2. The interpretation of this model is that ν_t is the (unobserved) trend component of the time series, and ξ_t is the irregular component. η_t affects the level of the trend, and ζ_t allows its slope to change.

Suppose now that $\sigma_\zeta^2 = 0$, then from (4.17) $\Delta\nu_t = \mu + \eta_t$, so that differencing (4.16) and substituting gives:

$$\Delta y_t = \mu + \eta_t + \Delta\xi_t,$$

which is the same as (4.15) when $v_t = \eta_t + \Delta\xi_t$, but now $\{v_t\}$ cannot be IID unless $\sigma_\xi^2 = 0$. Thus, the difference-stationary model is a structural time-series model in which there is no 'irregular' component (i.e., no measurement error), and the 'slope' does not change. In the next section, we show how the deterministic trend-stationary model can also be derived as a special case of the model set out in (4.16) and (4.17).

In reality, economic time series may be integrated of higher orders, and non-stationarity may emanate from regime shifts and structural breaks, which.may be better treated as deterministic in nature.[3] Trend-stationary models are discussed in section 4.5, and in section 4.6, unit root and trend-stationary processes are shown to be nested within the class of fractionally integrated (or fractionally differenced) processes.

Solving (4.15):

$$y_t = y_0 + \mu t + \sum_{i=1}^{t} v_i, \tag{4.18}$$

and hence past shocks persist indefinitely. Now, $\mathsf{E}[y_t] = y_0 + \mu t$, which trends over time, in contrast to the constant unconditional mean in the stationary case. However, the conditional mean of y_{T+1}, given y_T, retains the same form as in (4.3), namely $\mathsf{E}[y_{T+1}|y_T] = \mu + y_T$.

The conditional variance of y_t in (4.15) for known parameters is $\mathsf{V}[y_{T+1}|y_T] = \sigma_v^2$. However, the unconditional variance is $\mathsf{V}[y_t] = \sigma_v^2 t$, which increases linearly over time, making distant forecasts of the level increasingly uncertain.

4.4.2 *h*-step ahead forecasts

The h-step ahead forecast for known parameters, conditional on information available at time T is:

$$\widetilde{y}_{T+h} = \mu + y_{T+h-1} = \mu h + y_T. \tag{4.19}$$

Thus, the forecast is of a change in the variable from the forecast origin with a local trend, or slope, function. The conditional multi-period forecast error is:

$$e_{T+h} = y_{T+h} - \widetilde{y}_{T+h} = \mu h + y_T + \sum_{i=0}^{h-1} v_{T+h-i} - (\mu h + y_T) = \sum_{i=0}^{h-1} v_{T+h-i}. \tag{4.20}$$

[3] See the debate about whether US GNP has a unit root (e.g., Campbell and Mankiw, 1987, and references therein). Distinguishing between stochastic and deterministic non-stationarity is difficult in practice, not least because the debate turns on whether 'non-stationarity of economic time series is produced by the cumulation of permanent shocks at each observation point or by few large shocks occurring infrequently', Reichlin (1989, p.231).

This has a cumulative error, with a variance that increases at $O(h)$ in the horizon h:

$$\mathsf{V}\left[e_{T+h}\right] = h\sigma_v^2, \tag{4.21}$$

in contrast to the $O(1)$ stationary forecast-error variance in (4.10). Conversely, from (4.15), changes cannot be forecast more accurately than their unconditional mean μ.

Stationary combinations of non-stationary variables (e.g., due to cointegration or differencing) will have multi-period forecast-error variances that converge to the unconditional variance of the process (as in (4.10)): thus, section 4.3 reapplies for forecasting Δy_t. However, the forecast-error variances of the constituent series will increase with the forecast horizon (as in (4.21)). Engle and Yoo (1987) demonstrate these propositions using the vector moving average representation of a system of cointegrated variables (also see section 6.2.1).

The h-step forecast error for levels using estimated parameter values is:

$$\begin{aligned} \widehat{e}_{T+h} = y_{T+h} - \widehat{y}_{T+h} &= \mu h + y_T + \sum_{i=0}^{h-1} v_{T+h-i} - \left(\widehat{\mu} h + \widehat{\rho}^h y_T\right) \\ &= \left(\mu - \widehat{\mu}\right) h + \left(1 - \widehat{\rho}^h\right) y_T + \sum_{i=0}^{h-1} v_{T+h-i}. \end{aligned} \tag{4.22}$$

We neglect the coefficient biases, treating such conditional forecasts as unbiased.

Generally, for estimated parameters in I(1) processes, the variance of the forecast error is hard to derive due to the non-standard nature of the distribution: chapter 11 discusses the derivations. However, the limiting distribution is normal when the unit-root model is estimated unrestrictedly for non-zero μ (see West, 1988): the estimate of ρ converges at a rate of $T^{\frac{3}{2}}$ (so its variance can be neglected), whereas $\mathsf{V}[\widehat{\mu}] = 4\sigma_v^2 T^{-1}$ emphasizing the importance of accurately estimating the local trend.

We concentrate on the case in which ρ is correctly imposed as unity. Then, the forecast-error variance increases quadratically in the forecast horizon, h, for fixed T:

$$\mathsf{V}\left[\widehat{e}_{T+h}\right] = h\left(\sigma_v^2 + h\mathsf{V}\left[\widehat{\mu}\right]\right) \simeq h\sigma_v^2\left(1 + h/T\right). \tag{4.23}$$

If we control the rate at which T and h go to infinity by (see Sampson, 1991):

$$T = Ah^{\tau} \tag{4.24}$$

where $\tau \geq 0$, then:

$$\mathsf{V}\left[\widehat{e}_{T+h}\right] \simeq h\sigma_v^2\left(1 + A^{-1}h^{1-\tau}\right) \tag{4.25}$$

which is $O(h^2)$ for $\tau = 0$, $O(h^{2-\tau})$ for $0 < \tau < 1$ and $O(h)$ for $\tau \geq 1$ (see Sampson, 1991, eqn. 12).

4.5 Deterministic non-stationarity

The trend-stationary DGP is given by:

$$y_t = \phi + \gamma t + u_t \qquad (4.26)$$

where we maintain the assumption that the disturbance term is an independently distributed random variable with a constant mean and variance, $u_t \sim \mathsf{ID}(0, \sigma_u^2)$. This model can be obtained as a special case of the structural time-series model defined in (4.16) and (4.17) of section 4.4, by setting $\sigma_\eta^2 = \sigma_\zeta^2 = 0$, so that (4.17) becomes:

$$\nu_t = \nu_{t-1} + \mu = \nu_0 + \mu t. \qquad (4.27)$$

(4.27) indicates that the trend has a constant 'slope' ($\sigma_\zeta^2 = 0$), and the 'level' is not subject to stochastic shocks ($\sigma_\eta^2 = 0$). Substituting into (4.16) results in:

$$y_t = \nu_0 + \mu t + \xi_t$$

which is identical to (4.26) when $\nu_0 = \phi$, $\mu = \gamma$ and $\xi_t = u_t$. Thus, the trend-stationary model is a limiting case of the structural time-series model in which the level and the slope of the trend component are constant over time. From the relationship between such models and the difference-stationary model in section 4.4, structural time-series models essentially comprise functions of time with time-varying parameters.

The h-step ahead forecast for known parameters from (4.26), conditional on information available at time T is:

$$\widetilde{y}_{T+h} = \phi + \gamma (T + h), \qquad (4.28)$$

with multi-period forecast error:

$$e_{T+h} = y_{T+h} - \widetilde{y}_{T+h} = u_{T+h}. \qquad (4.29)$$

The conditional forecast-error variance is the variance of the disturbance term:

$$\mathsf{V}[e_{T+h}] = \sigma_u^2. \qquad (4.30)$$

When parameters have to be estimated, (4.28) becomes:

$$\widehat{y}_{T+h} = \widehat{\phi} + \widehat{\gamma} (T + h), \qquad (4.31)$$

and the multi-period forecast error and error variance are given respectively by:

$$\widehat{e}_{T+h} = \left(\phi - \widehat{\phi}\right) + (\gamma - \widehat{\gamma})(T + h) + u_{T+h}, \qquad (4.32)$$

with:

$$\mathsf{V}[\widehat{e}_{T+h}] = \mathsf{V}\left[\widehat{\phi}\right] + (T + h)^2 \mathsf{V}[\widehat{\gamma}] + 2(T + h)\,\mathsf{C}\left[\widehat{\phi}, \widehat{\gamma}\right] + \sigma_u^2. \qquad (4.33)$$

Thus, we need to evaluate $\mathsf{V}[\widehat{\boldsymbol{\theta}}]$, where $\widehat{\boldsymbol{\theta}} = [\widehat{\phi} : \widehat{\gamma}]'$:

$$\begin{aligned}\mathsf{V}\left[\widehat{\boldsymbol{\theta}}\right] = \mathsf{V}\left[\begin{array}{c}\widehat{\phi}\\ \widehat{\gamma}\end{array}\right] &= \sigma_u^2\left[\left(\begin{array}{cc}T & \frac{1}{2}T(T+1)\\ \frac{1}{2}T(T+1) & \frac{1}{6}T(T+1)(2T+1)\end{array}\right)^{-1}\right] \\ &= \sigma_u^2 T^{-1}(T-1)^{-1}\left[\begin{array}{cc}2(2T+1) & -6\\ -6 & 12(T+1)^{-1}\end{array}\right]. \end{aligned} \tag{4.34}$$

Substituting from (4.34) into (4.33), and simplifying by approximating $(T+1) \simeq T$ gives:

$$\begin{aligned}\mathsf{V}\left[\widehat{e}_{T+h}\right] &\simeq 4\sigma_u^2 T^{-1} - 12(T+h)\sigma_u^2 T^{-2} + 12(T+h)^2\sigma_u^2 T^{-3} + \sigma_u^2 \\ &= \sigma_u^2\left[1 + 4T^{-1} + 12hT^{-2} + 12h^2 T^{-3}\right].\end{aligned} \tag{4.35}$$

From (4.35), the forecast-error variance grows with the square of the forecast horizon, for fixed T. We can again use (4.24) to determine the behaviour of (4.35) as h and T go to infinity:

$$\mathsf{V}\left[\widehat{e}_{T+h}\right] \simeq \sigma_u^2\left[1 + 4A^{-1}h^{-\tau} + 12A^{-2}h^{1-2\tau} + 12A^{-3}h^{2-3\tau}\right]. \tag{4.36}$$

Thus, we find that (4.36) is $O(h^2)$ for $\tau = 0$, $O(h^{2-3\tau})$ for $0 < \tau < \frac{2}{3}$, and $O(1)$ for $\tau \geq \frac{2}{3}$ (see Sampson, 1991, eqn. 18). To more easily compare (4.35) for the trend-stationary model (TS) with (4.23) for the difference-stationary model (DS), when T is not assumed fixed, we calculate the ratio of the two, and eliminating T using (4.24):

$$\frac{\mathsf{V}_{\mathsf{ds}}}{\mathsf{V}_{\mathsf{ts}}} = \left(h + A^{-1}h^{2-\tau}\right)\left(1 + 4A^{-1}h^{-\tau} + 12A^{-2}h^{1-2\tau} + 12A^{-3}h^{2-3\tau}\right)^{-1}. \tag{4.37}$$

From examination of (4.37) it is apparent that $\mathsf{V}_{\mathsf{ds}}/\mathsf{V}_{\mathsf{ts}} \to \infty$ as $h \to \infty$ (and T approaches ∞ at the rate determined by (4.24)) for all values of τ other than $\tau = 0$. In fact, $\tau = 0$ corresponds to a fixed T, and in that case $\mathsf{V}_{\mathsf{ds}}/\mathsf{V}_{\mathsf{ts}} \to A^2/12$ as $h \to \infty$. When we allow T to grow as h increases, no matter how slowly (τ close to but not equal to zero), then $\mathsf{V}_{\mathsf{ds}}/\mathsf{V}_{\mathsf{ts}} \to \infty$ and the forecast-error variance of the DS model swamps that of the TS model in the limit. Thus, only when T is fixed will the DS and TS models be asymptotically indistinguishable, even allowing for parameter uncertainty.

Sampson (1991) argues that allowing for parameter uncertainty leads to forecast-error variances which grow with the square of the forecast horizon for both the DS and TS models, so that asymptotically the two are indistinguishable in terms of their implications for forecastability. As shown, this result requires that the estimation sample T remains fixed while the forecast horizon h goes to infinity.

These two models of non-stationarity have radically different implications for forecastability when the parameters of the models are known: forecast-error variances grow linearly in the forecast horizon for the DS model, but are bounded for the TS model.

This is perhaps an unsurprising conclusion given that the unit-root model accumulates indefinitely the effect of previous disturbance terms, but in the TS model with known parameters, the conditional h-step ahead forecast error is simply the disturbance term in period $T+h$. Uncertainty plays an add-on role in the TS model, but is integral to the DS model. However, when the error term on the TS model becomes highly autocorrelated – as tends to be the case in practice – the two models more closely mimic each other.

4.6 Fractionally integrated processes

Hitherto, the order of integration has been assumed to be either zero or a positive integer – in section 4.4, $d = 1$ so that the process defined by (4.15) is integrated of order 1 ($\mathsf{I}(1)$). Granger and Joyeux (1980) and Hosking (1981) generalized the ARIMA(p, d, q) family of processes by allowing the order of integration (alternatively, the degree of differencing) d, to take fractional values. It can be shown that the resulting models are stationary for $d < 0.5$, and have the advantage of being able to model the 'long-term persistence' in a process. Such models have the feature that the autocorrelations decay at a hyperbolic rate rather than the exponential decay characteristic of stationary ARMA processes, and are therefore capable of capturing dependence between distant observations. In fractional models, the value of d can be chosen to match the low-frequency behaviour of the data leaving the behaviour of the process at higher frequencies largely unrestricted, and capable of being modelled in the usual way by the ARMA parameters (where the roots of the AR and MA polynomials are strictly outside the unit circle). Sowell (1992, figure 1, p.280) shows that the spectral densities at higher frequencies for a range of d from -0.5 to 0.5 for a fractionally integrated white-noise process are relatively flat but vary greatly at low frequencies, consistent with the view that the two parts of the model, the degree of fractional differencing and the ARMA parameters can be used to capture the long- and short-run behaviour of the process.

The fractional white-noise model is given by:

$$(1 - L)^d x_t = \epsilon_t \tag{4.38}$$

for non-integer d, where ϵ_t can be taken to be a unit-variance innovation. Further details, including the derivation of the Wold representation by binomial expansion, and the autocorrelation function, are given in the cited literature. In the remainder of this section we describe how the difference-stationary and trend-stationary models can be nested within a model that allows fractional differencing, following Sowell (1992), allowing each to be tested against the more general model.

The general fractional ARIMA model is:

$$(1 + \phi_1 L + \cdots + \phi_p L^p)\,(1 - L)^d x_t = (1 + \theta_1 L + \cdots + \theta_q L^q)\,\epsilon_t. \tag{4.39}$$

The simple difference-stationary model, discussed in section 4.4 and given by equation

(4.15), for $x_t = \Delta y_t - \mu$ is:

$$x_t = v_t$$

which is (4.39) with $p = q = 0$ and $d = 0$.

First differencing the trend-stationary model (4.26) in section 4.5 gives:

$$\Delta y_t = \gamma + \Delta u_t$$

which we can write in the form of (4.39) for $x_t = \Delta y_t - \gamma$ as:

$$(1 - L)^{-1} x_t = u_t, \tag{4.40}$$

where $p = q = 0$, but now $d = -1$, in contrast to $d = 0$ for the difference-stationary model. Sowell (1992) suggests testing between the two models by estimating a fractional ARIMA. A value of d close to zero would lend support to the unit-root model, and conversely a value close to -1 would be more consistent with the trend-stationary model. This test was applied to postwar US quarterly real GNP. The results indicated that the estimate of d is not significantly different from either 0 or -1, so that the data are unable to distinguish between the two models of trend.

4.7 Forecasting with non-linear models

There has been a rapid development in non-linear time-series analysis in recent years. Tong (1995) provides a comprehensive account, and De Gooijer and Kumar (1992) focus on some of the practical issues that arise in using such models for forecasting. De Gooijer and Kumar (1992) believe the jury is still out on the question of whether such models forecast better than linear models, even in those instances when they appear to fit the data better within sample. Moreover, non-linear multiple time-series modelling is very much in its infancy, which limits the usefulness of the non-linear approach for economic forecasting where the interdependencies within the economic system strongly point toward a multivariate approach.[4]

The meaning of linear (and therefore non-linear) depends on the context: processes are linear when they can be expressed as a linear function of independent errors, and models are linear when they are invariant under linear transforms and have constant derivatives (see, e.g., Harvey, 1993, chapter 8). Thus, the Wold representation is linear only when the errors are independent (so ARMA with ARCH errors is non-linear: see section 4.8), and $y = a + bx^2$ is linear in $z = x^2$, whereas $y = ax + bx^2$ is non-linear.

Our discussion will provide a brief overview of the complications that arise when non-linear models are used for forecasting. We begin in section 4.7.1 with some of the difficulties involved in obtaining multi-step forecasts from non-linear models, and

[4] However, non-linear threshold terms can be incorporated into traditional econometric specifications.

describe the methods that have been suggested in the literature. In section 4.7.2 we introduce two classes of non-linear model that have become popular for modelling economics data, and report on recent research on the usefulness of such models from a forecasting perspective. Multi-period forecasts from one of the models (the SETAR) have to be obtained using the methods described in section 4.7.1, while the other forecasts can be calculated analytically but model estimation is more complicated. Finally, in section 4.7.3 we consider data which appear unpredictable using linear models but may not be once we allow for non-linear generating mechanisms.

4.7.1 Calculating multi-step forecasts

Granger and Teräsvirta (1993) illustrate the issues that arise once we consider non-linear models. Our discussion of methods of forecasting is based directly on Granger and Teräsvirta (1993, section 8.1).[5] The following bivariate model is considered:

$$y_t = g\left(x_{t-1}\right) + \varepsilon_t, \tag{4.41}$$

where $g(x) = x^2$, say, x_t is AR(1):

$$x_t = \alpha x_{t-1} + e_t \tag{4.42}$$

and ε_t and e_t are both zero-mean, IID, the latter with distribution function $\Phi(\cdot)$. Assuming $g(\cdot)$ is known, the MMSFE 1-step predictor is the conditional expectation, as in the linear case:

$$\widetilde{y}_{T+1} = g\left(x_T\right). \tag{4.43}$$

To form the 2-step forecast, we need a forecast of x_{T+1}, $\widetilde{x}_{T+1} = \alpha x_T$. Complications arise, relative to the linear case, because when $g(\cdot)$ is a non-linear function:

$$\mathsf{E}\left[g\left(\cdot\right)\right] \neq g\left(\mathsf{E}\left[\cdot\right]\right).$$

Thus:

$$\mathsf{E}\left[g\left(\widetilde{x}_{T+1} + e_{T+1}\right)\right] \neq g\left(\mathsf{E}\left[\widetilde{x}_{T+1} + e_{T+1}\right]\right) = g\left(\widetilde{x}_{T+1}\right). \tag{4.44}$$

Then, four alternative methods for forecasting 2-steps ahead, based on:

$$\widetilde{y}_{T+2} = \mathsf{E}\left[g\left(\widetilde{x}_{T+1} + e_{T+1}\right)\right] \tag{4.45}$$

are:

(i) deterministic:

$$\widetilde{y}_{n,T+2} = g\left(\widetilde{x}_{T+1}\right);$$

[5] See Tong (1995, chapter 6) for a discussion of the basic methods of obtaining multi-period predictions from non-linear models using the Chapman–Kolmogorov relation; and his chapter 4, section 2, for a discussion of numerical integration routines, given that analytical solutions generally are not available.

(ii) exact:

$$\widetilde{y}_{e,T+2} = \int_{-\infty}^{\infty} g\left(\widetilde{x}_{T+1} + z\right) \mathrm{d}\Phi\left(z\right),$$

where $\Phi(z)$ is the distribution function of e:

(iii) Monte Carlo:

$$\widetilde{y}_{m,T+2} = \frac{1}{N} \sum_{j=1}^{N} g\left(\widetilde{x}_{T+1} + z_j\right),$$

where z_j are random numbers, drawn from $\Phi(z)$:

(iv) bootstrap:

$$\widetilde{y}_{b,T+2} = \frac{1}{n-1} \sum_{j=1}^{n-1} g\left(\widetilde{x}_{T+1} + e_j\right),$$

where the e_j are the sample period residuals from (4.42).

Finally, y_t could be modelled directly on x_{t-2} for a 2-step forecast, in the spirit of multi-step, or dynamic, estimation (see chapter 11).

The deterministic (or naive) method can be viewed as either ignoring the problem in (4.44), or setting $e_{T+1} = 0$ (rather than just setting its expected value to zero). As N increases the Monte Carlo [6] method will provide increasingly good approximations to the exact case. Granger and Teräsvirta (1993) briefly discuss the relative advantages of the methods when $g(\cdot)$ has to be estimated, and an incorrect distribution $\Phi(\cdot)$ is assumed. Brown and Mariano (1984, 1989) provide a detailed analysis.

The difficulties of calculating multi-step forecasts are exacerbated at 3-steps:

$$\widetilde{y}_{T+3} = \mathsf{E}\left[g\left(\widetilde{x}_{T+2} + e_{T+2}\right)\right] = \mathsf{E}\left[g\left(\alpha\left(\widetilde{x}_{T+1} + e_{T+1}\right) + e_{T+2}\right)\right]$$

since the exact method now involves a double integral. Smaller complications arise for the Monte Carlo and bootstrap methods, while the deterministic method is simply:

$$\widetilde{y}_{T+3} = g\left(\widetilde{x}_{T+2}\right) = g\left(\alpha^2 x_T\right) = \alpha^4 x_T^2.$$

Finally, consider models which are autoregressive, such as

$$y_t = g\left(y_{t-1}\right) + \varepsilon_t,$$

where $x_t = y_t$ in (4.41). Then (4.43) and (4.45) become:

$$\widetilde{y}_{T+1} = g\left(y_T\right), \tag{4.46}$$

[6] An introduction to basic Monte Carlo theory is given in chapter 5.

and the 2-step forecast is based on :

$$\begin{aligned} \widetilde{y}_{T+2} &= \mathsf{E}\left[g\left(\widetilde{y}_{T+1}+\varepsilon_{T+1}\right)\right] \\ &= \mathsf{E}\left[g\left(g\left(y_T\right)+\varepsilon_{T+1}\right)\right]. \end{aligned} \tag{4.47}$$

The exact 3-step will again involve a double integral, being based upon:

$$\begin{aligned} \widetilde{y}_{T+3} &= \mathsf{E}\left[g\left(\widetilde{y}_{T+2}+\varepsilon_{T+2}\right)\right] \\ &= \mathsf{E}\left[g\left(g\left(g\left(y_T\right)+\varepsilon_{T+1}\right)+\varepsilon_{T+2}\right)\right]. \end{aligned} \tag{4.48}$$

We can view the derivation of multi-step forecasts, such as (4.47) and (4.48) as an application of the law of iterated expectations (see Harvey, 1993, chapter 8.2) since:

$$\widetilde{y}_{T+h} \equiv \mathsf{E}_T\left[y_{T+h}\right] = \mathsf{E}_T\mathsf{E}_{T+1}\ldots\mathsf{E}_{T+h-1}\left[y_{T+h}\right],$$

where the subscripts denote the information set on which expectations are being based (hitherto, implicitly T). Thus we can obtain (4.47), for example, from:

$$\mathsf{E}_{T+1}\left[y_{T+2}\right] = \mathsf{E}_{T+1}\left[g\left(y_{T+1}\right)+\varepsilon_{T+1}\right] = g\left(y_{T+1}\right)+\varepsilon_{T+1}$$

so that:

$$\begin{aligned} \widetilde{y}_{T+2} &\equiv \mathsf{E}_T\left[y_{T+2}\right] \\ &= \mathsf{E}_T\mathsf{E}_{T+1}\left[y_{T+2}\right] \\ &= \mathsf{E}_T\left[g\left(y_{T+1}\right)+\varepsilon_{T+1}\right] \\ &= \mathsf{E}_T\left[g\left(g\left(y_T\right)+\varepsilon_{T+1}\right)\right]. \end{aligned}$$

4.7.2 SETAR and MS-AR models

The two classes of non-linear model we consider are the self-exciting threshold autoregressive (SETAR) models first proposed by Tong (1978), Tong and Lim (1980) and Tong (1983) (and see also Tong, 1995, for a detailed account),[7] and the Markov-switching autoregressive model (MS-AR) popularised by Hamilton (1989) as a way of characterizing the US business cycle.[8]

The models are described below. However, from a forecasting perspective there appears to be no clear consensus on whether allowing for non-linearities of these types leads to a much improved forecast performance. Clements and Krolzig (1998) carry out

[7] This model has been used to analyse exchange rates, and there are an increasing number of applications to output variables, e.g., Tiao and Tsay (1994), Potter (1995) and Hansen (1996).

[8] See *inter alia* Albert and Chib (1993), Diebold, Lee and Weinbach (1994), Ghysels (1994), Goodwin (1993), Hamilton (1994), Kähler and Marnet (1994), Kim (1994), Krolzig and Lütkepohl (1995), Krolzig (1996), Lam (1990), McCulloch and Tsay (1994), Phillips (1991) and Sensier (1996).

an empirical forecast accuracy comparison of the two models for post-War US GNP, and a Monte Carlo study to assess the costs of using the 'wrong' non-linear model. They find that while both the MS-AR and SETAR models are superior to linear models in capturing certain features of the business cycle, their superiority from a forecasting perspective is less convincing.

4.7.2.1 *Self-exciting threshold autoregressive models*

A SETAR model characterises a variable as being governed by a series of distinct linear autoregressions, where the linear autoregression that generates the values of the time series at any instant depends upon the value taken by the process d periods earlier, where d is known as the length of the delay.

Formally, x_{t-d} is continuous on $\mathbb{R}$, so that partitioning the real line defines the number of distinct regimes, say N_r, where the process is in the ith regime when $r_{i-1} \leq x_{t-d} < r_i$, and in that case the pth order linear AR is defined by:

$$x_t = \phi_0^{\{i\}} + \phi_1^{\{i\}} x_{t-1} + \cdots + \phi_p^{\{i\}} x_{t-p} + \epsilon_t^{\{i\}}, \quad i = 1, 2, \ldots, N_r, \tag{4.49}$$

where $\epsilon_t^{\{i\}} \sim \mathsf{IID}[0, \sigma^{2\{i\}}]$, and the parameters superscripted by $\{i\}$ may vary across regimes. This model is sometimes written as a SETAR$(N_r; p, \ldots, p)$. A lag order that varies over regimes can be accommodated within this framework by defining p as the maximum lag order across the regimes, and noting that some of the $\phi_j^{\{i\}}$ may be zero.

Conditional on the number of regimes, the regime r (assuming $N_r = 2$), and the delay, *d*, the sample can simply be split into two and an OLS regression can be estimated from the observations belonging to each regime separately, or indicator functions can be used in a single regression, constraining the residual error variance to be constant across regimes (see, e.g., Potter, 1995, p.113.)

In practice r is unknown, and the model is estimated by searching over r and d: r is allowed to take on each of the sample period values of x_{t-d} in turn,[9] and d typically takes on the values $0, 1, 2, \ldots$ up to the maximum lag length allowed. The choice of p will also typically be data based.

As presaged in section 4.7.1, exact analytical solutions are not available for multi-period forecasts. Numerical solutions require sequences of numerical integrations (see, e.g., Tong, 1995, sections 4.2.4 and 6.2) based on the Chapman–Kolmogorov relation. Clements and Smith (1997) compare a number of alternative methods of obtaining multi-period forecasts, including the normal forecast-error method (NFE) suggested by Al-Qassam and Lane (1989) for the exponential-autoregressive model, and adapted by De Gooijer and De Bruin (1997) to forecasting SETAR models. They conclude that the Monte Carlo method performs reasonably well.

[9] In practice the range of values of x_{t-d} is restricted to those between the 15th and 85th percentile of the empirical distribution, following Andrews (1993) and Hansen (1996).

4.7.2.2 Markov-switching autoregressive models

In MS-AR processes, contractions and expansions are modelled as switching regimes of the stochastic process generating the growth rate of GNP. The regimes are associated with different conditional distributions of the growth rate of real GNP, where, for example, the mean is positive in the first regime ('expansion') and negative in the second regime ('contraction').

The Hamilton (1989) model of the US business cycle fits a fourth-order autoregression ($p = 4$) to the quarterly percentage change in US real GNP from 1953 to 1984:

$$\Delta y_t - \mu(s_t) = \alpha_1 (\Delta y_{t-1} - \mu(s_{t-1})) + \cdots + \alpha_4 (\Delta y_{t-p} - \mu(s_{t-4})) + u_t, \quad (4.50)$$

where $u_t \sim \mathsf{IN}[0, \sigma_u^2]$. The mean $\mu(s_t)$ switches between two states ($M = 2$):

$$\mu(s_t) = \begin{cases} \mu_1 > 0 & \text{if } s_t = 1 \text{ ('expansion' or 'boom')}, \\ \mu_2 < 0 & \text{if } s_t = 2 \text{ ('contraction' or 'recession')}. \end{cases} \quad (4.51)$$

The description of a MS-AR model is completed by the specification of a model for the stochastic and unobservable regimes on which the parameters of the conditional process depend. Once a law has been specified for the states s_t, the evolution of regimes can be inferred from the data. The regime-generating process is assumed to be an ergodic Markov chain with a finite number of states $s_t = 1, 2$ (for a two-regime model), defined by the transition probabilities:

$$p_{ij} = \mathsf{P}(s_{t+1} = j \mid s_t = i), \quad \sum_{j=1}^{2} p_{ij} = 1 \quad \forall i, j \in \{1, 2\}. \quad (4.52)$$

The assumption of fixed transition probabilities p_{ij} can be relaxed (see, for example, Diebold, Rudebusch and Sichel, 1993, Diebold *et al.*, 1994, Filardo, 1994, Lahiri and Wang, 1994 and Durland and McCurdy, 1994).

The derivation of an optimal predictor can often be quite complicated in empirical work for non-linear time-series models, but forecasts can be easily obtained for MS-AR models. In contrast to linear models, the MMSFE predictor does not have the property of being a linear predictor, but the conditional mean can be derived analytically, unlike for many non-linear models (including the SETAR model).

For the Hamilton model, we need to solve the recursion:

$$\widehat{\Delta y}_{T+h|T} = \widehat{\mu}_{T+h|T} + \sum_{k=1}^{4} \alpha_k \left(\widehat{\Delta y}_{T+h-k|T} - \widehat{\mu}_{T+h-k|T} \right) \quad (4.53)$$

with initial values $\widehat{\Delta y}_{T+h|T} = \Delta y_{T+h}$ for $h \leq 0$, and where the predicted mean is:

$$\widehat{\mu}_{T+h|T} = \sum_{j=1}^{2} \mu_j \mathsf{P}(s_{T+h} = j \mid Y_T).$$

The predicted regime probabilities:

$$\mathsf{P}\left(s_{T+h}=j \mid Y_T\right)=\sum_{i=1}^{2} \mathsf{P}\left(s_{T+h}=j \mid s_T=i\right) \mathsf{P}\left(s_T=i \mid Y_T\right)$$

only depend on the transition probabilities $\mathsf{P}(s_t = j|s_{t-1} = i) = p_{ij}$, $i, j = 1, 2$ and the filtered regime probability $\mathsf{P}(s_T = i|Y_T)$.

The model can be estimated using the expectation-maximization (EM) algorithm – see Hamilton (1990) and Krolzig (1996). The EM algorithm introduced by Dempster, Laird and Rubin (1977) is designed for models where the observed time series depends on some unobservable stochastic variables – for MS-AR models these are the s_t.

In conjunction with the filtering algorithm of Hamilton (1988, 1989) and the smoothing algorithms of Kim (1994), we can conduct optimal inference on the latent state of the economy by assigning probabilities to the unobserved regimes 'expansion' and 'contraction' conditional on the available information set.

4.7.3 Non-linear data generating mechanisms

Turning now to non-linear data generating mechanisms, Harvey (1993) produces an example in which a series generated from a non-linear mechanism is weak white noise (WN): the random variables are uncorrelated, zero mean and constant variance, but are not independent (that is, not strict WN). Therefore, linear models will have no predictive power, but as the process is not independent, it may still be possible to predict future values of the series from current and past values using non-linear models. The DGP is:

$$y_t = \varepsilon_t + \beta \varepsilon_{t-1} \varepsilon_{t-2}, \quad \text{where } \varepsilon_t \sim \mathsf{IID}\left[0, \sigma_\varepsilon^2\right], \varepsilon_0 = \varepsilon_{-1} = 0. \tag{4.54}$$

y_t has a zero mean, a constant variance and zero autocovariances. Calculating the current and lagged values of the εs recursively, the MMSFE 1-step predictor is:

$$\widetilde{y}_{T+1} = \beta \varepsilon_T \varepsilon_{T-1} \tag{4.55}$$

which has a smaller forecast-error variance than the variance of the process, (σ_ε^2 compared to $(1 + \beta^2 \sigma_\varepsilon^2)\sigma_\varepsilon^2$: see Harvey, 1993, pp.267–8 for details).

A martingale difference series (MDS) has the property that its expectation, conditional on the past of the process, is zero, which implies (*i*) that it also has a zero unconditional mean; and (*ii*) it is uncorrelated with any (possibly non-linear) function of the past of the process. Following Harvey (1993), we note that:

(a) A MDS is serially uncorrelated. Not all serially uncorrelated series are MDS – in (4.55), ε_T and ε_{T-1} can be written as functions of past values of y. A MDS need not have a constant variance, but if it does, then it is (weak) WN.
(b) All zero-mean independent series are MDS, but the converse does not hold.

A MDS is characterized by the property that past information does not help predict future values of the series. Since (4.54) does not possess this property, it is not a MDS. In the next section, we briefly discuss a class of models which have the MDS property, but which are not strict WN. Series which are MDS, but not strict WN (i.e., not independent) are non-linear in a way in which only higher moments, such as variances are affected. This has implications for forecast uncertainty, but not first-moment concepts such as point forecasts.

4.8 Forecasting with ARCH errors

In this section, we discuss the implications for forecasting of autoregressive conditional heteroscedasticity (ARCH). The ARCH model of Engle (1982) and its generalizations have become almost indispensable in the modelling of financial series, which are typically characterized by thick-tailed unconditional distributions, variances that change over time, and a clustering of large (small) changes in the series. There are a number of good surveys available of the vast literature on ARCH and related models: see Engle and Bollerslev (1987), Bollerslev *et al.* (1992), Bera and Higgins (1993) and Shephard (1996); Engle (1995) contains an edited selection of some of the key papers. We concentrate on the implications for forecasting, following the treatment in Bera and Higgins (1993); Baillie and Bollerslev (1992) contains additional details.

ARCH implies that the ability to predict future values of a series may vary over time. In previous sections, we showed how the ability to predict the future might vary with the forecast horizon. ARCH effects imply that there may be periods of relatively high volatility associated with wide prediction intervals (or low volatility and narrow bands) so that the forecast origin is important.

In general, the optimal forecast from an ARMA process is not affected by ARCH, so that the method of construction of the point forecast outlined in (2.10) is unaltered. Section 4.9 qualifies this statement for asymmetric loss functions. ARCH will affect the uncertainty in the point forecast and therefore the construction of prediction intervals.

For the ARMA process in section 2.7.1, we derived the unconditional forecast-error variance (equation (2.15)) as a measure of the uncertainty in the forecast. Since $\mathsf{E}[v_{T+j}^2|\mathcal{I}_T] = \mathsf{E}[v_{T+j}^2] = \sigma_v^2$ when the errors are homoscedastic, the conditional and unconditional forecast-error variances coincide. In place of (2.15), we now write the expression for the conditional forecast-error variance as:

$$\mathsf{V}\left[e_{T+h} \mid \mathcal{I}_T\right] = \sum_{j=1}^{h} \psi_{h-j}^2 \mathsf{E}\left[v_{T+j}^2 \mid \mathcal{I}_T\right], \tag{4.56}$$

where we condition on the information used to construct the forecast, $\mathcal{I}_T$, to allow for the possibility of temporal dependence in the variances of the disturbances. Indeed, the hallmark of ARCH-type models is that $\mathsf{E}[v_{T+j}^2|\mathcal{I}_T]$ depends on $\mathcal{I}_T$. We can evaluate these expressions for general GARCH processes: we choose a GARCH(1,1) process for v_t in conjunction with an AR(1) process for y_t for illustrative purposes. For the AR(1) model, we established in section 2.7.1 that $\psi_i^2 = \phi_1^{2i}$, $i = 0, \ldots, h-1$, so (4.56) becomes:

$$\mathsf{V}\left[e_{T+h} \mid \mathcal{I}_T\right] = \sum_{j=0}^{h-1} \phi_1^{2j} \mathsf{E}\left[v_{T+h-j}^2 \mid \mathcal{I}_T\right]. \tag{4.57}$$

A GARCH$(1,1)$ model for v_t has the form:

$$v_t \mid \mathcal{I}_{t-1} \sim \mathsf{N}\left[0, h_t\right],$$

where:

$$h_t = \alpha_0 + \alpha_1 v_{t-1}^2 + \beta_1 h_{t-1}. \tag{4.58}$$

An ARCH(p) process would be of the form:

$$h_t = \alpha_0 + \alpha_1 v_{t-1}^2 + \cdots + \alpha_p v_{t-p}^2.$$

Since we can write (4.58) as:

$$h_t = \frac{\alpha_0}{1-\beta_1} + \frac{\alpha_1 L}{1-\beta_1 L} v_t^2$$

then a GARCH model is simply an infinite order ARCH process with a rational lag structure.

Letting $\nu_t = v_t^2 - h_t$, v_t^2 has the ARMA$(1,1)$ representation:

$$v_t^2 = \alpha_0 + \left(\alpha_1 + \beta_1\right) v_{t-1}^2 - \beta_1 \nu_{t-1} + \nu_t. \tag{4.59}$$

Taking conditional expectations of (4.59), we obtain a recursive formula for computing the relevant second moments:

$$\mathsf{E}\left[v_{T+h}^2 \mid \mathcal{I}_T\right] = \alpha_0 + \left(\alpha_1 + \beta_1\right) \mathsf{E}\left[v_{T+h-1}^2 \mid \mathcal{I}_T\right], \quad h > 1 \tag{4.60}$$

with:

$$\mathsf{E}\left[v_{T+1}^2 \mid \mathcal{I}_T\right] = \alpha_0 + \alpha_1 v_T^2 + \beta_1 h_T$$

which can then be substituted into (4.57).

There are two important points to make about (4.60), concerning the starting point of the process and its dynamics. Firstly, $\mathsf{E}[v_{T+h}^2|\mathcal{I}_T]$ depends on T. If T is a tranquil period, this quantity is likely to increase monotonically in h. But if T is a volatile period then it may initially decline. Forecast accuracy may be increasing in h due to the effects of ARCH for some forecast origins: as the period of high volatility gives way to a more tranquil period, the inherent uncertainty in predicting the process is reduced and prediction intervals shrink.

We have argued that $\mathsf{E}[v^2_{T+h}|\mathcal{I}_T]$ may initially rise or fall as we increase h, depending on T. Suppose the root of $1-(\alpha_1+\beta_1)Z$ lies outside the unit circle, then:

$$\lim_{h\to\infty} \mathsf{E}\left[v^2_{T+h} \mid \mathcal{I}_T\right] = \frac{\alpha_0}{1-(\alpha_1+\beta_1)}$$

which is the unconditional variance of the process. But, if there is a unit root, $\alpha_1+\beta_1 = 1$, (known as integrated ARCH or IGARCH) then:

$$\mathsf{E}\left[v^2_{T+h} \mid \mathcal{I}_T\right] = h\alpha_0 + \mathsf{E}\left[v^2_T \mid \mathcal{I}_T\right]$$

so that the conditional variance does not converge, but grows linearly in h. Then, the influence of $\mathcal{I}_T$ persists via $\mathsf{E}[v^2_T|\mathcal{I}_T]$.

In terms of the discussion in section 4.7, all (G)ARCH models are MDS, since the v_t are zero-mean and uncorrelated. When the unconditional variance of v_t is constant, they are also WN (requiring $\alpha_1+\beta_1<1$, for GARCH(1,1), so that IGARCH is not WN). However the v_t are not independent due to the dependence in the squares of the series, and so such processes are not strict WN, and hence non-linear.

In economics, processes such as $y_t = v_t$ are uncommon since economic variables are likely to be autoregressive (e.g., $\phi_1 \neq 0$ in the AR(1) model). The prediction intervals for AR models are constructed by summing the conditional variances (4.60) with declining weights (for stationary models), as in (4.56) and (4.57). For such processes, forecast uncertainty will be non-decreasing in h.

Finally, ARCH can be given a random-coefficient model interpretation, and so the preceding analysis applies, for example, to a model such as:

$$y_t = \phi_t y_{t-1} + \epsilon_t,$$

where $\phi_t \sim \mathsf{D}_\phi(\phi, \sigma^2_\phi)$ is the random coefficient, and $\epsilon_t \sim \mathsf{D}_\epsilon(0, \sigma^2_\epsilon)$. When the ϕ_t are unknown:

$$\mathsf{E}\left[y_{T+1} \mid \mathcal{I}_T\right] = \phi y_T$$

and:

$$\mathsf{V}\left[y_{T+1} \mid \mathcal{I}_T\right] = \sigma^2_\epsilon + \sigma^2_\phi y^2_T.$$

The point forecast is unaffected by the random coefficient, and the conditional variance of the process is first-order ARCH.

4.9 Second-moment dependence and asymmetric loss

In section 4.3, we demonstrated that the conditional expectation (the mean of the conditional distribution of the process) is the MMSFE, so that the conditional expectation is optimal if the loss function is quadratic in the forecast error. Loss functions are discussed in some detail in chapter 3, but in this section we demonstrate that when loss is asymmetric ARCH effects as discussed in section 4.8 may affect optimal point predictions as well as prediction intervals.

In the absence of ARCH effects, so that the prediction-error variance is homoscedastic (equivalently, the conditional prediction-error variance equals the unconditional prediction-error variance) as in (2.15), Granger (1969) has shown that although the conditional mean predictor is not optimal for asymmetric loss, a simple fixed adjustment of it is, where the adjustment depends only on the form of the loss function and the prediction-error variance. This theorem requires that the process is Gaussian, and that the loss function is defined over forecast errors, rather than the realizations and forecasts more generally. An immediate implication of the conditional expectation being non-optimal (given the loss function) is that biased predictions are consistent with rational behaviour: see Zellner (1986).

Christoffersen and Diebold (1996) generalize the theorem to allow for processes which are only conditionally Gaussian, which include the ARCH-type processes discussed in section 4.8. They show that if the prediction-error variance is time varying, then the adjustment to the mean predictor will not be constant since it depends on the conditional error variance. Thus, temporal dependence in the second moments of the process will affect the optimal point predictions and in a way which will depend on the degree of temporal dependence.

The argument can be illustrated with a simple asymmetric loss function which can be solved analytically for the optimal predictor. Following Christoffersen and Diebold (1996), who extend the analysis of Zellner (1986), we consider the 'linex' loss function of Varian (1975), defined by:

$$\mathsf{C}(e) = b\left[\exp(ae) - ae - 1\right], \quad a \neq 0, b \geq 0,$$

where for $a > 0$, the loss function is approximately linear for $e < 0$ ('over-predictions'), and exponential for $e > 0$, ('under-predictions'). For small a, the loss function is approximately quadratic:

$$\mathsf{C}(e) \simeq \frac{ba}{2}e^2$$

from the first two terms of the Taylor-series expansion. The optimal predictor h-steps ahead solves:

$$\underset{\widehat{y}_{T+h}}{\operatorname{argmin}}\ \mathsf{E}_T\left[b\left\{\exp(ae_h) - ae_h - 1\right\}\right], \tag{4.61}$$

where $e_h = y_{T+h} - \widehat{y}_{T+h}$, $\widehat{y}_{T+h}$ is the optimal predictor, and is assumed to have the form $\widehat{y}_{T+h} = \mu_{T+h} + \alpha_{T+h}$, where the process is conditionally Gaussian:

$$y_{T+h} \mid \mathcal{I}_T \sim \mathsf{N}\left[\mu_{T+h}, \sigma^2_{T+h}\right],$$

so that μ_{T+h} is the conditional mean predictor and σ^2_{T+h} is the conditional variance. Substituting for $e_h = y_{T+h} - \mu_{T+h} - \alpha_{T+h}$ in (4.61) and using the result that:

$$\mathsf{E}_T\left[\exp(ay_{T+h})\right] = \exp\left[a\mu_{T+h} + \frac{a^2\sigma^2_{T+h}}{2}\right],$$

gives:

$$\underset{\alpha_{T+h}}{\operatorname{argmin}} \mathsf{E}_T \left[b \left\{ \exp\left(\frac{a^2\sigma^2_{T+h}}{2} - a\alpha_{T+h} \right) - a\left(y_{T+h} - \mu_{T+h} - \alpha_{T+h}\right) - 1 \right\} \right]. \tag{4.62}$$

The first-order condition is satisfied by:

$$\alpha_{T+h} = \frac{a}{2}\sigma^2_{T+h}$$

so that the optimal predictor becomes:

$$y_{T+h} = \mu_{T+h} + \frac{a}{2}\sigma^2_{T+h}. \tag{4.63}$$

To interpret (4.63), assume that $a \gg 0$, so that a is not close to zero, and being positive implies that costs to under-prediction are weighted more heavily than those to over-prediction. The optimal predictor then exceeds the conditional expectation, so that the conditionally expected error will on average be negative, that is, there will be a tendency to over-predict. The greater the conditionally expected variation around the conditional expectation the greater the tendency to over-predict. As the degree of asymmetry lessens ($a \to 0$) so the optimal predictor approaches the conditional expectation.

Christoffersen and Diebold (1996) also derive the optimal predictor for 'linlin' loss (linear on both sides of the origin but with different slopes). In general though, analytic solutions are not available and those authors suggest some numerical methods for computing the optimal predictor.

4.10 Overview

We have considered forecasting in simple linear autoregressive models, and have found that the properties of forecasts and prediction intervals derived from such models depend crucially on the time-series properties of the variables. In practice, it may be difficult to discriminate between a trend-stationary and difference-stationary DGP, although the implications of the two for how accurately the process can be forecast are quite different. We also discussed two classes of non-linear model, the SETAR and MS-AR models, which have been used to model (univariate) economic time series. The SETAR model is an example of a piece-wise linear model, in that the model is linear within a regime but moves between regimes depending upon the realized value of the process a number of periods previously. The MS-AR model is also linear conditional upon the regime that the process is in, but now the regime-determining variable is an unobservable variable assumed to follow a Markov chain. While such models possess certain attractive features in terms of characterizing the history of the process, their forecast performance is not clearly superior.

We have also discussed the impact of ARCH on the calculation of measures of uncertainty around point forecasts, and how ARCH in conjunction with asymmetric loss can affect point forecasts.

Some of the material in this chapter will be further developed in subsequent chapters (e.g., the extension to systems of cointegrated-integrated variables in chapter 6), but read on its own, provides an introduction to forecasting with univariate time-series models that stresses the implications for forecasting of the time-series properties of the variables.

4.11 Appendix: Approximating powers of estimates

We use a number of approximations to obtain tractable expressions for variances of powers of estimated parameters, following Schmidt (1977), Baillie (1979b, 1979a) and Chong and Hendry (1986). Ericsson and Marquez (1989, 1996) and Campos (1992) provide good expositions and unifying treatments. We consider the stationary AR(1) model in (4.1):

$$y_t = \mu + \rho y_{t-1} + v_t \quad v_t \sim \mathsf{IN}\left[0, \sigma_v^2\right],$$

where estimation is by OLS. Let:

$$\widehat{\rho} = \rho + \delta, \tag{4.64}$$

where δ is $O_p(1/\sqrt{T})$, so that powers of δ are asymptotically negligible. Then the first approximation is:

$$\widehat{\rho}^h = (\rho + \delta)^h \simeq \rho^h + h\delta\rho^{h-1} = \rho^h + h\rho^{h-1}(\widehat{\rho} - \rho). \tag{4.65}$$

Consequently:

$$\mathsf{E}\left[\widehat{\rho}^h\right] \simeq \rho^h + h\rho^{h-1}\mathsf{E}\left[\widehat{\rho} - \rho\right] \simeq \rho^h$$

by the approximation that $\mathsf{E}[\widehat{\rho} - \rho] = 0$. Higher-order approximations can be calculated if needed. Next:

$$\mathsf{V}\left[\left(\widehat{\rho}^h - \rho^h\right)\right] \simeq \mathsf{V}\left[h\rho^{h-1}(\widehat{\rho} - \rho)\right] = h^2\rho^{2(h-1)}\mathsf{V}\left[\widehat{\rho}\right]. \tag{4.66}$$

This result also follows from the usual formula for a non-linear estimation function:

$$\mathsf{V}\left[\widehat{\rho}^h\right] \simeq \frac{\partial \rho^h}{\partial \rho}\mathsf{V}\left[\widehat{\rho}\right]\frac{\partial \rho^h}{\partial \rho}. \tag{4.67}$$

Further:

$$\mu\rho^j - \widehat{\mu}\widehat{\rho}^j = \rho^j(\mu - \widehat{\mu}) + \mu\left(\rho^j - \widehat{\rho}^j\right) - (\mu - \widehat{\mu})\left(\rho^j - \widehat{\rho}^j\right), \tag{4.68}$$

where the final term is negligible relative to the first two as $T \rightarrow \infty$. The second main approximation comes in ignoring that term, so that from (4.65):

$$
\begin{aligned}
\sum_{j=0}^{h-1}\left(\mu\rho^{j}-\widehat{\mu}\widehat{\rho}^{j}\right) &\simeq (\mu-\widehat{\mu})\sum_{j=0}^{h-1}\rho^{j}+\mu\left(\rho-\widehat{\rho}\right)\sum_{j=1}^{h-1}j\rho^{j-1} \\
&= (\mu-\widehat{\mu})\frac{\left(1-\rho^{h}\right)}{(1-\rho)}+\left(\rho-\widehat{\rho}\right)\mu\frac{\left(1-h\rho^{h-1}(1-\rho)-\rho^{h}\right)}{(1-\rho)^{2}} \\
&= \left(\boldsymbol{\theta}-\widehat{\boldsymbol{\theta}}\right)'\mathbf{b},
\end{aligned}
\tag{4.69}
$$

say, where:

$$
\mathbf{b}'=\left[\frac{\left(1-\rho^{h}\right)}{(1-\rho)}:\mu\frac{\left(1-h\rho^{h-1}(1-\rho)-\rho^{h}\right)}{(1-\rho)^{2}}\right].
$$

Then:

$$
\mathsf{E}\left[\left\{\sum_{j=0}^{h-1}\left(\mu\rho^{j}-\widehat{\mu}\widehat{\rho}^{j}\right)\right\}^{2}\right]=\mathbf{b}'\mathsf{V}\left[\widehat{\boldsymbol{\theta}}\right]\mathbf{b}. \tag{4.70}
$$

Finally, using (4.65) and (4.69):

$$
\begin{aligned}
\mathsf{E}\left[\left\{\sum_{j=0}^{h-1}\left(\mu\rho^{j}-\widehat{\mu}\widehat{\rho}^{j}\right)\right\}\left(\rho^{h}-\widehat{\rho}^{h}\right)\right]y_{T} &= h\rho^{h-1}\mathbf{b}'\mathsf{E}\left[\left(\boldsymbol{\theta}-\widehat{\boldsymbol{\theta}}\right)\left(\rho-\widehat{\rho}\right)\right]y_{T} \\
&= h\rho^{h-1}\mathbf{b}'\mathsf{V}\left[\widehat{\boldsymbol{\theta}}\right]\mathbf{s}y_{T},
\end{aligned}
\tag{4.71}
$$

where $\mathbf{s}'=(0:1)$. Letting $h\rho^{h-1}y_{T}\mathbf{s}=\mathbf{c}$ and $\mathbf{d}=\mathbf{b}+\mathbf{c}$, (4.13) becomes:

$$
\mathsf{V}\left[\widehat{e}_{T+h}\mid y_{T}\right]=\sigma_{v}^{2}\frac{1-\rho^{2h}}{1-\rho^{2}}+\mathbf{d}'\mathsf{V}\left[\widehat{\boldsymbol{\theta}}\right]\mathbf{d}, \tag{4.72}
$$

where:

$$
\mathsf{V}\left[\widehat{\boldsymbol{\theta}}\right]=T^{-1}\begin{bmatrix}\sigma_{v}^{2}+\mu^{2}\frac{(1+\rho)}{(1-\rho)} & -\mu(1+\rho)\\ -\mu(1+\rho) & \left(1-\rho^{2}\right)\end{bmatrix} \tag{4.73}
$$

from which our analytical approximations in the text are calculated.

Chapter 5

Monte Carlo techniques

This chapter provides an introduction to the use of simulation techniques, such as Monte Carlo, in forecasting theory. We begin by presenting a basic theorem that underlies Monte Carlo experimentation. That statistical theorem establishes a link between the Monte Carlo simulation results and the population values of the parameters. An application of the theorem follows in chapter 6, where we consider the relationship between the Monte Carlo estimates of the forecast second-moment measures and their population values (given by asymptotic formulae in section 6.4). The theorem is first illustrated in the context of a simple example, then demonstrated for the example in chapter 6. We next consider ways in which Monte Carlo studies can be made more informative. First, control variates are described, as well as how these can be incorporated into Monte Carlo computations as a method of variance reduction. Secondly, we explain the role of antithetic variates which are also a variance-reduction method intended to make a Monte Carlo more efficient than distribution sampling. Antithetic variates exploit the fact that the random numbers are known to the investigator, and can be re-used so that the uncertainty in the experiment is reduced: the random numbers are selected in sets to offset each other's variability. However, the technique of antithetic variates can also be used as an analytical tool to establish various properties concerning the bias of the forecasts and the impact of deterministic components (such as a constant) in the DGP. We show that unbiased forecasts may result even though the parameter estimates of the models from which they are generated are biased.

5.1 Introduction

Stochastic simulation, or Monte Carlo, has been used in many ways in econometrics. Perhaps the earliest use of Monte Carlo was in calculating the small-sample distributions of estimators and tests whose asymptotic behaviour was known. The usefulness of the large-sample results could then be gauged for samples of the size typically available to the applied researcher, and the questions of 'how large is large?' and 'how small is small?' could be addressed. In chapter 6, we use Monte Carlo methods for this purpose.

An alternative use of Monte Carlo is in obtaining a reference distribution for a test statistic. Suppose an investigator calculates a given test, but the small-sample distribution of the test statistic is not known. A reference distribution for the statistic can be obtained by simulating the model under the null hypothesis to produce a number of samples (of appropriate size) of artificial data. Each sample of artificial data is generated by replacing the model's errors by random variates from a random number generator (or by sampling with replacement from the estimated model's errors, called the bootstrap – see, for example, the surveys by Hinkley, 1988 and Hall, 1994). The actual test statistic value can then be compared to critical values from that reference distribution. An early reference is Williams (1970). A recent example is Pesaran and Pesaran (1993), who use a simulation method to calculate the numerator of the Cox statistic (Cox, 1961b, 1962) for testing non-nested models.

Monte Carlo methods have also been used to solve difficult problems of numerical integration,[1] particularly in the field of Bayesian econometrics: see, inter alia, Geman and Geman (1984), Geweke (1988a, 1988b) and Richard and Zhang (1996b, 1996a). Such methods have important applications to estimation in latent-variable models (see, e.g., Pakes and Pollard, 1989, Hendry and Richard, 1991 and Hajivassiliou and Ruud, 1994), but we will not consider that literature here.

The remainder of this chapter is organized as follows. In section 5.2, we introduce basic Monte Carlo theory, which underlies the use of the Monte Carlo method in the first mode outlined above. Control variates and antithetic variables are discussed in section 5.3 and section 5.4 as a means of improving the efficiency of the Monte Carlo, and the latter are also used to obtain a number of properties of the forecasts and measures of forecast accuracy. General references to Monte Carlo methods include Hammersley and Handscomb (1964), Hendry (1984), Ripley (1987) and Davidson and MacKinnon (1993).

5.2 Basic Monte Carlo theory

Consider a random variable y, identically and independently distributed with mean $\mathsf{E}[y] = \mu$ and variance $\mathsf{E}[(y-\mu)^2] = \sigma^2$, where both parameters are unknown. We wish to calculate these first two moments of y. When we observe the $\{y_i\}$, where $y_i \sim \mathsf{IID}(\mu, \sigma^2)$, the statistical theory of the distribution of the sample mean and variance as estimators of μ and σ^2 is well developed. A similar theory applies when we can construct appropriate quantities as functions of pseudo-random variates (from a random number generator) which have the same unknown distribution, mean and variance as the $\{y_i\}$. In either case, y_i is viewed as the value of y on replication i of R replications (sampling or Monte Carlo). There are many settings where we know that $y_i \sim \mathsf{IID}(\mu, \sigma^2)$ but cannot derive $\mathsf{E}[y]$ or $\mathsf{E}[(y-\mu)^2]$ analytically. Nevertheless, we

[1] For example, in section 4.7.1 and section 4.7.2 we came across the use of Monte Carlo to calculate multi-period forecasts from non-linear models.

might be able to obtain drawings of y_i from an artificial experiment, and use the sample statistics of that experiment to estimate the unknown moments. It is surprisingly easy to set up experiments that deliver appropriate drawings of y_i even though μ and σ^2 are unknown: we will explain how in specific contexts shortly. When the y_i are constructed quantities, we are in effect substituting a stochastic problem for an (assumed intractable) deterministic analytical problem (calculating the first two population moments of y), and then solving the stochastic problem by simulation. The stochastic problem has to be set up such that we are certain in advance that it has the same solution as the deterministic one.

The basic statistical theorem is that the Monte Carlo sample mean:

$$\widetilde{y} = R^{-1} \sum_{i=1}^{R} y_i, \tag{5.1}$$

is an unbiased estimator of the population mean, that is $\mathbb{E}[\widetilde{y}] = \mu$, with a variance around the population mean given by:

$$\mathbb{E}\left[\left(\widetilde{y} - \mu\right)^2\right] = \frac{\sigma^2}{R} = \mathcal{V}\left[\widetilde{y}\right], \tag{5.2}$$

where $\mathbb{E}$ and $\mathcal{V}$ denote an expectation and a variance with respect to the random variables in the Monte Carlo. When the number of replications, R, is large, $\widetilde{y} \underset{app}{\sim} \mathsf{N}[\mu, \sigma^2/R]$, where $\underset{app}{\sim}$ denotes 'is approximately distributed as'. Finally, the sample variance defined by (its square root, $\widetilde{\sigma}$, is the Monte Carlo standard deviation, MCSD):

$$\widetilde{\sigma}^2 = (R-1)^{-1} \sum_{i=1}^{R} \left(y_i - \widetilde{y}\right)^2, \tag{5.3}$$

is an unbiased estimator of the unknown population variance $\mathbb{E}[\widetilde{\sigma}^2] = \sigma^2$. Hence, providing we can obtain suitable y_i, we can calculate all the required estimates together with a measure of the uncertainty in the experiment, which, from the expression for $\mathcal{V}[\widetilde{y}]$, is seen to tend to zero as R increases. From a sufficiently large number of random replications, essentially precise results can be obtained.

Examples of the use of Monte Carlo to obtain estimates of measures of forecast accuracy for particular models estimated from small samples are reported in section 6.7 and section 6.8. There we estimate trace mean-square forecast errors (TMSFEs) and generalized forecast-error second-moment measures (GFESMs). The properties of these measures of forecast accuracy are established formally in chapter 3.

To obtain the TMSFE, we simulate the unconditional forecast-error second-moment matrices (termed $\mathsf{M}[\mathbf{e}_{T+h}]$ in section 2.1) by:

$$\overline{\mathbf{M}} = R^{-1} \sum_{i=1}^{R} \widehat{\mathbf{M}}_i = R^{-1} \sum_{i=1}^{R} \left[\widehat{\mathbf{e}}_{T+h,i} \widehat{\mathbf{e}}'_{T+h,i}\right], \tag{5.4}$$

where the summation is over the number of replications ($R = 1000$), and $\widehat{\mathbf{e}}_{T+h,i}$ is the h-step ahead forecast error on the ith replication from using a particular model. The TMSFE is then the trace of (5.4) (or, equivalently, the average over replications of the $tr(\widehat{\mathbf{M}}_i)$). In terms of the theorem outlined above, we simply let $y_i = tr[\mathbf{e}_{T+h,i}\widehat{\mathbf{e}}'_{T+h,i}]$, then calculate $\widetilde{y}$, the sample mean of the Monte Carlo (5.1), which we know is an unbiased estimator of the population mean value of the TMSFE. When the forecasts are unbiased, (5.4) will also give the forecast-error covariance matrix. Zero-mean forecast errors can be shown to result under quite general conditions (see for example the formulae in section 6.4, Hendry and Trivedi, 1972 and Dufour, 1985).

As a measure of the precision of the Monte Carlo, we calculate the Monte Carlo standard errors (MCSEs) of the TMSFEs. From (5.3), the sample variance of the Monte Carlo is:

$$\begin{aligned}\widehat{\sigma}^2 &= R^{-1}\sum_{i=1}^{R}\left[tr\left(\widehat{\mathbf{M}}_i\right) - tr\left(\overline{\mathbf{M}}\right)\right]^2 \\ &= R^{-1}\sum_{i=1}^{R}\left[tr\left(\widehat{\mathbf{M}}_i\right)\right]^2 - \left[tr\left(\overline{\mathbf{M}}\right)\right]^2, \end{aligned} \tag{5.5}$$

so that $\widehat{\sigma}^2/R$ is an unbiased estimator of the variance of $\overline{\mathbf{M}}$ around the population value, and the MCSEs quoted in table 6.2 of section 6.8 are given by $\widehat{\sigma}/\sqrt{R}$.

As described in section 3.6, the GFESM is formed by stacking the forecast errors from all previous step ahead forecasts as in (5.6):

$$|\mathbf{\Phi}_h| = \left|\mathsf{E}\left[\mathbf{E}\mathbf{E}'\right]\right|, \tag{5.6}$$

where $\mathbf{E}' = [\mathbf{e}'_{T+1}, \mathbf{e}'_{T+2}, \ldots, \mathbf{e}'_{T+h-1}, \mathbf{e}'_{T+h}]$. It is the determinant of an expectation. The expectation of the stacked matrix of forecast errors is simulated by averaging over replications, before calculating its determinant. Denoting by $\mathbf{E}_{h,j}$ the outcome on the jth of R replications (a column vector of dimension nh), $|\sum \mathbf{E}_{h,i}\mathbf{E}'_{h,i}|$ estimates $|\mathbf{\Phi}_h|$, not $\sum |\mathbf{E}_{h,i}\mathbf{E}'_{h,i}|$: we cannot set $y_i = |\mathbf{E}_{h,i}\mathbf{E}'_{h,i}|$ then calculate $\sum y_i$, since $|\mathbf{E}_{h,i}\mathbf{E}'_{h,i}| \equiv 0$ for each individual replication. It is impossible to obtain a measure of the sampling variability in the same way as for the TMSFE.

The appropriate distributional theory for the GFESM is available in the statistics literature. As the Monte Carlo delivers independent replications of $\mathbf{E}_h$:

$$\mathbf{E}_{h,j} \underset{\widetilde{app}}{} \mathsf{IN}_{nh}\left[\mathbf{0}, \mathbf{\Phi}_h\right], \tag{5.7}$$

for $T \to \infty$, so that:

$$R \cdot \widehat{\mathbf{\Phi}}_h = \sum_{j=1}^{R} \mathbf{E}_{h,j}\mathbf{E}'_{h,j} \underset{\widetilde{app}}{} \mathsf{W}_{nh}\left[R, \mathbf{\Phi}_h\right], \tag{5.8}$$

when $\mathsf{W}_{nh}[R, \mathbf{\Phi}_h]$ denotes a central Wishart distribution with R degrees of freedom. Also, $|\widehat{\mathbf{\Phi}}_h|$ provides a consistent estimator of $|\mathbf{\Phi}_h|$ (see Rao, 1965, chapter 8). Anderson (1984, chapter 7) shows that for n equations, an h-step forecast horizon, and R independent replications, using $\underset{a}{\sim}$ to denote 'is asymptotically distributed as $R \to \infty$':

$$\sqrt{R}\left(\frac{|\widehat{\mathbf{\Phi}}_h|}{|\mathbf{\Phi}_h|} - 1\right) \underset{a}{\sim} \mathsf{N}\left[0, 2nh\right]. \tag{5.9}$$

For moderate sample sizes, $(\{|\widehat{\mathbf{\Phi}}_h|/|\mathbf{\Phi}_h|\} - 1)$ will be close to $\ln(|\widehat{\mathbf{\Phi}}_h|/|\mathbf{\Phi}_h|)$. From (5.9), it is apparent that the uncertainty in the Monte Carlo rankings based on $|\widehat{\mathbf{\Phi}}_h|$ will be $O(4h)$ in the forecast horizon for the bivariate case.

In practice, we report estimates of the quantity $|\widehat{\mathbf{\Phi}}_h|^{1/h}$. This power transform will not affect the qualitative outcome of between-estimator comparisons, but will serve to stabilize estimates of GFESM for large h when $|\mathbf{\Phi}_1|$ differs from unity.

The inherent uncertainty in Monte Carlo simulations can be reduced by a number of techniques. These include:

(1) common sets of random numbers;
(2) control variates;
(3) antithetic variates;
(4) invariance arguments.

For example, in a Monte Carlo comparison of a number of econometric estimators, it is natural to use the same set of random numbers for the calculation of each estimator for a given experimental design, and also to use that same set as the experimental design is altered. By using common random numbers in this way, the variance of between-estimator comparisons, and of comparisons over different experimental designs, will be reduced. The potential gains from using control variates are considered in section 5.3 below.

In section 5.4 we consider antithetic variates. Antithetic variates can be incorporated into the scheme for sampling the random numbers to reduce variability (see, for example, Ericsson and Marquez, 1996), but we have not pursued that approach here. Instead the technique is used to establish various analytical properties of the forecast moments. The information gleaned from this source and from direct analysis may help to improve the efficiency of the Monte Carlo by allowing invariances to certain parameter combinations to be exploited at the design stage, reducing the dimension of the parameter space that needs to be explored.

5.3 Control variates for second-moment measures

Control variates are typically used to control for variation in the Monte Carlo due to the particular random numbers used (see, e.g., Hendry, 1984 and Hendry, Neale and

Ericsson, 1991: a similar approach is adopted by Ericsson and Marquez, 1989, 1996 and Chambers, 1993). Their use is best explained by an example. In sections 6.7 and 6.8, we utilize this technique in the Monte Carlo simulation of second-moment measures of forecast accuracy.

Consider the DGP:

$$\mathbf{x}_t = \mathbf{\Lambda x}_{t-1} + \boldsymbol{\epsilon}_t, \tag{5.10}$$

where $\boldsymbol{\epsilon}_t \sim \mathsf{IN}_n[\mathbf{0}, \boldsymbol{\Omega}]$. Let the Monte Carlo estimator of the forecast-error covariance matrix for known parameter values be denoted by $\mathbf{M}^*$:

$$\mathbf{M}^* = R^{-1}\sum_{i=1}^{R}\left[\mathbf{e}^*_{T+h,i}\mathbf{e}^{*\prime}_{T+h,i}\right], \tag{5.11}$$

where:

$$\mathbf{e}^*_{T+h} = \mathbf{x}_{T+h} - \mathbf{x}^*_{T+h} \tag{5.12}$$

and $\mathbf{x}^*_{T+h} = \mathbf{A}^h\mathbf{x}_T$, (compare (5.4), where $\widehat{\mathbf{e}}_{T+h} = \mathbf{x}_{T+h} - \widehat{\mathbf{x}}_{T+h}$ and $\widehat{\mathbf{x}}_{T+h} = \widehat{\mathbf{A}}^h\mathbf{x}_T$ when $\widehat{\mathbf{A}}$ is an estimate of $\mathbf{A}$ in (5.10)). We wish to obtain an estimate of the forecast-error covariance matrix when the forecasts are generated by an estimated model (using $\widehat{\mathbf{A}}$ instead of $\mathbf{A}$), but as shown below we can exploit the fact that $\mathbf{A}$ is known to the experimenter to increase the efficiency of the Monte Carlo. We construct the sophisticated Monte Carlo forecast-error covariance matrix estimator $\widetilde{\mathbf{M}}$ as:

$$\widetilde{\mathbf{M}} = \widehat{\mathbf{M}} - [\mathbf{M}^* - \mathbf{M}^a], \tag{5.13}$$

where $\mathbf{M}^a$ is the asymptotic value of the forecast-error covariance matrix.[2] The difference $\mathbf{M}^* - \mathbf{M}^a$ is due to Monte Carlo variation and tends to zero as $R \to \infty$. That is, $\mathbb{E}[\mathbf{M}^* - \mathbf{M}^a] = \mathbf{0}$ because $\mathbf{M}^*$ is an unbiased estimator of the population forecast-error covariance matrix $\mathbf{M}^a$. Thus, $\mathbb{E}[\widetilde{\mathbf{M}}] = \mathbb{E}[\widehat{\mathbf{M}}]$. Improved precision of (5.13) over (5.4) results when:

$$\mathcal{V}\left[\widetilde{\mathbf{M}}\right] = \mathcal{V}\left[\widehat{\mathbf{M}}\right] + \mathcal{V}\left[\mathbf{M}^* - \mathbf{M}^a\right] - 2\mathcal{C}\left[\widehat{\mathbf{M}}, (\mathbf{M}^* - \mathbf{M}^a)\right] < \mathcal{V}\left[\widehat{\mathbf{M}}\right], \tag{5.14}$$

so that the covariance term exceeds the second variance term on the right-hand side of the equality. We could also calculate MCSEs for (5.13) similarly to (5.5). Specifically:

$$\begin{aligned}\widetilde{\sigma}^2 &= R^{-1}\sum_{i=1}^{R}\left[tr\left(\widetilde{\mathbf{M}}_i\right) - tr\left(\widetilde{\mathbf{M}}\right)\right]^2 \\ &= R^{-1}\sum_{i=1}^{R}\left[tr\left(\widehat{\mathbf{M}}_i - \mathbf{M}^*_i\right)\right]^2 - \left[tr\left(\widehat{\mathbf{M}} - \mathbf{M}^*\right)\right]^2,\end{aligned}$$

since $\widetilde{\mathbf{M}}_i = \widehat{\mathbf{M}}_i - [\mathbf{M}^*_i - \mathbf{M}^a]$.

---

[2] In terms of the actual Monte Carlo undertaken in sections 6.7 and 6.8, $\mathbf{M}^a$ corresponds to one of (6.19), (6.20) or (6.24).

5.4 Antithetic variates: single-equation forecast biases

A number of authors have studied the properties of least-squares predictors in the scalar AR(1) process, both for stationary and I(1) processes. Symmetry arguments based on the notion of antithetic variates are used to establish the conditions under which forecasts are unbiased. When the process contains an intercept, unbiasedness of the least-squares predictor requires that the process is mean stationary, so the initial condition is drawn from a distribution with the same mean as that of the process. Under mean stationarity, we can deduce that the forecast bias for a process with no intercept is zero. However, any mean-stationary process with a non-zero intercept can be transformed to a zero-intercept mean-stationary process without loss of generality. Since we make extensive use of this idea, and of the invariance of linear models to linear transformations, the supporting analysis is given in detail for the scalar case.

We then derive the properties of forecasts from an econometric model that imposes a unit root. This links in with the analyses in chapters 6 and 12. We find that the unit-root model yields unbiased forecasts under the assumption of mean stationarity whether or not the unit-root model implies a zero growth rate of the variable. The importance of the start-up assumption becomes apparent when we contrast the results for mean stationarity with those for fixed start-up.

In section 6.5 the notions and ideas developed here for scalar models are extended to the systems case. As will be seen, additional issues arise when we consider cointegrated systems.

We begin with a scalar AR(1) process, which has been the focus of much attention in the literature. The model is thus:

$$y_t = \alpha y_{t-1} + \varphi + u_t \text{ where } u_t \sim \mathsf{IN}\left[0, \sigma_u^2\right]. \tag{5.15}$$

Some care is required over the specification of the initial condition, y_0. We consider two possibilities:

(1) the fixed start-up model: $y_0 = 0$; and,
(2) the strictly stationary model: $y_0 = (1-\alpha^2)^{-\frac{1}{2}} u_0 + (1-\alpha)^{-1}\varphi$.

In the latter case, $\mathsf{E}[y_t] = (1-\alpha)^{-1}\varphi$ and $\mathsf{V}[y_t] = (1-\alpha^2)^{-1}\sigma_u^2$ for all t (including $t = 0$). This list of alternatives concerning the initial condition is by no means exhaustive: see for example Magnus and Pesaran (1991).

Malinvaud (1970) establishes that the least-squares predictor is unbiased when $\varphi = 0$, and Fuller and Hasza (1980) show that the more general least-squares predictor with (α, φ) unknown is also unbiased for the strictly stationary model. These results can be established using antithetic variates as follows. Suppose to begin with that $\varphi = 0$ in (5.15), although an intercept is estimated by OLS. Then we have that:

$$y_{T+h} = \alpha^h y_T + \sum_{j=0}^{h-1} \alpha^j u_{T+h-j} = \alpha^{T+h} y_0 + \sum_{j=0}^{T+h-1} \alpha^j u_{T+h-j} \tag{5.16}$$

and:

$$\widehat{y}_{T+h} = \widehat{\alpha}^h y_T + \widehat{\varphi} \sum_{j=0}^{h-1} \widehat{\alpha}^j, \tag{5.17}$$

where (5.17) gives the h-step least-squares forecasts. Suppose that the series $\{y_t\}$, $t = 0, \ldots, T+h$ is generated by $\{u_t\}$ $t = 0, \ldots, T+h$ from (5.16). Now, let $\{y_t^-\}$ denote the series generated by $\{-u_t\}$ $t = 0, \ldots, T+h$. The series $\{-u_t\}$ is a legitimate choice, and is as equally likely as $\{u_t\}$ given symmetry. From (5.16) and $y_0 = (1-\alpha^2)^{-\frac{1}{2}} u_0$, it is clear that $\{y_t^-\} = -\{y_t\}$. Moreover, from the least-squares formulae for $\widehat{\alpha}$ and $\widehat{\varphi}$:

$$\widehat{\alpha} = \frac{\sum_{t=1}^{T} y_t y_{t-1} - T^{-1} \sum_{t=1}^{T} y_{t-1} \sum_{t=1}^{T} y_t}{\sum_{t=1}^{T} y_{t-1}^2 - T^{-1} \left(\sum_{t=1}^{T} y_{t-1} \right)^2} \tag{5.18}$$

and:

$$\widehat{\varphi} = T^{-1} \left(\sum_{t=1}^{T} y_t - \widehat{\alpha} \sum_{t=1}^{T} y_{t-1} \right) \tag{5.19}$$

it is apparent that $\widehat{\alpha}^- = \widehat{\alpha}$, and $\widehat{\varphi}^- = -\widehat{\varphi}$, where $\widehat{\alpha}^-$ and $\widehat{\varphi}^-$ are the estimates obtained from $\{y_t^-\}$.

Now, consider the average forecast error of the antithetic pair:

$$\frac{1}{2}\left[\widehat{e}_{T+h} + \widehat{e}_{T+h}^-\right] = \frac{1}{2}\left[\left(y_{T+h} + y_{T+h}^-\right) - \left(\widehat{y}_{T+h} + \widehat{y}_{T+h}^-\right)\right] = 0 \tag{5.20}$$

since $y_{T+h} = -y_{T+h}^-$ and $\widehat{y}_{T+h} = -\widehat{y}_{T+h}^-$ from (5.17). Since every possible pair of matched forecast errors averages to zero, the expected forecast error is zero also, and hence the forecasts are unbiased even though the parameter estimates are not.

The assumption that $\varphi = 0$ is without loss of generality under the strict stationarity assumption for y_0. Suppose $\varphi \neq 0$. We can subtract the mean from the series so that:

$$y_t^* = y_t - \mu, \quad \text{where} \quad \mu = (1-\alpha)^{-1}\varphi \tag{5.21}$$

and thus:

$$y_t^* = \alpha y_{t-1}^* + \varphi^* + u_t \quad \text{where} \quad \varphi^* = 0. \tag{5.22}$$

Consider the estimators of α and φ^* in (5.22), denoted by $\widetilde{\alpha}$ and $\widetilde{\varphi}$. Firstly, notice that:

$$\widetilde{\alpha} = \frac{\sum_{t=1}^{T} y_t^* y_{t-1}^* - T^{-1} \sum_{t=1}^{T} y_{t-1}^* \sum_{t=1}^{T} y_t^*}{\sum_{t=1}^{T} y_{t-1}^{*2} - T^{-1} \left(\sum_{t=1}^{T} y_{t-1}^* \right)^2} = \widehat{\alpha} \tag{5.23}$$

so that the estimator of α is invariant to φ as long as a constant term is estimated. Now consider the estimator of the constant term in (5.22):

$$\widetilde{\varphi} = T^{-1}\left(\sum_{t=1}^{T} y_t^* - \widehat{\alpha}\sum_{t=1}^{T} y_{t-1}^*\right) = \widehat{\varphi} - (1-\widehat{\alpha})\,\mu \tag{5.24}$$

and:

$$\widetilde{\varphi}^- = T^{-1}\left(\sum_{t=1}^{T} y_t^{*-} - \widehat{\alpha}\sum_{t=1}^{T} y_{t-1}^{*-}\right) = \widehat{\varphi}^- - (1-\widehat{\alpha})\,\mu. \tag{5.25}$$

When $\varphi \neq 0$, $\widehat{\varphi}^- \neq \widehat{\varphi}$, but it is apparent from (5.24) and (5.25) that $\widetilde{\varphi}^- = -\widetilde{\varphi}$. This is because from (5.22):

$$y_t^* = \alpha^t y_0^* + \sum_{j=0}^{t-1} \alpha^j u_{t-j} = \alpha^t \left(1-\alpha^2\right)^{-\frac{1}{2}} u_0 + \sum_{j=0}^{t-1} \alpha^j u_{t-j},$$

since:

$$y_0^* = y_0 - \mu = \left(1-\alpha^2\right)^{-\frac{1}{2}} u_0.$$

Therefore $y_t^{*-} = -y_t^*$, and the relationship that $\widetilde{\varphi} = -\widetilde{\varphi}^-$ follows immediately. Furthermore:

$$\widetilde{\varphi}^- = -\widetilde{\varphi} \text{ implies } \widehat{\varphi} = -\widehat{\varphi}^- + 2\,(1-\widehat{\alpha})\,\mu,$$

so that the long-run mean μ is unbiasedly estimated by $\widehat{\varphi}/(1-\widehat{\alpha})$. In terms of the y^*s, the forecasts are seen to be unbiased, analogously to the forecasts in terms of y_t when $\varphi = 0$ in (5.20):

$$\frac{1}{2}\left[\left(y_{T+h}^* + y_{T+h}^{*-}\right) - \left(\widehat{y}_{T+h}^* + \widehat{y}_{T+h}^{*-}\right)\right] = \frac{1}{2}\,[0-0] = 0. \tag{5.26}$$

Since the forecasts in terms of the y^*s are unbiased, and the y^*s are a linear transform of the ys, then forecasts in the original variables are also unbiased. We can demonstrate this proposition explicitly as follows. Consider y_t when $\varphi \neq 0$:

$$y_t = \alpha^t y_0 + \varphi \sum_{j=0}^{t-1} \alpha^j + \sum_{j=0}^{t-1} \alpha^j u_{t-j} \tag{5.27}$$

so under mean stationarity:

$$y_t + y_t^- = 2\alpha^t \mu + 2\varphi \sum_{j=0}^{t-1} \alpha^j = 2\mu. \tag{5.28}$$

Now, consider the sum of the forecasts, taking $\widehat{\alpha} \neq 1$:

$$\widehat{y}_{T+h} + \widehat{y}_{T+h}^- = \widehat{\alpha}^h \left(y_T + y_T^-\right) + \left(\widehat{\varphi} + \widehat{\varphi}^-\right) \sum_{j=0}^{h-1} \widehat{\alpha}^j = 2\widehat{\alpha}^h \mu + 2\mu\left(1-\widehat{\alpha}^h\right) = 2\mu, \tag{5.29}$$

so from (5.28) and (5.29), $(y_{T+h} + y^-_{T+h}) - (\widehat{y}_{T+h} + \widehat{y}^-_{T+h}) = 0$, demonstrating unbiasedness. Thus least-squares forecasts are unbiased under strict stationarity.[3] The problem with the fixed start-up model is clear in this context: the resulting process will not have a constant mean over time (unless $\varphi = 0$ so that $\mu = 0$) and thus a transformation of the process to a zero-mean process is not possible. In terms of the algebra above, the transformation in (5.21) is not defined.

If $\varphi = 0$, then unbiasedness results under the fixed start-up condition. The above discussion implicitly assumes that the process is stationary ($-1 < \alpha < 1$). Otherwise the process does not have a constant mean, and only the fixed start-up assumption is possible. In that case, forecasts are unbiased if $\varphi = 0$, but not otherwise (notice that the proof of the unbiasedness of OLS when $\varphi = 0$ makes no reference to the actual value of α, and does not therefore exclude α on the unit circle).

We shall also consider a predictor where the parameter of y_{t-1} is imposed at 1, but $-1 < \alpha < 1$ in (5.15). This model will be referred to as the unit-root model (and the DV model – 'differenced VAR' – in the multivariate context). For the unit-root model it is relatively straightforward to obtain explicit expressions for the size of the bias.

We begin with the stationary start-up assumption, so that from (5.28) we have $y_i + y_i^- = 2\mu$. The unit-root model predictor is defined by:

$$\Delta\widetilde{y}_{T+h} = \widetilde{\varphi}, \quad \text{and so} \quad \widetilde{y}_{T+h} = y_T + h\widetilde{\varphi},$$

where:

$$\widetilde{\varphi} = T^{-1}\sum_{s=1}^{T}\Delta y_s = T^{-1}\left(y_T - y_0\right). \tag{5.30}$$

Thus:

$$\widetilde{y}_{T+h} + \widetilde{y}^-_{T+h} = 2\mu + hT^{-1}\left(2\mu - 2\mu\right) = 2\mu \tag{5.31}$$

which in conjunction with (5.28) implies that the average forecast error for the antithetic pair is zero. When a constant term is not estimated, so that the unit-root predictor is simply:

$$\widetilde{y}_{T+h} = \widetilde{y}_{T+h-1} = \cdots = \widetilde{y}_T,$$

then (5.31) is unchanged and therefore forecasts from the unit-root model remain unbiased even though a unit root is imposed. The bias of the parameter 'estimate' of α for the unit-root model is $1 - \alpha$.

Now consider the fixed start-up model. From (5.27) with $y_0 = 0$:

$$y_i + y_i^- = 2\varphi\sum_{j=0}^{i-1}\alpha^j = 2\varphi\frac{1-\alpha^i}{1-\alpha} \tag{5.32}$$

[3] To be precise, we require mean stationarity rather than strict stationarity. That is u_0 can have a different variance from that of subsequent u_ts.

and (5.31) becomes:

$$\widetilde{y}_{T+h} + \widetilde{y}_{T+h}^{-} = 2\varphi \left(1 + hT^{-1}\right) \frac{1-\alpha^T}{1-\alpha}. \tag{5.33}$$

The average forecast error for the antithetic pair is:

$$\varphi \frac{1-\alpha^{T+h}}{1-\alpha} - \varphi \left(1 + hT^{-1}\right) \frac{1-\alpha^T}{1-\alpha} = \varphi \left(\alpha^T \frac{1-\alpha^h}{1-\alpha} - hT^{-1} \frac{1-\alpha^T}{1-\alpha} \right). \tag{5.34}$$

By L'Hôpital's rule, as $\alpha \to 1$, $(1-\alpha^j)/(1-\alpha) \to j$, so that, as $\alpha \to 1$, (5.34) goes to:

$$\varphi \left(1 \times h - hT^{-1} \times T\right) = 0.$$

If, however, $\alpha = 0$, then (5.34) becomes $-\varphi h T^{-1}$, which is increasing in h.

Contrast the case when a constant term is not estimated. Then, the expression corresponding to (5.33) is:

$$\widetilde{y}_{T+h} + \widetilde{y}_{T+h}^{-} = y_T + y_T^{-} = 2\varphi \frac{1-\alpha^T}{1-\alpha} \tag{5.35}$$

so that the bias from (5.32) and (5.35) is:

$$\varphi \alpha^T \frac{1-\alpha^h}{1-\alpha} \approx \varphi h \quad \text{as } \alpha \to 1, \text{ and } 0 \text{ for } \alpha = 0. \tag{5.36}$$

Thus, the bias will be smaller for the 'no change' forecasts ($\widetilde{y}_{T+h} = y_T$, $\forall h$) than for the unit-root model with a constant estimated when α is close to zero and/or the sample size is small.

If $\alpha = 1$ so that $y_t \sim \mathsf{I}(1)$, then with $y_0 = 0$ from (5.27) we obtain:

$$y_i + y_i^{-} = 2\varphi i.$$

From (5.30), $\widetilde{\varphi} + \widetilde{\varphi}^{-} = 2T^{-1}\varphi T = 2\varphi$, so that:

$$\widetilde{y}_{T+h} + \widetilde{y}_{T+h}^{-} = 2\varphi T + 2\varphi h = 2\varphi(T+h)$$

establishing unbiasedness when a constant is estimated, but a bias of φh otherwise, consistent with (5.34) and (5.36).

To summarize: forecasts from the model estimated by OLS and from the (misspecified) unit-root model are unbiased when the process is mean stationary. Related results can be established in dynamic systems, but to do so we first need to develop the notation and relationships involved. Thus we return to apply antithetic variates to the biases in dynamic system forecasts in section 6.5.

5.5 Overview

Stochastic simulation or Monte Carlo is now used extensively in econometrics. It can be used to calculate the small-sample distribution of an estimator or test statistics when the asymptotic distribution is known, to obtain the reference or empirical null distribution of a test statistic (even when the asymptotic distribution is unknown), or to solve difficult problems of numerical integration. This chapter can be read as a self-contained introduction to the use of Monte Carlo in econometrics. It provides the necessary background material to understand the Monte Carlo applications in chapters 6 and 11.

We review sophisticated Monte Carlo techniques such as control variables and antithetic variates. The latter is viewed as both a means of improving efficiency and a way of establishing useful properties of forecasts, such as that of unbiasedness, using symmetry arguments. We return to this use of antithetic variates in section 6.5 when we consider forecasting in cointegrated systems.

Chapter 6

Forecasting in cointegrated systems

In chapter 4, we considered forecasting in univariate processes using simple time-series models. The properties of forecasts and prediction intervals derived from such models were found to depend crucially on the time-series properties of the variables. This chapter considers forecasting with systems of integrated variables. This is a non-trivial extension of the univariate analysis of forecasting with an integrated variable because of cointegration, whereby a linear combination of individually integrated variables may be non-integrated $\mathsf{I}(0)$ variable, with potentially important consequences for forecasting. We first establish a number of representations of integrated-cointegrated systems, which highlight the relevant features of variables for forecasting. We then derive expressions for the asymptotic forecast-error variances or prediction intervals for multi-step forecasts. A particular form of model mis-specification is considered, that is, the implications for forecast accuracy of not imposing the restrictions implied by cointegration on the forecasting model. Antithetic variates establish conditions for unbiased forecasts. We then address the implications for forecast accuracy of small-sample parameter estimation uncertainty in a Monte Carlo, and compare the outcomes with those obtained using control variates.

6.1 Introduction

We showed in chapter 4 that whether economic time series are $\mathsf{I}(1)$ or stationary has important implications for their forecastability. Although $\mathsf{I}(1)$ variables can only be forecast with increasingly wide confidence intervals, cointegrating linear combinations of such variables have finite prediction intervals as the horizon grows. A central theme of this chapter concerns the relative merits of imposing cointegrating restrictions as against the elimination of unit roots by differencing the variables individually. To this end, we derive analytical formulae for forecast-error variances, as a natural extension to the formulae derived in chapter 4. The analytical formulae correspond to the known parameter case, and can be viewed as the asymptotic outcomes. The role of parameter estimation uncertainty is also investigated.

Before tackling such issues, we consider the restrictions on a general system of equations implied by cointegration, recalling that cointegration and equilibrium-correction are isomorphic (see Engle and Granger, 1987).

We begin in section 6.2 with the moving-average representation of a vector of variables, as a generalization of the Wold decomposition for a scalar process, and discuss the restrictions on the coefficients of the MA lag polynomial implied by cointegration. The approach to forecasting in cointegrated processes of Engle and Yoo (1987) is based on this formulation, and we discuss it to bring out the valuable insights that it affords. We then turn to the vector autoregressive representation (VAR), and outline three equivalent representations of a cointegrated system. Beginning with a VAR in levels, an equivalent representation of the system has the (vector of) differences of the variables as the regressand, or alternatively, in an $\mathsf{I}(0)$ transformation of the vector of variables, the regressand is made up of both cointegrating combinations and differences of the original variables. Section 6.3 establishes that the representations are equivalent, since the transformations on which they are based are members of a general class of non-singular linear transformations to which linear models are invariant.

Section 6.4 derives the asymptotic-variance formulae, and demonstrates the importance of the linear transformation on which forecast accuracy is assessed for MSFEs, building on chapter 3. Section 6.5 extends the antithetic-variate analysis of section 5.4 to establish the conditions for unbiased forecasts in cointegrated and differenced systems. In section 6.6, we discuss theoretical results on estimation in small samples for integrated-cointegrated variables, and on the impact of estimation uncertainty on forecast-error variances, before turning to a Monte Carlo study, making use of the ideas discussed in chapter 5. Sections 6.7 and 6.8 discuss the experimental design and present the results. Section 6.9 provides an empirical illustration, based on the forecast performance of models of the demand for UK M1. The implications and recommendations that follow from the analysis in this chapter are brought together in section 6.10.

6.2 Systems for non-stationary variables

In chapter 4, we noted the conditions for a scalar process to be integrated of order one: namely, the occurrence of a unit root in the autoregressive lag polynomial of the ARMA representation. Cointegration is a relationship that may hold between a number of integrated economic time series, and implies that some of the series have common unit-root components that cancel when we take appropriate linear combinations. Thus, cointegration implies restrictions on systems of equations. The basis is the Granger representation theorem in Engle and Granger (1987); Hylleberg and Mizon (1989) and Engle and Yoo (1991) provide extensions and simplified proofs using Smith–McMillan–Yoo forms; and Clements (1990) uses these to compare the mathematical formulations of the restrictions in Davidson (1988) and Johansen (1988b). A number of representations of the system, based on the vector moving-average (VMA) and VAR representations of the system are possible. We begin by expositing the theory of forecasting in cointegrated systems, as developed by Engle and Yoo (1987), in a VMA.

6.2.1 Forecasting based on the VMA representation

Suppose the data are generated by:

$$\Delta \mathbf{x}_t = \boldsymbol{\mu} + \mathbf{C}(L)\boldsymbol{\epsilon}_t, \tag{6.1}$$

where $\boldsymbol{\epsilon}_t \sim \mathsf{IN}_n[\mathbf{0}, \boldsymbol{\Omega}]$, $\mathbf{x}_t$ is an $n \times 1$ vector, and $\mathbf{C}(L)$ is the matrix lag polynomial:

$$\mathbf{C}(L) = \mathbf{C}_0 + \mathbf{C}_1 L + \mathbf{C}_2 L^2 + \cdots .$$

Cointegration implies that in the representation of $\mathbf{C}(L)$ as:

$$\mathbf{C}(L) = \mathbf{C}(1) + \Delta\mathbf{C}^*(L), \quad \text{where } \Delta = 1 - L,$$

and $\mathbf{C}(1) = \sum_{i=0}^{\infty} \mathbf{C}_i$ (consistent with evaluating $\mathbf{C}(L)$ at $L = 1$), then $\boldsymbol{\beta}'\mathbf{C}(1) = \mathbf{0}$ for $\boldsymbol{\beta}$ an $n \times r$ matrix of rank r whose columns span the cointegrating space. Thus, $\mathbf{C}(1)$ is of rank $n - r$. We allow deterministic components in the form of $\boldsymbol{\mu}$, and thus require the additional condition for cointegration that $\boldsymbol{\beta}'\boldsymbol{\mu} = \mathbf{0}$. A more formal treatment including discussion of additional auxiliary assumptions and proofs can be found in the references cited above. If we assume that $\boldsymbol{\epsilon}_j = \mathbf{0}\, \forall j \leq 0$, and $\mathbf{x}_0 = \mathbf{0}$, then we can limit the dependence of the process on the past, and by backward substitution in (6.1), obtain:

$$\mathbf{x}_t = \boldsymbol{\mu} t + \sum_{i=1}^{t} \sum_{j=0}^{t-i} \mathbf{C}_j \boldsymbol{\epsilon}_i. \tag{6.2}$$

Thus the actual value of the process in period $T + h$ is:

$$\begin{aligned}
\mathbf{x}_{T+h} &= \boldsymbol{\mu}(T+h) + \sum_{i=1}^{T+h} \sum_{j=0}^{T+h-i} \mathbf{C}_j \boldsymbol{\epsilon}_i \\
&= \boldsymbol{\mu}(T+h) + \sum_{i=1}^{T} \sum_{j=0}^{T+h-i} \mathbf{C}_j \boldsymbol{\epsilon}_i + \sum_{i=T+1}^{T+h} \sum_{j=0}^{T+h-i} \mathbf{C}_j \boldsymbol{\epsilon}_i \qquad (6.3) \\
&= \boldsymbol{\mu}(T+h) + \sum_{i=1}^{T} \sum_{j=0}^{T+h-i} \mathbf{C}_j \boldsymbol{\epsilon}_i + \sum_{i=1}^{h} \sum_{j=0}^{h-i} \mathbf{C}_j \boldsymbol{\epsilon}_{T+i},
\end{aligned}$$

where the last two lines of (6.3) separate the $\boldsymbol{\epsilon}_i$ into those known at time T, $i \leq T$, and those with an expected value of zero at time T ($i > T$). From this formulation, the conditional expectation of the process at $T + h$, based on time T, is:

$$\mathsf{E}\left[\mathbf{x}_{T+h} \mid \mathbf{x}_T\right] = \widehat{\mathbf{x}}_{T+h} = \boldsymbol{\mu}(T+h) + \sum_{i=1}^{T} \sum_{j=0}^{T+h-i} \mathbf{C}_j \boldsymbol{\epsilon}_i. \tag{6.4}$$

Since the $\mathbf{C}_i$ may be expected to decay rapidly as i becomes large, the approximation:

$$\sum_{j=0}^{T+h-i} \mathbf{C}_j \simeq \mathbf{C}(1) \tag{6.5}$$

should be reasonable for large h, since in the limit:

$$\lim_{h\to\infty} \sum_{j=0}^{T+h-i} \mathbf{C}_j = \mathbf{C}(1).$$

Thus, we can approximate (6.4) by:

$$\widehat{\mathbf{x}}_{T+h} = \boldsymbol{\mu}\,(T+h) + \mathbf{C}(1) \sum_{i=1}^{T} \boldsymbol{\epsilon}_i \tag{6.6}$$

from which it is clear that the forecasts are generated by $n-r$ stochastic trends. These are sometimes known as 'common trends' (see Stock and Watson, 1988). The long-run forecasts are tied together in the sense that for large h:

$$\boldsymbol{\beta}'\widehat{\mathbf{x}}_{T+h} \simeq \boldsymbol{\beta}'\boldsymbol{\mu}\,(T+h) + \boldsymbol{\beta}'\mathbf{C}(1) \sum_{i=1}^{T} \boldsymbol{\epsilon}_i = \mathbf{0}.$$

This is a property of the process (6.1), not dependent on the econometrician knowing about, or imposing, cointegration. From (6.3) and (6.4), the forecast error is:

$$\mathbf{e}_{T+h} = \mathbf{x}_{T+h} - \widehat{\mathbf{x}}_{T+h} = \sum_{i=1}^{h} \sum_{j=0}^{h-i} \mathbf{C}_j \boldsymbol{\epsilon}_{T+i},$$

and the forecast-error variance by:

$$\mathsf{V}\left[\mathbf{e}_{T+h}\right] = \sum_{i=1}^{h} \left[\left(\sum_{j=0}^{h-i} \mathbf{C}_j \right) \boldsymbol{\Omega} \left(\sum_{j=0}^{h-i} \mathbf{C}'_j \right) \right],$$

which is $O(h)$ for large h.

Some intuition into the behaviour of the forecast-error variances for the stationary linear combinations can be obtained by splitting the relevant formula as:

$$\begin{aligned} \mathsf{V}\left[\boldsymbol{\beta}'\mathbf{e}_{T+h}\right] &= \sum_{i=1}^{h_1} \left[\boldsymbol{\beta}' \left(\sum_{j=0}^{h_1-i} \mathbf{C}_j \right) \boldsymbol{\Omega} \left(\sum_{j=0}^{h_1-i} \mathbf{C}'_j \right) \boldsymbol{\beta} \right] \\ &\quad + \sum_{i=h_1+1}^{h} \left[\boldsymbol{\beta}' \left(\sum_{j=0}^{h-i} \mathbf{C}_j \right) \boldsymbol{\Omega} \left(\sum_{j=0}^{h-i} \mathbf{C}'_j \right) \boldsymbol{\beta} \right], \end{aligned}$$

where h_1 is defined such that for $h > h_1$, $\sum_{j=0}^{h-i} \mathbf{C}_j \to \mathbf{C}(1)$, so that the second term is negligible. Thus the value of $\mathsf{V}[\boldsymbol{\beta}'\mathbf{e}_{T+h}]$ is approximately given by the first term as h increases past h_1, which is independent of h, so $\mathsf{V}[\boldsymbol{\beta}'\mathbf{e}_{T+h}]$ is $O(1)$. These results parallel the behaviour of the forecast-error variances derived for the stationary and integrated univariate processes in chapter 4, and formally establish that error variances increase without bound for the individual $\mathsf{I}(1)$ series, but are bounded for $\mathsf{I}(0)$ linear combinations of the series.

6.2.2 Forecasting based on the VAR

Engle and Yoo (1991), following on from Engle and Granger (1987), show how the VAR (or more generally, the VARMA) representation can be derived from the Wold representation, and deduce the relationship between the restrictions on the lag polynomials of the two formulations. For our purposes, little additional intuition into forecasting would be obtained by detailing this analysis, which is relatively straightforward when Smith–McMillan–Yoo forms are used, and we proceed by writing down a first-order VAR. In section 2.7.1, we showed that the MA component of a VARMA model complicates the mechanics of forecasting with such models, since the MA errors have to be solved for recursively whether or not the parameters of the VARMA are assumed known. Estimation and inference is also easier in the absence of MA components. For these reasons, we will concentrate on autoregressive representations of the data process.

Let $\mathbf{x}_t$ be an $n \times 1$ vector of time-series variables, then a first-order dynamic linear system can be written as:

$$\mathbf{x}_t = \boldsymbol{\Upsilon}\mathbf{x}_{t-1} + \boldsymbol{\Psi}\mathbf{D}_t + \mathbf{v}_t, \tag{6.7}$$

where $\mathbf{v}_t \sim \mathsf{IN}_n[\mathbf{0}, \boldsymbol{\Omega}]$ for $t = 1, 2, \ldots, T$. $\mathbf{D}_t$ contains deterministic components, and the initial value $\mathbf{x}_0$ is fixed. $\boldsymbol{\Upsilon}$ is an $n \times n$ matrix of coefficients. Equation (6.7) can be reparameterized as:

$$\Delta\mathbf{x}_t = \boldsymbol{\Pi}\mathbf{x}_{t-1} + \boldsymbol{\Psi}\mathbf{D}_t + \mathbf{v}_t, \tag{6.8}$$

where $\boldsymbol{\Pi} = \boldsymbol{\Upsilon} - \mathbf{I}_n = \boldsymbol{\alpha}\boldsymbol{\beta}'$ and $\boldsymbol{\alpha}$ and $\boldsymbol{\beta}$ are $n \times r$ of rank $r < n$ when $\mathbf{x}_t \sim \mathsf{I}(1)$ and the cointegrating rank is r. Imposing cointegration, the vector equilibrium-correction form (VEqCM) is:

$$\Delta\mathbf{x}_t = \boldsymbol{\alpha}\left(\boldsymbol{\beta}'\mathbf{x}_{t-1}\right) + \boldsymbol{\Psi}\mathbf{D}_t + \mathbf{v}_t.$$

Lag systems of an arbitrary order can be stacked into a first-order form after a suitable change of notation. This is well known for (6.7) (namely the companion form), and as shown in, for example, Hendry and Mizon (1993), the system in (6.8) becomes:

$$\begin{aligned}\mathbf{f}_t &= \begin{pmatrix}\Delta\mathbf{x}_t \\ \boldsymbol{\beta}'\mathbf{x}_{t-1}\end{pmatrix} = \begin{pmatrix}\boldsymbol{\Pi} & \boldsymbol{\alpha} \\ \boldsymbol{\beta}' & \mathbf{I}_r\end{pmatrix}\begin{pmatrix}\Delta\mathbf{x}_{t-1} \\ \boldsymbol{\beta}'\mathbf{x}_{t-2}\end{pmatrix} + \begin{pmatrix}\boldsymbol{\Psi} \\ \mathbf{0}\end{pmatrix}\mathbf{D}_t + \begin{pmatrix}\mathbf{v}_t \\ \mathbf{0}\end{pmatrix} \\ &= \boldsymbol{\Pi}^*\mathbf{f}_{t-1} + \underline{\mathbf{v}}_t.\end{aligned} \tag{6.9}$$

Further terms in $\Delta \mathbf{x}_{t-i}$ merely extend $\mathbf{f}_t$, so there is no loss of generality in analysing (6.9). However, that notation is inconvenient since the rank of $\mathbf{\Pi}^*$ differs from that of $\mathbf{\Pi}$ by $pn + r$ (for p lags), and so we work with the first-order systems (6.7) and (6.8).

We exclude explosive variables by assuming that none of the roots of $|\mathbf{I}_n - \mathbf{\Upsilon} L| = 0$ lie inside the unit circle, and also rule out $\mathbf{x}_t$ being integrated of order 2. Thus, we assume that $\boldsymbol{\alpha}'_{\perp}\mathbf{\Theta}\boldsymbol{\beta}_{\perp}$ is full rank, where $\mathbf{\Theta}$ is the mean-lag matrix (here, simply $\mathbf{\Upsilon}$), and $\boldsymbol{\alpha}_{\perp}$ and $\boldsymbol{\beta}_{\perp}$ are full column rank $n \times (n-r)$ matrices such that $\boldsymbol{\alpha}'\boldsymbol{\alpha}_{\perp} = \boldsymbol{\beta}'\boldsymbol{\beta}_{\perp} = \mathbf{0}$ (see Johansen, 1992a).

A reformulation of (6.7) that is sometimes more convenient may be obtained by partitioning $\mathbf{x}_t$ into $(\mathbf{x}'_{a,t} : \mathbf{x}'_{b,t})'$ where $\boldsymbol{\beta}'\mathbf{x}_t$ and $\Delta \mathbf{x}_{b,t} = \boldsymbol{\beta}'_{\perp}\Delta \mathbf{x}_t$ are I(0) by construction. $\boldsymbol{\beta}$ is normalized such that its first r rows are the identity matrix, i.e., $\boldsymbol{\beta} = (\mathbf{I}_r : \boldsymbol{\beta}'_2)'$. This ensures that the transformation from $\mathbf{x}_t$ to $\mathbf{w}'_t = (\mathbf{x}'_t\boldsymbol{\beta} : \Delta \mathbf{x}'_{b,t}) = (\mathbf{w}'_{a,t} : \mathbf{w}'_{b,t})'$ is scale-preserving. Partitioning conformably, $\boldsymbol{\alpha}' = (\boldsymbol{\alpha}'_a : \boldsymbol{\alpha}'_b)$, which is $(r \times r : r \times (n-r))$, then we can write:

$$\mathbf{w}_t = \mathbf{G}\mathbf{w}_{t-1} + \mathbf{\Psi}_0 \mathbf{D}_t + \boldsymbol{\epsilon}_t, \tag{6.10}$$

where $\boldsymbol{\epsilon}_t \sim \mathsf{IN}_n[\mathbf{0}, \mathbf{\Sigma}]$. In (6.10), $\mathbf{\Psi}_0 = (\mathbf{\Psi}'\boldsymbol{\beta} : \mathbf{\Psi}'_b)' = \mathbf{Q}\mathbf{\Psi}$ where $\mathbf{\Psi}_b = \mathbf{J}'\mathbf{\Psi}$ when $\mathbf{J}' = (\mathbf{0} : \mathbf{I}_{n-r})$ and:

$$\mathbf{Q} = \begin{pmatrix} \boldsymbol{\beta}' \\ \mathbf{J}' \end{pmatrix}, \; \mathbf{G} = \begin{pmatrix} (\mathbf{I}_r + \boldsymbol{\beta}'\boldsymbol{\alpha}) & \mathbf{0} \\ \boldsymbol{\alpha}_b & \mathbf{0} \end{pmatrix} = \begin{pmatrix} \boldsymbol{\lambda} & \mathbf{0} \\ \boldsymbol{\alpha}_b & \mathbf{0} \end{pmatrix} \tag{6.11}$$

and:

$$\mathbf{\Sigma} = \begin{pmatrix} \boldsymbol{\beta}'\mathbf{\Omega}\boldsymbol{\beta} & \boldsymbol{\beta}'\mathbf{\Omega}\mathbf{J} \\ \mathbf{J}'\mathbf{\Omega}\boldsymbol{\beta} & \mathbf{J}'\mathbf{\Omega}\mathbf{J} \end{pmatrix}.$$

The system in (6.10) determines both the conditional and unconditional means and variances of all the I(0) variables. When $D_t = 1$ (a constant term), $\mathbf{\Psi}$ is denoted by the $n \times 1$ vector $\boldsymbol{\tau}$. Then, for $\boldsymbol{\alpha} \neq \mathbf{0}$, the long-run solution for the system is defined by:

$$\mathsf{E}[\mathbf{w}_t] = (\mathbf{I}_n - \mathbf{G})^{-1} \mathbf{Q}\boldsymbol{\tau} = \begin{pmatrix} -(\boldsymbol{\beta}'\boldsymbol{\alpha})^{-1}\boldsymbol{\beta}'\boldsymbol{\tau} \\ \boldsymbol{\alpha}_b(\boldsymbol{\beta}'\boldsymbol{\alpha})^{-1}\boldsymbol{\beta}'\boldsymbol{\tau} + \boldsymbol{\tau}_b \end{pmatrix}. \tag{6.12}$$

Also, the expectation of $\Delta \mathbf{x}_t$ is:

$$\begin{aligned} \mathsf{E}[\Delta \mathbf{x}_t] &= \mathsf{E}[\boldsymbol{\alpha}\boldsymbol{\beta}'\mathbf{x}_{t-1} + \boldsymbol{\tau} + \mathbf{v}_t] \\ &= \boldsymbol{\alpha}\mathsf{E}[\mathbf{w}_{a,t-1}] + \boldsymbol{\tau} \\ &= \left(\mathbf{I}_r - \boldsymbol{\alpha}(\boldsymbol{\beta}'\boldsymbol{\alpha})^{-1}\boldsymbol{\beta}'\right)\boldsymbol{\tau} \\ &= \mathbf{K}\boldsymbol{\tau} = \mathbf{g}_x, \end{aligned} \tag{6.13}$$

which defines the growth in the system. The matrix $\mathbf{K}$ is non-symmetric, but idempotent, with $\boldsymbol{\beta}'\mathbf{K} = \mathbf{0}'$ and $\mathbf{K}\boldsymbol{\alpha} = \mathbf{0}$, so $\mathbf{\Upsilon}\mathbf{K} = \mathbf{K}$ and $\boldsymbol{\beta}'\mathbf{K}\boldsymbol{\tau} = \boldsymbol{\beta}'\mathbf{g}_x = 0$. Also from (6.12):

$$\mathsf{E}[\boldsymbol{\beta}'\mathbf{x}_t] = -(\boldsymbol{\beta}'\boldsymbol{\alpha})^{-1}\boldsymbol{\beta}'\boldsymbol{\tau}.$$

The condition that $\boldsymbol{\tau}$ falls in the cointegrating space is that $\boldsymbol{\tau} = \boldsymbol{\alpha}\boldsymbol{\tau}^*$ where $\boldsymbol{\tau}^*$ is $r \times 1$ (see Johansen and Juselius, 1990). If so, from (6.13):

$$\mathsf{E}\left[\Delta\mathbf{x}_t\right] = \mathsf{E}\left[\boldsymbol{\alpha}\left(\boldsymbol{\beta}' : \boldsymbol{\tau}^*\right)\begin{pmatrix} \mathbf{x}_{t-1} \\ 1 \end{pmatrix} + \mathbf{v}_t\right] = \mathbf{K}\boldsymbol{\alpha}\boldsymbol{\tau}^* = \mathbf{0}, \tag{6.14}$$

demonstrating the absence of linear trends in the elements of $\mathbf{x}_t$. Consequently, $\mathsf{E}[\boldsymbol{\beta}'\mathbf{x}_t] = \boldsymbol{\tau}^*$.

6.3 Linear transformations of the AR representation

In this section, we use the notation from section 3.5.2 for isomorphic representations of linear systems. The linear forecasting system is written as:

$$\boldsymbol{\Phi}\mathbf{s}_t = \mathbf{u}_t, \tag{6.15}$$

where $\mathbf{u}_t \sim \mathsf{ID}_n[\mathbf{0}, \boldsymbol{\Omega}]$, $\mathbf{s}_t' = (\mathbf{x}_t' : \mathbf{z}_t')$, $\mathbf{x}_t$ are the n variables to be forecast and $\mathbf{z}_t$ are k available predetermined variables (perhaps just $\mathbf{x}_{t-1}$) with $\boldsymbol{\Phi} = (\mathbf{I}_n : -\mathbf{B})$. The parameters are $(\mathbf{B} : \boldsymbol{\Omega})$ and $\boldsymbol{\Omega}$ is symmetric, positive semi-definite.

It is straightforward to establish that the transformations from $\mathbf{x}_t$ to $\Delta\mathbf{x}_t$, and to $\mathbf{w}_t$, are both examples of the $\mathbf{P}$-class of transformation, and thus have the property that they leave linear models unchanged. Consider the transformation from $\mathbf{x}_t$ to $\Delta\mathbf{x}_t$ for the system given by (6.7) with $\boldsymbol{\Psi} = \mathbf{0}$ (ignoring the deterministic components without loss of generality). Then the $\mathbf{z}_t$ variables in (6.15) are just $\mathbf{x}_{t-1}$ (so that $k = n$). Thus, $\mathbf{s}_t' = (\mathbf{x}_t' : \mathbf{x}_{t-1}')$, and $\boldsymbol{\Phi} = (\mathbf{I}_n : -\boldsymbol{\Upsilon})$. The transformation to first differences is achieved by pre-multiplying $\mathbf{s}_t$ by $\mathbf{P}$:

$$\mathbf{s}_t^* = \mathbf{P}\mathbf{s}_t = \begin{pmatrix} \Delta\mathbf{x}_t \\ \mathbf{x}_{t-1} \end{pmatrix} \quad \text{where } \mathbf{P} = \begin{pmatrix} \mathbf{I}_n & -\mathbf{I}_n \\ \mathbf{0} & \mathbf{I}_n \end{pmatrix},$$

as the blocks are of dimension n. Then:

$$\mathbf{P}^{-1} = \begin{pmatrix} \mathbf{I}_n & \mathbf{I}_n \\ \mathbf{0} & \mathbf{I}_n \end{pmatrix},$$

so that $\boldsymbol{\Phi}^* \equiv \boldsymbol{\Phi}\mathbf{P}^{-1} = (\mathbf{I}_n : \mathbf{I}_n - \boldsymbol{\Upsilon})$, and:

$$\boldsymbol{\Phi}^*\mathbf{s}_t^* = \Delta\mathbf{x}_t + (\mathbf{I}_n - \boldsymbol{\Upsilon})\,\mathbf{x}_{t-1} = \mathbf{v}_t$$

which is equivalent to (6.8) noting that $\boldsymbol{\Pi} = \boldsymbol{\Upsilon} - \mathbf{I}_n$. The error term is invariant to the $\mathbf{P}$-transform.

The form of $\mathbf{P}$ that generates $\mathbf{w}_t$ from $\mathbf{x}_t$ is slightly more involved, and is given by:

$$\mathbf{P} = \begin{pmatrix} \boldsymbol{\beta}' & \mathbf{0}_{r\times n} \\ \mathbf{J} & -\mathbf{J} \\ \mathbf{0}_n & \mathbf{I}_n \end{pmatrix},$$

where $\boldsymbol{\beta}$ is an $n \times r$ matrix as above, $\mathbf{J} = (\mathbf{0}_{(n-r)\times r} : \mathbf{I}_{n-r})$, an $(n-r) \times n$ matrix, so that $\mathbf{P}$ is $2n \times 2n$. Then:

$$\mathbf{s}_t^* = \mathbf{P}\mathbf{s}_t = \begin{pmatrix} \boldsymbol{\beta}'\mathbf{x}_t \\ \mathbf{J}\Delta\mathbf{x}_t \\ \mathbf{x}_{t-1} \end{pmatrix}.$$

Next, in order to calculate $\boldsymbol{\Phi}^* = \boldsymbol{\Phi}\mathbf{P}^{-1}$ we need $\mathbf{P}^{-1}$. Writing $\mathbf{P}$ as the partitioned matrix of $n \times n$ blocks:

$$\begin{pmatrix} \mathbf{P}_1 & \mathbf{P}_2 \\ \mathbf{0} & \mathbf{I}_n \end{pmatrix},$$

partitioned inversion yields:

$$\mathbf{P}^{-1} = \begin{pmatrix} \mathbf{P}_1^{-1} & -\mathbf{P}_1^{-1}\mathbf{P}_2 \\ \mathbf{0} & \mathbf{I}_n \end{pmatrix}.$$

Thus:

$$\boldsymbol{\Phi}^* = \left(\mathbf{P}_1^{-1} : -\mathbf{P}_1^{-1}\mathbf{P}_2 - \boldsymbol{\Upsilon}\right),$$

from which the system can be written as:

$$\begin{aligned} \boldsymbol{\Phi}^*\mathbf{s}_t^* &= \mathbf{P}_1^{-1}\mathbf{w}_t - \left(\mathbf{P}_1^{-1}\mathbf{P}_2 + \boldsymbol{\Upsilon}\right)\mathbf{x}_{t-1} &&= \mathbf{v}_t \\ \mathbf{P}_1\boldsymbol{\Phi}^*\mathbf{s}_t^* &= \mathbf{w}_t - \left[\mathbf{P}_2 + \mathbf{P}_1\boldsymbol{\Upsilon}\right]\mathbf{x}_{t-1} &&= \mathbf{P}_1\mathbf{v}_t \\ \mathbf{P}_1\boldsymbol{\Phi}^*\mathbf{s}_t^* &= \mathbf{w}_t - \begin{pmatrix} (\mathbf{I}_r + \boldsymbol{\beta}'\boldsymbol{\alpha}) & \mathbf{0} \\ \boldsymbol{\alpha}_b & \mathbf{0} \end{pmatrix}\mathbf{w}_{t-1} &&= \mathbf{P}_1\mathbf{v}_t. \end{aligned} \tag{6.16}$$

The last line of (6.16) is the representation for $\mathbf{w}_t$ given by (6.10) and (6.11), and is obtained by substituting for $\mathbf{P}_2$, $\mathbf{P}_1$ and $\boldsymbol{\Upsilon}$, and manipulating the resulting expression.

The form of the model (6.10) and (6.11) and above suggests that:

$$\mathbf{P}_1\mathbf{v}_t = \boldsymbol{\epsilon}_t = \left(\boldsymbol{\beta} : \mathbf{J}'\right)'\mathbf{v}_t \neq \mathbf{v}_t,$$

so that the $\mathbf{P}$-transform appears to have changed the error term. However, an alternative (and equivalent) representation of the model in terms of $\mathbf{w}_t$ leaves the error term unaffected. To see this, let $\mathbf{w}_t' = (\mathbf{x}_t'\boldsymbol{\beta} : \Delta\mathbf{x}_{b,t}') = (\mathbf{w}_{a,t}' : \mathbf{w}_{b,t}')'$, partition $\boldsymbol{\epsilon}_t$ conformably, and note that $\boldsymbol{\beta}' = (\mathbf{I}_r : \boldsymbol{\beta}_b')$. Then the disturbance term in the $\mathbf{w}_{a,t}$ equation is given by, $\boldsymbol{\beta}'\mathbf{v}_t = \mathbf{v}_{a,t} + \boldsymbol{\beta}_b'\mathbf{v}_{b,t}$. From the equation for $\mathbf{w}_{b,t}$, pre-multiplying by $\boldsymbol{\beta}_b'$ yields:

$$\boldsymbol{\beta}_b'\mathbf{v}_{b,t} = \boldsymbol{\beta}_b'\mathbf{w}_t - \boldsymbol{\beta}_b'\boldsymbol{\alpha}_b\mathbf{w}_{a,t-1},$$

so that substituting into the $\mathbf{w}_{a,t}$ equation allows us to write the system with:

$$\mathbf{G} = \begin{pmatrix} \mathbf{I}_r + \boldsymbol{\beta}'\boldsymbol{\alpha} - \boldsymbol{\beta}_b'\boldsymbol{\alpha}_b & \boldsymbol{\beta}' \\ \boldsymbol{\alpha}_b & \mathbf{0} \end{pmatrix} = \begin{pmatrix} \mathbf{I}_r + \boldsymbol{\alpha}_a & \boldsymbol{\beta}' \\ \boldsymbol{\alpha}_b & \mathbf{0} \end{pmatrix},$$

and $\boldsymbol{\epsilon}_t = \mathbf{v}_t$.

6.4 Asymptotic variance formulae

In this section, we abstract from parameter uncertainty and derive asymptotic formulae for the h-step ahead forecast uncertainty. We also abstract from many of the other sources of forecast error that are likely to arise in practice: these are discussed in chapter 7. We first consider the case in which the DGP and econometric model coincide: that is, the econometric model is correctly specified. The relationships between the forecast second moments for the transformations of the model discussed in section 6.3 are established. Secondly, since one of our objectives is to examine the role of imposing unit roots and cointegrating restrictions, we derive the analogous forecast-variance formulae when the econometric model is a VAR in differences, denoted by DV (differenced VAR), where the variables are all individually $\mathsf{I}(0)$ by virtue of being differenced prior to modelling. This model incorrectly imposes unit roots when there is cointegration, but its parameter values can be deduced from the DGP. A study of its forecasting properties is of more than theoretical interest since such models are routinely used in empirical time-series analysis.

There are three main types of forecast moments that could be analysed. These are $\mathsf{M}[\mathbf{e}_{T+h}]$, $\mathsf{M}[\mathbf{e}_{T+h}|\mathbf{x}_T]$ and $\mathsf{M}[\mathbf{e}_{T+h}|\mathbf{X}_T^1]$, where $\mathsf{M}[\mathbf{z}] \equiv \mathsf{E}[\mathbf{zz}']$ and $\mathbf{X}_T^1 = (\mathbf{x}_1, \ldots, \mathbf{x}_T)$. The first of these is an unconditional moment, and corresponds to resampling $\mathbf{X}_{T+h}^1$ on each replication in a Monte Carlo; the last involves conditional forecasting after parameter estimation, and would correspond to a Monte Carlo where only one set $\mathbf{X}_T^1$ is drawn from which sets of independent forecasts are then generated. The middle is a hybrid, albeit one which is regularly used for computing forecast-variance formulae, where taking expectations over $\mathbf{x}_T$ will yield the first. We consider the first two types of forecast moment.

6.4.1 Correctly specified econometric model

From (6.7), denoting by $\widehat{\mathbf{x}}_{T+j}$ the conditional j-step ahead expectation (conditional on period T) we have:

$$\widehat{\mathbf{x}}_{T+h} = \boldsymbol{\Upsilon}\widehat{\mathbf{x}}_{T+h-1} + \boldsymbol{\Psi}\mathbf{D}_{T+h},$$

so that by backward substitution when there is only an intercept and $\boldsymbol{\Psi}\mathbf{D}_{T+h} = \boldsymbol{\tau}$:

$$\widehat{\mathbf{x}}_{T+h} = \boldsymbol{\Upsilon}^h\widehat{\mathbf{x}}_T + \sum_{i=0}^{h-1}\boldsymbol{\Upsilon}^i\boldsymbol{\tau},$$

with $\widehat{\mathbf{x}}_T = \mathbf{x}_T$. The actual value of the process is:

$$\mathbf{x}_{T+h} = \boldsymbol{\Upsilon}^h\mathbf{x}_T + \sum_{i=0}^{h-1}\boldsymbol{\Upsilon}^i\boldsymbol{\tau} + \sum_{i=0}^{h-1}\boldsymbol{\Upsilon}^i\mathbf{v}_{T+h-i}. \tag{6.17}$$

Define the h-step ahead forecast error for the levels as $\mathbf{e}_{x,T+h} = \mathbf{x}_{T+h} - \widehat{\mathbf{x}}_{T+h}$, then the forecasts are (conditionally and unconditionally) unbiased:

$$\mathsf{E}\left[\mathbf{e}_{x,T+h}\right] = \mathsf{E}\left[\mathbf{e}_{x,T+h} \mid \mathbf{x}_T\right] = \mathsf{E}\left[\sum_{i=0}^{h-1} \boldsymbol{\Upsilon}^i \mathbf{v}_{T+h-i}\right] = \mathbf{0}, \tag{6.18}$$

and the second-moment matrix $\mathsf{E}[\mathbf{e}_{x,T+h}\mathbf{e}'_{x,T+h}]$ is given by:

$$\mathbf{V}_{x,h} \equiv \mathsf{M}\left[\mathbf{e}_{x,T+h}\right] = \mathsf{M}\left[\mathbf{e}_{x,T+h} \mid \mathbf{x}_T\right] = \sum_{i=0}^{h-1} \boldsymbol{\Upsilon}^i \boldsymbol{\Omega} \boldsymbol{\Upsilon}^{i\prime}. \tag{6.19}$$

The conditional and unconditional moments again coincide, and $\mathbf{V}_{x,h}$ is the mean squared forecast-error matrix (MSFEM).

An equivalent expression holds in terms of $\mathbf{G}$ and $\boldsymbol{\Sigma}$ for the model defined in (6.10) using $\mathbf{w}_t$:

$$\mathbf{V}_{w,h} \equiv \mathsf{M}\left[\mathbf{e}_{w,T+h}\right] = \mathsf{M}\left[\mathbf{e}_{w,T+h} \mid \mathbf{x}_T\right] = \sum_{i=0}^{h-1} \mathbf{G}^i \boldsymbol{\Sigma} \mathbf{G}^{i\prime}. \tag{6.20}$$

Alternatively, an expression for the forecast variance for $\mathbf{w}_t$ can be found by combining the expressions for $\mathbf{x}_t$ and $\Delta\mathbf{x}_t$ from (6.19) and (6.24) (see below), since:

$$\mathbf{e}_{w,T+h} = \left(\mathbf{e}'_{x,T+h}\boldsymbol{\beta} : \mathbf{e}'_{\Delta x,T+h}\mathbf{J}\right)',$$

so that the forecast-error second-moment matrix of $\mathbf{w}_t$ is:

$$\mathsf{V}\left[\mathbf{e}_{w,T+h}\right] = \begin{bmatrix} \boldsymbol{\beta}'\mathsf{M}\left[\mathbf{e}_{x,T+h}\right]\boldsymbol{\beta} & \boldsymbol{\beta}'\mathsf{E}\left[\mathbf{e}_{x,T+h}\mathbf{e}'_{\Delta x,T+h}\right]\mathbf{J} \\ \mathbf{J}'\mathsf{E}\left[\mathbf{e}_{x,T+h}\mathbf{e}'_{\Delta x,T+h}\right]\boldsymbol{\beta} & \mathbf{J}'\mathsf{M}\left[\mathbf{e}_{\Delta x,T+h}\right]\mathbf{J} \end{bmatrix}$$

which can be shown to be equivalent to (6.20) because:

$$\boldsymbol{\beta}'\mathsf{V}\left[\mathbf{e}_{x,T+h}\right]\boldsymbol{\beta} = \mathsf{V}\left[\boldsymbol{\beta}'\mathbf{e}_{x,T+h}\right] = \mathsf{V}\left[\sum_{i=0}^{h-1} \boldsymbol{\beta}'\boldsymbol{\Upsilon}^i \mathbf{v}_{T+h-i}\right] = \mathsf{V}\left[\sum_{i=0}^{h-1} \boldsymbol{\lambda}^i \boldsymbol{\beta}' \mathbf{v}_{T+h-i}\right],$$

from (6.18), as:

$$\boldsymbol{\beta}'\boldsymbol{\Upsilon}^i = \left(\boldsymbol{\beta}' + \boldsymbol{\beta}'\boldsymbol{\alpha}\boldsymbol{\beta}'\right)\boldsymbol{\Upsilon}^{i-1} = \left(\mathbf{I}_r + \boldsymbol{\beta}'\boldsymbol{\alpha}\right)\boldsymbol{\beta}'\boldsymbol{\Upsilon}^{i-1} = \boldsymbol{\lambda}\boldsymbol{\beta}'\boldsymbol{\Upsilon}^{i-1} = \cdots = \boldsymbol{\lambda}^i\boldsymbol{\beta}',$$

where $\boldsymbol{\lambda} = (\mathbf{I}_r + \boldsymbol{\beta}'\boldsymbol{\alpha})$ which has no unit roots.

Despite their similarity of form, (6.19) and (6.20) are fundamentally different. Since $\boldsymbol{\Upsilon} = (\mathbf{I}_n + \boldsymbol{\alpha}\boldsymbol{\beta}')$ has roots equal to unity, the TMSFE, given by the trace of the forecast-error second-moment matrix, for $\mathbf{x}_t$ from (6.19) is $O(h)$, while the TMSFE for $\mathbf{w}_t$ from (6.20) is $O(1)$ in h, reflecting the fact that $\mathbf{x}_t \sim \mathsf{I}(1)$ but $\mathbf{w}_t \sim \mathsf{I}(0)$ (see Engle and Yoo, 1987 and Lütkepohl, 1991, sections 3.5 and 11.3, and section 6.2).

When the system is expressed in differences, lag equation (6.17) once to give:

$$\mathbf{x}_{T+h-1} = \boldsymbol{\Upsilon}^{h-1}\mathbf{x}_T + \sum_{i=0}^{h-2} \boldsymbol{\Upsilon}^i \boldsymbol{\tau} + \sum_{i=0}^{h-2} \boldsymbol{\Upsilon}^i \mathbf{v}_{T+h-i-1},$$

and subtract from (6.17) to write $\Delta\mathbf{x}_t$, the actual h-step ahead change, as:

$$\Delta\mathbf{x}_{T+h} = \boldsymbol{\Upsilon}^{h-1}\left(\boldsymbol{\alpha\beta}'\mathbf{x}_T + \boldsymbol{\tau}\right) + \mathbf{v}_{T+h} + \sum_{i=0}^{h-2} \boldsymbol{\Upsilon}^i \boldsymbol{\alpha\beta}'\mathbf{v}_{T+h-i-1}. \tag{6.21}$$

The forecasts are obtained by setting $\mathsf{E}[\mathbf{v}_{T+i}] = \mathbf{0}\ \forall i$, so the conditional expectation is:

$$\widehat{\Delta\mathbf{x}}_{T+h} = \boldsymbol{\Upsilon}^{h-1}\left(\boldsymbol{\alpha\beta}'\mathbf{x}_T + \boldsymbol{\tau}\right), \tag{6.22}$$

with expected forecast error:

$$\mathsf{E}\left[\mathbf{e}_{\Delta x,T+h}\right] = \mathsf{E}\left[\Delta\mathbf{x}_{T+h} - \widehat{\Delta\mathbf{x}}_{T+h}\right] = \mathsf{E}\left[\mathbf{v}_{T+h} + \sum_{i=0}^{h-2} \boldsymbol{\Upsilon}^i \boldsymbol{\alpha\beta}'\mathbf{v}_{T+h-i-1}\right] = \mathbf{0}. \tag{6.23}$$

The resulting general variance formula is:

$$\mathbf{V}_{\Delta x,h} \equiv \mathsf{M}\left[\mathbf{e}_{\Delta x,T+h}\right] = \mathsf{M}\left[\mathbf{e}_{\Delta x,T+h} \mid \mathbf{x}_T\right] = \boldsymbol{\Omega} + \sum_{i=0}^{h-2} \boldsymbol{\Upsilon}^i \boldsymbol{\alpha\beta}'\boldsymbol{\Omega\beta\alpha}'\boldsymbol{\Upsilon}^{i\prime}, \tag{6.24}$$

which collapses to $\boldsymbol{\Omega}$ when $h = 1$.

Since $\boldsymbol{\Upsilon} = (\mathbf{I}_n + \boldsymbol{\alpha\beta}')$, then $\boldsymbol{\Upsilon\alpha} = \boldsymbol{\alpha}(\mathbf{I}_r + \boldsymbol{\beta}'\boldsymbol{\alpha}) = \boldsymbol{\alpha\lambda}$, and hence $\boldsymbol{\Upsilon}^s\boldsymbol{\alpha} = \boldsymbol{\alpha\lambda}^s$. Thus, the MSFE in (6.24) is $O(1)$ despite the terms in $\boldsymbol{\Upsilon}^s$. In a bivariate cointegrated system, λ is the eigenvalue of $\boldsymbol{\Upsilon}$ strictly less than unity in absolute value so $\boldsymbol{\alpha\lambda}^s \to \mathbf{0}$ as $s \to \infty$.

6.4.2 Incorrectly specified DV model

The asymptotic variance expressions for the DV model in terms of $\mathbf{x}_t$, $\mathbf{w}_t$ and $\Delta\mathbf{x}_t$ are derived below because the DV model is mis-specified when $r \neq 0$. The derivation of these expressions again ignores sampling variability. The forecasts from the DV model for $\Delta\mathbf{x}_t$ are calculated by setting $\Delta\mathbf{x}_{T+h}$ equal to the population growth rate $\mathbf{K}\boldsymbol{\tau}$ (defined by (6.13)), so that:

$$\widetilde{\Delta\mathbf{x}}_{T+h} = \mathbf{K}\boldsymbol{\tau}. \tag{6.25}$$

From (6.21) and (6.25), the expression for the forecast error $\widetilde{\mathbf{e}}_{\Delta x,T+h}$ is:

$$\widetilde{\mathbf{e}}_{\Delta x,T+h} = \boldsymbol{\Upsilon}^{h-1}\left(\boldsymbol{\alpha\beta}'\mathbf{x}_T + \boldsymbol{\tau}\right) - \mathbf{K}\boldsymbol{\tau} + \mathbf{v}_{T+h} + \sum_{i=0}^{h-2} \boldsymbol{\Upsilon}^i \boldsymbol{\alpha\beta}'\mathbf{v}_{T+h-i-1}, \tag{6.26}$$

so that for $\boldsymbol{\alpha} \neq \mathbf{0}$ and using (6.12):

$$\begin{aligned} \mathsf{E}\left[\widetilde{\mathbf{e}}_{\Delta x,T+h} \mid \mathbf{x}_T\right] &= \boldsymbol{\Upsilon}^{h-1}\left(\boldsymbol{\alpha\beta}'\mathbf{x}_T + \boldsymbol{\tau}\right) - \mathbf{K}\boldsymbol{\tau} \\ &= \boldsymbol{\alpha\lambda}^{h-1}\boldsymbol{\beta}'\mathbf{x}_T + \boldsymbol{\Upsilon}^{h-1}\left(\mathbf{I}_n - \mathbf{K}\right)\boldsymbol{\tau} \\ &= \boldsymbol{\alpha\lambda}^{h-1}\left(\mathbf{w}_{a,T} - \mathsf{E}\left[\mathbf{w}_{a,T}\right]\right). \end{aligned} \tag{6.27}$$

Equation (6.24) continues to hold for $\mathsf{V}[\widetilde{\mathbf{e}}_{\Delta x,T+h}|\mathbf{x}_T]$. Thus, for $\Delta\mathbf{x}_t$ from a DV, the conditional forecasts are biased unless $\boldsymbol{\alpha} = \mathbf{0}$, but tend to zero for large h, and the MSFE is $O(1)$.

To obtain expressions for the unconditional expectations and forecast-error variance, take the unconditional expectation in (6.27):

$$\mathsf{E}\left[\widetilde{\mathbf{e}}_{\Delta x,T+h}\right] = \boldsymbol{\alpha\lambda}^{h-1}\mathsf{E}\left[\mathbf{w}_{a,T} - \mathsf{E}\left[\mathbf{w}_{a,T}\right]\right] = \mathbf{0}, \tag{6.28}$$

so the unconditional forecasts from the DV are unbiased when the average growth rate is used as the forecast. However, they would be biased by $-\boldsymbol{\alpha}(\boldsymbol{\beta}'\boldsymbol{\alpha})^{-1}\boldsymbol{\beta}'\boldsymbol{\tau}$ if $\mathbf{K} = \mathbf{I}_n$ was used in (6.25), so that the forecast was $\boldsymbol{\tau}$, as might be incorrectly assumed on setting $\mathbf{\Pi}$ to zero in (6.8).

From (6.10), the unconditional variance matrix of $\mathbf{w}_t$, $\mathsf{M}[\mathbf{w}_t]$, is $\mathbf{H} = \mathbf{GHG}' + \boldsymbol{\Sigma}$ so that from (6.11):

$$\begin{pmatrix} \mathbf{H}_{aa} & \mathbf{H}_{ab} \\ \mathbf{H}_{ba} & \mathbf{H}_{bb} \end{pmatrix} = \begin{pmatrix} \boldsymbol{\lambda}\mathbf{H}_{aa}\boldsymbol{\lambda}' & \boldsymbol{\lambda}\mathbf{H}_{aa}\boldsymbol{\alpha}_b' \\ \boldsymbol{\alpha}_b\mathbf{H}_{aa}\boldsymbol{\lambda}' & \boldsymbol{\alpha}_b\mathbf{H}_{aa}\boldsymbol{\alpha}_b' \end{pmatrix} + \begin{pmatrix} \boldsymbol{\Sigma}_{aa} & \boldsymbol{\Sigma}_{ab} \\ \boldsymbol{\Sigma}_{ba} & \boldsymbol{\Sigma}_{bb} \end{pmatrix}. \tag{6.29}$$

Consequently, from (6.26) for $\boldsymbol{\alpha} \neq \mathbf{0}$ (the last term on the first line is present only for $h > 1$):

$$\begin{aligned} \mathsf{M}\left[\widetilde{\mathbf{e}}_{\Delta x,T+h}\right] &= \boldsymbol{\alpha\lambda}^{h-1}\mathsf{M}\left[\mathbf{w}_{a,T}\right]\boldsymbol{\lambda}^{h-1\prime}\boldsymbol{\alpha}' + \boldsymbol{\Omega} + \sum_{i=0}^{h-2}\boldsymbol{\alpha\lambda}^i\boldsymbol{\beta}'\boldsymbol{\Omega\beta\lambda}^{i\prime}\boldsymbol{\alpha}' \\ &= \boldsymbol{\Omega} + \boldsymbol{\alpha}\mathsf{M}\left[\mathbf{w}_{a,T}\right]\boldsymbol{\alpha}'. \end{aligned} \tag{6.30}$$

The last expression in (6.30) follows because $\mathbf{H}_{aa} = \boldsymbol{\lambda}\mathbf{H}_{aa}\boldsymbol{\lambda}' + \boldsymbol{\beta}'\boldsymbol{\Omega\beta}$ from (6.29) and (6.11), so we can write the first line of (6.30) as:

$$\begin{aligned} &\boldsymbol{\alpha\lambda}^{h-2}\left[\boldsymbol{\lambda}\mathbf{H}_{aa}\boldsymbol{\lambda}' + \boldsymbol{\beta}'\boldsymbol{\Omega\beta}\right]\boldsymbol{\lambda}^{h-2\prime}\boldsymbol{\alpha}' + \boldsymbol{\Omega} + \sum_{i=0}^{h-3}\boldsymbol{\alpha\lambda}^i\boldsymbol{\beta}'\boldsymbol{\Omega\beta\lambda}^{i\prime}\boldsymbol{\alpha}' \\ =\; &\boldsymbol{\alpha\lambda}^{h-2}\mathbf{H}_{aa}\boldsymbol{\lambda}^{h-2\prime}\boldsymbol{\alpha}' + \boldsymbol{\Omega} + \sum_{i=0}^{h-3}\boldsymbol{\alpha\lambda}^i\boldsymbol{\beta}'\boldsymbol{\Omega\beta\lambda}^{i\prime}\boldsymbol{\alpha}', \end{aligned} \tag{6.31}$$

and so on. Thus, (6.30) is independent of h. In the bivariate case, λ is the scalar $(1 + \boldsymbol{\beta}'\boldsymbol{\alpha})$ and so $\boldsymbol{\alpha}\mathsf{M}[\mathbf{w}_{a,T}]\boldsymbol{\alpha}' = \boldsymbol{\alpha\beta}'\boldsymbol{\Omega\beta\alpha}'(1-\lambda^2)^{-1}$, using (6.29). From (6.30), therefore:

$$\sum_{i=0}^{h-2}\boldsymbol{\alpha\lambda}^i\boldsymbol{\beta}'\boldsymbol{\Omega\beta\lambda}^{i\prime}\boldsymbol{\alpha}' = \boldsymbol{\alpha}\mathsf{M}\left[\mathbf{w}_{a,T}\right]\boldsymbol{\alpha}' - \boldsymbol{\alpha\lambda}^{h-1}\mathsf{M}\left[\mathbf{w}_{a,T}\right]\boldsymbol{\lambda}^{h-1\prime}\boldsymbol{\alpha}', \tag{6.32}$$

and substituting this into (6.24):

$$\mathbf{V}_{\Delta x,h} = \boldsymbol{\Omega} + \boldsymbol{\alpha}\mathsf{M}\left[\mathbf{w}_{a,T}\right]\boldsymbol{\alpha}' - \boldsymbol{\alpha}\boldsymbol{\lambda}^{h-1}\mathsf{M}\left[\mathbf{w}_{a,T}\right]\boldsymbol{\lambda}^{h-1\prime}\boldsymbol{\alpha}'. \tag{6.33}$$

Thus, the difference between the correct model and the DV model asymptotic variance formulae for $\Delta\mathbf{x}_t$ (6.33) and (6.30) is $\boldsymbol{\alpha}\boldsymbol{\lambda}^{h-1}\mathsf{M}[\mathbf{w}_{a,T}]\boldsymbol{\lambda}^{h-1\prime}\boldsymbol{\alpha}'$, which goes to zero in h. Hence, when assessing forecast accuracy using the second-moment matrix for $\Delta\mathbf{x}_t$, there is no measurable gain to using the correctly specified model at anything but the shortest forecast horizons.

The analogous expressions for forecasting levels using the DV model are based on forecasts of $\mathbf{x}_t$ derived by integrating the forecasts of $\Delta\mathbf{x}_t$ (given in (6.25)) from the forecast origin:

$$\widetilde{\mathbf{x}}_{T+h} = \widetilde{\mathbf{x}}_{T+h-1} + \mathbf{K}\boldsymbol{\tau} = \widetilde{\mathbf{x}}_T + h\mathbf{K}\boldsymbol{\tau}. \tag{6.34}$$

By subtracting (6.34) from (6.17) we obtain:

$$\widetilde{\mathbf{e}}_{x,T+h} = \left(\boldsymbol{\Upsilon}^h - \mathbf{I}_n\right)\mathbf{x}_T + \sum_{i=0}^{h-1}\left(\boldsymbol{\Upsilon}^i - \mathbf{K}\right)\boldsymbol{\tau} + \sum_{i=0}^{h-1}\boldsymbol{\Upsilon}^i\mathbf{v}_{T+h-i}. \tag{6.35}$$

Now, $\left(\boldsymbol{\Upsilon}^h - \mathbf{I}_n\right) = \boldsymbol{\alpha}\sum_{i=0}^{h-1}\boldsymbol{\lambda}^i\boldsymbol{\beta}'$ because:

$$\begin{aligned}
\boldsymbol{\Upsilon}^h - \mathbf{I}_n &= \boldsymbol{\Upsilon}^{h-1}\left(\mathbf{I}_n + \boldsymbol{\alpha}\boldsymbol{\beta}'\right) - \mathbf{I}_n \\
&= \boldsymbol{\Upsilon}^{h-1}\boldsymbol{\alpha}\boldsymbol{\beta}' + \boldsymbol{\Upsilon}^{h-1} - \mathbf{I}_n \\
&= \boldsymbol{\Upsilon}^{h-1}\boldsymbol{\alpha}\boldsymbol{\beta}' + \boldsymbol{\Upsilon}^{h-2}\boldsymbol{\alpha}\boldsymbol{\beta}' + \cdots + \boldsymbol{\Upsilon}^0\boldsymbol{\alpha}\boldsymbol{\beta}' + \boldsymbol{\Upsilon}^0 - \mathbf{I}_n \\
&= \sum_{i=0}^{h-1}\boldsymbol{\Upsilon}^i\boldsymbol{\alpha}\boldsymbol{\beta}',
\end{aligned} \tag{6.36}$$

and $\boldsymbol{\Upsilon}^i\boldsymbol{\alpha} = \boldsymbol{\alpha}(\mathbf{I}_r + \boldsymbol{\beta}'\boldsymbol{\alpha})^i = \boldsymbol{\alpha}\boldsymbol{\lambda}^i$. Also:

$$\sum_{i=0}^{h-1}\left(\boldsymbol{\Upsilon}^i - \mathbf{K}\right) = \sum_{i=0}^{h-1}\boldsymbol{\Upsilon}^i\left(\mathbf{I}_n - \mathbf{K}\right) = \sum_{i=0}^{h-1}\boldsymbol{\Upsilon}^i\boldsymbol{\alpha}\left(\boldsymbol{\beta}'\boldsymbol{\alpha}\right)^{-1}\boldsymbol{\beta}' = \sum_{i=0}^{h-1}\boldsymbol{\alpha}\boldsymbol{\lambda}^i\left(\boldsymbol{\beta}'\boldsymbol{\alpha}\right)^{-1}\boldsymbol{\beta}'.$$

Substituting in to (6.35) and using (6.12) results in the following expression for the conditional expectation:

$$\mathsf{E}\left[\widetilde{\mathbf{e}}_{x,T+h} \mid \mathbf{x}_T\right] = \sum_{i=0}^{h-1}\boldsymbol{\alpha}\boldsymbol{\lambda}^i\left(\boldsymbol{\beta}'\mathbf{x}_T - \mathsf{E}\left[\boldsymbol{\beta}'\mathbf{x}_T\right]\right). \tag{6.37}$$

The unconditional expectation implies unbiased DV-model levels' forecasts:

$$\mathsf{E}\left[\widetilde{\mathbf{e}}_{x,T+h}\right] = \sum_{i=0}^{h-1}\boldsymbol{\alpha}\boldsymbol{\lambda}^i\mathsf{E}\left[\mathbf{w}_{a,T} - \mathsf{E}\left[\mathbf{w}_{a,T}\right]\right] = \mathbf{0}. \tag{6.38}$$

The conditional variance $\mathsf{M}[\widetilde{\mathbf{e}}_{x,T+h}|\mathbf{x}_T]$ is equivalent to (6.19), but the unconditional variance for the DV forecast of $\mathbf{x}_t$ differs, and is given by:

$$\mathsf{M}\left[\widetilde{\mathbf{e}}_{x,T+h}\right]=\sum_{i=0}^{h-1}\sum_{q=0}^{h-1}\boldsymbol{\alpha}\boldsymbol{\lambda}^{i}\mathsf{M}\left[\mathbf{w}_{a,T}\right]\boldsymbol{\lambda}^{q\prime}\boldsymbol{\alpha}'+\sum_{s=0}^{h-1}\boldsymbol{\Upsilon}^{s}\boldsymbol{\Omega}\boldsymbol{\Upsilon}^{s\prime}. \tag{6.39}$$

Comparing (6.39) to (6.19), the unconditional variance will always exceed the conditional since the first term is a positive-definite matrix. However, it declines asymptotically in h. For example, in the bivariate case when λ is a scalar:

$$\begin{aligned}\sum_{i=0}^{h-1}\sum_{q=0}^{h-1}\boldsymbol{\alpha}\lambda^{i}\mathsf{M}\left[\mathbf{w}_{a,T}\right]\lambda^{q\prime}\boldsymbol{\alpha}' &= \boldsymbol{\alpha}\mathsf{M}\left[\mathbf{w}_{a,T}\right]\boldsymbol{\alpha}'\left(\sum_{i=0}^{h-1}\lambda^{i}\right)\left(\sum_{q=0}^{h-1}\lambda^{q}\right)\\ &= \boldsymbol{\alpha}\mathsf{M}\left[\mathbf{w}_{a,T}\right]\boldsymbol{\alpha}'\left(1-\lambda^{h}\right)^{2}\left(1-\lambda\right)^{-2}.\end{aligned} \tag{6.40}$$

The expressions for the forecast variances of $\mathbf{w}_t$ in the DV model can be found by combining the expressions for $\mathbf{x}_t$ and $\Delta\mathbf{x}_t$ from (6.35) and (6.26):

$$\widetilde{\mathbf{e}}_{w,T+h}=\left(\widetilde{\mathbf{e}}_{x,T+h}'\boldsymbol{\beta}:\widetilde{\mathbf{e}}_{\Delta x,T+h}'\mathbf{J}\right)', \tag{6.41}$$

so that the formula for the forecast-error second-moment matrix of $\mathbf{w}_t$ in the DV model is implicitly given by:

$$\mathsf{M}\left[\widetilde{\mathbf{e}}_{w,T+h}\right]=\begin{pmatrix}\boldsymbol{\beta}'\mathsf{M}\left[\widetilde{\mathbf{e}}_{x,T+h}\right]\boldsymbol{\beta} & \boldsymbol{\beta}'\mathsf{E}\left[\widetilde{\mathbf{e}}_{x,T+h}\widetilde{\mathbf{e}}_{\Delta x,T+h}'\right]\mathbf{J}\\ \mathbf{J}'\mathsf{E}\left[\widetilde{\mathbf{e}}_{x,T+h}\widetilde{\mathbf{e}}_{\Delta x,T+h}'\right]\boldsymbol{\beta} & \mathbf{J}'\mathsf{M}\left[\widetilde{\mathbf{e}}_{\Delta x,T+h}\right]\mathbf{J}\end{pmatrix} \tag{6.42}$$

These analytical formulae imply that, at anything other than the shortest horizons, the mis-specified model will fare just as well as the correctly specified model in terms of how well they are able to predict differences. This is shown dramatically by figure 6.1 which is based on a bivariate DGP with a cointegrating vector $\boldsymbol{\beta}'=(1:1)$, $\boldsymbol{\alpha}'=(-0.1:0.25)$, and uncorrelated, normally distributed disturbances with unit variance. The figure plots the ratio of the TMSFE for the DV to that for the correctly specified model, and also compares the two models in terms of their ability to predict the levels of the series and the (cointegrating) stationary transformation of the data. Thus, it summarizes the information in the analytical formulae. Forecast evaluation exercises based on MSFE comparisons of the ability to predict differences of variables may fail to reject the DV even when it is mis-specified due to omitting the variables which cointegrate. Moreover, the asymptotic formulae (again see figure 6.1) show that such an outcome would be less likely using MSFEs for cointegrating combinations. Rather than viewing this as a reason for favouring the second strategy, we argued in chapter 3 that it constitutes a limitation to using measures for assessing forecast accuracy such as MSFE which are not invariant to the linear transformation of the variables on which forecast accuracy is assessed.[1] In section 3.6, we discussed an invariant criterion.

[1] Ericsson (1993) demonstrates the empirical relevance of this limitation in an example of evaluating multi-period forecasts of the exchange rate.

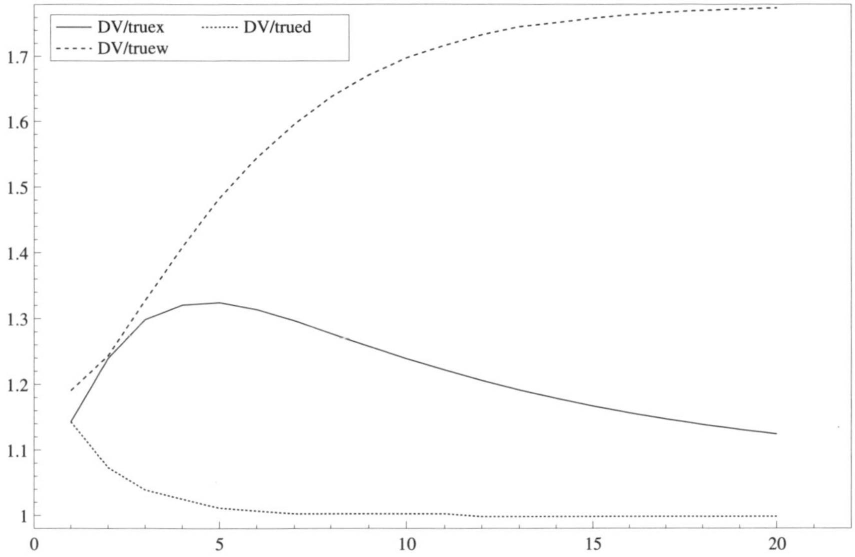

Figure 6.1 Ratio of TMSFE of the DV model to the correctly specified case

6.5 Forecast biases in systems

Section 5.4 developed the analysis of antithetic variates to establish the unbiasedness of forecasts in dynamic equations, even though parameter estimates are biased. We now extend that analysis to cointegrated and differenced systems. We consider both fixed ($\mathbf{x}_0 = \mathbf{0}$) and stationary start-up. The extension to the systems case raises additional issues when we consider cointegrated systems. In particular, we show that the issue of whether the constant terms in the system lie within the space spanned by the cointegrating vectors interacts with the assumptions we make about the initial conditions to determine the (first-order) properties of forecasts. OLS will yield unbiased predictors only under mean stationarity and the assumption that the constant terms lie in the cointegrating space. As well as systems analogues of OLS, we also consider the unit-root model.

Finally, we make use of the analysis to indicate when second-moment measures of forecast accuracy (such as MSFEs) will be invariant to drift in the system. Again using symmetry arguments, we establish that under mean stationarity systems analogues of OLS will yield forecasts with MSFEs invariant to the drift terms when the constants lie in the cointegrating space, but that for the unit-root model this result holds more generally. These results are particularly useful in illuminating the role played by deterministic terms in affecting the forecast accuracy of econometric models.

6.5.1 Fixed start-up

The systems case is based on the DGP of section 6.2:

$$\mathbf{x}_t = \boldsymbol{\Upsilon}\mathbf{x}_{t-1} + \boldsymbol{\tau} + \mathbf{v}_t \tag{6.43}$$

for $\mathbf{v}_t \sim \mathsf{IN}_n[\mathbf{0}, \boldsymbol{\Omega}]$. By backward induction we obtain:

$$\mathbf{x}_i = \boldsymbol{\Upsilon}^i\mathbf{x}_0 + \sum_{j=0}^{i-1}\boldsymbol{\Upsilon}^j\boldsymbol{\tau} + \sum_{j=0}^{i-1}\boldsymbol{\Upsilon}^j\mathbf{v}_{i-j} \quad \forall i. \tag{6.44}$$

Many of the results are direct analogues of the scalar case. For instance, the least-squares predictor is unbiased under the assumption of fixed start-up ($\mathbf{x}_0 = \mathbf{0}$) provided $\boldsymbol{\tau} = \mathbf{0}$, but not otherwise. When $\boldsymbol{\tau} = \mathbf{0}$, switching the sign of the $\{\mathbf{v}_t\}$ switches the sign of $\{\mathbf{x}_t\}$; the estimated slope coefficients are invariant to the sign switch ($\widehat{\boldsymbol{\Upsilon}} = \widehat{\boldsymbol{\Upsilon}}^-$), and the sign on the constant term coefficient is reversed ($\widehat{\boldsymbol{\tau}} = -\widehat{\boldsymbol{\tau}}^-$) (if estimated). Consequently, the forecasts for the antithetic pair are of opposite signs, establishing unbiasedness.

For the unit-root predictor (or DV model in the systems case), a similar analysis applies, but with an additional interesting feature. The DV model forecasts of $\mathbf{x}_{T+h}$ are given by $\widetilde{\mathbf{x}}_{T+h}$:

$$\widetilde{\mathbf{x}}_{T+h} = \mathbf{x}_T + h\widetilde{\boldsymbol{\varphi}}, \tag{6.45}$$

where, as in the scalar case, $\widetilde{\boldsymbol{\varphi}}$, the estimated sample growth rate, is given by:

$$\begin{aligned}
\widetilde{\boldsymbol{\varphi}} &= T^{-1}\sum_{s=1}^{T}\Delta\mathbf{x}_s \\
&= T^{-1}\left(\mathbf{x}_T - \mathbf{x}_0\right) \\
&= T^{-1}\left(\boldsymbol{\Upsilon}^T\mathbf{x}_0 + \sum_{i=0}^{T-1}\boldsymbol{\Upsilon}^i\boldsymbol{\tau} + \sum_{i=0}^{T-1}\boldsymbol{\Upsilon}^i\mathbf{v}_{T-i} - \mathbf{x}_0\right).
\end{aligned} \tag{6.46}$$

Under the fixed start-up assumption, $\mathbf{x}_0 = \mathbf{0}$:

$$\widetilde{\boldsymbol{\varphi}} = T^{-1}\left(\sum_{i=0}^{T-1}\boldsymbol{\Upsilon}^i\boldsymbol{\tau} + \sum_{i=0}^{T-1}\boldsymbol{\Upsilon}^i\mathbf{v}_{T-i}\right).$$

Switching the signs of the random numbers gives:

$$\widetilde{\boldsymbol{\varphi}}^- = T^{-1}\left(\sum_{i=0}^{T-1}\boldsymbol{\Upsilon}^i\boldsymbol{\tau} - \sum_{i=0}^{T-1}\boldsymbol{\Upsilon}^i\mathbf{v}_{T-i}\right). \tag{6.47}$$

The average error of the antithetic pair is given by:

$$\begin{aligned}
&\tfrac{1}{2}\left[\left(\mathbf{x}_{T+h}+\mathbf{x}^{-}_{T+h}\right)-\left(\widetilde{\mathbf{x}}_{T+h}+\widetilde{\mathbf{x}}^{-}_{T+h}\right)\right] \\
&= \tfrac{1}{2}\left(2\sum_{i=0}^{T+h-1}\boldsymbol{\Upsilon}^{i}\boldsymbol{\tau}-2\sum_{i=0}^{T-1}\boldsymbol{\Upsilon}^{i}\boldsymbol{\tau}-2hT^{-1}\sum_{i=0}^{T-1}\boldsymbol{\Upsilon}^{i}\boldsymbol{\tau}\right) \\
&= \left(\sum_{i=0}^{h-1}\boldsymbol{\Upsilon}^{T+i}-hT^{-1}\sum_{i=0}^{T-1}\boldsymbol{\Upsilon}^{i}\right)\boldsymbol{\tau}
\end{aligned} \tag{6.48}$$

which is zero when $\boldsymbol{\tau}=\mathbf{0}$ or $\boldsymbol{\Upsilon}=\mathbf{I}_n$.

Further, using the result that $\boldsymbol{\Upsilon}^{r}\rightarrow\mathbf{K}$ as $r\rightarrow\infty$ (see appendix equation (6.63)), then the first term is approximately $h\mathbf{K}\boldsymbol{\tau}$ for large T. When $\boldsymbol{\alpha}=\mathbf{0}$, $\boldsymbol{\Upsilon}=\mathbf{I}_n$, so (6.48) becomes $(h\mathbf{I}_n-hT^{-1}T\mathbf{I}_n)\boldsymbol{\tau}=\mathbf{0}$, as noted. More generally, if a row of $\boldsymbol{\alpha}$ contains zeros (corresponding to an equation not being 'equilibrium-correcting'), for example, $\boldsymbol{\alpha}_1=\mathbf{0}$, (the first row or first s rows, without loss of generality), then:

$$\tfrac{1}{2}\left[\left(\mathbf{x}_{1,T+h}+\mathbf{x}^{-}_{1,T+h}\right)-\left(\widetilde{\mathbf{x}}_{1,T+h}+\widetilde{\mathbf{x}}^{-}_{1,T+h}\right)\right]=\mathbf{0},$$

where $\mathbf{x}_t=(\mathbf{x}'_{1t}:\mathbf{x}'_{2t})'$. This follows from (6.48) by noting that $(\boldsymbol{\Upsilon}^{r})_1=(\mathbf{I}_s:\mathbf{0})\ \forall r$ where $(\boldsymbol{\Upsilon}^{r})_1$ refers to the first s rows of $\boldsymbol{\Upsilon}^{r}$.

If we do not estimate the constant term, then (6.48) becomes:

$$\begin{aligned}
\tfrac{1}{2}\left[\left(\mathbf{x}_{T+h}+\mathbf{x}^{-}_{T+h}\right)-\left(\widetilde{\mathbf{x}}_{T+h}+\widetilde{\mathbf{x}}^{-}_{T+h}\right)\right] &= \tfrac{1}{2}\left[\left(\mathbf{x}_{T+h}+\mathbf{x}^{-}_{T+h}\right)-\left(\mathbf{x}_{T}+\mathbf{x}^{-}_{T}\right)\right] \\
&= \tfrac{1}{2}\left(2\sum_{i=0}^{T+h-1}\boldsymbol{\Upsilon}^{i}\boldsymbol{\tau}-2\sum_{i=0}^{T-1}\boldsymbol{\Upsilon}^{i}\boldsymbol{\tau}\right) \\
&= \sum_{i=0}^{h-1}\boldsymbol{\Upsilon}^{T+i}\boldsymbol{\tau} \\
&\simeq h\mathbf{K}\boldsymbol{\tau},
\end{aligned}$$

where we use (6.63) for the approximation in the last line.

Whether constant terms are estimated or not, forecasts from the DV model are unbiased if $\boldsymbol{\tau}=\mathbf{0}$. If that condition holds, the modelling of cointegration relationships amongst the $\mathbf{x}_t$ is not necessary for forecasts to be unbiased.

6.5.2 Stationary initial conditions

The initial conditions are chosen to satisfy (6.12) as:

$$\Delta\mathbf{x}_{b,0}=\boldsymbol{\alpha}_b\boldsymbol{\beta}'\mathbf{x}_{-1}+\boldsymbol{\tau}_b+\mathbf{v}_{b,0}$$

and:

$$\boldsymbol{\beta}'\mathbf{x}_0=\boldsymbol{\lambda}\boldsymbol{\beta}'\mathbf{x}_{-1}+\boldsymbol{\beta}'\boldsymbol{\tau}+\boldsymbol{\beta}'\mathbf{v}_0 \tag{6.49}$$

then:

$$\mathsf{E}\left[\mathbf{w}_0\right] = \mathsf{E}\left[\begin{array}{c} \boldsymbol{\beta}'\mathbf{x}_0 \\ \Delta\mathbf{x}_{b,0} \end{array}\right] = \left(\begin{array}{c} -\left(\boldsymbol{\beta}'\boldsymbol{\alpha}\right)^{-1}\boldsymbol{\beta}'\boldsymbol{\tau} \\ \boldsymbol{\alpha}_b(\boldsymbol{\beta}'\boldsymbol{\alpha})^{-1}\boldsymbol{\beta}'\boldsymbol{\tau} + \boldsymbol{\tau}_b \end{array}\right).$$

From (6.44), $\mathbf{x}_i$ is given by:

$$\begin{aligned} \mathbf{x}_i &= \boldsymbol{\Upsilon}^i\mathbf{x}_0 + \sum_{j=0}^{i-1}\boldsymbol{\Upsilon}^j\boldsymbol{\tau} + \sum_{j=0}^{i-1}\boldsymbol{\Upsilon}^j\mathbf{v}_{i-j} \\ &= \left(\mathbf{I}_n + \sum_{j=0}^{i-1}\boldsymbol{\Upsilon}^j\boldsymbol{\alpha}\boldsymbol{\beta}'\right)\mathbf{x}_0 + \sum_{j=0}^{i-1}\boldsymbol{\Upsilon}^j\boldsymbol{\tau} + \sum_{j=0}^{i-1}\boldsymbol{\Upsilon}^j\mathbf{v}_{i-j} \\ &= \mathbf{x}_0 + \sum_{j=0}^{i-1}\boldsymbol{\Upsilon}^j\left(\mathbf{I}_n - \boldsymbol{\alpha}\left(\boldsymbol{\beta}'\boldsymbol{\alpha}\right)^{-1}\boldsymbol{\beta}'\right)\boldsymbol{\tau} + \sum_{j=0}^{i-1}\boldsymbol{\Upsilon}^j\mathbf{v}_{i-j} + \boldsymbol{\Xi}\mathbf{v}_0 \\ &= \mathbf{x}_0 + i\mathbf{K}\boldsymbol{\tau} + \sum_{j=0}^{i-1}\boldsymbol{\Upsilon}^j\mathbf{v}_{i-j} + \boldsymbol{\Xi}\mathbf{v}_0, \end{aligned} \tag{6.50}$$

using (6.49), since $\boldsymbol{\Upsilon}^i = \mathbf{I}_n + \sum_{j=0}^{i-1}\boldsymbol{\Upsilon}^j\boldsymbol{\alpha}\boldsymbol{\beta}'$ and $\boldsymbol{\Upsilon}^r\mathbf{K} = \mathbf{K}$. Now if $\boldsymbol{\tau} = \boldsymbol{\alpha}\boldsymbol{\tau}^*$, so the intercept lies in the cointegration space and there is zero growth, since $\mathbf{K}\boldsymbol{\alpha} = \mathbf{0}$, then (6.50) simplifies to:

$$\mathbf{x}_i = \mathbf{x}_0 + \sum_{j=0}^{i-1}\boldsymbol{\Upsilon}^j\mathbf{v}_{i-j} + \boldsymbol{\Xi}\mathbf{v}_0.$$

We can write this special case as:

$$\mathbf{y}_i = \boldsymbol{\Upsilon}\mathbf{y}_{i-1} + \mathbf{v}_i = \boldsymbol{\Upsilon}^i\mathbf{y}_0 + \sum_{j=0}^{i-1}\boldsymbol{\Upsilon}^j\mathbf{v}_{i-j}, \tag{6.51}$$

where $\mathbf{y}_i = \mathbf{x}_i - \mathbf{x}_0$, so that $\mathbf{y}_0 = \mathbf{0}$. Thus, under these assumptions, we can transform the stationary start-up process to a mean-zero process with a fixed start-up condition: we have already seen that such processes yield unbiased forecasts. The importance of the condition that the constant terms lie in the cointegrating space should be apparent: otherwise from (6.50), $\mathsf{E}[\mathbf{x}_t] = \mathbf{x}_0 + t\mathbf{K}\boldsymbol{\tau}$ so that the process has a time variant mean and cannot be made stationary.

6.5.2.1 Unit-root predictor

From (6.50) we obtain:

$$\widetilde{\boldsymbol{\varphi}} = T^{-1}\left(\mathbf{x}_T - \mathbf{x}_0\right) = \mathbf{K}\boldsymbol{\tau} + T^{-1}\sum_{i=0}^{T-1}\boldsymbol{\Upsilon}^i\mathbf{v}_{T-i}. \tag{6.52}$$

Thus, $\widetilde{\varphi} + \widetilde{\varphi}^{-} = 2\mathbf{K}\boldsymbol{\tau}$. Substituting for the $\widetilde{\varphi}$s from (6.52) and for $\mathbf{x}_i$ from (6.50):

$$\begin{aligned} & \tfrac{1}{2}\left[\left(\mathbf{x}_{T+h} + \mathbf{x}^{-}_{T+h}\right) - \left(\widetilde{\mathbf{x}}_{T+h} + \widetilde{\mathbf{x}}^{-}_{T+h}\right)\right] \\ = & \tfrac{1}{2}\left[(2\mathbf{x}_0 + 2(T+h)\mathbf{K}\boldsymbol{\tau}) - (2\mathbf{x}_0 + 2T\mathbf{K}\boldsymbol{\tau} + 2h\mathbf{K}\boldsymbol{\tau})\right] = \mathbf{0}, \end{aligned}$$

so that unbiasedness results when constant terms are estimated. When constant terms are not estimated:

$$\begin{aligned} & \tfrac{1}{2}\left[\left(\mathbf{x}_{T+h} + \mathbf{x}^{-}_{T+h}\right) - \left(\mathbf{x}_{T} + \mathbf{x}^{-}_{T}\right)\right] \\ = & \tfrac{1}{2}\left[(2\mathbf{x}_0 + 2(T+h)\mathbf{K}\boldsymbol{\tau}) - (2\mathbf{x}_0 + 2T\mathbf{K}\boldsymbol{\tau})\right] \\ = & h\mathbf{K}\boldsymbol{\tau}, \end{aligned}$$

which equals zero when $\boldsymbol{\tau} = \boldsymbol{\alpha}\boldsymbol{\tau}^{*}$, since then $\mathbf{K}\boldsymbol{\tau} = \mathbf{0}$.

6.5.3 Invariance of MSFEs to constant terms in the DGP

Assuming mean stationarity and that constant terms are estimated in the econometric models, we can establish a number of results concerning the invariance of second-moment measures of forecast accuracy for the OLS and DV model forecasts to constant terms in the DGP. Beginning with the DV model, consider the forecast error $\mathbf{x}_{T+h} - \widetilde{\mathbf{x}}_{T+h}$, where $\mathbf{x}_{T+h}$ is given by (6.50), and the predictor by $\mathbf{x}_T + h\widetilde{\varphi}$, where $\widetilde{\varphi}$ is given by (6.52). The assumption of mean stationarity implies that $\mathbf{K}\boldsymbol{\alpha} = \mathbf{0}$, so that the analysis is effectively for the $\{\mathbf{y}_t\}$ process in (6.51), although we continue with the $\{\mathbf{x}_t\}$ notation. Then by substitution we obtain:

$$\widehat{\mathbf{e}}_{T+h} = \mathbf{x}_{T+h} - \widetilde{\mathbf{x}}_{T+h} = \sum_{j=0}^{T+h-1} \boldsymbol{\Upsilon}^{j}\mathbf{v}_{T+h-j} - \left(1 + hT^{-1}\right)\sum_{j=0}^{T-1} \boldsymbol{\Upsilon}^{j}\mathbf{v}_{T-j}.$$

Since $\widehat{\mathbf{e}}_{T+h} = -\widehat{\mathbf{e}}^{-}_{T+h}$ (establishing unbiasedness), $\mathsf{M}[\widehat{\mathbf{e}}_{T+h}] = \mathsf{M}[\widehat{\mathbf{e}}^{-}_{T+h}]$. The forecast errors are invariant to $\boldsymbol{\tau}$, and hence the MSFE is also invariant to $\boldsymbol{\tau}$.

This result sheds some light on the Monte Carlo study of forecast accuracy reported in section 6.8 below. In section 5.2, we noted that the Monte Carlo estimator of the MSFE was:

$$\widehat{\mathbf{M}} = R^{-1}\sum_{i=1}^{R}\left(\widehat{\mathbf{e}}_{T+h,i}\widehat{\mathbf{e}}'_{T+h,i}\right).$$

The R realizations can be approximately viewed as $R/2$ antithetic pairs. Then we have:

$$\begin{aligned} \widehat{\mathbf{M}} &= R^{-1}\sum_{i=1}^{R}\left(\widehat{\mathbf{e}}_{T+h,i}\widehat{\mathbf{e}}'_{T+h,i}\right) \\ &\approx R^{-1}\sum_{i=1}^{R/2}\left(\widehat{\mathbf{e}}_{T+h,i}\widehat{\mathbf{e}}'_{T+h,i} + \widehat{\mathbf{e}}^{-}_{T+h,i}\widehat{\mathbf{e}}^{-\prime}_{T+h,i}\right) \end{aligned}$$

$$= \left(\frac{R}{2}\right)^{-1} \sum_{i=1}^{R/2} \widehat{\mathbf{e}}_{T+h,i} \widehat{\mathbf{e}}'_{T+h,i}.$$

When the $\widehat{\mathbf{e}}_{T+h,i}$ are invariant to $\boldsymbol{\tau}$, then (approximately) so will $\widehat{\mathbf{M}}$.

Consider now the systems analogues of the OLS predictor. From (6.51) we have that:

$$\mathbf{y}_i = \sum_{j=0}^{i-1} \boldsymbol{\Upsilon}^j \mathbf{v}_{i-j}.$$

Then:

$$\mathbf{y}_{T+h} - \widehat{\mathbf{y}}_{T+h} = \sum_{j=0}^{T+h-1} \boldsymbol{\Upsilon}^j \mathbf{v}_{T+h-j} - \sum_{j=0}^{T+h-1} \widehat{\boldsymbol{\Upsilon}}^j \widehat{\boldsymbol{\tau}}. \tag{6.53}$$

Since (6.51) contains zero drift whatever the value of $\boldsymbol{\tau}$ as long as $\boldsymbol{\tau} = \boldsymbol{\alpha}\boldsymbol{\tau}^*$, then both $\widehat{\boldsymbol{\Upsilon}}$ and $\widehat{\boldsymbol{\tau}}$ are invariant to $\boldsymbol{\tau}$, and therefore (6.53) is as well. An argument analogous to that above for the unit-root model then implies that the Monte Carlo estimator of the MSFE for the OLS model will be approximately invariant to $\boldsymbol{\tau}$ when $\boldsymbol{\tau} = \boldsymbol{\alpha}\boldsymbol{\tau}^*$.

From the way in which the results have been derived, their qualitative nature does not depend on the estimation method used; in particular, imposing reduced-rank restrictions on the 'long-run' or 'cointegration matrix' is irrelevant to whether the resulting forecasts are biased or not. Thus the 'OLS predictor' could be either the unrestricted VAR (in levels) or the Johansen ML estimator (see Johansen, 1988a, and Johansen and Juselius, 1990). However, if we impose a cointegrating rank less than the true value, then the qualitative nature of the results differs, as indicated by analysis for the DV.

Here, mean stationarity requires that $\mathbf{x}_0$ be consistent with $\mathbf{w}_0$ being drawn from its unconditional distribution. This parallels the usual procedure of discarding an initial number of observations when dealing with non-stationary (integrated) systems. For the OLS predictor to be unbiased, we also require that the constants lie in the cointegrating space. The predictions from the DV model are unbiased without this additional assumption. In section 6.8, we gauge the usefulness of the antithetic variate analysis predictions of the dependence of forecast accuracy on the constant terms.

6.6 Small-sample estimation issues

When parameters are unknown and have to be estimated from small samples of observations, the forecast-error variance formulae derived above need to be augmented by a term that reflects parameter estimation uncertainty (see, for example, Schmidt, 1974, Ericsson and Marquez, 1989, and Lütkepohl, 1991, sections 3.5 and 11.3). However, since this additional term has a zero probability limit, whether or not $\mathbf{x}_t$ is an integrated process, the formulae for estimated parameters and known parameters (as derived above) coincide asymptotically. Various approximations to the parameter-uncertainty term are available (see the references quoted above,) but as Lütkepohl (1991, p.378) states 'little is known about the small sample properties of forecasts based on estimated unstable processes'. The following sections seek to address this issue, albeit for the specific case of a first-order bivariate DGP. We first note the roles of Monte Carlo and asymptotic analysis before examining the former in detail.

In the Monte Carlo, we categorize estimation methods in terms of the number of common trends (Stock and Watson, 1988) or unit roots, $n - r$, and cointegrating restrictions, r, imposed. OLS on each equation in the system in turn is referred to as the unrestricted VAR estimator (UV), and estimates $\mathbf{\Pi}$ as a full-rank matrix, that is, neither unit roots nor cointegrating restrictions are imposed. The polar case is the estimator of the VAR in differences (DV), for which $\mathbf{\Pi}$ is set to the null matrix so that n unit roots are imposed. The intermediate case is illustrated by the maximum likelihood (ML) estimator of Johansen (1988a) and Johansen and Juselius (1990). For comparison with other studies the two-step procedure of Engle and Granger (1987) (EG) is also used in some experiments. The results obtained are subject to the qualifications noted in the previous chapter, but throw light on several important issues.

A theory of inference in regressions with non-stationary variables has been developed, *inter alia*, by Phillips and his co-authors (see, e.g., Phillips, 1991, for references, and Johansen, 1988a, Johansen, 1991). Engle and Yoo (1991) provide a good exposition. In general, the asymptotic distributions of coefficient estimators in systems of $\mathsf{I}(1)$ variables will be non-standard, and involve functionals of Wiener processes, but will converge at rate T, faster than the $\sqrt{T}$ rate in regressions involving $\mathsf{I}(0)$ variables. Some results on the asymptotic distributions of estimators, and powers thereof, are given in chapter 11 for $\mathsf{I}(1)$ processes.

West (1988) demonstrates that an even faster rate of convergence holds when the differences of the $\mathsf{I}(1)$ variables have non-zero means. In that case, the coefficients on stochastic $\mathsf{I}(1)$ variables in OLS regressions will converge at the rate of $\sqrt{T^3}$ while estimates of the constant term converge at $\sqrt{T}$. Moreover, the distribution of the estimators will be asymptotically normal, in which case the major contribution to overall forecast uncertainty from estimating parameters will be from the constant term rather than from slope coefficients.

Notwithstanding these rates of convergence, the practical importance of imposing cointegration restrictions for forecast accuracy in small samples is worthy of study, and is the focus of our Monte Carlo. We do not consider testing for cointegration but contrast the costs of having too few cointegrating vectors versus including spurious combinations of levels terms. Brandner and Kunst (1990), for example, find a tendency to over-estimate r when the true value is low, and claim that the costs of incorrectly specifying r are greater for over-estimates (imposing too much 'cointegration'), so they recommend the use of VARs in differences for forecasting. We find little support for this prescription in our bivariate example, given the absence of deterministic non-stationarities such as structural breaks and regime shifts.

6.7 The Monte Carlo experimental design

The DGP in the Monte Carlo is a first-order bivariate system as in Engle and Yoo (1987), where $\mathbf{x}_t = (z_t : y_t)'$ so from (6.8):

$$\Delta\mathbf{x}_t = \mathbf{\Pi}\mathbf{x}_{t-1} + \boldsymbol{\tau} + \mathbf{v}_t, \tag{6.54}$$

where $\mathbf{v}_t \sim \mathsf{IN}_2[\mathbf{0}, \mathbf{\Omega}]$, with:

$$\mathbf{\Pi} = \begin{pmatrix} a_{11} & -a_{11}\beta \\ a_{22} & -a_{22}\beta \end{pmatrix}, \ \boldsymbol{\tau} = \begin{pmatrix} a_{10} \\ a_{20} \end{pmatrix} \ \text{and} \ \mathbf{\Omega} = \begin{pmatrix} 1 & \rho s \\ \rho s & s^2 \end{pmatrix}.$$

Hence $|\mathbf{\Pi}| = 0$, and $r = 1$ for either $a_{11} \neq 0$ or $a_{22} \neq 0$. Thus, up to a scale factor, the cointegrating vector is given by the corresponding row of $\mathbf{\Pi}$, that is, $z_t - \beta y_t \sim \mathsf{I}(0)$. Allowing constant terms in general induces non-zero steady-state rates of growth:

$$g_z \equiv \mathsf{E}[\Delta z_t] = \beta\left(a_{22}a_{10} - a_{11}a_{20}\right) / \left(a_{22}\beta - a_{11}\right) \tag{6.55}$$

$$g_y \equiv \mathsf{E}[\Delta y_t] = \beta^{-1} g_z. \tag{6.56}$$

When both equations are equilibrium correcting, then the condition that the constant terms may be restricted to the cointegrating space ($\boldsymbol{\tau} = \boldsymbol{\alpha}\boldsymbol{\tau}^*$) implies that $a_{22}a_{10} = a_{11}a_{20}$, so from (6.55) and (6.56), $g_y = g_z = 0$. Deriving the steady-state solution for $\{z_t - \beta y_t\}$ by substituting from (6.55) or (6.56) in (6.54) shows that the cointegrating combination will have a zero mean if either $a_{10} = a_{20} = 0$, or $a_{10} = a_{20}$ and $\beta = 1$.

In generating data from (6.54), $\mathbf{x}_0$ was set equal to zero for each replication. In order to lessen the influence of this non-random initial condition on the simulated data, time series of $\{\mathbf{x}_t\}$ were constructed to have 20 more observations than required for estimation and forecasting, and the initial 20 observations were then discarded.[2]

The TMSFEs are then calculated from (5.4), as described in section 5.2, for each of the four estimation methods (UV, ML, EG or DV), and for each of the three transformations of the model ($\mathbf{x}_t$, $\mathbf{w}_t$ and $\Delta\mathbf{x}_t$). We also report the Monte Carlo standard errors (MCSEs) of the TMSFEs given by (5.5). These are shown in table 6.2.

Section 5.2 outlined how we obtained the Monte Carlo estimates of the GFESM.

In terms of $\mathbf{w}_t$ (see (6.10)), the model can be represented as the first-order process:

$$\mathbf{w}_t = \mathbf{G}\mathbf{w}_{t-1} + \boldsymbol{\tau}_0 + \boldsymbol{\epsilon}_t, \tag{6.57}$$

where $\boldsymbol{\epsilon}_t \sim \mathsf{IN}_2[\mathbf{0}, \mathbf{\Sigma}]$, when:

$$\mathbf{G} = \begin{pmatrix} 1 + a_{11} - \beta a_{22} & 0 \\ a_{22} & 0 \end{pmatrix}, \ \boldsymbol{\tau}_0 = \begin{pmatrix} a_{10} - \beta a_{20} \\ a_{20} \end{pmatrix}, \ \boldsymbol{\epsilon}_t = \begin{pmatrix} v_{1t} - \beta v_{2t} \\ v_{2t} \end{pmatrix},$$

[2] Alternatively, we could have generated data from the stationary representation for $\mathbf{w}_t$ in (6.57), where $\mathbf{w}_0$ is drawn from a normal distribution with mean and variance given by the unconditional mean and variance of $\mathbf{w}_t$.

and:

$$\mathbf{\Sigma} = \begin{pmatrix} 1 - 2\beta\rho s + \beta^2 s^2 & \rho s - \beta s^2 \\ \rho s - \beta s^2 & s_2 \end{pmatrix}.$$

A range of experiments was used to explore the impact of various features of the experimental design on forecast accuracy for the estimation methods. Since the results are invariant to certain aspects of the design, such as equal multiples of the variances of the disturbance terms $\{v_{1t}, v_{2t}\}$, we could economize without loss on the number of experiments, but a limitation of any Monte Carlo is that the findings are specific to the experiments undertaken and may be a poor guide to performance at other points in the parameter space. Table 6.1 records the design parameter values.

Table 6.1 Monte Carlo experimental design

Experiment	ρ	s	a_{10}	a_{11}	a_{22}	β
0	0	1	0	0	0.25	1
1	0.5	1	0	0	0.25	1
2	0	2	0	0	0.25	1
3	0	1	1	0	0.25	1
4	0	1	0	-0.1	0.25	1
5	0	1	0	0	0	1
6	0	1	0	0	0.25	2
7	0.5	2	1	-0.1	0.25	2
8	-0.5	1	0	0	0.25	1
9	0	1	0	-0.5	0.25	1
10	0	1	0	-0.5	0	1
11	0	$\sqrt{2}$	0	0	0.25	1
12	0.5	$\sqrt{2}$	0	0	0.25	1

In this set of experiments, a_{20} is taken to be zero. For each experimental design, constants were estimated unrestrictedly in both equations for every econometric estimator. The experiments where $\boldsymbol{\tau} = \mathbf{0}$ (i.e., all except 3 and 7) were then repeated, not estimating the constant terms. In total, therefore, there were 24 experiments, each of which was replicated 1,000 times. Experiment 0 may be viewed as the 'central case', on which the others represent variations, while experiment 4 most closely resembles the design of Engle and Yoo (1987). All the simulation experiments were conducted using Gauss, and the response surfaces were estimated in PcGive (see Hendry and Doornik, 1996b).

6.8 Simulation results

The presentation of our Monte Carlo results takes two forms: TMSFE and GFESM calculations for isomorphic representations of the forecasts for the four econometric models; and the calculation of response surfaces for the Monte Carlo estimates of the GFESM, $|\widehat{\mathbf{\Phi}}|$, across the range of experimental designs.

To illustrate the findings, we present results for the single experiment 4 in table 6.1. This essentially reproduces the DGP of Engle and Yoo (1987), which in our notation is characterized by $\{\rho = 0,\ s = 1,\ a_{10} = 0, a_{11} = -0.4,\ a_{22} = 0.1,\ \beta = 2\}$. The equations for both variables exhibit feedback from the common cointegrating vector in such experiments, although the cointegrating parameter and speeds of adjustment differ, with the 'equilibrium-correcting' behaviour being quantitatively more important in Engle and Yoo's DGP. Notice that $\boldsymbol{\tau} = \mathbf{0}$, and we follow Engle and Yoo in not estimating constants in the equations. Table 6.2 shows the relationships between the Monte Carlo estimates for each estimator, the Monte Carlo control variable estimates (common to all estimators) and the asymptotic values, for both TMSFEs and GFESMs, for a selection of multi-step forecast horizons, and for two estimation sample sizes.

In the notation of section 5.3, columns 1 to 4 in panels A, B and C of table 6.2 record the estimates, $\widetilde{\mathbf{M}}_h$, given by (5.13). That condition (5.14) was generally satisfied was apparent from comparing the results for $\widetilde{\mathbf{M}}_h$ with those for $\widehat{\mathbf{M}}_h$ (not shown), and observing that the former were a smoother function of h. The TMSFEs for $\mathbf{x}_t$ are $O(h)$ in the forecast horizon, while the TMSFEs for $\mathbf{w}_t$ and $\Delta\mathbf{x}_t$ are both $O(1)$, as suggested by (6.19), (6.20) and (6.24).

In table 6.2, the second row of figures for each horizon are the MCSEs of the TMSFEs ($\widehat{\sigma}/\sqrt{R}$: see section 5.2). Panel D records the simulation results for the GFESM measure $|\widehat{\mathbf{\Phi}}_h|$ for each estimator, and for $|\mathbf{\Phi}_h^*|$ calculated for known parameters (the asymptotic value of the GFESM, $|\mathbf{\Phi}_h|$, is unity for all h, so is not reported).

For an estimation sample size of 100 (as used by Engle and Yoo), there is little to choose between EG and UV at the shortest horizons when forecast accuracy comparisons are based on $\mathbf{x}_t$. There is a clear advantage to using EG at longer horizons (observe the size of the MCSEs), matching the findings of Engle and Yoo, an effect which is accentuated for $T = 50$. The small differences in our results compared to those of Engle and Yoo reflect the imprecision of the Monte Carlo given the relatively small number of replications and the particular DGP parameter values selected.

Nevertheless, interpreting these results as indicating 'the importance of imposing long-run constraint rather than the restriction *per se*' (Engle and Yoo, 1987, p.151) is suspect, since the dominance of EG over UV is not robust to switching from $\mathbf{x}_t$ to $\mathbf{w}_t$ (see panel B of table 6.2), illustrating the importance of the particular common basis of comparison chosen for such a measure. In terms of $\mathbf{w}_t$, again noting the size of the MCSEs, there is little to choose between EG, UV and ML. The UV estimator appears to dominate EG for all but the shortest forecast horizons, with the gains coming from the improved accuracy of UV in predicting the I(0) combination. Figures 6.2 and 6.3 illustrate the lack of invariance of TMSFEs discussed in section 3.5.

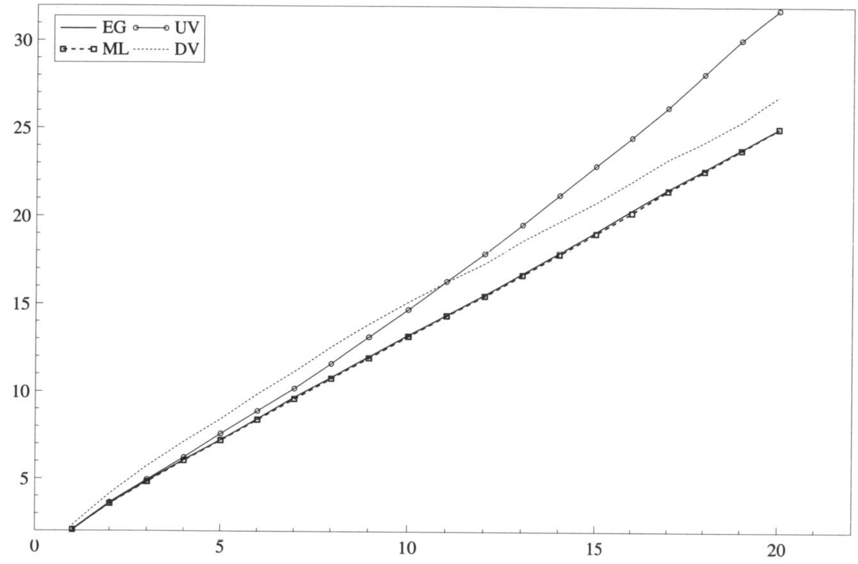

Figure 6.2 MSFE calculations for the levels of the variables

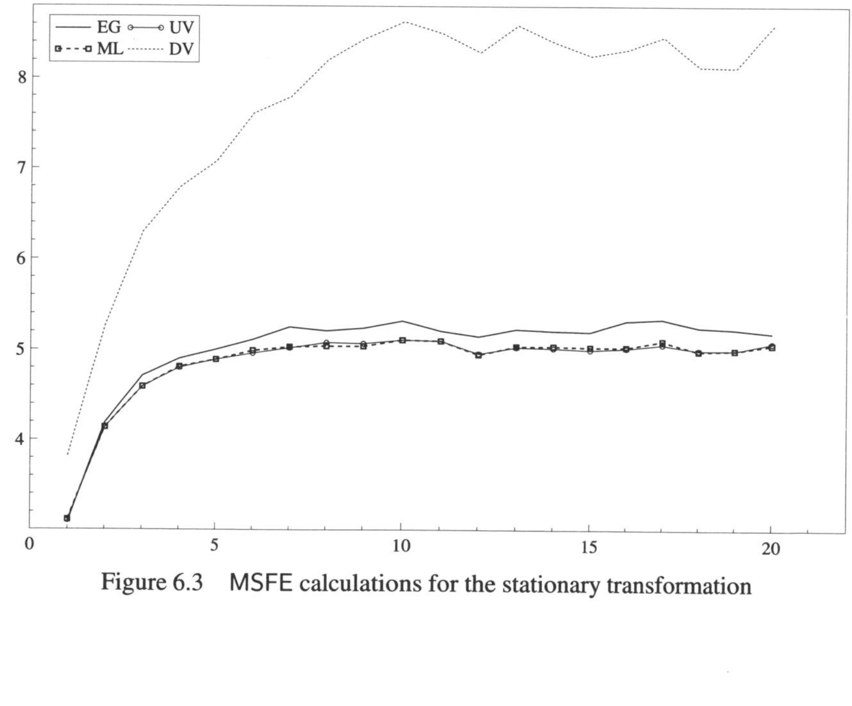

Figure 6.3 MSFE calculations for the stationary transformation

The ML is not appreciably better than EG when the comparison is in terms of $\mathbf{x}_t$. The DV estimator, which is mis-specified since the variables cointegrate, does not generate clearly inferior forecasts for comparisons on $\mathbf{x}_t$, and beats UV at long horizons. For an estimation sample size of $T = 50$, the superiority of DV over UV at longer horizons is even more marked. In terms of $\mathbf{w}_t$, though, the inferiority of DV is dramatic (about 40 percent worse than UV for $h = 20$).

The asymptotic forecast-error variance formulae in section 6.4 help explain these results. Viewing EG, UV and ML as correctly specified models, then (6.19), (6.20) and (6.24) explain the relationships between the results for these three models and those for the DV model across these isomorphic transformations of the variables. For example, DV is only appreciably worse at short horizons for comparisons in terms of $\mathbf{x}_t$ (see (6.39)) and $\Delta\mathbf{x}_t$ (see (6.24) and (6.30)), while numerical evaluation of (6.42) relative to (6.20) for $\mathbf{w}_t$ accurately predicts the poor performance of the DV model on this transformation of the variables.

The simulation results for GFESM, $|\widehat{\mathbf{\Phi}}_h|^{1/h}$, recorded in panel D of table 6.2 show little to choose between EG and UV. The ML is generally preferred to both EG and UV except at the shortest horizons, while the relative inferiority of DV is apparent.[3]

Table 6.3 highlights the information in table 6.2 on the gains and losses from each estimator relative to UV, for the three transformations of the model. The entries are calculated as $(UV/xx - 1) \times 100$, where *xx* is either EG, ML or DV. From tables 6.2 and 6.3, EG, ML and DV do relatively better than UV at $T = 50$ compared to $T = 100$, showing the importance of valid reduced-rank restrictions in EG and ML when there are fewer degrees of freedom.

Response surfaces were estimated for $|\widehat{\mathbf{\Phi}}|$ for each of the ML, UV and DV estimators for 1- and 8-step ahead forecast horizons. The results are summarized in tables 6.4 and 6.5 for 1- and 8-step ahead forecast horizons, respectively. The form of the dependent variable for UV and ML was suggested by (5.9), namely $\ln(|\widehat{\mathbf{\Phi}}||/|\mathbf{\Phi}^*|)$, where $\widehat{\mathbf{\Phi}}$ is the Monte Carlo estimator of $\mathbf{\Phi}$ for each estimator, and $\mathbf{\Phi}^*$ is the control variable which captures the variability emanating from the sampling of the Monte Carlo disturbances. In tables 6.4 and 6.5, $\ln(|\widehat{\mathbf{\Phi}}|/|\mathbf{\Phi}^*|)$ is referred to as $\ln(xx/cv)$, where *xx* denotes the estimation method. Equations are numbered as, for example, (2a) to distinguish them from numbered text formulae.

Explaining the deviations around the control variables is the correct approach in our experiments since the correlation between (the logs of) $|\widehat{\mathbf{\Phi}}|$ and $|\mathbf{\Phi}^*|$ for UV and ML exceeded 0.995 for $h = 1$, and 0.96 for $h = 8$. The correlation between $|\widehat{\mathbf{\Phi}}|$ for DV and $|\mathbf{\Phi}^*|$ was 0.947 for $h = 1$ and 0.97 for $h = 8$, compared to correlations with $|\widetilde{\mathbf{\Phi}}|$ (the DV model asymptotic value) of 0.996 and 0.981. A complication arises for the DV model when constants are not estimated, since the control variable for the DV model,

[3] A one percentage point gain or loss at large h is relatively larger than at small h due to raising $|\widehat{\mathbf{\Phi}}_{\mathbf{h}}|$ to the power of h^{-1}. The adjustment makes sense when parameters are known, but may down play differences when parameters are estimated.

$|\widetilde{\mathbf{\Phi}}^*|$, becomes the same as the DV model estimate. In such cases, we can either use the correctly specified model control variable to form the regressand (see equations (3a) and (6a) in tables 6.4 and 6.5), or $|\widetilde{\mathbf{\Phi}}|$ (equations (3b) and (6b)).

The regressand was related linearly to a constant term, an indicator variable taking the value unity for estimated constants and zero otherwise (D), the autoregressive parameters of $\mathbf{\Upsilon}$ and those defining the covariance structure of the disturbance terms (ρ, s). Other transformations of the basic design parameters that were tried typically included the inverse of the non-unit root of $|\Delta \mathbf{I}_2 - \mathbf{\Pi} L|$ (see (6.54)), namely $(1 + a_{11} - a_{22}\beta)$ as a measure of the 'degree of cointegration'. λ takes the value unity when there is no cointegration and is bounded by 0.25 in our experiments $(a_{11} = -0.5,\ a_{22} = 0.25)$. Also the approximation $\ln|\mathbf{\Phi}_h^*| - 2h\ln(s) \simeq h\ln(1 - \rho^2)$ is used, which is exact for $\ln|\mathbf{\Phi}_h|$. The reported response surfaces are the final simplified selections for the 24 experiments, based on sequentially deleting variables with low t-values.

Comparisons between methods (within panels) and between different horizons are revealing and are discussed below. Overall, the response surfaces seem well specified, fit well given that 1,000 replications were used (the best measure here of the success of the forecast variance control variables), and have interpretable coefficients.

Our preferred response surfaces for the 1-step ahead ML and UV forecasts have the same specification, as do the 8-step ahead response surfaces for these two estimators. This suggests that the effect of imposing reduced-rank cointegration restrictions is small in a bivariate system with a relatively large sample for estimation $(T = 100)$. For both UV and ML, the autoregressive design parameters enter in the form $(a_{11}a_{22})$ and a_{22}, both terms with positive coefficients. This indicates that the control variables work less well (in terms of explaining the outcomes in the econometric models when the coefficients are estimated) when the variables in the DGP are cointegrated. The multiplicative term is an offset to this when the cointegrating vector enters both equations. Apart from these terms, the response surfacc for 1-step ahead ML forecasts indicates that the parameter uncertainty on average increases the measure of forecast uncertainty by 3 percent (approximately $1/\sqrt{T}$), with a 2 percent increase from estimating constant terms and an additional 1 percent increase if there are non-zero intercepts in the DGP.

For UV, equation (2a) reveals that the constant term in the regression is greater than for ML, so that baseline parameter uncertainty with this estimator is around 4 percent, and the coefficients on D and a_{10} are larger, indicating that UV copes less well with constant terms in the DGP. The influences of the autoregressive parameters are similar.

Equation (3a) shows that forecast accuracy for the DV estimator is inversely related to the degree of cointegration, λ, and the large (negative) coefficient on $\ln(1 - \rho^2)$ reveals that the coefficient on $|\mathbf{\Phi}^*|$ differs markedly from unity, undoubtedly due to the mis-specification. Further, the negative coefficient on ρ shows improved forecast accuracy when the disturbances are positively correlated (rather than negatively correlated to the same degree). The important feature of equation (3b) (which uses the DV model asymptotic values in place of the correctly specified model control variable) is that it has a much smaller standard error than (3a). There are more regressors, not all of which are readily interpretable.

The response surfaces for 8-step ahead forecasts illustrate the theoretical result that forecast uncertainty is not a monotonically increasing function of the forecast horizon when parameters have to be estimated (see, *inter alia*, Chong and Hendry, 1986). The constant term and D coefficients for ML (equation 4a) increase approximately eight-fold, a_{10} four-fold, and the preferred combination of design parameters changes. The response surfaces in tables 6.4 and 6.5 are based on the raw GFESMs; raising the estimates for the estimators and the control variable to the power of the reciprocal of h is equivalent to dividing the estimated coefficients for the 8-step ahead response surfaces by 8 (with a commensurate adjustment to the regression standard errors which brings them more into line with those for the 1-step ahead forecasts). The baseline parameter uncertainty effect and that of estimating constant terms unrestrictedly are little altered.

There are increases of around 8-fold in the constant term and the coefficient of a_{10} in the equation for UV (equation 5a), and a role for the feedback coefficient a_{11} with a positive coefficient. However, the coefficient of D only increases by a factor of three relative to equation (2a), and hence is now smaller than in the ML equation.

Equation (6a) changes greatly for DV from 1-step ahead forecasts: virtually all the autoregressive and disturbance design parameters now enter. Relative to (3a) the equation standard error has doubled. Using the DV-model asymptotic values (6b) again greatly reduces the standard error of the equation, but now there is evidence of functional form mis-specification of the response surface.

The last set of results concerns restricting the constant to the cointegration space as shown in table 6.6. In panel A, columns 1, 3 and 5 report $|\widehat{\mathbf{\Phi}}|^{1/h}$ calculations for UV, ML and DV respectively, for experimental design 4 (reported in tables 6.2 and 6.3), for which $\boldsymbol{\tau} = \mathbf{0}$, but with intercepts estimated unrestrictedly in the econometric models. Columns 2, 4 and 6 are the percentage changes relative to table 6.2, panel D (when constants are not estimated). Panel B reports the results of two experiments, for which $\boldsymbol{\tau} \neq \mathbf{0}$ and constants are estimated, as percentage changes relative to the results given in columns 1, 3 and 5 in panel A. In the first experiment (columns 1, 3 and 5 of panel B) $\boldsymbol{\tau} = [1 : -1]' \neq \boldsymbol{\alpha}\boldsymbol{\tau}^*$ (labelled 'NEq' in the table), so that the variables contain linear trends. In the second experiment, $\boldsymbol{\tau} = [1 : -2.5]' = \boldsymbol{\alpha}\boldsymbol{\tau}^*$ (labelled Eq in the table), so that the constant falls within the cointegration space. In this case, there is the option with ML of imposing the restriction at the estimation stage: the results of doing so are given in column 4b.

The relative loss of forecast accuracy from estimating constant terms when they do not appear in the DGP increases in h for ML and DV (see panel A) but in comparison is smaller for UV except at very short horizons. This outcome is consistent with the coefficients on D in the response surfaces in tables 6.4 and 6.5. However, for UV the increase in $|\widehat{\mathbf{\Phi}}|^{1/h}$ is large relative to $\boldsymbol{\tau} = \mathbf{0}$ when $\boldsymbol{\tau} \neq \mathbf{0}$ and $\boldsymbol{\tau} \neq \boldsymbol{\alpha}\boldsymbol{\tau}^*$, while for ML there is no increase for $h = 20$, and for the DV model there is no significant change at any forecast horizon (see columns 1, 3 and 5 of Panel B). Indeed, as long as constants are estimated, then forecast accuracy using the DV model is invariant to the values of the intercepts in the DGP, at least to the degree of numerical accuracy reported in the table. Furthermore, the UV and ML estimators appear invariant when the constants lie in the cointegrating space (columns 2 and 4a), but not otherwise. When this condition holds and is correctly imposed by ML, there is a 2 percent gain in accuracy at the longer horizons. Some of these results were established analytically using antithetic variates.

6.9 An empirical illustration

In this section, we illustrate the preceding analysis by examining the forecast performance of models of the demand for UK M1, based on a simplified version of the approach in Hendry and Ericsson (1991), Hendry and Mizon (1993), Engle and Hendry (1993) and Hendry and Doornik (1994), *inter alia*.[4] We consider the bivariate system of the (inverse) velocity of circulation v and a learning-adjusted measure of the opportunity cost of holding money R_n (see Hendry and Ericsson, 1991, pp. 844–6 and pp. 850–3), where $v = m - p - y$ when m, p and y are the natural logarithms of nominal UK M1, the total final expenditure deflator and real total final expenditure respectively.

The data are quarterly, seasonally adjusted, and after the creation of lags, the estimation period runs from 1964:1 to 1984:2, with the 20 observations from 1984:3 to 1989:2 retained as the forecast period. For this small monetary system, we estimated three second-order models: an unrestricted VAR in the levels of (v, R_n) (termed UV earlier); the DV model imposing two unit roots; and the ML model. The Johansen procedure on the full sample indicated one cointegrating vector, which when normalized on v has the form: $w \equiv v + 7.7R_n$, and which we restricted to only enter the velocity equation. Ignoring the possible problems for inference caused by the presence of unit roots, the ML model represents a non-rejectable simplification of the UV (the likelihood ratio test of the three restrictions implicit in the ML relative to the UV yielded a test value of 6.6, which is $\chi^2(3)$ under the null in stationary processes), while the DV was clearly rejected against the UV (test statistic value of 37.4, compared to a $\chi^2(4)$).[5] These models were then used to generate 1-, 2-, 4-, 8- and 12-step ahead forecasts over the period 1984:3–1989:2. From which we calculated empirical MSFEs by averaging the 20 squared 1-step errors, the 19 squared 2-step errors, etc.

Root MSFEs (RMSFEs) are given in table 6.7. The asymptotic formulae in section 6.4 and the results of the Monte Carlo in section 6.8 are useful when interpreting the

[4] A sketch of the more general model is provided in sections 9.7 and 12.7.

[5] Sims, Stock and Watson (1990) show that tests of joint significance which include only cointegrated non-stationary regressors have their standard asymptotic distributions, while those that include non-stationary regressors will be non-standard. Thus, the test statistics quoted here have non-standard distributions. Consistent with this, the tests for the dimension of the cointegrating space in Johansen (1988a) have to be compared to non-standard critical values.

empirical RMSFEs in table 6.7. For example, equations (6.33) and (6.30) in section 6.4 suggest that for medium-term horizons there will be little gain from using the correctly-specified model (UV or ML) relative to the DV when forecast accuracy is assessed in terms of predicting differences (columns 1 and 2 of table 6.7). The column for Δv indicates that the losses from using the DV model are large for short horizons but have all but disappeared for 12-step ahead forecasts. The likelihood ratio statistics quoted earlier indicate that the DV model is mis-specified for v but not for R_n (the specification of the equations for R_n in the ML and DV models are identical) which explains the similar forecast accuracy of the models for all steps ahead for ΔR_n. In terms of forecasting the levels of the variables, the analysis in section 6.4 suggests that the DV model will continue to predict worse than the UV and ML as we increase h, and this is evident for v in table 6.7. Since the DV model is correctly specified for R_n on a single-equation basis, it is not surprising that it fares relatively better for predicting the level of R_n.

Finally, we relate these results to the Monte Carlo in section 6.8. The Monte Carlo indicates that for a bivariate model and for samples as large as $T = 100$, it may be difficult to choose between the ML and UV models. When $T = 50$ the relative differences are more evident, particularly for the levels of the series (see table 6.2, panel [A]). Our estimation sample size is 82 observations, and differs from the Monte Carlo DGP in that we are estimating second-order models where the 'error-correction' term enters only one equation. However, as in the Monte Carlo, the UV fares a little worse than the ML but generally better than the DV. An apparent anomaly between the empirical MSFEs and the Monte Carlo results is how well the DV model predicts w. Only at $h = 12$ is it outperformed by the UV and ML models.

6.10 Overview

In this chapter we have both extended and applied some of the ideas and concepts developed in earlier chapters. We have extended the univariate results of chapter 4, concerning the implications of the time-series properties of variables for the properties of forecast-error variances etc., to integrated-cointegrated systems of variables. We have also made extensive use of the Monte Carlo techniques, discussed in chapter 5, and the measures of forecast accuracy, discussed in chapter 3, to analyse the properties of forecasts from a number of econometric models for such a system.

Given the amount of ground we have covered, we comment briefly on the main implications of the material in this chapter. Forecast evaluation exercises based on MSFEs for differences of variables, may fail to reject the DV even when it is mis-specified due to ignoring cointegration. The asymptotic formulae show that MSFEs for cointegrating combinations may be more discriminating. Alternatively, as argued in chapter 3, invariant criteria seem preferable, especially in Monte Carlo evaluations of forecasting where evaluation may be done in levels or differences just for convenience.

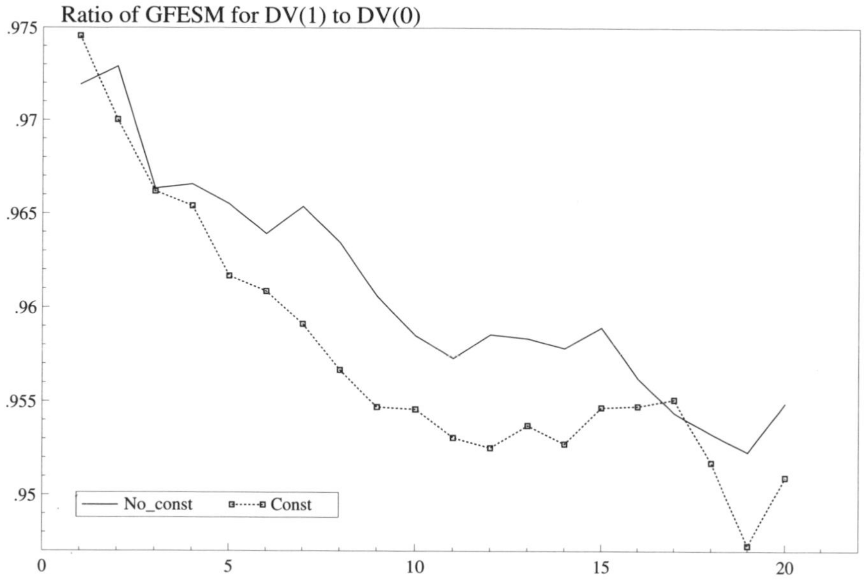

Figure 6.4 GFESM calculations for DV models

The invariant GFESM detected DV to be a poor model. Also, advocating the UV over the DV (on the GFESM) is the reverse of what one would suggest on the basis of MSFE comparisons on predictions of the levels of I(1) series.

While other methods of model evaluation exist (such as tests for serial correlation in the residuals) which might more frequently detect mis-specification, including the lagged difference as a regressor in the DV model had little effect on forecast performance in the Monte Carlo. This is perhaps unsurprising, since against the reduction in the forecast-error variance (from a better fit) must be set the effects of estimating more parameters. Figure 6.4 records the ratios for the (unscaled) GFESMs for the DV model with an additional lagged difference on each of the explanatory variables relative to the basic DV model, both when constants are estimated and not estimated. We have not investigated the impact on forecast accuracy of optimally choosing the lag order of the DV model according to a model-selection criterion. Chambers (1993) examines such an estimator using an average MSFE across horizons and finds it dominates UV for levels at long horizons, which is in accordance with our findings (see table 6.2, panel A).

The asymptotic forecast-error variance formulae in section 6.4 reveal a great deal about the behaviour of the various methods and models as forecast horizons increase. In particular, the extent of the dependence of the formulae on the length of the horizon is confirmed by, and clarifies, the Monte Carlo simulation findings, so that the formulae seem relevant for the sample sizes considered in the simulation.

The Monte Carlo is for a bivariate system, and suggests that there is little benefit from imposing reduced-rank cointegration restrictions (ML versus UV) unless the sample size is small. However, that conclusion is based on experiments where the number of cointegrating combinations is known. When the number of cointegration vectors has to be determined from the data, the performance of the outcome will reflect both under- and over-specification of the degree of cointegration. Thus, the outcome will reflect aspects of the various methods considered above. Conversely, the ML estimator might be expected to dominate the unrestricted VAR more decisively for larger systems of equations when a cointegration relation imposes many more restrictions.

The response surfaces highlighted the factors influencing performance between estimators and across horizons, especially the similarities between the UV and ML models. The control variates accounted for about 99 percent of the total variability in the GFESM, so the slight increase in the complexity of the Monte Carlo repaid handsome dividends in increased precision. The estimation of the intercepts plays an important role in the deviations of the finite sample outcomes from the asymptotic formulae.

In terms of empirical practice, there are three main conclusions. First, in bivariate systems, imposing too few cointegration vectors may impose greater costs in forecast accuracy than allowing the presence of too many levels terms, some of which do not cointegrate. Intuitively, the former exclude precisely the relationships which keep differentials between the levels of variables stationary, whereas the latter have parameter estimates on I(1) variables which converge at $O_p(T)$ against the growth in forecast-error variance at $O(h)$ for h-step ahead forecasts. We believe this result will hold for larger systems when there are no structural breaks: estimating and forecasting with an additional 'spurious' levels term is likely to be no more costly in terms of forecast accuracy than under-estimating the cointegrating rank by one. However, once breaks occur, as section 2.9 showed, differencing may play a robustifying role.

There may be a significant deterioration in forecast accuracy from allowing unrestricted constant terms in the ML procedure when the DGP has no drift. Nevertheless, we showed analytically that, when the constants fall within the cointegrating space, forecast accuracy using ML (or UV and DV as well) is invariant to their value: forecast accuracy improvements can result from correctly restricting the intercepts to the cointegration space. Doing so removes 'spurious' local trends in forecasts of I(1) variables, which may have an increasing cost in terms of forecast accuracy as h increases. However, in most empirical work, the researcher is unlikely to know that the intercepts can be so restricted, in which case the outcome in practice will depend upon the characteristics of tests for restricting the constant terms to the cointegrating space.

Finally, the asymptotic forecast-error variance formulae are useful guides to the finite-sample outcomes even in cointegrated I(1) systems. In some simulation studies of integrated data, a close match between theory and evidence has not been found in small samples (see, e.g., Banerjee, Dolado, Hendry and Smith, 1986), whereas in others, it has (see, e.g., Banerjee and Hendry, 1992). Such discrepancies appear to be linked to serial correlation in the residuals of estimated equations, with a closer match occurring when there is none. Here, the concordance also probably results from the large sample size relative to the number of unknown parameters, the reparameterization of the cointegrated I(1) system to I(0) space, as well as the convergence rate of $O_p(T)$ for the coefficients of I(1) variables in systems with innovation errors.

6.11 Appendix: Algebraic derivation

Proof of $(\mathbf{I}_n - \boldsymbol{\Upsilon}^h) = -\sum_{i=0}^{h-1} \boldsymbol{\Upsilon}^i \boldsymbol{\alpha}\boldsymbol{\beta}'$. Expand $(\mathbf{I}_n - \boldsymbol{\Upsilon}^h)$ as follows:

$$\begin{aligned} \mathbf{I}_n - \boldsymbol{\Upsilon}^h &= \mathbf{I}_n - \boldsymbol{\Upsilon}^{h-1}(\mathbf{I}_n + \boldsymbol{\alpha}\boldsymbol{\beta}') \\ &= \mathbf{I}_n - \boldsymbol{\Upsilon}^{h-1}\boldsymbol{\alpha}\boldsymbol{\beta}' - \boldsymbol{\Upsilon}^{h-1} \\ &= \mathbf{I}_n - \boldsymbol{\Upsilon}^{h-1}\boldsymbol{\alpha}\boldsymbol{\beta}' - \boldsymbol{\Upsilon}^{h-2}\boldsymbol{\alpha}\boldsymbol{\beta}' - \cdots - \boldsymbol{\Upsilon}^{0}\boldsymbol{\alpha}\boldsymbol{\beta}' - \boldsymbol{\Upsilon}^{0} \\ &= -\sum_{i=0}^{h-1} \boldsymbol{\Upsilon}^i \boldsymbol{\alpha}\boldsymbol{\beta}'. \end{aligned} \tag{6.58}$$

Proof that $\boldsymbol{\Upsilon}^h \to \mathbf{K}$ for large h. From (6.58):

$$\boldsymbol{\Upsilon}^h = \mathbf{I}_n + \sum_{i=0}^{h-1} \boldsymbol{\Upsilon}^i \boldsymbol{\alpha}\boldsymbol{\beta}'. \tag{6.59}$$

Now:

$$\begin{aligned} \boldsymbol{\Upsilon}^i \boldsymbol{\alpha}\boldsymbol{\beta}' &= \boldsymbol{\Upsilon}^{i-1}(\mathbf{I}_n + \boldsymbol{\alpha}\boldsymbol{\beta}')\boldsymbol{\alpha}\boldsymbol{\beta}' \\ &= \boldsymbol{\Upsilon}^{i-1}\boldsymbol{\alpha}(\mathbf{I}_n + \boldsymbol{\beta}'\boldsymbol{\alpha})\boldsymbol{\beta}' \\ &= \boldsymbol{\Upsilon}^{i-2}(\mathbf{I}_n + \boldsymbol{\alpha}\boldsymbol{\beta}')\boldsymbol{\alpha}(\mathbf{I}_r + \boldsymbol{\beta}'\boldsymbol{\alpha})\boldsymbol{\beta}' \\ &= \boldsymbol{\alpha}(\mathbf{I}_r + \boldsymbol{\beta}'\boldsymbol{\alpha})^i\boldsymbol{\beta}'. \end{aligned} \tag{6.60}$$

Substituting (6.60) into (6.59):

$$\boldsymbol{\Upsilon}^h = \mathbf{I}_n + \boldsymbol{\alpha}\sum_{i=0}^{h-1} (\mathbf{I}_r + \boldsymbol{\beta}'\boldsymbol{\alpha})^i \boldsymbol{\beta}'. \tag{6.61}$$

Since:

$$(\boldsymbol{\beta}'\boldsymbol{\alpha})^{-1} = -(\mathbf{I}_r - (\mathbf{I}_r + \boldsymbol{\beta}'\boldsymbol{\alpha}))^{-1} = -\sum_{i=0}^{\infty} (\mathbf{I}_r + \boldsymbol{\beta}'\boldsymbol{\alpha})^i$$

then we have the approximation for large h that:

$$\sum_{i=0}^{h-1} (\mathbf{I}_r + \boldsymbol{\beta}'\boldsymbol{\alpha})^i \approx -(\boldsymbol{\beta}'\boldsymbol{\alpha})^{-1}, \tag{6.62}$$

so that:

$$\boldsymbol{\Upsilon}^h \approx \mathbf{I}_n - \boldsymbol{\alpha}(\boldsymbol{\beta}'\boldsymbol{\alpha})^{-1}\boldsymbol{\beta}' = \mathbf{K}. \tag{6.63}$$

Table 6.2 Monte Carlo estimates of forecast accuracy of estimation methods

	EG		UV		ML		DV		trM_h^*		trM_h^a
h/T	100	50	100	50	100	50	100	50	100	50	
[A] MSFEs for $\mathbf{x}_t$											
1	2.04	2.10	2.07	2.13	2.06	2.09	2.32	2.28	1.96	2.07	2.00
	0.07	0.07	0.07	0.07	0.07	0.07	0.07	0.07	0.07	0.07	
5	7.24	7.54	7.60	8.35	7.21	7.43	8.44	8.50	6.90	7.30	7.01
	0.25	0.25	0.26	0.31	0.25	0.25	0.28	0.27	0.25	0.24	
10	13.30	13.70	14.70	17.10	13.20	13.50	15.20	14.50	12.10	13.60	12.90
	0.49	0.55	0.59	0.74	0.49	0.55	0.53	0.53	0.49	0.52	
20	25.10	25.80	31.80	41.60	25.00	25.60	26.90	26.60	22.80	24.50	24.70
	0.90	1.02	1.59	2.10	0.90	1.03	0.92	1.01	0.89	0.99	
[B] MSFEs for $\mathbf{w}_t$											
1	3.08	3.22	3.10	3.21	3.11	3.20	3.82	3.71	2.87	3.11	3.00
	0.12	0.13	0.12	0.13	0.12	0.13	0.15	0.15	0.12	0.12	
5	5.00	5.24	4.89	5.03	4.89	5.02	7.08	7.23	4.71	4.54	4.63
	0.18	0.18	0.18	0.18	0.18	0.18	0.26	0.28	0.17	0.16	
10	5.32	5.41	5.11	5.13	5.11	5.11	8.63	7.70	4.28	4.77	4.68
	0.19	0.20	0.18	0.19	0.18	0.18	0.33	0.29	0.15	0.17	
20	5.19	5.76	5.08	5.20	5.06	5.30	8.59	8.18	4.64	4.83	4.68
	0.18	0.23	0.17	0.19	0.17	0.21	0.34	0.33	0.16	0.17	
[C] MSFEs for Δx_t											
1	2.04	2.10	2.07	2.13	2.06	2.09	2.32	2.28	1.96	2.07	2.00
	0.07	0.07	0.07	0.07	0.07	0.07	0.07	0.07	0.07	0.07	
5	2.24	2.25	2.27	2.31	2.24	2.25	2.25	2.26	2.29	2.19	2.24
	0.07	0.07	0.07	0.07	0.07	0.07	0.07	0.07	0.07	0.07	
10	2.25	2.25	2.27	2.31	2.25	2.25	2.25	2.25	2.21	2.31	2.25
	0.07	0.08	0.07	0.08	0.07	0.07	0.07	0.08	0.07	0.07	
20	2.25	2.25	2.26	2.31	2.25	2.25	2.25	2.25	2.28	2.28	2.25
	0.07	0.07	0.07	0.07	0.07	0.07	0.07	0.07	0.07	0.07	

	EG		UV		ML		DV		$\lvert\Phi^*\rvert^{\frac{1}{h}}$	
[D] Determinant of generalized second moment matrix $\lvert\hat{\Phi}\rvert^{1/h}$										
1	1.00	1.17	1.03	1.21	1.01	1.17	1.28	1.36	0.96	1.07
5	1.03	1.03	1.03	1.05	1.02	1.02	1.16	1.14	0.99	0.97
10	1.00	1.04	1.00	1.05	0.99	1.02	1.09	1.11	0.96	0.99
20	0.99	1.00	1.00	1.01	0.98	0.99	1.05	1.05	0.96	0.96

Notes: DGP as experiment 4: $R = 1000, T = 50, 100$

Table 6.3 Forecast accuracy summary

	MSFE					
h/T	EG		ML		DV	
	100	50	100	50	100	50
[A] $\mathbf{x}_t$						
1	1.5	1.4	0.5	1.9	−10.8	−6.6
5	5.0	10.7	5.4	12.4	−10.0	−1.8
10	11.0	25.4	11.6	26.7	−2.8	18.0
20	27.0	61.1	27.1	62.4	18.3	56.3
[B] $\mathbf{w}_t$						
1	0.6	−0.3	−0.3	0.3	−18.8	−13.5
5	−2.2	−4.0	0.0	0.2	−30.9	−30.4
10	−3.9	−5.2	0.0	0.4	−40.8	−33.4
20	−2.1	−9.7	0.4	−1.9	−40.9	−36.4
[C] $\Delta\mathbf{x}_t$						
1	1.5	1.4	0.5	1.9	−10.8	−6.6
5	1.3	2.7	1.3	2.7	0.9	2.2
10	0.9	2.7	0.9	2.7	0.9	2.7
20	0.4	2.7	0.4	2.7	0.4	2.7
[D] $\lvert\hat{\mathbf{\Phi}}\rvert^{\frac{1}{h}}$						
1	3.0	3.4	2.0	3.4	−19.5	−11.0
5	0.0	1.9	1.0	2.9	−11.2	−7.9
10	0.0	1.0	1.0	2.9	−8.3	−5.4
20	1.0	1.0	2.0	2.0	−4.8	−3.8

Notes:
DGP as experiment 4: $R = 1000, T = 50, 100$
Entries are % gains or losses $(-)$ relative to the UV.

Table 6.4 Monte Carlo response surfaces for $|\widehat{\Phi}|$ when $T = 100$. 1-step ahead

$$\ln\left(\frac{ml}{cv}\right) = \underset{(0.003)}{0.03} + \underset{(0.002)}{0.02} D + \underset{(0.004)}{0.01} a_{10} + \underset{(0.03)}{0.15} a_{11}a_{22} + \underset{(0.01)}{0.09} a_{22}$$

$$\mathsf{R}^2 = 0.921 \quad \widehat{\sigma} = 0.0053 \quad \mathsf{F}(4,19) = 55.18 \quad SC = -10.04$$
$$\chi^2_n = 0.63 \; \mathsf{F}_{\mathsf{reset}}(1,18) = 1.97 \; \mathsf{F}_{\mathsf{het}}(5,13) = 1.22 \qquad \text{(1a)}$$

$$\ln\left(\frac{uv}{cv}\right) = \underset{(0.003)}{0.04} + \underset{(0.002)}{0.04} D + \underset{(0.004)}{0.03} a_{10} + \underset{(0.03)}{0.14} a_{11}a_{22} + \underset{(0.01)}{0.09} a_{22}$$

$$\mathsf{R}^2 = 0.958 \quad \widehat{\sigma} = 0.0056 \quad \mathsf{F}(4,19) = 109.1 \quad SC = -9.93$$
$$\chi^2_n = 2.77 \; \mathsf{F}_{\mathsf{reset}}(1,18) = 0.0001 \; \mathsf{F}_{\mathsf{het}}(5,13) = 0.35 \qquad \text{(2a)}$$

$$\ln\left(\frac{dv}{cv}\right) = \underset{(0.05)}{0.12} a_{10} - \underset{(0.05)}{0.32} \rho + \underset{(0.04)}{0.90} (1-\lambda) - \underset{(0.09)}{0.50} \ln\left(1-\rho^2\right)$$

$$\mathsf{R}^2 = 0.981 \quad \widehat{\sigma} = 0.058 \quad SC = -5.34$$
$$\chi^2_n = 1.38 \; \mathsf{F}_{\mathsf{reset}}(1,19) = 3.56 \qquad \text{(3a)}$$

$$\ln\left(\frac{dv}{as}\right) = -\underset{(0.01)}{0.06} + \underset{(0.003)}{0.01} D - \underset{(0.01)}{0.03} \rho + \underset{(0.01)}{0.10} \lambda$$
$$+ \underset{(0.07)}{0.23} a_{11}a_{22} - \underset{(0.02)}{0.09} a_{22}$$

$$\mathsf{R}^2 = 0.871 \quad \widehat{\sigma} = 0.008 \quad \mathsf{F}(5,18) = 24.32 \quad SC = -9.05$$
$$\chi^2_n = 1.44 \; \mathsf{F}_{\mathsf{reset}}(1,17) = 0.21 \; \mathsf{F}_{\mathsf{het}}(8,9) = 0.81 \qquad \text{(3b)}$$

Table 6.5 Monte Carlo response surfaces for $|\widehat{\Phi}|$ when $T = 100$. 8-step ahead

$$\ln\left(\frac{ml}{cv}\right) = \underset{(0.01)}{0.23} + \underset{(0.01)}{0.16}\, D + \underset{(0.02)}{0.24}\, a_{10} + \underset{(0.03)}{0.15}\, a_{11}$$

$$\begin{array}{l} \mathsf{R}^2 = 0.922 \quad \widehat{\sigma} = 0.029 \quad \mathsf{F}(3,20) = 78.82 \quad SC = -6.76 \\ \chi^2_n = 9.74 \; \mathsf{F}_{\mathsf{reset}}(1,19) = 0.46 \; \mathsf{F}_{\mathsf{het}}(4,15) = 0.17 \end{array} \qquad (4a)$$

$$\ln\left(\frac{uv}{cv}\right) = \underset{(0.01)}{0.34} + \underset{(0.01)}{0.10}\, D + \underset{(0.02)}{0.24}\, a_{10} + \underset{(0.03)}{0.21}\, a_{11}$$

$$\begin{array}{l} \mathsf{R}^2 = 0.937 \quad \widehat{\sigma} = 0.029 \quad \mathsf{F}(3,20) = 99.94 \quad SC = -6.74 \\ \chi^2_n = 4.31 \; \mathsf{F}_{\mathsf{reset}}(1,19) = 0.17 \; \mathsf{F}_{\mathsf{het}}(4,15) = 0.19 \end{array} \qquad (5a)$$

$$\begin{aligned} \ln\left(\frac{dv}{cv}\right) = {} & \underset{(0.04)}{0.14}\, D + \underset{(0.09)}{0.29}\, a_{10} - \underset{(0.06)}{3.4}\, a_{11} + \underset{(0.23)}{3.5}\, a_{22} - \underset{(0.04)}{0.83}\, \rho \\ & + \underset{(0.05)}{0.42}\, \beta + \underset{(0.48)}{8.2}\, a_{11}a_{22} - \underset{(0.05)}{0.41}\, \lambda - \underset{(0.17)}{1.1}\, \ln\left(1-\rho^2\right) \end{aligned}$$

$$\begin{array}{l} \mathsf{R}^2 = 0.997 \quad \widehat{\sigma} = 0.101 \quad SC = -3.86 \\ \chi^2_n = 5.96 \; \mathsf{F}_{\mathsf{reset}}(1,14) = 1.49 \end{array} \qquad (6a)$$

$$\begin{aligned} \ln\left(\frac{dv}{as}\right) = {} & \underset{(0.01)}{0.14} + \underset{(0.04)}{0.07}\, a_{11} - \underset{(0.03)}{0.17}\, a_{22} - \underset{(0.01)}{0.06}\, \beta \\ & - \underset{(0.01)}{0.18}\, \lambda + \underset{(0.02)}{0.40}\, a_{11}a_{22} \end{aligned}$$

$$\begin{array}{l} \mathsf{R}^2 = 0.995 \quad \widehat{\sigma} = 0.015 \quad SC = -7.88 \\ \chi^2_n = 1.30 \; \mathsf{F}_{\mathsf{reset}}(1,17) = 6.97 \; \mathsf{F}_{\mathsf{het}}(7,10) = 2.47 \end{array} \qquad (6b)$$

Notes:
$\mathsf{F}(\cdot,\cdot)$: F-test of joint significance of the regressors (other than the constant);
SC: Schwarz criterion;
χ^2_n: normality test, see Jarque and Bera (1980);
$\mathsf{F}_{\mathsf{reset}}$: Reset test of functional form, see Ramsey (1969);
$\mathsf{F}_{\mathsf{het}}$: Heteroscedasticity/functional form test, see White (1980).

Table 6.6 Impact of estimating intercepts

h	UV $\lvert\hat{\Phi}\rvert^{\frac{1}{h}}$	UV G/L	ML $\lvert\hat{\Phi}\rvert^{\frac{1}{h}}$	ML G/L	DV $\lvert\hat{\Phi}\rvert^{\frac{1}{h}}$	DV G/L
	1	2	3	4	5	6
[A] $\tau = 0$						
1	1.06	2.91	1.04	2.97	1.29	0.78
5	1.05	1.94	1.04	1.96	1.18	1.72
10	1.01	1.00	1.01	2.02	1.11	1.83
20	1.00	0.00	1.01	3.06	1.07	1.90

h	UV NEq	UV Eq	ML NEq	ML Eq	ML Eq	DV NEq	DV Eq
	1	2	3	4a	4b	5	6
[B] $\tau \neq 0$							
1	1.89	0.00	0.00	0.00	0.00	0.00	0.00
5	2.86	0.00	0.96	0.00	-1.90	0.00	0.00
10	3.96	0.00	0.99	0.00	-0.99	0.00	0.00
20	4.00	0.00	0.00	0.00	-1.98	0.00	0.00

Notes: Experiment 4: $R = 1000,\ T = 100$

Table 6.7 Empirical RMSFEs over 1984:3 to 1989:2

h	Δv	ΔR_n	v	R_n	w
[A] UV model					
1	0.020	0.017	0.020	0.017	0.12
2	0.026	0.017	0.038	0.028	0.18
4	0.031	0.015	0.083	0.049	0.30
8	0.031	0.008	0.20	0.067	0.32
12	0.023	0.008	0.31	0.071	0.25
[B] ML model					
1	0.019	0.015	0.019	0.015	0.10
2	0.023	0.014	0.033	0.022	0.14
4	0.026	0.014	0.067	0.037	0.22
8	0.028	0.008	0.17	0.056	0.27
12	0.023	0.008	0.28	0.068	0.25
[C] DV model					
1	0.034	0.015	0.034	0.015	0.10
2	0.035	0.014	0.066	0.021	0.13
4	0.036	0.013	0.13	0.034	0.20
8	0.033	0.008	0.26	0.049	0.25
12	0.026	0.008	0.39	0.060	0.28

Chapter 7

Forecasting with large-scale macroeconometric models

We now establish a framework for analysing some of the problems that arise in using large-scale macroeconometric models for forecasting. A number of facets of the real-world forecasting venture complicate the picture compared to the analyses of chapters 4 and 6, and each may contribute to forecast errors. A taxonomy of sources of forecast error is developed to enable a systematic treatment of these issues, along with the sources of error covered in earlier chapters. The taxonomy comprises five major categories, namely parameter non-constancy, model mis-specification, sampling variability, variable mis-measurement and error uncertainty, and suggests partial remedies. The potential impact of forecasts, or expectations, on outcomes (the 'bandwagon effect' of section 1.3) arises naturally in the taxonomy as a form of variable uncertainty. We also discuss some of the techniques commonly used to evaluate large-scale macroeconometric models.

7.1 Introduction

The large-scale macroeconometric models currently in use differ from the univariate and multivariate time-series models of chapters 4 and 6 in ways which have important implications for forecasting. Moreover, as argued in chapter 1, the process being forecast (that is, 'the economy') is perhaps best characterized as being a cointegrated-integrated system but subject to intermittent regime shifts and structural breaks of varying magnitudes.

The sizes of such models (hundreds of equations, relative to the two or three-equation models of the textbook illustration of simultaneous-equations estimation), and their non-linearity render the conventional econometric evaluation techniques largely inapplicable.[1] Consequently, large-scale models are often evaluated by their historical track records: how well the model describes or accounts for what has actually

[1] Clements and Mizon (1991) and Hendry and Mizon (1993) show how small systems of interdependent variables, or particular sectors of the model, can be tested by the validity of the implied (over-identifying) restrictions relative to the unrestricted reduced form.

happened. Such methods differ as to whether essentially 1-step or dynamic errors are considered. The limitations of this approach become evident once it is shown that these errors can be mapped into the disturbances of the structural model, casting doubt on whether any new information is provided. Such techniques also rely on (usually untested) exogeneity claims. An alternative approach to appraising large-scale models is that of forecast encompassing, explicitly developed by Chong and Hendry (1986) as a means of evaluating models in terms of their forecast performance, with minimal informational requirements (just the series of 1-step forecasts from the competing models). Traditional evaluation techniques are discussed in section 7.5, and the discussion of forecast encompassing is postponed until section 10.3.

In section 7.2, we discuss the nature of empirical econometric models, and their relation to the DGP. Section 7.3 develops the taxonomy of sources of forecast uncertainty that arises when we allow the system to exhibit non-constancy. The taxonomy comprises five major categories, namely parameter non-constancy, model mis-specification, sampling variability, variable mis-measurement and error uncertainty, with a number of sub-classes. In section 7.4, possible approaches to reducing the various sources of forecast uncertainty are noted, and some of these receive a more detailed treatment as part of the discussion of intercept corrections in chapter 8, and multi-step estimation in chapter 11.

7.2 The economic system and forecasting models

In any real-world forecasting exercise, many of the following factors will complicate matters. First, the parameters of the forecasting model may be non-constant over the forecast period, either because the process being modelled is non-constant although the model was 'correctly specified' (i.e., congruent: see Hendry, 1995a) in-sample, or the model is mis-specified and, while the modelled process is constant, non-modelled aspects are not and these impinge on the mis-specifications. Secondly, the parameters will be unknown and have to be estimated from available data; the model's size may induce the use of inappropriate estimators. Thirdly, the forecast origin may be subject to error and revision, or may not yet be available (see Wallis, Andrews, Fisher, Longbottom and Whitley, 1986, on the 'ragged edge' problem); since these constitute the baseline for the forecasts, considerable inaccuracy may result. Fourthly, there may be non-modelled variables which need to be separately forecast; variables like world trade, oil prices, etc., are often forecast 'off-line' and the resulting values treated as fixed numbers in forecasts. Fifthly, the model may not only fail to characterize the data to within an innovation error (model mis-specification), but the error process distribution may change over time (as in section 4.8). Next, the forecaster may have extraneous information about events not included in the model; anticipated strikes or announced future tax changes are examples, but sometimes 'gut-feelings' about likely macroeconomic evolution also enter. Finally, the costs of over- and under-predicting may differ (asymmetric loss), forecasts may need to be 'credible', or not too far from the consensus view, or not too different from previously published forecasts, etc., all of which lead to modifications of the pure model-based predictions.

We classify some of these facets within a general taxonomy of the factors that contribute to forecast error. However, in contrast to Wallis and Whitley (1991), we do not identify the 'judgemental element' which is often incorporated in the values set for the equation error terms over the future. Wallis and Whitley (1991) decompose a published forecast error into a 'model error', the contribution of residual adjustments, and the contribution of errors in setting the values of 'exogenous' variables. The model error is the realized value of the variable less the model-based forecast with no judgemental adjustments using the *ex post* values of the non-modelled variables. The contribution of residual adjustments is the difference between forecasts with the judgemental residual settings and without (pure model-based forecasts), in each case having substituted the *ex post* values of 'exogenous' variables. The final component is the difference between the judgemental forecasts with the *ex ante*, and with the *ex post*, values of the 'exogenous' variables. Our analysis is for purely model-based forecasts, and we utilize a closed system. The role of judgemental adjustments and intercept corrections is treated in chapter 8, where the latter are viewed as a remedy for certain sources of forecast error which are part of the composite 'model error'. Nor do we single out the 'exogenous' variables in the taxonomy, although the extension required is straightforward, and we sketch the additional sources of error that arise. Non-modelled variables also have to be forecast, although we recognize that the autoregressive schemes we adopt for these variables may not be appropriate for 'policy' variables. However, to the extent that the division is not based on econometrically relevant notions of exogeneity, such as in Engle, Hendry and Richard (1983), the model error is likely to be a decreasing function of the number of variables assigned to the 'exogenous' category. In practice, though, the Wallis–Whitley decomposition serves the useful purpose of highlighting whether errors in non-modelled variables and intercept corrections tend to compound or mitigate model errors.

To motivate the taxonomy, we begin with the linear dynamic system of (6.7), so that the vector of n $\mathsf{I}(1)$ variables of interest is denoted by $\mathbf{x}_t$, and its data generation process is taken to be the first-order vector autoregression:

$$\mathbf{x}_t = \boldsymbol{\tau} + \boldsymbol{\Upsilon}\mathbf{x}_{t-1} + \boldsymbol{\nu}_t, \tag{7.1}$$

where $\boldsymbol{\Upsilon}$ is an $n \times n$ matrix of coefficients, and $\boldsymbol{\tau}$ is an n dimensional vector of constant terms. The error $\boldsymbol{\nu}_t \sim \mathsf{IN}_n[\mathbf{0}, \boldsymbol{\Omega}]$, with expectation $\mathsf{E}[\boldsymbol{\nu}_t] = \mathbf{0}$, and variance matrix $\mathsf{V}[\boldsymbol{\nu}_t] = \boldsymbol{\Omega}$. Moreover, as in section 6.2, (7.1) satisfies $r < n$ cointegration relations such that:

$$\boldsymbol{\Upsilon} = \mathbf{I}_n + \boldsymbol{\alpha}\boldsymbol{\beta}', \tag{7.2}$$

where $\boldsymbol{\alpha}$ and $\boldsymbol{\beta}$ are $n \times r$ full rank matrices. Thus the equations have the equilibrium-correction representation:

$$\Delta \mathbf{x}_t = \boldsymbol{\tau} + \boldsymbol{\alpha}\boldsymbol{\beta}'\mathbf{x}_{t-1} + \boldsymbol{\nu}_t. \tag{7.3}$$

It will prove useful to write the constant vector in (7.3) as comprising two components:

$$\boldsymbol{\tau} = \boldsymbol{\gamma} - \boldsymbol{\alpha}\boldsymbol{\mu}. \tag{7.4}$$

We define $\boldsymbol{\gamma} \equiv \mathsf{E}[\Delta \mathbf{x}_t]$, so $\boldsymbol{\gamma}$ is the expected growth rate of the system. Then taking expectations through (7.3):

$$\boldsymbol{\gamma} = \boldsymbol{\alpha}\mathsf{E}\left[\boldsymbol{\beta}'\mathbf{x}_{t-1}\right] + \boldsymbol{\tau} \tag{7.5}$$

so that $\boldsymbol{\mu}$ is the equilibrium mean $\boldsymbol{\mu} \equiv \mathsf{E}[\boldsymbol{\beta}'\mathbf{x}_t]$. Thus, in (7.6), both $\Delta \mathbf{x}_t$ and $\boldsymbol{\beta}'\mathbf{x}_t$ are expressed as deviations about their means:

$$\Delta \mathbf{x}_t - \boldsymbol{\gamma} = \boldsymbol{\alpha}\left(\boldsymbol{\beta}'\mathbf{x}_{t-1} - \boldsymbol{\mu}\right) + \boldsymbol{\nu}_t. \tag{7.6}$$

There are, in fact, the same number of free parameters on both sides of (7.4). $\boldsymbol{\tau}$ is $n \times 1$, and from:

$$\boldsymbol{\beta}'\boldsymbol{\gamma} = \mathsf{E}\left[\boldsymbol{\beta}'\Delta \mathbf{x}_t\right] = \mathsf{E}\left[\Delta\boldsymbol{\beta}'\mathbf{x}_t\right] = \mathbf{0},$$

where $\boldsymbol{\beta}$ is $n \times r$, then $\boldsymbol{\gamma}$ consists of only $n-r$ free parameters. We can write $\boldsymbol{\gamma} = \boldsymbol{\beta}'_{\perp}\boldsymbol{\gamma}^*$, say, where $\boldsymbol{\beta}'_{\perp}$ is the orthogonal complement of $\boldsymbol{\beta}'$, and $\boldsymbol{\gamma}^*$ are the common linear trends (in the levels of the variables). Further, $\boldsymbol{\mu}$ is $r \times 1$, since there are r linearly independent cointegrating vectors.

This formulation is more general than it may seem, as the first-order VAR in (7.1) can be interpreted as the companion form to a qth order VAR, stacked as:

$$\begin{aligned}
\mathbf{x}_t &= \begin{pmatrix} \underline{\mathbf{x}}_t \\ \underline{\mathbf{x}}_{t-1} \\ \vdots \\ \underline{\mathbf{x}}_{t-q+1} \end{pmatrix} = \boldsymbol{\tau} + \boldsymbol{\Upsilon}\mathbf{x}_{t-1} + \boldsymbol{\nu}_t \\
&= \begin{pmatrix} \underline{\boldsymbol{\tau}} \\ \mathbf{0} \\ \vdots \\ \mathbf{0} \end{pmatrix} + \begin{pmatrix} \boldsymbol{\Upsilon}_{\{1\}} & \boldsymbol{\Upsilon}_{\{2\}} & \cdots & \boldsymbol{\Upsilon}_{\{q-1\}} & \boldsymbol{\Upsilon}_{\{q\}} \\ \mathbf{I}_n & \mathbf{0} & \cdots & \mathbf{0} & \mathbf{0} \\ \mathbf{0} & \mathbf{I}_n & \mathbf{0} & \mathbf{0} & \vdots \\ \vdots & \ddots & \ddots & \ddots & \vdots \\ \mathbf{0} & \cdots & \mathbf{0} & \mathbf{I}_n & \mathbf{0} \end{pmatrix} \begin{pmatrix} \underline{\mathbf{x}}_{t-1} \\ \underline{\mathbf{x}}_{t-2} \\ \vdots \\ \underline{\mathbf{x}}_{t-q} \end{pmatrix} + \begin{pmatrix} \underline{\boldsymbol{\nu}}_t \\ \mathbf{0} \\ \vdots \\ \mathbf{0} \end{pmatrix}.
\end{aligned}$$

Thus, the lag length assumption is not restrictive, although our main aim here is expository. Linearity is more constraining (see section 4.7, and Mariano and Brown, 1983), but we doubt if it is the main explanation of recent predictive failures. Conversely, as shown in section 6.2, (7.1) allows for integrated and cointegrated processes, and is a useful framework for considering sources of forecast errors.

Although the form of the model to be fitted coincides with (7.1), insofar as it is a linear representation linking elements of $\mathbf{x}_t$, its specification could differ in every important regard from that of the DGP, due to imposing invalid restrictions on the parameters. We write the model as:

$$\mathbf{x}_t = \boldsymbol{\tau}_p + \boldsymbol{\Upsilon}_p \mathbf{x}_{t-1} + \mathbf{u}_t, \tag{7.7}$$

where the parameter estimates $(\widehat{\boldsymbol{\tau}} : \widehat{\boldsymbol{\Upsilon}} : \widehat{\boldsymbol{\Omega}})$ are possibly inconsistent, with $\boldsymbol{\tau}_p \neq \boldsymbol{\tau}$ and $\boldsymbol{\Upsilon}_p \neq \boldsymbol{\Upsilon}$, because of model mis-specification. Given knowledge of the DGP, it is possible to deduce the values of the model's parameters and the properties of the model's error term $\mathbf{u}_t$. This is formalized in the theory of reduction, which explains the origin and status of empirical econometric models in terms of the implied information reductions relative to the process that generated the data. Reductions implicitly transform the parameters of the process. Thus, empirical models are reductions of the DGP, not numerically calibrated theoretical models, with error processes which are derived by reduction operations and are not autonomous; see Cook and Hendry (1993), Ericsson, Campos and Tran (1990), Florens, Mouchart and Rolin (1990), Gilbert (1986), Hendry (1987, 1993b, 1995a), Hendry and Mizon (1990, 1993), Hendry and Richard (1982, 1983) and Spanos (1986) among many others.

Schematically, if the empirical model is

$$\underset{\text{[observed]}}{y_t} = \underset{\text{[explanation]}}{g(z_t)} + \underset{\text{[remainder]}}{\epsilon_t} \tag{7.8}$$

then the left-hand side determines the right, rather than the other way round. Thus y_t can be decomposed into two components, $g(z_t)$ (a part which can be explained by z) and ϵ_t (a part which is unexplained). Such a partition is possible even when y_t does not depend on $g(z_t)$, but is determined by completely different factors $h(x_t)$, say. In econometrics:

$$\epsilon_t = y_t - g(z_t)$$

describes empirical models: changing the choice or specification of z_t on the right-hand side alters the left-hand side, so $\{\epsilon_t\}$ is a derived process. $\{\epsilon_t\}$ in (7.8) is not a random drawing from nature: it is what is left over from y_t after extracting $g(z_t)$ and must represent everything omitted from the model, including all the mistakes in formulating $g(\cdot)$ or selecting z.

The resulting error process could be autocorrelated and heteroscedastic. However, empirical models are susceptible to design to achieve desired criteria (such as white-noise errors). Statistics used in that design process become part of the selection criteria, perhaps as diagnostics used to check on the validity of the reduction, and hence cease to be tests in any useful sense. Thus, it will often be the case in (7.7) that:

$$\mathbf{u}_t = \mathbf{x}_t - \mathsf{E}_{\mathsf{M}}[\mathbf{x}_t \mid \mathbf{x}_{t-1}]$$

(where $\mathsf{E}_{\mathsf{M}}[\cdot|\cdot]$ denotes a conditional expectation with respect to the model) is an innovation process:

$$\mathsf{E}\left[\mathbf{u}_t \mid \mathbf{x}_{t-1}\right] = \mathbf{0}.$$

Two models we shall consider correspond to the correctly specified and DV models of section 6.4, defined by $(\boldsymbol{\tau}_p = \boldsymbol{\tau}, \boldsymbol{\Upsilon}_p = \boldsymbol{\Upsilon})$ and $(\boldsymbol{\tau}_p = \boldsymbol{\gamma}, \boldsymbol{\Upsilon}_p = \mathbf{I}_n)$. The first model is the data generation process, and analyses of economic forecasting have often been based on this assumption. However, empirical econometric models are invariably not facsimiles of the process that generated the data, and in this sense are false. In place of the notion of a 'true' model, the concept of a congruent model has been developed as an operational criterion for evaluating models (see Hendry, 1995a). A model is said to be congruent if it matches the data evidence in all measurable respects – which does not require that it is either complete or correct. Key elements of congruency include that the empirical model's error is a homoscedastic innovation against the available information; that the conditioning variables are weakly exogenous for the parameters of the model (see Engle *et al.*, 1983); and that those parameters are constant. In principle, it is possible to design models with all these characteristics which thereby exhaust the available information, and in essence represent the DGP, as observed so far, up to an innovation error.

As it stands, (7.4) specifies a relation between $\boldsymbol{\tau}$, $\boldsymbol{\gamma}$, $\boldsymbol{\alpha}$ and $\boldsymbol{\mu}$. However, in deducing the causal inter-relationships between the parameters, the economics' context is important. To a first approximation, we might assume that $\boldsymbol{\gamma}$, $\boldsymbol{\alpha}$ and $\boldsymbol{\mu}$ are variation free, although admit the possibility that $\boldsymbol{\mu}$ is a deterministic function of $\boldsymbol{\gamma}$. For example, Hendry and von Ungern-Sternberg (1981) show that the equilibrium value of the savings ratio ($\boldsymbol{\mu}$) may depend on the underlying growth rate of consumption and income ($\boldsymbol{\gamma}$). In general, the underlying growth rate, the equilibrium mean, and the speeds of adjustment to equilibrium ($\boldsymbol{\alpha}$) might be viewed as being determined independently by separate sets of factors. One consequence is that $(\boldsymbol{\tau}, \boldsymbol{\Upsilon})$ are not variation free. For $(\boldsymbol{\tau}, \boldsymbol{\Upsilon})$ to be variation free when $\boldsymbol{\alpha}$ changes, $\boldsymbol{\gamma}$, $\boldsymbol{\alpha}$ and $\boldsymbol{\mu}$ could not be.

In a stationary context, we can interpret whether or not $(\boldsymbol{\tau}, \boldsymbol{\Upsilon})$ are variation free in terms of whether the long-run mean of the process changes in response to shifts in $\boldsymbol{\Upsilon}$. From (7.1), under stationarity, the relationship between the long-run mean, $\boldsymbol{\pi} = \mathsf{E}[\mathbf{x}_t]$, and $\boldsymbol{\tau}$ is given by:

$$\boldsymbol{\tau} = (\mathbf{I}_n - \boldsymbol{\Upsilon})\,\boldsymbol{\pi}.$$

If $\boldsymbol{\pi}$ remains unaltered when speeds of adjustment, $\boldsymbol{\Upsilon}$, change, then $\boldsymbol{\tau}$ is forced to change: with a fixed long-run mean the assumption that $(\boldsymbol{\tau}, \boldsymbol{\Upsilon})$ are variation free is untenable. Equation (7.4) clarifies directly that changes in only one of $\boldsymbol{\gamma}$, $\boldsymbol{\alpha}$ or $\boldsymbol{\mu}$ must force $\boldsymbol{\tau}$ to alter. In general, when there are structural breaks, the properties of forecasts will depend on which other parameters alter and which are variation free. This is a property of the economy, not the model per se, and may only be discoverable by careful empirical work.

Equation (7.6) is isomorphic to (7.1). The first model ((7.7) with $\boldsymbol{\tau}_p = \boldsymbol{\tau}$, $\boldsymbol{\Upsilon}_p = \boldsymbol{\Upsilon}$) was correctly specified for (7.1), and therefore also coincides with (7.6). In terms of (7.6), the DV model is given by:

$$\Delta \mathbf{x}_t = \boldsymbol{\gamma} + \boldsymbol{\xi}_t$$

which is correctly specified when $\boldsymbol{\alpha} = \mathbf{0}$ in (7.6), in which case $\boldsymbol{\xi}_t = \boldsymbol{\nu}_t$. It is a VAR in the differences of the variables, and is mis-specified by omitting the cointegrating vectors. This model is not congruent when the series cointegrate, since its error will not be an innovation against the past of the process. However, it characterizes the type of model that would result from the Box–Jenkins time-series modelling tradition, where the data are differenced a sufficient number of times to remove unit roots (once, in this example) prior to modelling. It is a simple example in that the differenced series are then modelled as a constant, but little seems to gained for our analysis by allowing for further lags in differences.

7.3 A taxonomy of forecast errors

In this section, we develop a taxonomy of forecast errors when there is structural change over the forecast period, when the model and DGP may differ over the sample period, the parameters of the model have to be estimated from the data, and the forecast commences from a forecast origin (denoted by $\widehat{\mathbf{x}}_T$) which may differ from the 'true' value $\mathbf{x}_T$ due to poor provisional statistics, which are subject to revisions before being finalized (see, for example, Patterson, 1995). Then, h-step ahead forecasts are given by:

$$\widehat{\mathbf{x}}_{T+h} = \widehat{\boldsymbol{\tau}} + \widehat{\boldsymbol{\Upsilon}}\widehat{\mathbf{x}}_{T+h-1} = \sum_{i=0}^{h-1} \widehat{\boldsymbol{\Upsilon}}^i \widehat{\boldsymbol{\tau}} + \widehat{\boldsymbol{\Upsilon}}^h \widehat{\mathbf{x}}_T, \quad h = 1, \ldots, H, \tag{7.9}$$

under the possibly mistaken assumption of parameter constancy, where '^'s on parameters denote estimates, and on random variables, forecasts. The forecast errors are:

$$\widehat{\boldsymbol{\nu}}_{T+h} = \mathbf{x}_{T+h} - \widehat{\mathbf{x}}_{T+h}.$$

Suppose the system experiences a step change between the estimation and forecast periods, such that $(\boldsymbol{\tau} : \boldsymbol{\Upsilon})$ changes to $(\boldsymbol{\tau}^* : \boldsymbol{\Upsilon}^*)$ over $h = 1, \ldots, H$, and the variance, autocorrelation and distribution of the error may change to $\boldsymbol{\nu}_{T+h} \sim \mathsf{D}_n(\mathbf{0}, \boldsymbol{\Omega}^*)$. More complicated changes are obviously feasible empirically, but we have not found that their analysis yields useful insights, whereas the single break does reveal certain problems. Imposing $\mathsf{E}[\boldsymbol{\nu}_{T+h}] = \mathbf{0}$ is without loss of generality when $\boldsymbol{\tau}^* \neq \boldsymbol{\tau}$. Thus, the data actually generated by the process for the next H periods are given by:

$$\begin{aligned} \mathbf{x}_{T+h} &= \boldsymbol{\tau}^* + \boldsymbol{\Upsilon}^* \mathbf{x}_{T+h-1} + \boldsymbol{\nu}_{T+h} \\ &= \sum_{i=0}^{h-1} (\boldsymbol{\Upsilon}^*)^i \boldsymbol{\tau}^* + (\boldsymbol{\Upsilon}^*)^h \mathbf{x}_T + \sum_{i=0}^{h-1} (\boldsymbol{\Upsilon}^*)^i \boldsymbol{\nu}_{T+h-i}. \end{aligned} \tag{7.10}$$

To progress, we need to clarify the definitions we use of two mathematical operations: vectoring and Kronecker product. Let $(\cdot)^{\nu}$ denote forming a column vector, such that for an $n \times m$ matrix $\mathbf{A}$ if:

$$\mathbf{A} = \begin{pmatrix} \mathbf{a}_1 & \mathbf{a}_2 & \cdots & \mathbf{a}_m \end{pmatrix} \text{ then } \mathbf{A}^{\nu} = \begin{pmatrix} \mathbf{a}_1 \\ \mathbf{a}_2 \\ \vdots \\ \mathbf{a}_m \end{pmatrix},$$

which is an nm column vector obtained by stacking each $\mathbf{a}_i$ $(n \times 1)$. $\otimes$ denotes the Kronecker product of two matrices $\mathbf{A}$ and $\mathbf{B}$, which are $n \times m$ and $p \times q$, defined by:

$$\mathbf{A} \otimes \mathbf{B} = (b_{ij}\mathbf{A}) = \begin{pmatrix} b_{11}\mathbf{A} & b_{12}\mathbf{A} & \cdots & b_{1q}\mathbf{A} \\ b_{21}\mathbf{A} & b_{22}\mathbf{A} & \cdots & b_{2q}\mathbf{A} \\ \vdots & \vdots & \ddots & \vdots \\ b_{p1}\mathbf{A} & b_{p2}\mathbf{A} & \cdots & b_{pq}\mathbf{A} \end{pmatrix},$$

which is an $np \times mq$ matrix.

From (7.9) and (7.10), the h-step ahead forecast error is:

$$\widehat{\boldsymbol{\nu}}_{T+h} = \sum_{i=0}^{h-1} (\boldsymbol{\Upsilon}^*)^i \boldsymbol{\tau}^* - \sum_{i=0}^{h-1} \widehat{\boldsymbol{\Upsilon}}^i \widehat{\boldsymbol{\tau}} + (\boldsymbol{\Upsilon}^*)^h \mathbf{x}_T - \widehat{\boldsymbol{\Upsilon}}^h \widehat{\mathbf{x}}_T + \sum_{i=0}^{h-1} (\boldsymbol{\Upsilon}^*)^i \boldsymbol{\nu}_{T+h-i}. \tag{7.11}$$

We denote deviations between sample estimates and population parameters by $\boldsymbol{\delta}_{\tau} = \widehat{\boldsymbol{\tau}} - \boldsymbol{\tau}_p$ and $\boldsymbol{\delta}_{\Upsilon} = \widehat{\boldsymbol{\Upsilon}} - \boldsymbol{\Upsilon}_p$. Then, ignoring powers and cross-products in the $\boldsymbol{\delta}$s (which may induce variance-covariance effects), since:

$$\widehat{\boldsymbol{\Upsilon}}^i = (\boldsymbol{\Upsilon}_p + \boldsymbol{\delta}_{\Upsilon})^i \approx \boldsymbol{\Upsilon}_p^i + \sum_{j=0}^{i-1} \boldsymbol{\Upsilon}_p^j \boldsymbol{\delta}_{\Upsilon} \boldsymbol{\Upsilon}_p^{i-j-1} = \boldsymbol{\Upsilon}_p^i + \mathbf{C}_i, \tag{7.12}$$

we obtain:

$$\sum_{i=0}^{h-1} \left[(\boldsymbol{\Upsilon}^*)^i \boldsymbol{\tau}^* - \widehat{\boldsymbol{\Upsilon}}^i \widehat{\boldsymbol{\tau}} \right] \approx \sum_{i=0}^{h-1} \left[(\boldsymbol{\Upsilon}^*)^i \boldsymbol{\tau}^* - \left(\boldsymbol{\Upsilon}_p^i \boldsymbol{\tau}_p + \boldsymbol{\Upsilon}_p^i \boldsymbol{\delta}_{\tau} + \mathbf{D}_i \boldsymbol{\delta}_{\Upsilon}^{\nu} \right) \right]. \tag{7.13}$$

To see this, note that on vectoring (7.12):

$$\left(\widehat{\boldsymbol{\Upsilon}}^i \right)^{\nu} \approx \left(\boldsymbol{\Upsilon}_p^i \right)^{\nu} + \left(\sum_{j=0}^{i-1} \boldsymbol{\Upsilon}_p^j \otimes \boldsymbol{\Upsilon}_p^{i-j-1\prime} \right) \boldsymbol{\delta}_{\Upsilon}^{\nu},$$

and hence:

$$\widehat{\boldsymbol{\Upsilon}}^i \widehat{\boldsymbol{\tau}} \approx \left(\boldsymbol{\Upsilon}_p^i + \sum_{j=0}^{i-1} \boldsymbol{\Upsilon}_p^j \boldsymbol{\delta}_{\Upsilon} \boldsymbol{\Upsilon}_p^{i-j-1} \right) (\boldsymbol{\tau}_p + \boldsymbol{\delta}_{\tau})$$

$$= \sum_{j=0}^{i-1} \boldsymbol{\Upsilon}_p^j \boldsymbol{\delta}_\Upsilon \boldsymbol{\Upsilon}_p^{i-j-1} \boldsymbol{\tau}_p + \boldsymbol{\Upsilon}_p^i \boldsymbol{\tau}_p + \boldsymbol{\Upsilon}_p^i \boldsymbol{\delta}_\tau,$$

yielding:

$$\begin{aligned} \widehat{\boldsymbol{\Upsilon}}^i \widehat{\boldsymbol{\tau}} &\approx \boldsymbol{\Upsilon}_p^i \boldsymbol{\tau}_p + \boldsymbol{\Upsilon}_p^i \boldsymbol{\delta}_\tau + \left(\sum_{j=0}^{i-1} \boldsymbol{\Upsilon}_p^j \otimes \boldsymbol{\tau}_p' \boldsymbol{\Upsilon}_p^{i-j-1\prime} \right) \boldsymbol{\delta}_\Upsilon^\nu \\ &= \boldsymbol{\Upsilon}_p^i \boldsymbol{\tau}_p + \boldsymbol{\Upsilon}_p^i \boldsymbol{\delta}_\tau + \mathbf{D}_i \boldsymbol{\delta}_\Upsilon^\nu. \end{aligned}$$

It is informative to allow explicitly for the model being mis-specified, and hence to decompose the term $\sum_{i=0}^{h-1} [(\boldsymbol{\Upsilon}^*)^i \boldsymbol{\tau}^* - \widehat{\boldsymbol{\Upsilon}}^i \widehat{\boldsymbol{\tau}}]$ in (7.13) into:

$$\begin{aligned} &\sum_{i=0}^{h-1} \left[(\boldsymbol{\Upsilon}^*)^i (\boldsymbol{\tau}^* - \boldsymbol{\tau}) + (\boldsymbol{\Upsilon}^*)^i (\boldsymbol{\tau} - \boldsymbol{\tau}_p) + \left((\boldsymbol{\Upsilon}^*)^i - \boldsymbol{\Upsilon}^i \right) \boldsymbol{\tau}_p \right] \\ &+ \sum_{i=0}^{h-1} \left[\left(\boldsymbol{\Upsilon}^i - \boldsymbol{\Upsilon}_p^i \right) \boldsymbol{\tau}_p - \boldsymbol{\Upsilon}_p^i \boldsymbol{\delta}_\tau - \mathbf{D}_i \boldsymbol{\delta}_\Upsilon^\nu \right]. \end{aligned}$$

Similarly, for the terms in (7.11) post-multiplied by $\mathbf{x}_T$ or $\widehat{\mathbf{x}}_T$, using:

$$\mathbf{C}_h \mathbf{x}_T = \sum_{j=0}^{h-1} \boldsymbol{\Upsilon}_p^j \boldsymbol{\delta}_\Upsilon \boldsymbol{\Upsilon}_p^{h-j-1} \mathbf{x}_T = \left(\sum_{j=0}^{h-1} \boldsymbol{\Upsilon}_p^k \otimes \mathbf{x}_T' \boldsymbol{\Upsilon}_p^{h-j-1\prime} \right) \boldsymbol{\delta}_\Upsilon^\nu = \mathbf{F}_h \boldsymbol{\delta}_\Upsilon^\nu,$$

and letting $(\mathbf{x}_T - \widehat{\mathbf{x}}_T) = \boldsymbol{\delta}_x$:

$$(\boldsymbol{\Upsilon}^*)^h \mathbf{x}_T - \widehat{\boldsymbol{\Upsilon}}^h \widehat{\mathbf{x}}_T \approx \left((\boldsymbol{\Upsilon}^*)^h - \boldsymbol{\Upsilon}^h \right) \mathbf{x}_T + \left(\boldsymbol{\Upsilon}^h - \boldsymbol{\Upsilon}_p^h \right) \mathbf{x}_T - \mathbf{F}_h \boldsymbol{\delta}_\Upsilon^\nu + \left(\boldsymbol{\Upsilon}_p^h + \mathbf{C}_h \right) \boldsymbol{\delta}_x.$$

There is no necessity that cross products involving $\boldsymbol{\delta}_\Upsilon$ and $\boldsymbol{\delta}_x$ be negligible, so interaction terms may arise from the forecast origin. To this order of approximation, conditional on $\mathbf{x}_T$, one taxonomy of forecast errors in (7.11) is shown in table 7.1.

At first sight, the expression is both somewhat daunting and not suggestive of positive implications. However, the decomposition supports a meaningful interpretation of the forecast error. Conditional on $\mathbf{x}_T$, the first four rows only have bias effects, whereas the remainder may also affect forecast-error variances. Further, the decomposition simplifies in various states of nature, and these correspond to various elements vanishing in table 7.1. For example, (*iiia*)–(*iiib*) vanish if the model is 'correctly specified' in sample, but otherwise the formula remains intact on replacing $(\boldsymbol{\Upsilon}_p, \boldsymbol{\tau}_p)$ by $(\boldsymbol{\Upsilon}, \boldsymbol{\tau})$. Similarly, if parameters remain constant, (*i*)–(*ii*) disappear, and the formula applies with $(\boldsymbol{\Upsilon}^*, \boldsymbol{\tau}^*) = (\boldsymbol{\Upsilon}, \boldsymbol{\tau})$. When $\mathbf{x}_T = \widehat{\mathbf{x}}_T$, (*v*) vanishes. If parameter values are imposed rather than estimated, (*iva*)–(*ivb*) disappear, and so does $\mathbf{C}_h$ in (*v*). However, (*vi*) will only vanish under omniscience.

Table 7.1 Forecast error $\widehat{\nu}_{T+h}$

$\sum_{i=0}^{h-1}\left(\left(\boldsymbol{\Upsilon}^*\right)^i - \boldsymbol{\Upsilon}^i\right)\boldsymbol{\tau}_p + \left(\left(\boldsymbol{\Upsilon}^*\right)^h - \boldsymbol{\Upsilon}^h\right)\mathbf{x}_T$	(*i*) slope change
$+\sum_{i=0}^{h-1}\left(\boldsymbol{\Upsilon}^*\right)^i\left(\boldsymbol{\tau}^* - \boldsymbol{\tau}\right)$	(*ii*) intercept change
$+\sum_{i=1}^{h-1}\left(\boldsymbol{\Upsilon}^i - \boldsymbol{\Upsilon}_p^i\right)\boldsymbol{\tau}_p + \left(\boldsymbol{\Upsilon}^h - \boldsymbol{\Upsilon}_p^h\right)\mathbf{x}_T$	(*iiia*) slope mis-specification
$+\sum_{i=0}^{h-1}\left(\boldsymbol{\Upsilon}^*\right)^i\left(\boldsymbol{\tau} - \boldsymbol{\tau}_p\right)$	(*iiib*) intercept mis-specification
$-\sum_{i=0}^{h-1}\left(\mathbf{D}_i - \mathbf{F}_i\right)\boldsymbol{\delta}_{\Upsilon}^{\nu}$	(*iva*) slope estimation
$-\sum_{i=0}^{h-1}\boldsymbol{\Upsilon}_p^i\boldsymbol{\delta}_{\tau}$	(*ivb*) intercept estimation
$+\left(\boldsymbol{\Upsilon}_p^h + \mathbf{C}_h\right)\boldsymbol{\delta}_x$	(*v*) initial condition
$+\sum_{i=0}^{h-1}\left(\boldsymbol{\Upsilon}^*\right)^i\boldsymbol{\nu}_{T+h-i}$	(*vi*) error accumulation.

Typical analyses of forecast errors only entertain (*iv*) and (*vi*). Thus, in deriving second-moment measures of forecast accuracy, and assuming that parameter estimators are $\sqrt{T}$ consistent, the impact of estimation uncertainty appears to be of order T^{-1} and the impact of the accumulation of future disturbances dominates. Asymptotically, forecasts are only uncertain to the extent that the process generating the data is stochastic and forecasting accumulates the inherent uncertainty at each point in time. Before discussing the taxonomy in detail, we note the corresponding outcome for an open system.

7.3.1 Open systems

Suppose now that in place of the closed system (7.1), we admit non-modelled variables, and we have a simultaneous structural linear stochastic econometric model of m endogenous variables $\mathbf{y}_t$ conditional on k non-modelled regressors $\mathbf{z}_t$:

$$\mathbf{B}_0\mathbf{y}_t + \mathbf{B}_1\mathbf{y}_{t-1} + \cdots + \mathbf{B}_r\mathbf{y}_{t-r} = \mathbf{C}_0\mathbf{z}_t + \mathbf{C}_1\mathbf{z}_{t-1} + \cdots + \mathbf{C}_s\mathbf{z}_{t-s} + \epsilon_t \quad (7.14)$$

where $\epsilon_t \sim \mathsf{IN}_m[\mathbf{0}, \boldsymbol{\Sigma}]$. The $\mathbf{B}_i$ are the $m \times m$ coefficient matrices of the m vector of endogenous variables lagged i periods, and the $\mathbf{C}_i$ are the $m \times k$ coefficient matrices on the non-modelled and policy variables $\mathbf{z}_t$. Assuming that $\mathbf{B}_0$ is non-singular, the reduced form is:

$$\begin{aligned}\mathbf{y}_t &= \mathbf{B}_0^{-1}\mathbf{C}_0\mathbf{z}_t + \cdots + \mathbf{B}_0^{-1}\mathbf{C}_s\mathbf{z}_{t-s} - \mathbf{B}_0^{-1}\left(\mathbf{B}_1\mathbf{y}_{t-1} + \cdots + \mathbf{B}_r\mathbf{y}_{t-r} + \boldsymbol{\epsilon}_t\right) \\ &= \boldsymbol{\Gamma}_0\mathbf{z}_t + \cdots + \boldsymbol{\Gamma}_s\mathbf{z}_{t-s} + \boldsymbol{\Phi}_1\mathbf{y}_{t-1} + \cdots + \boldsymbol{\Phi}_r\mathbf{y}_{t-r} + \boldsymbol{\eta}_t.\end{aligned} \tag{7.15}$$

One lag on the dependent variables is fully general – a first-order system can be viewed as a companion form to a system of arbitrary order. Hence we need only consider:

$$\mathbf{B}_0\mathbf{y}_t + \mathbf{B}_1\mathbf{y}_{t-1} = \mathbf{C}\mathbf{z}_t + \boldsymbol{\epsilon}_t \tag{7.16}$$

with reduced form:

$$\mathbf{y}_t = \boldsymbol{\Gamma}\mathbf{z}_t + \boldsymbol{\Phi}\mathbf{y}_{t-1} + \boldsymbol{\eta}_t, \tag{7.17}$$

where $\boldsymbol{\eta}_t \sim \mathsf{IN}_m[\mathbf{0}, \boldsymbol{\Omega}]$ and $\boldsymbol{\Gamma} = \mathbf{B}_0^{-1}\mathbf{C}$, with $\boldsymbol{\Phi} = -\mathbf{B}_0^{-1}\mathbf{B}_1$. If the autoregressive component of the model is dynamically stable, $\boldsymbol{\Phi}^j \to \mathbf{0}$ as $j \to \infty$, so by backward substitution:

$$\mathbf{y}_t = \sum_{i=0}^{\infty} \boldsymbol{\Phi}^i\boldsymbol{\Gamma}\mathbf{z}_{t-i} + \sum_{i=0}^{\infty} \boldsymbol{\Phi}^i\boldsymbol{\eta}_{t-i}, \tag{7.18}$$

so that $\mathbf{y}_t$ is the cumulation of all past zs and disturbances, with declining weights. If we let $\mathbf{w}_t' = (\mathbf{z}_t' : \mathbf{y}_{t-1}')$ and $\boldsymbol{\Pi} = (\boldsymbol{\Gamma} : \boldsymbol{\Phi})$, then the system (7.17) becomes:

$$\mathbf{y}_t = \boldsymbol{\Pi}\mathbf{w}_t + \boldsymbol{\eta}_t. \tag{7.19}$$

(7.19) will prove useful for section 7.5 when we consider evaluating large-scale models by their historical tracking performance.

In the case of open systems like (7.17), with off-line forecasts denoted by $\check{\mathbf{z}}_{T+h}$, the 1-step ahead error in forecasting the value of $\mathbf{y}_{T+h}$ for $\widehat{\boldsymbol{\eta}}_{T+h} = \mathbf{y}_{T+h} - \widehat{\mathbf{y}}_{T+h}$ is:

$$\begin{aligned}\widehat{\boldsymbol{\eta}}_{T+h} &= \boldsymbol{\Gamma}_h^*\mathbf{z}_{T+h} - \widehat{\boldsymbol{\Gamma}}\check{\mathbf{z}}_{T+h} + \boldsymbol{\Phi}_h^*\mathbf{y}_{T+h-1} - \widehat{\boldsymbol{\Phi}}\widehat{\mathbf{y}}_{T+h-1} + \boldsymbol{\eta}_{T+h} \\ &= \left(\boldsymbol{\Gamma}_h^* - \boldsymbol{\Gamma}\right)\mathbf{z}_{T+h} + \left(\boldsymbol{\Gamma} - \boldsymbol{\Gamma}_p\right)\mathbf{z}_{T+h} + \left(\boldsymbol{\Gamma}_p - \widehat{\boldsymbol{\Gamma}}\right)\mathbf{z}_{T+h} + \widehat{\boldsymbol{\Gamma}}\left(\mathbf{z}_{T+h} - \check{\mathbf{z}}_{T+h}\right) \\ &\quad + \left(\boldsymbol{\Phi}_h^* - \boldsymbol{\Phi}\right)\mathbf{y}_{T+h-1} + \left(\boldsymbol{\Phi} - \boldsymbol{\Phi}_p\right)\mathbf{y}_{T+h-1} + \left(\boldsymbol{\Phi}_p - \widehat{\boldsymbol{\Phi}}\right)\mathbf{y}_{T+h-1} \\ &\quad + \widehat{\boldsymbol{\Phi}}\left(\mathbf{y}_{T+h-1} - \widehat{\mathbf{y}}_{T+h-1}\right) + \boldsymbol{\eta}_{T+h}.\end{aligned} \tag{7.20}$$

There is a multi-step ahead expression for (7.20) analogous to (7.11), but it adds little insight for our purposes. Relative to (7.11) and table 7.1 for the closed system, (7.20) indicates additional sources of uncertainty from parameter change in the way the zs affect the ys, from the effect of the zs on the ys being mis-specified, from estimation uncertainty in quantifying the effect of the zs on the ys, and from errors in projecting the zs (the four terms in the second line of (7.20)).

7.4 Sources of forecast uncertainty

For both (7.11), the closed system, and (7.20), the open system, an aggregated five-fold partition of sources of forecast error, where $\boldsymbol{\tau}$ and $\boldsymbol{\Upsilon}$, or $\boldsymbol{\Gamma}$ and $\boldsymbol{\Phi}$, are treated as subsets of a generic parameter vector $\boldsymbol{\theta}$, can be expressed as:

I parameter change: $\boldsymbol{\theta}^* \neq \boldsymbol{\theta}$;
II model mis-specification: $\boldsymbol{\theta} \neq \boldsymbol{\theta}_p$;
III estimation uncertainty: $\mathsf{E}[(\widehat{\boldsymbol{\theta}} - \boldsymbol{\theta}_p)(\widehat{\boldsymbol{\theta}} - \boldsymbol{\theta}_p)'] \neq \mathbf{0}$;
IV variable mis-measurement: $\mathbf{x}_T \neq \widehat{\mathbf{x}}_T$; or in the open system:
(i) initial condition uncertainty: $\mathbf{y}_T \neq \widehat{\mathbf{y}}_T$;
(ii) non-modelled variable uncertainty: $\mathbf{z}_{T+h} \neq \check{\mathbf{z}}_{T+h}$ for $h = 0, \ldots, H$;
(iii) incorrect categorization of some variables as exogenous;
(iv) lack of invariance to policy changes in exogenous variables;
V error accumulation due to $\mathsf{M}[\sum_{i=0}^{h-1} (\boldsymbol{\Upsilon}^*)^i \boldsymbol{\nu}_{T+h-i}] \neq \mathbf{0}$.

7.4.1 Parameter change

This can take many forms, and is probably the main cause of serious forecasting errors when models are used operationally. For example, the closed system model-based forecasts implicitly assume that $\boldsymbol{\tau}$ and $\boldsymbol{\Upsilon}$ remain constant, when in fact they may alter (as in (7.10)) to $\boldsymbol{\tau}_h^*$ and $\boldsymbol{\Upsilon}_h^*$ ($\boldsymbol{\tau}_h^*$ subsumes any change from the zero mean of the error distribution). The subscript h denotes the lead over time T, and generalizes the above analysis by allowing these parameters to change each period.

Many analyses of forecasting are based on the premise that the data are generated by a constant, time-invariant process. This would appear to be an inappropriate assumption in reality, as the DGP appears to be non-constant, with its evolution characterized by both structural change and regime shifts. The historical record of periods of dramatic predictive failure suggests, not surprisingly, a close association between poor forecast performance and episodes of economic turbulence.[2] An econometric theory of economic forecasting must recognize the role of non-constancy to deliver relevant conclusions about empirical forecasting. Otherwise, it is predicated on assumptions concerning the state of nature which do not adequately capture certain key aspects of the real world to be forecast. In the absence of an explicit recognition of the impact of structural breaks on purely model-based forecasts traditional, textbook analyses cannot easily account for the historical records of forecasting performance (Cook, 1995 discusses the track record of the UK Treasury model forecasts).

[2] A (non-exhaustive) catalogue would probably include: the under-prediction of postwar consumption (see Spanos, 1989), the failure to predict the 1974–5 and 1979–81 recessions (see Wallis, 1989), the poor performance in predicting the consumer boom in the late 1980s, and also the depth and duration of the recession in the 1990s.

Parameter change and model mis-specification can sometimes be hard to disentangle. When models are not congruent specifications of the economic mechanism, changes in one part of a system can induce apparent parameter change in other equations (see Hendry, 1979b). Simulation evidence in Favero and Hendry (1992) suggests that this can produce important predictive failures. Thus, predictive failure may result from model mis-specification coupled with changes in relevant variables, and does not necessarily imply that a structural break has occurred in the underlying behavioural equations. Nor does the absence of predictive failure imply that models are not mis-specified: under unchanged structure, incorrect models will perform as expected.

We now isolate the main impacts of parameter change in the closed system. From table 7.1, the h-step ahead forecast error is:

$$\widehat{\boldsymbol{\nu}}_{T+h} = \sum_{i=0}^{h-1} (\boldsymbol{\Upsilon}^*)^i \boldsymbol{\tau}^* - \sum_{i=0}^{h-1} \boldsymbol{\Upsilon}^i \boldsymbol{\tau} + (\boldsymbol{\Upsilon}^*)^h \mathbf{x}_T - \boldsymbol{\Upsilon}^h \mathbf{x}_T + \sum_{i=0}^{h-1} (\boldsymbol{\Upsilon}^*)^i \boldsymbol{\nu}_{T+h-i} \quad (7.21)$$

with the further simplification, when only the intercept is non-constant, to:

$$\widehat{\boldsymbol{\nu}}_{T+h} = \sum_{i=0}^{h-1} \boldsymbol{\Upsilon}^i (\boldsymbol{\tau}^* - \boldsymbol{\tau}) + \sum_{i=0}^{h-1} \boldsymbol{\Upsilon}^i \boldsymbol{\nu}_{T+h-i}. \quad (7.22)$$

This more tractable expression highlights a major effect due to parameter change, namely a persistent, and usually increasing, bias (when $(\boldsymbol{\tau}^* - \boldsymbol{\tau}) > \mathbf{0}$, say). In fact, the dominant error source is the change in the equilibrium mean, either directly from a change in $\boldsymbol{\tau}$, or indirectly from the change in $\boldsymbol{\Upsilon}$. This proposition can be demonstrated once the system is expressed in I(0) space, so for simplicity we treat the original system in (7.1) as stationary, with long-run mean $\boldsymbol{\pi} = \mathsf{E}[\mathbf{x}_t]$, given by:

$$\boldsymbol{\pi} = (\mathbf{I}_n - \boldsymbol{\Upsilon})^{-1} \boldsymbol{\tau}.$$

Using the definition of $\boldsymbol{\pi}$, rewrite the system in (7.1) as:

$$\mathbf{x}_t - \boldsymbol{\pi} = \boldsymbol{\Upsilon} (\mathbf{x}_{t-1} - \boldsymbol{\pi}) + \boldsymbol{\nu}_t.$$

Assuming known parameters, to focus on change effects alone, the h-step ahead forecasts at time T are:

$$\widehat{\mathbf{x}}_{T+h} - \boldsymbol{\pi} = \boldsymbol{\Upsilon} (\widehat{\mathbf{x}}_{T+h-1} - \boldsymbol{\pi}) = \boldsymbol{\Upsilon}^h (\mathbf{x}_T - \boldsymbol{\pi}). \quad (7.23)$$

Once $(\boldsymbol{\tau} : \boldsymbol{\Upsilon})$ changes to $(\boldsymbol{\tau}^* : \boldsymbol{\Upsilon}^*)$, where $\boldsymbol{\Upsilon}^*$ still has all its eigenvalues less than unity in absolute value, letting $\boldsymbol{\tau}^* = (\mathbf{I}_n - \boldsymbol{\Upsilon}^*)\boldsymbol{\pi}^*$:[3]

$$\begin{aligned} \mathbf{x}_{T+h} - \boldsymbol{\pi}^* &= \boldsymbol{\Upsilon}^* (\mathbf{x}_{T+h-1} - \boldsymbol{\pi}^*) + \boldsymbol{\nu}_{T+h} \\ &= (\boldsymbol{\Upsilon}^*)^h (\mathbf{x}_T - \boldsymbol{\pi}^*) + \sum_{i=0}^{h-1} (\boldsymbol{\Upsilon}^*)^i \boldsymbol{\nu}_{T+h-i}. \end{aligned} \quad (7.24)$$

[3] We construe blips (such as 1968(1)–(2) for consumers' expenditure in the UK), to be the above change, followed by a second shift superimposed thereon.

The h-step ahead forecast error $\widehat{\boldsymbol{\nu}}_{T+h} = \mathbf{x}_{T+h} - \widehat{\mathbf{x}}_{T+h}$ is:

$$\begin{aligned}\widehat{\boldsymbol{\nu}}_{T+h} &= \boldsymbol{\pi}^* - \boldsymbol{\pi} + (\boldsymbol{\Upsilon}^*)^h (\mathbf{x}_T - \boldsymbol{\pi}^*) - \boldsymbol{\Upsilon}^h (\mathbf{x}_T - \boldsymbol{\pi}) + \sum_{i=0}^{h-1} (\boldsymbol{\Upsilon}^*)^i \boldsymbol{\nu}_{T+h-i} \\ &= \left(\mathbf{I}_n - (\boldsymbol{\Upsilon}^*)^h\right)(\boldsymbol{\pi}^* - \boldsymbol{\pi}) + \left((\boldsymbol{\Upsilon}^*)^h - \boldsymbol{\Upsilon}^h\right)(\mathbf{x}_T - \boldsymbol{\pi}) \\ &\quad + \sum_{i=0}^{h-1} (\boldsymbol{\Upsilon}^*)^i \boldsymbol{\nu}_{T+h-i}. \end{aligned} \tag{7.25}$$

Taking expectations, noting that:

$$\mathsf{E}\left[\mathbf{x}_T - \boldsymbol{\pi}\right] = \mathbf{0},$$

then:

$$\mathsf{E}\left[\widehat{\boldsymbol{\nu}}_{T+h}\right] = \left(\mathbf{I}_n - (\boldsymbol{\Upsilon}^*)^h\right)(\boldsymbol{\pi}^* - \boldsymbol{\pi}). \tag{7.26}$$

Thus, forecasts are biased only to the extent that the long-run mean shifts from the in-sample value, and are unbiased for mean-zero processes ($\boldsymbol{\pi} = \boldsymbol{\pi}^* = \mathbf{0}$), or when shifts in $\boldsymbol{\tau}^*$ offset those in $\boldsymbol{\Upsilon}^*$ to leave $\boldsymbol{\pi}$ unaffected ($\boldsymbol{\pi}^* = \boldsymbol{\pi}$). As the horizon increases, such effects converge to the full impact of the shift ($\boldsymbol{\pi}^* - \boldsymbol{\pi}$). There are variance effects as well when $\boldsymbol{\Upsilon}$ changes, which are detrimental on a MSFE basis; and the *ex ante* forecast-error variance estimates will mis-estimate those ruling *ex post*, but these problems seem likely to be secondary to mean-shift structural breaks. Although non-linearities, asymmetric errors, or roots moving onto the unit circle could generate more complicated outcomes, the basic finding points up a key requirement for eliminating systematic forecast-error biases.

By way of contrast, changes in the dynamics (and in fact, dynamic parameter mis-specifications), are multiplied by mean-zero terms, so vanish on average. Surprisingly, table 7.1 can be written such that they would have no effect at all on the forecast errors if the initial condition equalled the equilibrium mean. Conversely, the larger the dis-equilibrium at the time of a shift in slope, the larger the resulting impact; but as $\boldsymbol{\Upsilon}^*$ and $\boldsymbol{\Upsilon}$ (by assumption) have all their roots inside the unit circle, these effects die out as the horizon expands.

When only the deterministic components of the process change, the conditional forecast-error variances have the same form as that observed in-sample. For example, from (7.21):

$$\mathsf{M}\left[\widehat{\boldsymbol{\nu}}_{T+h} \mid \mathbf{x}_T\right] = \sum_{i=0}^{h-1} (\boldsymbol{\Upsilon}^*)^i \boldsymbol{\Omega} (\boldsymbol{\Upsilon}^*)'^i,$$

assuming the future disturbances are temporally uncorrelated, and retain their in-sample contemporaneous covariance structure, while from (7.22):

$$\mathsf{M}\left[\widehat{\boldsymbol{\nu}}_{T+h} \mid \mathbf{x}_T\right] = \sum_{i=0}^{h-1} \boldsymbol{\Upsilon}^i \boldsymbol{\Omega} \boldsymbol{\Upsilon}'^i.$$

There are a number of ways in which forecasts may be robustified against some non-constant features of the DGP. Clements and Hendry (1996b) consider the consequences of a shift in the equilibrium mean (μ in (7.4)) and show that forecasts from the DV model will be unconditionally unbiased when the long-run equilibrium mean has changed prior to forecasting, and the underlying growth rate of the system is unchanged. The correctly specified VEqCM (prior to the parameter shift over the forecast period), however, will produce biased forecasts: the equilibrium-correction terms tend to pull the forecasts towards the now inappropriate 'equilibrium'.[4] This does not necessarily entail that DV models should be used in preference to VEqCMs. In chapter 6, we showed that the DV model will have larger forecast-error variances when there is cointegration, although we also established that the extent to which this.is so is dependent on the linear transformation of the data being forecast. However, for a sufficiently large structural change, the bias component will dominate the forecast error-variance component, so the DV model will have the smaller MSFE in the face of a shift in the equilibrium mean.

Many macroeconometric systems are in VEqCM form. The historical coincidence of serious forecast errors and apparent regime shifts may be due in part to the adverse effects of equilibrium-correction mechanisms in such states of nature (for example, the OPEC oil-price hike and the 1974–5 recession; OPEC II, the Thatcher government's policies, and the 1979–81 recession; financial deregulation and the consumer boom in the late 1980s; etc.).

In Clements and Hendry (1996b), we investigate other ways in which forecasts may be robustified to parameter change over the forecast period, and report on this work in chapter 8.

7.4.2 Model mis-specification

In section 7.2, we discussed the nature of empirical econometric models. The theory of reduction indicates that models are derived constructs and are susceptible to being designed to satisfy certain criteria. The notion of congruency is the operational benchmark that replaces the assumption of 'truth' in the absence of omniscience or assumed knowledge of the DGP. Since models are unlikely to be 'complete', the requirement that models are parameterized so that the included variables are relatively orthogonal would appear to be particularly important. To the extent that the regressors are orthogonal to wrongly excluded influences, the parameter estimates will be consistent. Orthogonal-parameter, congruent econometric models seem one of the more likely classes to deliver consistent, reliable estimates. An example is provided by the series of

[4] Following Davidson, Hendry, Srba and Yeo (1978), these terms have been known as 'error-corrections'. The recognition that they may play the opposite role when the equilibrium changes accounts for the change in terminology to 'equilibrium-correction'. Fortunately the acronym is unchanged.

studies attempting to model the behaviour of aggregate consumers' expenditure in the UK. From Davidson *et al.* (1978), through Hendry, Muellbauer and Murphy (1990), to Harvey and Scott (1994), the initial dynamic and equilibrium-correction parameters recur over extended information sets and time periods, notwithstanding the considerable regime shifts which contributed to the predictive failures of the consumption function in the second half of the 1980s.

It is believed that there are good reasons to place a premium on parsimony to counter-balance a tendency towards 'over-fitting' when selecting models from the available data sample, whereby accidental or irrelevant data features may become embodied in the model. We discuss the role of parsimony and the associated effects of collinearity in chapter 12: the general issues of 'over-fitting' and capturing accidental data features in empirical models are discussed in Hendry (1995a). Such transient features will detract from the forecast performance of the model if at a later date their behaviour changes. Some preliminary results on model selection when forecasting for simple AR models are also discussed in chapter 12.

In the context of forecasting, it may pay to omit 'genuine' features of models which are likely to be particularly susceptible to structural breaks if their omission is not particularly deleterious in fit (see the case referred to in section 7.4.1). This suggests a tension between the choice of models for forecasting as opposed to policy analysis (which might dictate using the model that provides the best characterization of the historical data) in a world characterized by parameter non-constancy: see Clements and Hendry (1995b) and Banerjee, Hendry and Mizon (1996) for discussion of these issues.

7.4.3 Estimation uncertainty

Estimation uncertainty is dependent on the size and information content of the sample, the quality of the model, the innovation-error variance, the choice of the parameterization, and the selection of the estimator. The degree of integration of the data and whether unit roots are imposed or implicitly estimated also interact with these factors. We reported the results of research into the impact of estimation uncertainty on forecast accuracy in cointegrated systems in section 6.8, and asymptotic forecast-error variances for VARs in levels and differences in section 6.4.

Many of the problems just noted can be ameliorated by efficient specification, modelling and estimation strategies (see, e.g., Banerjee, Dolado, Galbraith and Hendry, 1993, on the implications of non-stationarity for modelling practice).

Somewhat surprisingly, when parameter values are uncertain, the h-step forecast confidence intervals do not always increase monotonically as the horizon of the forecast increases, but may first expand then contract. Since the forecast variance eventually equals the unconditional data variance for weakly stationary processes, but must allow for parameter uncertainty at intermediate horizons, conditional dynamic forecasts can have larger variances than unconditional. The calculations in Hendry (1986) suggest that this can occur within the policy-relevant forecast horizon, which would allow scope for pooling forecasts. We take this idea up as an example of an intercept correction in section 8.4, and again in section 10.4 in the discussion of the combination of forecasts. Alternatively, there is scope for imposing parameter values rather than estimating them, since forecast-error variances will fall when restrictions are nearly satisfied by the data: parsimonious, yet valid, parameterizations can pay dividends here. Issues of estimating parameters versus imposing values are addressed in chapter 12 on model selection when forecasting.

There is a growing literature on estimating models by minimizing (in-sample) squared multi-step errors. The idea is that when the model is mis-specified, estimation techniques based on in-sample minimization of 1-step errors (e.g., ordinary least squares and maximum likelihood), may not be too bad at short leads, but could produce forecasts which go awry at longer horizons. On the other hand, estimating the model by minimizing the in-sample counterpart of the desired out-of-sample forecast horizon may yield better forecasts at those horizons. We address these issues in chapter 11 where we delineate the conditions under which multi-step estimation might yield gains. That chapter constructs an important bridge between model mis-specification and parameter estimation, since multi-step estimation permits the implicit model class to change, and it is a change in the degree of model mis–specification at longer leads that is instrumental in securing overall gains in terms of enhanced forecast accuracy.

7.4.4 Variable uncertainty

Incorrectly measured initial values. A badly measured forecast origin may impart an important source of error to short-term forecasts. The frequency with which preliminary data are subsequently revised suggests that forecasts may often be conditioned on data measured with a substantial degree of error. In section 8.3, we consider several ways of making an allowance for measurement errors. Survey information has a potentially useful role in improving initial values estimates. The 'ragged edge' problem of information reliability spanning several periods is discussed by Wallis *et al.* (1986).

Projections of non-modelled variables. In open systems, off-line projections of non-modelled variables have to be made, and in generating future paths for these variables the forecaster will be engaged in the sorts of activities noted in section 1.5. It is conceivable that mistakes in extrapolating non-modelled variables may be compensated for by other 'corrections' (see Wallis and Whitley, 1991). Non-modelled variable uncertainty can only be reduced by devoting greater resources to modelling the 'exogenous' and policy variables; having a better feel for what the future will bring forth; and taking account of extraneous information on their likely evolution.

Feedbacks on to non-modelled variables. Another form of variable-based forecast error is hidden in (7.20) which is based on the legitimacy of treating the $\mathbf{z}$ variables as strongly exogenous (see Engle *et al.*, 1983). Whereas weak exogeneity is sufficient at the estimation stage to justify ignoring the marginal process generating the $\mathbf{z}$s, the generation of multi-step ahead forecasts from equations with conditioning variables such as (7.17) requires the absence of lagged feedback from the $\mathbf{y}$s on to the $\mathbf{z}$s. Such feedbacks violate conditioning on future non-modelled variables, but are testable from sample information. The absence of feedback is the condition that the $\mathbf{y}$s do not Granger cause the $\mathbf{z}$s (see Granger, 1969). Intuitively, one may expect misleading forecasts to result in the worst instances of this form of mis-specification: for example, suppose nominal wages are forecast assuming a fixed future trajectory for prices.

Invariance to policy changes. To support policy analysis, when the $\mathbf{z}$s are policy instruments, we require the super exogeneity of the $\mathbf{z}$s for the parameters of the forecasting system, and not just their weak exogeneity: this issue is analysed in Engle and Hendry (1993) and Favero and Hendry (1992). A failure of super exogeneity may arise if agents alter the way they form expectations (the 'critique' in Lucas, 1976), or if regime shifts occur out of sample. The Lucas critique does not of itself condemn the forecasting enterprise to failure. In any specific instance, the critique is testable, and in general may lack force (Favero and Hendry, 1992). In other cases, potential effects from regime shifts can be determined *ex ante*: see Hendry and Ericsson (1991) for a model of financial innovation which could have been implemented in part prior to the change having its effect. In general, if anticipated future changes in policy are reasonably correlated with past episodes, then previous *ex post* errors may suggest a pattern of adjustments to the model-based forecasts. Nevertheless, if it is desired to use a model across policy regimes, either the relevant parameters must be invariant, or the effect of the policy change must be incorporated.

The impact of forecasts on outcomes (the bandwagon effect) is only a problem to the extent that it is capricious and cannot be modelled as part of the forecasting device. For some discussion of the historical background, see section 1.3. Many models explicitly incorporate terms to capture agents' expectations concerning future values of variables, so that in principle at least this effect can be controlled. Models can be solved to ensure model-consistent expectations, whereby the expectations of the future values of the variables coincide with the values for those variables generated by the model. For example, suppose that in the simple example:

$$y_t = \alpha_1 \widehat{y}_{t+1} + \boldsymbol{\alpha}_2' \mathbf{x}_t + v_t,$$

where the solution y in period t depends on the forecast of its value in period $t+1$, $\widehat{y}_{t+1} = \mathsf{E}[y_{t+1}|\mathcal{I}_t]$. A model-consistent series of forecasts satisfies:

$$\widehat{y}_\tau = \alpha_1 \widehat{y}_{\tau+1} + \boldsymbol{\alpha}_2' \mathbf{x}_\tau \qquad \text{for } \tau = T+1, \ldots T+H.$$

There is an infinite-regress problem, in that in order to obtain a solution for period $T+H$ a forecast for period $T+H+1$ is required, which is typically dealt with by imposing a terminal condition. This form of model solution 'internalizes' the 'bandwagon effect' since the outcome is (in part) determined by expectations of what it will be.

Within this framework, $\mathsf{E}[y_{t+1}|\mathcal{I}_t]$ is the mathematical expectation with respect to the whole structure of the model. This is sometimes known as the strong form of the rational expectations hypothesis, and has been criticized on the grounds that it makes unrealistic demands on what agents are required to know, when viewed as a behavioural hypothesis. Although the formation of expectations, and the rational expectations hypothesis in particular, is a contentious issue, it is apparent that expectations can be incorporated into model solutions in one form or another (see Hall, 1995, pp.977–80, for a recent review and references).

7.4.5 Error accumulation

The inherent uncertainty in the DGP places a limit on the predictability of non-stationary dynamic mechanisms, although no empirical model is likely to attain such a bound. For $\mathsf{I}(0)$ transforms, such an error source is bounded by the unconditional variance, but for the level of the economy we suspect that the variance is unbounded over time. Put simply, anything is possible in the indefinite future: imagine the level and composition of GNP today had the Industrial Revolution not occurred, or if a nuclear war had. Fortunately, only a few periods ahead are usually necessary for economic stabilization policy (e.g., 4–8 quarters), and only medium-term averages are needed for growth and investment strategies, such as education and infra-structure.

In practice, many models have errors which are not even innovations against their own information sets, and hence they can be improved by better modelling (e.g., by not imposing 'theoretically plausible', but data-rejected, constraints); better methodology (e.g., general-to-simple); and higher-quality databanks of information. The innovation error in a model is not a given, but is derived from the design of the model, so congruent, encompassing models should out-perform others on this aspect, especially against models with autocorrelated residuals.

Asymmetric error distributions potentially induce biased forecasts. Positive inflation shocks might be more likely than negative, so models which assumed mean-zero forecast errors would on average underpredict inflation. Also, error-variance changes (e.g., heteroscedasticity) will lead to increased average squared errors, which will be reflected in many measures of forecast inaccuracy.

7.5 Large-scale model evaluation techniques

A mainstay of large-scale model evaluation has been a consideration of how well the model tracks the past. Fisher and Wallis (1990) provide a comprehensive bibliography of studies of historical tracking performance, from which it is evident that most of the main macroeconomic modelling groups have undertaken such exercises. For historical tracking exercises, we can define the static solution to the model from the reduced form (7.19), by using known values of the parameters, and non-modelled and lagged endogenous variables, as well as known forecast origin $\mathbf{y}_0$:

$$\widehat{\mathbf{y}}_t = \mathbf{\Pi}\mathbf{w}_t, \qquad t = 1, \ldots, T.$$

The resulting 'static' prediction errors are $\mathbf{e}_t = \mathbf{y}_t - \widehat{\mathbf{y}}_t = \boldsymbol{\eta}_t$, that is, the reduced-form residuals, where from (7.16) and (7.17), $\boldsymbol{\eta}_t = \mathbf{B}_0^{-1}\boldsymbol{\epsilon}_t$. Thus, $\mathbf{e}_t \sim \mathsf{IN}_m[\mathbf{0}, \mathbf{B}_0^{-1}\mathbf{\Sigma}\mathbf{B}_0^{-1\prime}]$. Given that the structural disturbances are zero mean and homoscedastic, so are the static errors.

Alternatively, the dynamic simulation approach to historical tracking generates a solution by solving the model forward from the initial conditions, using the values of the endogenous variables from one period as the input to the next (but the true values of the $\mathbf{z}_t$), thus satisfying the recursion (for the one-lag illustration):

$$\mathbf{B}_0\widetilde{\mathbf{y}}_t + \mathbf{B}_1\widetilde{\mathbf{y}}_{t-1} = \mathbf{C}\mathbf{z}_t, \qquad t = 1, \ldots, T, \quad \widetilde{\mathbf{y}}_0 = \mathbf{y}_0. \tag{7.27}$$

From (7.27) and section 7.3.1:

$$\widetilde{\mathbf{y}}_t = \mathbf{\Phi}^t\mathbf{y}_0 + \sum_{i=0}^{t-1} \mathbf{\Phi}^i\mathbf{\Gamma}\mathbf{z}_{t-i}$$

so the historical dynamic simulation errors are:

$$\mathbf{v}_t = \mathbf{y}_t - \widetilde{\mathbf{y}}_t = \sum_{i=0}^{t-1} \mathbf{\Phi}^i\mathbf{B}_0^{-1}\boldsymbol{\epsilon}_{t-i}.$$

While the dynamic errors also inherit the zero-mean property of the simultaneous model errors, they lose the homoscedastic and serially uncorrelated properties, and hence may be difficult to interpret.

Once we allow for coefficient estimation uncertainty, the above results only hold asymptotically for well-specified models (see Pagan, 1989, for more details, and a general analysis of the role of simulation in the statistical evaluation of large-scale models). In particular, if the simulation period coincides exactly with the estimation period, and the structural residuals $\{\widehat{\boldsymbol{\epsilon}}_t\}$ sum to zero (as will be true for most econometric estimators), then the $\mathbf{e}_t$ will also sum to zero, and the $\mathbf{v}_t$ will sum to approximately zero. Thus, the unbiasedness of the static or dynamic errors in historical tracking exercises will not be a powerful way of discovering 'good' models: the property of unbiasedness more or less follows automatically.

Fisher and Wallis (1990) argue for using the static residuals as a measure of system performance, rather than the heteroscedastic dynamic residuals. They recognize the link between the zero-mean structural residuals and the static residuals, but believe that this result may be of limited applicability (see Fisher and Wallis, 1990, p.181), and suggest that a non-zero mean for the reduced-form errors at the very least is indicative of model failure. Finally, we note the Hendry and Richard (1982) and Chong and Hendry (1986) criticisms of dynamic simulation as a means of model evaluation. They are concerned that comparisons of historical track records will favour the model which 'attributes data variance to factors that it treats as being outside of the model, irrespective of the justification for doing so' (Fisher and Wallis, 1990, p.181). Exogeneity claims need to be tested. This criticism of dynamic simulation would appear to apply equally well to some comparisons of *ex post* 1-step forecast errors (the static residuals): treating average earnings (or wages) and import prices as exogenous should produce superior *ex post* forecasts of domestic prices. A common set of 'exogeneity' assumptions across models may yield fairer comparisons, but if the assumptions are invalid, then the exercise will tend to flatter all the models. The 'best' may be of little value.

Finally, the step from backward analyses of historical tracking to the analysis of forecasts is conceptual rather than substantive, since the static and dynamic simulation errors have counterparts in 1-step and h-step forecast errors. Thus, 1-step forecasts for time $T+i$, made at $T+i-1$, with known data but estimated parameters – as used in testing parameter constancy – are:

$$\widehat{\mathbf{y}}_{T+i} = \widehat{\mathbf{\Pi}}\mathbf{w}_{T+i}, \tag{7.28}$$

with forecast errors $\mathbf{y}_{T+i} - \widehat{\mathbf{y}}_{T+i} = \widehat{\mathbf{e}}_{T+i}$, where:

$$\widehat{\mathbf{e}}_{T+i} = \left(\mathbf{\Pi} - \widehat{\mathbf{\Pi}}\right)\mathbf{w}_{T+i} + \boldsymbol{\eta}_{T+i} = \left(\mathbf{I}\otimes\mathbf{w}'_{T+i}\right)\left(\mathbf{\Pi} - \widehat{\mathbf{\Pi}}\right)^{\nu} + \boldsymbol{\eta}_{T+i}. \tag{7.29}$$

When $\widehat{\mathbf{\Pi}}$ is unbiased for $\mathbf{\Pi}$, or the errors are symmetric, to a first approximation, $\mathsf{E}[\widehat{\mathbf{e}}_{T+i}] = \mathbf{0}$ and:

$$\mathsf{V}\left[\widehat{\mathbf{e}}_{T+i}\right] = \mathbf{\Omega} + \left(\mathbf{I}_{k+m}\otimes\mathbf{w}'_{T+i}\right)\mathsf{V}\left[\widehat{\mathbf{\Pi}}^{v}\right]\left(\mathbf{I}_{k+m}\otimes\mathbf{w}_{T+i}\right) = \mathbf{\Theta}_i, \tag{7.30}$$

so that (see Calzolari, 1981 and Chong and Hendry, 1986):

$$\widehat{\mathbf{e}}_{T+i} \underset{app}{\sim} \mathsf{IN}_m\left[\mathbf{0}, \mathbf{\Theta}_i\right], \tag{7.31}$$

where $\mathbf{\Theta}_i$ reflects both parameter and innovation-error uncertainty. *Ex post*, for model evaluation over H periods, on the null of correct specification and parameter constancy:

$$\sum_{j=1}^{H}\widehat{\mathbf{e}}'_{T+j}\widehat{\mathbf{\Theta}}_j^{-1}\widehat{\mathbf{e}}_{T+j} \underset{app}{\sim} \chi^2\left(\left(k+m\right)H\right). \tag{7.32}$$

Next, we derive the vector analogues of the h-step ahead conditional forecast errors and error variances for the univariate processes given by (4.10), (4.13), (4.21) and (4.23) in chapter 4. To begin with, we assume that parameters are constant, and their values, forecast origin and future **z**s are known and correct. The h-step ahead forecasts for time $T+h$, based on knowledge of $\mathbf{y}$ up to period $\mathbf{y}_T$, are defined recursively from (7.17) as:

$$\widetilde{\mathbf{y}}_{T+h} = \mathbf{\Phi}\widetilde{\mathbf{y}}_{T+h-1} + \mathbf{\Gamma}\mathbf{z}_{T+h}, \quad h = 1, \ldots \tag{7.33}$$

so that the forecast errors are defined recursively by:

$$\widetilde{\boldsymbol{\eta}}_{T+j} = \mathbf{y}_{T+j} - \widetilde{\mathbf{y}}_{T+j} = \mathbf{\Phi}\left(\mathbf{y}_{T+j-1} - \widetilde{\mathbf{y}}_{T+j-1}\right) + \boldsymbol{\eta}_{T+j} = \mathbf{\Phi}\widetilde{\boldsymbol{\eta}}_{T+j-1} + \boldsymbol{\eta}_{T+j} \tag{7.34}$$

and by backward substitution:

$$\widetilde{\boldsymbol{\eta}}_{T+h} = \sum_{i=0}^{h-1} \mathbf{\Phi}^i \boldsymbol{\eta}_{T+h-i} + \mathbf{\Phi}^h \widetilde{\boldsymbol{\eta}}_T = \sum_{i=0}^{h-1} \mathbf{\Phi}^i \boldsymbol{\eta}_{T+h-i}, \tag{7.35}$$

since $\widetilde{\mathbf{y}}_T = \mathbf{y}_T$ implies that $\widetilde{\boldsymbol{\eta}}_T = \mathbf{0}$. (Compare the $\widetilde{\boldsymbol{\eta}}_{T+h}$ with the dynamic simulation errors $\mathbf{v}_t$). Hence the h-step ahead conditional forecast error can be expressed as a weighted average of all previous 1-step ahead errors (which are just the future realizations of the underlying error process, given our assumptions). Some of these errors will cumulate indefinitely when $\mathbf{\Phi}$ has a root of unity.

The forecast errors defined by (7.35) are heteroscedastic in h (like the dynamic simulation errors), with the forecast-error variances given by:

$$\mathsf{E}\left[\widetilde{\boldsymbol{\eta}}_{T+h}\widetilde{\boldsymbol{\eta}}'_{T+h} \mid \mathbf{y}_T\right] = \mathsf{E}\left[\sum_{i=0}^{h-1}\sum_{j=0}^{h-1} \mathbf{\Phi}^i \boldsymbol{\eta}_{T+h-i}\boldsymbol{\eta}'_{T+h-j}\mathbf{\Phi}^{j\prime}\right] = \sum_{i=0}^{h-1} \mathbf{\Phi}^i \mathbf{\Omega} \mathbf{\Phi}^{i\prime}. \tag{7.36}$$

The forecast standard errors increase with the horizon ahead, but converge to the variance of $\mathbf{y}_t$, given current and past $\mathbf{z}_t$, when all the latent roots of $\mathbf{\Phi}$ lie inside the unit circle, and otherwise diverge indefinitely. Given stationarity, the variance of $\mathbf{y}_t$ can be derived from (7.18) as:

$$\mathsf{E}\left[\left(\mathbf{y}_T - \mathsf{E}\left[\mathbf{y}_T\right]\right)\left(\mathbf{y}_T - \mathsf{E}\left[\mathbf{y}_T\right]\right)'\right] = \sum_{j=0}^{\infty} \mathbf{\Phi}^j \mathbf{\Omega} \mathbf{\Phi}^{j\prime}. \tag{7.37}$$

When parameters are estimated, but the model coincides with a constant DGP, (7.36) can be generalized to account for parameter uncertainty (see Schmidt, 1977, Spitzer and Baillie, 1983, Chong and Hendry, 1986 and Calzolari, 1987). The case with unit roots is analysed in chapter 11.

7.6 Overview

In this chapter we have developed a formal framework to account for the various forecast errors that arise when large-scale macroeconometric models are used for forecasting. It is essentially an 'accounting' framework, where forecast errors are decomposed into elements attributable to parameter non-constancy, model mis-specification, sampling variability, variable mis-measurement and error uncertainty. The taxonomy enables a systematic treatment of the sources of forecast error, and ordering the information in this way suggests areas where improvements may be made. We suspect that parameter change is responsible for some of the more dramatic episodes of predictive failure, and we return to this in chapter 8. Parameter estimation uncertainty is often accorded a primary role in this regard, to the detriment of the other components of the taxonomy that we have discussed in this chapter. In chapter 11 we discuss parameter estimation uncertainty specifically in the context of forecasting integrated processes.

We also presented a critique of some of the techniques commonly used to evaluate large-scale macroeconometric models, as a prelude to the discussion of forecast encompassing in chapter 10.

Chapter 8

A theory of intercept corrections: beyond mechanistic forecasts

We outline a general framework for analysing the adjustments typically made to model-based forecasts. Published forecasts based on large-scale macroeconometric models reflect to varying degrees the properties of the models and the adjustments made by their proprietors in arriving at a final forecast. The scope for, and importance of, such adjustments has long been recognized, and recent work by the ESRC Macroeconomic Modelling Bureau suggests that the adjustments made by the main UK forecasting groups to their model-based forecasts usually result in improved forecast accuracy. Our theory of intercept corrections is based on the relationships between the data generating process, the estimated econometric model, the mechanics of the forecasting technique, the data accuracy and any information about future events held at the beginning of the forecast period. It indicates a variety of situations under which intercept corrections will enhance forecast accuracy. The resulting forms of intercept correction differ, and in any practical setting would have to be combined, although we do not explicitly consider interactions between them. Intercept corrections are shown to offer some protection against structural breaks, and as such are an important aspect of a general approach to the theory of economic forecasting which explicitly recognizes that the model is not the mechanism, and that the mechanism is subject to change.

8.1 Introduction

Any account of practical forecasting with large-scale macroeconometric models has to recognize that published forecasts reflect in varying degree the properties of the models and the skills of the models' proprietors. In chapter 7, we dealt with the first part of this union, but left until now the role of the forecaster in 'shaping' the model-based predictions. This aspect of the forecasting venture is potentially important. Forecasts are rarely based on the estimated model alone. Rather, adjustments (sometimes extensive) are often made to the model-based predictions in arriving at a final forecast, typically to the constant terms or intercepts in the models' equations. Thus, they are known as intercept corrections, or alternatively as residual adjustments, add-factors, or, somewhat more emotively, *ad hoc* factors or con adjustments. We shall adopt the first pseudonym in this chapter to denote the setting of non-zero equation residuals over the forecast period, irrespective of the source of the correction.

The importance of adjusting model-based forecasts has long been recognized. For example, Marris (1954) warned against the 'mechanistic' adherence to models in the generation of forecasts when the economic system changes:

> the danger of its operators becoming wedded to belief in the stability of relationships (parameters) which are not in fact stable. (Marris, 1954, p.772)

The recognition of the scope for, and importance of, adjusting purely model-based forecasts has a long lineage (see, *inter alia*, Theil, 1961, p.57, Klein, 1971, Klein, Howrey and MacCarthy, 1974; the sequence of reviews by the UK ESRC Macroeconomic Modelling Bureau in Wallis, Andrews, Bell, Fisher and Whitley, 1984, 1985, Wallis, Andrews, Fisher, Longbottom and Whitley, 1986, Wallis, Fisher, Longbottom, Turner and Whitley, 1987, Turner, 1990, and Wallis and Whitley, 1991). Forecasters' adjustments appear to improve forecast accuracy empirically, as documented by Wallis *et al.* (1986, table 4.8), Wallis *et al.* (1987, figures 4.3 and 4.4) and Wallis and Whitley (1991).

Intercept corrections are typically divided into two broad categories in the literature:

(a) those which represent the influence of anticipated future events that are not explicitly incorporated in the specification of the model; and
(b) projecting into the future past errors based on apparent model mis-specification, or non-constancy, of an unknown source which is nevertheless expected to persist (see Young, 1979 and Turner, 1990). This is sometimes known as setting the model 'back on track'.

Wallis and Whitley (1991) refer to the second group of adjustments as 'automatic' in that they represent a quick-fix solution to perceived model inadequacy (relative to model re-specifications and re-estimation), while the former are termed 'discretionary'. Discretionary adjustments require the exercise of judgement by the forecaster, while the role of judgement in automatic adjustments is less clear. Typically, an average of some of the most recent errors is used to adjust forecasts by a constant amount. If the adjustments were applied to the model immediately prior to the forecast period, then these errors would be approximately removed (by construction), so this is the sense in which forecasts are set 'back on track'. In an analysis of published forecasts based on four UK models, Wallis and Whitley (1991) isolate the mechanical and judgemental components of intercept corrections by generating two variant forecasts. In the first, all the intercept corrections are set to zero to produce a pure, model-based forecast. In the second variant, the residuals are set according to a mechanical adjustment rule. Comparing these two variants with the published forecasts, Wallis and Whitley conclude that the evidence of improved forecast accuracy is more persuasive from the automatic adjustments.

Whatever the forecasters own motivations for making the adjustments, whether in response to perceived model inadequacy, or to incorporate new information, it is possible to establish a general framework for the analysis of adjustments to model-based forecasts. In this chapter, we seek to furnish a general theory of intercept corrections, which is founded upon the relationships between the DGP, the econometric model, the mechanics of the forecasting technique, the data accuracy and any information about future events held at the beginning of the forecast period. We use the taxonomy of information suggested by Hendry and Richard (1982) and Hendry and Richard (1983) (see also Gilbert, 1986) in the context of evaluating models within which to couch our theory of intercept corrections. This should help to ensure that our theory is reasonably exhaustive in coverage. The strata of the information taxonomy are:

(1) The relative past;
(2) The relative present;
(3) The relative future;
(4) Theory information;
(5) Measurement information;
(6) Rival models.

The temporal segregation here is relative to time T, the beginning of the forecast period, although we will also consider the possibility that the split is relative to T^e, the end of the estimation sample period, where $T \geq T^e$.

(1) The relative past may convey evidence of model mis-specification, exactly as in the context of model evaluation. The first-best solution would be to improve the model, at least up to the point where its error is a homoscedastic innovation process, and the within-sample parameters are constant (see section 7.2). In practice, this option may be ruled out by deadlines which do not permit such in-depth analysis. In such a case, there is a *prima facie* argument for adjusting the future values of the equation intercept in an attempt to make some allowance for the perceived problems with the equation. Typically, it is not just the equation intercept term which is thought to be incorrect; for example, Turner (1990) outlines the form of intercept correction implied by a perceived change in the coefficient of an exogenous variable. Intercept corrections motivated by apparent model mis-specification over the estimation period (or the period prior to the forecast) as evidenced by the (estimated) residuals are discussed in sections 8.6 and 8.7.
(2) The relative present will include information on how well the equation performs around time T or T^e: the relevance of that information in the current context is that the data observations on which the most recent residuals are calculated may be measured subject to substantial error. Indeed, Wallis (1989, p.32) attributes an important role to measurement-error related issues in justifying a role for intercept corrections: 'the continuing presence of data discrepancies and delays is one reason why there remains a role for informed judgement in forecasting'. In

section 7.4.4, we identified a badly measured forecast origin as an example of variable uncertainty in our taxonomy of sources of forecast error. In section 8.3, we discuss the implications for intercept corrections of near-contemporaneous equation errors resulting from measurement errors.

(3) The relative future may indicate a role for intercept corrections if it is thought that the underlying DGP may change, so that a hitherto reasonably congruent econometric model will cease to be so. Of course, model failure may arise when the correlations between variables change but the DGP is unaltered: such epochs can be useful in detecting model mis-specification and discriminating between contending models which were hitherto nearly observationally equivalent. Conceptually at least, the situation we have in mind is distinct from (a) above: we conjecture a change in the underlying relationships rather than, say, changes in tax rates/allowances in an otherwise unchanged world. This distinction will be blurred in practice, particularly if changing the value of certain policy variables causes economic agents to behave in a fundamentally different way (the so-called Lucas, 1976 'critique' discussed in section 7.4.4, where we noted that Engle and Hendry, 1993, Favero and Hendry, 1992 and Ericsson and Irons, 1995, developed a theory of testing for its applicability, and reported empirical evidence as to its relevance). In section 8.6, we discuss some of these considerations, and whether intercept corrections offer some insurance against parameter change.

(4) Theory information, in the context of intercept corrections, concerns the properties of different methods of prediction based on statistical theory. One example (which we shall discuss in section 8.4) is the relationship between conditional and unconditional forecasts of stationary processes that may be exploited to reduce forecast-error variance in some circumstances. Following from section 4.3, we show how parameter estimation uncertainty in the case of the conditional forecast creates the possibility that the unconditional forecast may have a lower MSFE for certain horizons and parameter values. This is a small-sample result since (in general, in the stationary case) the impact of parameter estimation uncertainty is of order T^{-1}. Another example of a small-sample result arises when adding the previous period's forecast error (in the case of 1-step ahead forecasts) to the current forecast value may improve forecast accuracy. This can occur even if the model is not obviously mis-specified, with the possible exception of the parameter estimate having an inordinately large variance. An illustration is given in section 8.5.

(5) Measurement information relates to 'data admissibility' and data accuracy, as in the context of model evaluation. However, for forecasting, this source is closely related to (2) above, and is also discussed in section 8.3.

(6) Finally, rival model information can formally encapsulate knowledge about the future from other sources, which gives rise to the rationale for intercept corrections described in (a) above.

This taxonomy is comprehensive in coverage, and nests many of the justifications for intercept corrections that have been advanced in the literature on a more *ad hoc* basis. For example: 'where a model is not well specified or structurally stable' (Turner, 1990, p.315), is an example of (1) or possibly (3); mis-specification in terms of omitted variables (Young, 1979, p.269), is an example of (1) but again may involve (3) if sample correlations change in the future; and measurement errors (Young, 1979 and Wallis, 1989) fall under (5). In particular, Turner (1990) examines a number of key residual adjustments in forecasts produced by the National Institute of Economic and Social Research (NIESR) and the London Business School (LBS), and concludes that the adjustments are made in response to systematic past errors in the equations (termed automatic adjustments above), suggesting a single type of rationale, namely (1). However, the failure to account for the rise in consumers' expenditure in the second half of the 1980s may in part represent measurement error in terms of the under-recording of income, or could be a structural break due to financial innovation, suggesting that the richer classification may in some instances be more informative. In particular, 'mechanistic' adjustments of the setting the forecast 'back on track' variety are seen as a possible counter to structural breaks or parameter change, and not just as corrections to model mis-specification. Although parameter change may induce model mis-specification, conceptually the two are distinct.

We show below that the nature of the required intercept correction depends upon its rationale, so that the theory of intercept corrections furnishes positive prescriptions. We treat each source in isolation and do not consider interactions between the possible sources.

It is illuminating to contrast our approach to the understanding of intercept corrections with that of Artis, Moss and Ormerod (1992) who seek to develop an expert system to replace the judgmental role of the forecaster in generating final forecasts from macroeconometric models. That is, they try to codify the judgmental role exercised by the forecaster in a set of computer-implementable rules. In so doing, Artis *et al.* are essentially describing and formalizing what expert forecasters actually do, rather than attempting to explain why what forecasters do works.

The above justifications for modifying model-based forecasts via intercept corrections are analysed in a number of simple examples. Either first-order scalar or vector autoregressive DGPs suffice for the most part to illustrate the arguments. However, to highlight the connection between an intercept correction (IC) and differencing, we first consider the simplest possible setting, namely, an IID process with a non-zero mean as its only parameter. Thus, let y_t be generated by:

$$y_t = \mu + \epsilon_t \text{ where } \epsilon_t \sim \mathsf{IN}\left[0, \sigma_\epsilon^2\right], \tag{8.1}$$

estimated in-sample by least squares. The conventional forecast is:

$$\widehat{y}_{T+1} = \widehat{\mu}. \tag{8.2}$$

At T, there was a residual of $\widehat{\epsilon}_T = y_T - \widehat{\mu}$, so to set the model 'back on track' (i.e., fit the last observation perfectly), the intercept correction $\widehat{\epsilon}_T$ is added to (8.2) to yield:

$$\widehat{y}_{\iota,T+1} = \widehat{\mu} + \widehat{\epsilon}_T = y_T.$$

Thus, in this instance, the IC forecast is identical to that based on a random walk, which could have been obtained by differencing (8.1) and ignoring the resulting (negative) moving-average error.

We next consider the issue of basing the analysis on linear equations as approximations to the large non-linear systems to which forecasters actually apply intercept corrections, drawing on the results developed in chapter 4.

8.2 Intercept corrections in non-linear equations

Our outline of the commonly used methods of forecasting in large-scale models will follow the account given in Young (1979), and aims to highlight the role played by intercept corrections. Such models can be characterized as a system of non-linear equations of the form:

$$f_i\left(\mathbf{y}_t, \mathbf{Y}_{t-1}, \mathbf{X}_t; \boldsymbol{\psi}\right) = \epsilon_{i,t} \tag{8.3}$$

for $i = 1, \ldots, m$, where $\mathbf{y}_t$ is a $m \times 1$ vector of current dated endogenous (i.e., modelled) variables, $\mathbf{Y}_{t-1}$ contains all lagged values of endogenous variables, $\mathbf{X}_t$ contains current and lagged values of non-modelled variables, and $\boldsymbol{\psi}$ denotes the vector of parameters. Then the forecast is constructed as follows. Suppose we have a set of estimates of the parameters from the sample period 1 to T, denoted $\widehat{\boldsymbol{\psi}}$, and projections for the future values of $\mathbf{X}_{T+h}$, given by $\widetilde{\mathbf{X}}_{T+h}$. For a forecast at period $T+h$, then:

$$\widetilde{\mathbf{X}}_{T+h} = \left[\mathbf{X}_T^1 : \widetilde{\mathbf{X}}_{T+h}^{T+1}\right],$$

so that the variables in the first part of the partition refer to variables known at time T, and those in the second part are projections. In practice, as noted above, there is a 'ragged edge' (see Wallis *et al.*, 1986), and we return to this below when analysing the related idea that measurement errors are likely to be larger for more recent data. The forecasts for $\mathbf{y}_{T+h}$, denoted $\widehat{\mathbf{y}}_{T+h}$, solve:

$$f_i\left(\widehat{\mathbf{y}}_{T+h}, \widehat{\mathbf{Y}}_{T+h-1}, \widetilde{\mathbf{X}}_{T+h}; \widehat{\boldsymbol{\psi}}\right) = \widetilde{\epsilon}_{i,T+h} \tag{8.4}$$

for $i = 1, \ldots, m$, and for $h > 0$, where the $\wedge$ on $\mathbf{Y}_{T+h-1}$ indicates that the lagged values of the endogenous variables will themselves be forecasts for $h > 1$, and the $\sim$ on the disturbance terms indicates that these variables are also projections, in much the same way as 'exogenous' variables. Mechanistic deterministic forecasts satisfy (8.4), but with the right-hand side of the expression set to zero, that is $\widetilde{\boldsymbol{\epsilon}}_{T+h} = \mathbf{0}$. The rationale for this is straightforward: the underlying equation disturbance terms are generally assumed to be zero mean, $\mathsf{E}[\epsilon_{i,T+h}] = 0$, and most econometric estimators have the property that the estimated residuals sum to zero over the sample period. Thus, *ceteris paribus*, it seems natural to set the equation error terms to zero over the future.

The $\{\epsilon_{i,t}\}$ in equation (8.3) for the estimation period 1 to T are denoted by $\widehat{\epsilon}_{i,t}$ to indicate an estimated residual. The intercept corrections that are commonly projected into the future are defined by:

$$r_{i,t} = y_{i,t} - \widehat{y}_{i,t} \tag{8.5}$$

for $t = 1, \ldots, T$, where $\widehat{y}_{i,t}$ is the fitted value for $y_{i,t}$ implicitly defined in equation (8.3). Thus, $r_{i,t}$ will not coincide with the disturbances in (8.3) or (8.4) when $f_i(\cdot)$ is non-linear. Several authors have questioned the deterministic solution of (8.3) as described by (8.4) when the equations are non-linear, since this will result in biased forecasts: see, for example, Ericsson and Marquez (1996), and section 4.7.1 where this issue is addressed for non-linear extensions of Box–Jenkins time series models. The asymptotic bias from deterministic solution will be of first order, $O(1)$, when the model parameters are consistently estimated, but the asymptotic bias can be reduced to being $O(T^{-1})$ for a stochastic predictor based on a Monte Carlo average. In that case, an estimated (stochastic) prediction is obtained by averaging over predictions calculated by solving the model for different realizations of the disturbance terms drawn from a specified distribution. Ericsson and Marquez (1996) calculates the bias of deterministic forecasts for a number of empirical models of the US external trade balance. The Monte Carlo estimator of the conditional expectation is calculated to allow for the parameter estimates to be stochastic (as well as the disturbance terms), and the variance-reduction technique of antithetic variates is used, with a considerable efficiency gain in estimating the non-linearity bias compared to naive Monte Carlo (see section 5.4).

Whilst these issues are clearly of interest, they are not of central concern to the subject matter of this chapter. Mariano and Brown (1983) observed that most forecasts from non-linear systems were deterministic, and this still appears to be true of recent practice. Of interest here would be whether such considerations suggest benefits from using intercept corrections in deterministic solutions, but there do not seem to be any general prescriptions as to the required form of corrections. Moreover, whether we have a deterministic or a stochastic solution, the issue of intercept corrections would appear to be the same: in the stochastic case, the intercept correction would be implemented either by taking realizations from a distribution with a non-zero mean, or from a zero-mean distribution and adding on an additional (deterministic) factor.

The importance (at least in principle) of the non-linear model deterministic solution bias has been established for the evaluation of econometric (non-linear) models by comparison to time-series models. Wallis (1984) argues that finding in favour of a time-series model over an econometric model in MSFE comparisons, in the non-linear case, does not necessarily imply the inadequacy of the latter (as in the linear case). Wallis advocates obtaining the conditional expectation of the non-linear model by simulation and using this as the basis for between-model forecast-error comparisons.

Following Young (1979) and Kennedy (1983), we can deduce the relationship between $\{r_{i,t}\}$ and $\{\epsilon_{i,t}\}$ when the equation is in log-linear form (in the sense that the additive error in this form is normal). This is a typical case in time-series econometrics. Some of the formulations below assume that the variables are stationary. In principle, this allows for I(1) variables but assumes that a certain number of linear combinations of these variables cointegrate, and that the models in this chapter are already expressed in differences and cointegrating combinations (the transformation from the I(1) levels of the variables to the I(0) representation is described in section 6.3).

For the ith equation we can write:

$$\ln y_{i,t} = \ln \widehat{y}_{i,t} + \widehat{\epsilon}_{i,t}. \tag{8.6}$$

We assume that $\widehat{\epsilon}_{i,t} = \epsilon_{i,t} + o_p(1)$ (so consistent estimates have been used), and neglect the $o_p(1)$ term for the remainder of this section. Then:

$$y_{i,t} = \widehat{y}_{i,t} \cdot \exp\left(\epsilon_{i,t}\right) \tag{8.7}$$

so that from (8.5) and (8.7):

$$r_{i,t} = \widehat{y}_{i,t}\left(\exp\left(\epsilon_{i,t}\right) - 1\right). \tag{8.8}$$

Hence, even assuming that $\epsilon_{i,t} \sim \mathsf{IN}[0, \sigma_\epsilon^2]$, $r_{i,t}$ is the product of a log-normal variate and $\widehat{y}_{i,t}$. However, using the expansion of the exponential

$$\exp\left(\epsilon_{i,t}\right) = 1 + \epsilon_{i,t} + \tfrac{1}{2}\,\epsilon_{i,t}^2 + \cdots,$$

then:

$$r_{i,t} = \widehat{y}_{i,t}\epsilon_{i,t} + \tfrac{1}{2}\,\widehat{y}_{i,t}\epsilon_{i,t}^2 + \cdots \tag{8.9}$$

and so $\mathsf{E}[r_{i,t}] \approx \frac{1}{2}\widehat{y}_{i,t}\sigma_\epsilon^2$. This is a reasonable approximation because $\widehat{y}_{i,t}$ should be independent of $\epsilon_{i,t}$ and under the normality of $\epsilon_{i,t}$, the next term in the expansion (being the third moment of a normally distributed variate) would disappear. Since $\epsilon_{i,t}$ is the error on a log-linear equation, $100\sigma_\epsilon$ will be approximately a percentage of $y_{i,t}$ (such as 1 – 5 percent for most economic time series), so $\mathsf{E}[r_{i,t}]$ will usually be small.

For log-linear equations, practitioners often use multiplicative (rather than additive) factors so (8.5) becomes:

$$r_{i,t}^* = \frac{y_{i,t}}{\widehat{y}_{i,t}} \tag{8.10}$$

and the relationship between the intercept correction $r_{i,t}^*$ and the disturbance in (8.6) is given by:

$$r_{i,t}^* = \exp\left(\epsilon_{i,t}\right) \tag{8.11}$$

which is now independent of the level of the variable. The mean of $r_{i,t}^*$ exceeds unity by a small amount:

$$\mathsf{E}\left[r_{i,t}^*\right] = \exp\left(\mathsf{E}\left[\epsilon_{i,t}\right] + \tfrac{1}{2}\,\sigma_\epsilon^2\right) = \exp\left(\tfrac{1}{2}\,\sigma_\epsilon^2\right) \approx 1 + \tfrac{1}{2}\,\sigma_\epsilon^2, \tag{8.12}$$

which yields a similar relative error to (8.9) (see Aitchison and Brown, 1957, on the log-normal distribution). As before, σ_ϵ is less than 0.05, so the expressions for $(y_{i,t} - \widehat{y}_{i,t})/\widehat{y}_{i,t}$ in (8.9) and (8.12) are close to zero. Consequently, we focus on the linear case without much loss of generality, and with a considerable gain in tractability.

8.3 Measurement errors and data revisions

The effects of measurement errors on the properties of parameter estimates are well known for regressions involving stationary variables, and are discussed in standard econometrics textbooks. For the consequences of measurement errors on regression estimators when variables are non-stationary and integrated, see for example Stock (1988) and Banerjee, Dolado, Galbraith and Hendry (1993). Our interest is in the potential role for intercept corrections as a means of mitigating the forecast errors that may result from conditioning the forecast on the most recent observations when these are assumed to be measured with substantial error. Typically, a number of 'estimates' are released (such as the preliminary or provisional, followed by the revised figures) before the 'final' data are made available. Gallo (1996) describes an approach which eschews all but the final data as 'purist' compared to the 'naive' approach which treats all published data as if it were 'true'. Gallo (1996) treats the estimates that become available as forecasts of the 'true' value based on different information sets. If later estimates do not fully encapsulate all the information in earlier ones, then the potential for pooling arises to extract a better 'signal' from the noisy observations.

A full discussion of pooling, or the combination of, forecasts is the subject matter of chapter 10. In this section, we consider two situations. In the first, we have a single estimate of the value of a variable, which we assume is measured with error. Forecasts can either be conditioned on this value (naive approach), or on the model prediction for this period (the purist approach), or on a combination of the two. We show how the combination option leads to a form of intercept correction. Secondly, we consider a richer scheme of data revisions, by allowing for preliminary and revised estimates before the final data become known. The conditions under which the preliminary estimates are informative, given that the revised estimates are available, can be established, and indicate when it may pay to use the two estimates in conjunction. As a straightforward extension of the results in the first part of this section, these estimates can be combined with the model's prediction of the forecast origin (based on its latest data).

8.3.1 Measurement errors

It is well known that measurement errors in dynamic models lead to autocorrelated residuals. In analysing measurement errors, we abstract from the effects on parameter estimates by using known parameters: we are only concerned with a few badly measured observations at the end of the sample period which have a relatively negligible effect on full-sample parameter estimates. Whole-sample tests for autocorrelation will usually fail to detect this problem. However, careful end-of-sample residual analysis might prove useful. The simple conceptualization we adopt below divides time into three non-overlapping periods: the estimation period $(1, \ldots, T^e)$ during which the data are observed without error; a period during which the data are observed with error $(T^e + 1, \ldots, T)$, followed by the forecast period $(T + 1, \ldots, T + H)$. That the estimation period does not extend to the beginning of the forecast period reflects the sizes of models currently in use, which makes it expensive to re-estimate all equations each time a new data point becomes available, and possibly undesirable if the latest data are unreliable. To emphasize the main implications, we will later consider uncertainty in the forecast origin only, so the period T observations alone are observed with error.

The DGP is deliberately simple to highlight the logic of the analysis, namely:

$$y_t = \psi y_{t-1} + v_t, \tag{8.13}$$

for $t = 1, \ldots, T + H$, where $v_t \sim \mathsf{IN}[0, \sigma_v^2]$ and $|\psi| < 1$.

In the absence of measurement errors, and assuming a correctly specified model with known parameters, the model coincides with (8.13) for $t = 1, \ldots, T^e$. Over $s = T^e + 1, \ldots, T$, the observed series is the actual y_s measured with an error η_s:

$$y_s^* = y_s + \eta_s, \tag{8.14}$$

where $\eta_s \sim \mathsf{IN}[0, \sigma_s^2]$ and $\mathsf{E}[y_s \eta_t] = 0$ for all t, s. Thus, the measurement error is independent of the 'true' value. By construction, $\sigma_s^2 = 0$ for $s = 1, \ldots, T^e$ and $\sigma_s^2 > 0$ for $s > T^e$. Substituting (8.14) into (8.13):

$$y_s^* - \eta_s = \psi \left(y_{s-1}^* - \eta_{s-1} \right) + v_s, \tag{8.15}$$

so for $s = T^e + 1, \ldots, T$, the model becomes:

$$y_s^* = \psi y_{s-1}^* + e_s, \tag{8.16}$$

where the disturbance e_s denotes that (8.16) is not a regression residual once the parameter 'estimation period' ends at T^e. When the parameters are estimated, e_s and v_s also differ by the term $(\widehat{\psi} - \psi) y_{s-1}^*$. Hence:

$$e_s = v_s + \eta_s - \psi \eta_{s-1}.$$

Thus, the observed residual series here should exhibit the following properties over the period immediately prior to forecasting:

$$\mathsf{E}\left[e_s\right] = 0 \tag{8.17}$$

as both the measurement and DGP errors are assumed to have zero mean; and

$$\mathsf{V}\left[e_s\right] = \sigma_v^2 + \sigma_s^2 + \psi^2 \sigma_{s-1}^2. \tag{8.18}$$

Also:

$$\mathsf{E}\left[e_s e_{s-1}\right] = -\psi\sigma^2_{s-1} \tag{8.19}$$

corresponding to error autocorrelation ρ_s of the form:

$$\rho_s = \frac{\mathsf{E}\left[e_s e_{s-1}\right]}{\sqrt{\mathsf{V}\left[e_s\right]\mathsf{V}\left[e_{s-1}\right]}}. \tag{8.20}$$

Although heteroscedastic measurement errors seem likely (with σ^2_s increasing as time T approaches), we will assume a constant $\sigma^2_s = \sigma^2$ where this permits more useful analytical formulae. With that homoscedasticity assumption, we have:

$$\rho_s = \frac{-\psi\sigma^2}{\sigma^2_v + (\psi^2 + 1)\,\sigma^2}. \tag{8.21}$$

Further, if we assume that $\sigma^2_v = \sigma^2$, so that the variance of the DGP disturbance term and the variance of the measurement error are equal, then $\rho_s = -\psi/(2 + \psi^2)$ so $|\rho_s| < \frac{1}{3}$. For $\psi > 0$, $\rho_s < 0$ so measurement errors imply that the adjacent residuals observed by the forecaster will be negatively correlated in simple dynamic models. Heteroscedasticity would lead to changing autocorrelation, and smaller measurement errors would lead to less (absolute) autocorrelation. However, the importance of recent measurement errors for forecast accuracy does not depend only on this end-of-sample autocorrelation.

To derive the implications of measurement errors for intercept corrections, we make use of the literature on 'signal-extraction' popularized in macroeconomics by Lucas (1973) in his 'islands model'. The problem is to derive the optimal predictor of y_{T+h} given information available at period T. To highlight the main issue, we assume that only the last observation y^*_T is error ridden, which is the case of forecast origin uncertainty. Thus, the information set (denoted by $\mathcal{I}^*_T$) contains the values of y_s for $s < T$ and knowledge of the model given by (8.13) (jointly denoted by $\mathcal{I}^1_T$); and the relationship between y^*_T and y_T given by (8.14) (denoted by $\mathcal{I}^2_T$). Then, the optimal predictor is given by $\mathsf{E}[y_{T+h}|\mathcal{I}^*_T]$, which must be inferior relative to the predictor in the absence of measurement error, namely $\mathsf{E}[y_{T+h}|\mathcal{I}_T]$, where $\mathcal{I}_T$ replaces y^*_T by y_T (relative to $\mathcal{I}^*_T$).

From (8.13):

$$y_{T+h} = \psi^h y_T + \sum_{i=0}^{h-1} \psi^i v_{T+h-i}, \tag{8.22}$$

where the expectation of the last term is zero for all forecast horizons. Consequently, we can view the forecasting task as a '2-stage' procedure: first, obtain the best estimate of y_T, which we denote by $\breve{y}_T$, and then forecast y_{T+h} from $\psi^h \breve{y}_T$. The first stage is of interest when there are measurement errors (and the parameters of the model are assumed known), since then the problem requires estimating $\mathsf{E}[y_T|\mathcal{I}^*_T]$.

We consider the optimal predictor of y_T given the information sets $\mathcal{I}^1_T$ and $\mathcal{I}^2_T$ in turn, and then combine the two predictors in an optimal fashion by choosing weights that minimize the squared prediction error. Survey based information could be incorporated in a similar way. Appendix 8.9 records the details, where we show that the composite 'signal' has the form:

$$\mathsf{E}\left[y_T \mid \mathcal{I}_T^*\right] = (1-\mu)\,\widehat{y}_T + \mu\widetilde{y}_T, \tag{8.23}$$

where μ weights the two components, with $\widetilde{y}_T = \psi y_{T-1}$ and $\widehat{y}_T = k_T y_T^*$, where $k_T = (1 + \sigma_T^2/\sigma_y^2)^{-1}$ depends on the relative variance of the measurement-error component ($\sigma_T^2 = \mathsf{E}[\eta_T^2]$) to the underlying uncertainty in the DGP ($\sigma_y^2 = \sigma_v^2/(1-\psi^2)$). Minimizing the squared prediction error from (8.23) yields a value of μ, say μ^*, so that the optimal predictor becomes:

$$\breve{y}_T = \widehat{y}_T - \mu^*\left(\widehat{y}_T - \widetilde{y}_T\right) = y_T^* - (1-\mu^*)\,(1-k_T)\,y_T^* - \mu^* e_T, \tag{8.24}$$

where we use the second expression below. When measurement error is confined to period T, so that $\widehat{y}_{T-1} = y_{T-1}$, this formula has a straightforward interpretation since μ^* varies positively with the variability of the measurement error (see appendix 8.9). Thus, the noisier the measurement error, the greater the reliance on the model-based predictor. In the limit, as $\sigma_T^2 \to \infty$, $\mu^* \to 1$, and hence $\breve{y}_T = \psi y_{T-1}$, so the model-based predictor of the initial condition is the 1-step ahead conditional expectation, based on the model (8.13) at $T-1$, completely ignoring the period T observation. The converse holds if $\sigma_T^2 = 0$.

The second-stage forecast of y_{T+h} using the first-stage estimate $\breve{y}_T$ yields:

$$\breve{y}_{T+h} = \psi^h \breve{y}_T = \psi^h y_T^* - \psi^h\left[(1-\mu^*)\,(1-k_T)\,y_T^* + \mu^* e_T\right]. \tag{8.25}$$

When predicting using $\psi^h y_T^*$ rather than $\psi^h y_T$, the required intercept correction is given by the second term in (8.25). For example, when $k_T \approx 1$, the last term is approximately $-\mu^*\psi^h e_T$, which diminishes in h under the assumption that $\{y_t\}$ is stationary.

8.3.2 Data revisions

Suppose that instead of a single estimate of y_T measured with error (y_T^*), preliminary and revised estimates are available, y_T^p and y_T^r, respectively.[1] The preliminary data were available first, but both are available at time T, when the forecast of y_{T+1} is to be made (different dating conventions would not alter the logic of the analysis). We allow for the possibility that y_T^p is informative about y_T (in a sense we make precise below) even when y_T^r is available. The forecast (or measurement) errors are defined by:

$$\begin{aligned} y_T^p &= y_T + e_T^p \\ y_T^r &= y_T + e_T^r. \end{aligned}$$

[1] The impact of data revisions on $\mathsf{I}(1)$ variables is discussed in Hendry (1995a).

Consider combining the two estimates as $y^c_T = \mu y^r_T + (1-\mu) y^p_T$, where the weights sum to one since we are assuming the estimates are unbiased. Then choose μ to minimize $\mathsf{E}[(y_T - y^c_T)^2]$, which yields:

$$\mu^* = \frac{\sigma^2_p - \sigma_{rp}}{\sigma^2_p + \sigma^2_r - 2\sigma_{rp}}, \tag{8.26}$$

where $\sigma^2_i = \mathsf{E}[(e^i_T)^2]$, for $i = r, p$, and $\sigma_{rp} = \mathsf{E}[e^r_T e^p_T]$.

For 'rational' preliminary estimates (see the discussion of rationality and related concepts in section 3.2.2), we can deduce that $\lambda = 1$ in:

$$e^p_T = \lambda e^r_T + u_T,$$

where $\mathsf{E}[e^r_T u_T] = 0$, so that the error in the preliminary estimate is equal to the error in the revised estimate plus an orthogonal component, and:

$$\sigma^2_p = \sigma^2_r + \sigma^2_u.$$

Thus, $\sigma^2_p > \sigma^2_r$, given that y^p_T is based on a subset of the information underlying y^r_T. Hence $\sigma_{rp} = \sigma^2_r$ and so $\mu^* = 1$, and no weight is attached to the preliminary forecast. When $\sigma_{rp} = 0$, so that the two measurement errors are uncorrelated, then from (8.26) it is apparent that the two estimates should be weighted according to their relative variability. When the informational content of the preliminary estimate is not wholly subsumed in the revised estimate ($\sigma_{rp} \neq \sigma^2_r$) then both the preliminary and revised estimates will have a role to play.

8.4 Conditional and unconditional predictors

Forecasts from macroeconomic models are conditional forecasts given the initial values of the variables as well as the projected future time paths of any non-modelled variables. One rationale for intercept corrections is, somewhat paradoxically, to exploit the potential information in unconditional forecasts. In section 4.3, we derived the conditional and unconditional forecast-error variances for a stationary process. In this section, we demonstrate that the conditional error variance can exceed the unconditional variance of the process when we allow for parameter estimation uncertainty. Furthermore, we develop the suggestion of Chong and Hendry (1986) that a weighted average of the conditional and unconditional predictors may have a smaller variance than either alone, and that this might be exploited to improve forecast accuracy. We show that combination with the unconditional predictor can be implemented as a form of intercept correction in large-scale macroeconometric models.

These ideas are illustrated with the simple first-order scalar autoregressive process given by (8.13), with the coefficient value assumed unknown. We continue to assume stationarity and no measurement errors. The h-step ahead conditional MSFE_h is:

$$\mathsf{E}\left[\widehat{e}_{T+h}^2 \mid y_T\right] = \mathsf{MSFE}_h = \frac{\sigma_v^2\left(1-\psi^{2h}\right)}{\left(1-\psi^2\right)} + \mathsf{E}\left[\left(\psi^h - \widehat{\psi}^h\right)^2\right] y_T^2. \qquad (8.27)$$

The first term is the contribution of future disturbances, and the second is due to parameter uncertainty, which we evaluate using the asymptotic formula in Baillie (1979a, equation 1.6, p.676):

$$\mathsf{MSFE}_h = \frac{\sigma_v^2\left(1-\psi^{2h}\right)}{\left(1-\psi^2\right)} + h^2\psi^{2(h-1)}T^{-1}\left(1-\psi^2\right) y_T^2. \qquad (8.28)$$

Details of this derivation are provided by Ericsson and Marquez (1989, p.5), and as a special case of appendix 4.11, by setting $\mu = 0$ in (4.13). The first term is monotonically increasing in h, approaching the unconditional variance of y_T asymptotically:

$$\frac{\sigma_v^2\left(1-\psi^{2h}\right)}{\left(1-\psi^2\right)} \to \mathsf{V}\left[y_T^2\right] = \frac{\sigma_v^2}{\left(1-\psi^2\right)} \quad \text{as } h \to \infty.$$

Chong and Hendry (1986) note that $h^2\psi^{2(h-1)}$ in the second term of (8.28) has a maximum at $h = -1/\ln\psi$, and so is not monotonic. Thus, when parameters have to be estimated, the resulting expressions for forecast uncertainty may not be monotonic in the forecast horizon, h, so that prediction intervals may contract over certain ranges of h. Hence, for sufficiently large values of y_T^2 (standardized relative to σ_y^2), and appropriate values of the parameters, the outcome in (8.28) will exceed the unconditional variance, namely when:

$$\frac{y_T^2}{\sigma_y^2} > \frac{T\psi^2}{h^2\left(1-\psi^2\right)} = h^{-2}\tau_{\psi=0}^2,$$

where $\tau_{\psi=0}^2 = T\psi^2/(1-\psi^2)$ is the non-centrality of the t-test of $\psi = 0$ (see chapter 12 where we discuss the role such terms play in deciding whether to impose or estimate parameters when selecting models for forecasting).

Consider the behaviour of a composite predictor formed by combining linearly the conditional predictor $\widehat{y}_{T+h}$ and $\overline{y}$, where the latter does not depend on time, and is a function of the information set at time T; for example, $\overline{y}$ could be the mean of a long sample of historical data. There is no benefit to using the same sample to calculate $\overline{y}$. Since the model is expressed in $\mathsf{I}(0)$ space, y_t can be thought of as a growth rate, so that $\overline{y}$ is the historical average growth rate, although we treat it as having zero variance. For models where y_t is an acceleration (e.g., the second difference of the logarithm of a variable), $\overline{y} = 0$ is a natural choice.

There is a large literature on the combination of forecasts and the related notion of forecast encompassing, which forms the subject matter of chapter 10. We shall return to this issue in section 10.4 in the wider context of the combination of forecasts.

In the above example, the y_t process has a zero mean, so that we set $\overline{y} = 0$. The composite predictor is then given by:

$$\widetilde{y}_{T+h} = \alpha \overline{y} + (1 - \alpha) \widehat{y}_{T+h} = (1 - \alpha) \widehat{y}_{T+h}, \tag{8.29}$$

where $0 \leq \alpha \leq 1$, and the associated h-step ahead composite forecast error is:

$$\widetilde{e}_{T+h} = y_{T+h} - \widetilde{y}_{T+h} = \alpha \overline{e}_{T+h} + (1 - \alpha) e_{T+h}, \tag{8.30}$$

where $e_{T+h} \equiv y_{T+h} - \widehat{y}_{T+h}$ and $\overline{e}_{T+h} \equiv y_{T+h} - \overline{y} = y_{T+h}$. As (8.29) reveals, the benefit (if any) is due to 'shrinkage': the conditional forecast is shrunk toward zero by a weight of $(1-\alpha)$, although zero is a sensible shrinkage point only because we assumed that $\mathsf{E}[y_t] = 0$.

Consider the conditional MSFE, $\mathsf{E}[\widetilde{e}^2_{T+h} | y_T]$, for the composite predictor:[2]

$$\begin{aligned} & \alpha^2 \mathsf{E}\left[\overline{e}^2_{T+h}\right] + (1-\alpha)^2 \mathsf{E}\left[e^2_{T+h}\right] + 2\alpha(1-\alpha)\mathsf{E}\left[\overline{e}_{T+h} e_{T+h}\right] \quad (8.31) \\ = \; & \alpha^2 \mathsf{E}\left[y^2_{T+h}\right] + (1-\alpha)^2 \mathsf{E}\left[e^2_{T+h}\right] + 2\alpha(1-\alpha)\mathsf{E}\left[y_{T+h} e_{T+h}\right]. \end{aligned}$$

Expanding the third term in (8.31) using (8.22) and:

$$e_{T+h} = \left(\psi^h - \widehat{\psi}^h\right) y_T + \sum_{i=0}^{h-1} \psi^i v_{T+h-i},$$

we obtain:

$$\begin{aligned} \mathsf{E}\left[y_{T+h} e_{T+h} \mid y_T\right] &= \mathsf{E}\left[\psi^h \left(\psi^h - \widehat{\psi}^h\right) y^2_T\right] + \mathsf{E}\left[\sum_{i=0}^{h-1} \psi^i v_{T+h-i}\right]^2 \\ &\quad + \mathsf{E}\left[\left(\psi^h + \left(\psi^h - \widehat{\psi}^h\right)\right) y_T \sum_{i=0}^{h-1} \psi^i v_{T+h-i}\right] \\ &\simeq \sigma^2_v \frac{\left(1 - \psi^{2h}\right)}{\left(1 - \psi^2\right)}, \end{aligned} \tag{8.32}$$

since the first and third terms are essentially zero. Hence, using (8.32), and (8.28) for $\mathsf{E}[e^2_{T+h} \mid y_T]$, (8.31) becomes:

$$\begin{aligned} \mathsf{E}\left[\widetilde{e}^2_{T+h} \mid y_T\right] &\simeq \alpha^2 \mathsf{E}\left[y^2_{T+h}\right] + \sigma^2_v \left(1 - \alpha^2\right) \frac{\left(1 - \psi^{2h}\right)}{\left(1 - \psi^2\right)} \\ &\quad + (1-\alpha)^2 h^2 \psi^{2(h-1)} T^{-1} \left(1 - \psi^2\right) y^2_T \\ &= \alpha^2 \psi^{2h} y^2_T + \sigma^2_v \frac{\left(1 - \psi^{2h}\right)}{\left(1 - \psi^2\right)} \\ &\quad + (1-\alpha)^2 h^2 \psi^{2(h-1)} T^{-1} \left(1 - \psi^2\right) y^2_T \end{aligned} \tag{8.33}$$

[2] Although not explicit in (8.31), (8.32) and (8.33), the expectations operators on the right-hand sides of the equations are conditional on period T.

since:

$$\mathsf{E}\left[y_{T+h}^2 \mid y_T\right] = \sigma_v^2 \frac{\left(1-\psi^{2h}\right)}{\left(1-\psi^2\right)} + \psi^{2h} y_T^2.$$

Minimizing (8.33) with respect to α yields:

$$\alpha_h^* = \left(1 + \frac{T\psi^2}{h^2\left(1-\psi^2\right)}\right)^{-1} = \left(1 + \frac{\tau_{\psi=0}^2}{h^2}\right)^{-1}. \tag{8.34}$$

Notice that (8.34) does not depend on y_T^2. From (8.34), the overall MSFE may be reduced by using the composite predictor defined in (8.29). However, α_h^* will be close to zero unless h is large and/or $T\psi^2$ is small, so the gains may not be large, and may be lost by estimating the long-run mean. Typically, the conditional variance will be less than the unconditional initially, and then rise above it as h increases, suggesting increasing α_h^* from 0 to 1 as h increases (or from zero rising to a maximum and then back to zero, since the conditional and unconditional forecast-error variances converge). From (8.29), this implies an intercept correction that adjusts the model prediction towards the long-run mean (of zero in this case) by an increasing amount as the number of steps ahead increases. Eventually, the conditional predictor will converge towards the unconditional predictor anyway, so that the intercept correction can be tailed off after some point to leave the 'pure' model forecasts.

8.5 Setting the forecast back on track

Forecasters often set models 'back on track', so that under- (over-)prediction of an equation in the past leads to a commensurate adjustment in the future. In this section, we assume that the model is not mis-specified. We can make the analysis of this behaviour operational by assuming that the forecaster adds in the residual of the current period to the next period's forecast for 1-step ahead forecasts. Hence, the adjustment to the forecast is based only on the forecast error in the current period. This formulation lets us establish conditions under which such behaviour will improve forecast accuracy, as well as relate the potential gains to the properties of the DGP and the econometric model being used for forecasting.

We continue to consider only the DGP given by (8.13) so the forecast for period $T+1$ based on period T information is:

$$\widehat{y}_{T+1} = \widehat{\psi} y_T, \tag{8.35}$$

with a forecast error given by:

$$e_{T+1} = y_{T+1} - \widehat{y}_{T+1} = \left(\psi - \widehat{\psi}\right) y_T + v_{T+1}. \tag{8.36}$$

The forecast from setting the model 'back on track' is:

$$\widehat{y}_{T+1}^* = \widehat{\psi} y_T + e_T, \tag{8.37}$$

with a forecast error $\widehat{e}_{T+1}$ given by:

$$\widehat{e}_{T+1} = y_{T+1} - \widehat{y}^{*}_{T+1} = \left(\psi - \widehat{\psi}\right) y_T + v_{T+1} - e_T = e_{T+1} - e_T, \tag{8.38}$$

using (8.36). Hence:

$$\widehat{e}_{T+1} = \Delta e_{T+1} \tag{8.39}$$

so that resetting forecasts has the property of inducing the difference in the original forecast error, as with our first illustration. Thus:

$$\mathsf{V}\left[\widehat{e}_{T+1}\right] = \mathsf{V}\left[\Delta e_{T+1}\right] = \mathsf{V}\left[e_{T+1}\right] + \mathsf{V}\left[e_T\right] - 2\mathsf{C}\left[e_{T+1}e_T\right]. \tag{8.40}$$

and assuming weak stationarity, so that $\mathsf{V}[e_j] = \mathsf{V}[e_t]\ \forall j$:

$$\mathsf{V}\left[\widehat{e}_{T+1}\right] = 2\mathsf{V}\left[e_t\right] - 2\rho_e\mathsf{V}\left[e_t\right] = 2\left(1-\rho_e\right)\mathsf{V}\left[e_t\right], \tag{8.41}$$

where ρ_e is the correlation coefficient between adjacent (ordinary) forecast errors, $\{e_t\}$. Hence, setting the forecast back on track reduces the expected squared forecast error if $\rho_e > 1/2$. This condition is in terms of the estimated residuals. To express the implications in terms of the parameters of the DGP and the estimator of the econometric model, from (8.36):

$$\begin{aligned}
\mathsf{V}\left[e_{T+1}\right] &= \mathsf{E}\left[\left\{\left(\psi - \widehat{\psi}\right) y_T + v_{T+1} - \mathsf{E}\left[\left(\psi - \widehat{\psi}\right) y_T + v_{T+1}\right]\right\}^2\right] \\
&\simeq \mathsf{V}\left[\widehat{\psi}\right]\sigma_y^2 + \sigma_v^2,
\end{aligned} \tag{8.42}$$

where we have assumed that the estimator is unbiased, $\mathsf{E}[\psi - \widehat{\psi}] = 0$, and ignored the (small) correlation between $(\psi - \widehat{\psi})$ and y_T. Now, $\mathsf{E}[e_{T+1}e_T]$ is given by

$$\begin{aligned}
&\mathsf{E}\left[\left(\psi - \widehat{\psi}\right)^2 \left(\psi y_{T-1} + v_T\right) y_{T-1}\right] + \mathsf{E}\left[\left(\psi - \widehat{\psi}\right)\left(\psi y_{T-1} + v_T\right) v_T\right] \\
&+ \mathsf{E}\left[\left(\psi - \widehat{\psi}\right) y_{T-1} v_{T+1}\right] + \mathsf{E}\left[v_{T+1}v_T\right].
\end{aligned} \tag{8.43}$$

Absence of serial correlation in $\{v_t\}$, due to its being an innovation process with respect to the information available to the forecaster, implies that the last two terms are zero. The second term is also negligible ($\mathsf{E}[\psi - \widehat{\psi}] = 0$), so that (8.43) becomes:

$$\mathsf{E}\left[e_{T+1}e_T\right] \simeq \mathsf{E}\left[\left(\psi - \widehat{\psi}\right)^2\right]\psi\mathsf{E}\left[y_{T-1}^2\right] \simeq \mathsf{V}\left[\widehat{\psi}\right]\psi\sigma_y^2. \tag{8.44}$$

From (8.42) and (8.44):

$$\rho_e = \frac{\mathsf{V}\left[\widehat{\psi}\right]\psi\sigma_y^2}{\mathsf{V}\left[\widehat{\psi}\right]\sigma_y^2 + \sigma_v^2}. \tag{8.45}$$

From (8.13), $\sigma_y^2 = \sigma_v^2/(1-\psi^2)$, so that:

$$\rho_e = \psi \left[1 + \frac{(1-\psi^2)}{\mathsf{V}\left[\widehat{\psi}\right]} \right]^{-1} \simeq \psi \left[1+T\right]^{-1}, \tag{8.46}$$

where the last expression uses the asymptotic approximation $\mathsf{V}[\widehat{\psi}] = (1-\psi^2)/T$. For a given value of $\psi > 1/2$, $\rho_e > 1/2$ will hold for a sufficiently imprecise estimator of ψ, but would not hold for the asymptotic approximation. A necessary condition for this form of residual adjustment to work is that ψ is positive. This parallels the requirement that the estimated residuals are at least positively correlated.

By itself, the above small-sample rationale for an intercept correction is not overly interesting. However, particular forms of structural breaks may generate positive autocorrelation in post-estimation sample residuals, so this form of correction may well be effective in those circumstances. This issue is discussed in the following section.

8.6 Structural change during the forecast period

We can distinguish a number of different cases of structural change. Suppose future changes in policy are anticipated, and that these are reasonably well correlated with past episodes. If in the past the model exhibited a lack of invariance to such policy changes, then these previous *ex-post* errors may suggest a pattern for future intercept corrections. Thus the model is expected to be mis-specified for the state of nature that is foreseen. Periods over which forecasts perform badly highlight areas of general model weakness (not just lack of invariance to certain interventions), and provide an impetus to model development. Wallis (1989) documents the new avenues of research opened up by poor track records during the 1974–5 and 1979–81 recessions.

An example is documented by Turner (1990). Turner quotes Haache and Townend (1981) who stated that for forecasting the exchange rate 'we are left without any stable empirical relationship which might be used'. In terms of our taxonomy of information, the exchange rate equation is mis-specified, but to such an extent that past errors are not believed to provide any useful indication as to how the equation might perform in the future. Turner (1990) states that the NIESR forecasters impose a time-path for the exchange rate in their forecast based upon their view of the rate of depreciation of sterling that the Government would be prepared to countenance. Thus, the intercept correction here is due to information based on the relative future, albeit that over-riding an equation completely is a polar extreme of intercept correction. The NIESR forecasters' view about the Treasury's reaction to likely downward pressure on sterling during the forecast period was probably formed on the basis of information from a variety of sources. An important strand would presumably be the way in which the Government had reacted in the past to similar circumstances, although this clearly had not proved amenable to formal modelling, and is itself subject to changing again in the future.

In the remainder of this section, we consider structural breaks that have occurred prior to the forecast period, between periods $T-1$ and T, say, but of which the forecaster is ignorant for whatever reason. The analysis extends that of section 7.4.1, and the point of departure is the model given by (7.1). We abstract from considerations of parameter uncertainty. The actual values of the process are given by:

$$\mathbf{x}_{T+h} = \boldsymbol{\tau}^* + \boldsymbol{\Upsilon}^* \mathbf{x}_{T+h-1} + \boldsymbol{\nu}_{T+h} \quad \text{for } h = 0, \ldots, H, \tag{8.47}$$

where the in-sample parameters are $(\boldsymbol{\tau} : \boldsymbol{\Upsilon})$. The timing of the break is important, because the forecaster observes the period T residual given by:

$$\mathbf{e}_T^* = \mathbf{x}_T - \widehat{\mathbf{x}}_T = \boldsymbol{\tau}^* - \boldsymbol{\tau} + (\boldsymbol{\Upsilon}^* - \boldsymbol{\Upsilon})\, \mathbf{x}_{T-1} + \boldsymbol{\nu}_T \tag{8.48}$$

where $\widehat{\mathbf{x}}_T = \boldsymbol{\tau} + \boldsymbol{\Upsilon}\mathbf{x}_{T-1}$. To forecast period $T+1$, there are two options: (*i*) use $\widehat{\mathbf{x}}_{T+1} = \boldsymbol{\tau} + \boldsymbol{\Upsilon}\mathbf{x}_T$ so the period T error is ignored with an associated forecast error of:

$$\mathbf{e}_{T+1}^* = \boldsymbol{\tau}^* - \boldsymbol{\tau} + (\boldsymbol{\Upsilon}^* - \boldsymbol{\Upsilon})\, \mathbf{x}_T + \boldsymbol{\nu}_{T+1}, \tag{8.49}$$

or, (*ii*) set the forecast back on track by adding in the period T residual. Thus the forecast value will be given by $\widetilde{\mathbf{x}}_{T+1} = \widehat{\mathbf{x}}_{T+1} + \mathbf{e}_T^*$, which produces the forecast error:

$$\begin{aligned} \widetilde{\mathbf{e}}_{T+1} &= \boldsymbol{\tau}^* - \boldsymbol{\tau} + (\boldsymbol{\Upsilon}^* - \boldsymbol{\Upsilon})\, \mathbf{x}_T + \boldsymbol{\nu}_{T+1} - \mathbf{e}_T^* \\ &= (\boldsymbol{\Upsilon}^* - \boldsymbol{\Upsilon})\, \Delta\mathbf{x}_T + \Delta\boldsymbol{\nu}_{T+1} = \Delta\mathbf{e}_{T+1}^*, \end{aligned} \tag{8.50}$$

where the second equality follows from substituting for $\mathbf{e}_T^*$ from (8.48).

In terms of bias, neither strategy produces unbiased forecasts, although (8.50) suggests that the intercept correction will reduce the bias, and will completely remove it when only $\boldsymbol{\tau}$ changes (so that $\boldsymbol{\Upsilon}^* = \boldsymbol{\Upsilon}$):

$$\begin{aligned} \mathsf{E}\left[\mathbf{e}_{T+1}^* \mid \mathbf{x}_T\right] &= (\boldsymbol{\tau}^* - \boldsymbol{\tau}) + (\boldsymbol{\Upsilon}^* - \boldsymbol{\Upsilon})\, \mathbf{x}_T \\ \mathsf{E}\left[\widetilde{\mathbf{e}}_{T+1} \mid \mathbf{x}_T\right] &= (\boldsymbol{\Upsilon}^* - \boldsymbol{\Upsilon})\, \Delta\mathbf{x}_T. \end{aligned}$$

From (8.49) and (8.50), the conditional forecast-error variances are given by:

$$\mathsf{V}\left[\mathbf{e}_{T+1}^* \mid \mathbf{x}_T\right] = \boldsymbol{\Omega} \quad \text{and} \quad \mathsf{V}\left[\widetilde{\mathbf{e}}_{T+1} \mid \mathbf{x}_T\right] = 2\boldsymbol{\Omega},$$

where $\mathsf{V}[\mathbf{z}_t] = \mathsf{M}[\mathbf{z}_t] - (\mathsf{E}[\mathbf{z}_t])^2$. Thus, the conditional MSFEs are:

$$\begin{aligned} \mathsf{M}\left[\mathbf{e}_{T+1}^* \mid \mathbf{x}_T\right] &= \boldsymbol{\Omega} + \left[(\boldsymbol{\tau}^* - \boldsymbol{\tau}) + (\boldsymbol{\Upsilon}^* - \boldsymbol{\Upsilon})\, \mathbf{x}_T\right]\left[(\boldsymbol{\tau}^* - \boldsymbol{\tau}) + (\boldsymbol{\Upsilon}^* - \boldsymbol{\Upsilon})\, \mathbf{x}_T\right]' \\ \mathsf{M}\left[\widetilde{\mathbf{e}}_{T+1} \mid \mathbf{x}_T\right] &= 2\boldsymbol{\Omega} + (\boldsymbol{\Upsilon}^* - \boldsymbol{\Upsilon})\, \Delta\mathbf{x}_T \Delta\mathbf{x}_T' \,(\boldsymbol{\Upsilon}^* - \boldsymbol{\Upsilon})'. \end{aligned}$$

These expressions simplify considerably if we assume that only $\boldsymbol{\tau}$ changes:

$$\begin{aligned} \mathsf{M}\left[\mathbf{e}_{T+1}^* \mid \mathbf{x}_T\right] &= \boldsymbol{\Omega} + (\boldsymbol{\tau}^* - \boldsymbol{\tau})\,(\boldsymbol{\tau}^* - \boldsymbol{\tau})' \\ \mathsf{M}\left[\widetilde{\mathbf{e}}_{T+1} \mid \mathbf{x}_T\right] &= 2\boldsymbol{\Omega}, \end{aligned}$$

so that intercept correcting pays if $\boldsymbol{\Omega} \prec (\boldsymbol{\tau}^* - \boldsymbol{\tau})(\boldsymbol{\tau}^* - \boldsymbol{\tau})'$, where '$\prec$' denotes smaller by a positive definite matrix. The increase in the variance must be smaller than the squared bias of the 'mechanistic' predictor induced by the structural break.

In practice, the forecaster may be interested in forecasting h-steps ahead, and a number of alternatives then exist. From (8.47), the actual value of the process (for a one-off change in $(\boldsymbol{\tau} : \boldsymbol{\Upsilon})$) is:

$$\mathbf{x}_{T+h} = \sum_{i=0}^{h-1} (\boldsymbol{\Upsilon}^*)^i \boldsymbol{\tau}^* + (\boldsymbol{\Upsilon}^*)^h \mathbf{x}_T + \sum_{i=0}^{h-1} (\boldsymbol{\Upsilon}^*)^i \boldsymbol{\nu}_{T+h-i} \tag{8.51}$$

which simplifies to:

$$\mathbf{x}_{T+h} = \sum_{i=0}^{h-1} \boldsymbol{\Upsilon}^i \boldsymbol{\tau}^* + \boldsymbol{\Upsilon}^h \mathbf{x}_T + \sum_{i=0}^{h-1} \boldsymbol{\Upsilon}^i \boldsymbol{\nu}_{T+h-i} \tag{8.52}$$

when only $\boldsymbol{\tau}$ changes.

We consider four methods of forecasting the value of $\mathbf{x}_{T+h}$. The first is simply the conditional expectation (based on the, now incorrect, in-sample model). The h-step generalization of $\widehat{\mathbf{x}}_{T+1}$ is:

$$\widehat{\mathbf{x}}_{T+h} = \sum_{i=0}^{h-1} \boldsymbol{\Upsilon}^i \boldsymbol{\tau} + \boldsymbol{\Upsilon}^h \mathbf{x}_T. \tag{8.53}$$

Secondly, we can hold the intercept correction constant over the forecast period, so that the period T error is added in at each step ahead. This is perhaps the most commonly used form of intercept correction, where the adjustment over the future is held constant at an average of the most recent errors (in our example, just the period T error). This amounts to solving:

$$\widetilde{\mathbf{x}}_{T+h} = \boldsymbol{\tau} + \boldsymbol{\Upsilon} \widetilde{\mathbf{x}}_{T+h-1} + \mathbf{e}_T^* \tag{8.54}$$

so that:

$$\widetilde{\mathbf{x}}_{T+h} = \widehat{\mathbf{x}}_{T+h} + \sum_{i=0}^{h-1} \boldsymbol{\Upsilon}^i \mathbf{e}_T^*. \tag{8.55}$$

Thirdly, only adjust the 1-step forecast:

$$\overrightarrow{\mathbf{x}}_{T+h} = \boldsymbol{\tau} + \boldsymbol{\Upsilon} \overrightarrow{\mathbf{x}}_{T+h-1}, \quad \overrightarrow{\mathbf{x}}_{T+1} = \widetilde{\mathbf{x}}_{T+1} \tag{8.56}$$

which implies that:

$$\overrightarrow{\mathbf{x}}_{T+h} = \widehat{\mathbf{x}}_{T+h} + \boldsymbol{\Upsilon}^{h-1} \mathbf{e}_T^*. \tag{8.57}$$

Finally, adjust the h-step forecast by the full amount of the period T error:

$$\overleftrightarrow{\mathbf{x}}_{T+h} = \widehat{\mathbf{x}}_{T+h} + \mathbf{e}_T^*. \tag{8.58}$$

We now compare these four strategies when only $\boldsymbol{\tau}$ changes, starting with the biases. These are given by:

$$\mathsf{E}\left[\mathbf{e}^{*}_{T+h} \mid \mathbf{x}_T\right] = \mathbf{x}_{T+h} - \widehat{\mathbf{x}}_{T+h} = \sum_{i=0}^{h-1} \boldsymbol{\Upsilon}^i \left(\boldsymbol{\tau}^* - \boldsymbol{\tau}\right) \tag{8.59}$$

$$\mathsf{E}\left[\widetilde{\mathbf{e}}_{T+h} \mid \mathbf{x}_T\right] = \mathbf{x}_{T+h} - \widetilde{\mathbf{x}}_{T+h} = \sum_{i=0}^{h-1} \boldsymbol{\Upsilon}^i \left(\boldsymbol{\tau}^* - \boldsymbol{\tau}\right) - \sum_{i=0}^{h-1} \boldsymbol{\Upsilon}^i \mathbf{e}^{*}_{T} = \mathbf{0} \tag{8.60}$$

$$\mathsf{E}\left[\overrightarrow{\mathbf{e}}_{T+h} \mid \mathbf{x}_T\right] = \mathbf{x}_{T+h} - \overrightarrow{\mathbf{x}}_{T+h} = \sum_{i=0}^{h-1} \boldsymbol{\Upsilon}^i \left(\boldsymbol{\tau}^* - \boldsymbol{\tau}\right) - \boldsymbol{\Upsilon}^{h-1} \mathbf{e}^{*}_{T} = \sum_{i=0}^{h-2} \boldsymbol{\Upsilon}^i \left(\boldsymbol{\tau}^* - \boldsymbol{\tau}\right) \tag{8.61}$$

$$\begin{aligned}\mathsf{E}\left[\overleftrightarrow{\mathbf{e}}_{T+h} \mid \mathbf{x}_T\right] &= \mathbf{x}_{T+h} - \overleftrightarrow{\mathbf{x}}_{T+h} = \sum_{i=0}^{h-1} \boldsymbol{\Upsilon}^i \left(\boldsymbol{\tau}^* - \boldsymbol{\tau}\right) - \mathbf{e}^{*}_{T} \\ &= \sum_{i=1}^{h-1} \boldsymbol{\Upsilon}^i \left(\boldsymbol{\tau}^* - \boldsymbol{\tau}\right).\end{aligned} \tag{8.62}$$

The second strategy yields unbiased forecasts for this form of structural break. When $\boldsymbol{\Upsilon} = \mathbf{0}$, so that $\mathsf{E}[\mathbf{x}_t] = \boldsymbol{\tau}, t < T$ and $\mathsf{E}[\mathbf{x}_t] = \boldsymbol{\tau}^*, t \geq T$, the fourth strategy (8.62) also yields unbiased forecasts.

For a scalar process y_t with parameter ρ and $0 < \rho < 1$:

$$\mathsf{E}\left[e^{*}_{T+h} \mid y_T\right] = \frac{\left(\tau^* - \tau\right)\left(1 - \rho^h\right)}{1 - \rho},$$

$$\mathsf{E}\left[\overrightarrow{e}_{T+h} \mid y_T\right] = \frac{\left(\tau^* - \tau\right)\left(1 - \rho^{h-1}\right)}{1 - \rho},$$

and:

$$\mathsf{E}\left[\overleftrightarrow{e}_{T+h} \mid y_T\right] = \frac{\left(\tau^* - \tau\right)\left(\rho - \rho^h\right)}{1 - \rho},$$

so that the ordering is:

$$\mathsf{E}\left[e^{*}_{T+h} \mid y_T\right] > \mathsf{E}\left[\overrightarrow{e}_{T+h} \mid y_T\right] > \mathsf{E}\left[\overleftrightarrow{e}_{T+h} \mid y_T\right].$$

Although the difference between (8.59) and (8.61) is only $o(h)$, all three forms of intercept correction result in smaller biases than the mechanistic predictor. Moreover, even if the process remains unchanged ($\boldsymbol{\tau}^* = \boldsymbol{\tau}$), there is no penalty in terms of bias from using one of the three forms of intercept correction.

As we now show, the penalty to intercept correcting when the process is unchanged is in terms of increased uncertainty. Consider now the conditional forecast-error variances of these four strategies in the vector case. These are straightforward to derive and are given by:

$$\mathsf{V}\left[\mathbf{e}^{*}_{T+h} \mid \mathbf{x}_T\right] = \sum_{i=0}^{h-1} \boldsymbol{\Upsilon}^i \boldsymbol{\Omega} \boldsymbol{\Upsilon}^{i\prime} \tag{8.63}$$

$$\mathsf{V}\left[\widetilde{\mathbf{e}}_{T+h} \mid \mathbf{x}_T\right] = 2\sum_{i=0}^{h-1} \boldsymbol{\Upsilon}^i \boldsymbol{\Omega} \boldsymbol{\Upsilon}^{i\prime} \tag{8.64}$$

$$\mathsf{V}\left[\overrightarrow{\mathbf{e}}_{T+h} \mid \mathbf{x}_T\right] = \sum_{i=0}^{h-1} \boldsymbol{\Upsilon}^i \boldsymbol{\Omega} \boldsymbol{\Upsilon}^{i\prime} + \boldsymbol{\Upsilon}^{h-1} \boldsymbol{\Omega} \boldsymbol{\Upsilon}^{h-1\prime} \tag{8.65}$$

$$\mathsf{V}\left[\overleftrightarrow{\mathbf{e}}_{T+h} \mid \mathbf{x}_T\right] = \sum_{i=0}^{h-1} \boldsymbol{\Upsilon}^i \boldsymbol{\Omega} \boldsymbol{\Upsilon}^{i\prime} + \boldsymbol{\Omega} \tag{8.66}$$

so that 'intercept correcting' results in larger forecast-error variances. The MSFE weights the biases and variances, and for the scalar process are given by:

$$\mathsf{E}\left[e^{*2}_{T+h} \mid y_T\right] = \left(\sum_{i=0}^{h-1} \rho^i \left(\tau^* - \tau\right)\right)^2 + \sigma^2_\epsilon \frac{1-\rho^{2h}}{1-\rho^2} \tag{8.67}$$

$$\mathsf{E}\left[\widetilde{e}^{2}_{T+h} \mid y_T\right] = 2\sigma^2_\epsilon \frac{1-\rho^{2h}}{1-\rho^2} \tag{8.68}$$

$$\mathsf{E}\left[\overrightarrow{e}^{2}_{T+h} \mid y_T\right] = \left(\sum_{i=0}^{h-2} \rho^i \left(\tau^* - \tau\right)\right)^2 + \sigma^2_\epsilon \frac{1-2\rho^{2h}+\rho^{2(h-1)}}{1-\rho^2} \tag{8.69}$$

$$\mathsf{E}\left[\overleftrightarrow{e}^{2}_{T+h} \mid y_T\right] = \left(\sum_{i=1}^{h-1} \rho^i \left(\tau^* - \tau\right)\right)^2 + \sigma^2_\epsilon \frac{2-\rho^{2h}-\rho^2}{1-\rho^2}. \tag{8.70}$$

From (8.67)–(8.70), for a sufficiently large value of $(\tau^* - \tau)$, holding the adjustment constant over the forecast period will result in the smallest MSFE.

Suppose now that there is only a one-off change in $\boldsymbol{\Upsilon}$ to $\boldsymbol{\Upsilon}^*$ (for $T, \ldots, T+H$). If we further assume that $\boldsymbol{\tau} = \mathbf{0}$, we can derive some interpretable conditions under which intercept corrections improve forecast accuracy. From (8.51) the actual value of the process in period $T+h$ is:

$$\mathbf{x}_{T+h} = \left(\boldsymbol{\Upsilon}^*\right)^h \mathbf{x}_T + \sum_{i=0}^{h-1} \left(\boldsymbol{\Upsilon}^*\right)^i \boldsymbol{\nu}_{T+h-i}. \tag{8.71}$$

The biases of the four forecasting methods in (8.53) to (8.58) are given by:

$$\mathsf{E}\left[\mathbf{e}^*_{T+h} \mid \mathbf{x}_T\right] = \left((\boldsymbol{\Upsilon}^*)^h - \boldsymbol{\Upsilon}^h\right)\mathbf{x}_T \tag{8.72}$$

$$\mathsf{E}\left[\widetilde{\mathbf{e}}_{T+h} \mid \mathbf{x}_T\right] = \left((\boldsymbol{\Upsilon}^*)^h - \boldsymbol{\Upsilon}^h - \sum_{i=0}^{h-1}\boldsymbol{\Upsilon}^i\left(\boldsymbol{\Upsilon}^* - \boldsymbol{\Upsilon}\right)\right)\mathbf{x}_T \tag{8.73}$$

$$\begin{aligned}\mathsf{E}\left[\overrightarrow{\mathbf{e}}_{T+h} \mid \mathbf{x}_T\right] &= \left((\boldsymbol{\Upsilon}^*)^h - \boldsymbol{\Upsilon}^h - \boldsymbol{\Upsilon}^{h-1}\left(\boldsymbol{\Upsilon}^* - \boldsymbol{\Upsilon}\right)\right)\mathbf{x}_T \\ &= \left((\boldsymbol{\Upsilon}^*)^h - \boldsymbol{\Upsilon}^{h-1}\boldsymbol{\Upsilon}^*\right)\mathbf{x}_T \end{aligned} \tag{8.74}$$

$$\mathsf{E}\left[\overleftrightarrow{\mathbf{e}}_{T+h} \mid \mathbf{x}_T\right] = \left((\boldsymbol{\Upsilon}^*)^h - \boldsymbol{\Upsilon}^h - \left(\boldsymbol{\Upsilon}^* - \boldsymbol{\Upsilon}\right)\right)\mathbf{x}_T. \tag{8.75}$$

We can obtain some insight into (8.72)–(8.75) by again considering the scalar case with $0 < \rho < 1$. The bias of the conditional expectation is $o(h)$, despite the change in the slope, and although (8.75) yields unbiased forecasts for $h = 1$, the limiting value of the bias is $(\rho^* - \rho)y_T$, which is the value of the adjustment. (8.74) is also unbiased for $h = 1$, and like the conditional expectation (8.72), is $o(h)$. We can write:

$$\mathsf{E}\left[\overrightarrow{e}_{T+h} \mid y_T\right] = \mathsf{E}\left[e^*_{T+h} \mid y_T\right] - \rho^{h-1}\left(\rho^* - \rho\right)y_T,$$

where $(\rho^* - \rho) > 0$, so that for $h > 1$ this intercept correction reduces the bias if:

$$\left|\rho^{h-1}\left(\rho^* - \rho\right)y_T\right| < 2\left|\mathsf{E}\left[e^*_{T+h} \mid y_T\right]\right|.$$

Finally, (8.73) is unbiased for $h = 1$ but has a limiting bias of $(\rho^* - \rho)/(1 - \rho)$. Thus, the three types of intercept correction yield unbiased predictors for 1-step ahead, but only (8.74) is unbiased as $h \to \infty$ (along with the conditional expectation).

Lastly, consider the behaviour of the forecast-error variances and MSFEs:

$$\mathsf{V}\left[\mathbf{e}^*_{T+h} \mid \mathbf{x}_T\right] = \sum_{i=0}^{h-1}\left(\boldsymbol{\Upsilon}^*\right)^i\boldsymbol{\Omega}\left(\boldsymbol{\Upsilon}^*\right)^{i\prime} \tag{8.76}$$

$$\mathsf{V}\left[\widetilde{\mathbf{e}}_{T+h} \mid \mathbf{x}_T\right] = \sum_{i=0}^{h-1}\left(\boldsymbol{\Upsilon}^*\right)^i\boldsymbol{\Omega}\left(\boldsymbol{\Upsilon}^*\right)^{i\prime} + \sum_{i=0}^{h-1}\boldsymbol{\Upsilon}^i\boldsymbol{\Omega}\boldsymbol{\Upsilon}^{i\prime} \tag{8.77}$$

$$\mathsf{V}\left[\overrightarrow{\mathbf{e}}_{T+h} \mid \mathbf{x}_T\right] = \sum_{i=0}^{h-1}\left(\boldsymbol{\Upsilon}^*\right)^i\boldsymbol{\Omega}\left(\boldsymbol{\Upsilon}^*\right)^{i\prime} + \boldsymbol{\Upsilon}^{h-1}\boldsymbol{\Omega}\boldsymbol{\Upsilon}^{h-1\prime} \tag{8.78}$$

$$\mathsf{V}\left[\overleftrightarrow{\mathbf{e}}_{T+h} \mid \mathbf{x}_T\right] = \sum_{i=0}^{h-1}\left(\boldsymbol{\Upsilon}^*\right)^i\boldsymbol{\Omega}\left(\boldsymbol{\Upsilon}^*\right)^{i\prime} + \boldsymbol{\Omega}. \tag{8.79}$$

As in the case of a changed intercept, 'intercept correcting' results in larger forecast-error variances. The MSFEs are obtained by combining the squares of the biases in (8.72)–(8.75) with the forecast-error variances in (8.76)–(8.79). The resulting formulae are somewhat hard to interpret, so we focus on comparisons which might be of particular interest. Only the first and third strategies (the conditional expectation, and adjusting only the 1- step forecast) are unbiased as $h \to \infty$, and a comparison of the two on MSFE may be useful. For the scalar process, the MSFEs are given by:

$$\mathsf{E}\left[e^{*2}_{T+h} \mid y_T\right] = \left((\rho^*)^h - \rho^h\right)^2 y_T^2 + \sigma_\epsilon^2 \frac{1-(\rho^*)^{2h}}{1-(\rho^*)^2} \tag{8.80}$$

$$\mathsf{E}\left[\overrightarrow{e}^{\,2}_{T+h} \mid y_T\right] = \left((\rho^*)^h - \rho^{h-1}\rho^*\right)^2 y_T^2 + \sigma_\epsilon^2 \left(\frac{1-(\rho^*)^{2h}}{1-(\rho^*)^2} + \rho^{2(h-1)}\right). \tag{8.81}$$

For $h = 1$, the adjusted forecast has a smaller MSFE than the mechanistic predictor. For $h > 1$ we calculate the relative gain/loss to intercept correcting as (8.80) less (8.81) divided by the error variance:

$$\begin{aligned}\mathsf{R}_l\left[e^*_{T+h}, \overrightarrow{e}_{T+h}\right] &= \sigma_\epsilon^{-2}\left(\rho^{2h} - \rho^{2(h-1)}(\rho^*)^2 - 2\rho^h(\rho^*)^h + 2\rho^{h-1}(\rho^*)^{h+1}\right) \\ &\quad -\rho^{2(h-1)} \\ &= \sigma_\epsilon^{-2}\rho^{h-1}\left(\rho^{h+1} - \rho^{h-1}(\rho^*)^2 - 2\rho(\rho^*)^h + 2(\rho^*)^{h+1}\right) \\ &\quad -\rho^{2(h-1)}\end{aligned}$$

which could take either sign. As $h \to \infty$, $\mathsf{R}_l[\cdot] \to 0$; when $\rho = 0$, $\mathsf{R}_l[\cdot] = 0$; and when $\rho \simeq 1$, $\mathsf{R}_l[\cdot] \doteqdot \sigma_\epsilon^{-2}(1-(\rho^*)^2) - 1$, so that for $\rho^* < 1$ intercept correcting will pay for a sufficiently small error variance.

In this section, we have shown that appropriate forms of intercept corrections can partially robustify (h-step) forecasts against structural breaks. For changes in intercepts, the appropriate correction will often be to hold the adjustment constant over the forecast period. For changes in slope parameters, a one-off adjustment to the 1-step forecast will yield unbiased forecasts for $h = 1$ and for large h, but the results for comparisons to the mechanistic predictor for medium h were inconclusive.

Clements and Hendry (1996b) present an empirical illustration of the modelling of UK wages, prices and unemployment which demonstrates the bias reductions that can be achieved by the use of intercept corrections, although only at the cost of a considerable increase in forecast-error variance.

8.7 Model mis-specification

Suspected model mis-specification is perhaps the most obvious and best understood rationale for extrapolating non-zero residuals into the future. The examples in the previous sections can either be adapted to allow for model mis-specification, or directly indicate the implications for intercept corrections of certain types of model mis-specification. In section 8.6, for example, we analysed the consequences of a changed DGP and an unchanged model. The analysis could be adapted so that the DGP is unchanged and the model mis-specified. In the analysis of setting the forecast 'back on track' in section 8.5, model mis-specification could be incorporated by amending the assumption of an innovation disturbance term, allowing for serial correlation, etc. For example, suppose that the econometric model is such that v_t in (8.13) is not a serially uncorrelated innovation relative to y_{t-1}, then (8.43) becomes:

$$\mathsf{E}\left[e_{T+1}e_T\right] = \mathsf{V}\left[\widehat{\psi}\right]\psi\sigma_y^2 + \mathsf{V}\left[\widehat{\psi}\right]\mathsf{E}\left[v_T y_{T-1}\right] + \mathsf{E}\left[v_{T+1}v_T\right], \qquad (8.82)$$

so that setting the forecast back on track is more likely to be successful if $\mathsf{E}[v_T y_{T-1}] > 0$ and $\mathsf{E}[v_{T+1}v_T] > 0$.

8.8 Overview

Forecasters' adjustments to model-based forecasts are endemic. Published forecasts based on large-scale macroeconometric models reflect to varying degrees the properties of the models and the adjustments made by their proprietors in arriving at a final forecast. In this chapter, we have sought to provide a general framework for analysing why such adjustments might work. We suggest a number of rationales for intercept corrections, which dovetail with the sources of forecast error expounded in the taxonomy of chapter 7. For example, parameter change or structural breaks may be partly mitigated by appropriate adjustments, and we have analysed the likely costs and benefits of so doing in terms of the properties of the resulting forecast errors. Another example we considered countered the impact of parameter estimation uncertainty by combining the estimated model forecast with predictions based on the unconditional first moment of the process.

8.9 Appendix: Estimating the forecast origin

First, consider estimating y_T from $\mathcal{I}_T^2$. From (8.14):

$$\mathsf{E}\left[y_T \mid y_T^*\right] = \mathsf{E}\left[y_T^* \mid y_T^*\right] - \mathsf{E}\left[\eta_T \mid y_T^*\right]. \qquad (8.83)$$

Define λ_T by:

$$\mathsf{E}\left[\eta_T \mid y_T^*\right] = \lambda_T y_T^*, \qquad (8.84)$$

where $u_T = \eta_T - \lambda_T y_T^*$ is orthogonal to y_T^* by construction. Then for $\sigma_T^2 = \mathsf{E}[\eta_T^2]$:

$$\lambda_T = \frac{\mathsf{E}\left[\eta_T y_T^*\right]}{\mathsf{E}\left[\left(y_T^*\right)^2\right]} = \frac{\sigma_T^2}{\mathsf{E}\left[y_T^2\right] + \sigma_T^2} = \frac{\sigma_T^2}{\sigma_y^2 + \sigma_T^2}, \qquad (8.85)$$

where $\sigma_y^2 = \sigma_v^2/(1-\psi^2)$, so $0 \leq \lambda_T \leq 1$. Then (8.83) becomes:

$$\mathsf{E}\left[y_T \mid y_T^*\right] = y_T^* - \lambda_T y_T^* = (1-\lambda_T)\, y_T^* \equiv k_T y_T^*. \tag{8.86}$$

Next, from $\mathcal{I}_T^1$ (allowing $\sigma_s^2 \neq 0$, $s = T^e+1, \ldots, T$, so the last $T - T^e$ observations are assumed to be measured with error):

$$\begin{aligned}
\mathsf{E}\left[y_T \mid \mathcal{I}_T^1\right] &= \psi\mathsf{E}\left[y_{T-1} \mid \mathcal{I}_T^1\right] + \mathsf{E}\left[v_T \mid \mathcal{I}_T^1\right] \\
&= \psi\mathsf{E}\left[y_{T-1}^* \mid \mathcal{I}_T^1\right] - \psi\mathsf{E}\left[\eta_{T-1} \mid \mathcal{I}_T^1\right] \\
&= \psi y_{T-1}^* - \psi\lambda_{T-1} y_{T-1}^* \\
&= \psi k_{T-1} y_{T-1}^*.
\end{aligned} \tag{8.87}$$

Underlying (8.87) is the relation $y_T = \psi y_{T-1}^* - \psi\eta_{T-1} + v_T$, and underlying (8.83) is $y_T = y_T^* - \eta_T$, so that taking a convex combination of these:

$$y_T = \mu\psi y_{T-1}^* - \mu\psi\eta_{T-1} + \mu v_T + (1-\mu)\, y_T^* - (1-\mu)\,\eta_T. \tag{8.88}$$

Thus, the composite predictor formed from that combination is $\mathsf{E}[y_T|\mathcal{I}_T^*]$ with:

$$\begin{aligned}
\widetilde{y}_T &= \mu\psi k_{T-1} y_{T-1}^* + (1-\mu)\, k_T y_T^* \\
&= \widehat{y}_T - \mu\left(\widehat{y}_T - \psi\widehat{y}_{T-1}\right),
\end{aligned} \tag{8.89}$$

where $\widehat{y}_T = k_T y_T^*$. This leads to (8.23) in section 8.3 when $\widehat{y}_{T-1} = y_{T-1}$ (which assumes $\sigma_{T-1}^2 = 0$, so that (8.87) is simply $\mathsf{E}[y_T|\mathcal{I}_T^1] = \psi y_{T-1}$).

To calculate the optimal value of μ, form the prediction error from (8.88) and (8.89), and use $1 - k_{T-1} = \lambda_{T-1}$:

$$\begin{aligned}
y_T - \widetilde{y}_T &= -\mu\psi\eta_{T-1} + \mu v_T + (1-\mu)\, y_T^* - (1-\mu)\,\eta_T \\
&\quad +\mu\psi\lambda_{T-1} y_{T-1}^* - (1-\mu)\, k_T y_T^* \\
&= \mu v_T - \mu\psi\eta_{T-1} - (1-\mu)\,\eta_T + \mu\psi\lambda_{T-1} y_{T-1}^* + (1-\mu)\,\lambda_T y_T^* \\
&= \mu v_T - \mu\psi u_{T-1} - (1-\mu)\, u_T
\end{aligned} \tag{8.90}$$

then minimize $\mathsf{E}[(y_T - \widetilde{y}_T)^2]$ with respect to μ, to give μ^*, say. From (8.89):

$$\breve{y}_T = \widehat{y}_T - \mu^*\left(\widehat{y}_T - \psi\widehat{y}_{T-1}\right). \tag{8.91}$$

For the special case in the text, $\sigma_{T-1}^2 = 0$, so from (8.83) and (8.84):

$$\sigma_T^2 = \lambda_T^2(\sigma_y^2 + \sigma_T^2) + \sigma_{u_T}^2$$

and hence:

$$\sigma_{u_T}^2 = \left(1 - \lambda_T^2\right)\sigma_T^2 - \lambda_T^2\sigma_y^2 = \sigma_y^2\frac{\sigma_T^2}{\sigma_y^2 + \sigma_T^2} = \frac{\sigma_y^2}{1 + \sigma_y^2/\sigma_T^2}$$

using (8.85). Thus:

$$\mathsf{E}\left[\left(y_T - \widetilde{y}_T\right)^2\right] = \mathsf{E}\left[\left(\mu v_T - (1-\mu)\, u_T\right)^2\right] = \mu^2\sigma_v^2 + (1-\mu)^2\,\sigma_{u_T}^2. \tag{8.92}$$

Then, minimizing $\mathsf{E}[(y_T - \widetilde{y}_T)^2]$ with respect to μ implies:

$$\frac{\partial\left(\mu^2\sigma_v^2 + (1-\mu)^2\,\sigma_{u_T}^2\right)}{\partial\mu} = 2\mu\sigma_v^2 - 2\,(1-\mu)\,\sigma_{u_T}^2 = 0 \tag{8.93}$$

yielding:

$$\mu^* = \frac{\sigma_{u_T}^2}{\left(\sigma_v^2 + \sigma_{u_T}^2\right)} = \frac{\sigma_T^2}{\left((2-\psi^2)\,\sigma_T^2 + \sigma_v^2\right)}. \tag{8.94}$$

From (8.94), $\mu^* = 0$ when the period T observation is error free ($\sigma_T^2 = 0$ and $\lambda_T = 0$), and since $\lambda_T \rightarrow 1$ as $\sigma_T^2 \rightarrow \infty$, $\mu^* \rightarrow 1$ when there is no useful information in the period T observation.

Chapter 9

Forecasting using leading indicators

We now consider the use of indices of leading indicators in forecasting and macroeconomic modelling. The procedures used to select the components and construct the indices are examined, noting that the composition of indicator systems gets altered frequently. Cointegration within the indices, and between their components and macroeconomic variables are considered as well as the role of co-breaking to mitigate regime shifts. Issues of model choice and data-based restrictions are investigated. A framework is proposed for index analysis and selecting indices, and applied to the UK longer-leading indicator. The effects of adding leading indicators to macro models are considered theoretically and for UK data.[1]

9.1 Introduction

An indicator is any variable believed informative about another variable of interest. An index is a weighted average of a set of component indicators. The weights may be fixed as in a Laspeyres index for (say) real gross national product (GNP), or changing over time as in a Divisia index, such as that for retail prices (RPI). The weights may be based on 'natural' choices such as value shares (like the RPI or FTSE100), or *ad hoc* (as when weighting, say, consumer credit, retail sales and new car registrations, to produce an index of 'consumer activity', or inflation and unemployment, for a 'misery' index).

Next, a leading indicator is any variable whose outcome is known in advance of a related variable that it is desired to forecast. A composite leading index (denoted CLI) is a combination of such variables. We will discuss the selection of indicators, methods of constructing indices from these, and the theoretical forecasting properties such indicators and indexes may have. Their use in isolation, and as a component time series in another forecasting procedure, such as VAR, will be considered.

There has been a recent revival of interest in using CLIs of economic activity in forecasting the state of the economy: see, *inter alia*, Artis, Bladen-Hovell, Osborn, Smith and Zhang (1995), Diebold and Rudebusch (1989, 1991a, 1991b), Koch and

[1] This chapter is co-authored with Rebecca A. Emerson, and is based on Emerson and Hendry (1996).

Rasche (1988), Lahiri and Moore (1991), Neftci (1979), Parigi and Schlitzer (1995), Samuelson (1987), Stock and Watson (1989, 1992), Weller (1979) and Zarnowitz and Braun (1992). The revival seems partly in response to perceived forecasting failures by macroeconometric systems, but in part is also due to developments in leading-indicator theory. Most work has been done on the US indicator system, perhaps due to the importance placed on leading indicators in the US by their popular press. For earlier work, see, e.g., Moore (1961) and Shiskin and Moore (1968). The analysis in Emerson and Hendry (1996) was prompted by the 'real-time' evaluations of leading indicators in forecasting by Diebold and Rudebusch (1991b) and Stock and Watson (1992) who show a marked deterioration for CLIs of post-sample performance relative to within-sample findings. Such an outcome might be anticipated in non-stationary time series (both integrated and subject to regime shifts), and suggests there may be dangers in including CLIs as a part of other forecasting procedures. Indeed, the composition of CLIs gets altered frequently in practice, so variables do not seem to lead systematically for prolonged periods. The many publications by the UK Central Statistical Office (CSO; now ONS denoting Office for National Statistics) document the regular changes to their system since 1975; many changes also occurred in the CLIs of other countries (see Emerson, 1994, for details, background and bibliographic perspective).

Although CLIs may nevertheless have a role in providing estimates of the current state of the economy, we do not investigate that issue further here (see section 8.3, where they may be usable in formulating appropriate intercept corrections; and section 7.4.4 where they could be incorporated into determining a better estimate of the initial state of the economy). Nor is the claim that CLIs specifically predict business cycle 'turning points' considered here: we are concerned with systematic 'leading' (or lagging) at all points of the cycle.

The Harvard A-B-C curves were the earliest forecasting system (see Persons, 1924), but fell into disrepute after claims that they failed to predict the 1929 crash and subsequent depression (but see Samuelson, 1987). Indicators that occurred in early work included such variables as the output of pig-iron and ton-miles of rail shipments, neither of which would be selected today: the dangers in using the largest *ex post* lagged correlations to forecast are well illustrated by Coen, Gomme and Kendall (1969). The current system of business-cycle indicators began with the seminal work of Mitchell and Burns (1938) and Burns and Mitchell (1946). The criticism in Koopmans (1947) that Burns and Mitchell's work on business cycles and their indicators lacked a microeconomic theory basis often recurs (see, e.g., Auerbach, 1982), as does Koopmans' complaint that the notion of the reference cycle lacked a secure definition. Although Vining (1949) offered a robust defence of the Burns–Mitchell approach in terms of model discovery, his arguments did not carry the day (see Hendry and Morgan, 1995).

As presaged in chapter 1, the basis for our evaluation of leading indicators in forecasting is an integrated-cointegrated economy subject to regime shifts. The analysis of CLIs begins in section 9.2 by describing the current CLIs in the UK, their components and their method of construction. Next, section 9.3 considers the theoretical foundations for the indices, the procedures used to select their components and methods of constructing CLIs. When the economy is an integrated dynamic system, information losses may arise from ignoring cointegration within the indices (i.e., between the indicators) and between indices and target variables, leading to inefficient forecasts. Perhaps more seriously, as the economy seems subject to intermittent structural breaks and indicators do not seek to embody causal links (one interpretation of the Koopmans, 1947, critique), CLIs seem almost bound to fail. Here our analysis introduces the concept of co-breaking, whereby breaks are eliminated by linear combinations of variables, analogous to cointegration removing unit roots. We believe co-breaking is unlikely for CLIs, and helps explain the non-systematic nature of the data correlations. Section 9.4 presents a framework for constant-parameter processes: generalizations to non-linear processes, longer lags and non-constant parameters were considered by Emerson and Hendry (1996).

We then investigate the use of CLIs in macroeconomic modelling and forecasting. Section 9.5 undertakes an empirical analysis of the UK longer-leading indicator, focusing on the degree of integration of the indicators and of cointegration between the components. Section 9.6 analyses the addition of LIs to econometric models for forecasting, and section 9.7 applies that analysis to a small monetary model of the UK.

9.2 Current UK CLIs

As of January 1994, cyclical indicators for the UK had been unaltered since July 1993. The CSO calculates two leading indicators for the UK economy: the first is constructed to lead by a year or more (called the longer-leading indicator, LLI); the other is intended to have a median lead of six months (the shorter-leading indicator, SLI). They are published monthly in *Economic Trends*.

Using GDP as the measure of aggregate economic activity, the individual indicators are chosen using a computer program developed by Moore and Shiskin (1967) for the National Bureau of Economic Research (NBER) in the United States. For the exact list of criteria, which are similar to those used in the US, see Central Statistical Office (1975). In the US, the NBER computer program selects a set of indicators based on a scoring system giving points for (to quote):

> cyclical timing, economic significance, statistical adequacy, conformity to the business cycle, smoothness, prompt availability (currency), and revisions.

The system of 'scoring' economic variables to select components of the UK CLIs entails giving each economic series points out of 100, based on six broad categories. A possible maximum 20 points is awarded for each of the categories of economic significance, statistical adequacy, conformity (to the business cycle) and timing. A possible maximum of 10 points is awarded for each of the categories of currency and smoothness. Although this system of scoring economic variables is implemented with the aim of using the highest scoring variables, in practice human judgement may be needed to make the final selection of variables (see, e.g., Zarnowitz and Boschan, 1977b).

The current components of the UK LLI, denoted $I_{L,t}^{UK}$, are the three-month rate of interest on prime bank bills (inverted), denoted R_{3t}; total dwelling starts for Great Britain (the UK excluding Northern Ireland), S_t; the inverted yield curve ($R_{3t}-R_{bt}$, where R_{bt} is the 20-year bond rate); the financial surplus/deficit of industrial and commercial companies in 1990 prices (deflated by the GDP deflator), D_t; and the optimism balance from the Confederation of British Industry (CBI) survey, O_t. The quarterly components of the longer-leading indicator are shown in figures 9.1a–d and reveal quite disparate time-series behaviour.

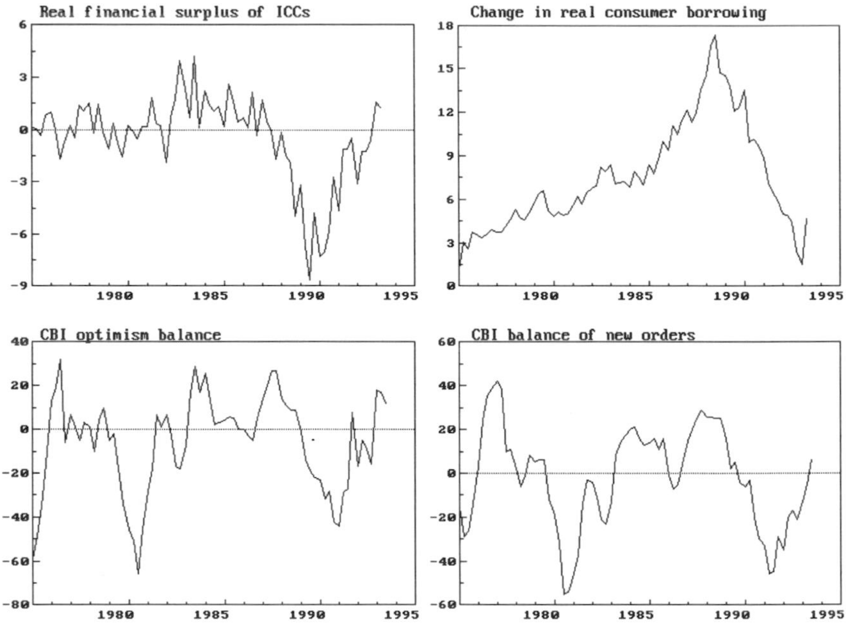

Figure 9.1 Time series of UK quarterly leading indicators

The components of the UK SLI, $I_{S,t}^{UK}$, are new car registrations, N_t; the balance of new orders from the past four months from the CBI survey, B_t; the consumer confidence index from the EC/Gallup survey, G_t; the change in consumers' outstanding borrowing in 1990 prices (deflated by the GDP deflator), L_t; and *The Financial Times* Actuaries' 500-share index of common stock prices, F_t. The monthly components of the indices, shown in figures 9.2a–d, have similar 'cyclical' patterns but are not modelled here as the macroeconomic system we use is quarterly: the higher frequency of the SLI is obviously one of its advantages. Figure 9.3 compares the time series of the UK and US composite leading indices to illustrate the considerable differences in their trajectories. They are set to the value of 100 in their base month (mid 1991 for the LLI and mid 1992 for the SLI). The method of construction of the CLIs from their components is noted in Emerson and Hendry (1996); Central Statistical Office (1983) and Moore (1993) provide more exact descriptions.

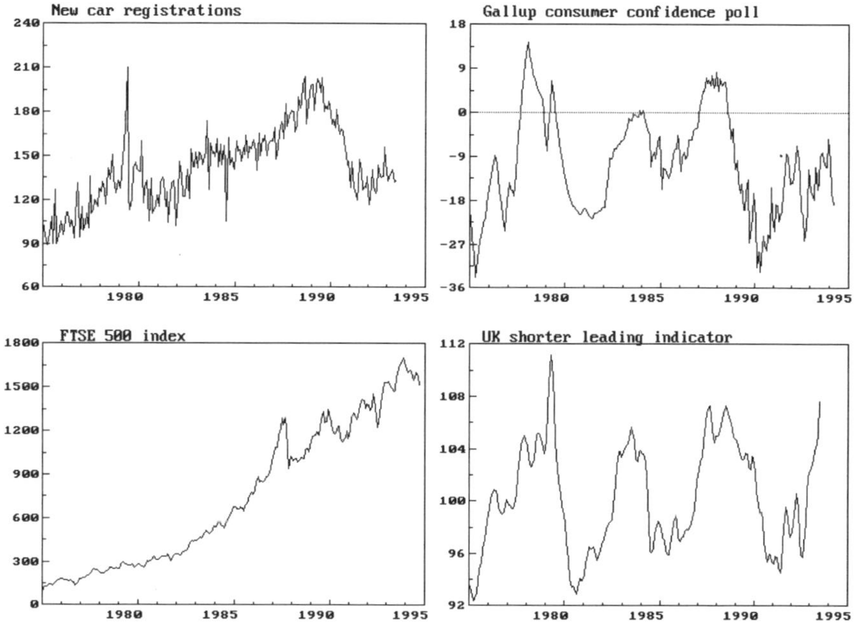

Figure 9.2 Time series of UK monthly leading indicators

9.3 Analysis of CLIs

Emerson and Hendry (1996) examine the foundations for CLIs, noting their attempt to eliminate the noise in individual indicators by averaging across many series and sectors of the economy to reflect different causes of cyclical fluctuations (see, e.g., Zarnowitz and Boschan, 1977a, p.173). Components of CLIs are usually chosen for having high bivariate correlations with the variable they are intended to lead, although the robustness of correlations to structural change has been doubted since Koopmans (1937). Despite emphasizing their systematically leading, the construction process for CLIs otherwise ignores the time-series properties of the components, including dynamics and cointegration. Thus, the autoregressive nature of aggregate economic activity, which makes it forecastable in part, is ignored. Alternatively expressed, CLIs sometimes impose strong

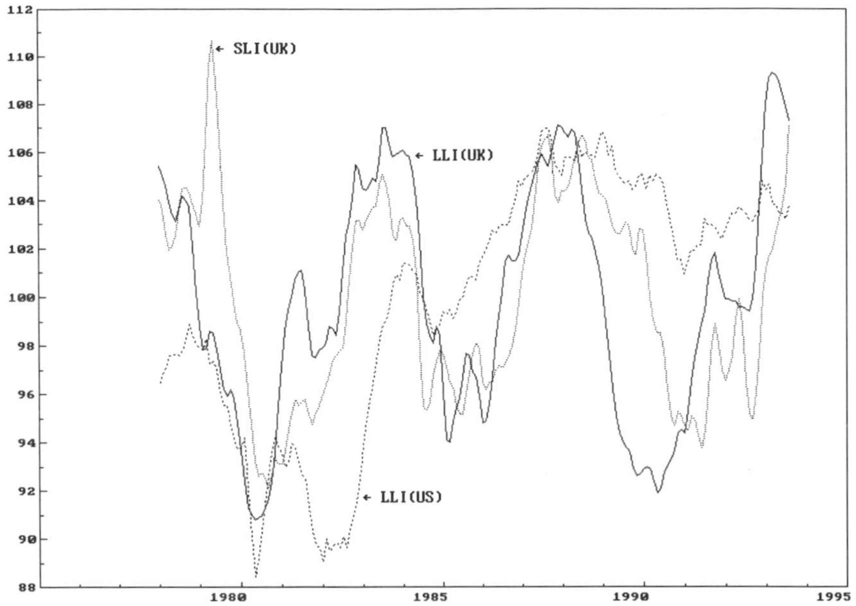

Figure 9.3 Shorter (SLI) and longer (LLI) UK and US leading indicators

restrictions on dynamic systems relative to macroeconomic forecasting methods, an issue analysed in section 9.4.2.

By construction, CLIs aim to be *ex-post* efficient, although *ex-ante* efficiency is needed for prediction. If the correlation structure remained constant, the latter aim would be achieved, but the frequent alterations in the composition of CLIs due to a deteriorating predictive performance suggests it does not. For example, Diebold and Rudebusch (1991a, 1991b) demonstrate that the current and past US CLIs are not efficient *ex ante* due to this difficulty. Also, Stock and Watson (1989, 1992) demonstrated that some alternative CLIs constructed for real-time forecasting by a more formal probabilistic approach were also *ex-post* inefficient.

9.3.1 Integration and cointegration

The construction of CLIs rarely takes account of the possibly different orders of integration of the components (I(1), I(0), or perhaps I(2)): Nelson and Plosser (1982) and Campbell and Mankiw (1987) discuss the empirical frequency of unit roots in aggregate economic time series. The presence of mixtures of I(0) and I(1) variables can complicate inference (including the choice of appropriate critical values: see, e.g., Sims, Stock and Watson, 1990), and remains potentially prone to 'nonsense regressions' problems in the absence of cointegration (see Hendry, 1980 and Banerjee, Dolado, Galbraith and Hendry, 1993). This suggests reducing all components of indicators to a common degree of integration, perhaps selected to ensure cointegration with the target.

Further, the construction process rarely involves formal tests for cointegration between the components, or with aggregate economic activity. For example, if a CLI is cointegrated with the levels of a set of variables such as consumption and income (c and y), then it cannot be cointegrated with $\mathsf{I}(0)$ linear combinations of these (e.g., $s = y - c$) when c and y are $\mathsf{I}(1)$, and s is $\mathsf{I}(0)$. Once data are integrated, care is required in specifying precisely what variable the CLI is intended to lead if the forecasts are not to be inefficient – or even irrelevant – for a given choice. Our framework allows for integrated-cointegrated time series, since we have shown above that these attributes influence how the target process is forecast. A well-known result (see Granger, 1986) is that an efficient forecast must be cointegrated with the outcome, and hence there must be Granger (1969) causality in at least one direction. If a forecast is not cointegrated with the outcome, it cannot be efficient at any horizon, so CLIs that are not cointegrated with targets must be inefficient, and their automatic inclusion potentially detracts from forecast accuracy. Conversely, if CLIs are cointegrated with targets, they must be related by Granger causality in one direction. These seem valuable attributes even if no unique MSFE ranking is possible at short horizons between cointegrated and non-cointegrated indicators (see chapters 3 and 6). Below, we consider whether cointegrating vectors may be useful leading indicators.

The UK SLIs and LLIs are mainly constructed from differenced data, but contain series which might be integrated of order one. In section 9.5 we consider whether the information contained in the UK components is efficiently used, and find that, empirically, both the UK indices allow the unit-root hypothesis to be rejected. This is also true of the cointegrating vectors, but the latter seem to produce better forecasts for the data set used here.

9.3.2 Co-breaking

The evidence in Diebold and Rudebusch (1989, 1991a, 1991b) and Stock and Watson (1989, 1992), and the changes made to the UK CLIs, suggest that the relationships within and between aggregate economic activity and indicators are not constant over time. Parameter non-constancy within-sample is testable, but present methods of constructing CLIs do not appear to check this key aspect.

Structural breaks in relationships may or may not be related across variables, in an analogous way to cointegration. When breaks between series in a forecast relation and their target are unrelated, predictive failure will ensue, so to avoid this significant problem, the breaks must be accounted for by the forecasting procedure. The concept of co-breaking in Hendry (1995c) considers conditions under which regime shifts cancel across linear combinations of variables, such that the transformed sets do not depend on the breaks. Cancellation of breaks could occur because of coincidentally offsetting effects. However across many breaks, luck seems unlikely to persist, leading to poor forecasts. A genuine relationship may fare better, highlighting the key distinction between an indicator – which is non-causal of, and non-caused by, the target – and a causally related variable. The former is unlikely to systematically experience the same shifts as the target. While non-constant processes pose problems for all forecasting devices, an important use of an econometric system is to explain why breaks occur, and to progress towards a more robust (deeper) parameterization than that which characterizes phenomena directly.

The converse difficulty for CLIs is that breaks can occur for reasons that would not affect an econometric model with co-breaking relations. For example, the demand for M2 depends on relative rates of return, and hence alters for portfolio reasons as well as transactions changes: the demand function could be stable for a regime shift in interest rate policy, even though the correlation with GNP was unstable. Indeed, the 1989–90 US recession was not preceded by a large downturn in monetary variables and thus CLIs which relied heavily on that relationship had problems picking up the downturn (see Stock and Watson, 1992). The behaviour of unemployment in the UK leading the 1991–92 recovery may be another example of a change in structure (usually it is a 'lagging indicator').

The absence of co-breaking may be the main reason for predictive failure in indicators that lack a causal relation to the target. Indicators with a causal basis, that are both cointegrated with and co-break with the target, will maintain constant relationships with that target and hence provide a useful forecasting procedure, but one that is tantamount to an econometric model.

9.4 A constant-parameter framework for index analysis

Being a weighted linear function of a set of indicators, a CLI can be interpreted as a restriction on the vector of aggregate economic time series. We now consider an integrated dynamic system with constant parameters to investigate the consequences of constructing CLIs using only contemporaneous values of variables.

As before, $\mathbf{x}_t$ denotes the vector of n observable economic variables, and $\mathbf{i}_t$ is a $p \times 1$ vector of individual leading indicators, formed into the CLI g_t, to lead an index of economic activity, $a_t = \boldsymbol{\lambda}'\mathbf{x}_t$, where $\boldsymbol{\lambda}$ is an $n \times 1$ vector of coefficients. We assume that the index weights are fixed for simplicity, so:

$$g_t = \boldsymbol{\phi}'\mathbf{i}_t, \tag{9.1}$$

where $\boldsymbol{\phi}$ is a $p \times 1$ vector of weights. Finally, $\mathbf{i}_t$ is a subset of $\mathbf{x}_t$ given by $\mathbf{i}_t = \mathbf{S}\mathbf{x}_t$ where $\mathbf{S}$ is $p \times n$. Empirically, the highest frequency involved in the $\mathbf{i}_t$ exceeds that at which most of the $\mathbf{x}_t$ are observed, but we assume a common time unit of a quarter, so the $\mathbf{i}_t$ here may be time aggregated.

The DGP is our usual first-order $\mathsf{I}(1)$ VAR:

$$\mathbf{x}_t = \boldsymbol{\tau} + \boldsymbol{\Upsilon}\mathbf{x}_{t-1} + \mathbf{v}_t, \tag{9.2}$$

where $\mathbf{v}_t \sim \mathsf{IN}_n[\mathbf{0}, \boldsymbol{\Omega}]$, and $\boldsymbol{\Upsilon}$ has no eigenvalues outside the unit circle.[2] As in section 7.2, $\boldsymbol{\Upsilon} = \mathbf{I}_n + \boldsymbol{\alpha}\boldsymbol{\beta}'$, such that $\boldsymbol{\beta}'\mathbf{x}_t$ is $\mathsf{I}(0)$. Letting $\boldsymbol{\tau} = \boldsymbol{\gamma} - \boldsymbol{\alpha}\boldsymbol{\mu}$:

$$\Delta\mathbf{x}_t = \boldsymbol{\gamma} + \boldsymbol{\alpha}\left(\boldsymbol{\beta}'\mathbf{x}_{t-1} - \boldsymbol{\mu}\right) + \mathbf{v}_t, \tag{9.3}$$

where $\mathsf{E}[\Delta\mathbf{x}_t] = \boldsymbol{\gamma}$ $(n \times 1)$ and $\mathsf{E}[\boldsymbol{\beta}'\mathbf{x}_t] = \boldsymbol{\mu}$ $(r \times 1)$ so that $\boldsymbol{\beta}'\boldsymbol{\gamma} = \mathbf{0}$ (which imposes $(n - r$ restrictions). The VEqCM in (9.3) is the focus of our analysis, but we briefly consider the issues that arise when $(\boldsymbol{\tau}, \boldsymbol{\Upsilon}, \boldsymbol{\Omega})$ are not constant over time.

9.4.1 Activity index

Given $\boldsymbol{\lambda}$, a_t is a reparameterization and reduction of $\mathbf{x}_t$ defined from (9.2) by:

$$a_t = \boldsymbol{\lambda}'\mathbf{x}_t = \boldsymbol{\lambda}'\boldsymbol{\tau} + \boldsymbol{\lambda}'\boldsymbol{\Upsilon}\mathbf{x}_{t-1} + \boldsymbol{\lambda}'\mathbf{v}_t = \mu_0 + \mu_1 a_{t-1} + \eta_t, \tag{9.4}$$

where $\mu_0 = \boldsymbol{\lambda}'\boldsymbol{\tau}$, and η_t is:

$$\eta_t = \boldsymbol{\lambda}'\left(\boldsymbol{\Upsilon} - \mu_1\mathbf{I}_n\right)\mathbf{x}_{t-1} + \boldsymbol{\lambda}'\mathbf{v}_t = \boldsymbol{\lambda}'\left(\left[1 - \mu_1\right]\mathbf{I}_n + \boldsymbol{\alpha}\boldsymbol{\beta}'\right)\mathbf{x}_{t-1} + \boldsymbol{\lambda}'\mathbf{v}_t \tag{9.5}$$

when μ_1 is determined by $\mathsf{E}[a_{t-1}\eta_t] = 0$:

$$\begin{aligned} \mathsf{E}\left[a_{t-1}\eta_t\right] &= \mathsf{E}\left[\boldsymbol{\lambda}'\mathbf{x}_{t-1}\left(\mathbf{x}_{t-1}'\left(\left[1 - \mu_1\right]\mathbf{I}_n + \boldsymbol{\beta}\boldsymbol{\alpha}'\right)\boldsymbol{\lambda} + \mathbf{v}_t'\boldsymbol{\lambda}\right)\right] \\ &= \mathsf{E}\left[\boldsymbol{\lambda}'\mathbf{x}_{t-1}\mathbf{x}_{t-1}'\left(\left[1 - \mu_1\right]\boldsymbol{\lambda} + \boldsymbol{\beta}\boldsymbol{\alpha}'\boldsymbol{\lambda}\right)\right]. \end{aligned} \tag{9.6}$$

We consider two possibilities, first, $\boldsymbol{\lambda} = \boldsymbol{\beta}\mathbf{k}$ where $\mathbf{k}$ is $n \times 1$; and, second, when $\boldsymbol{\lambda}$ cannot be expressed as a linear function of $\boldsymbol{\beta}$. Then, in the cointegrated case:

$$\begin{aligned} \mathsf{E}\left[a_{t-1}\eta_t\right] &= \mathsf{E}\left[\mathbf{k}'\boldsymbol{\beta}'\mathbf{x}_{t-1}\mathbf{x}_{t-1}'\left(\left[1 - \mu_1\right]\boldsymbol{\beta}\mathbf{k} + \boldsymbol{\beta}\boldsymbol{\alpha}'\boldsymbol{\beta}\mathbf{k}\right)\right] \\ &= \mathbf{k}'\mathsf{E}\left[\boldsymbol{\beta}'\mathbf{x}_{t-1}\mathbf{x}_{t-1}'\boldsymbol{\beta}\right]\left(\boldsymbol{\alpha}'\boldsymbol{\beta} + \left(1 - \mu_1\right)\mathbf{I}_r\right)\mathbf{k}. \end{aligned}$$

For this to be zero, as $\mathsf{E}[\boldsymbol{\beta}'\mathbf{x}_{t-1}\mathbf{x}_{t-1}'\boldsymbol{\beta}] = \mathbf{M}$ is $r \times r$ non-singular, and $\boldsymbol{\beta}\mathbf{k} \neq \mathbf{0}$, then:

$$\mathbf{k}'\mathbf{M}\left(\boldsymbol{\alpha}'\boldsymbol{\beta} + \left(1 - \mu_1\right)\mathbf{I}_r\right)\mathbf{k} = 0.$$

Since all the roots of $(\mathbf{I}_r + \boldsymbol{\alpha}'\boldsymbol{\beta})$ are inside the unit circle (see chapter 6), this requires $|\mu_1| < 1$. Then, from (9.5):

$$\begin{aligned} \eta_t &= \mathbf{k}'\boldsymbol{\beta}'\left(\left[1 - \mu_1\right]\mathbf{I}_n + \boldsymbol{\alpha}\boldsymbol{\beta}'\right)\mathbf{x}_{t-1} + \boldsymbol{\lambda}'\mathbf{v}_t \\ &= \mathbf{k}'\left(\left[1 - \mu_1\right]\mathbf{I}_r + \boldsymbol{\beta}'\boldsymbol{\alpha}\right)\boldsymbol{\beta}'\mathbf{x}_{t-1} + \boldsymbol{\lambda}'\mathbf{v}_t, \end{aligned}$$

and hence is stationary.

---

[2] Longer lags complicate, but do not alter, the principles of the analysis.

Secondly, when $\boldsymbol{\lambda} \neq \boldsymbol{\beta}\mathbf{k}$, from (9.5) $\{\eta_t\}$ will depend on non-cointegrating combinations of $\mathbf{x}_{t-1}$ unless $\mu_1 = 1$, so will be stationary only if the activity index is a random walk with drift (plus a potentially autocorrelated error). Thus, either the items in the index cointegrate using the weights $\boldsymbol{\lambda}$ so $\{a_t\}$ is stationary, or the index will be $\mathsf{I}(1)$: this result is unaffected by continually resetting $a_t = 100$ in a base period.

Such an outcome restricts the admissible combinations of levels of variables that can be used in any stationary index: otherwise only the change in the index will be $\mathsf{I}(0)$. When stationarity is desired, recent multivariate cointegration approaches could be used to determine the activity index. Detrending a_t (removing a linear deterministic trend) will not suffice to remove the unit root, which induces a stochastic – not a deterministic – trend: see Phillips and Durlauf (1986). Of course, differencing a_t is sufficient for it to be $\mathsf{I}(0)$ when the DGP is $\mathsf{I}(1)$, but will over-difference when $\boldsymbol{\lambda} = \boldsymbol{\beta}\mathbf{k}$.

The covariance of the activity index with any element $x_{it} = \mathbf{j}_i'\mathbf{x}_t$ of $\mathbf{x}_t$ is given by (ignoring means):

$$\mathsf{E}\left[a_t x_{it}\right] = \mathsf{E}\left[\boldsymbol{\lambda}'\mathbf{x}_t\mathbf{x}_t'\mathbf{j}_i\right].$$

This is well defined only when $\boldsymbol{\lambda} = \boldsymbol{\beta}\mathbf{k}$ and x_{it} is stationary, or when a_t and x_{it} are both $\mathsf{I}(1)$ but cointegrate. A constant correlation seems most unlikely unless such conditions are fulfilled.

9.4.2 Leading index

We now use the same approach to analyse the CLI. From (9.2), since $\mathbf{i}_t = \mathbf{S}\mathbf{x}_t$:

$$\mathbf{i}_t = \mathbf{S}\mathbf{x}_t = \mathbf{S}\boldsymbol{\tau} + \mathbf{S}\boldsymbol{\Upsilon}\mathbf{x}_{t-1} + \mathbf{S}\mathbf{v}_t = \boldsymbol{\gamma} + \boldsymbol{\Gamma}\mathbf{i}_{t-1} + \mathbf{u}_t, \tag{9.7}$$

where $\boldsymbol{\gamma} = \mathbf{S}\boldsymbol{\tau}$, and $\boldsymbol{\Gamma}$ derives from 'minimizing' the expected matrix sum of squares of $\{\mathbf{u}_t\}$ in:

$$\mathbf{u}_t = \left(\left[\mathbf{I}_p - \boldsymbol{\Gamma}\right]\mathbf{S} + \mathbf{S}\boldsymbol{\alpha}\boldsymbol{\beta}'\right)\mathbf{x}_{t-1} + \mathbf{S}\mathbf{v}_t. \tag{9.8}$$

The choice of indicators could retain or lose cointegration, and could have a VAR or a VARMA representation accordingly. For simplicity, we assume that a good choice of $\mathbf{S}$ has been made ($\mathbf{S}\boldsymbol{\Upsilon} = \boldsymbol{\Gamma}\mathbf{S}$), and so (9.7) is the VAR:

$$\mathbf{i}_t = \boldsymbol{\gamma} + \boldsymbol{\Gamma}\mathbf{i}_{t-1} + \mathbf{u}_t, \tag{9.9}$$

where $\mathbf{u}_t \sim \mathsf{IN}_p[\mathbf{0}, \boldsymbol{\Sigma}]$ with $\boldsymbol{\Sigma} = \mathbf{S}\boldsymbol{\Omega}\mathbf{S}'$.

Since:

$$g_t = \boldsymbol{\phi}'\mathbf{i}_t = \boldsymbol{\phi}'\mathbf{S}\mathbf{x}_t = \boldsymbol{\varphi}'\mathbf{x}_t \tag{9.10}$$

is a reparameterization and reduction of $\mathbf{x}_t$, when a stationary CLI is desired, $\boldsymbol{\varphi} = \boldsymbol{\beta}\mathbf{h}$ (where $\mathbf{h}$ is $n \times 1$) is required. From the Granger representation theorem (see, e.g., Engle and Granger, 1987), cointegration entails Granger (1969) causality in at least one direction, so some predictability must result from the use of cointegrating combinations. Indeed, from (9.3) when $\varphi = \boldsymbol{\beta}\mathbf{h}$, for $\Delta\mathbf{x}_t$:

$$\mathsf{E}\left[g_{t-1}\Delta x_{it}\right] = \mathbf{h}'\mathsf{E}\left[\boldsymbol{\beta}'\mathbf{x}_{t-1}\Delta\mathbf{x}_t'\right]\mathbf{j}_i = \mathbf{h}'\mathsf{E}\left[\boldsymbol{\beta}'\mathbf{x}_{t-1}\mathbf{x}_{t-1}'\boldsymbol{\beta}\boldsymbol{\alpha}'\right]\mathbf{j}_i = \mathbf{h}'\mathbf{M}\boldsymbol{\alpha}_i.$$

This is well defined, and delivers a constant correlation, but the covariance need not be the best that can be achieved.

When $\mathbf{i}_t$ satisfies the VAR in (9.9), we next consider the conditions under which g_t is a sufficient summary of the component indices. Then we analyse its role relative to the original VAR, and consider its ability to predict future variables or indexes. Let $\mathbf{Q}$ be a $p \times p$ non-singular matrix such that:

$$\mathbf{Q} = \begin{pmatrix} \boldsymbol{\phi}' \\ \mathbf{Q}^* \end{pmatrix} \quad \text{and so} \quad \mathbf{Q}\mathbf{i}_t = \begin{pmatrix} g_t \\ \mathbf{i}_t^* \end{pmatrix},$$

where $\mathbf{Q}^*$ is $(p-1) \times p$. From (9.9):

$$\mathbf{Q}\mathbf{i}_t = \mathbf{Q}\boldsymbol{\gamma} + \mathbf{Q}\boldsymbol{\Gamma}\mathbf{i}_{t-1} + \mathbf{Q}\mathbf{u}_t = \boldsymbol{\gamma}^* + \mathbf{C}\mathbf{Q}\mathbf{i}_{t-1} + \mathbf{Q}\mathbf{u}_t, \tag{9.11}$$

where $\mathbf{Q}\boldsymbol{\Gamma}\mathbf{Q}^{-1} = \mathbf{C}$. Then:

$$\begin{pmatrix} g_t \\ \mathbf{i}_t^* \end{pmatrix} = \boldsymbol{\gamma}^* + \begin{pmatrix} c_{11} & \mathbf{c}_{12}' \\ \mathbf{c}_{21} & \mathbf{c}_{22} \end{pmatrix} \begin{pmatrix} g_{t-1} \\ \mathbf{i}_{t-1}^* \end{pmatrix} + \mathbf{u}_t^*. \tag{9.12}$$

Thus, g_t is a sufficient summary of $\mathbf{i}_t$ for prediction if $\mathbf{c}_{12} = \mathbf{0}$ and $\mathbf{c}_{22} = \mathbf{0}$, and otherwise, $\mathbf{i}_{t-1}^*$ also contains relevant information for predicting $\mathbf{i}_t$. These are testable conditions. Conversely, necessary conditions for g_{t-1} to predict elements of $\mathbf{i}_t$ are that $c_{11} \neq 0$ and/or $\mathbf{c}_{21} \neq \mathbf{0}$. Generalizations of this approach will apply below.

Next, without loss of generality, $\mathbf{x}_t$ can be reparameterized in terms of the (non-overlapping) items for the putative CLI, the remaining indicators, the activity index and the rest of the (perhaps combinations of) $\mathbf{x}_t$ as:

$$\mathbf{P}\mathbf{x}_t = \begin{pmatrix} \mathbf{QS} \\ \boldsymbol{\lambda}' \\ \boldsymbol{\Psi} \end{pmatrix} \mathbf{x}_t = \begin{pmatrix} \mathbf{Q}\mathbf{i}_t \\ a_t \\ \boldsymbol{\Psi}\mathbf{x}_t \end{pmatrix} = \begin{pmatrix} \boldsymbol{\varphi}' \\ \mathbf{Q}^*\mathbf{S} \\ \boldsymbol{\lambda}' \\ \boldsymbol{\Psi} \end{pmatrix} \mathbf{x}_t = \begin{pmatrix} g_t \\ \mathbf{i}_t^* \\ a_t \\ \boldsymbol{\Psi}\mathbf{x}_t \end{pmatrix}, \tag{9.13}$$

where $\mathbf{P}$ is an $n \times n$ non-singular matrix such that $|\mathbf{P}| = 1$, and $\boldsymbol{\Psi}$ is $(n-p-1) \times n$. Substituting (9.2) into (9.13) yields:

$$\begin{aligned} \mathbf{P}\mathbf{x}_t &= \mathbf{P}\boldsymbol{\tau} + \mathbf{P}\boldsymbol{\Upsilon}\mathbf{x}_{t-1} + \mathbf{P}\mathbf{v}_t \\ &= \mathbf{P}\boldsymbol{\tau} + \left(\mathbf{P}\boldsymbol{\Upsilon}\mathbf{P}^{-1}\right)\mathbf{P}\mathbf{x}_{t-1} + \mathbf{P}\mathbf{v}_t \\ &= \boldsymbol{\tau}^* + \boldsymbol{\Xi}\mathbf{P}\mathbf{x}_{t-1} + \boldsymbol{\omega}_t, \end{aligned} \tag{9.14}$$

where $\mathbf{P\Upsilon P}^{-1} = \mathbf{I}_n + \mathbf{P}\boldsymbol{\alpha\beta}'\mathbf{P}^{-1}$ so that $\boldsymbol{\Xi} - \mathbf{I}_n = \mathbf{P}\boldsymbol{\alpha\beta}'\mathbf{P}^{-1} = \boldsymbol{\alpha}^*\boldsymbol{\beta}^{*\prime} = \boldsymbol{\Theta}$ where $\boldsymbol{\beta}^* = \mathbf{P}^{-1\prime}\boldsymbol{\beta}$. Consequently, in levels:

$$\begin{pmatrix} g_t \\ \mathbf{i}_t^* \\ a_t \\ \boldsymbol{\Psi}\mathbf{x}_t \end{pmatrix} = \begin{pmatrix} \tau_1^* \\ \boldsymbol{\tau}_2^* \\ \tau_3^* \\ \boldsymbol{\tau}_4^* \end{pmatrix} + \begin{pmatrix} \xi_{11} & \boldsymbol{\xi}_{12}' & \xi_{13} & \boldsymbol{\xi}_{14}' \\ \boldsymbol{\xi}_{21} & \boldsymbol{\xi}_{22} & \boldsymbol{\xi}_{23} & \boldsymbol{\xi}_{24} \\ \xi_{31} & \boldsymbol{\xi}_{32}' & \xi_{33} & \boldsymbol{\xi}_{34}' \\ \boldsymbol{\xi}_{41} & \boldsymbol{\xi}_{42} & \boldsymbol{\xi}_{43} & \boldsymbol{\xi}_{44} \end{pmatrix} \begin{pmatrix} g_{t-1} \\ \mathbf{i}_{t-1}^* \\ a_{t-1} \\ \boldsymbol{\Psi}\mathbf{x}_{t-1} \end{pmatrix} + \begin{pmatrix} \omega_{1t} \\ \boldsymbol{\omega}_{2t} \\ \omega_{3t} \\ \boldsymbol{\omega}_{4t} \end{pmatrix} \tag{9.15}$$

and hence in I(0) form:

$$\begin{pmatrix} \Delta g_t \\ \Delta \mathbf{i}_t^* \\ \Delta a_t \\ \boldsymbol{\Psi}\Delta\mathbf{x}_t \end{pmatrix} = \begin{pmatrix} \tau_1^* \\ \boldsymbol{\tau}_2^* \\ \tau_3^* \\ \boldsymbol{\tau}_4^* \end{pmatrix} + \begin{pmatrix} \theta_{11}g_{t-1} + \boldsymbol{\theta}_{12}'\mathbf{i}_{t-1}^* + \theta_{13}a_{t-1} + \boldsymbol{\theta}_{14}'\boldsymbol{\Psi}\mathbf{x}_{t-1} \\ \boldsymbol{\theta}_{21}g_{t-1} + \boldsymbol{\theta}_{22}\mathbf{i}_{t-1}^* + \boldsymbol{\theta}_{23}a_{t-1} + \boldsymbol{\theta}_{24}\boldsymbol{\Psi}\mathbf{x}_{t-1} \\ \theta_{31}g_{t-1} + \boldsymbol{\theta}_{32}'\mathbf{i}_{t-1}^* + \theta_{33}a_{t-1} + \boldsymbol{\theta}_{34}'\boldsymbol{\Psi}\mathbf{x}_{t-1} \\ \boldsymbol{\theta}_{41}g_{t-1} + \boldsymbol{\theta}_{42}\mathbf{i}_{t-1}^* + \boldsymbol{\theta}_{43}a_{t-1} + \boldsymbol{\theta}_{44}\boldsymbol{\Psi}\mathbf{x}_{t-1} \end{pmatrix} + \begin{pmatrix} \omega_{1t} \\ \boldsymbol{\omega}_{2t} \\ \omega_{3t} \\ \boldsymbol{\omega}_{4t} \end{pmatrix}. \tag{9.16}$$

The forecasting objective may be to predict future values of levels or changes in a_t or elements of $\mathbf{x}_t$ (or functions thereof), including $\mathbf{i}_t$. Any or all of $\mathbf{x}_{t-1}$, or the linear combinations $\mathbf{i}_{t-1}^*$, a_{t-1} or g_{t-1} could be used for forecasting. We consider the various possibilities in turn, focusing on predicting changes, from which levels can be obtained by integration. For 1-step forecasts, the results are invariant but it matters which functions are selected for longer horizons (see section 3.5).

From (9.16), the index g_t is a possible CLI for future values of elements derivable from $\boldsymbol{\Psi}\Delta\mathbf{x}_t$ when the relevant elements of $\boldsymbol{\theta}_{41} \neq \mathbf{0}$. The CLI is a sufficient statistic for future $\boldsymbol{\Psi}\Delta\mathbf{x}_t$ when $\boldsymbol{\theta}_{42} = \mathbf{0}$, $\boldsymbol{\theta}_{43} = \mathbf{0}$, and $\boldsymbol{\theta}_{44}\boldsymbol{\Psi} = \mathbf{0}$ as well, which are testable hypotheses. However, when $\boldsymbol{\theta}_{42} \neq \mathbf{0}$, $\boldsymbol{\theta}_{43} \neq \mathbf{0}$ and/or $\boldsymbol{\theta}_{44}\boldsymbol{\Psi} \neq \mathbf{0}$, the omitted variables may attenuate or enhance the marginal predictive value of g_{t-1} when it alone is used.

Similar comments apply to forecasting Δa_t: g_t is potentially a CLI when $\theta_{31} \neq 0$. Using only the index g_{t-1} instead of the entire vector $\mathbf{x}_{t-1}$ involves no loss of information for predicting future Δa_t when $\boldsymbol{\theta}_{32} = \mathbf{0}$, $\theta_{33} = 0$ and $\boldsymbol{\theta}_{34}'\boldsymbol{\Psi} = \mathbf{0}'$ which again are testable assumptions given a specification of a_t and g_t. In general, strong exclusion restrictions are imposed by regarding a CLI as a sufficient predictor. While there certainly exist grounds for wishing to use parsimonious models (see Box and Jenkins, 1976, and Hendry and Clements, 1993 and chapter 12), the methods for selecting CLIs and their component indicators described above suggest that the resulting (untested) reductions may lose information of value in forecasting.

Suppose that the DGP is given by (9.2), all of the elements of $\mathbf{x}_t$ are stationary, but $\boldsymbol{\xi}_{32} \neq \mathbf{0}$, $\xi_{33} \neq 0$ and $\boldsymbol{\xi}_{34}'\boldsymbol{\Psi} \neq \mathbf{0}'$, yet the modeller estimates:

$$a_t = d_0 + d_1 g_{t-1} + e_t \tag{9.17}$$

and uses it to forecast future values of the activity index; we consider 1-step ahead forecasts. We assume that the modeller knows the value of $\mathbf{d} = (d_0 : d_1)'$, and let $\widetilde{a_{T+1}}$ be the conditional-expectation forecast of a_{T+1} given by:

$$\widetilde{a_{T+1}} = \mathsf{E}\left[a_{T+1} \mid g_T\right] = d_0 + d_1 g_T. \tag{9.18}$$

The optimal conditional forecast of $\mathbf{x}_{T+1}$ from (9.2) is:

$$\mathsf{E}\left[\mathbf{x}_{T+1} \mid \mathbf{x}_T\right] = \boldsymbol{\tau} + \boldsymbol{\Upsilon}\mathbf{x}_T \tag{9.19}$$

and thus of a_{T+1} is:

$$\mathsf{E}\left[a_{T+1} \mid \mathbf{x}_T\right] = \tau_3^* + \xi_{31} g_T + \boldsymbol{\xi}_{32}' \mathbf{i}_T^* + \xi_{33} a_T + \boldsymbol{\xi}_{34}' \boldsymbol{\Psi} \mathbf{x}_T. \tag{9.20}$$

The forecast error from using (9.18) with known parameters is:

$$e_{T+1} = a_{T+1} - \widetilde{a_{T+1}} = \tau_3^* + \xi_{31} g_T + \boldsymbol{\xi}_{32}' \mathbf{i}_T^* + \xi_{33} a_T + \boldsymbol{\xi}_{34}' \boldsymbol{\Psi} \mathbf{x}_T - d_0 - d_1 g_T + \omega_{3t} \tag{9.21}$$

and therefore the conditional expected forecast error is:

$$\mathsf{E}\left[e_{T+1} \mid \mathbf{x}_T\right] = \left(\tau_3^* - d_0\right) + \left(\xi_{31} - d_1\right) g_T + \boldsymbol{\xi}_{32}' \mathbf{i}_T^* + \xi_{33} a_T + \boldsymbol{\xi}_{34}' \boldsymbol{\Psi} \mathbf{x}_T \tag{9.22}$$

which is non-zero unless considerable (chance) cancellation occurs. The resulting biases are due to the restrictions on how the component indices enter the CLI, the absence of lagged values of the activity index, and the omission of useful predictors $\boldsymbol{\Psi}\mathbf{x}_T$, together with the consequentially biased coefficients in (9.17).

9.4.3 Selecting a CLI

An alternative application of the present framework is to select the 'optimal' CLI for forecasting a_t. Since $a_t = \boldsymbol{\lambda}'\mathbf{x}_t$, consider the linear transformation of $\mathbf{x}_{t-1}$ from (9.2) that maximizes predictability. From (9.4), this is:

$$a_t = \mu_0 + \boldsymbol{\psi}'\mathbf{x}_{t-1} + e_t = \mu_0 + \ell_{t-1} + e_t^*, \tag{9.23}$$

where $\boldsymbol{\psi} = \boldsymbol{\Upsilon}'\boldsymbol{\lambda}$ and $\ell_{t-1} = \boldsymbol{\psi}'\mathbf{x}_{t-1}$ is defined to be the 'best' leading indicator of a_t as it leaves an innovation error $\{e_t^*\}$ relative to $\mathbf{x}_{t-1}$:

$$\mathsf{E}\left[e_t^* \mid \mathbf{x}_{t-1}\right] = 0 \text{ with } \mathsf{E}\left[\left(e_t^*\right)^2 \mid \mathbf{x}_{t-1}\right] = \boldsymbol{\lambda}'\boldsymbol{\Omega}\boldsymbol{\lambda}. \tag{9.24}$$

This formulation reveals that the sampling uncertainty of the weights $\boldsymbol{\psi}$ should be included in measures of forecast uncertainty associated with any CLI method.

9.5 An empirical analysis of the UK LLI

We first investigate the UK LLI, as a prelude to studying its role in VAR modelling. Since the data set for the econometric model is only available quarterly, we converted the three monthly indicators, and the CLI, to quarterly data by selecting the last monthly outcome of each quarter. The resulting time series closely resemble the corresponding monthly variables, and, as shown in (9.25), 87 percent of the variance of quarterly changes in the CLI is explained by the quarterly change in its components. More precisely, over the available quarterly sample 1975(2)–1993(2), regressing $\Delta I_{L,t}^{UK}$ on its synthetic components yields:

$$\widehat{\Delta I_{L,t}^{UK}} = -\underset{(0.14)}{0.75}\ \Delta R_{3t} + \underset{(0.07)}{0.64}\ \Delta S_t - \underset{(0.18)}{0.62}\ \Delta\left(R_{bt} - R_{3t}\right)$$
$$+ \underset{(0.06)}{0.17}\ \Delta D_t - \underset{(0.01)}{0.01}\ \Delta O_t \qquad (9.25)$$
$$\mathsf{R}^2 = 0.87,\ \hat{\sigma} = 0.84,\ DW = 1.58.$$

This is far from an identity, but nevertheless explains much of the variance of the changes in the index. The main 'explanatory' variables all have the correct sign and are highly significant, other than ΔO_t.

Next, we apply the analysis in section 9.4.2. The VAR for the component indicators is a five-dimensional system for ΔR_{3t}, ΔS_t, $\Delta(R_{bt} - R_{3t})$, ΔD_t and ΔO_t. This was tested for cointegration using the Johansen (1988a) approach in PcFiml (see Doornik and Hendry, 1997), using two lags on every variable plus an intercept. Table 9.1 shows the outcome for the cointegration test statistics for 1975(4)–1993(2).

Table 9.1 Cointegration analysis

r	1	2	3	4	5
μ	0.36	0.32	0.14	0.08	0.04
Max.	27.1	23.6†	9.4	5.3	2.6
Tr.	68.0†	40.9†	17.3	7.9	2.6

Note:† Unadjusted test significant at 5 percent.

Strictly, no test is significant at the 5 percent level, but that may be due to the small sample size: two of the eigenvalues are quite large at over 0.3. Next, table 9.2 shows the two eigenvectors corresponding to the two largest eigenvalues. The vector estimated in (9.25) does not lie in the cointegration space, as assuming there are two cointegration vectors, $\chi^2(3) = 16.9$.

The feedback coefficients for the first two eigenvectors are shown in table 9.3. Figure 9.4 shows the time series of $I_{L,t}^{UK}$ and the first 'cointegrating combination' denoted $I_{C,t}^{UK}$:

$$I_{C,t}^{UK} = R_3 - 1.01S + 0.02\left(R_b - R_3\right) - 0.68D + 0.25O.$$

Table 9.2 Cointegration vectors

$\hat{\beta}'$	R_3	S	$R_b - R_3$	D	O
1	1	−1.01	0.02	−0.68	0.25
2	0.79	1	−0.08	0.18	0.05

$I_{C,t}^{UK}$ and $I_{L,t}^{UK}$ are not highly correlated, and often not in phase.

Table 9.3 Feedback coefficients

$\hat{\alpha}$	1	2
R_3	−0.02	0.11
S	0.03	−0.28
$R_b - R_3$	−0.01	0.13
D	−0.03	−0.14
O	−1.80	−1.08

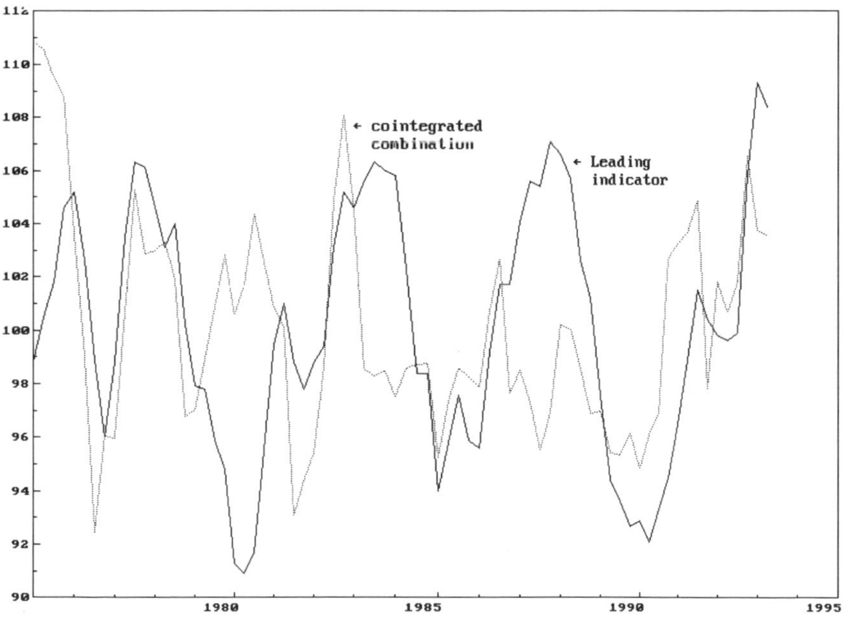

Figure 9.4 Cointegrating combination of indicators and UK longer-leading index

Finally, we consider the restrictions placed on the leading indicators by their combination in $I_{L,t}^{UK}$, as in (9.12). If the five-dimensional VAR is modelled parsimoniously, it becomes nearly diagonal, so no single vector with all of its components non-zero could capture all the available information for predicting the component indicators. Replacing R_3 by $I_{L,t}^{UK}$, the test of $\mathbf{c}_{12} = \mathbf{0}$ accepts, so no additional variables help predict the CLI. However, $\mathbf{c}_{22} = \mathbf{0}$ is strongly rejected, with seven coefficients having t-values in excess of 2.7 in absolute value, so the CLI is not fully informative. Conversely, both $c_{11} = 0$ and $\mathbf{c}_{21} = \mathbf{0}$ are strongly rejected so the CLI does capture some of the dynamic behaviour.

9.6 Adding CLIs to macroeconomic models

We now consider the use of indices, or CLIs, in macroeconomic modelling and forecasting (see, e.g., Bladen-Hovell and Zhang, 1992 and Marsland and Weale, 1992). When modellers use an index, instead of all of the components separately, they are assuming that the way in which the index enters the model matches the way the components also enter the model. Testing the significance of an index involves testing the joint hypothesis of the components entering the model, and having the same relationship in the model as in the index. Thus, the insignificance of the index does not preclude that some (or all) of the components of the index belong in the model, albeit with different coefficients than those in the index, as in section 9.4.

Consider the role of a CLI in a VAR in differences (DVAR) for the DGP:

$$\Delta \mathbf{x}_t = \boldsymbol{\gamma} + \boldsymbol{\alpha} \left(\boldsymbol{\beta}' \mathbf{x}_{t-1} - \boldsymbol{\mu} \right) + \mathbf{v}_t \tag{9.26}$$

which is thereby approximated by:

$$\Delta \mathbf{x}_t = \boldsymbol{\lambda} + \boldsymbol{\Gamma} \Delta \mathbf{x}_{t-1} + \boldsymbol{\xi}_t. \tag{9.27}$$

Such approximations can be robust to regime shifts, particularly in $\boldsymbol{\mu}$ (see Clements and Hendry, 1996b and section 7.4.1). First, consider adding $g_{t-1} = \boldsymbol{\varphi}' \mathbf{x}_{t-1}$ to (9.27) when $\boldsymbol{\Gamma} = \mathbf{0}$ (for simplicity), so that:

$$\Delta \mathbf{x}_t = \boldsymbol{\delta} + \boldsymbol{\rho} g_{t-1} + \mathbf{e}_t \tag{9.28}$$

and testing $\boldsymbol{\rho} = \mathbf{0}$. From (9.26), therefore:

$$\mathbf{e}_t = (\boldsymbol{\gamma} - \boldsymbol{\alpha\mu} - \boldsymbol{\delta}) + \left(\boldsymbol{\alpha\beta}' - \boldsymbol{\rho\varphi}' \right) \mathbf{x}_{t-1} + \mathbf{v}_t. \tag{9.29}$$

When $\boldsymbol{\varphi}' = \mathbf{h}' \boldsymbol{\beta}'$ (where $\mathbf{h}$ is $r \times 1$), the CLI is a cointegrating combination, and the error $\{\mathbf{e}_t\}$ will be stationary. For $\boldsymbol{\rho}$ selected to minimize the deviation of $\boldsymbol{\alpha}$ from $\boldsymbol{\rho}\mathbf{h}'$, $\boldsymbol{\rho} \neq \mathbf{0}$ even though $\boldsymbol{\rho\varphi}'$ is only rank 1, so $\mathsf{E}[g_t] = \mathbf{h}' \boldsymbol{\mu}$, with $\boldsymbol{\delta} = \boldsymbol{\gamma} - \boldsymbol{\rho}\mathbf{h}' \boldsymbol{\mu}$. Otherwise, when $\boldsymbol{\varphi}'$ does not cointegrate $\mathbf{x}_t$, $\{\mathbf{e}_t\}$ will not be stationary unless $\boldsymbol{\rho} = \mathbf{0}$. When $\boldsymbol{\Gamma} \neq \mathbf{0}$, both $\Delta \mathbf{x}_{t-1}$ and g_{t-1} will proxy the omitted cointegrating vectors, reducing the significance of the latter. However, if g_{t-1} does enter empirically, the intercept will depend on $\boldsymbol{\mu}$ so the robustness of (9.27) to shifts in the equilibrium mean will be lost.

Second, consider a CLI based on differenced data, replacing g_{t-1} in (9.28) by $g^*_{t-1} = \boldsymbol{\psi}'\Delta\mathbf{x}_{t-1}$. Now in place of (9.29):

$$\mathbf{e}_t = \left(\left[\mathbf{I}_n - \rho\boldsymbol{\psi}'\right]\boldsymbol{\gamma} - \boldsymbol{\delta}\right) + \boldsymbol{\alpha}\left(\boldsymbol{\beta}'\mathbf{x}_{t-1} - \boldsymbol{\mu}\right) - \rho\boldsymbol{\psi}'\left(\Delta\mathbf{x}_{t-1} - \boldsymbol{\gamma}\right) + \mathbf{v}_t. \quad (9.30)$$

Again, the error $\{\mathbf{e}_t\}$ will be stationary, and the minimizing value of ρ will usually be non-zero, due to the autocorrelated nature of the cointegrating vectors. There is no additional role for g^*_{t-1} when $\Delta\mathbf{x}_{t-1}$ is included unrestrictedly in (9.27). In practice, only a subset $\mathbf{y}_t$ of $\mathbf{x}_t$ will be analysed, so the analysis of section 9.4 applies, and the CLI may proxy omitted effects.

There are interesting implications of this analysis under regime shifts in $\boldsymbol{\gamma}$ and $\boldsymbol{\mu}$. The CLI will improve forecasting performance relative to the DVAR only if co-breaking occurs using the CLI's weights. Since $\boldsymbol{\beta}$ is co-breaking for shifts in the growth rate $\boldsymbol{\gamma}$ when the cointegrating vectors do not trend (so $\boldsymbol{\beta}'\boldsymbol{\gamma} = \mathbf{0}$: see Hendry, 1997), whereas $\{\mathbf{e}_t\}$ depends on $\boldsymbol{\gamma}$ in both (9.29) and (9.30), a CLI will be a poor proxy in such a state of nature relative to the correct cointegrating vectors. Further, although the DVAR is little affected by changes in $\boldsymbol{\mu}$ (because the deviations of the cointegrating vectors from their means are omitted), the CLI-based model in (9.29) depends on $\boldsymbol{\mu}$ and will experience similar predictive failure to the VEqCM. Thus, robustness is lost in both leading cases.

9.7 The role of the UK LLI in a small monetary model

To illustrate the role of a leading indicator in a linear dynamic system, we now consider the four-equation monetary model analysed by Hendry and Mizon (1993) and Hendry and Doornik (1994), and also investigated by Boswijk (1992), Ericsson, Campos and Tran (1990) and Johansen (1992b) *inter alia*. This is an extension of the two-equation model in section 6.9 using the same data set M, Y, P and R_n (nominal M_1, real total final expenditure, at 1985 prices, its deflator and the learning-adjusted-opportunity cost of holding M_1: see Hendry and Ericsson, 1991, for details). Money and expenditure are in £million, the deflator is unity in 1985, and the interest rate is annual, in fractions. Lower-case letters denote logs of the corresponding capitals. The data are quarterly, seasonally adjusted and, after allowing for the leading-indicator sample period, estimation is usually over 1976(1)–1989(2). We adopted the specification in Hendry and Doornik (1994), so analysed $m-p$, y, Δp, and R_n, adding $I^{UK}_{L,t}$ to create a five-variable VAR with a lag length of two.

Figure 9.5 shows the time-series graph of $I^{UK}_{L,t}$ and the two cointegration vectors of the econometric system (denoted by c_{1t} and c_{2t}) defined by Hendry and Doornik (1994) as:

$$c_{1t} = (m_t - p_t) - y_t + 7.0\left(\Delta p_t + R_{nt}\right) \quad \text{and} \quad c_{2t} = y_t - 0.0063t - 3.4\Delta p_t + 1.8R_{nt}. \quad (9.31)$$

The first is the deviation from the long-run money-demand equation, interpreted as the excess demand for money. The second is the deviation of output from trend as a function of the 'real' interest rate (which would require $1.8(R_{nt} - 4\Delta p_t)$), interpreted as the excess demand for goods. The overall pattern of behaviour of these series is similar to the CLI, the correlations of $I_{L,t}^{UK}$ with c_{1t} and c_{2t} being about 0.55.

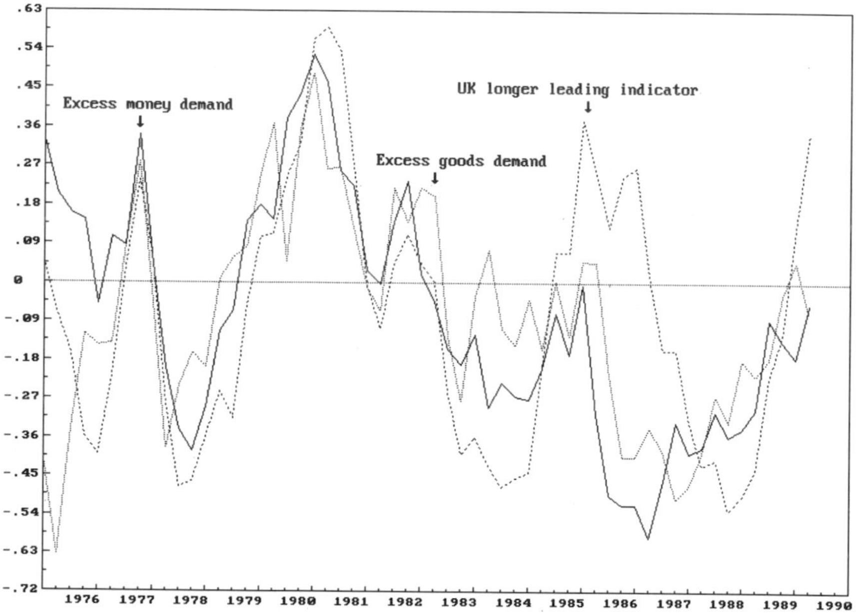

Figure 9.5 UK longer-leading index and cointegration vectors

Following a similar reduction sequence to Hendry and Doornik (1994) leads to the parsimonious VEqCM representation shown in table 9.4, where D_{out} and D_{oil} are dummy variables for output and oil-price shocks. The likelihood-ratio test of the over-identifying restrictions on the original VAR yields $\chi^2(39) = 39.9$, which is insignificant at the 5 percent level. Thus, the reductions are valid, and lead to a specification in which the CLI is not significant in the output equation (y_t), although 'leading' it is one of the main rationales for the CLI. However, the CLI is significant in the inflation equation, and induces the additional significance of c_{1t-1}, thereby violating weak exogeneity of $\Delta^2 p_t$ for a conditional money-demand model (see Engle, Hendry and Richard, 1983, and Johansen, 1992b). The parameter estimates in the money-demand equation become less well determined, but the impact of c_{2t-1} on both Δy_t and $\Delta^2 p_t$ is now stronger.

Table 9.5 records the residual standard deviations, which are generally smaller than in Hendry and Doornik (1994). Thus, there is some information in the longer-leading

Table 9.4 FIML estimates with $I_{L,t}^{UK}$

$$\Delta(m-p)_t = -\underset{(0.41)}{1.18}\ \Delta^2 p_t - \underset{(0.37)}{0.74}\ \Delta R_{nt} - \underset{(0.007)}{0.09}\ c_{1t-1} + \underset{(0.002)}{0.01}$$

$$\Delta y_t = \underset{(0.007)}{0.06}\ D_{out} - \underset{(0.023)}{0.17}\ c_{2t-1} + \underset{(0.001)}{0.01}$$

$$\Delta^2 p_t = \underset{(0.005)}{0.01}\ D_{oil} + \underset{(0.028)}{0.12}\ c_{2t-1} - \underset{(0.009)}{0.03}\ I_{L,t-1}^{UK} - \underset{(0.005)}{0.02}\ c_{1t-1}$$

$$\Delta R_{nt} = \underset{(0.10)}{0.27}\ \Delta R_{nt-1} - \underset{(0.036)}{0.07}\ c_{2t-1}$$

$$I_{L,t}^{UK} = \underset{(0.09)}{1.33}\ I_{L,t-1}^{UK} - \underset{(0.09)}{0.45}\ I_{L,t-2}^{UK} + \underset{(0.005)}{0.01}$$

index that explains the previous error in the inflation equation, but otherwise does not greatly influence the system. The sample is too short to sustain unrestricted modelling of the component indicators as well as the monetary data, so we are unable to determine which individual indicator variables contribute most.

Table 9.5 Residual standard deviations

$\Delta(m-p)_t$	Δy_t	$\Delta^2 p_t$	ΔR_{nt}	$I_{L,t}^{UK}$
1.30 %	0.78 %	0.63 %	0.016	0.002

The final selection is little changed by using $I_{C,t}^{UK}$ in place of $I_{L,t}^{UK}$. The significance of c_{2t-1} is emphasized, but most other coefficients are about the same.

If we allow both $I_{C,t}^{UK}$ and $I_{L,t}^{UK}$ to be elements of a VAR, only the former enters significantly as a level, forcing $I_{L,t}^{UK}$ to insignificance. This supports the idea of using cointegration analysis to select a CLI when stationarity is desired.

A dramatically different answer ensues if the economic cointegration vectors (c_{1t} and c_{2t}) are deleted from the VEqCM, which becomes a VAR in differences, but both forms of CLI are used. Now $I_{L,t-1}^{UK}$ is significant in every equation, and $I_{C,t}^{UK}$ is irrelevant. This may reflect the method of selecting the CLI to lead within sample. However, it seems as if a DVAR can benefit from adding a CLI as a proxy for omitted cointegration vectors, even when a VEqCM cannot be much improved. Of course, the over-identification test for dropping c_{1t} and c_{2t} is highly significant against the original cointegrated VAR, and a valid reduction is hard to obtain.

Such results on the use of CLIs in DVARs are in line with the analysis in section 9.6. *Ex post*, an apparent improvement is seen, but appears to derive from proxying the cointegration vectors. *Ex ante*, however, regime shifts will cause the DVAR with only proxy CLIs to lose its relative robustness (see Clements and Hendry, 1996b). Thus, the augmented DVAR may get the worst of both worlds, and could perform worse than a pure DVAR against a shift in the long-run equilibrium or in the growth rate.

9.8 Overview

Leading indicator systems are altered sufficiently frequently to suggest they do not systematically lead for long. Our empirical evidence confirms the earlier theoretical analysis in that information was lost by restricting the way the component indicators entered the CLI, and their weights did not lie in the cointegration space. Nevertheless, the UK LLI seemed to be stationary, and helped explain some of the variance of inflation in a VEqCM. Its significance in every equation of a DVAR showed it could act as a proxy (albeit poor) for omitted cointegration effects. As the causes of business cycles change over time, and as successful forecasting requires modelling such evolution, CLIs seem at best an adjunct to, and not a substitute for, econometric modelling. Since both the size and timing of economic relationships alter, and co-breaking seems unlikely for non-causal relations, we believe the latter is the dominant strategy.

We argued in section 2.9 that it is impossible to prove that causal information is superior to non-causal information when the model is mis-specified for the DGP and the DGP is non-constant, in the sense that it cannot be shown that adding (subtracting) causally relevant variables to (from) such a model will improve (worsen) forecast performance. Consequently, we cannot establish formally that the addition of LIs or CLIs to forecasting models will not improve forecasts, even when the former do not 'lead' (in any useful sense) the target to be forecast (provided, as will typically be the case, the forecasting models are mis-specified for a non-constant DGP). However, a case can be made for the pre-eminence of causal information on the grounds that the likelihood of models based on causally relevant variables capturing persistent relationships between variables exceeds the likelihood of bivariate correlations between variables persisting. Co-breaking on a systematic basis must depend on causal links.

Chapter 10

Combining forecasts

The combination of forecasts may be superior (on MSFE, say) to each of the constituents. However, forecast combination runs counter to the concept of encompassing viewed as part of a progressive research strategy. The latter would suggest that a better approach is to refine a model when it is found to be wanting in some dimensions: here, the inability to predict some aspects of a process as well as a rival. The goal is a model which encompasses its competitors by forecasting the process better than its rivals. A test for forecast encompassing is the same as that for whether there is any benefit to combination, although conceptually the encompassing approach is different from the ethos behind the combination of forecasts. When models do not draw on a common information pool, and are essentially of a different nature or type, or when models are differentially susceptible to structural breaks, then the case for combination is more persuasive.

10.1 Introduction

The basic idea behind the combination, or 'pooling', of forecasts is that, although one forecast may be superior to another (on some criterion), nevertheless a combined forecast based on the two may be better than either alone. We distinguish between the combination of forecasts where each is based on a common pool of information, and where the forecasts are of an essentially different type or nature, or are differentially susceptible to mis-specification (see Hendry, 1979a). When forecasts are all based on econometric models, each of which has access to the same information set, then combining the resulting forecasts will rarely be a good idea. It is better to sort out the individual models – to derive a preferred model that contains the useful features of the original models. Our discussion of combining forecasts loosely follows the historical development of the subject: see Clemen (1989) for a review and bibliography.

In section 10.2, we outline two methods of combining forecasts. Section 10.3 discusses these ideas in terms of the principle of encompassing, which is the requirement that an empirical model be able to account for the findings of rival models (see, Hendry and Richard, 1982, Mizon, 1984, Mizon and Richard, 1986 and Hendry and Richard, 1989). There are many aspects of a rival model that one might wish to account for.

Forecast encompassing concerns the forecast performance of the models, and, while it is not in general a good way to evaluate models, it was recommended by Chong and Hendry (1986) as a feasible method for evaluating the forecasts from large-scale macro-econometric models for which standard methods may not be operational. We will note the drawbacks with forecast encompassing.

Testing for forecast encompassing is formally equivalent to the procedure for computing 'conditional efficiency' of Nelson (1972) and Granger and Newbold (1973). A forecast is said to be conditionally efficient if the variance of the forecast error from a combination of that forecast and a rival forecast is not significantly less than that of the original forecast alone. We concur with Granger and Newbold (1977) when they state that they regard 'the conditional efficiency criterion as being of great potential value in actual forecast evaluation' (p.283), but have less sympathy with the combining of sample-period fitted values from different models in an attempt to improve forecasts. Rather, the principle of encompassing suggests it is better to sort out the two models since a combination of two mis-specified models is unlikely to systematically produce good forecasts. We provide an illustration of the pooling of two forecasts from mis-specified models based on the example introduced in section 3.6.

In section 10.4, we consider the combination of forecasts which are essentially different in nature, so that the original forecasts in this case can be thought of as being based on different sources of information. We focus on pooling conditional and unconditional forecasts, as discussed in section 8.4.

Finally, we consider pooling for DGPs which are subject to structural breaks when models are affected in different ways by the break. In practice, one may not know how the models are affected, but it may nevertheless be possible to enhance robustness at the cost of increased variance (see section 10.5).

10.2 The combination of forecasts

One of the earliest examples of the combination of forecasts is Barnard (1963). A simple average of a Box–Jenkins model and an exponential smoothing model is shown to have an error variance less than either alone, for 1-step forecasts of world airline passenger miles per month over the period 1951–1960. A more sophisticated approach to combination was suggested by Bates and Granger (1969) where two (or more) predictors are used in the convex combination:

$$P_{c,T+j} = \alpha P_{1,T+j} + (1-\alpha) P_{2,T+j}. \tag{10.1}$$

$P_{x,T+j}$ is the h-step ahead forecast of the value of the series made j periods ago, using model M_x. Unless otherwise specified, h will be taken to be 1. Furthermore, j runs over the period for which predictions and outcomes are available, $j = 1, \ldots, H$, which is sometimes referred to as the within-sample period, and can be used to calculate the optimal combining weights. The out-of-sample period is then $H+1, \ldots, H+L$, $L > 1$, over which the combined predictor is used to forecast.

The weights are chosen to minimize the MSFE of the combined predictor. This formulation assumes that the two predictors are both unbiased, otherwise the implicit restriction that the coefficients on the predictors sum to one is invalid. It also assumes that they both have a constant relation to the outcome, and that we know the unique transform of interest (see section 3.4.1). However, Bates and Granger allow for the possibility that the performance of the predictors may change over time, that is, the forecast-error variances are not stationary. In that case, improved forecast performance may be achieved by adopting varying weights, α_τ. A number of ways are suggested of calculating α_τ, $\tau = T+2, \ldots, T+H$, based on the past errors of the predictor series for periods prior to τ. The performance of the various combination methods is assessed for the airline passenger traffic data, and is generally found to lead to some improvement. Subsequently, a large literature has grown up on combining forecasts, see, *inter alia*, Nelson (1972), who combines forecasts from a large-scale macroeconometric model (the FRB–MIT–PENN model of the US economy) with those from ARIMA models; Newbold and Granger (1974), who combine 1-step ahead Box–Jenkins, Holt–Winters (Holt, 1957, Winters, 1960), and stepwise autoregressive forecasts; and Granger and Newbold (1975), who combine econometric model and Box–Jenkins forecasts.

10.2.1 The regression method

We outline what has been termed the regression method of Granger and Ramanathan (1984) by Diebold (1988), in contrast to the variance-covariance method of Bates and Granger (1969) (discussed below). Both approaches yield identical estimates of the combination parameter. A sample estimate of α can be obtained from OLS on:

$$A_{T+j} = \alpha P_{1,T+j} + (1-\alpha) P_{2,T+j} + e_{c,T+j}, \tag{10.2}$$

since OLS minimizes $\sum_{j=T+1}^{T+H} \widehat{e}_{c,j}^2$ over α. The restriction that the weights on $P_{1,T+j}$ and $P_{2,T+j}$ sum to unity can be conveniently imposed by rewriting (10.2) as:

$$e_{2,T+j} = \alpha (P_{1,T+j} - P_{2,T+j}) + e_{c,T+j}, \tag{10.3}$$

where $e_{2,T+j} \equiv A_{T+j} - P_{2,T+j}$. Then α is given by the regression of the M_2 errors on the difference between the M_1 and M_2 model predictions, and α has the appealing property that the greater the explanatory power of the difference between the two predictors for the M_2 errors, then the greater the weight accorded to M_1 in the composite predictor.

10.2.2 The variance-covariance approach

The variance-covariance approach is based on the relationship between the prediction errors given by (for $t = T + j$):

$$e_{c,t} = \alpha e_{1,t} + (1-\alpha) e_{2,t}, \tag{10.4}$$

and the variance of the combined forecast error:

$$\mathsf{V}\left[e_{c,t}\right]=\alpha^{2}\mathsf{V}\left[e_{1,t}\right]+\left(1-\alpha\right)^{2}\mathsf{V}\left[e_{2,t}\right]+2\alpha\left(1-\alpha\right)\mathsf{C}\left[e_{1,t},e_{2,t}\right]. \tag{10.5}$$

Minimizing $\mathsf{V}[e_{c,t}]$ over α leads to:

$$\alpha^{*}=\frac{\mathsf{V}\left[e_{2,t}\right]-\mathsf{C}\left[e_{1,t},e_{2,t}\right]}{\mathsf{V}\left[e_{1,t}\right]+\mathsf{V}\left[e_{2,t}\right]-2\mathsf{C}\left[e_{1,t},e_{2,t}\right]}. \tag{10.6}$$

Substituting (10.6) into (10.5) we can obtain:

$$\mathsf{V}\left[e_{c,t}\right]_{\rfloor\,\min}=\frac{\left(1-\rho^{2}\right)\mathsf{V}_{1}\mathsf{V}_{2}}{\mathsf{V}_{1}+\mathsf{V}_{2}-2\rho\sqrt{\mathsf{V}_{1}\mathsf{V}_{2}}},$$

where $\mathsf{V}_1=\mathsf{V}[e_{1,t}]$, etc., and $\rho=\mathsf{C}[e_{1,t},e_{2,t}]/\sqrt{\mathsf{V}_1\mathsf{V}_2}$. Thus, using the optimal weight α^* leads to the inequality:

$$\mathsf{MSFE}\left(P_{c,t}\right)\leq\min\left\{\mathsf{MSFE}\left(P_{1,t}\right),\mathsf{MSFE}\left(P_{2,t}\right)\right\}, \tag{10.7}$$

so that combining cannot cost, in that the MSFE of the combined forecast is no larger than the smaller of the individual forecasts' MSFEs. In the unlikely event that the forecast errors are uncorrelated with one another (because the forecasts are uncorrelated), then $\mathsf{C}[e_{1,t},e_{2,t}]=0$, and (10.6) specializes to:

$$\alpha^{*}=\frac{\mathsf{V}\left[e_{2,t}\right]}{\mathsf{V}\left[e_{1,t}\right]+\mathsf{V}\left[e_{2,t}\right]}$$

which has the natural interpretation that the weights only depend (inversely) on the sizes of the relative forecast-error variances.

In practice, the population second-moment matrices of the errors are replaced by their sample counterparts. It is then straightforward to establish that the estimates of α obtained from (10.3) and (10.6) are identical. From (10.3), the OLS estimator $\widehat{\alpha}$ is:

$$\begin{aligned}\widehat{\alpha} &= \frac{\sum_{t=T+1}^{T+H}\left(P_{1,t}-P_{2,t}\right)e_{2,t}}{\sum_{t=T+1}^{T+H}\left(P_{1,t}-P_{2,t}\right)^{2}}\\ &= \frac{H^{-1}\sum_{t=T+1}^{T+H}e_{2,t}^{2}-H^{-1}\sum_{t=T+1}^{T+H}e_{1,t}e_{2,t}}{H^{-1}\sum_{t=T+1}^{T+H}e_{1,t}^{2}+H^{-1}\sum_{t=T+1}^{T+H}e_{2,t}^{2}-2H^{-1}\sum_{t=T+1}^{T+H}e_{1,t}e_{2,t}},\end{aligned} \tag{10.8}$$

where the summation is over the sample for which we have predictions, and we have divided the numerator and denominator by H to give sample estimates. The right-hand side of (10.8) can be compared to (10.6).

The combination of forecasts can be extended to an arbitrary number of forecasts of the same variable (Reid, 1969), and is applicable to forecasts of an arbitrary number of steps ahead (h).

10.2.3 Serial correlation in the combining equation

As Diebold (1988) points out for the regression-based approach, the relaxation of the implicit zero intercept assumption in (10.2) and of the summing to unity of the weights cannot worsen the within-sample mean square loss, since imposing restrictions will always increase the residual sum of squares. In the variance-covariance approach, these restrictions are automatically imposed. Diebold (1988) considers the relative merits of the variance-covariance approach and the unrestricted regression methods from the view point of the serial correlation properties of combined regression residuals. Generalizing (10.2) to an unrestricted combination equation we have:

$$A_{T+j} = \alpha_0 + \alpha_1 P_{1,T+j} + \alpha_2 P_{2,T+j} + e_{c,T+j} \tag{10.9}$$

with combined forecast given by:

$$P_{c,T\,|\,j} = \widehat{\alpha}_0 + \widehat{\alpha}_1 P_{1,T+j} + \widehat{\alpha}_2 P_{2,T+j}. \tag{10.10}$$

From (10.9) and (10.10), and after some rearrangement, we can write the within-sample prediction-error as:

$$\begin{aligned} A_{T+j} - P_{c,T+j} &= -\widehat{\alpha}_0 + \left(1 - \sum_{i=1}^{2} \widehat{\alpha}_i\right) A_{T+j} + \sum_{i=1}^{2} \widehat{\alpha}_i \left(A_{T+j} - P_{i,T+j}\right) \\ &= -\widehat{\alpha}_0 + \left(1 - \sum_{i=1}^{2} \widehat{\alpha}_i\right) A_{T+j} + \eta_{T+j}, \end{aligned} \tag{10.11}$$

where:

$$\eta_{T+j} = \sum_{i=1}^{2} \widehat{\alpha}_i (A_{T+j} - P_{i,T+j}) = \sum_{i=1}^{2} \widehat{\alpha}_i \widehat{e}_{i,T+j}.$$

From (10.11), it is apparent that the prediction errors will only be serially uncorrelated in the unrestricted approach ($\sum_{i=1}^{2} \widehat{\alpha}_i \neq 1$) if both A_{T+j} is serially uncorrelated and the $\widehat{e}_{i,T+j}$ are uncorrelated. Diebold argues that we may reasonably suppose that the individual model errors will be approximately white noise, so that the serial correlation in the combined prediction errors will be due to the serial correlation in the series itself.

This can be removed by imposing the summing-up constraint at the cost of a larger within-sample squared error.

These considerations led Diebold to propose estimating dynamic combining equations of the form (for example, for an AR(1) error):

$$\begin{aligned} A_{T+j} &= \alpha_0 + \sum_{i=1}^{2} \alpha_i P_{i,T+j} + e_{c,T+j} \\ e_{c,T+j} &= \rho e_{c,T+j-1} + \xi_{T+j} \end{aligned} \tag{10.12}$$

with combined forecast given by:

$$P_{c,T+j} = \widehat{\alpha}_0 + \sum_{i=1}^{2} \widehat{\alpha}_i P_{i,T+j} + \widehat{\rho}\widehat{e}_{c,T+j-1}. \tag{10.13}$$

Coulson and Robins (1993) seek to generalize the approach of Diebold by stressing the importance of testing the implicit common-factor restriction in (10.12) (see Hendry and Mizon, 1978), initially allowing more general dynamic structures. For example, for the system given in (10.12), the unrestricted dynamic counterpart is:

$$A_{T+j} = \alpha_0 + \sum_{i=1}^{2} \alpha_i P_{i,T+j} + \sum_{i=3}^{4} \alpha_i P_{i,T+j-1} + \alpha_5 A_{T+j-1} + \xi_{T+j}. \tag{10.14}$$

Since competing forecasts will often be collinear, they stress the importance of imposing restrictions to improve the precision of the estimates. Rather than testing the common-factor restriction, they favour testing the hypothesis that $\alpha_3 = \alpha_4 = 0$, on the grounds that for 'good' forecasts $P_{i,T+j}$ should contain all the information in $P_{i,T+j-1}$. Thus, the lagged terms in $P_{i,T+j}$ probably should not play a role, and it will often be data admissible to set them to zero, leaving the combined forecast:

$$P_{c,T+j} = \widehat{\alpha}_0 + \sum_{i=1}^{2} \widehat{\alpha}_i P_{i,T+j} + \widehat{\alpha}_5 A_{T+j-1}.$$

10.3 Forecast encompassing

In this section, we describe the concept of encompassing in section 10.3.1 , and its practical implementation in the context of evaluating large-scale macroeconometric models as forecast encompassing in section 10.3.2. We contrast the econometric methodologies underlying the combination and encompassing approaches. Typical of tests based on 1-step ahead forecast errors, tests of forecast encompassing are invariant, in the sense described in section 10.3.3. We then consider the logical relations that exist between some of the measures and tests of forecast accuracy. Finally, we give an example of the pooling of forecasts from two mis-specified models.

10.3.1 Encompassing

The concept of encompassing in econometrics can be motivated by considering a world in which the investigator knows the actual mechanism that gave rise to the observed data series. It would not be necessary to run a regression to learn about a particular (mis-specified) model: the properties of such a model could simply be deduced given knowledge of the DGP (see Hendry and Richard, 1983). In reality, the DGP is not known, although the above thought-experiment indicates that from any empirical model that is claimed to closely approximate the DGP, it should be possible to deduce the properties of other models. This is the property of encompassing. Each model can in turn be assumed to be the DGP, and we can then assess how well it does at explaining certain features of the other models. Formal tests of encompassing can be found in the papers referenced in the introduction to this chapter, and tests of the forecast variant of encompassing are outlined below.

Encompassing is part of a progressive research strategy where at each stage, models are subjected to tests, which may result in further refinements if the model is found wanting in certain dimensions. The goal is to arrive at a model which encompasses its competitors, in the sense of being able to explain their results, and hence characterize the properties of the data series at least as well as its rivals. Conceptually and operationally, the encompassing approach is different from the ethos behind the combination of forecasts, as will be emphasized in section 10.3.2. Various forms of encompassing can be defined depending upon which aspects of a rival model's performance one is seeking to explain (see section 10.3.4). Forecast encompassing is particularly relevant for assessing the performance of large-scale macroeconometric models where size considerations may rule out the use of more standard econometric tests.

10.3.2 Forecast encompassing and conditional efficiency

Forecast encompassing concerns whether the 1-step forecasts of one model can explain the forecast errors made by another. Such tests were proposed as a feasible way to evaluate large-scale econometric models by Chong and Hendry (1986), who establish that any need to pool forecasts from disparate sources indicates model mis-specification. Diebold (1989) attempts to reconcile the pooling and encompassing approaches.

When $\widehat{x}_j$ denotes the 1-step ahead forecast of x_j from M_1, and $\widetilde{x}_j$ a corresponding forecast from M_2, the pooled forecast is given by (10.1) reproduced here as:

$$\overline{x}_j = (1 - \alpha)\,\widehat{x}_j + \alpha\widetilde{x}_j. \tag{10.15}$$

If the MMSFE value of α is neither zero nor unity, then both forecasts are valuable in forecasting x_j but neither is sufficient. However, the linear combination of forecasts in (10.15) generally is not a sensible way to handle information: two models which individually fail to capture the salient features of the data are unlikely to combine on a systematic basis to produce good forecasts. Howrey (1993) provides a simple example which illustrates some of the pitfalls of uncritically combining forecasts, and another example based on the DGP in section 3.6 is provided at the end of this section. It seems wiser to sort out the models. A different prescription comes from the early literature on combining forecasts, typified by the following quotation from Nelson (1972, p.916):

> if the bum on the street corner offers free tips to the decision maker on his way to the office, these will be incorporated in composite predictions if they result in any reduction in expected loss.

One can gauge the effect on within-sample predictions of such tips, but their casual nature does not instill confidence in their reliability in the future.

Although the prescriptions for modelling practice differ radically, the combination and encompassing approaches are equivalent at the testing stage: testing for forecast encompassing is formally equivalent to Nelson (1972)'s procedure for computing 'conditional efficiency', as in Granger and Newbold (1973), although Nelson only applied the procedure to within-sample predictions, rather than forecasts. As described in section 3.2, a forecast is said to be conditionally efficient (CE) if the variance of the forecast error from a combination of that forecast and a rival forecast is not significantly less than that of the original forecast alone.

If the forecast error from M_1 is given by $x_j - \widehat{x}_j = \widehat{u}_j$, from (10.15):

$$x_j - \overline{x}_j = x_j - \widehat{x}_j + \alpha\left(\widehat{x}_j - \widetilde{x}_j\right) = \widehat{u}_j - \alpha\left(\widehat{u}_j - \widetilde{u}_j\right) = \overline{u}_j \tag{10.16}$$

(say), so that $\mathsf{V}[\overline{u}_j] < \mathsf{V}[\widehat{u}_j]$ only if $\alpha \neq 0$. The condition for the CE of the forecast from M_1 is that $\alpha = 0$, which is the same as the condition for forecast encompassing. If $\alpha \neq 0$, then the difference between the forecast errors of the two models can help explain the forecast errors of M_1, so that M_1 could be improved by incorporating some of the features of M_2. The forecast encompassing test is implemented by regressing $\widehat{u}_j$ on $\widehat{x}_j - \widetilde{x}_j$ (see (10.3)):

$$x_j - \widehat{x}_j = \alpha\left(\widehat{x}_j - \widetilde{x}_j\right) + \zeta_j \tag{10.17}$$

and using a t-test of H_0: $\alpha = 0$. This is equivalent to the regression:[1]

$$x_j = (1+\alpha)\widehat{x}_j - \alpha\widetilde{x}_j + \zeta_j. \tag{10.18}$$

This is a variant of the test due to Chong and Hendry (1986) of forecast encompassing (suggested to us by Stephen Hall), which had the form of:

$$x_j - \widehat{x}_j = \delta\widetilde{x}_j + \xi_j \tag{10.19}$$

and tested $\delta = 0$. Ericsson (1993) notes that both are special cases of:

$$x_j = \alpha_1\widehat{x}_j - \alpha_2\widetilde{x}_j + \vartheta_j, \tag{10.20}$$

[1] We are grateful to Howrey (1993) for drawing to our attention that (10.17) is identical to a regression equation proposed by Hoel (1947): also see Williams and Kloot (1953).

where (10.17) tests $\alpha_1 = 1$ (or $\alpha_2 = 0$) conditional on $\alpha_1 + \alpha_2 = 1$, whereas (10.19) tests $\alpha_2 = 0$ conditional on $\alpha_1 = 1$ only. Thus the null hypotheses are the same, but the alternatives differ. This small change in formulation may be important when the series are integrated. When $x_j \sim \mathsf{I}(1)$, so long as the two models are sufficiently well specified that $x_j - \widehat{x}_j \sim \mathsf{I}(0)$ and $x_j - \widetilde{x}_j \sim \mathsf{I}(0)$, then:

$$-(x_j - \widehat{x}_j) + (x_j - \widetilde{x}_j) = (\widehat{x}_j - \widetilde{x}_j) \sim \mathsf{I}(0),$$

so that both the regressand and regressor are $\mathsf{I}(0)$ in (10.17) under both the null and alternative, but this is only the case under the null for (10.19). The second implication of the change from (10.17) to (10.19) will become apparent in the following subsection.

If there are several competing models and a sufficiently rich parameterization, the F-test of the joint null can be used. If there is a vector of variables, the following multi-equation regression is needed:

$$\mathbf{x}_j - \widehat{\mathbf{x}}_j = \boldsymbol{\Gamma}(\widehat{\mathbf{x}}_j - \widetilde{\mathbf{x}}_j) + \boldsymbol{\zeta}_j. \qquad (10.21)$$

When $\boldsymbol{\Gamma} = \mathbf{0}$, the first system forecast encompasses the second, but it fails to do so if $\boldsymbol{\Gamma} \neq \mathbf{0}$. Such a forecast encompassing test seems useful only for large systems where more conventional tests are inapplicable.

10.3.3 Invariance of forecast encompassing tests

In section 3.5, we suggested that invariance to linear transformations is a potentially desirable property for a measure of forecast accuracy. It is straightforward to establish that forecast encompassing tests are invariant, and that tests based on 1-step forecasts typically are invariant to non-singular linear transforms.

For example, a switch from $\mathbf{x}_j$ to $\Delta\mathbf{x}_j$ leaves the test unaffected due to the homogeneity of (10.21):

$$\Delta\mathbf{x}_j - \Delta\widehat{\mathbf{x}}_j = \boldsymbol{\Gamma}(\Delta\widehat{\mathbf{x}}_j - \Delta\widetilde{\mathbf{x}}_j) + \boldsymbol{\zeta}_j \qquad (10.22)$$

since the $\mathbf{x}_{j-1}$ cancel. However, (10.19) (and system equivalents) are not homogeneous, so will be affected by non-singular linear transformations. Further, suppose that forecast encompassing holds for a set of variables in a linear system, so $\boldsymbol{\Gamma} = \mathbf{0}$ in (10.22). Then forecast encompassing must hold for any linear combination of that set of variables (with the usual *caveat* about the possibility of conflicts from finite sample tests at fixed significance levels). Consequently, despite its limitations, if forecast encompassing can be established for all relevant variables, that will ensure population MSFE dominance for all linear combinations such that $|\mathbf{M}| = 1$ (see section 3.5).

10.3.4 Forecast encompassing, MSFE and GFESM

Ericsson (1992) discusses forecast-based measures of model adequacy within the taxonomy of information sets for evaluating and designing models of Hendry and Richard (1982). The four information sets are:

A data of the model;
B measurement system of the data;
C economic theory;
D rival models' data.

Of relevance here are the first and last categories, each of which can be further sub-divided into:

1 relative past;
2 relative present;
3 relative future.

See, *inter alia*, Ericsson (1992, table 2) and section 8.1 where this taxonomy is used as the framework for a theory of intercept corrections. Lu and Mizon (1991) provide a detailed and insightful analysis of the relationships between constancy, encompassing and the implications that can be drawn from various forecast encompassing tests.

A3 can be used to generate testable hypotheses about parameter constancy and predictive accuracy (see chapter 13).

Under D1, we can distinguish three concepts that are testable: variance dominance, variance encompassing and parameter encompassing. Briefly, M_1 variance encompasses M_2 if it correctly predicts what the error variance of M_2 is; M_1 variance dominates M_2 if it has a smaller error variance than M_2, and, finally, M_1 parameter encompasses M_2 if it correctly predicts the parameters of M_2. Variance dominance is necessary but not sufficient for variance encompassing, which in turn is necessary but not sufficient for parameter encompassing (see, inter alia, Ericsson, 1992).

Ericsson suggests that a parallel structure holds under D3, relating MSFE dominance (or MMSFE), forecast encompassing, and forecast-model encompassing. M_1 forecast encompasses M_2 if it correctly predicts M_2's MSFE; it dominates M_2 on MSFE if it has a smaller MSFE; and, finally, it 'forecast-model' encompasses M_2 if M_2's regressors do not help to explain M_1's forecast errors. The same logical relations that hold at level D1 are also present for D3: MSFE dominance is necessary but not sufficient for forecast encompassing, which in turn is necessary but not sufficient for forecast-model encompassing.

The position of GFESM in this hierarchy is clear once we note that 1-step GFESM and MSFE are equivalent: thus forecast encompassing is sufficient to ensure 1-step GFESM dominance, but the model which performs best on $|\widehat{\mathbf{\Phi}}|$ need not be able to encompass all the contending models. The forecast-model encompassing concept suggested by Ericsson (1992) is required to avoid conflicts.

10.3.5 An example of pooling

Suppose the DGP is an MA(1) process, and that the two rival models are an AR(1) process and a white-noise process, as in section 3.6. Reproducing the DGP and models here for convenience, we have:

$$\begin{array}{llll} \mathsf{DGP}: & y_t = \epsilon_t + \theta\epsilon_{t-1} & \text{where} & \epsilon_t \sim \mathsf{IN}\left[0, \sigma_\epsilon^2\right] \\ \mathsf{M}_1: & y_t = \rho y_{t-1} + \nu_t & \text{where} & \nu_t \underset{h}{\sim} \mathsf{IN}\left[0, \sigma_v^2\right] \\ \mathsf{M}_2: & y_t = \eta_t & \text{where} & \eta_t \underset{h}{\sim} \mathsf{IN}\left[0, \sigma_\eta^2\right]. \end{array}$$

We established that M_1 (denoted by$\widehat{\ }$) 'wins' for 1-step forecasts using MSFE on levels (or differences), since:

$$\mathsf{M}_1\text{: } \mathsf{V}\left[\widehat{u}_{T+1}\right] = \sigma_\epsilon^2 \left(1+\theta^2\right)\left(1-\rho^2\right),$$

whereas:

$$\mathsf{M}_2\text{: } \mathsf{V}\left[\widetilde{u}_{T+1}\right] = \sigma_\epsilon^2 \left(1+\theta^2\right).$$

Suppose an investigator decides to combine the forecasts from the two models, rather than attempting to learn about the DGP. To simplify notation without loss of generality, we set $\sigma_\epsilon^2 = 1$ in what follows. The 1-step forecasts are combined according to (10.15) giving the relationship between the forecast errors as in (10.16):

$$\overline{u}_{T+1} = \widehat{u}_{T+1} - \alpha\left(\widehat{u}_{T+1} - \widetilde{u}_{T+1}\right),$$

so that :

$$\mathsf{V}\left[\overline{u}_{T+1}\right] = (1-\alpha)^2 \mathsf{V}\left[\widehat{u}_{T+1}\right] + \alpha^2 \mathsf{V}\left[\widetilde{u}_{T+1}\right] + 2\alpha(1-\alpha)\mathsf{E}\left[\widehat{u}_{T+1}\widetilde{u}_{T+1}\right]. \quad (10.23)$$

The covariance term is:

$$\mathsf{E}\left[\widehat{u}_{T+1}\widetilde{u}_{T+1}\right] = \left[1+\theta(\theta-\rho)\right] = \left(1+\theta^2\right)\left(1-\rho^2\right) = \mathsf{V}\left[\widehat{u}_{T+1}\right].$$

Substituting into (10.23) and simplifying yields:

$$\mathsf{V}\left[\overline{u}_{T+1}\right] = \left(1+\theta^2\right)\left(1-\rho^2\left(1-\alpha^2\right)\right)$$

which is minimized by $\alpha^* = 0$, so that for $0 < \alpha < 1$:

$$\mathsf{V}\left[\widehat{u}_{T+1}\right] < \mathsf{V}\left[\overline{u}_{T+1}\right] < \mathsf{V}\left[\widetilde{u}_{T+1}\right].$$

Thus, the combined forecast error always exceeds that of M_1 for a strictly convex combination, which in turn exceeds the conditional 1-step ahead DGP error variance (which is the minimum attainable if we knew the DGP).[2] That both M_1 and M_2 are

[2] In obtaining (10.7), we allowed the combination parameter α to lie in the closed interval $[0,1]$ rather than restricting it to the open interval $(0,1)$.

mis-specified would be readily apparent (at the population level, at least) from an examination of the temporal dependence in the residuals or forecast errors.

Suppose now we are interested in 2-step forecasts. We already have the individual 2-step forecast-error variances, and the covariance term is:

$$\mathsf{E}\left[\widehat{u}_{T+2}\widetilde{u}_{T+2}\right] = \mathsf{V}\left[\widetilde{u}_{T+1}\right].$$

Since:

$$\mathsf{V}\left[\overline{u}_{T+2}\right] = \left(1+\theta^2\right)\left(1+\rho^4\left(1-\alpha\right)^2\right)$$

which is minimized by $\alpha^* = 1$, then for $0 < \alpha < 1$:

$$\mathsf{V}\left[\widetilde{u}_{T+1}\right] < \mathsf{V}\left[\overline{u}_{T+1}\right] < \mathsf{V}\left[\widehat{u}_{T+1}\right]$$

reversing the ordering for $h = 1$.

In the above example, combination is worse than picking the best individual model. One would hope that the mis-specification in the 'best' model might be detectable by a careful econometric analysis so that it might be possible to arrive at a better model still. The example is merely illustrative, and little can be inferred from specific instances about how best to proceed in general: we rest our support for the position taken in this chapter regarding encompassing versus combination on the methodological principles outlined in Hendry (1995a).

10.4 Combining conditional and unconditional forecasts

In section 8.4, we showed that a linear combination of a conditional and unconditional predictor could have a smaller MSFE than either alone. In this section, we will interpret that result in the wider context of the combination of forecasts, and as an example of combining forecasts from restricted and unrestricted models. There is a more thorough treatment of estimation versus imposing parameter values for forecasting in chapter 12.

The DGP is again given by the stationary AR(1) process:

$$y_t = \psi y_{t-1} + v_t \quad \text{where } v_t \sim \mathsf{IN}\left[0, \sigma_v^2\right]. \tag{10.24}$$

We defined the composite predictor as (see (10.1)) as:

$$\widetilde{y}_{T+h} = \alpha\overline{y} + (1-\alpha)\,\widehat{y}_{T+h} = (1-\alpha)\,\widehat{y}_{T+h}, \tag{10.25}$$

where $\widehat{y}_{T+h} = \widehat{\psi}^h y_T$ is the conditional predictor and $\overline{y} = 0$ the unconditional, with respective h-step ahead conditional forecast errors given by $\widehat{e}_{T+h}$ and $\overline{e}_{T+h}$. Then the conditional MSFE for the composite predictor is:

$$\begin{aligned}\mathsf{E}\left[\widetilde{e}^2_{T+h} \mid y_T\right] &= \alpha^2\mathsf{E}\left[\overline{e}^2_{T+h} \mid y_T\right] + (1-\alpha)^2\,\mathsf{E}\left[\widehat{e}^2_{T+h} \mid y_T\right] \\ &\quad + 2\alpha(1-\alpha)\,\mathsf{E}\left[\overline{e}_{T+h}\widehat{e}_{T+h} \mid y_T\right],\end{aligned} \tag{10.26}$$

which was minimized by (8.34), as:

$$\alpha^* = \left(1 + \frac{T\psi^2}{h^2\left(1-\psi^2\right)}\right)^{-1}. \tag{10.27}$$

Alternatively, from (10.6), the value of α that minimizes (10.26) is given by:

$$\alpha^* = \frac{\mathsf{V}\left[\widehat{e}\right] - \mathsf{C}\left[\widehat{e}, \overline{e}\right]}{\mathsf{V}\left[\overline{e}\right] + \mathsf{V}\left[\widehat{e}\right] - 2\mathsf{C}\left[\overline{e}, \widehat{e}\right]}$$

with an obvious simplification to the notation. Substituting for $\mathsf{V}[\widehat{e}]$ from (8.28) and noting that:

$$\mathsf{V}\left[\overline{e}\right] = \mathsf{V}\left[y_{T+h} \mid y_T\right] = \sigma_v^2 \frac{\left(1-\psi^{2h}\right)}{\left(1-\psi^2\right)} + \psi^{2h} y_T^2$$

and:

$$\mathsf{C}\left[\widehat{e}, \overline{e}\right] = \sigma_v^2 \frac{\left(1-\psi^{2h}\right)}{\left(1-\psi^2\right)} + y_T^2 \mathsf{E}\left[\psi^h \left(\psi^h - \widehat{\psi}^h\right)\right] \simeq \sigma_v^2 \frac{\left(1-\psi^{2h}\right)}{\left(1-\psi^2\right)}$$

will also yield (10.27). This is the variance-covariance approach of section 10.2. The regression method based on:

$$\widehat{e}_{T+h} = \alpha\left(\overline{y} - \widehat{y}_{T+h}\right) + \widetilde{e}_{T+h} = \alpha\left(\overline{e}_{T+h} - \widehat{e}_{T+h}\right) + \widetilde{e}_{T+h}$$

(see (10.3)) yields the same outcome. Thus, the analysis in section 8.4 is just an example of the general framework established in this chapter.

10.4.1 Numerical analysis of the gains from combination

A simple numerical illustration may be useful in demonstrating the magnitudes of the potential gains. We shall compare the performance of the predictors in terms of unconditional forecast-error second moments. The conditional predictions are given by the forecasts from the unrestricted OLS estimation of (10.24). We can obtain the unconditional forecast-error second moment from (8.28) by averaging over the initial conditional:

$$\mathsf{V}\left[\widehat{e}_{T+h}\right] \approx \frac{\sigma_v^2\left(1-\psi^{2h}\right)}{1-\psi^2} + \sigma_v^2 T^{-1} h^2 \psi^{2(h-1)} \tag{10.28}$$

(replacing y_T^2 by $\mathsf{E}[y_T^2] = \sigma_v^2(1-\psi^2)^{-1}$). For $h = 1$ (and $\sigma^2 = 1$), (10.28) is simply $1 + T^{-1}$ and therefore independent of ψ. When $h > 1$, the MSFEs are bowl-shaped attaining their minimum at $\psi = 0$.

We can think of the unconditional predictor as a restricted regression model with $\psi = 0$, yielding the 'zero' forecast:

$$\overline{y}_{T+h} = 0 \quad \forall\, h \tag{10.29}$$

which has an unconditional forecast-error variance of:

$$\mathsf{V}\left[\overline{e}_{T+h}\right] = \mathsf{V}\left[y_{T+h}\right] = \frac{\sigma_v^2}{1-\psi^2} \tag{10.30}$$

which is independent of h. By substituting the optimal weights given by (10.27) into (8.33) and averaging over the initial condition, we can obtain the unconditional-error variance of the combined forecast. This is not given analytically, but the results of numerically evaluating (10.28), (10.30) and the combined unconditional forecast-error variance formulae are given in table 10.1.

Table 10.1 The gains from pooling conditional and unconditional forecasts

h	1	1	2	2
ψ	0.25	0.5	0.25	0.5
OLS: conditional	1.04	1.04	1.0725	1.29
Restricted: unconditional	1.0667	1.3333	1.0667	1.3333
Combined	1.0250	1.0375	1.0654	1.2770
percent gain relative to conditional	1.44	0.24	0.66	1.01

Thus, the gains are relatively small in magnitude.

In this model, we can view the Coulson and Robins (1993) suggestion for combining forecasts as combination of the OLS unrestricted forecasts with forecasts from a restricted, 'no-change' model. To see this, notice that the Coulson and Robins composite predictor based on (10.14) is given by:

$$\ddot{y}_{T+1} = \alpha_1\widehat{y}_{T+1} + \alpha_2\overline{y}_{T+1} + (1-\alpha_1-\alpha_2)\,y_T, \tag{10.31}$$

where $P_{1,T+1}$ and $P_{2,T+1}$ are replaced by $\widehat{y}_{T+1}$ and $\overline{y}_{T+1}$, $A_T = y_T$, $\alpha_3 = \alpha_4 = 0$ and $\sum\alpha_i = 0$. We deal only with $h = 1$ for simplicity. Noting that $\overline{y}_{T+1} = 0$, we can economize on notation by setting $\alpha_1 = \alpha$, so that (10.31) becomes:

$$\ddot{y}_{T+1} = \alpha\widehat{y}_{T+1} + (1-\alpha)\,y_T. \tag{10.32}$$

The y_T term can be viewed as the forecast value from a no-change predictor of the form:

$$\check{y}_{T+1} = y_T.$$

In terms of the forecast errors:

$$\ddot{e}_{T+1} = y_{T+1} - \ddot{y}_{T+1} = (1-\alpha)\,\check{e}_{T+1} + \alpha\widehat{e}_{T+1}, \tag{10.33}$$

where $\breve{e}_{T+1} = y_{T+1} - y_T$. The combined forecast-error variance (for $\sigma_v^2 = 1$) is:

$$\begin{aligned}
\mathsf{V}\left[\ddot{e}_{T+1} \mid y_T\right] &= \alpha^2 \mathsf{V}\left[\widehat{e}^2_{T+1} \mid y_T\right] + (1-\alpha)^2 \mathsf{V}\left[\breve{e}^2_{T+1} \mid y_T\right] \\
&\quad +2\alpha(1-\alpha)\mathsf{E}\left[\widehat{e}_{T+1}\breve{e}_{T+1} \mid y_T\right] \\
&\simeq \alpha^2\left(1+T^{-1}y_T^2\left(1-\psi^2\right)\right) + (1-\alpha)^2\left(1+y_T^2(1-\psi)^2\right) \\
&\quad +2\alpha(1-\alpha)
\end{aligned} \tag{10.34}$$

so:

$$\mathsf{V}\left[\ddot{e}_{T+1}\right] = \alpha^2\left(T^{-1}-1\right) + 2\alpha + (1+\psi)^{-1}\left(2-4\alpha+2\alpha^2\right)$$

taking expectations over y_T. Minimizing over α gives:

$$\ddot{\alpha} = \frac{1-\psi}{1-\psi+T^{-1}(1+\psi)} \tag{10.35}$$

so that $0 \leq \ddot{\alpha} \leq 1$, as required.

In the following table we compare the performance of the unrestricted forecasts ($\widehat{y}_{T+1} = \widehat{\psi} y_T$, labelled 'OLS'), the restricted forecasts ($\overline{y}_{T+1} = 0$, labelled 'Zero'), those formed from the 'optimal' combination using (10.27) (which we abbreviate to OC), and those from Coulson and Robins (CR) combination (using (10.35)), for $h = 1$.

Table 10.2 Forecast combination: OC versus CR

ψ	0	0.1	0.2	0.3	0.4	0.5	0.6	0.7	0.8	0.9
OLS	1.04	1.04	1.04	1.04	1.04	1.04	1.04	1.04	1.04	1.04
Zero	1.00	1.01	1.04	1.10	1.19	1.33	1.56	1.96	2.78	5.26
OC	1.00	1.01	1.02	1.03	1.03	1.04	1.047	1.04	1.039	1.040
CR	1.04	1.04	1.04	1.04	1.04	1.04	1.04	1.04	1.03	1.02

Not surprisingly, OC beats CR for $\psi < \frac{1}{2}$, loses to it for $\psi > \frac{1}{2}$, and they are equal for $\psi = \frac{1}{2}$. This is because CR effectively combines the 'no-change' with the unrestricted forecast, while OC combines the 'zero forecast' with the unrestricted forecasts. The no-change forecast is optimal when $\psi = 1$, and the zero forecast is when $\psi = 0$. If we were to calculate the MSFE for the no-change forecast, then the CR combination would be everywhere smaller than the minimum of it and the unrestricted forecast.

We will return to these issues in chapter 12 when we discuss model selection for forecasting, and in particular the gains to be had from imposing (incorrect) parameter values versus estimating the parameters.

10.5 Pooling of models differentially susceptible to breaks

Structural change that occurs over the forecast period will in general induce model misspecification : see sections 7.4.1 and 8.6. Clements and Hendry (1996b) show that the

VEqCM and DV model, for instance, will be differentially susceptible to certain types of structural break. Intercept corrections were proposed as a partial remedy for the VEqCM in section 8.6, but an alternative approach would be to pool forecasts.

Hendry and Clements (1994a) illustrate the usefulness of this approach for artificial data subject to a structural break. They find that pooling the VEqCM and DV model forecasts fares as well as any single forecasting device, particularly for predicting levels and cointegrating combinations of the data.

10.6 Overview

A combination of forecasts may be superior to any of the individual forecasts alone. Therefore, if the objective is narrowly defined as obtaining the best predictions (e.g., MMSFE predictions) in a particular instance, then combination may serve this purpose. However, if the aim of an econometric modelling exercise is viewed more broadly as discovering forecasting models that can be reliably used to forecast on an ongoing basis, then combination might be viewed as a convenient stop-gap measure. The concept of encompassing, viewed as part of a progressive research strategy, would suggest trying to refine a model to incorporate the superior features of rivals which account for their 'value-added' relative to our model.

Testing whether there are gains to combination is exactly the same as testing whether one model forecast-encompasses another. Given the problems with some large-scale model evaluation techniques (see section 7.5), testing for gains to combination, viewed as an encompassing-based model diagnostic test, may prove useful.

Chapter 11

Multi-step estimation

In this chapter, we evaluate the impact of parameter-estimation uncertainty on forecast-error uncertainty, from the perspective of multi-step (or dynamic) estimation (DE). Advocates of DE argue that when a model is mis-specified, minimization of 1-step errors may not deliver reliable forecasts at longer lead times, so that estimation by minimizing the in-sample counterpart of the desired step-ahead horizon may be advantageous. We delineate conditions which favour DE for multi-step forecasting. An analytical example shows how DE may accommodate incorrectly-specified models as the forecast lead alters, improving forecast performance for some mis-specifications. However, in well-specified models, reducing finite-sample biases does not justify DE. In a Monte Carlo forecasting study for integrated processes, estimating a unit root in the presence of a neglected negative moving-average error may favour DE, though other solutions exist to that scenario. A second Monte Carlo study obtains the estimator biases and explains these using asymptotic approximations.

11.1 Introduction

Minimizing multi-step, in-sample criteria for estimating unknown parameters has a long pedigree, although the method does not seem to have been subject to many formal analyses (see, e.g., Klein, 1971). Cox (1961a) applied this idea to the exponentially weighted moving average (EWMA) or integrated moving-average IMA(1,1) model, and Findley (1983) and Weiss (1991) among others considered multi-step estimation criteria for autoregressive (AR) models. The intuition is that when a model is not well specified, minimization of 1-step errors need not deliver reliable forecasts at longer lead times, so estimation by minimizing the in-sample counterpart of the desired step-ahead horizon may yield better forecasts.

When models are mis-specified for the DGP, MSFE rankings can alter as the forecast horizon h increases. Indeed, a necessary condition for such a result in large samples is that the models under consideration are mis-specified. However, mis-specification is not sufficient for reversals of forecast-accuracy ranking to occur, since model selection based on MSFE is not invariant under linear transformations when $h > 1$, as shown in section 3.5. This implication depends only on the DGP providing the correct conditional expectation, which is the minimum MSFE predictor. As it is not possible to prove that 1-step estimation is optimal when models are mis-specified, DE (also called 'adaptive forecasting': Tsay, 1993, and Lin and Tsay, 1996) could improve multi-period forecast accuracy.

Here, we investigate model mis-specifications which may sustain DE. Empirical studies have been used by some authors (e.g., Lin and Tsay, 1996) to gauge the practical usefulness of DE, from which it is difficult to deduce precisely which characteristics are responsible for the outcomes. We consider a simple analytic example to illustrate some of the issues involved, before presenting a Monte Carlo study to identify features which might favour DE for multi-step forecasting.

The basic formulation is as follows. Consider an h-period ahead forecast from a VAR for the n variables $\mathbf{x}_t$:

$$\mathbf{x}_t = \boldsymbol{\Upsilon}\mathbf{x}_{t-1} + \boldsymbol{\epsilon}_t, \tag{11.1}$$

where we omit the intercept for simplicity, and only specify that $\mathsf{E}[\boldsymbol{\epsilon}_t] = \mathbf{0}$. Then, h-periods ahead from an end-of-sample point T:

$$\mathbf{x}_{T+h} = \boldsymbol{\Upsilon}^h\mathbf{x}_T + \sum_{i=0}^{h-1}\boldsymbol{\Upsilon}^i\boldsymbol{\epsilon}_{T+h-i}. \tag{11.2}$$

A corresponding forecast is made, either from a 'powered-up' 1-step parameter estimator or using an h-step estimator. The 1-step estimator is defined by:

$$\widehat{\boldsymbol{\Upsilon}} = \underset{\boldsymbol{\Upsilon}}{\operatorname{argmin}}\left|\sum_{t=1}^{T}(\mathbf{x}_t - \boldsymbol{\Upsilon}\mathbf{x}_{t-1})(\mathbf{x}_t - \boldsymbol{\Upsilon}\mathbf{x}_{t-1})'\right| \tag{11.3}$$

$$= \sum_{t=1}^{T}\mathbf{x}_t\mathbf{x}_{t-1}'\left(\sum_{t=1}^{T}\mathbf{x}_{t-1}\mathbf{x}_{t-1}'\right)^{-1} \tag{11.4}$$

with forecasts given by:

$$\widehat{\mathbf{x}}_{T+h} = \widehat{\boldsymbol{\Upsilon}}^h\mathbf{x}_T \tag{11.5}$$

and average conditional error:

$$\mathsf{E}\left[\mathbf{x}_{T+h} - \widehat{\mathbf{x}}_{T+h} \mid \mathbf{x}_T\right] = \left(\boldsymbol{\Upsilon}^h - \mathsf{E}\left[\widehat{\boldsymbol{\Upsilon}}^h\right]\right)\mathbf{x}_T. \tag{11.6}$$

The h-step estimator is defined by the relation:

$$\mathbf{x}_{T+h} = \boldsymbol{\Upsilon}_h\mathbf{x}_T + \mathbf{u}_{T+h},$$

where $\boldsymbol{\Upsilon}_h$ is selected by:

$$\widetilde{\boldsymbol{\Upsilon}_h} = \underset{\boldsymbol{\Upsilon}_h}{\operatorname{argmin}}\left|\sum_{t=1}^{T}(\mathbf{x}_t - \boldsymbol{\Upsilon}_h\mathbf{x}_{t-h})(\mathbf{x}_t - \boldsymbol{\Upsilon}_h\mathbf{x}_{t-h})'\right| \tag{11.7}$$

$$= \sum_{t=1}^{T} \mathbf{x}_t \mathbf{x}'_{t-h} \left(\sum_{t=1}^{T} \mathbf{x}_{t-h} \mathbf{x}'_{t-h} \right)^{-1} \tag{11.8}$$

so that using the h-step estimator of the 'powered-up' parameter directly:

$$\widetilde{\mathbf{x}}_{T+h} = \widetilde{\mathbf{\Upsilon}}_h \mathbf{x}_T, \tag{11.9}$$

with average conditional error:

$$\mathsf{E}\left[\mathbf{x}_{T+h} - \widetilde{\mathbf{x}}_{T+h} \mid \mathbf{x}_T\right] = \left(\mathbf{\Upsilon}^h - \mathsf{E}\left[\widetilde{\mathbf{\Upsilon}_h}\right]\right) \mathbf{x}_T. \tag{11.10}$$

The relative accuracy of the multi-step forecast procedure (11.9) compared to (11.5) is determined by that of the powered estimate versus the estimated power. When $\widehat{\mathbf{\Upsilon}}$ is badly biased for $\mathbf{\Upsilon}$, powered estimated values will deviate increasingly from the powered 'true' values, in which case, direct estimation of $\mathbf{\Upsilon}_h$ may have potential. Generally, when:

$$\mathsf{E}\left[\mathbf{x}_{T+1} \mid \mathbf{x}_T\right] = \mathbf{\Upsilon} \mathbf{x}_T,$$

but:

$$\mathsf{E}\left[\mathbf{x}_{T+h} \mid \mathbf{x}_T\right] = \mathbf{\Upsilon}_h \mathbf{x}_T \neq \mathbf{\Upsilon}^h \mathbf{x}_T,$$

powering up $\widehat{\mathbf{\Upsilon}}$ may prove a poor strategy, no matter how precisely it is estimated.

However, the issue is more subtle than this. First, in stationary processes, dynamic mis-specification *per se* is not sufficient to ensure poor multi-step forecasts since 1-step estimation of $\mathbf{\Upsilon}$ in (11.1) yields the least-squares approximation, and h-step forecasts converge on the unconditional expectation with both $\mathbf{\Upsilon}^h$ and $\mathbf{\Upsilon}_h$ tending to zero. Since increasing divergence from powered estimates seems unlikely (except perhaps from accidentally estimating stationary roots as unit roots), we focus on integrated processes.

Secondly, when $\boldsymbol{\epsilon}_t \sim \mathsf{IN}_n[\mathbf{0}, \mathbf{\Omega}]$, finite-sample biases in OLS are unlikely to be large enough to offset the inefficiency of DE (see section 11.5). Thus, mis-specification seems required, so we consider the third possibility of unmodelled dynamics, using an omitted moving-average (MA) error in the DGP, such that in (11.1):

$$\boldsymbol{\epsilon}_t = \boldsymbol{\theta}(L) \boldsymbol{\zeta}_t, \quad \text{where} \quad \boldsymbol{\zeta}_t \sim \mathsf{IN}_n[\mathbf{0}, \mathbf{\Sigma}],$$

where $\boldsymbol{\theta}_0 = \mathbf{I}_n$. When $\boldsymbol{\theta}(L) = \mathbf{I}_n + \boldsymbol{\theta}_1 L$:

$$\begin{aligned}
\mathsf{E}\left[\mathbf{x}_{T+1} \mid \mathbf{x}_T\right] &= \mathbf{\Upsilon}\mathbf{x}_T + \boldsymbol{\theta}_1 \mathsf{E}\left[\boldsymbol{\zeta}_T \mid \mathbf{x}_T\right] \\
&= \left(\mathbf{\Upsilon} + \boldsymbol{\theta}_1 \mathbf{\Lambda}\right) \mathbf{x}_T \\
&= \mathbf{\Psi} \mathbf{x}_T,
\end{aligned}$$

where $\mathsf{E}[\boldsymbol{\zeta}_t | \mathbf{x}_t] = \mathbf{\Lambda}\mathbf{x}_t$, but:

$$\begin{aligned}
\mathsf{E}\left[\mathbf{x}_{T+h} \mid \mathbf{x}_T\right] &= \mathbf{\Upsilon}^h \mathbf{x}_T + \mathbf{\Upsilon}^{h-1} \boldsymbol{\theta}_1 \mathsf{E}\left[\boldsymbol{\zeta}_T \mid \mathbf{x}_T\right] \\
&= \mathbf{\Upsilon}^{h-1} \left(\mathbf{\Upsilon} + \boldsymbol{\theta}_1 \mathbf{\Lambda}\right) \mathbf{x}_T \\
&= \mathbf{\Upsilon}^{h-1} \mathbf{\Psi} \mathbf{x}_T.
\end{aligned}$$

Defining:

$$\mathsf{E}\left[\mathbf{x}_{T+h} \mid \mathbf{x}_T\right] = \boldsymbol{\Psi}_h \mathbf{x}_T$$

then $\boldsymbol{\Psi}_h = \boldsymbol{\Psi}^h$ only if $\boldsymbol{\theta}(L) = \mathbf{I}_n$, in which case $\boldsymbol{\Psi} = \boldsymbol{\Upsilon}$. (11.6) and (11.10) remain intact upon replacing $\boldsymbol{\Upsilon}^h$ by $\boldsymbol{\Psi}_h$, but $\mathsf{E}[\widehat{\boldsymbol{\Psi}}^h] \neq \boldsymbol{\Psi}_h$. This analysis suggests it is worth examining whether the substantive biases due to the interaction between estimated unit roots and neglected negative MA errors, discussed (*inter alia*) by Molinas (1986) and Schwert (1989), could justify DE over 1-step estimation. Such transpires to be the case, but we also consider other solutions to that cause of mis-specification, including using 1-step instrumental-variables (IV) estimators following Hall (1989).

The plan of this chapter is as follows. Section 11.2 describes the relationships between estimation criteria and forecast evaluation. Section 11.3 outlines a simplified version of the forecast-error taxonomy of section 7.3 to delineate the roles of estimation and model mis-specification for 1-step and DE. Section 11.4 analyses the application of DE in a simple setting. Section 11.5 shows that for correctly specified models, there is little finite-sample bias reduction from 2-step estimation versus squaring the 1-step estimator in a first-order AR. Section 11.6 reports the Monte Carlo forecasting study, showing that neglected moving-average errors have relatively benign effects on forecast performance using OLS, except in the presence of unit roots, paralleling the poor performance of unit-root tests in this situation. In section 11.7, we consider the IV estimator of Hall (1989), and a hybrid IV multi-step estimator. Their asymptotic distributions are derived for h-step forecasts, together with a Monte Carlo study. Section 11.8 provides an overview.

11.2 Estimation and evaluation criteria

Granger (1993) suggests that, at least asymptotically, the criterion used to evaluate forecasts (C_F) should also be used to estimate the parameters of the forecasting model (C_E). In the context of assessing multi-step forecasts, Weiss (1991) shows that (in large samples) parameter estimation based on minimizing squared in-sample h-step forecast errors is optimal if C_F is a squared-error loss function defined over h-step forecast errors. His Monte Carlo evidence of small-sample performance in stationary DGPs indicates that OLS is generally as good as DE. Stoica and Nehorai (1989) give similar asymptotic results for ARMA processes, and their Monte Carlo also shows small gains from DE (a possible exception being when the model is 'under-parameterized' for the DGP).[1] They conjecture that EWMA schemes may yield gains from DE because the processes to be predicted are higher order than an IMA(1,1) model. More recently, Tsay (1993) and Lin and Tsay (1996) offer an upbeat assessment of DE based on empirical studies. Weiss (1996) explores procedures which base estimation on the forecast

[1] Based on simulating an ARMA(2,2) DGP and an AR(1) model.

criterion function for a variety of forecast criteria, such as asymmetric quadratic loss: also see Christoffersen and Diebold (1996).

We consider the gains (if any) from matching estimation and evaluation criteria, taking C_F as the MSFE loss function. Unfortunately, as in chapter 3, rankings by such C_F-measures, for a given C_E, depend on the selected linear transformations of the C_F arguments (levels, differences, etc.), so a different DE is needed in each instance: see section 11.4.

11.3 A partial taxonomy of forecast errors

In this section, we present variants of the taxonomy of forecast errors developed in section 7.3 that focus on the issue of estimation uncertainty. We consider a forecast for a vector of variables $\mathbf{x}_t$ at horizon h from an estimated model M based on the conditional expectation with respect to the model where the information set is $\mathcal{I}_t$:[2]

$$\mathbf{x}_{M,T+h} = \mathsf{E}_{\mathsf{M}}\left[\mathbf{x}_{T+h} \mid \mathcal{I}_T\right].$$

Typically M will contain unknown parameters, $\mathbf{\Phi}$, which need to be estimated, so a complete description of the forecast-generation process will require both the specification of the model and the estimation criterion C_E. Using estimates $\widehat{\mathbf{\Phi}}$, the operational forecast errors are:

$$\widehat{\boldsymbol{\nu}}_{T+h} = \mathbf{x}_{T+h} - \widehat{\mathbf{x}}_{M,T+h}.$$

To contrast 1-step and multi-step estimation, we consider the special case of the forecast-error taxonomy in chapter 7 where the DGP is constant with accurate forecast origin $\mathbf{x}_T$. The degree of integration of the data, and whether unit roots are imposed or estimated, also matters: see Clements and Hendry (1995a) and Lin and Tsay (1996).

The issues are easily seen in a stationary first-order univariate AR model with an intercept when the DGP is the ARMA(1,q):

$$\begin{aligned} y_{T+h} &= \phi + \rho\left(y_{T+h-1} - \phi\right) + \nu_{T+h} \\ &= \phi + \rho^h\left(y_T - \phi\right) + \sum_{i=0}^{h-1} \rho^i \nu_{T+h-i}, \end{aligned} \qquad (11.11)$$

where $\nu_t = \theta(L)\zeta_t$ and $\zeta_t \sim \mathsf{IN}[0, \sigma_\zeta^2]$. The model is:

$$\mathsf{M}\colon y_t = \mu_p + \rho_p y_{t-1} + u_t = \phi + \rho_p\left(y_{t-1} - \phi\right) + u_t \qquad (11.12)$$

because:

$$\mathsf{E}\left[y_t\right] = \frac{\mu}{1-\rho} = \frac{\mu_p}{1-\rho_p} = \phi$$

[2] In some states of nature it may be desirable to 'correct' the conditional expectation: see chapter 8.

providing an intercept is included in (11.12), so $\mathbf{\Phi} = (\mu_p : \rho_p)$. We allow $\mu_p \neq \mu$ and $\rho_p \neq \rho$, because $\theta(L) \neq 1$ but v_t is treated as white noise. The 1-step parameter estimates $(\widehat{\mu}_p : \widehat{\rho}_p)$ yield the h-step ahead forecasts:

$$\widehat{y}_{T+h} = \widehat{\phi} + \widehat{\rho}_p^h \left(y_T - \widehat{\phi} \right). \tag{11.13}$$

From (11.11) and (11.13), the h-step ahead forecast errors are:

$$\widehat{\nu}_{T+h} = \left(1 - \rho^h\right) \phi - \left(1 - \widehat{\rho}_p^h\right) \widehat{\phi} + \left(\rho^h - \widehat{\rho}_p^h\right) y_T + \sum_{i=0}^{h-1} \rho^i \nu_{T+h-i}. \tag{11.14}$$

Denote deviations between sample estimates and population parameters by $\delta_\phi = \widehat{\phi} - \phi$ and $\delta_\rho = \widehat{\rho}_p - \rho_p$. We neglect powers of, and interactions between, δ_k, as well as any finite-sample biases in $\widehat{\phi}$ and $\widehat{\rho}_p$ around their plims, using the approximation described in section 4.11:

$$\widehat{\rho}_p^h = (\rho_p + \delta_\rho)^h \approx \rho_p^h + h\rho_p^{h-1}\delta_\rho = \rho_p^h + C_h,$$

to obtain:

$$\widehat{\rho}_p^h \widehat{\phi} \approx \left(\rho_p^h + h\rho_p^{h-1}\delta_\rho\right)(\phi + \delta_\phi) \approx \rho_p^h \phi + C_h \phi + \rho_p^h \delta_\phi,$$

so the first two terms in (11.14) are:

$$\phi - \widehat{\phi} - \rho^h \phi + \widehat{\rho}_p^h \widehat{\phi} = -\left(\rho^h - \rho_p^h\right)\phi + C_h \phi - \left(1 - \rho_p^h\right)\delta_\phi.$$

The term multiplied by y_T is approximated by:

$$\left(\rho^h - \widehat{\rho}_p^h\right) y_T = \left(\rho^h - \rho_p^h\right) y_T + \left(\rho_p^h - \widehat{\rho}_p^h\right) y_T \approx \left(\rho^h - \rho_p^h\right) y_T - C_h y_T. \tag{11.15}$$

This leads to the decomposition in table 11.1.

Table 11.1 Forecast-error taxonomy for stationary 1-step estimation

$\widehat{\nu}_{T+h}$	$\simeq$	$\left(\rho^h - \rho_p^h\right)(y_T - \phi)$	slope mis-specification
	$+$	0	intercept mis-specification
	$-$	$C_h (y_T - \phi)$	slope estimation
	$-$	$\left(1 - \rho_p^h\right)\delta_\phi$	intercept estimation
	$+$	$\sum_{i=0}^{h-1} \rho^i \nu_{T+h-i}$	error accumulation

Unconditionally, the first rows has an expectation of zero, and the second is zero, so there are no bias effects, and the remaining rows only affect forecast-error variances.

Consider the alternative of estimating ϕ and $\rho_h = \rho^h$ by DE in:

$$y_t = \phi + \rho_h (y_{t-h} - \phi) + u_t,$$

and forecasting by:

$$\widetilde{y}_{T+h} = \widetilde{\phi} + \widetilde{\rho_h}\left(y_T - \widetilde{\phi}\right). \tag{11.16}$$

From (11.11) and (11.16), the h-step ahead forecast error is:

$$\begin{aligned}\widetilde{\nu}_{T+h} &= \left(\phi - \widetilde{\phi}\right) + \rho_h (y_{t-h} - \phi) - \widetilde{\rho_h}\left(y_T - \widetilde{\phi}\right) + \sum_{i=0}^{h-1} \rho^i \nu_{T+h-i} \qquad (11.17)\\ &= -\left(1 - \rho_h^*\right)\lambda_\phi + \left(\rho_h - \rho_h^*\right)(y_{t-h} - \phi) - \lambda_\rho (y_T - \phi) + \sum_{i=0}^{h-1} \rho^i \nu_{T+h-i},\end{aligned}$$

denoting deviations between multi-step sample estimates and population parameters by $\lambda_\phi = \widetilde{\phi} - \phi$ and $\lambda_\rho = \widetilde{\rho_h} - \rho_h^*$, and neglecting powers of λ_k and finite-sample biases in $\widetilde{\phi}$ and $\widetilde{\rho_h}$ around their plims ϕ and ρ_h^*. Then, the corresponding forecast-error taxonomy for DE is shown in table 11.2.

Table 11.2 Forecast-error taxonomy for stationary multi-step estimation

$\widetilde{\nu}_{T+h}$	$\simeq$	$\left(\rho_h - \rho_h^*\right)(y_T - \phi)$	slope mis-specification
	$+$	0	intercept mis-specification
	$-$	$\lambda_\rho (y_T - \phi)$	slope estimation
	$-$	$\left(1 - \rho_h^*\right)\lambda_\phi$	intercept estimation
	$+$	$\sum_{i=0}^{h-1} \rho^i \nu_{T+h-i}$	error accumulation

The outcomes are clearly very similar when the process is stationary, the only differences being in the biases and variances for the respective estimators of ρ^h.

By way of contrast, table 11.3 shows the outcome when the process has a unit root, so $\rho = 1$. The derivation is similar to that in (11.11)–(11.15), where:

$$\sum_{i=0}^{h-1} \rho_p^i = \rho_p^{\{h\}}.$$

Similarly, for DE, when $\rho = 1$, we have table 11.4. Only the last row is in common with table 11.3, and there are no interactions between slope and intercept as in table 11.3: any of the remaining terms could be larger or smaller in mean and/or variance depending upon the specific example.

The example in section 11.4 extends this analysis to show that DE may even change the implicit model class. The Monte Carlo in section 11.6 calculates the relative magnitudes of the mis-specification and estimation effects for a number of examples.

Table 11.3 Forecast-error taxonomy for unit-root 1-step estimation

$\widehat{\nu}_{T+h}$	$\simeq$	$\left(1-\rho_p^{\{h\}}\right)\mu_p+\left(1-\rho_p^h\right)y_T$	slope mis-specification
	$+$	$(\mu-\mu_p)$	intercept mis-specification
	$-$	$C_i^{\{h\}}\mu_p-C_h y_T$	slope estimation
	$-$	$\rho_p^{\{h\}}\delta_\mu$	intercept estimation
	$+$	$\sum_{i=0}^{h-1}\nu_{T+h-i}$	error accumulation

Table 11.4 Forecast-error taxonomy for unit-root multi-step estimation

$\widetilde{\nu}_{T+h}$	$\simeq$	$(1-\rho_h^*)\,y_T$	slope mis-specification
	$+$	$(\mu_h-\mu_h^*)$	intercept mis-specification
	$-$	$\lambda_\rho y_T$	slope estimation
	$-$	λ_μ	intercept estimation
	$+$	$\sum_{i=0}^{h-1}\nu_{T+h-i}$	error accumulation

11.4 An analytical example

In section 3.6, we showed that forecast-accuracy rankings may switch across forecast horizons between models on one MSFE measure yet not on another, when parameter values are known. Here we extend the example of that section to allow for the additional impact of parameter estimation, and compare both 1-step and 2-step estimation criteria.

Thus the DGP and model are (ignoring M_2, the white-noise process):

$$\mathsf{M}_0\colon y_t=\epsilon_t+\theta\epsilon_{t-1},\quad \text{where}\quad \epsilon_t\sim\mathsf{IN}[0,\sigma_\epsilon^2],\tag{11.18}$$

and:

$$\mathsf{M}_1\colon y_t=\rho y_{t-1}+\nu_t,\qquad \text{where}\quad \nu_t\underset{h}{\sim}\mathsf{IN}\left[0,\sigma_\nu^2\right],$$

where $\underset{h}{\sim}$ denotes 'is hypothesized to be distributed as'. We consider four alternative strategies for 2-step forecasting, namely, estimating the M_1 parameter using 1-step and 2-step error minimization, and predicting levels or changes.

11.4.1 1-step minimization for levels

First, 1-step in-sample fitting of the model in levels yields $\widehat{\rho}$:

$$\widehat{\rho}=\underset{\rho}{\operatorname{argmin}}\sum_{t=1}^{T}(y_t-\rho y_{t-1})^2=\sum_{t=1}^{T}y_t y_{t-1}\left(\sum_{t=1}^{T}y_{t-1}^2\right)^{-1}\tag{11.19}$$

as the scalar version of (11.3). To a first approximation:

$$\mathsf{E}\left[\widehat{\rho}\right] \simeq \frac{\theta}{(1+\theta^2)} = \rho. \tag{11.20}$$

Then forecasts of y_{T+2} from M_1 are given by:

$$\widehat{y}_{T+2} = \widehat{\rho}^2 y_T.$$

Since both estimation criterion and forecast horizon affect the outcome, we denote MSFEs by (e.g.) $\mathsf{MSFE}^{\Delta:2}_{\mathsf{L}:1}$, where the superscripts denote predicting the differences (Δ, using L for levels) 2-steps ahead, and subscripts denote estimation to minimize errors in levels (L) 1-step ahead. Then for $h = 2$:

$$\mathsf{E}\left[\widehat{y}_{T+2} \mid y_T\right] = \mathsf{E}\left[\widehat{\rho}^2\right] y_T \simeq \rho^2 y_T$$

so that:

$$\begin{aligned}\mathsf{MSFE}^{\mathsf{L}:2}_{\mathsf{L}:1} &= \mathsf{E}\left[\left(y_{T+2} - \widehat{\rho}^2 y_T\right)^2 \mid y_T\right] \\ &\simeq \left(1+\theta^2\right)\sigma^2_\epsilon + \left(\mathsf{V}\left[\widehat{\rho}^2\right] + \rho^4\right) y^2_T.\end{aligned}$$

11.4.2 2-step minimization for levels

The second strategy is to write the model as:

$$y_t = \rho^2 y_{t-2} + \nu_t + \rho\nu_{t-1} = \phi y_{t-2} + v_t$$

and estimate ϕ by minimizing 2-step errors in levels (see (11.7)):

$$\widetilde{\phi} = \underset{\phi}{\operatorname{argmin}} \sum_{t=1}^{T} \left(y_t - \phi y_{t-2}\right)^2 = \sum_{t=1}^{T} y_t y_{t-2} \left(\sum_{t=1}^{T} y^2_{t-2}\right)^{-1}, \tag{11.21}$$

where to a first approximation under M_0, $\mathsf{E}[\widetilde{\phi}] \simeq 0$. Thus, forecasts of y_{T+2} using 2-step minimization of M_1 under M_0 are given by the white-noise process:

$$\widetilde{y}_{T+2} = \widetilde{\phi} y_T \simeq 0,$$

so that:

$$\begin{aligned}\mathsf{MSFE}^{\mathsf{L}:2}_{\mathsf{L}:2} &= \mathsf{E}\left[\left(y_{T+2} - \widetilde{\phi} y_T\right)^2 \mid y_T\right] \\ &\simeq \left(1+\theta^2\right)\sigma^2_\epsilon + \mathsf{V}\left[\widetilde{\phi}\right] y^2_T.\end{aligned}$$

Providing $\mathsf{V}[\widetilde{\phi}] \leq (\mathsf{V}[\widehat{\rho}^2] + \rho^4)$, the second strategy (in (11.21)) will produce a smaller MSFE than the first ((11.19)). A necessary condition for this outcome is that

M_1 is mis-specified for M_0 since otherwise, $\widetilde{\phi} = \widehat{\rho^2}$ is an inefficient estimator of ρ^2 relative to $(\widehat{\rho})^2$, as there is no further information to exploit beyond that contained in the 1-step forecasts. When 2-step estimation is used, the conventionally reported coefficient standard errors are biased and inconsistent, so autocorrelation-consistent standard errors should be calculated.

Implicitly, the multi-step criterion has induced a change in model class from an autoregression to a moving average, represented at 2-steps ahead by white noise. Conversely, in large samples, switching the class of model is symptomatic of mis-specification. In finite samples, however, the non-monotonicity of forecast confidence intervals provides a possible alternative rationale (see Hendry, 1986 and section 8.4).

11.4.3 1-step minimization for differences

For 1-step minimization using Δy_t, define $\widehat{\rho}_{\Delta}$ by:

$$\widehat{\rho}_{\Delta} = \underset{\rho_{\Delta}}{\operatorname{argmin}} \sum_{t=1}^{T} \left(\Delta y_t - \rho_{\Delta} y_{t-1}\right)^2 \tag{11.22}$$

then $\widehat{\rho}_{\Delta} = \widehat{\rho} - 1$, so that $\mathsf{E}[\widehat{\rho}_{\Delta}] \simeq \rho - 1$. Since M_1 assumes:

$$\Delta y_{T+2} = \rho_{\Delta} \left(\rho_{\Delta} - 1\right) y_T + \nu_{T+2} + \left(\rho - 1\right) \nu_{T+1}$$

then:

$$\widehat{\Delta y}_{T+2} = \widehat{\rho}_{\Delta} \left(\widehat{\rho}_{\Delta} - 1\right) y_T = \widehat{\rho} \left(\widehat{\rho} - 1\right) y_T = \Delta \widehat{y}_{T+2},$$

so that $\mathsf{MSFE}_{\Delta:1}^{\Delta:2} = \mathsf{MSFE}_{\mathsf{L}:1}^{\Delta:2}$, and hence there is no difference between predicting from fitting 1-step to levels or to changes.[3] Since:

$$\Delta y_{T+2} = \epsilon_{T+2} + \left(\theta - 1\right) \epsilon_{T+1} - \theta \epsilon_T \tag{11.23}$$

then since $\mathsf{E}[\epsilon_T | y_T] = (1 + \theta^2)^{-1} y_T$ as $\mathsf{E}[\epsilon_T y_T] = \sigma_\epsilon^2$ and $\mathsf{E}[y_T^2] = (1 + \theta^2)\sigma_\epsilon^2$:

$$\begin{aligned} \mathsf{MSFE}_{\Delta:1}^{\Delta:2} &= \mathsf{E}\left[\left(\Delta y_{T+2} - \widehat{\Delta y}_{T+2}\right)^2 \mid y_T\right] \\ &\simeq \left[1 + (\theta - 1)^2\right] \sigma_\epsilon^2 + \theta^2 \mathsf{E}\left[\epsilon_T^2 \mid y_T\right] \\ &\quad + \left[(1 + 2\rho) \mathsf{V}\left[\widehat{\rho}^2\right] + \mathsf{V}\left[\widehat{\rho}\right]\right] y_T^2. \end{aligned} \tag{11.24}$$

11.4.4 2-step minimization for differences

For 2-step errors, the model-based prediction of Δy_t is:

$$\widetilde{\Delta y}_t = \rho \left(\rho - 1\right) y_{t-2} = \phi_{\Delta} y_{t-2}$$

[3] However, replacing $\rho_{\Delta} y_{t-1}$ by $\rho_{\Delta} \Delta y_{t-1}$ in (11.22) would alter the model class by imposing a unit root.

suggesting estimation of the parameter from:

$$\widetilde{\phi}_{\Delta} = \underset{\phi_{\Delta}}{\operatorname{argmin}} \sum_{t=1}^{T} (\Delta y_t - \phi_{\Delta} y_{t-2})^2 = \sum_{t=1}^{T} \Delta y_t y_{t-2} \left(\sum_{t=1}^{T} y_{t-2}^2 \right)^{-1}. \quad (11.25)$$

Under M_0:

$$\mathsf{E}\left[\widetilde{\phi}_{\Delta}\right] = \frac{-\theta}{1+\theta^2} = -\rho$$

noting from (11.23) that:

$$\mathsf{E}\left[\Delta y_{T+2} \mid y_T\right] = -\theta \mathsf{E}\left[\epsilon_T \mid y_T\right] = -\theta \left(1+\theta^2\right)^{-1} y_T = -\rho y_T$$

hence 2-step minimization for differences picks up the appropriate model. Forecasts of Δy_{T+2} become:

$$\widetilde{\Delta y}_{T+2} = \widetilde{\phi}_{\Delta} y_T.$$

Thus:

$$\begin{aligned} \mathsf{MSFE}_{\Delta:2}^{\Delta:2} &= \mathsf{E}\left[\left(\Delta y_{T+2} - \widetilde{\phi}_{\Delta} y_T\right)^2 \mid y_T\right] \\ &\simeq \left[1 + (\theta-1)^2\right]\sigma_{\epsilon}^2 + \theta^2 \mathsf{E}\left[\epsilon_T^2 \mid y_T\right] + \left(\mathsf{V}\left[\widetilde{\phi}_{\Delta}\right] - \rho^2\right) y_T^2 \end{aligned}$$

which is likely to be smaller than (11.24).

Forecasts of Δy_{T+2}, using 2-step estimation of the levels, under M_0, are given by the difference between the 2-step levels estimator, and the 1-step levels (or differences) estimator:

$$\widetilde{\Delta y}_{T+2} = \widetilde{\phi} y_T - \widehat{\rho} y_T = \left(\widetilde{\phi} - \widehat{\rho}\right) y_T$$

so that $\mathsf{MSFE}_{\Delta:2}^{\Delta:2} \neq \mathsf{MSFE}_{\mathsf{L}:2}^{\Delta:2}$. In section 11.6, we quantify the gains from matching the linear transformation in estimation to that used in forecast evaluation by simulating $\mathsf{MSFE}_{\Delta:h}^{\Delta:h}$ and $\mathsf{MSFE}_{\mathsf{L}:h}^{\Delta:h}$ for $h = 1, \ldots, 4$, over a variety of experiments.

11.5 Finite-sample behaviour under correct specification

An alternative reason for minimizing a 2-step criterion when 2-step forecasts are desired in dynamic models is the possible reduction in finite-sample bias that might result from doing so even when the models are correctly specified. As an illustration, suppose that the model is correctly specified for a stationary AR(1) with an intercept. Then (see White, 1961), we obtain a finite-sample bias for 1-step estimation of the AR parameter, ρ, given by:

$$\mathsf{E}\left[\widehat{\rho}\right] \simeq \rho - \frac{1+3\rho}{T}. \quad (11.26)$$

The analysis of the bias in $\widetilde{\rho^2}$ (the 2-step estimator) is close in form to that for the bias in the 1-step estimator (see e.g., Hendry, 1984, for an exposition), and to $O(1/T)$ suggests that $\mathsf{E}[\widetilde{\rho^2}]$ is the square of (11.26). When $\rho = 0$, retaining terms of $O(1/T)$ only, it is straightforward to show that (see section 11.9):

$$\mathsf{E}\left[\widetilde{\rho^2} \mid \rho = 0\right] \simeq -\frac{1}{T},$$

as indicated in figure 11.1. For OLS, from:

$$\mathsf{E}\left[\widehat{\rho}^2 \mid \rho = 0\right] = \left(\mathsf{E}\left[\widehat{\rho} \mid \rho = 0\right]\right)^2 + \mathsf{V}\left[\widehat{\rho} \mid \rho = 0\right] = \frac{1}{T^2} + \frac{1}{T},$$

we obtain a bias of roughly equal magnitude but opposite sign.

This result can be confirmed by Monte Carlo simulationusing PcNaive (see Hendry, Neale and Ericsson, 1991). We selected $\rho = 0, 0.4, 0.8, 1.0$ and $T = 100$, and conducted the simulations recursively from $t = 10, \ldots, 100$ with 10,000 replications. Figure 11.1 plots $\mathsf{E}[\widehat{\rho}^2 - \rho^2]$ (the dotted lines) and $\mathsf{E}[\widetilde{\rho^2} - \rho^2]$ (the solid lines) for the four values of ρ. Thus, BDE0 denotes the bias in DE for $\rho = 0$; BOLS4sq is the bias in OLS for ρ^2 when $\rho = 0.4$, etc. The two approaches are similarly biased at large values of ρ and all sample sizes, so there is no gain in terms of finite-sample bias from direct 2-step estimation. Biases are smaller at smaller ρ, but OLS still dominates, except perhaps at $\rho = 0$. The case of $\rho = 1$ is analysed in section 11.7.

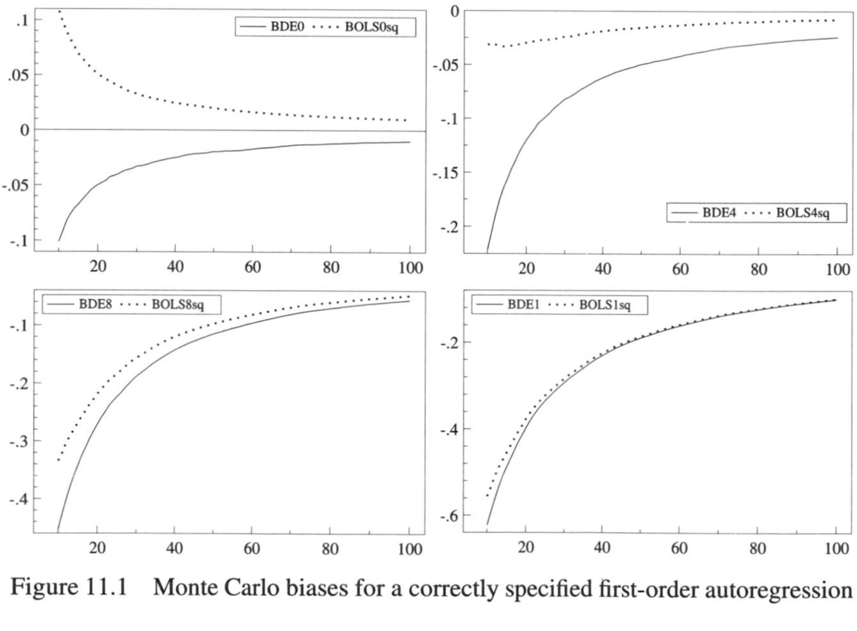

Figure 11.1 Monte Carlo biases for a correctly specified first-order autoregression

11.6 A Monte Carlo study of multi-step forecasting

On the basis of these results, we conjecture that neither sampling variability (where 1-step should do best), nor (stationary) finite-sample bias are likely to indicate a role for DE. Alternatively, any divergence between $(\mathbf{\Psi}_h - \mathbf{\Upsilon}_p^h)$, on the one hand, versus $(\mathbf{\Psi}_h - \mathbf{\Upsilon}_h^*)$, on the other, might be important, particularly for integrated data where not all the terms are tending to zero in the forecast horizon. Recall $\mathbf{\Psi}_h$ is defined by $\mathsf{E}[\mathbf{x}_{T+h}|\mathbf{x}_T] = \mathbf{\Psi}_h \mathbf{x}_T$, and $\mathbf{\Psi}_h = \mathbf{\Upsilon}^h$ only when the DGP can be represented as a VAR (ruling out MA errors). Thus, we designed the Monte Carlo to highlight potential biases when estimating unit-root processes yet neglecting negative moving-average errors.

The DGP is the scalar 'nonseasonal Holt model' (see, among others, Ord, 1988, and Harvey, 1989), generating the data as the sum of unobserved components for the trend, intercept, and irregular elements:

$$y_t = \mu_t + \epsilon_t \tag{11.27}$$

$$\mu_t = \mu_{t-1} + \beta_t + \delta_{1t} \tag{11.28}$$

$$\beta_t = \beta_{t-1} + \delta_{2t}. \tag{11.29}$$

In (11.27)–(11.29), the disturbances ϵ_t, δ_{1t} and δ_{2t} are assumed to be normal, independent through time and of each other (at all lags and leads), with zero means and variances $\sigma_\epsilon^2, \sigma_{\delta_1}^2, \sigma_{\delta_2}^2$. The 'reduced form' implies the restricted ARIMA(0,2,2) model:

$$(1-L)^2 y_t = (1 - \theta_1 L - \theta_2 L^2) a_t, \tag{11.30}$$

where the θ_i can be deduced by matching moments in (11.30) and (11.31), the latter obtained directly from (11.27)–(11.29) (see Harvey, 1989):

$$(1-L)^2 y_t = \epsilon_t + \delta_{1t} + \delta_{2t} - 2\epsilon_{t-1} - \delta_{1t-1} + \epsilon_{t-2}. \tag{11.31}$$

Zero restrictions on the variances $\sigma_\epsilon^2, \sigma_{\delta_1}^2, \sigma_{\delta_2}^2$ enable data with different orders of integration to be generated from (11.27)–(11.29). These are summarized in table 11.5.

We consider six AR forecasting models. M_1 is an AR(2) process for the levels, formulated in differences (i.e., with a unit root imposed):

$$\mathsf{M}_1\text{: } \Delta y_t = \alpha_0 + \alpha_1 \Delta y_{t-1} + \nu_t \tag{11.32}$$

and M_1^* is the same model but with $\alpha_0 = 0$. M_2 is the same AR(2) model, but in levels without the unit root imposed, and M_2^* is M_2 without a constant term. Finally, we consider an AR(1) model in levels, with a constant term (M_3), and without (M_3^*).

Minimizing the in-sample h-step errors is non-linear in the parameters of the original models, but can be approximated by a linear projection (and thus by OLS).[4] For

[4] While linear projection is not in general equivalent to non-linear minimization, the two coincide here for multi-step estimation, but would not do so for models with explanatory variables where there are restrictions on the parameters.

Table 11.5 Monte Carlo design

	Parameter restrictions	DGP	Description
I	None	See (11.30)	ARIMA(0,2,2)
	$\sigma_\epsilon^2 \quad \sigma_{\delta_1}^2 \quad \sigma_{\delta_2}^2$		
(i)	$1 \quad 1 \quad 1$		
(ii)	$1 \quad .5 \quad 1$		
(iii)	$1 \quad 1 \quad .5$		
II	$\sigma_{\delta_2}^2 = 0, \quad \beta_t = \beta \neq 0$	$\Delta y_t = \beta + \delta_{1t} + \Delta\epsilon_t$	ARIMA(0,1,1) plus drift
III	$\sigma_{\delta_2}^2 = 0, \quad \beta_t = \beta = 0$	$\Delta y_t = \delta_{1t} + \Delta\epsilon_t$	ARIMA(0,1,1)
IV	$\sigma_{\delta_2}^2 = 0,$ $\beta_t = \beta \neq 0, \sigma_\epsilon^2 = 0$	$\Delta y_t = \beta + \delta_{1t}$	ARIMA(0,1,0) plus drift
V	$\sigma_{\delta_2}^2 = 0,$ $\beta_t = \beta = 0, \sigma_\epsilon^2 = 0$	$\Delta y_t = \delta_{1t}$	ARIMA(0,1,0)
VI	$\sigma_{\delta_2}^2 = \sigma_{\delta_1}^2 = 0, \quad \beta \neq 0$	$y_t = \beta t + \epsilon_t$	Linear trend
VII	$\sigma_{\delta_2}^2 = \sigma_{\delta_1}^2 = 0, \quad \beta = 0$	$y_t = \epsilon_t$	White noise
VIII	$\sigma_{\delta_1}^2 = 0, \quad \sigma_\epsilon^2 = 0$	$(1 - \tau_1 L)(1 - \tau_2 L) y_t = \delta_{2t}$	
(i)	$\lvert\tau_1\rvert = \lvert\tau_2\rvert = 1$		ARIMA(0,2,0)
(ii)	$\lvert\tau_1\rvert = 1, \lvert\tau_2\rvert < 1$		ARIMA(1,1,0)
(iii)	$\lvert\tau_1\rvert < 1, \lvert\tau_2\rvert < 1$		ARIMA(2,0,0)
IX		$\Delta y_t = \tau_1 \Delta y_{t-1} + \delta_{2t} + \Delta\delta_{1t}$	
(i)	$\sigma_{\delta_1}^2 = \sigma_{\delta_2}^2 = 1, \sigma_\epsilon^2 = 0,$ $\tau_1 = 0.5, \tau_2 = 1$		ARIMA(1,1,1)
(ii)	$\sigma_{\delta_1}^2 = \sigma_{\delta_2}^2 = 1, \sigma_\epsilon^2 = 0,$ $\tau_1 = 0.1, \tau_2 = 1$		ARIMA(1,1,1)

example, M_1 in (11.32) implies h-step errors ($\nu_{h,t}$) of the form:

$$\Delta y_t = \alpha_0 \sum_{i=0}^{h-1} \alpha_1^i + \alpha_1^h \Delta y_{t-h} + \sum_{i=0}^{h-1} \alpha_1^i \nu_{t-i} \tag{11.33}$$

$$= \alpha_{0,h} + \alpha_{1,h} \Delta y_{t-h} + \nu_{h,t}. \tag{11.34}$$

We estimate $\boldsymbol{\alpha} = [\alpha_0 : \alpha_1]'$ by minimizing the sums of squares of $\nu_{h,t}$ with respect to the parameters:

$$\underset{\boldsymbol{\alpha}}{\operatorname{argmin}} \sum_{t=h+1}^{T} \left(\Delta y_t - \alpha_0 \sum_{i=0}^{h-1} \alpha_1^i - \alpha_1^h \Delta y_{t-h} \right)^2 \tag{11.35}$$

yielding a function which is non-linear in the parameters α_0 and α_1. The same outcome results by projecting Δy_t on a constant and Δy_{t-h} by OLS, defining $\boldsymbol{\alpha} = [\alpha_{0,h} : \alpha_{1,h}]'$

as in (11.33), since for this model, the form of (11.35) does not impose any restrictions on $[\alpha_{0,h} : \alpha_{1,h}]$ for h-step estimation. However, the parameters of the 1-period model $(\alpha_0 : \alpha_1)$ are not necessarily uniquely identifiable from the OLS projection (consider $h = 2$).

In all cases we use OLS to estimate the models, and calculate 1- to h-step MSFEs for 1-step estimation but only h-period MSFEs for h-step estimation.

11.6.1 Analysis of results

There are three basic sets of results: (a) table 11.9 reports MSFEs for predicting Δy_t using models M_1 and M_1^*; (b) table 11.10 shows MSFEs for predicting y_t using models M_2, M_2^* and M_3, M_3^* (the AR(2) and AR(1) models); and (c) table 11.11 compares estimation in differences with levels for predicting Δy_t using an AR(2) model (including a constant term).

First, tables 11.9 and 11.10 are summarized in tables 11.6 and 11.7 using response surfaces to highlight the conditions which favoured DE over OLS. The dependent variable is the log of the ratio of the MSFE for DE to that for OLS: in table 11.6 for 2-steps ahead, and in table 11.7 for 4-step ahead forecasts. Four regressions are reported in each table. The first pools results from table 11.9 (MSFEs for predicting Δy_t using M_1, labelled experiments 1–14) and table 11.10 (MSFEs for predicting y_t using model M_2, labelled experiments 15–28, and using M_3, labelled experiments 29–42). The other regressions are specific to the results for a particular model.

The explanatory variables are a constant, a dummy which is unity if at least one unit root is estimated and zero otherwise (Dur), a dummy which is unity if there is a moving-average term and zero otherwise (Dma), an interaction dummy for these two effects (Dur×Dma) and, finally, Dcanc, which is unity for DGP (IXi), M_2 and M_3 when the MA root is approximately cancelled by an AR root.

Table 11.6 Response surfaces for log(DE/OLS) for 2-step forecasts

	All experiments	Exp. 1–14	Exp. 15–28	Exp. 29–42
Constant	−0.011	0.003	−0.025	−0.015
	(0.017)	(0.015)	(0.038)	(0.017)
Dur	0.017	−0.003	0.032	0.021
	(0.024)	(0.034)	(0.051)	(0.023)
Dma	−0.013	−0.026		
	(0.027)	(0.020)		
Dur×Dma	−0.065	−0.121	−0.102	−0.019
	(0.035)	(0.040)	(0.043)	(0.019)
Dcanc	0.078		0.101	0.018
	(0.040)		(0.072)	(0.032)
R^2	0.301	0.829	0.400	0.123

Table 11.7 Response surfaces for log(DE/OLS) for 4-step forecasts

	All experiments	Exp. 1–14	Exp. 15–28	Exp. 29–42
Constant	−0.028	0.007	−0.029	−0.072
	(0.040)	(0.027)	(0.090)	(0.055)
Dur	0.047	0.001	0.050	0.094
	(0.058)	(0.060)	(0.119)	(0.072)
Dma	0.038	0.004		
	(0.065)	(0.035)		
Dur×Dma	−0.233	−0.355	−0.248	−0.062
	(0.084)	(0.071)	(0.101)	(0.061)
Dcanc	0.192		0.246	0.054
	(0.094)		(0.168)	(0.102)
R^2	0.347	0.911	0.431	0.169

The tables report coefficient estimates and standard errors (in brackets). Dcanc is zero for all observations for the first sub-sample, and Dma and Dur×Dma are collinear for the second and third, so the former is omitted. In no case are the constant, Dur and Dma significantly different from zero: in general, therefore, there is little gain (loss) from DE, and either estimating unit roots or neglecting MA components, in the absence of the other, does not alter this.

The conjunction of the two (signalled by Dur×Dma), on the other hand, significantly favours DE, particularly at 4-steps (table 11.7), except for the third sub-sample where the model is under-parameterized for many of the DGPs. Finally, the coefficient on Dcanc is always approximately equal magnitude and opposite sign to Dur×Dma, so that there is no gain to DE when the MA term is effectively cancelled by an AR root (see section 11.6.1.3).

We now discuss the contributions to forecast errors of stochastic uncertainty, model mis-specification and estimation uncertainty.

11.6.1.1 Stochastic uncertainty

The uncertainty from accumulating future disturbances in the DGP sets a baseline level which cannot be improved upon by stochastic models. This source of forecast uncertainty, as measured by MSFE, is $O(1)$ in the forecast horizon for $\mathsf{I}(0)$ processes, and $O(h)$ for $\mathsf{I}(1)$ processes (see, e.g., Engle and Yoo, 1987, and chapter 4), as is reflected in our results. For example, from the first column of MSFEs in table 11.10, the MSFE for DGP (VIIIi) is $O(h^2)$ in the forecast horizon, since y_t is $\mathsf{I}(2)$; for DGP (VIIIii), it is $O(h)$ in the forecast horizon, since y_t is $\mathsf{I}(1)$; and for DGP (VIIIiii), it is $O(1)$, since y_t is $\mathsf{I}(0)$. Table 11.9 conveys the same information for Δy_t where the orders of integration and their rates of increase are reduced by unity.

Although the effects of this source of uncertainty can be obtained analytically, the figures in the tables are Monte Carlo estimates calculated numerically by simulating forecasts from (11.27)–(11.29) with the disturbances set to zero over the forecast period. Such estimates reflect Monte Carlo variability, but this is small for 10,000 replications. For example, when the process is a linear trend or white noise (DGPs (VI,VII)), the theoretical conditional forecast-error variances for predicting Δy_t are 1 for $h = 1$ and 2 for $h > 1$ compared with Monte Carlo estimates for the 1- to 4-step horizons of $[1, 1.99, 2.04, 2.01]$: see table 11.9.

11.6.1.2 Model mis-specification

To gauge the impact of model mis-specification in the absence of parameter-estimation uncertainty, we generated forecasts using the pseudo-true values of the models' parameters under the DGP (referred to as $[\mu_p : \rho_p]$ for 1-step, and $[\mu_h^* : \rho_h^*]$ for h-step, in section 11.3). These values are derived analytically. We computed this source of uncertainty including the stochastic element from the future disturbances, so these forecasts can be compared against the actual realizations.

Table 11.9 reveals the main points. First, when the model is correctly specified, the 'true model' and 'control' (for estimation uncertainty) columns are identical (DGPs (IV,V,VIIIi&ii) in table 11.9). Failure to impose a valid unit root does not constitute model mis-specification (table 11.9, DGP (VIIIi)), but imposing an invalid unit root does (table 11.9, DGP (VIIIiii)) as over-parameterization is not a form of mis-specification, but under-parameterization is.

Secondly, abstracting from DGP (I), the impact of model mis-specification is largest at 1-step horizons and is typically small at longer horizons (see the '1-step control' in table 11.9, for DGPs (II,III,VI,VII)). An exception is where the model is mis-specified in terms of omitting a constant (e.g., M_1^* for DGP (II)). In DGP (VIIIiii), the model incorrectly imposes a unit root for a stationary AR(2) process, so the impact of model mis-specification is more persistent in the forecast horizon.

For DGPs (VI,VII,IXii), there is a marked improvement at $h = 2$ from the DE control ('h-step control': ρ_h^* and μ_h^*) relative to the 1-period control. Using DGP (VII) as an example, since $y_t = \epsilon_t$ then $\Delta y_t = \Delta\epsilon_t$ when the model is:

$$\Delta y_t = \alpha_1 \Delta y_{t-1} + \nu_t.$$

Thus, the DGP has a non-invertible MA error which is imperfectly captured by Δy_{t-1} in the model: the disturbance $\Delta\epsilon_t$ has autocorrelations of $-1/2$ then zero at longer lags, whereas the mis-specified model has α_1, α_1^2, etc. This affects OLS but not DE, since for $h > 1$ estimation, the pseudo-true value ρ_h^* of α_1 is zero, and the forecast of the change $\widehat{\Delta y}_{T+h} = 0$ for $h > 1$, with MSFE $\mathsf{E}[\epsilon_{T+h} - \epsilon_{T+h-1}]^2 = 2\sigma_\epsilon^2$. Thus the $h > 1$ control is a white-noise model, while the $h = 1$ control is autoregressive (with $\alpha_1 = -1/2$). The forecast for $h = 2$ using the $h = 1$ control is:

$$\widehat{\Delta y}_{T+2} = \left(-\tfrac{1}{2}\right)^2 \Delta y_T$$

so:

$$\mathsf{E}\left[\left(\Delta y_{T+2} - \widehat{\Delta y}_{T+2}\right)^2\right] = \mathsf{E}\left[\left(\epsilon_{T+2} - \epsilon_{T+1} - \frac{1}{4}\left(\epsilon_T - \epsilon_{T-1}\right)\right)^2\right] = 2.125\sigma_\epsilon^2.$$

The h-step control allows the model to change in response to Δy_t being unpredictable (white noise) at more than 1-step ahead. Including the Δy_{t-1} term simply inflates the forecast error. The forecast for $h = 4$ using the $h = 1$ control is:

$$\widehat{\Delta y}_{T+4} = \left(-\tfrac{1}{2}\right)^4 \Delta y_T = \frac{1}{16}\Delta y_T \simeq 0,$$

so that the cost of using the 1-step control has all but disappeared for $h = 4$.

A similar analysis holds for DGPs (II,III), except that the 'cost' of using the 1-step control for forecasting $T + 2$ is quantitatively smaller: the 1-step control model has a coefficient of $-1/3$ rather than $-1/2$ and the base-line uncertainty is larger at $2\sigma_\epsilon^2 + \sigma_{\delta_1}^2$.

Comparing results for DGPs (VIIIi) and (I) suggests that neglecting the MA error is responsible for the large increase in forecast uncertainty relative to that inherent in predicting an $\mathsf{I}(2)$ process. The 1-step and multi-step controls for DGP (I) have all had the slope parameter set to unity (the constant, where estimated, is zero). This is only correct asymptotically, but is a reasonable approximation unless the MA roots are close to minus one. DGP (IXi&ii) table 11.9 has only a first-order MA and a stationary root, compared to the second-order MA and unit root in DGP (I). The impact of model mis-specification is largest at a 1-step horizon, and is more persistent than for DGPs (II,III), due to the interaction of the omitted MA error with the autoregressive dynamics. Nevertheless, that the AR dynamics are stationary implies that the impact of the MA mis-specification dies out in the horizon: this is not the case when the AR dynamics have a unit root as in DGP (I). The AR component in DGP (IXi) relative to DGP (VII), reduces the gains from the multi-step control characteristic of processes with MAs.

11.6.1.3 Estimation uncertainty: 1-*step and multi-step criteria*

The impact of 1-step estimation uncertainty is generally fairly small apart from DGPs (I,VIIIi), table 11.9, when a unit root is being estimated. DE is significantly better for DGP (I), when a unit root is being estimated in conjunction with omitted MA errors, but not in the absence of MA mis-specification as in DGP (VIIIi). An omitted MA error in the absence of implicit unit-root estimation (table 11.9, DGP (IXi&ii)) leads to only a small increase in overall forecast uncertainty above that due to model mis-specification, and no significant benefit from multi-step estimation. In summary, unit-root AR dynamics together with omitted MA errors seem necessary here for gains from multi-step over 1-step estimation.

In table 11.10, DGP (VIII), the AR(2) model is correctly specified, and so the 1- and h-step estimation columns measure the impact of estimation uncertainty, such that estimating the unit roots (two for VIIIi, one for VIIIii) significantly inflates the forecast-error variances, but there is no gain to DE.

1-step estimation is also better here than DE when there are unit roots and the model is under-parameterized (table 11.10, DGPs (VIIIi&ii) and AR(1) model), although there is little between the two when the model is under-parameterized and unit roots are not being implicitly estimated (table 11.10, DGP (VIIIiii), AR(1) model).

Further evidence that DE appears to be most advantageous when unit roots are being estimated and there are omitted MA components is provided by table 11.10, DGPs (II,III), the AR(1) model. However, merely over-parameterizing the autoregressive part of the model largely removes the gains from DE and yields a lower forecast-error variance: the extra autoregression corrects the missing MA error. Table 11.10 DGP (I), AR(2) model shows gains from DE when MA components are present and a *double* unit root is being estimated (but not when the AR component is under-parameterized).

At first sight, table 11.10, DGP (IXi) is an anomaly since the DGP is an ARIMA$(1,1,1)$, and the models are AR(2) and AR(1) in levels. Thus, a unit root is being estimated with a neglected MA error, but 1-step estimation is preferred. The reason is that the second autoregressive root approximately cancels the MA term so that the DGP is nearly ARIMA$(0,1,0)$. The implied value of θ is:

$$\theta = \frac{\sqrt{(q^2+4q)}-2-q}{2} \quad \text{where} \quad q = \frac{\sigma^2_{\delta_2}}{\sigma^2_{\delta_1}},$$

(see Harvey, 1993). For DGP (IXi), $\theta \simeq -0.382$, so that the AR and MA polynomials are $(1-L)(1-0.5L)$ and $(1-0.382L)$, leading to near cancellation of the MA root with the second AR root. For DGP (IXii), $\theta \simeq -0.605$ but $\mu_1 = 0.1$, ensuring that the process is ARIMA$(1,1,1)$, and delivering the expected gains from DE for both the AR(2) and under-parameterized AR(1) model (see table 11.10).

11.6.1.4 Matching the linear transforms of estimation and forecast criteria

Table 11.11 compares DE based on minimizing in-sample errors in predicting multi-period differences of the data and multi-period levels of the data, when the evaluation criterion is in terms of predicting differences.

There are benefits to be had from matching the linear transformation in estimation with that used in evaluation for DGPs (I,VIIIi), where two unit roots are being estimated in the AR(2) model, and in those cases the gain is increasing in the forecast horizon. In all other cases, the MSFEs are very similar.

11.6.1.5 Explaining other researchers' findings

Our results help explain some other researchers' findings. First, Stoica and Nehorai (1989) find that in the ARMA$(2, 2)$ DGP given by:

$$y_t - 0.98y_{t-2} = e_t - 0.87e_{t-1} - 0.775e_{t-2},$$

DE yields superior forecasts to OLS when the forecasting model is an AR(1). They interpret this as being due to the model being under-parameterized and only poorly approximating the true process. Consistent with this, the gains to DE disappear for an AR(6) model. However, the process has a near-unit root and negative MA errors, precisely the circumstances under which DE performs well. If we set the AR coefficient to -0.90 instead of -0.98, and re-run their simulations, the gains to DE disappear, suggesting that the relevant feature is not under-parameterization *per se*. However, over-parameterization is likely to lessen the gains to DE (see section 11.6.1.3).

Secondly, Weiss (1991) considers a stationary second-order autoregressive-distributed lag process with a strongly exogenous $\mathsf{I}(0)$ variable. Various mis-specified models are estimated by OLS and DE, and forecast performances are compared. Our analysis indicates little gain to DE in these circumstances, and indeed Weiss finds the differences between DE and OLS MSFEs are small.

11.7 Unit roots and neglected moving-average errors

We have established that neglecting MA errors in unit-root processes provides a rationale for DE at short horizons due to 'model mis-specification effects' (table 11.9, DGPs VI,VII,IXii). In this section, we derive the asymptotic distributions of the estimators, and perform a Monte Carlo to compare the empirical distributions of the unit-root estimates from OLS and DE to check whether the divergence between parameter estimates accounts for the forecast differences. The Monte Carlo examines a range of values of the MA parameter, namely $\theta = \{-0.9, -0.5, -0.1, 0, 0.1, 0.5, 0.9\}$ and sample sizes $T = \{25, 50, 100\}$, using 50,000 replications. We include the IV estimator suggested by Hall (1989) in the comparison, and a fourth estimator, obtained by applying IV to DE (IVDE), which is motivated below. The DGP is:

$$\begin{aligned} y_t &= y_{t-1} + u_t \\ u_t &= \epsilon_t + \theta\epsilon_{t-1} \\ \epsilon_t &\sim \mathsf{IN}\left[0, \sigma_\epsilon^2\right], \end{aligned}$$

where $\sigma_\epsilon^2 = 1$ and the h-step forecast function is:

$$\widehat{y}_{T+h} = \widetilde{\rho}_{(h)} y_T,$$

where $\widetilde{\rho}_{(h)}$ is alternatively $(\widehat{\rho}_{\mathrm{OLS}})^h$, $\widehat{\rho}_{\mathrm{DE}_h}$, $(\widehat{\rho}_{\mathrm{IV}})^h$ and $\widehat{\rho}_{\mathrm{IVDE}_h}$ for OLS, DE, IV and IVDE. The first two are defined by the scalar versions of (11.3) to the power h and

(11.7) at h lags, and the last two by:

$$\text{IV: } (\widehat{\rho}_{\text{IV}})^h = \left(\frac{\sum y_t y_{t-2}}{\sum y_{t-1} y_{t-2}} \right)^h$$

$$\text{IVDE: } \widehat{\rho}_{\text{IVDE}_h} = \frac{\sum y_t y_{t-h-1}}{\sum y_{t-h} y_{t-h-1}}.$$

Hall (1989) shows that in an I(1) process, the IV estimator of ρ in $y_t = \rho y_{t-1} + e_t$ has the Dickey–Fuller (DF) distribution when an instrument dated y_{t-k}, $k > 1$, is used (or, more generally, when u_t follows an MA(q) process, for $k > q$). $\widehat{\rho}_{\text{OLS}}$ will not have the DF distribution because of the bias induced by the correlation between y_{t-1} and u_t. IV is valid because the unit root in the process implies that y_t is correlated with y_s for all s, but y_s ($s < t$) will not be correlated with u_t for $t - s$ sufficiently large (depending on the order of the MA), and thus are valid instruments. Below, we derive limiting distributions for any h of the four estimators to examine the impact of estimation on multi-step forecasting of a neglected first-order MA error process.

First, for the IV estimator at $h = 1$:

$$T(\widehat{\rho}_{\text{IV}} - 1) = \left(T^{-2} \sum_{t=1}^{T} y_{t-1} y_{t-2} \right)^{-1} T^{-1} \sum_{t=1}^{T} y_{t-2} u_t. \tag{11.36}$$

Using the usual notation that:

$$S_t = \sum_{s=1}^{t} u_s,$$

and:

$$\sigma^2 = \lim_{T\to\infty} T^{-1} \mathsf{E}\left(S_T^2\right), \quad \sigma_u^2 = \lim_{T\to\infty} T^{-1} \sum_{t=1}^{T} u_t^2$$

then:

$$\sigma^2 = (1+\theta)^2 \sigma_\epsilon^2 \quad \text{and} \quad \sigma_u^2 = \left(1+\theta^2\right) \sigma_\epsilon^2.$$

The denominator in (11.36) is:

$$T^{-2} \sum_{t=1}^{T} y_{t-1} y_{t-2} \Rightarrow \sigma^2 \int_0^1 W(r)^2 \, \mathrm{d}r, \tag{11.37}$$

where $\Rightarrow$ denotes weak convergence (see, e.g., Banerjee, Dolado, Galbraith and Hendry, 1993, Hendry, 1995a and Johansen, 1995). In (11.37), $W(r)$ is the Wiener process associated with $\{u_t\}$. Since:

$$T^{-1} \sum_{t=1}^{T} y_{t-1} u_t \Rightarrow \frac{\sigma^2}{2} \left[W(1)^2 - 1 \right] + \frac{\sigma^2 - \sigma_u^2}{2} \tag{11.38}$$

and:

$$T^{-1}\sum_{t=1}^{T} u_t u_{t-1} \Rightarrow \theta\sigma_\epsilon^2.$$

The numerator:

$$\begin{aligned} T^{-1}\sum_{t=1}^{T} y_{t-2}u_t &= T^{-1}\sum_{t=1}^{T} y_{t-1}u_t - T^{-1}\sum_{t=1}^{T} u_t u_{t-1} \\ &\Rightarrow \frac{\sigma^2}{2}\left(W(1)^2 - 1\right) \end{aligned} \tag{11.39}$$

and hence:

$$T(\widehat{\rho}_{\mathrm{IV}} - 1) \Rightarrow \tfrac{1}{2}\left(W(1)^2 - 1\right)\left(\int_0^1 W(r)^2\,\mathrm{d}r\right)^{-1} \tag{11.40}$$

which is the Dickey–Fuller distribution (see Dickey and Fuller, 1979, 1981) for testing for a unit root in a univariate process, independently of the residual autocorrelation. The numerator in (11.40) is (see Fuller, 1976):

$$\int_0^1 W(r)\,\mathrm{d}W(r) = \tfrac{1}{2}\left(W(1)^2 - 1\right) \sim \tfrac{1}{2}\left(\chi^2(1) - 1\right),$$

and as $\mathsf{P}(\chi^2(1) \leq 1) \simeq 0.7$, this imparts a negative shift to the distribution.

The outcome in (11.40) contrasts with:

$$T(\widehat{\rho}_{\mathrm{OLS}} - 1) = \left(T^{-2}\sum_{t=1}^{T} y_{t-1}^2\right)^{-1} T^{-1}\sum_{t=1}^{T} y_{t-1}u_t. \tag{11.41}$$

The denominator converges to the same limit as (11.37), and the numerator is given by (11.38). Hence:

$$T(\widehat{\rho}_{\mathrm{OLS}} - 1) \Rightarrow \left(\int_0^1 W(r)^2\,\mathrm{d}r\right)^{-1}\left[\tfrac{1}{2}\left(W(1)^2 - 1\right) + \frac{\theta}{(1+\theta)^2}\right]. \tag{11.42}$$

Consequently, the appropriately normalized distribution is non-central; in particular, when $\theta < 0$, the leftward shift of the limiting distribution is exacerbated. For $\theta > -0.2$, the non-centrality is minor (≤ -0.3), but, when $-1 < \theta < -0.73$, the non-centrality exceeds 10, and for $\theta < -0.9$, it is very large (≥ -90).

To compare the performance of the estimators for multi-step forecasting, we need the asymptotic distributions of $(\widehat{\rho}_{\mathrm{OLS}})^h$ and $(\widehat{\rho}_{\mathrm{IV}})^h$ (appendix 11.10 provides details). For OLS:

$$T\left((\widehat{\rho}_{\mathrm{OLS}})^h - 1\right) \Rightarrow \left(\int_0^1 W(r)^2\,\mathrm{d}r\right)^{-1} h\left[\tfrac{1}{2}\left(W(1)^2 - 1\right) + \frac{\theta}{(1+\theta)^2}\right] \tag{11.43}$$

indicating a bias h times as large as for $\widehat{\rho}_{\mathrm{OLS}}$. However, a better approximation in finite samples takes account of lower-order biases:

$$T\left((\widehat{\rho}_{\mathrm{OLS}})^h - 1\right) \Rightarrow \left[\sum_{i=0}^{h-1}\left(1 + T^{-1}B\right)^i\right] B \simeq h\left[1 + \frac{(h-1)}{2T}B\right] B, \tag{11.44}$$

where B is (11.42). Thus, the increase in the bias for finite T should be less than h times that of the 1-step.

For IV, appendix 11.10 shows that:

$$T\left((\widehat{\rho}_{\mathrm{IV}})^h - 1\right) \Rightarrow \left(\int_0^1 W(r)^2 \,\mathrm{d}r\right)^{-1} \frac{h}{2}\left(W(1)^2 - 1\right) \simeq \left[1 + \frac{(h-1)}{2T}C\right] C, \tag{11.45}$$

taking account of lower-order biases as for OLS, where C is given by (11.40) and replaces B from (11.42).

Appendix 11.10 also derives the asymptotic bias for the h-step DE:

$$T\left(\widehat{\rho}_{\mathrm{DE}_h} - 1\right) \Rightarrow \left(\int_0^1 W(r)^2 \,\mathrm{d}r\right)^{-1} h\left[\tfrac{1}{2}\left(W(1)^2 - 1\right) + \frac{\theta}{h(1+\theta)^2}\right]. \tag{11.46}$$

Thc IVDE estimator is motivated by noting that in the DE estimator the regressor is correlated with the disturbance term, but when u_t is MA(1), y_{t-h-1} is a suitable instrument. Thus, for the h-step IVDE:

$$T\left(\widehat{\rho}_{\mathrm{IVDE}_h} - 1\right) = \frac{T^{-1}\sum_{t=1}^{T} y_{t-h-1}\sum_{s=0}^{h-1} u_{t-s}}{T^{-2}\sum_{t=1}^{T} y_{t-h}y_{t-h-1}}. \tag{11.47}$$

Similar arguments to those set out in appendix 11.10 for the DE estimator show that:

$$T\left(\widehat{\rho}_{\mathrm{IVDE}_h} - 1\right) \Rightarrow \left(\int_0^1 W(r)^2 \,\mathrm{d}r\right)^{-1} \frac{h}{2}\left[\left(W(1)^2 - 1\right)\right],$$

which is the same as the h-step IV limiting distribution (11.45).

Thus, for OLS, the leftward non-centrality due to $\theta < 0$ increases in h, whereas for DE it does not, and their limiting distributions coincide if $\theta = 0$, suggesting no gain to DE in that case (as borne out by our Monte Carlo). IV is better still, and asymptotically the distributions of IV and IVDE coincide.

11.7.1 A Monte Carlo study of the estimators

The results of the simulations are given in table 11.12. The IV methods (IV and IVDE) have no moments of any order for any value of θ, but this does not prevent apparently sensible values of the mean and variance being obtained by simulation for some values of θ (see Sargan, 1982 and Hendry, 1990). Moreover, moments would exist if more than one lag were used as an instrument (e.g., $y_{t-k}, \ldots, y_{t-k-p}$, where $k > q, p > 0$) . For those values of θ for which the estimator is poorly behaved (θ large and negative)[5] extreme values can be discarded. Here, we signal estimates of the mean in excess of 10 by a '–' in the tables, and report selected percentiles of the empirical distributions, including the median.

Table 11.8 Estimates of $\mathsf{E}\,[\widehat{\rho}^{\,j}_{OLS}]$ for $T = 100$

		$\theta = -0.9$	$\theta = -0.5$
$j = 2$	MC estimate	0.288	0.890
	(11.43)	−0.066	0.880
	(11.44)	0.218	0.884
$j = 4$	MC estimate	0.145	0.810
	(11.43)	−1.132	0.760
	(11.44)	0.048	0.781

A striking feature of the results, in line with the asymptotic bias formulae, is the marked increase in bias for OLS as h increases, when there is a negative moving-average error, and the correspondingly much smaller increase in bias for DE. This is illustrated graphically in figure 11.2 which shows the histograms of OLS and DE at powers of 2 and 4 ($(\widehat{\rho}_{\mathrm{OLS}})^h$ and $\widehat{\rho}_{\mathrm{DE}_h}$, $h = 2, 4$) for $\theta = \{-0.9, -0.5, 0, 0.9\}$ at $T = 100$. In the presence of negative MAs, OLS and DE are median biased for both $h = 2$ and $h = 4$, their means and medians being roughly similar otherwise.

Figure 11.3 plots the histograms of the resulting 2- and 4-step forecast errors for OLS and DE corresponding to the estimates plotted in figure 11.2. These are visually much better behaved, due to the relatively dominant role played by error accumulation even in the face of the very disperse and biased distributions shown in figure 11.2.

As expected, Hall's IV estimator is approximately median unbiased for all θ, as is IVDE, but for $\theta \geq 0$, IV generally has a smaller Monte Carlo variance than IVDE. The inter-quartile ranges (25–75 percent) for the two IV estimators are similar except when $\theta = -0.9$.

Table 11.8 compares the values of $(\widehat{\rho}_{\mathrm{OLS}})^h$ for $h = 2, 4$ as predicted by (11.43) and (11.44) (taking account of lower-order biases), with the means of the Monte Carlo.[6] The asymptotic formulae use estimates of B (see (11.42)) from the same set of replications. The table illustrates the usefulness of the asymptotic formulae for OLS for $T = 100$

[5] As $\theta \to -1$, the correlations between successive ys go to zero, so the instruments become useless.

[6] The Monte Carlo estimates in table 11.8 were produced from 5,000 replications, and differ slightly from those reported in table 11.12.

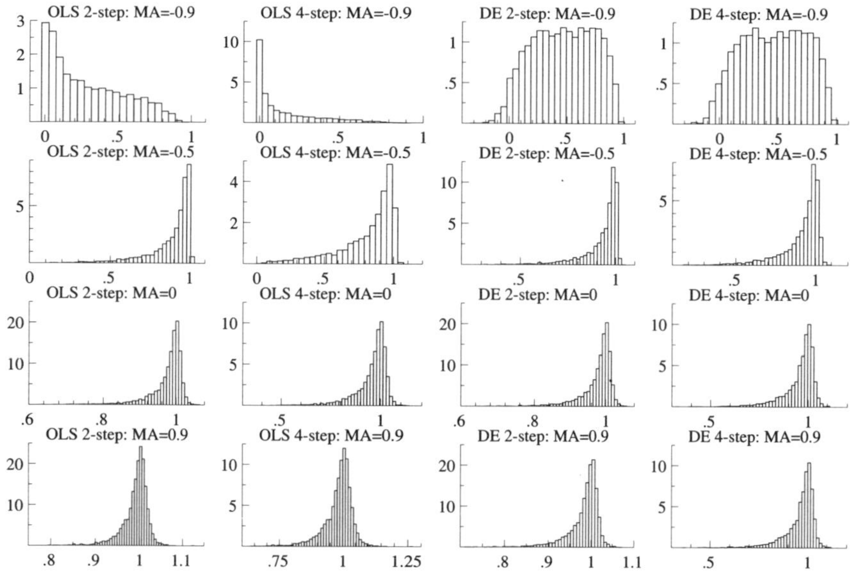

Figure 11.2 Histograms of OLS and DE at powers of 2 and 4

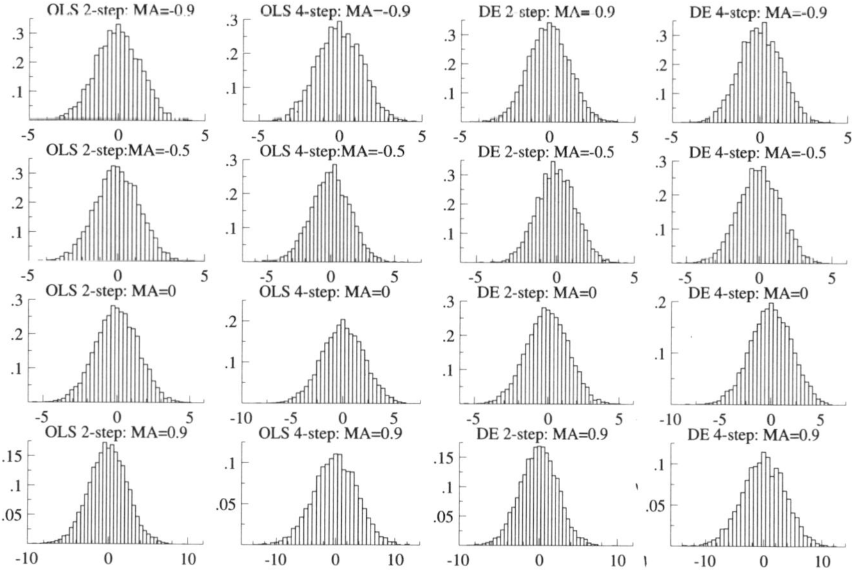

Figure 11.3 Histograms of the OLS and DE 2 and 4-step forecast errors

and $\theta = -0.9, -0.5$. The rows (11.43) are calculated as $hBT^{-1} + 1$, where $B = T(\widehat{\rho}_{\mathrm{OLS}} - 1)$, and the rows (11.44) as $BT^{-1}(\sum_{i=0}^{h-1}(1+T^{-1}B)^i)+1$. Thus, allowing for the approximation to the lower-order biases is essential for the accuracy of the formulae when $\theta = -0.9$, and quite important for values of $\theta \leq -0.5$.

11.8 Overview

Model mis-specification is necessary but not sufficient to justify DE. Multi-step estimation criteria can lead to different parameter estimators from 1-step, and can even alter the implicit model class. Conversely, a switch in the implicit model class implies model mis-specification. In stationary processes, DE, approximated by OLS projection, maintains the pseudo-true values of AR parameters when the step-ahead error horizons being optimized over are larger than the degree of the MA process, and results in enhanced forecast accuracy. However, the gains will typically fade rapidly in the forecast horizon. For example, if an AR(1) model is used to approximate an MA(1) process, the pseudo-true value of the AR parameter for 2-step projection is zero, yielding the optimal 2-step forecast of zero: the 1-step AR parameter will be non-zero, but will rapidly approach zero as it is powered up.

When the process contains unit roots, forecast success depends upon how accurately these are estimated. Here, large negative MA errors are pernicious since they exacerbate the downward bias of OLS. A separate Monte Carlo assessed the usefulness of DE in these circumstances, and the results bore out the hypothesis that the improved forecast accuracy from DE, when unit roots are estimated in the presence of neglected negative MA errors, stems from better estimates of the unit roots. The properties of two other estimators were also explored.

We have only considered $\mathsf{E}[\mathbf{x}_{T+1}|\mathbf{x}_T] = \boldsymbol{\Upsilon}\mathbf{x}_T$ yet $\mathsf{E}[\mathbf{x}_{T+h}|\mathbf{x}_T] \neq \boldsymbol{\Upsilon}^h\mathbf{x}_T$ because of neglected moving-average terms. However, our analysis is more generally applicable because moving averages will arise as a result of a variety of forms of mis-specification, for example: non-linearity due to the DGP being fractionally integrated (see Tiao and Tsay, 1994, who show the benefits to DE of linear models of such processes); infinite-order autoregression DGPs (see Bhansali (1996)); measurement errors; and omitted variables.

Outliers have also been proposed as a reason for preferring DE to OLS (see Peña, 1994). In unit-root processes, outliers will generate similar effects to a negative moving-average error in that they will downwards bias the estimate of the unit root. However, they would need to be quite large to induce sizeable effects, in which case they should be detectable from a careful analysis of the residuals. Thus, in most instances, we suspect reasonable alternatives to DE exist; for example, mean absolute deviation estimators for outliers, or modelling them.

Few economic time series seem likely to exhibit negative moving-average error autocorrelation of the size liable to cause really serious problems for OLS when a model builder strives to develop congruent representations. Nevertheless, some economic variables may be $\mathsf{I}(2)$, represented as $\mathsf{I}(1)$ in differences with negative moving averages (as in our DGP I), resulting in poor forecasts of growth rates. Strictly, there is a redundant unit root which should cancel, but now outliers due to differencing step shifts in means (thereby converting them to 'blips', or apparent outliers) will bias the negative moving-average coefficient away from -1, so the scenario will be similar to our Monte Carlo. In such a state of nature, DE may be beneficial – but there are sensible alternatives. The analysis in section 11.7 indicates that IV may be a better solution. Indeed, the limiting distributions of IVDE and IV coincide, so that once the correlation between the regressor and the error has been taken care of by IV, no additional gains accrue to DE.

A final drawback of DE is that it is not invariant to linear transformations since it is dependent on the exact criterion selected for minimization. Consequently, different decisions could result for levels versus first differences.

11.9 Appendix: Finite-sample bias

Consider the zero-mean stationary AR(1):

$$y_t = \rho y_{t-1} + \nu_t,$$

where $|\rho| < 1$ and $v_t \sim \mathsf{IN}[0, \sigma_\nu^2]$. When $\rho = 0$, $y_t = \nu_t$ so that setting

$$\bar{\nu} = T^{-1} \sum_{t=1}^{T} \nu_t \simeq T^{-1} \sum_{t-1}^{T} \nu_{t-2},$$

we have:

$$\begin{aligned} \mathsf{E}\left[\widetilde{\rho^2} \mid \rho = 0\right] &= \mathsf{E}\left[\frac{T^{-1}\sum_{t=1}^{T}(\nu_t - \bar{\nu})(\nu_{t-2} - \bar{\nu})}{T^{-1}\sum_{t=1}^{T}(\nu_{t-2} - \bar{\nu})^2}\right] \\ &\simeq \mathsf{E}\left[\frac{\left(T^{-1}\sum_{t=1}^{T}\nu_t\nu_{t-2} - \bar{\nu}^2\right)/\sigma_\nu^2}{1 + \left(T^{-1}\sum_{t=1}^{T}(\nu_{t-2} - \bar{\nu})^2/\sigma_\nu^2 - 1\right)}\right]. \end{aligned}$$

Expanding the denominator as a power series and retaining terms of $O(1/T)$:

$$\mathsf{E}\left[\widetilde{\rho^2} \mid \rho = 0\right] \simeq \mathsf{E}\left[\left(\frac{\left(T^{-1}\sum_{t=1}^{T}\nu_t\nu_{t-2} - \bar{\nu}^2\right)}{\sigma_\nu^2}\right)\left(2 - \frac{T^{-1}\sum_{t=1}^{T}\nu_{t-2}^2 - \bar{\nu}^2}{\sigma_\nu^2}\right)\right].$$

Multiplying out:

$$\mathsf{E}\left[\widetilde{\rho^2} \mid \rho = 0\right] \simeq \mathsf{E}\left[\left(\frac{-2\bar{\nu}^2}{\sigma_\nu^2}\right) + \frac{\left(\sum_{t=1}^{T}\nu_t\right)^2 \sum_{t=1}^{T}\nu_{t-2}^2}{T^3\sigma_\nu^4} - \frac{\bar{\nu}^4}{\sigma_\nu^4}\right],$$

where the middle term is:

$$\begin{aligned}
\mathsf{E}\left[\sum_t\sum_s\sum_r \nu_t\nu_s\nu_{r-2}^2\right] &= \sum_{t=s}\sum_r \mathsf{E}\left[\nu_t^2\right]\mathsf{E}\left[\nu_{r-2}^2\right] \\
&\quad +2\sum_{t=s=r-2}\mathsf{E}\left[\nu_t\nu_{r-2}\right]\mathsf{E}\left[\nu_s\nu_{r-2}\right] \\
&\simeq T^2\sigma_\nu^4,
\end{aligned}$$

and noting that:

$$\mathsf{E}\left[\frac{\overline{\nu}^2}{\sigma_\nu^2}\right] = \frac{1}{T} \text{ and } \mathsf{E}\left[\frac{\overline{\nu}^4}{\sigma_\nu^4}\right] = \frac{3}{T^3},$$

then, again retaining terms of $O(1/T)$:

$$\mathsf{E}\left[\widetilde{\widehat{\rho}^2} \mid \rho = 0\right] \simeq -\frac{1}{T}.$$

This matches the Monte Carlo finding (section 11.5).

11.10 Appendix: Limiting distributions of estimators

To derive the asymptotic distribution of $(\widehat{\rho}_{\rm OLS})^h$ when $\rho = 1$, first consider $(\widehat{\rho}_{\rm OLS})^2$.

$$\begin{aligned}
(\widehat{\rho}_{\rm OLS})^2 &= \left[1 + T^{-1}\left(T^{-1}\sum_{t=1}^T u_t y_{t-1}\right)\left(T^{-2}\sum_{t=1}^T y_{t-1}^2\right)^{-1}\right]^2 \\
&= \left(1 + T^{-1}\overline{B}\right)^2.
\end{aligned}$$

Then:

$$T\left((\widehat{\rho}_{\rm OLS})^2 - 1\right) = \left(2 + T^{-1}\overline{B}\right)\overline{B} \Rightarrow \left(2 + T^{-1}B\right)B,$$

where B is given by (11.42). A direct generalization yields (11.44):

$$T\left((\widehat{\rho}_{\rm OLS})^h - 1\right) \Rightarrow \left(\sum_{i=0}^{h-1}\left(1 + T^{-1}B\right)^i\right)B.$$

The derivation of the asymptotic distribution of $(\widehat{\rho}_{\rm IV})^h$ follows in a similar vein. For $(\widehat{\rho}_{\rm IV})^2$:

$$\begin{aligned}
(\widehat{\rho}_{\rm IV})^2 &= \left[1 + T^{-1}\left(T^{-1}\sum_{t=1}^T u_t y_{t-2}\right)\left(T^{-2}\sum_{t=1}^T y_{t-1}y_{t-2}\right)^{-1}\right]^2 \\
&= \left(1 + T^{-1}\overline{C}\right)^2,
\end{aligned}$$

so:

$$T\left((\widehat{\rho}_{\mathrm{IV}})^2 - 1\right) = \left(2 + T^{-1}\overline{C}\right)\overline{C} \Rightarrow \left(2 + T^{-1}C\right)C,$$

where C is given by (11.40). Thus (11.45) results:

$$T\left((\widehat{\rho}_{\mathrm{IV}})^h - 1\right) \Rightarrow \left(\sum_{i=0}^{h-1}\left(1 + T^{-1}C\right)^i\right)C.$$

For the h-step DE:

$$T\left(\widehat{\rho}_{\mathrm{DE}_h} - 1\right) = \frac{T^{-1}\sum_{t=1}^{T} y_{t-h}\left(\sum_{i=0}^{h-1} u_{t-i}\right)}{T^{-2}\sum_{t=1}^{T} y_{t-h}^2}. \tag{11.48}$$

The denominator is again (11.37). For the numerator, the various terms are:

$$T^{-1}\sum_{t=1}^{T} y_{t-h}u_{t-h+1} \Rightarrow \frac{\sigma^2}{2}\left[W(1)^2 - 1\right] + \frac{\sigma^2 - \sigma_u^2}{2},$$

whereas for $j = 2, \ldots, h$:

$$\begin{aligned} T^{-1}\sum_{t=1}^{T} y_{t-h}u_{t-h+j} &= T^{-1}\sum_{t=1}^{T} y_{t-h+1}u_{t-h+j} - T^{-1}\sum_{t=1}^{T} u_{t-h+1}u_{t-h+j} \\ &\Rightarrow \frac{\sigma^2}{2}\left[W(1)^2 - 1\right] + \frac{\sigma^2 - \sigma_u^2}{2} - \theta\sigma_\epsilon^2, \end{aligned}$$

so that:

$$T^{-1}\sum_{t=1}^{T} y_{t-h}\sum_{i=0}^{h-1} u_{t-i} \Rightarrow \sigma^2\left[\frac{h}{2}\left(W(1)^2 - 1\right) + h\frac{\sigma^2 - \sigma_u^2}{2\sigma^2} - (h-1)\theta\frac{\sigma_\epsilon^2}{\sigma^2}\right] \tag{11.49}$$

and hence we obtain equation (11.46).

Table 11.9 AR(2) unit root model: MSFE differences

DGP	True model	Constant 1-step Control	Constant 1-step Est.	Constant h-step Control	Constant h-step Est.	No Constant 1-step Control	No Constant 1-step Est.	No Constant h-step Control	No Constant h-step Est.
Ii	3.08	8.97	8.82	-	-	8.97	8.88	-	-
	5.03	8.02	10.76	8.02	8.00	8.02	9.07	8.02	8.06
	6.06	9.09	14.23	9.09	9.21	9.09	11.26	9.09	9.17
	6.93	9.96	17.05	9.96	10.12	9.96	13.37	9.96	10.05
Iii	2.30	7.47	7.46	-	-	7.47	7.45	-	-
	4.25	6.45	8.91	6.45	6.53	6.45	7.32	6.45	6.51
	5.32	7.58	12.13	7.58	7.80	7.58	9.35	7.58	7.70
	6.21	8.46	14.77	8.46	8.77	8.46	11.23	8.46	8.61
Iiii	2.30	8.19	6.85	-	-	8.19	7.59	-	-
	3.52	6.53	7.75	6.53	5.71	6.53	7.69	6.53	6.26
	3.80	6.82	8.99	6.82	6.03	6.82	9.15	6.82	6.50
	3.97	6.99	9.78	6.99	6.15	6.99	10.78	6.99	6.66
II	2.02	2.72	2.78	-	-	3.12	3.15	-	-
	3.00	3.04	3.07	3.02	3.06	3.24	3.25	3.24	3.28
	3.02	3.03	3.04	3.04	3.09	3.30	3.31	3.27	3.32
	2.99	2.99	3.00	3.01	3.04	3.25	3.25	3.23	3.27
III	2.02	2.72	2.78	-	-	2.72	2.75	-	-
	3.00	3.04	3.07	3.00	3.06	3.04	3.06	3.00	3.05
	3.02	3.03	3.04	3.02	3.09	3.03	3.03	3.02	3.08
	2.99	2.99	3.00	2.99	3.04	2.99	2.99	2.99	3.03
IV	1.03	1.03	1.06	-	-	1.23	1.25	-	-
	0.98	0.98	0.99	1.04	1.00	1.21	1.21	1.18	1.19
	0.98	0.98	0.99	1.05	1.00	1.25	1.24	1.19	1.21
	1.01	1.01	1.02	1.07	1.03	1.26	1.26	1.21	1.22
V	1.03	1.03	1.06	-	-	1.03	1.05	-	-
	0.98	0.98	0.99	0.98	1.00	0.98	0.98	0.98	0.99
	0.98	0.98	0.99	0.98	1.00	0.98	0.98	0.98	0.99
	1.01	1.01	1.02	1.01	1.03	1.01	1.01	1.01	1.02
VI	1.00	1.51	1.54	-	-	2.00	2.01	-	-
	1.99	2.11	2.12	2.02	2.02	2.22	2.22	2.22	2.24
	2.04	2.06	2.07	2.06	2.08	2.31	2.31	2.27	2.30
	2.01	2.02	2.03	2.04	2.05	2.27	2.27	2.25	2.28
VII	1.00	1.51	1.54	-	-	1.51	1.53	-	-
	1.99	2.11	2.12	1.99	2.02	2.11	2.12	1.99	2.02
	2.04	2.06	2.07	2.04	2.08	2.06	2.07	2.04	2.08
	2.01	2.02	2.03	2.01	2.05	2.02	2.03	2.01	2.05
VIIIi	1.02	1.02	1.05	-	-	1.02	1.03	-	-
	1.99	1.99	2.12	1.99	2.13	1.99	2.06	1.99	2.06
	2.98	2.98	3.22	2.98	3.28	2.98	3.12	2.98	3.13
	3.96	3.96	4.33	3.96	4.48	3.96	4.19	3.96	4.22
VIIIii	1.02	1.02	1.04	-	-	1.02	1.03	-	-
	1.23	1.23	1.26	1.23	1.28	1.23	1.24	1.23	1.25
	1.28	1.28	1.30	1.28	1.32	1.28	1.28	1.28	1.30
	1.32	1.32	1.35	1.32	1.38	1.32	1.33	1.32	1.35
VIIIiii	1.02	1.17	1.20	-	-	1.17	1.19	-	-
	0.98	1.16	1.18	1.19	1.17	1.16	1.17	1.19	1.15
	1.02	1.14	1.16	1.17	1.14	1.14	1.15	1.17	1.12
	1.14	1.20	1.21	1.21	1.20	1.20	1.20	1.21	1.19
IXi	2.08	2.68	2.74	-	-	2.68	2.71	-	-
	2.52	2.70	2.73	2.69	2.76	2.70	2.70	2.69	2.72
	2.56	2.60	2.63	2.60	2.66	2.60	2.60	2.60	2.63
	2.67	2.69	2.72	2.69	2.74	2.69	2.69	2.69	2.71
IXii	10.41	14.58	14.83	-	-	14.58	14.69	-	-
	17.32	17.99	18.45	17.38	17.61	17.99	18.41	17.38	17.58
	16.98	17.02	17.13	16.98	17.28	17.02	17.12	16.98	17.26
	17.58	17.59	17.65	17.58	17.81	17.59	17.64	17.58	17.80

Table 11.10 AR(2) model and AR(1) model: MSFE levels

		AR(2)				**AR(1)**			
		Constant		No constant		Constant		No constant	
DGP	True	1-step	h-step	1-step	h-step	1-step	h-step	1-step	h-step
Ii	3.08	8.79	-	9.16	-	21.28	-	50.32	-
	8.18	29.68	24.83	30.01	25.49	78.78	81.46	196	200
	18.36	73.35	54.99	74.77	55.32	179	192	452	467
	35.10	144	103	151	101	324	359	824	864
Iii	2.30	7.47	-	7.71	-	20.43	-	49.51	-
	6.60	25.28	20.79	24.89	21.05	76.96	79.63	195	198
	15.97	63.62	46.60	62.51	46.15	176	189	450	465
	32.03	128	88.67	128	85.51	320	355	821	861
Iiii	2.30	6.33	-	7.39	-	7.71	-	15.00	-
	4.33	17.64	15.48	22.29	18.50	23.01	23.62	52.10	52.85
	7.68	38.59	31.38	52.67	37.49	49.32	52.40	117	121
	12.56	69.41	54.60	101	64.61	86.44	95.15	211	221
II	2.02	2.86	-	2.84	-	3.14	-	3.10	-
	3.00	4.01	4.00	3.96	3.97	4.38	4.24	4.21	4.19
	4.02	5.35	5.31	5.21	5.23	5.87	5.52	5.46	5.42
	4.97	6.72	6.65	6.49	6.52	7.43	6.82	6.72	6.67
III	2.02	2.83	-	2.77	-	3.09	-	3.03	-
	3.00	3.92	3.91	3.78	3.78	4.50	4.13	4.10	4.01
	4.02	5.16	5.08	4.93	4.91	6.13	5.29	5.39	5.13
	4.97	6.35	6.29	6.01	5.99	7.75	6.45	6.60	6.18
IV	1.03	1.09	-	1.09	-	1.07	-	1.07	-
	2.04	2.22	2.24	2.22	2.24	2.20	2.20	2.20	2.20
	3.01	3.43	3.47	3.40	3.43	3.40	3.42	3.38	3.39
	3.96	4.70	4.79	4.66	4.72	4.67	4.71	4.65	4.66
V	1.03	1.08	-	1.06	-	1.06	-	1.04	-
	2.04	2.16	2.19	2.11	2.12	2.14	2.15	2.09	2.09
	3.01	3.24	3.31	3.16	3.19	3.20	3.26	3.13	3.14
	3.96	4.35	4.51	4.21	4.27	4.29	4.44	4.17	4.21
VI	1.00	1.59	-	1.61	-	2.10	-	2.08	-
	1.00	1.74	1.59	1.78	1.69	2.19	2.07	2.14	2.12
	1.02	1.73	1.62	1.89	1.85	2.39	2.12	2.32	2.28
	1.00	1.81	1.59	2.06	2.01	2.57	2.10	2.46	2.41
VII	1.00	1.04	-	1.02	-	1.03	-	1.02	-
	1.00	1.02	1.03	1.01	1.02	1.01	1.02	1.00	1.01
	1.02	1.03	1.06	1.02	1.04	1.03	1.05	1.02	1.03
	1.00	1.01	1.04	1.00	1.03	1.01	1.02	1.00	1.01
VIIIi	1.02	1.08	-	1.06	-	18.02	-	46.85	-
	5.03	5.59	5.70	5.42	5.46	74.28	77.01	192	196
	14.04	16.16	16.99	15.58	15.86	172	185	447	461
	29.91	35.53	38.89	34.15	35.30	316	351	818	859
VIIIii	1.02	1.06	-	1.04	-	1.40	-	1.38	-
	3.26	3.51	3.54	3.40	3.42	4.26	4.38	4.18	4.21
	6.30	6.95	7.10	6.67	6.75	7.89	8.29	7.73	7.85
	9.74	10.95	11.36	10.44	10.64	11.91	12.78	11.67	11.91
VIIIiii	1.02	1.05	-	1.04	-	1.11	-	1.09	-
	1.99	2.10	2.11	2.05	2.06	2.14	2.15	2.10	2.10
	2.53	2.67	2.71	2.60	2.62	2.72	2.72	2.67	2.64
	2.78	2.94	3.00	2.85	2.89	3.01	2.98	2.94	2.87
IXi	2.08	2.80	-	2.75	-	2.81	-	2.77	-
	4.60	6.45	6.50	6.26	6.30	6.46	6.55	6.30	6.33
	7.69	10.53	10.76	10.13	10.26	10.48	10.81	10.19	10.28
	11.03	14.72	15.34	14.15	14.43	14.58	15.36	14.21	14.41
IXii	10.41	14.60	-	14.57	-	16.41	-	16.86	-
	11.33	17.73	16.81	17.66	16.80	21.93	19.07	21.29	19.87
	12.43	20.30	18.16	19.10	18.00	26.53	20.41	24.61	21.07
	13.64	22.90	19.53	21.16	19.36	30.78	21.73	28.29	22.41

Table 11.11 DE in differences versus levels

DGP	True	Est. differences	Est. levels
Ii	3.08	8.79	8.79
	5.03	8.11	8.24
	6.06	9.66	10.32
	6.93	10.91	12.19
Iii	2.30	7.47	7.47
	4.25	6.67	6.76
	5.32	8.22	8.79
	6.21	9.54	10.66
Iiii	2.30	6.33	6.33
	3.52	5.44	5.57
	3.80	5.95	6.36
	3.97	6.12	6.79
II	2.02	2.86	2.86
	3.00	3.09	3.10
	3.02	3.13	3.14
	2.99	3.08	3.10
III	2.02	2.83	2.83
	3.00	3.06	3.07
	3.02	3.10	3.11
	2.99	3.07	3.09
IV	1.03	1.09	1.09
	0.98	1.03	1.03
	0.98	1.04	1.05
	1.01	1.07	1.08
V	1.03	1.08	1.08
	0.98	1.01	1.02
	0.98	1.02	1.02
	1.01	1.05	1.06
VI	1.00	1.59	1.59
	1.99	2.02	2.02
	2.04	2.08	2.08
	2.01	2.05	2.05
VII	1.00	1.04	1.04
	1.99	2.03	2.03
	2.04	2.09	2.09
	2.01	2.06	2.06
VIIIi	1.02	1.08	1.08
	1.99	2.28	2.32
	2.98	3.63	3.81
	3.96	5.21	5.67
VIIIii	1.02	1.06	1.06
	1.23	1.33	1.34
	1.28	1.40	1.42
	1.32	1.45	1.49
VIIIiii	1.02	1.05	1.05
	0.98	1.02	1.02
	1.02	1.04	1.05
	1.14	1.17	1.17
IXi	2.08	2.80	2.80
	2.52	2.84	2.85
	2.56	2.74	2.77
	2.67	2.80	2.85
IXii	10.41	14.60	14.60
	17.32	17.70	17.71
	16.98	17.31	17.33
	17.58	17.89	17.88

The MSFEs shown are for the differences.

Table 11.12 Mean, variance and percentiles of empirical distributions of $\widetilde{\mathsf{f}}(\widetilde{\rho}_h)$

	Mean	Variance	1 %	5 %	10 %	25 %	50 %	75 %	90 %	95 %	99 %
$T = 25$											
$\theta = -0.9$											
$h = 2$											
OLS	0.257	0.062	0.00	0.00	0.01	0.03	0.17	0.44	0.65	0.74	0.86
IV	-	-	0.00	0.05	0.16	0.60	0.98	1.60	6.59	24.51	559
DE	0.392	0.104	-0.33	-0.15	-0.05	0.15	0.41	0.66	0.81	0.87	0.94
IVDE	0.572	4077	-12.06	-2.03	-0.69	0.50	0.95	1.15	1.78	2.97	12.78
$h = 4$											
OLS	0.128	0.035	0.00	0.00	0.00	0.00	0.03	0.19	0.43	0.55	0.74
IV	-	-	0.00	0.00	0.03	0.36	0.97	2.55	43.44	601	312047
DE	0.387	0.111	-0.35	-0.17	-0.07	0.13	0.40	0.67	0.82	0.88	0.97
IVDE	-	-	-12.73	-2.04	-0.71	0.45	0.94	1.17	1.85	3.16	12.96
$\theta = -0.5$											
$h = 2$											
OLS	0.819	0.057	0.05	0.26	0.44	0.74	0.92	0.98	1.01	1.02	1.05
IV	-	-	0.18	0.61	0.78	0.93	0.99	1.03	1.08	1.16	2.15
DE	0.872	0.041	0.11	0.42	0.59	0.83	0.95	1.00	1.02	1.04	1.07
IVDE	0.940	2.42	0.06	0.63	0.79	0.93	0.99	1.02	1.06	1.11	1.37
$h = 4$											
OLS	0.727	0.094	0.00	0.07	0.19	0.55	0.84	0.96	1.02	1.05	1.11
IV	-	-	0.03	0.37	0.61	0.86	0.98	1.06	1.17	1.35	4.62
DE	0.843	0.070	-0.07	0.25	0.45	0.76	0.94	1.01	1.06	1.10	1.19
IVDE	0.942	16.7	-0.41	0.36	0.61	0.86	0.98	1.05	1.13	1.20	1.57
$\theta = -0.1$											
$h = 2$											
OLS	0.938	0.018	0.41	0.66	0.78	0.91	0.98	1.01	1.04	1.06	1.11
IV	0.952	0.130	0.38	0.68	0.80	0.93	0.99	1.02	1.05	1.07	1.15
DE	0.942	0.018	0.40	0.67	0.79	0.92	0.98	1.01	1.04	1.06	1.12
IVDE	0.945	0.024	0.32	0.67	0.80	0.92	0.99	1.02	1.05	1.07	1.15
$h = 4$											
OLS	0.897	0.045	0.16	0.43	0.60	0.83	0.96	1.02	1.08	1.12	1.23
IV	1.036	582	0.14	0.47	0.65	0.86	0.97	1.04	1.10	1.15	1.33
DE	0.903	0.054	0.04	0.41	0.61	0.84	0.97	1.03	1.09	1.14	1.27
IVDE	0.906	0.084	-0.14	0.39	0.61	0.85	0.97	1.04	1.11	1.17	1.33
$\theta = 0.0$											
$h = 2$											
OLS	0.950	0.014	0.48	0.70	0.81	0.92	0.98	1.02	1.04	1.06	1.12
IV	0.949	0.019	0.39	0.68	0.80	0.92	0.99	1.02	1.05	1.07	1.14
DE	0.948	0.016	0.44	0.69	0.80	0.92	0.98	1.02	1.04	1.07	1.12
IVDE	0.945	0.023	0.33	0.67	0.79	0.92	0.99	1.02	1.05	1.07	1.14
$h = 4$											
OLS	0.916	0.039	0.23	0.50	0.65	0.85	0.97	1.03	1.09	1.13	1.26
IV	0.919	0.062	0.15	0.47	0.65	0.85	0.97	1.04	1.10	1.15	1.30
DE	0.909	0.052	0.05	0.43	0.62	0.85	0.97	1.04	1.10	1.15	1.28
IVDE	0.906	0.088	-0.13	0.39	0.61	0.85	0.97	1.04	1.11	1.16	1.32

(continued)

Table 11.12 (continued)

	Mean	Variance	1 %	5 %	10 %	25 %	50 %	75 %	90 %	95 %	99 %
$\theta = 0.1$											
$h = 2$											
OLS	0.958	0.012	0.53	0.74	0.83	0.93	0.99	1.02	1.05	1.07	1.13
IV	0.948	0.018	0.40	0.68	0.80	0.92	0.99	1.02	1.05	1.07	1.14
DE	0.952	0.015	0.46	0.71	0.81	0.93	0.99	1.02	1.05	1.07	1.13
IVDE	0.958	0.022	0.33	0.67	0.79	0.92	0.99	1.02	1.05	1.07	1.14
$h = 4$											
OLS	0.9317	0.035	0.28	0.55	0.69	0.87	0.98	1.04	1.09	1.14	1.28
IV	0.917	0.045	0.16	0.47	0.64	0.85	0.97	1.03	1.09	1.14	1.29
DE	0.912	0.051	0.06	0.44	0.63	0.85	0.97	1.04	1.10	1.15	1.29
IVDE	0.905	0.070	-0.12	0.39	0.61	0.85	0.97	1.04	1.11	1.16	1.31
$\theta = 0.5$											
$h = 2$											
OLS	0.975	0.008	0.64	0.80	0.87	0.95	0.99	1.02	1.05	1.08	1.15
IV	0.948	0.017	0.41	0.68	0.80	0.92	0.99	1.02	1.05	1.07	1.13
DE	0.960	0.013	0.51	0.74	0.83	0.93	0.99	1.02	1.05	1.07	1.14
IVDE	0.945	0.021	0.34	0.67	0.79	0.92	0.99	1.02	1.05	1.07	1.13
$h = 4$											
OLS	0.958	0.027	0.40	0.64	0.75	0.90	0.99	1.05	1.11	1.17	1.33
IV	0.915	0.043	0.17	0.47	0.64	0.85	0.97	1.03	1.09	1.14	1.27
DE	0.919	0.050	0.07	0.46	0.64	0.86	0.98	1.04	1.10	1.16	1.30
IVDE	0.905	0.067	-0.10	0.39	0.61	0.85	0.97	1.04	1.11	1.16	1.31
$\theta = 0.9$											
$h = 2$											
OLS	0.978	0.008	0.66	0.81	0.88	0.95	0.99	1.02	1.06	1.08	1.16
IV	0.948	0.017	0.41	0.68	0.80	0.92	0.99	1.02	1.04	1.07	1.13
DE	0.962	0.013	0.52	0.74	0.84	0.94	0.99	1.02	1.05	1.08	1.14
IVDE	0.945	0.021	0.34	0.67	0.79	0.92	0.99	1.02	1.05	1.07	1.13
$h = 4$											
OLS	0.964	0.026	0.43	0.66	0.77	0.90	0.99	1.05	1.11	1.17	1.34
IV	0.915	0.043	0.17	0.47	0.64	0.85	0.97	1.03	1.09	1.14	1.27
DE	0.920	0.050	0.07	0.47	0.65	0.86	0.98	1.04	1.11	1.16	1.30
IVDE	0.905	0.066	-0.10	0.39	0.60	0.85	0.97	1.04	1.11	1.16	1.31
$T = 50$											
$\theta = -0.9$											
$h = 2$											
OLS	0.264	0.063	0.00	0.00	0.01	0.04	0.19	0.45	0.65	0.74	0.85
IV	-	-	0.00	0.08	0.25	0.71	0.99	1.36	3.97	12.94	330
DE	0.423	0.085	-0.18	-0.05	0.03	0.19	0.43	0.67	0.81	0.86	0.92
IVDE	0.241	625	-8.53	-1.14	-0.08	0.73	0.98	1.11	1.55	2.34	9.05
$h = 4$											
OLS	0.131	0.034	0.00	0.00	0.00	0.00	0.03	0.20	0.43	0.55	0.71
IV	-	-	0.00	0.01	0.06	0.51	0.98	1.86	15.73	168	108577
DE	0.417	0.089	-0.20	-0.06	0.02	0.18	0.42	0.67	0.82	0.87	0.94
IVDE	0.577	7398	-8.21	-1.17	-0.13	0.70	0.97	1.12	1.56	2.45	9.35
$\theta = -0.5$											
$h = 2$											
OLS	0.852	0.035	0.20	0.43	0.58	0.79	0.93	0.98	1.00	1.01	1.02
IV	0.995	23.9	0.50	0.78	0.86	0.95	0.99	1.01	1.04	1.06	1.20
DE	0.902	0.021	0.35	0.59	0.71	0.87	0.96	0.99	1.01	1.02	1.03
IVDE	0.966	0.035	0.55	0.79	0.87	0.95	0.99	1.01	1.03	1.05	1.10
$h = 4$											
OLS	0.762	0.068	0.04	0.18	0.33	0.63	0.86	0.96	1.00	1.02	1.05
IV	-	-	0.25	0.60	0.75	0.90	0.98	1.03	1.08	1.13	1.44
DE	0.877	0.036	0.20	0.46	0.61	0.82	0.95	1.00	1.03	1.05	1.09
IVDE	0.935	0.189	0.26	0.61	0.75	0.90	0.98	1.02	1.06	1.09	1.17

(continued)

Table 11.12 (continued)

$\theta = -0.1$											
$h = 2$											
OLS	0.956	0.008	0.61	0.78	0.85	0.94	0.98	1.01	1.02	1.03	1.06
IV	0.964	0.007	0.63	0.80	0.87	0.95	0.99	1.01	1.03	1.04	1.07
DE	0.960	0.007	0.62	0.79	0.86	0.94	0.99	1.01	1.02	1.03	1.06
IVDE	0.963	0.007	0.62	0.80	0.87	0.95	0.99	1.01	1.03	1.04	1.07
$h = 4$											
OLS	0.921	0.023	0.37	0.61	0.73	0.88	0.97	1.01	1.04	1.06	1.12
IV	0.937	0.020	0.40	0.65	0.76	0.90	0.98	1.02	1.05	1.08	1.14
DE	0.929	0.022	0.37	0.62	0.74	0.89	0.97	1.02	1.05	1.07	1.13
IVDE	0.932	0.024	0.32	0.62	0.75	0.89	0.98	1.02	1.06	1.08	1.14
$\theta = 0.0$											
$h = 2$											
OLS	0.965	0.006	0.67	0.81	0.88	0.95	0.99	1.01	1.02	1.04	1.06
IV	0.964	0.007	0.64	0.81	0.87	0.95	0.99	1.01	1.03	1.04	1.07
DE	0.964	0.006	0.65	0.81	0.87	0.95	0.99	1.01	1.02	1.04	1.06
IVDE	0.963	0.007	0.62	0.80	0.87	0.95	0.99	1.01	1.03	1.04	1.07
$h = 4$											
OLS	0.937	0.018	0.45	0.66	0.77	0.90	0.98	1.02	1.05	1.07	1.13
IV	0.936	0.019	0.41	0.65	0.76	0.90	0.98	1.02	1.05	1.08	1.14
DE	0.933	0.021	0.38	0.64	0.75	0.89	0.98	1.02	1.05	1.08	1.13
IVDE	0.932	0.024	0.33	0.62	0.75	0.89	0.98	1.02	1.06	1.08	1.14
$\theta = 0.1$											
$h = 2$											
OLS	0.972	0.005	0.71	0.84	0.89	0.95	0.99	1.01	1.03	1.04	1.07
IV	0.964	0.007	0.64	0.81	0.87	0.95	0.99	1.01	1.03	1.04	1.07
DE	0.968	0.006	0.67	0.82	0.88	0.95	0.99	1.01	1.03	1.04	1.07
IVDE	0.963	0.007	0.63	0.80	0.87	0.95	0.99	1.01	1.03	1.04	1.07
$h = 4$											
OLS	0.949	0.015	0.50	0.70	0.80	0.91	0.98	1.02	1.05	1.08	1.14
IV	0.936	0.019	0.41	0.65	0.76	0.90	0.98	1.02	1.05	1.08	1.14
DE	0.936	0.020	0.40	0.65	0.76	0.90	0.98	1.02	1.05	1.08	1.14
IVDE	0.932	0.024	0.33	0.62	0.75	0.89	0.98	1.02	1.06	1.08	1.14
$\theta = 0.5$											
$h = 2$											
OLS	0.983	0.003	0.78	0.88	0.92	0.97	1.00	1.01	1.03	1.05	1.08
IV	0.964	0.006	0.64	0.81	0.87	0.95	0.99	1.01	1.03	1.04	1.06
DE	0.973	0.005	0.71	0.84	0.90	0.96	0.99	1.01	1.03	1.04	1.07
IVDE	0.963	0.007	0.63	0.80	0.87	0.95	0.99	1.01	1.03	1.04	1.07
$h = 4$											
OLS	0.970	0.010	0.61	0.77	0.85	0.93	0.99	1.03	1.06	1.09	1.17
IV	0.936	0.019	0.42	0.65	0.76	0.90	0.98	1.02	1.05	1.07	1.13
DE	0.941	0.019	0.42	0.67	0.77	0.90	0.98	1.02	1.06	1.08	1.14
IVDE	0.932	0.024	0.34	0.62	0.75	0.89	0.98	1.02	1.06	1.08	1.14
$\theta = 0.9$											
$h = 2$											
OLS	0.986	0.003	0.80	0.89	0.92	0.97	1.00	1.01	1.03	1.05	1.08
IV	0.964	0.006	0.65	0.81	0.87	0.95	0.99	1.01	1.03	1.04	1.06
DE	0.974	0.004	0.72	0.85	0.90	0.96	0.99	1.01	1.03	1.04	1.07
IVDE	0.963	0.007	0.63	0.80	0.87	0.95	0.99	1.01	1.03	1.04	1.07
$h = 4$											
OLS	0.974	0.010	0.64	0.79	0.85	0.94	0.99	1.03	1.07	1.10	1.17
IV	0.936	0.019	0.42	0.65	0.76	0.90	0.98	1.02	1.05	1.07	1.13
DE	0.942	0.019	0.43	0.67	0.78	0.90	0.98	1.02	1.06	1.08	1.14
IVDE	0.932	0.024	0.34	0.62	0.75	0.89	0.98	1.02	1.06	1.08	1.14

(continued)

Table 11.12 (continued)

	Mean	Variance	1 %	5 %	10 %	25 %	50 %	75 %	90 %	95 %	99 %
$T = 100$											
$\theta = -0.9$											
$h = 2$											
OLS	0.292	0.063	0.00	0.00	0.01	0.06	0.23	0.49	0.68	0.76	0.85
IV	-	-	0.01	0.20	0.45	0.82	1.00	1.19	2.12	4.92	78.06
DE	0.469	0.0727	-0.07	0.04	0.11	0.25	0.48	0.70	0.83	0.87	0.92
IVDE	0.438	30679	-3.53	0.09	0.54	0.88	1.00	1.08	1.35	1.81	5.39
$h = 4$											
OLS	0.148	0.037	0.00	0.00	0.00	0.00	0.05	0.24	0.46	0.57	0.72
IV	-	-	0.00	0.00	0.04	0.20	0.67	0.99	1.41	4.51	24.16
DE	0.464	0.074	-0.08	0.03	0.10	0.24	0.47	0.70	0.83	0.88	0.93
IVDE	1.22	623	-3.40	0.01	0.49	0.86	0.99	1.08	1.34	1.79	5.42
$\theta = -0.5$											
$h = 2$											
OLS	0.892	0.018	0.40	0.60	0.71	0.85	0.94	0.98	1.00	1.00	1.01
IV	0.979	0.003	0.75	0.88	0.92	0.97	0.99	1.01	1.02	1.03	1.06
DE	0.932	0.009	0.56	0.73	0.81	0.91	0.97	0.99	1.00	1.01	1.02
IVDE	0.978	0.003	0.77	0.88	0.92	0.97	0.99	1.01	1.02	1.02	1.04
$h = 4$											
OLS	0.813	0.042	0.16	0.36	0.50	0.73	0.89	0.96	0.99	1.00	1.02
IV	0.961	0.011	0.56	0.77	0.85	0.94	0.99	1.01	1.04	1.05	1.12
DE	0.914	0.016	0.44	0.65	0.75	0.88	0.96	1.00	1.02	1.03	1.05
IVDE	0.957	0.009	0.59	0.78	0.85	0.93	0.98	1.01	1.03	1.04	1.08
$\theta = -0.1$											
$h = 2$											
OLS	0.972	0.003	0.77	0.87	0.91	0.96	0.99	1.00	1.01	1.02	1.03
IV	0.978	0.002	0.80	0.89	0.93	0.97	0.99	1.00	1.01	1.02	1.04
DE	0.975	0.002	0.78	0.88	0.92	0.96	0.99	1.00	1.01	1.02	1.03
IVDE	0.978	0.002	0.79	0.89	0.92	0.97	0.99	1.00	1.01	1.02	1.03
$h = 4$											
OLS	0.947	0.009	0.59	0.76	0.83	0.92	0.98	1.01	1.02	1.04	1.06
IV	0.958	0.007	0.63	0.79	0.86	0.93	0.98	1.01	1.03	1.04	1.07
DE	0.954	0.008	0.61	0.78	0.85	0.93	0.98	1.01	1.03	1.04	1.07
IVDE	0.957	0.008	0.61	0.78	0.85	0.93	0.98	1.01	1.03	1.04	1.07
$\theta = 0.0$											
$h = 2$											
OLS	0.978	0.002	0.81	0.89	0.93	0.97	0.99	1.00	1.01	1.02	1.03
IV	0.978	0.002	0.80	0.89	0.93	0.97	0.99	1.00	1.01	1.02	1.03
DE	0.978	0.002	0.80	0.89	0.93	0.97	0.99	1.00	1.01	1.02	1.03
IVDE	0.978	0.002	0.79	0.89	0.92	0.97	0.99	1.00	1.01	1.02	1.03
$h = 4$											
OLS	0.959	0.007	0.65	0.79	0.86	0.93	0.98	1.01	1.03	1.04	1.07
IV	0.958	0.007	0.63	0.79	0.86	0.93	0.98	1.01	1.03	1.04	1.07
DE	0.957	0.007	0.63	0.79	0.85	0.93	0.98	1.01	1.03	1.04	1.07
IVDE	0.957	0.008	0.61	0.78	0.85	0.93	0.98	1.01	1.03	1.04	1.07

(continued)

Table 11.12 (continued)

$\theta = 0.1$											
$h = 2$											
OLS	0.982	0.001	0.83	0.91	0.94	0.97	0.99	1.01	1.01	1.02	1.04
IV	0.978	0.002	0.80	0.89	0.92	0.97	0.99	1.00	1.01	1.02	1.03
DE	0.980	0.002	0.82	0.90	0.93	0.97	0.99	1.01	1.01	1.02	1.03
IVDE	0.978	0.002	0.79	0.89	0.92	0.97	0.99	1.00	1.01	1.02	1.03
$h = 4$											
OLS	0.967	0.005	0.70	0.82	0.88	0.94	0.99	1.01	1.03	1.04	1.07
IV	0.958	0.007	0.64	0.79	0.86	0.93	0.98	1.01	1.03	1.04	1.07
DE	0.959	0.007	0.64	0.79	0.86	0.93	0.98	1.01	1.03	1.04	1.07
IVDE	0.957	0.008	0.61	0.78	0.85	0.93	0.98	1.01	1.03	1.04	1.07
$\theta = 0.5$											
$h = 2$											
OLS	0.990	0.001	0.88	0.93	0.95	0.98	1.00	1.01	1.02	1.02	1.04
IV	0.978	0.002	0.80	0.89	0.92	0.97	0.99	1.00	1.01	1.02	1.03
DE	0.984	0.001	0.84	0.91	0.94	0.97	0.99	1.01	1.02	1.02	1.04
IVDE	0.978	0.002	0.79	0.89	0.92	0.97	0.99	1.00	1.01	1.02	1.03
$h = 4$											
OLS	0.981	0.003	0.78	0.87	0.91	0.96	0.99	1.02	1.04	1.05	1.08
IV	0.958	0.007	0.64	0.79	0.86	0.93	0.98	1.01	1.03	1.04	1.07
DE	0.963	0.006	0.66	0.81	0.87	0.94	0.98	1.01	1.03	1.04	1.07
IVDE	0.957	0.008	0.62	0.78	0.85	0.93	0.98	1.01	1.03	1.04	1.07
$\theta = 0.9$											
$h = 2$											
OLS	0.992	0.001	0.89	0.94	0.96	0.98	1.00	1.01	1.02	1.03	1.04
IV	0.978	0.002	0.80	0.89	0.92	0.97	0.99	1.00	1.01	1.02	1.03
DE	0.985	0.001	0.84	0.91	0.94	0.97	0.99	1.01	1.02	1.02	1.04
IVDE	0.977	0.002	0.79	0.89	0.92	0.97	0.99	1.00	1.01	1.02	1.03
$h = 4$											
OLS	0.984	0.003	0.79	0.88	0.92	0.96	0.99	1.02	1.04	1.05	1.09
IV	0.958	0.007	0.64	0.79	0.86	0.93	0.98	1.01	1.03	1.04	1.07
DE	0.963	0.006	0.66	0.81	0.87	0.94	0.99	1.01	1.03	1.04	1.07
IVDE	0.957	0.008	0.62	0.78	0.85	0.93	0.98	1.01	1.03	1.04	1.07

Chapter 12

Parsimony

We have addressed many issues arising in selecting models for forecasting, including selection criteria, the roles of causal information and indicators, the sources of error, forecast combinations, and the role of stationarity transformations. Both asymptotic analyses and small-sample evidence have been presented. However, the topic of parsimony remains to be analysed, and that is the focus of this chapter. Although most forecasters seem to believe that parsimony is important, and profligate parameterizations do not help multi-step forecasting, a formal theory has not yet been developed. After noting the large literature on model-selection criteria, we consider decisions based on values of the t-test of a coefficient on a variable being zero, and relate the outcome to our earlier result on non-monotonic forecast confidence intervals. However, it is hard to generalize this analysis to vector processes, as the powering up of a matrix can have odd effects on the importance of individual coefficients. Next, we establish that collinearity between regressors cannot be a strong justification for parsimony in stationary processes, but may play a role in systems subject to structural breaks. Finally, simplification in model selection is considered to establish whether it exacerbates or attenuates dependence on accidental aspects of a data set.

12.1 Introduction

There is a large literature on methods of selecting models for within-sample accuracy or fit, usually focused on the 1-step within-sample prediction errors (see, e.g., Judge, Griffiths, Hill, Lütkepohl and Lee, 1985, and Lütkepohl, 1991, for good summaries). There are many formal model-selection criteria, such as AIC, or the closely related final prediction error (FPE: see, e.g., Akaike, 1985), Schwartz (Schwartz, 1978), Hannan–Quinn (Hannan and Quinn, 1979), or PIC (Phillips, 1994). All of these criteria emphasize parsimony over improved fit more strongly than (say) maximizing R^2 or likelihood. However, it is well known that for single-variable exclusion decisions, most can be translated into conventional approaches in terms of whether the t^2-test on the restriction exceeds a given value, dependent on sample and model size. Such a value is often not much larger than two, favouring profligacy as against the value of four that is rampant in empirical economics, but more stringent than unity, which minimizes the residual standard deviation (adjusted for degrees of freedom). Policy analysis will often require a relatively detailed characterization of the channels of influence of the policy variables on the behavioural variables in the macroeconometric model, while a good forecasting performance may only be obtained from a model containing fewer parameters. Thus, the proprietors of large-scale models who routinely forecast and undertake policy analysis may find they require different models for each of these exercises.

In this chapter, we explore whether parsimony considerations apply in the same way when selecting models for multi-step forecasting. We find that the usual criteria based on t- or F-tests are not applicable when models are to be chosen on the basis of their ability to multi-step forecast. If the purpose of econometric modelling is forecasting, then our simple example suggests that there may be a greater premium on parsimony than other considerations would dictate. In particular, we find that parsimony becomes more important the further ahead one forecasts: larger 't-values' are required to justify retaining a regressor for h-step ahead forecasts. However, the effect is not large. More generally, parameter uncertainty is of the order $O(T^{-1})$ as against other errors of $O(1)$ in stationary processes, and even smaller when there are unit roots. Thus, considerable parameter uncertainty would seem necessary for parsimony in forecasting to be of much importance in practice. However, high-dimensional VARs may be a counter example, with parsimony in forecasting being a factor behind the recent popularity of Bayesian VARs (BVARs) in forecasting the main macro-aggregates (see, e.g., Doan, Litterman and Sims, 1984). While we present vector generalizations of the simple-case result, these do not sustain decisions about individual parameters in systems: powering up of a matrix can have odd effects on the importance of individual coefficients.

Next, we consider whether severe collinearity could justify parsimony in forecasting, but draw a blank. The more likely explanation for the harmful effects believed associated with collinearity, seems to be the need to exclude transient or non-constant features in a world of intermittent regime shifts. Finally, we examine the role of simplification in model selection to determine whether accidental data features are more likely to be attenuated or enhanced by simplification. The outcome is inconclusive – both could occur – but the latter should be revealed in a progressive research strategy over time by the falling significance of such variables, which would have had t-values increasing at $\sqrt{T}$ had they really mattered. The multi-step forecasts resulting from the empirical example differ little after the imposition of valid restrictions.

Overall, the analysis suggests some other route may be needed to explain the 'folklore' that parsimony is essential to accurate forecasts. Historically, Box and Jenkins (1976) provided no formal theorems to sustain their advocacy of parsimony in modelling – rather, parsimony in their model class is essential for uniqueness of the representation. Consider a simple ARIMA(1,1) model:

$$\Delta y_t = \mu + \rho \Delta y_{t-1} + \epsilon_t - \lambda \epsilon_{t-1} \text{ where } \epsilon_t \sim \mathsf{IN}\left[0, \sigma_\epsilon^2\right], \tag{12.1}$$

when $\rho \neq \lambda$. This can be written in lag operator notation as:

$$(1 - \rho L)\,\Delta y_t = \mu + (1 - \lambda L)\,\epsilon_t, \tag{12.2}$$

and so multiplying both side by the arbitrary factor $(1 - \gamma L)$:

$$(1 - \gamma L)\,(1 - \rho L)\,\Delta y_t = \mu^* + (1 - \gamma L)\,(1 - \lambda L)\,\epsilon_t \tag{12.3}$$

(where $\mu^* = (1 - \gamma)\mu$) which is not identified. Thus, the ARIMA(2,2) is not unique when an ARIMA(1,1) generated the data, and parsimony is needed for uniqueness, not accuracy. Such problems do not afflict other model classes, though related problems might.

The plan of this chapter is as follows. We first consider 1-step forecasts from correctly specified static models and investigate the selection of a subset of variables (section 12.2). In the following section, we examine dynamic models in the form of scalar autoregressive processes. The results show that the values of the forecast origin can matter but for the most part, the results of section 12.2 hold for 1-step forecasts from dynamic models. The anticipated forecast performance of an econometric and an autoregressive model are then compared, when the former is the DGP, to explore the role of parsimony in conditional forecasting. The selection criterion reveals potential advantages to differencing even when the process does not have a unit root. This matches the analysis of the Lucas (1976) critique in Favero and Hendry (1992), and the role in robustifying forecasts of intercept corrections which induce differencing (see chapter 8). Further, we show that care is required in interpreting the results of the interesting approach advocated by Granger and Deutsch (1992).

Section 12.4 examines the loss from estimating parameters when making h-step ahead forecasts ($h > 1$) from scalar dynamic models. We find that larger 't-values' than '$\mathrm{t}^2 > 1$' are required to justify retaining regressors. The results in section 12.2 transpire to be misleading: in many situations: it is not necessarily wise to select a model for forecasting using the criterion that '$\mathrm{t}^2 > 1$' – even when the model is not mis-specified in any way. We show that using the DGP can be deleterious despite the correctly included regressors being 'statistically significant'. We obtain an explanation for the non-monotonicity of forecast confidence intervals discussed in Chong and Hendry (1986), Hendry (1986) and Ericsson and Marquez (1989, 1996), and noted in chapter 8. Indeed, the 'best' model on 1-step forecasts need not dominate at longer horizons. Section 12.5 considers vector processes, section 12.6 demonstrates that collinearity cannot be a justification for parsimony in forecasting, and section 12.7 considers the role of simplification in model selection. Finally, section 12.8 concludes by using the analysis to explain why members of the univariate Box and Jenkins (1976) ARIMA predictors might beat econometric forecasts, even if the ARIMA model is mis-specified for the DGP, and the econometric model is not.

12.2 Selecting variables for forecasting in static models

To illustrate the analysis, the DGP is a linear regression model with k strongly exogenous stochastic regressors (see Engle, Hendry and Richard, 1983), and an independent, identically distributed error for $t = 1, ..., T$:

$$y_t = \boldsymbol{\beta}'\mathbf{x}_t + \nu_t \text{ where } \nu_t \sim \mathsf{IN}\left[0, \sigma_v^2\right]. \tag{12.4}$$

For simplicity, we assume that $\mathbf{x}_t \sim \mathsf{IN}_k[\mathbf{0}, \boldsymbol{\Omega}]$, independently of $\{\nu_t\}$. The disturbance term $\{\nu_t\}$ is an innovation against all available information.

First consider forecasting y_{T+1} when $\boldsymbol{\beta}$ and $\mathbf{x}_{T+1}$ are known. The minimum MSFE 1-step forecast $\overline{y}_{T+1}$ of y_{T+1} is the conditional expectation:

$$\mathsf{E}\left[y_{T+1} \mid \mathcal{I}_T\right] = \overline{y}_{T+1} = \boldsymbol{\beta}'\mathbf{x}_{T+1}, \tag{12.5}$$

where $\mathcal{I}_T$ denotes available information. From (12.4), $\overline{y}_{T+1}$ leaves an unpredictable forecast error of ν_{T+1} with a MSFE of:

$$\mathsf{E}\left[\nu_{T+1}^2 \mid \mathbf{x}_{T+1}\right] = \sigma_v^2. \tag{12.6}$$

In (12.5), $\overline{y}_{T+1}$ is the MMSFE forecast of y_{T+1} because if any other predictor $\widetilde{y}_{T+1} = \boldsymbol{\beta}^{*\prime}\mathbf{x}_{T+1}$ is used, the additional squared forecast error of $(\boldsymbol{\lambda}'\mathbf{x}_{T+1})^2$, where $\boldsymbol{\lambda} = (\boldsymbol{\beta}^* - \boldsymbol{\beta})$, is incurred. In such a setting, the DGP is the dominant forecasting mechanism, and this outcome is invariant to seeking to predict y_{T+1} or $\Delta y_{T+1} = y_{T+1} - y_T$ or $y_{T+1} - \mathbf{c}'\mathbf{x}_{T+1}$, for any known constant vector $\mathbf{c}$.

In practice, however, $\boldsymbol{\beta}$ is unknown and has to be estimated from previous sample evidence. When OLS is used to estimate $\boldsymbol{\beta}$ conditional on $\mathbf{X}' = (\mathbf{x}_1 \dots \mathbf{x}_T)$:

$$\widehat{\boldsymbol{\beta}} = (\mathbf{X}'\mathbf{X})^{-1}(\mathbf{X}'\mathbf{y}) \sim \mathsf{N}_k\left[\boldsymbol{\beta}, \sigma_v^2 (\mathbf{X}'\mathbf{X})^{-1}\right], \tag{12.7}$$

and:

$$\widehat{\sigma}_v^2 = (T-k)^{-1}\sum_{t=1}^{T}\left(y_t - \widehat{\boldsymbol{\beta}}'\mathbf{x}_t\right)^2 \sim \sigma_v^2 \frac{\chi_{T-k}^2}{(T-k)}. \tag{12.8}$$

Letting $\widehat{\boldsymbol{\Omega}} = T^{-1}(\mathbf{X}'\mathbf{X})$, from (12.7) and (12.8):

$$\frac{T\left(\widehat{\boldsymbol{\beta}} - \boldsymbol{\beta}\right)'\widehat{\boldsymbol{\Omega}}\left(\widehat{\boldsymbol{\beta}} - \boldsymbol{\beta}\right)}{k\widehat{\sigma}_v^2} \sim \mathsf{F}_{T-k}^k(0).$$

Hence, $T\widehat{\boldsymbol{\beta}}'\widehat{\boldsymbol{\Omega}}\widehat{\boldsymbol{\beta}}/k\widehat{\sigma}_v^2$ is distributed as a (singly) non-central $\mathsf{F}_{T-k}^k(\phi_{\boldsymbol{\beta}=\mathbf{0}}^2)$ with non-centrality parameter $\phi_{\boldsymbol{\beta}=\mathbf{0}}^2 = T\boldsymbol{\beta}'\boldsymbol{\Omega}\boldsymbol{\beta}/\sigma_v^2$. As we are interested in the average outcome, we replace $\widehat{\boldsymbol{\Omega}}$ by $\boldsymbol{\Omega} = \mathsf{E}[\widehat{\boldsymbol{\Omega}}]$, and use the result that for $T > k+2$ (see Johnson and Kotz, 1970, chapter 30):

$$\mathsf{E}\left[\mathsf{F}_{T-k}^k\left(\phi_{\boldsymbol{\beta}=\mathbf{0}}^2\right)\right] = \frac{(T-k)\left(k + \phi_{\boldsymbol{\beta}=\mathbf{0}}^2\right)}{k(T-k-2)} \simeq 1 + \phi_{\boldsymbol{\beta}=\mathbf{0}}^2/k = 1 + \Phi_{\boldsymbol{\beta}=\mathbf{0}}^2. \tag{12.9}$$

When $k=1$, we denote $\boldsymbol{\Omega}$ by σ_x^2 in which case $T\widehat{\beta}^2\widehat{\sigma}_x^2/\widehat{\sigma}_v^2 = \mathsf{t}_{T-1}^2(\cdot)$. The condition that $\mathsf{E}[\mathsf{t}_{T-1}^2(\phi_{\beta=0}^2)] > c^2$ will be interpreted to entail $1+\phi_{\beta=0}^2 > c^2$. Some writers interpret $\phi_{\beta=0}^2 > c^2$ as corresponding to $\mathsf{t}_{T-1}^2(\phi_{\beta=0}^2) > c^2$ directly (see, e.g., Judge *et al.*, 1985, chapter 21.2); (12.9) suggests this underestimates the required penalty.

When $\mathbf{x}_{T+1}$ is known, the conventional forecasting equation is:

$$\widehat{y}_{T+1} = \widehat{\boldsymbol{\beta}}'\mathbf{x}_{T+1}, \tag{12.10}$$

leading to the forecast error:

$$\widehat{\nu}_{T+1} = \left(\boldsymbol{\beta} - \widehat{\boldsymbol{\beta}}\right)'\mathbf{x}_{T+1} + \nu_{T+1}. \tag{12.11}$$

For large T:

$$\sqrt{T}\left(\widehat{\boldsymbol{\beta}} - \boldsymbol{\beta}\right) \sim \mathsf{N}_k\left[\mathbf{0}, \sigma_v^2\boldsymbol{\Omega}^{-1}\right],$$

and since $\mathsf{E}[\widehat{\nu}_{T+1}|\mathcal{I}_T] = 0$, then $\widehat{\nu}_{T+1}$ has the expected squared error:

$$\mathsf{E}\left[\widehat{\nu}_{T+1}^2 \mid \mathbf{x}_{T+1}\right] = \sigma_v^2 + \mathbf{x}_{T+1}'\mathsf{V}\left[\widehat{\boldsymbol{\beta}}\right]\mathbf{x}_{T+1} \simeq T^{-1}\sigma_v^2\left[T + \left(\mathbf{x}_{T+1}'\boldsymbol{\Omega}^{-1}\mathbf{x}_{T+1}\right)\right], \tag{12.12}$$

where $\mathsf{V}[\widehat{\boldsymbol{\beta}}]$ is the variance of $\widehat{\boldsymbol{\beta}}$. The component $(\mathbf{x}_{T+1}'\boldsymbol{\Omega}^{-1}\mathbf{x}_{T+1})$ has an expectation of k:

$$tr\left(\mathsf{E}\left[\mathbf{x}_{T+1}'\boldsymbol{\Omega}^{-1}\mathbf{x}_{T+1}\right]\right) = tr\left(\boldsymbol{\Omega}^{-1}\mathsf{E}\left[\mathbf{x}_{T+1}\mathbf{x}_{T+1}'\right]\right) = tr\left(\mathbf{I}_k\right) = k.$$

When $k=1$, as x_{T+1}/σ_x increases, then $\mathsf{E}[\widehat{\nu}_{T+1}^2|x_{T+1}]$ increases quadratically, matching the conventional textbook picture when forecasting from a bivariate regression.

Next, we compare the squared error in (12.12) to that arising when forecasting using a restricted value of $\boldsymbol{\beta}$. Consider the set of restrictions $\mathbf{F}\boldsymbol{\beta} = \mathbf{r}$, where $\mathbf{r}$ is $l \times 1$ such that:

$$\widetilde{\boldsymbol{\beta}} = \widehat{\boldsymbol{\beta}} - \left(\mathbf{X}'\mathbf{X}\right)^{-1}\mathbf{F}'\left(\mathbf{F}\left(\mathbf{X}'\mathbf{X}\right)^{-1}\mathbf{F}'\right)^{-1}\left(\mathbf{F}\widehat{\boldsymbol{\beta}} - \mathbf{r}\right),$$

where conditional on $\mathbf{X}$:

$$\mathsf{E}\left[\widetilde{\boldsymbol{\beta}}\right] \simeq \boldsymbol{\beta} - \left(\mathbf{X}'\mathbf{X}\right)^{-1}\mathbf{F}'\left(\mathbf{F}\left(\mathbf{X}'\mathbf{X}\right)^{-1}\mathbf{F}'\right)^{-1}\left(\mathbf{F}\boldsymbol{\beta} - \mathbf{r}\right) = \boldsymbol{\beta}^* \tag{12.13}$$

say, and for large T:

$$\sqrt{T}\left(\widetilde{\boldsymbol{\beta}} - \boldsymbol{\beta}^*\right) \sim \mathsf{N}_k\left[\mathbf{0}, \sigma_v^2\left(\boldsymbol{\Omega}^{-1} - \mathbf{Q}\right)\right],$$

when:

$$\mathbf{Q} = \boldsymbol{\Omega}^{-1}\mathbf{F}'\left(\mathbf{F}\boldsymbol{\Omega}^{-1}\mathbf{F}'\right)^{-1}\mathbf{F}\boldsymbol{\Omega}^{-1}.$$

Using the predictor $\widetilde{y}_{T+1} = \widetilde{\boldsymbol{\beta}}'\mathbf{x}_{T+1}$, when $\widetilde{\nu}_{T+1} = y_{T+1} - \widetilde{y}_{T+1}$ then:

$$\widetilde{\nu}_{T+1} = \boldsymbol{\lambda}'\mathbf{x}_{T+1} - \left(\widetilde{\boldsymbol{\beta}} - \boldsymbol{\beta}^*\right)'\mathbf{x}_{T+1} + \nu_{T+1},$$

where $\boldsymbol{\lambda} = (\boldsymbol{\beta} - \boldsymbol{\beta}^*)$ so that:

$$\mathsf{E}\left[\widetilde{\nu}_{T+1}^2 \mid \mathbf{x}_{T+1}\right] \simeq T^{-1}\sigma_v^2\left(T + \mathbf{x}_{T+1}'\left[T\boldsymbol{\lambda}\boldsymbol{\lambda}'/\sigma_v^2 + \boldsymbol{\Omega}^{-1} - \mathbf{Q}\right]\mathbf{x}_{T+1}\right). \quad (12.14)$$

To compare the two squared forecast errors in (12.12) and (12.14), we compute the relative loss, namely the difference in the conditional mean-square forecast errors relative to the innovation variance, denoted by $\mathsf{R}_\ell(\cdot,\cdot,h)$ for an h-step forecast, so that:

$$\mathsf{R}_\ell\left(\widetilde{\nu},\widehat{\nu},1\right) = \frac{\left(\mathsf{E}\left[\widetilde{\nu}_{T+1}^2|\mathcal{I}_T\right] - \mathsf{E}\left[\widehat{\nu}_{T+1}^2|\mathcal{I}_T\right]\right)}{\sigma_v^2}. \quad (12.15)$$

Then:

$$\mathsf{R}_\ell\left(\widetilde{\nu},\widehat{\nu},1\right) \simeq T^{-1}\mathbf{x}_{T+1}'\left[\frac{T\boldsymbol{\lambda}\boldsymbol{\lambda}'}{\sigma_v^2} - \mathbf{Q}\right]\mathbf{x}_{T+1}. \quad (12.16)$$

Unsurprisingly, the outcome depends on the trade-off between squared inconsistency (the first term inside the square brackets) and sampling variance (the second term). Although $\mathsf{R}_\ell(\cdot)$ is usually only $O(T^{-1})$, it determines the choice of variable given available information, and can be large when $\boldsymbol{\lambda}$ is large.

In large samples, replacing $T^{-1}(\mathbf{X}'\mathbf{X})$ in (12.13) by $\boldsymbol{\Omega}$, then:

$$\boldsymbol{\lambda} = \boldsymbol{\Omega}^{-1}\mathbf{F}'\left(\mathbf{F}\boldsymbol{\Omega}^{-1}\mathbf{F}'\right)^{-1}(\mathbf{F}\boldsymbol{\beta} - \mathbf{r}) = \boldsymbol{\Omega}^{-1}\mathbf{F}'\left(\mathbf{F}\boldsymbol{\Omega}^{-1}\mathbf{F}'\right)^{-1}\boldsymbol{\delta},$$

where $\boldsymbol{\delta} = \mathbf{F}\boldsymbol{\beta} - \mathbf{r}$, a measure of how closely the constraints are to being satisfied (holding exactly when $\boldsymbol{\delta} = \mathbf{0}$). To obtain a more useful expression than (12.16), we exploit the fact that since $\mathsf{R}_\ell(\cdot)$ is a scalar, it equals its trace, so on average we have:

$$\begin{aligned}
\mathsf{E}\left[\mathsf{R}_\ell\left(\widetilde{\nu},\widehat{\nu},1\right)\right] &\simeq T^{-1}tr\left\{\left(T\boldsymbol{\lambda}\boldsymbol{\lambda}'/\sigma_v^2 - \mathbf{Q}\right)\mathsf{E}\left[\mathbf{x}_{T+1}\mathbf{x}_{T+1}'\right]\right\} \\
&= T^{-1}tr\left\{\left(T\boldsymbol{\lambda}\boldsymbol{\lambda}'/\sigma_v^2 - \boldsymbol{\Omega}^{-1}\mathbf{F}'\left(\mathbf{F}\boldsymbol{\Omega}^{-1}\mathbf{F}'\right)^{-1}\mathbf{F}\boldsymbol{\Omega}^{-1}\right)\boldsymbol{\Omega}\right\} \\
&= T^{-1}tr\left\{T\boldsymbol{\delta}'\left(\mathbf{F}\boldsymbol{\Omega}^{-1}\mathbf{F}'\right)^{-1}\boldsymbol{\delta}/\sigma_v^2 - \mathbf{I}_l\right\} \\
&= T^{-1}l\left(\Phi_{\boldsymbol{\delta}=\mathbf{0}}^2 - 1\right),
\end{aligned} \quad (12.17)$$

where $\phi_{\boldsymbol{\delta}=\mathbf{0}}^2 = T\boldsymbol{\delta}'(\mathbf{F}\boldsymbol{\Omega}^{-1}\mathbf{F}')^{-1}\boldsymbol{\delta}/\sigma_v^2 = l\Phi_{\boldsymbol{\delta}=\mathbf{0}}^2$ is the non-centrality of the F_{T-k}^l-test of H: $\mathbf{F}\boldsymbol{\beta} = \mathbf{r}$. From (12.17), on average, it pays to impose restrictions if the F-test non-centrality is less than unity.

Two special cases of interest are when $\boldsymbol{\beta}$ is fixed at $\boldsymbol{\beta}^*$, corresponding to $\mathbf{F} = \mathbf{I}_k$ and $\boldsymbol{\beta}^* = \mathbf{r}$; and when imposing a subset $\boldsymbol{\beta}_2$ of $\boldsymbol{\beta}$ at zero (as in a model simplification exercise), corresponding to $\mathbf{F} = (\mathbf{0}\colon \mathbf{I}_{k_2})$ and $\mathbf{r} = \mathbf{0}$.

First, let $\overline{y}_{T+1} = \boldsymbol{\beta}^{*\prime}\mathbf{x}_{T+1}$, then:

$$\mathsf{E}\left[\overline{\nu}_{T+1}^2\right] = \sigma_v^2 + \left(\boldsymbol{\lambda}'\mathbf{x}_{T+1}\right)^2,$$

for $\boldsymbol{\lambda} = (\boldsymbol{\beta} - \boldsymbol{\beta}^*)$ so that:

$$\mathsf{R}_\ell\left(\overline{\nu},\widehat{\nu},1\right) \simeq T^{-1}\mathbf{x}_{T+1}'\left(T\boldsymbol{\lambda}\boldsymbol{\lambda}'/\sigma_v^2 - \boldsymbol{\Omega}^{-1}\right)\mathbf{x}_{T+1}. \quad (12.18)$$

and hence:

$$\begin{aligned} \mathsf{E}\left[\mathsf{R}_\ell\left(\overline{\nu}, \widehat{\nu}, 1\right)\right] &\simeq T^{-1} tr\left\{\left(T\boldsymbol{\lambda}\boldsymbol{\lambda}'/\sigma_v^2 - \boldsymbol{\Omega}^{-1}\right)\boldsymbol{\Omega}\right\} \\ &= T^{-1}k\left(\Phi^2_{\boldsymbol{\lambda}=\mathbf{0}} - 1\right), \end{aligned} \tag{12.19}$$

where $\phi^2_{\boldsymbol{\lambda}=\mathbf{0}} = T\boldsymbol{\lambda}'\boldsymbol{\Omega}\boldsymbol{\lambda}/\sigma_v^2 = k\Phi^2_{\boldsymbol{\lambda}=\mathbf{0}}$ is now the non-centrality of the F^k_{T-k}-test of H: $\boldsymbol{\beta} = \boldsymbol{\beta}^*$.

When $k = 1$:

$$\mathsf{R}_\ell\left(\widetilde{\nu}, \widehat{\nu}, 1\right) = T^{-1}\left(x^2_{T+1}/\sigma_x^2\right)\left[\phi^2_{\beta=\beta*} - 1\right], \tag{12.20}$$

where $\phi^2_{\beta=\beta*} = T(\beta - \beta^*)^2(\sigma_x^2/\sigma_v^2)$ is the non-centrality of the squared t-test of H: $\beta = \beta^*$. Thus, $\phi^2_{\beta=\beta*} > 1$, or an expected t^2-value greater than two, entails improved forecasting accuracy from estimating rather than imposing β, for a 1-step forecast, or at any finite horizon for which data on future xs is available. For a smaller t^2-value, it would pay to impose the coefficient β at β^* and use that for forecasting.

Next let $\boldsymbol{\beta}' = (\boldsymbol{\beta}_1' : \boldsymbol{\beta}_2')$ in (12.4), and conformably partition $\mathbf{x}_t' = (\mathbf{x}_{1,t}' : \mathbf{x}_{2,t}')$, so the simplified model is:

$$y_t = \boldsymbol{\gamma}_1'\mathbf{x}_{1,t} + u_t \text{ where } u_t \sim \mathsf{IN}\left[0, \sigma_u^2\right]. \tag{12.21}$$

Without loss of generality, take $\mathbf{x}_{1,t}$ and $\mathbf{x}_{2,t}$ to be orthogonal, since an appropriate reparameterization will always yield this case. Consequently, $\boldsymbol{\gamma}_1 = \boldsymbol{\beta}_1$ and $\sigma_u^2 = \sigma_v^2 + \boldsymbol{\beta}_2'\boldsymbol{\Omega}_{22.1}\boldsymbol{\beta}_2$ in (12.21), where under orthogonality:

$$\boldsymbol{\Omega}_{22.1} = \boldsymbol{\Omega}_{22} - \boldsymbol{\Omega}_{21}\boldsymbol{\Omega}_{11}^{-1}\boldsymbol{\Omega}_{12} = \boldsymbol{\Omega}_{22}.$$

The MSFE from (12.21) is:

$$\mathsf{E}\left[\widetilde{u}^2_{T+1} \mid \mathbf{x}_{T+1}\right] = \sigma_v^2 + \boldsymbol{\beta}_2'\mathbf{x}_{2,T+1}\mathbf{x}_{2,T+1}'\boldsymbol{\beta}_2 + T^{-1}\sigma_u^2\mathbf{x}_{1,T+1}'\boldsymbol{\Omega}_{11}^{-1}\mathbf{x}_{1,T+1}. \tag{12.22}$$

The $\mathsf{F}^{k_2}_{T-k}$-test of $\boldsymbol{\beta}_2 = \mathbf{0}$ has a non-centrality parameter of $\phi^2_{\boldsymbol{\beta}_2=\mathbf{0}} = T\boldsymbol{\beta}_2'\boldsymbol{\Omega}_{22.1}\boldsymbol{\beta}_2/\sigma_v^2$. Hence, from (12.12) and (12.22), $\mathsf{R}_\ell(\widetilde{u}, \widehat{\nu}, 1)$ is given by:

$$\begin{aligned} & T^{-1}\left(T\sigma_v^{-2}\boldsymbol{\beta}_2'\mathbf{x}_{2,T+1}\mathbf{x}_{2,T+1}'\boldsymbol{\beta}_2 + \sigma_u^2\sigma_v^{-2}\mathbf{x}_{1,T+1}'\boldsymbol{\Omega}_{11}^{-1}\mathbf{x}_{1,T+1} - \mathbf{x}_{T+1}'\boldsymbol{\Omega}^{-1}\mathbf{x}_{T+1}\right) \\ &= T^{-1}\left(T^{-1}\phi^2_{\boldsymbol{\beta}_2=\mathbf{0}}\mathbf{x}_{1,T+1}'\boldsymbol{\Omega}_{11}^{-1}\mathbf{x}_{1,T+1} + \mathbf{x}_{2,T+1}'\left[T\boldsymbol{\beta}_2\boldsymbol{\beta}_2'/\sigma_v^2 - \boldsymbol{\Omega}_{22}^{-1}\right]\mathbf{x}_{2,T+1}\right), \end{aligned} \tag{12.23}$$

where the last line follows by substituting for σ_u^2 and noting that under orthogonality:

$$\mathbf{x}_{T+1}'\boldsymbol{\Omega}^{-1}\mathbf{x}_{T+1} = \mathbf{x}_{1,T+1}'\boldsymbol{\Omega}_{11}^{-1}\mathbf{x}_{1,T+1} + \mathbf{x}_{2,T+1}'\boldsymbol{\Omega}_{22}^{-1}\mathbf{x}_{2,T+1}.$$

Using $\mathsf{E}[\mathbf{x}_{i,T+1}'\boldsymbol{\Omega}_{ii}^{-1}\mathbf{x}_{i,T+1}] = k_i \ \forall i = 1, 2$:

$$\begin{aligned} \mathsf{E}\left[\mathsf{R}_\ell\left(\widetilde{u}, \widehat{\nu}, 1\right)\right] &= T^{-1}\left(T^{-1}k_1\phi^2_{\boldsymbol{\beta}_2=\mathbf{0}} + tr\left[T\boldsymbol{\beta}_2'\boldsymbol{\Omega}_{22}\boldsymbol{\beta}_2/\sigma_v^2 - \mathbf{I}_{k_2}\right]\right) \\ &= T^{-1}k_2\left(\left(1 + T^{-1}k_1\right)\Phi^2_{\boldsymbol{\beta}_2=\mathbf{0}} - 1\right) \simeq T^{-1}k_2\left(\Phi^2_{\boldsymbol{\beta}_2=\mathbf{0}} - 1\right), \end{aligned} \tag{12.24}$$

dropping terms of $O(T^{-2})$. Equation (12.24) is the natural generalization of earlier formulae in that $\Phi^2_{\boldsymbol{\beta}_2=\mathbf{0}} > 1$ is required for a gain on average. When $k_2 = 1$, we replicate (12.20), so that result holds for a partial t-test in a regression equation.

The result in (12.20) for forecasting accuracy is related to the usual criterion of in-sample goodness of fit, since the residual standard deviation will rise (fall) if a deleted regressor has a t^2-value greater (smaller) than unity. However, there is one important difference: forecast accuracy will improve (worsen) depending on whether the deleted regressor has a t^2- value greater (smaller) than 2. From (12.20), it is apparent that there is a trade-off between squared inconsistency (given by $(\beta - \beta^*)^2$) and estimation uncertainty (given by $T^{-1}\sigma_x^2/\sigma_v^2$). Since the analysis is conditional on $(\mathbf{x}_1, \ldots, \mathbf{x}_T)$, replacing $\boldsymbol{\Omega}$ by $\widehat{\boldsymbol{\Omega}}$ has no substantive implications.

12.3 1-step forecasts in dynamic models

The result in (12.23) assumes known future values of regressors. We first consider a dynamic model with a deterministic regressor. Again the criterion for model choice depends directly on a criterion of the form $\phi^2 > 1$. Thus, the type of formula in (12.20) is robust to introducing dynamics, estimation of unknown parameters and additional explanatory variables for 1-step forecasts from correctly specified equations.

Consider a stationary first-order autoregression with intercept μ and autoregressive parameter ρ, where $-1 < \rho < 1$:

$$y_t = \mu + \rho y_{t-1} + \epsilon_t \text{ where } \epsilon_t \sim \mathsf{IN}\left[0, \sigma_\epsilon^2\right], \tag{12.25}$$

and $y_0 \sim \mathsf{IN}[\mu_y, \sigma_y^2]$, when $\mu_y = \mu/(1-\rho)$ and $\sigma_y^2 = \sigma_\epsilon^2/(1-\rho^2)$. Denote the standardized variate by $y_t^* = (y_t - \mu_y)/\sigma_\epsilon$, so that:

$$y_t^* = \mu^* + \rho y_{t-1}^* + \epsilon_t^*, \tag{12.26}$$

where $\epsilon_t^* \sim \mathsf{IN}[0,1]$, and now $\mu^* = 0$. The form in (12.26) provides a canonical representation. Due to the presence of dynamics, the results rely on asymptotic approximations (as in (12.27) following, and as discussed in section 4.3).

The estimate of $\boldsymbol{\theta} = (\mu : \rho)'$ in (12.25) is:

$$\begin{pmatrix} \sqrt{T}\left(\widehat{\mu} - \mu\right) \\ \sqrt{T}\left(\widehat{\rho} - \rho\right) \end{pmatrix} \xrightarrow{d} \mathsf{N}_2\left[\begin{pmatrix} 0 \\ 0 \end{pmatrix}, \left(1-\rho^2\right)\begin{pmatrix} \sigma_y^2 + \mu_y^2 & -\mu_y \\ -\mu_y & 1 \end{pmatrix}\right]. \tag{12.27}$$

The covariance matrix of $\widehat{\boldsymbol{\theta}}$ is obtained from:

$$\begin{aligned} \mathsf{V}\left[\widehat{\boldsymbol{\theta}}\right] &= \sigma_\epsilon^2 \mathsf{E}\left[\begin{array}{cc} T & \sum y_{t-1} \\ \sum y_{t-1} & \sum y_{t-1}^2 \end{array}\right]^{-1} \\ &\simeq \sigma_\epsilon^2 \begin{pmatrix} T & T\mu_y \\ T\mu_y & T\left(\sigma_y^2 + \mu_y^2\right) \end{pmatrix}^{-1} \end{aligned}$$

$$= \frac{\sigma_\epsilon^2}{\sigma_y^2} T^{-1} \begin{pmatrix} \sigma_y^2 + \mu_y^2 & -\mu_y \\ -\mu_y & 1 \end{pmatrix}$$

(see equation (4.7)). Let $\mathbf{x}'_T = (1 : y_T)$, then $\widehat{y}_{T+1} = \widehat{\boldsymbol{\theta}}'\mathbf{x}_T$, and hence for $\widehat{\epsilon}_{T+1} = y_{T+1} - \widehat{y}_{T+1}$:

$$\begin{aligned} \mathsf{E}\left[\widehat{\epsilon}^2_{T+1} \mid \mathbf{x}_T\right] &\simeq \left(\sigma_\epsilon^2 + \mathbf{x}'_T \mathsf{V}\left[\widehat{\boldsymbol{\theta}}\right]\mathbf{x}_T\right) \\ &= \sigma_\epsilon^2 + T^{-1}\left[\sigma_\epsilon^2 + (y_T - \mu_y)^2\left(1-\rho^2\right)\right] \\ &= T^{-1}\sigma_\epsilon^2\left(T + 1 + y_T^{\dagger 2}\right), \end{aligned} \tag{12.28}$$

where $y_T^\dagger = (y_T - \mu_y)/\sigma_y$. The analysis could use the canonical form in (12.26), since both the model and the estimator are invariant under linear transformations.

Any potential loss from estimating parameters rather than fixing them depends on whether μ, or ρ, or both, are fixed. The simplest case is where $(\mu : \rho)$ are set to $(0, 1)$, so that the loss from using zero as the forecast for Δy_{T+1} is calculated. Since:

$$\Delta y_t = \mu + (\rho - 1)\, y_{t-1} + \epsilon_t = (\rho - 1)\,(y_{t-1} - \mu_y) + \epsilon_t, \tag{12.29}$$

using $\Delta\check{y}_{T+1} = 0$, then $\check{\epsilon}_{T+1} = (\rho - 1)(y_T - \mu_y) + \epsilon_{T+1}$ so that:

$$\mathsf{E}\left[\check{\epsilon}^2_{T+1} \mid y_T\right] = \sigma_\epsilon^2 + (\rho-1)^2\,\sigma_y^2 y_T^{\dagger 2} = \sigma_\epsilon^2\left(1 + \left[\frac{1-\rho}{1+\rho}\right] y_T^{\dagger 2}\right). \tag{12.30}$$

Thus, from (12.28) and (12.30), the relative loss from imposing $(\mu : \rho)$ at $(0, 1)$ rather than estimating $\boldsymbol{\theta}$ is:

$$\begin{aligned} \mathsf{R}_\ell\left(\check{\epsilon}, \widehat{\epsilon}, 1\right) &= \left[\tfrac{1-\rho}{1+\rho}\right] y_T^{\dagger 2} - T^{-1}\left(1 + y_T^{\dagger 2}\right) \\ &= T^{-1}\left\{\left[T\left(\tfrac{1-\rho}{1+\rho}\right) - 1\right] y_T^{\dagger 2} - 1\right\} \\ &= T^{-1}\left[\left(\phi^2_{\rho=1} - 1\right) y_T^{\dagger 2} - 1\right], \end{aligned} \tag{12.31}$$

where $\phi^2_{\rho=1}$ is the non-centrality of the F^1_{T-2} test of H: $\rho = 1$ assuming stationarity. When μ is known to be zero, the formula becomes $T^{-1}(\phi^2_{\rho=1} - 1)y_T^{\dagger 2}$.

It is surprising that (12.31) does not depend directly on the value of μ, and the only cost to imposing it at zero is T^{-1}. However, this is due to the form of (12.29), not to expressing the formulae in differences, since MSFEs for 1-step forecasts are invariant to levels or differences (see section 3.5). Since $\mathsf{E}[y_T^{\dagger 2}] = 1$, when $|\rho| < 1$, then $\phi^2_{\rho=1} > 2$ is needed on average before the first-difference model loses to the estimated DGP.

Since (12.25) is stationary, an alternative predictor is the unconditional mean μ_y. To highlight the issue of model choice, as in our analysis of intercept corrections in section 8.4, we assume that μ_y is based on a large sample of historical data, such that its variance is negligible. This yields the forecast $\overline{y}_{T+1} = \mu_y$ with forecast error:

$$\overline{\epsilon}_{T+1} = \mu + \rho y_T + \epsilon_{T+1} - \mu_y = \rho\,(y_T - \mu_y) + \epsilon_{T+1},$$

and forecast-error second moment:

$$\mathsf{E}\left[\overline{\epsilon}^2_{T+1} \mid y_T\right] = \sigma^2_\epsilon + \rho^2\sigma^2_y y^{\dagger 2}_T = \sigma^2_\epsilon\left(1 + \left[\frac{\rho^2}{1-\rho^2}\right] y^{\dagger 2}_T\right). \tag{12.32}$$

In comparison to (12.30), the relative loss is:

$$\mathsf{R}_\ell\left(\overline{\epsilon}, \check{\epsilon}, 1\right) = \left(\frac{\rho^2 - (1-\rho)^2}{1-\rho^2}\right) y^{\dagger 2}_T = \frac{2}{1-\rho^2}\left(\rho - \tfrac{1}{2}\right) y^{\dagger 2}_T.$$

Thus, differencing will dominate in the well-known case that $\rho > 1/2$. Estimating μ_y will lower the required value of ρ for differencing to dominate irrespective of the value of μ, so forecasting the first difference as zero can have the smallest MSFE over a range of values of $0 < \rho < 1$ against both the DGP and the unconditional mean.

When the underlying process has $\rho = 1$, so there is a unit root, then the first-difference specification (which imposes the root at unity) is obviously preferable, but we can describe the loss from estimating ρ. It is well known (see Phillips, 1987, and Banerjee, Dolado, Galbraith and Hendry, 1993) that when $\rho = 1$ and $y_0 = \mu = 0$:

$$\begin{aligned} T\left(\widehat{\rho} - 1\right) &= \left(T^{-2}\sum_{t=1}^{T} y^2_{t-1}\right)^{-1}\left(T^{-1}\sum_{t=1}^{T} y_{t-1}\epsilon_t\right) \\ &\Rightarrow \left(\int_0^1 V(r)^2 \mathrm{d}r\right)^{-1}\left(\int_0^1 V(r)\mathrm{d}V(r)\right), \end{aligned}$$

where $V(r) \sim \mathsf{N}[0, r]$ (see section 11.7). Thus, $T(\widehat{\rho} - 1) \sim \mathsf{D}(\psi, \omega^2)$ (say). The variance of $\widehat{\rho}$ is approximately $T^{-2}\omega^2$, but $\mathsf{E}[y^2_T] = T\sigma^2_\epsilon$. Hence:

$$\mathsf{E}\left[\widehat{\epsilon}^2_{T+1} \mid y_T\right] \simeq \sigma^2_\epsilon + \left(T^{-1}\psi^2 + T^{-2}\omega^2\right) y^2_T \simeq \sigma^2_\epsilon\left[1 + \left(\psi^2 + T^{-1}\omega^2\right)\right].$$

The second term in $[\cdot]$ is the expected relative loss from estimating the unit root when forecasting, and compared to imposing $\rho = 1$ is given approximately by $(\psi^2 + \omega^2/T)$.

To summarize, model choice for 1-step forecasting, in the simple stationary process considered so far, mainly involves whether or not the relevant non-centrality ϕ^2 exceeds unity. A possible operational criterion is that the corresponding average t^2-statistic exceeds 2, but this can occur when $\phi^2 < 1$, or fail to occur when $\phi^2 > 1$.

To illustrate the issues arising in dynamic models with non-modelled regressors, consider a scalar first-order autoregressive process with an additional lagged white-noise explanatory variable z_{t-1}:

$$y_t = \gamma z_{t-1} + \alpha y_{t-1} + v_t, \tag{12.33}$$

where $-1 < \alpha < 1$ and $v_t \sim \mathsf{IN}[0, \sigma^2_v]$. The process generating z_t is:

$$z_t = u_t \text{ where } u_t \sim \mathsf{IN}\left[0, \sigma^2_u\right], \tag{12.34}$$

and $\mathsf{E}[u_t v_s] = 0$ for all t, s. We assume that $y_0 \sim \mathsf{IN}[0, (\sigma_v^2 + \gamma^2\sigma_u^2)/(1 - \alpha^2)]$ so the process defined by (12.33) and (12.34) is stationary. Let $\mathbf{x}_t = (z_t : y_t)'$ and $\boldsymbol{\theta} = (\gamma : \alpha)'$. Consider two investigators who respectively fit (12.33) (denoted M_1) and the following time-series model, denoted M_2:

$$y_t = \lambda y_{t-1} + \epsilon_t, \tag{12.35}$$

where $-1 < \lambda < 1$ and ϵ_t is asserted to be distributed as $\mathsf{IN}[0, \sigma_\epsilon^2]$.

Given (12.33) and (12.34), $\epsilon_t = \gamma u_{t-1} + v_t$ and hence $\mathsf{E}[\epsilon_t] = 0$, with $\sigma_\epsilon^2 = \sigma_v^2 + \gamma^2\sigma_u^2$, so that $\lambda = \alpha$. Both investigators use least squares for a sample of size T to estimate the parameters of their models, then seek to forecast y_{T+1} given information up to and including time T.

When the respective parameters are known, the choice of model is simple. Given the information available at time T, for known parameters, the conditional mean delivers the MMSFE in the next period, so for M_1:

$$\mathsf{E}\left[y_{T+1} \mid \mathbf{x}_T\right] = \widehat{y}_{T+1} = \gamma z_T + \alpha y_T, \tag{12.36}$$

with a forecast error of $y_{T+1} - \widehat{y}_{T+1} = v_{T+1}$ so that:

$$\mathsf{E}\left[v_{T+1} \mid \mathbf{x}_T\right] = 0 \;\text{ and }\; \mathsf{E}\left[v_{T+1}^2 \mid \mathbf{x}_T\right] = \sigma_v^2. \tag{12.37}$$

Correspondingly, M_2 uses:

$$\widetilde{y}_{T+1} = \lambda y_T \tag{12.38}$$

with a forecast error of $\epsilon_{T+1} = y_{T+1} - \widetilde{y}_{T+1} = v_{T+1} + \gamma z_T$, (since $\lambda = \alpha$) so that:

$$\mathsf{E}\left[\epsilon_{T+1} \mid y_T\right] = \gamma z_T \;\text{ and }\; \mathsf{E}\left[\epsilon_{T+1}^2 \mid y_T\right] = \sigma_v^2 + \gamma^2 z_T^2. \tag{12.39}$$

Consequently:

$$\mathsf{E}\left[\epsilon_{T+1}^2 \mid y_T\right] - \mathsf{E}\left[v_{T+1}^2 \mid y_T, z_T\right] = \sigma_v^2 + \gamma^2 z_T^2 - \sigma_v^2 = \gamma^2 z_T^2 \geq 0, \tag{12.40}$$

yielding the relative loss:

$$\mathsf{R}_\ell\left(\epsilon, v, 1\right) = \frac{\gamma^2 z_T^2}{\sigma_v^2}. \tag{12.41}$$

It pays to use the more informative model.

The two forecast errors for estimated parameter values become (for M_1, where $\widehat{v}_{T+1} = y_{T+1} - \widehat{y}_{T+1}$):

$$\widehat{v}_{T+1} = v_{T+1} + (\gamma - \widehat{\gamma})\, z_T + (\alpha - \widehat{\alpha})\, y_T = v_{T+1} + \left(\boldsymbol{\theta} - \widehat{\boldsymbol{\theta}}\right)' \mathbf{x}_T, \tag{12.42}$$

and for M_2:

$$\widetilde{\epsilon}_{T+1} = y_{T+1} - \widetilde{y}_{T+1} = v_{T+1} + \gamma z_T + \left(\lambda - \widetilde{\lambda}\right) y_T. \tag{12.43}$$

Although parameter estimates in dynamic models are in general biased to $O(T^{-1})$, we will ignore that in what follows. The variances of the forecast errors are (also ignoring a slight dependence on $\mathbf{x}_T$):

$$\mathsf{E}\left[\widehat{v}_{T+1}^2 \mid \mathbf{x}_T\right] = \sigma_v^2 + \mathbf{x}_T'\mathsf{V}\left[\widehat{\boldsymbol{\theta}}\right]\mathbf{x}_T, \tag{12.44}$$

and:

$$\mathsf{E}\left[\widetilde{\epsilon}_{T+1}^2 \mid y_T\right] = \sigma_v^2 + \gamma^2 z_T^2 + \mathsf{V}\left[\widetilde{\lambda}\right] y_T^2, \tag{12.45}$$

so that:

$$\mathsf{E}\left[\widetilde{\epsilon}_{T+1}^2 \mid y_T\right] - \mathsf{E}\left[\widehat{v}_{T+1}^2 \mid \mathbf{x}_T\right] = \gamma^2 z_T^2 + \mathsf{V}\left[\widetilde{\lambda}\right] y_T^2 - \mathbf{x}_T'\mathsf{V}\left[\widehat{\boldsymbol{\theta}}\right]\mathbf{x}_T. \tag{12.46}$$

From (12.33) (assuming the first observations are available for simplicity):

$$\begin{aligned}\mathsf{V}\left[\widehat{\boldsymbol{\theta}}\right] = \mathsf{V}\left[\begin{pmatrix}\widehat{\gamma}\\ \widehat{\alpha}\end{pmatrix}\right] &= \sigma_v^2\mathsf{E}\left[\begin{pmatrix}\sum_{t=1}^T z_{t-1}^2 & \sum_{t=1}^T z_{t-1}y_{t-1}\\ \sum_{t=1}^T y_{t-1}z_{t-1} & \sum_{t=1}^T y_{t-1}^2\end{pmatrix}^{-1}\right]\\ &\simeq \sigma_v^2 T^{-1}\begin{pmatrix}\sigma_u^2 & \delta\\ \delta & \sigma_\epsilon^2/\left(1-\alpha^2\right)\end{pmatrix}^{-1},\end{aligned} \tag{12.47}$$

where δ denotes the value of the covariance, but for (12.33) and (12.34), $\delta = 0$. The last approximation is valid asymptotically, so that we will take:

$$\mathsf{V}\left[\widehat{\boldsymbol{\theta}}\right] \simeq \sigma_v^2 T^{-1}\begin{bmatrix}1/\sigma_u^2 & 0\\ 0 & \left(1-\alpha^2\right)/\sigma_\epsilon^2\end{bmatrix}. \tag{12.48}$$

Similarly:

$$\mathsf{V}\left[\widetilde{\lambda}\right] \simeq T^{-1}\left(1-\alpha^2\right). \tag{12.49}$$

Thus, substituting (12.48) and (12.49) into (12.46) and scaling by σ_v^2:

$$\begin{aligned}\mathsf{R}_\ell\left(\widetilde{\epsilon},\widehat{v},1\right) &\simeq T^{-1}\sigma_v^{-2}\left[T\gamma^2 z_T^2 + \left(1-\alpha^2\right)y_T^2 - \left(\frac{\sigma_v^2}{\sigma_u^2}\right)z_T^2\right]\\ &\quad -T^{-1}\sigma_v^{-2}\left(\frac{\sigma_v^2}{\sigma_\epsilon^2}\right)\left(1-\alpha^2\right)y_T^2\\ &= T^{-1}\sigma_v^{-2}\left[\left(T\gamma^2 - \sigma_v^2/\sigma_u^2\right)z_T^2 + \left(\sigma_\epsilon^2-\sigma_v^2\right)\left(y_T^2/\sigma_y^2\right)\right]\\ &= T^{-1}\left[\left(\phi_{\gamma=0}^2 - 1\right)\left(z_T^2/\sigma_u^2\right) + T^{-1}\phi_{\gamma=0}^2\left(y_T^2/\sigma_y^2\right)\right],\end{aligned} \tag{12.50}$$

where $\phi_{\gamma=0}^2 = T\gamma^2\sigma_u^2/\sigma_v^2$ is the non-centrality of the F_{T-2}^1 test of $\gamma = 0$ when estimating (12.33). Hence from (12.50) since $\mathsf{E}[y_T^2/\sigma_y^2] = 1$ and $\mathsf{E}[z_T^2/\sigma_u^2] = 1$:

$$\mathsf{E}\left[\mathsf{R}_\ell\left(\widetilde{\epsilon},\widehat{v},1\right)\right] \simeq T^{-1}\left[\left(1+T^{-1}\right)\phi_{\gamma=0}^2 - 1\right] \simeq T^{-1}\left(\phi_{\gamma=0}^2 - 1\right), \tag{12.51}$$

to $O(T^{-1})$. On the basis of (12.51), the relative loss can go in either direction, and $\phi^2_{\gamma=0} > 1$ is required for an improvement from retaining z_{t-1}. If $\mathsf{t}^2_{T-k}(\phi^2_{\gamma=0}) = 4$ (a conventional criterion), then in units of $\sqrt{|\mathsf{R}_\ell(\cdot)|}$, when $T = 100$, there is a 14 percent loss for M_2 over M_1, and for $\mathsf{t}^2_{98}(\phi^2_{\gamma=0}) = 12$, then $\sqrt{|\mathsf{R}_\ell(\cdot)|}$ rises to 32 percent. Thus, variables must contribute noticeably to the explanation if even 1-step forecasts are to be markedly improved. When regressors are correlated, there may appear to be an offset from the covariance, but the estimated parameter variances are larger. Overall, there are potential gains from imposing, rather than estimating, coefficients if the absolute value of the 't'-test of the imposed restriction does not exceed $\sqrt{2}$ (approximately corresponding to $\phi^2_{\gamma=0} = 1$).

The comparison in (12.51) was between the estimated DGP and an estimated autoregressive model. However, we showed above that imposing the autoregressive parameter at unity could yield gains over estimating it, so a simple first-difference could well have a smaller MSFE than the estimated DGP. Indeed, from (12.35), if λ is fixed at unity, and $\breve{\epsilon}$ denotes the forecast error from predicting Δy_{T+1} as zero, then as in (12.30):

$$\mathsf{E}\left[\breve{\epsilon}^2_{T+1} \mid y_T\right] = \sigma^2_v + \gamma^2 z^2_T + (\alpha - 1)^2 y^2_T. \tag{12.52}$$

Comparing (12.52) to (12.44) given (12.48):

$$\begin{aligned}
\mathsf{R}_\ell(\breve{\epsilon}, \widehat{v}, 1) &\simeq \frac{1}{\sigma^2_v}\left[\gamma^2 z^2_T + (1-\alpha)^2 y^2_T - T^{-1}\sigma^2_v\left(\frac{z^2_T}{\sigma^2_u}\right) - T^{-1}\sigma^2_v\left(\frac{y^2_T}{\sigma^2_y}\right)\right] \\
&= T^{-1}\left[\left(\phi^2_{\gamma=0} - 1\right)\left(z^2_T/\sigma^2_u\right) + \left\{T\sigma^2_y(1-\alpha)^2/\sigma^2_v - 1\right\}\left(y^2_T/\sigma^2_y\right)\right] \\
&\simeq T^{-1}\left[\left(\phi^2_{\gamma=0} - 1\right)\left(z^2_T/\sigma^2_u\right) + \left(\phi^2_{\alpha=1} - 1\right)\left(y^2_T/\sigma^2_y\right)\right],
\end{aligned} \tag{12.53}$$

where $\phi^2_{\alpha=1} = T(1-\alpha)^2/(1-\alpha^2)$, using:

$$\frac{\sigma^2_y\left(1-\alpha^2\right)}{\sigma^2_v} = \frac{\sigma^2_\epsilon}{\sigma^2_v} = \left(1 + T^{-1}\phi^2_{\gamma=0}\right),$$

and dropping the term of $O(T^{-1})$. The result in (12.53) has a number of interesting features.

First, if $\phi^2_{\gamma=0} < 1$ but z^2_T/σ^2_u is large, a poor forecast could result from the estimated DGP relative to the false autoregressive model. Secondly, the relative importance of the forecast origins affects the potential ranking of the two predictors. Finally:

$$\mathsf{E}\left[\mathsf{R}_\ell(\breve{\epsilon}, \widehat{v}, 1)\right] \simeq T^{-1}\left[\left(\phi^2_{\gamma=0} + \phi^2_{\alpha=1}\right) - 2\right] \simeq (2T)^{-1}\left(\Phi^2_{\boldsymbol{\beta}=\mathbf{0}} - 1\right), \tag{12.54}$$

where $\boldsymbol{\beta} = (\gamma : \alpha - 1)'$, using (12.23) for orthogonal regressors, and retaining stationarity. This replicates our earlier results.

Thus, in comparing the anticipated forecast performance of estimated econometric and autoregressive models, even when the former is the DGP, it need not be the optimal predictor for 1-step ahead forecasts. The result also reveals potential advantages to differencing when α is close to unity. This matches the analysis of the critique of Lucas (1976) in Favero and Hendry (1992), and the role in robustifying forecasts against unknown structural breaks of intercept corrections which induce differencing (see chapter 8). Further, we see that care is required in interpreting the results of the approach advocated by Granger and Deutsch (1992). The model (12.33) is the DGP, yet forecasting accuracy could be improved by dropping z_{t-1} or imposing $\alpha = 1$. However, even if (12.35) predicted better than (12.33) in practice, it would be incorrect to conclude that policies based on changing z_{t-1} would not be effective, since their impact depends on the size of γ, and not on how precisely γ is estimated.

12.4 *h*-step ahead forecasts

12.4.1 OLS, 'no-change' and 'zero' forecasts

The previous sections focused on 1-step forecasts and we now consider whether or not the implications extend to h-step forecasts. We first examine h-step forecasts from the simple autoregression $y_t = \rho y_{t-1} + \epsilon_t$, where $|\rho| < 1$, to see the cumulative effect on forecasting of estimating ρ relative to imposing it. Since:

$$y_{T+h} = \rho^h y_T + \sum_{j=0}^{h-1} \rho^j \epsilon_{T+h-j}, \tag{12.55}$$

the h-step conditional forecast error from the estimated model using $\widehat{y}_{T+h} = \widehat{\rho}^h y_T$ given (12.55) is:

$$\widehat{\epsilon}_{T+h} = y_{T+h} - \widehat{y}_{T+h} = \left(\rho^h - \widehat{\rho}^h\right) y_T + \sum_{j=0}^{h-1} \rho^j \epsilon_{T+h-j}, \tag{12.56}$$

so that for forecasting the level y_{T+h} (see section 4.11):

$$\begin{aligned} \mathsf{E}\left[\widehat{\epsilon}^2_{T+h} \mid y_T\right] &\simeq \sigma^2_\epsilon \left(1 - \rho^{2h}\right)\left(1 - \rho^2\right)^{-1} + T^{-1} h^2 \rho^{2(h-1)} \left(1 - \rho^2\right) y^2_T \\ &= \sigma^2_y \left[\left(1 - \rho^{2h}\right) + T^{-1} h^2 \rho^{2(h-1)} \left(1 - \rho^2\right) y^{\dagger 2}_T\right]. \end{aligned} \tag{12.57}$$

When a forecast of zero is used, so $\widetilde{y}_{T+h} = 0 \; \forall h$, then:

$$\begin{aligned} \mathsf{E}\left[\widetilde{\epsilon}^2_{T+h} \mid y_T\right] &= \sigma^2_\epsilon \left(1 - \rho^{2h}\right)\left(1 - \rho^2\right)^{-1} + \rho^{2h} y^2_T \\ &= \sigma^2_y \left[\left(1 - \rho^{2h}\right) + \rho^{2h} y^{\dagger 2}_T\right]. \end{aligned} \tag{12.58}$$

Hence:

$$\begin{aligned} \mathsf{R}_\ell\left(\widetilde{\epsilon}, \widehat{\epsilon}, h\right) &= T^{-1} \rho^{2(h-1)} \left[T\rho^2 \left(1 - \rho^2\right)^{-1} - h^2\right] y^{\dagger 2}_T \\ &= T^{-1} \rho^{2(h-1)} \left(\phi^2_{\rho=0} - h^2\right) y^{\dagger 2}_T. \end{aligned} \tag{12.59}$$

Thus, the condition for retaining the estimated coefficient rather than imposing it arbitrarily at zero becomes increasingly stringent as h increases, although the term as a whole is tending to zero. In fact, if $\mathsf{R}_{\ell}(\cdot)$ is ever positive, a cross-over of sign must occur at some h, so there always exists an h at which negative values occur. The formula in (12.59) explains why forecast confidence bands are non-monotonic in h and can exceed the unconditional forecast uncertainty (see Chong and Hendry, 1986, Ericsson and Marquez, 1989, 1996, and chapter 8). Further, when $\phi^2_{\rho=0} > 1$, a weighted average of the estimated and imposed models will outperform either, matching the optimal weight for pooling the models obtained in section 8.4 and section 10.4. (See in particular (8.34), noting that $(1-\alpha^*_h)$, the weight on the estimated-model forecast, is non-zero whenever $\mathsf{t}^2_{T-1}(\phi^2_{\rho=0}) > 0$.)

If, instead of $\widetilde{y}_{T+h} = 0$, a forecast of no-change is used, so that:

$$\breve{y}_{T+h} = y_T \ \forall h, \tag{12.60}$$

then:

$$\breve{\epsilon}_{T+h} = y_{T+h} - \breve{y}_{T+h} = \left(\rho^h - 1\right) y_T + \sum_{j=0}^{h-1} \rho^j \epsilon_{T+h-j}, \tag{12.61}$$

and hence:

$$\begin{aligned} \mathsf{E}\left[\breve{\epsilon}^2_{T+h} \mid y_T\right] &= \sigma^2_{\epsilon}\left(1-\rho^{2h}\right)\left(1-\rho^2\right)^{-1} + \left(\rho^h - 1\right)^2 y^2_T \\ &= \sigma^2_y \left[\left(1-\rho^{2h}\right) + \left(1-\rho^h\right)^2 y^{\dagger 2}_T\right]. \end{aligned} \tag{12.62}$$

First, comparing zero against no-change yields a simple outcome:

$$\begin{aligned} \mathsf{R}_{\ell}\left(\widetilde{\epsilon}, \breve{\epsilon}, h\right) &= \left(1-\rho^2\right)^{-1}\left[\rho^{2h} - \left(1-\rho^h\right)^2\right] y^{\dagger 2}_T \\ &= 2\left(1-\rho^2\right)^{-1}\left(\rho^h - \tfrac{1}{2}\right) y^{\dagger 2}_T. \end{aligned} \tag{12.63}$$

On average, for further ahead forecasts, a no-change forecast will only dominate a forecast of the unconditional mean when ρ is ever closer to unity. Consequently, when $\rho = 0.7$, say, a switch in model choice could occur when going from 1-step to 2-step ahead forecasts between a no-change forecast and a zero forecast. The model that is best at one horizon, need not be best for all forecast horizons.

Lest it be thought that assuming a known unconditional mean is unreasonable, most models in, for example, second differences of the variables will have means of essentially zero. Further, for models in first differences, the analysis of section 12.3 revealed that imposing the mean at zero may yield benefits.

Next, comparing the no-change forecast against that from the fitted model:

$$
\begin{aligned}
\mathsf{R}_\ell\left(\breve{\epsilon},\widehat{\epsilon},h\right) &= \left[\left(1-\rho^h\right)^2 - T^{-1}h^2\rho^{2(h-1)}\left(1-\rho^2\right)\right]\left(y_T^2/\sigma_\epsilon^2\right) \\
&= T^{-1}\left[T\left(1-\rho^h\right)^2\left(1-\rho^2\right)^{-1} - h^2\rho^{2(h-1)}\right]y_T^{\dagger 2} \\
&= T^{-1}\left[\rho^{2(h-1)}\left(\phi_{\rho=0}^2 - h^2\right) - 2T\frac{\left(\rho^h - \frac{1}{2}\right)}{\left(1-\rho^2\right)}\right]y_T^{\dagger 2}.
\end{aligned} \tag{12.64}
$$

The result is expressed as the difference between $\mathsf{R}_\ell(\widetilde{\epsilon},\widehat{\epsilon},h)$ and $\mathsf{R}_\ell(\widetilde{\epsilon},\breve{\epsilon},h)$ with the two factors pulling in opposite directions, so the sign depends on the magnitudes of all the terms involved. However, the outcome is easily computed numerically to check the ordering in any instance. For ρ close to zero, a no-change forecast will never dominate a forecast using the estimated model. For ρ close to unity, let $\rho = e^{-\lambda}$ so that $\rho^{2h} = e^{-2h\lambda} \simeq 1 - 2h\lambda$, then:

$$
\begin{aligned}
\mathsf{R}_\ell\left(\breve{\epsilon},\widehat{\epsilon},h\right) &= T^{-1}\left[T\left(e^{-2h\lambda} - 2e^{-h\lambda} + 1\right)\left(1-e^{-2\lambda}\right)^{-1} - h^2 e^{-2(h-1)\lambda}\right]y_T^{\dagger 2} \\
&\simeq \left[\left(1 - 2h\lambda - 2 + 2h\lambda + 1\right)\left(2\lambda\right)^{-1} - T^{-1}h^2\left(1 - 2\left(h-1\right)\lambda\right)\right]y_T^{\dagger 2} \\
&= -T^{-1}h^2\left[1 - 2\left(h-1\right)\lambda\right]y_T^{\dagger 2}.
\end{aligned} \tag{12.65}
$$

For $h > 1 + (2\lambda)^{-1}$, the $[\cdot]$ term will become negative, so a sign switch will occur making $\mathsf{R}_\ell(\cdot)$ positive, but until that (perhaps distant) horizon, the no change forecast will dominate: however, these approximations are useful only if $h\lambda$ is small.

12.4.2 Monte Carlo illustration

A simple Monte Carlo was undertaken to illustrate the consequences of parameter estimation versus the imposition of parameter values as we change the forecast horizon. We make use of the AR(1) model, where the $\{\varepsilon_t\}$ are replaced by pseudo-random numbers drawn from a standard normal distribution. Two sample sizes were chosen, $T = 25$ and $T = 50$, and y_0 was drawn from $\mathsf{N}[\mu(1-\rho)^{-1}, \sigma_\varepsilon^2(1-\rho)^{-2}]$ so that the process $\{y_t\}$ is strictly stationary (as compared to fixed-start up models where $y_0 = 0$). We set $\mu = 0$ and $\sigma_\varepsilon^2 = 1$. Four values were chosen for the autoregressive parameter, ρ, $\{\rho = 0.1, 0.4, 0.9, 0.95\}$. The maximum forecast horizon considered was 10, given the finding by Hoque, Magnus and Pesaran (1988) that the MSFE for the model estimated by OLS only exists for $h \leq (T-2)/2$. The properties of forecasts obtained from the AR(1) model estimated by OLS have been studied by a number of authors (see Hoque *et al.*, 1988, for references, and section 5.4 for a review of the properties that can be derived from the use of antithetic variates).

We are able to confirm the findings of Hoque *et al.* (1988) that the MSFE for OLS is a decreasing function of T for all ρ and h (see below), and moreover, as suggested by section 8.4, the MSFE is not a monotonically increasing function of h: Hoque *et al.* (1988) find that this is particularly true for small ρ.

Our results are based on 50, 000 replications. We calculate MSFEs for the forecasts produced by OLS estimation of the model, for forecasts produced by setting $\rho = 1$ (no-change), and by setting $\rho = 0$ (zero forecast). Intercepts were not estimated.

The main findings are summarized in figures 12.1 and 12.2.

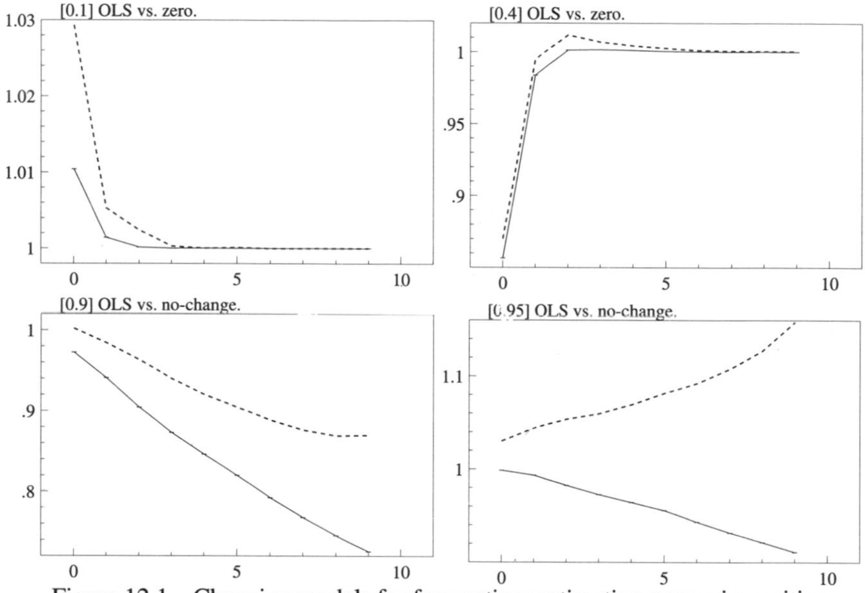

Figure 12.1 Choosing models for forecasting: estimation versus imposition

Each of the four graphs in figure 12.1 is for a different value of ρ. The top two (for $\rho = 0.1$ and $\rho = 0.4$ respectively), display the ratio of the MSFEs for OLS and zero forecasts for the two sample sizes, $T = 25, 50$: thus, values greater than unity imply OLS 'loses'. The top line in each panel, shown as dashed rather than solid, corresponds to $T = 25$. The bottom two graphs convey the same information for the MSFEs for OLS relative to those for the no-change forecasts: we have interchanged the zero comparison with the no-change because, for ρ close to 1, the no-change are more interesting, and more likely to be data selected.

The top-left graph of figure 12.1 shows that for ρ close to 0 (here $\rho = 0.1$), OLS is worse than the zero forecast for both sample sizes for small h. However, the difference between the two forecast errors goes to zero in h (the factor $\rho^{2(h-1)}$ in (12.59)). While the MSFE for the OLS model is $O(T^{-1})$ in T, the zero-forecast model (and the no-change) are $O(T^0)$, or largely independent of T. In the top-right graph, $\rho = 0.4$. The non-centrality parameter $\phi^2_{\rho=0}$ is increasing in ρ (recall, $\phi^2_{\rho=0} = T\rho^2(1-\rho^2)^{-1}$), and for these parameter values, we find that for short horizons, OLS wins. However, as

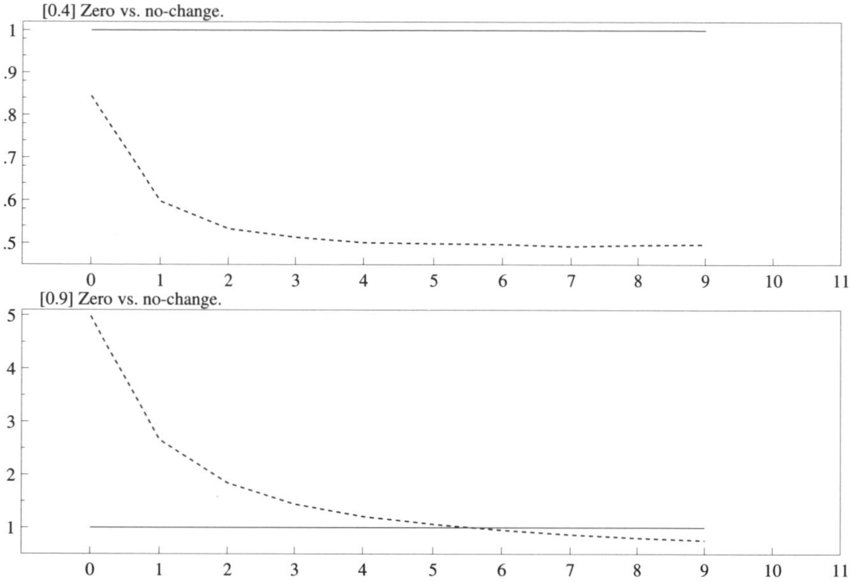

Figure 12.2 Choosing models for forecasting: 'zero' versus 'no-change'

(12.59) implies, when we increase h, there is a reversal for $T = 25$ before the whole term goes to zero.

The bottom two graphs in figure 12.1 indicate that OLS decisively beats no-change as h increases for $\rho = 0.9$, but that $\rho = 0.95$ is sufficiently close to 1 for no change to outperform OLS for $T = 25$ (but not $T = 50$).

Finally, figure 12.2 compares zero and no change for $\rho = 0.4$ and $\rho = 0.9$ (notice that the comparison does not depend on T). In the former case, the zero forecast wins at all h. In the latter, the no-change wins at small h, but by $h = 6$ or 7, the zero forecast dominates.

The results of this Monte Carlo are intended to illuminate the formulae derived in the previous section, and to provide some idea of the orders of magnitude involved.

12.4.3 MSFE calculations on differences of y_t

Since MSFEs are not invariant for h-step forecasts when $h > 1$, even for scalar processes (see chapter 3), we now consider forecasting the changes in y, namely Δy_{T+h}. From (12.55):

$$\begin{aligned} \Delta y_{T+h} &= \rho^h y_T + \sum_{j=1}^{h} \rho^{h-j} \epsilon_{T+j} - \left(\rho^{h-1} y_T + \sum_{j=1}^{h-1} \rho^{h-1-j} \epsilon_{T+j} \right) \\ &= (\rho - 1) \rho^{h-1} y_T + \epsilon_{T+h} + (\rho - 1) \sum_{j=1}^{h-1} \rho^{h-j-1} \epsilon_{T+j}. \end{aligned} \tag{12.66}$$

Using $\widehat{\Delta y}_{T+h} = \widehat{y}_{T+h} - \widehat{y}_{T+h-1} = (\widehat{\rho}-1)\widehat{\rho}^{h-1}y_T$, so that $\vec{e}_{T+h} = \Delta y_{T+h} - \widehat{\Delta y}_{T+h}$:

$$\vec{e}_{T+h} = \left\{ \epsilon_{T+h} + (\rho-1)\sum_{j=1}^{h-1} \rho^{h-j-1}\epsilon_{T+j} \right\} + \left((\rho-1)\,\rho^{h-1} - (\widehat{\rho}-1)\,\widehat{\rho}^{h-1} \right) y_T. \tag{12.67}$$

The term in $\{\cdot\}$ is common to the forecast error when using $\widetilde{\Delta y}_{T+h} = 0$, so we first consider the MSFE of $\overline{e}_{T+h} = \Delta y_{T+h} - \widetilde{\Delta y}_{T+h}$:

$$\overline{e}_{T+h} = \epsilon_{T+h} + (\rho-1)\sum_{j=1}^{h-1} \rho^{h-j-1}\epsilon_{T+j} + (\rho-1)\,\rho^{h-1}y_T,$$

so that:

$$\begin{aligned} \mathsf{E}\left[\overline{e}^2_{T+h} \mid y_T\right] &= \sigma^2_\epsilon \left[1 + (1-\rho)^2 \left(\frac{\left[1-\rho^{2(h-1)}\right]}{(1-\rho^2)} + \rho^{2(h-1)} \left(\frac{y_T^2}{\sigma_\epsilon^2} \right) \right) \right] \\ &= \sigma^2_y \left[(1-\rho^2) + (1-\rho)^2 - (1-\rho)^2 \rho^{2(h-1)} \left[1 - y_T^{\dagger 2} \right] \right] \\ &\simeq \sigma^2_\epsilon \left[2/(1+\rho) - T^{-1}\phi^2_{\rho=1}\rho^{2(h-1)} \left(1 - y_T^{\dagger 2} \right) \right], \end{aligned} \tag{12.68}$$

where the last line simplifies using the unconditional expectation $\mathsf{E}[y_T^{\dagger 2}] = 1$.

Next, we approximate the variance $\mathsf{V}[\cdot]$ of $(\widehat{\rho}-1)\widehat{\rho}^{h-1}$ in (12.67). Let $\widehat{\rho} = \rho + \delta$ where δ is $O_p(1/\sqrt{T})$ so that powers of δ are asymptotically negligible, then, as before:

$$\widehat{\rho}^h = (\rho+\delta)^h \simeq \rho^h + h\delta\rho^{h-1} = \rho^h + h\rho^{h-1}(\widehat{\rho}-\rho), \tag{12.69}$$

so that for $h \geq 1$:

$$\begin{aligned} \widehat{\rho}^h - \widehat{\rho}^{h-1} &\simeq \rho^h + h\rho^{h-1}(\widehat{\rho}-\rho) - \rho^{h-1} - (h-1)\,\rho^{h-2}(\widehat{\rho}-\rho) \\ &= -\rho^{h-1}(1-\rho) + \rho^{h-2}\left[1 + h(\rho-1)\right](\widehat{\rho}-\rho), \end{aligned} \tag{12.70}$$

and hence:

$$\begin{aligned} \mathsf{V}\left[(\widehat{\rho}-1)\,\widehat{\rho}^{h-1}\right] &\simeq \mathsf{E}\left[\left[\rho^{h-2}(1 + h(\rho-1))(\widehat{\rho}-\rho) \right]^2 \right] \\ &= (1 + h(\rho-1))^2 \rho^{2(h-2)} \mathsf{V}[\widehat{\rho}] \\ &\simeq T^{-1}(1 + h(\rho-1))^2 \rho^{2(h-2)} (1-\rho^2), \end{aligned}$$

where the last approximation holds for large T (based on $\mathsf{V}[\widehat{\rho}] \simeq T^{-1}(1-\rho^2)$). Further $\mathsf{E}[\vec{e}^2_{T+h}|y_T]$ is approximately:

$$\begin{aligned} &\sigma^2_\epsilon \left[1 + (1-\rho)^2 \frac{1-\rho^{2(h-1)}}{1-\rho^2} + T^{-1}(1 + h(\rho-1))^2 \rho^{2(h-2)} y_T^{\dagger 2} \right] \\ &= \sigma^2_\epsilon \left[2/(1+\rho) - T^{-1}\rho^{2(h-2)} \left\{ \phi^2_{\rho=1}\rho^2 - (1 + h(\rho-1))^2 y_T^{\dagger 2} \right\} \right] \end{aligned} \tag{12.71}$$

which again simplifies using $\mathsf{E}[y_T^{\dagger 2}] = 1$. Consequently:

$$\begin{aligned}\mathsf{R}_\ell(\bar{e}, \vec{e}, h) &= -T^{-1}\phi^2_{\rho=1}\rho^{2(h-1)}\left(1 - y_T^{\dagger 2}\right) \\ &\quad + T^{-1}\rho^{2(h-2)}\left[\phi^2_{\rho=1}\rho^2 - (1 + h(\rho - 1))^2 y_T^{\dagger 2}\right] \\ &= T^{-1}\rho^{2(h-2)}\left[\left(\phi^2_{\rho=0} - h^2\right)(1-\rho)^2 + 2h(1-\rho) - 1\right] y_T^{\dagger 2},\end{aligned} \tag{12.72}$$

since $\phi^2_{\rho=1}\rho^2 = \phi^2_{\rho=0}(1-\rho)^2$. Different outcomes from (12.64) may result merely from changing the metric to MSFE for differences once $h > 1$: the differenced model outperforms the estimated model at different values of ρ and h.

Overall, large t-values are necessary, but insufficient, for an additional regressor to improve forecast performance on h-step forecasts judged by MSFE.

12.5 Vector processes

The above analyses of variable selection also apply to VARs. We consider forecasts from a first-order VAR in n variables $\mathbf{x}_t$ with a known zero intercept:

$$\mathbf{x}_t = \mathbf{\Psi}\mathbf{x}_{t-1} + \boldsymbol{\epsilon}_t \;\text{ where }\; \boldsymbol{\epsilon}_t \sim \mathsf{IN}_n[\mathbf{0}, \mathbf{\Omega}], \tag{12.73}$$

and the h-step ahead outcome is given by:

$$\mathbf{x}_{T+h} = \mathbf{\Psi}^h\mathbf{x}_T + \sum_{j=0}^{h-1}\mathbf{\Psi}^j\boldsymbol{\epsilon}_{T+h-j}. \tag{12.74}$$

From (12.74), using $\widehat{\mathbf{x}}_{T+1} = \widehat{\mathbf{\Psi}}\mathbf{x}_T$: and defining $\widehat{\mathbf{e}}_{T+1} = \mathbf{x}_{T+1} - \widehat{\mathbf{x}}_{T+1}$ then:

$$\begin{aligned}\widehat{\mathbf{e}}_{T+1} &= \left(\mathbf{\Psi} - \widehat{\mathbf{\Psi}}\right)\mathbf{x}_T + \boldsymbol{\epsilon}_{T+1} \\ &= \left(\mathbf{I}_n \otimes \mathbf{x}_T'\right)\left(\mathbf{\Psi} - \widehat{\mathbf{\Psi}}\right)^v + \boldsymbol{\epsilon}_{T+1} = \mathbf{X}_T\left(\boldsymbol{\psi} - \widehat{\boldsymbol{\psi}}\right) + \boldsymbol{\epsilon}_{T+1},\end{aligned}$$

where $(\cdot)^v$ denotes vectoring, $\mathbf{X}_T = (\mathbf{I}_n \otimes \mathbf{x}_T')$, and $\boldsymbol{\psi} = \mathbf{\Psi}^v$ so that:

$$\mathsf{E}\left[\widehat{\mathbf{e}}_{T+1}\widehat{\mathbf{e}}_{T+1}'\right] = \mathbf{X}_T\mathsf{V}\left[\widehat{\boldsymbol{\psi}}\right]\mathbf{X}_T' + \mathbf{\Omega}. \tag{12.75}$$

In contrast, when $\mathbf{\Psi}$ is fixed at $\mathbf{\Psi}^*$, with $\boldsymbol{\delta} = \boldsymbol{\psi} - \boldsymbol{\psi}^*$:

$$\mathsf{E}\left[\widetilde{\mathbf{e}}_{T+1}\widetilde{\mathbf{e}}_{T+1}'\right] = \mathbf{X}_T\boldsymbol{\delta}\boldsymbol{\delta}'\mathbf{X}_T' + \mathbf{\Omega}. \tag{12.76}$$

Under stationarity:

$$\sqrt{T}\left(\widehat{\boldsymbol{\psi}} - \boldsymbol{\psi}\right) \xrightarrow{d} \mathsf{N}_{n^2}\left[\mathbf{0}, \mathbf{\Omega} \otimes \mathbf{Q}^{-1}\right] = \mathsf{N}_{n^2}[\mathbf{0}, \mathbf{H}], \tag{12.77}$$

where $\mathbf{Q} = \mathsf{E}[\mathbf{x}_t\mathbf{x}_t']$ so that:

$$T\left(\widehat{\psi}-\psi\right)'\widehat{\mathbf{H}}^{-1}\left(\widehat{\psi}-\psi\right) \xrightarrow{d} \chi^2_{n^2}\left(\phi^2_{\boldsymbol{\delta}=\mathbf{0}}\right), \tag{12.78}$$

when $\phi^2_{\boldsymbol{\delta}=\mathbf{0}}$ is the non-centrality parameter $T\boldsymbol{\delta}'\mathbf{H}^{-1}\boldsymbol{\delta}$ and $\Phi^2_{\boldsymbol{\delta}=\mathbf{0}} = T\boldsymbol{\delta}'\mathbf{H}^{-1}\boldsymbol{\delta}/n^2$. Thus:

$$\begin{aligned}\mathsf{E}\left[\widetilde{\mathbf{e}}_{T+1}\widetilde{\mathbf{e}}_{T+1}'\right]-\mathsf{E}\left[\widehat{\mathbf{e}}_{T+1}\widehat{\mathbf{e}}_{T+1}'\right] &= \mathbf{X}_T\left(\boldsymbol{\delta}\boldsymbol{\delta}'-\mathsf{V}\left[\widehat{\psi}\right]\right)\mathbf{X}_T' \\ &= \mathbf{X}_T\left(\boldsymbol{\delta}\boldsymbol{\delta}'-T^{-1}\mathbf{H}\right)\mathbf{X}_T'.\end{aligned} \tag{12.79}$$

Then $\boldsymbol{\delta}\boldsymbol{\delta}'-T^{-1}\mathbf{H}$ being positive (negative) definite implies the same for $\mathsf{E}[\widetilde{\mathbf{e}}_{T+1}\widetilde{\mathbf{e}}_{T+1}'] - \mathsf{E}[\widehat{\mathbf{e}}_{T+1}\widehat{\mathbf{e}}_{T+1}']$, but otherwise, little can be said. However, if we consider the expected trace of the relative loss, denoted L_1:

$$\begin{aligned}\mathsf{L}_1 &= tr\left(\boldsymbol{\Omega}^{-1}\mathsf{E}\left[\mathsf{E}\left[\widetilde{\mathbf{e}}_{T+1}\widetilde{\mathbf{e}}_{T+1}'\right]-\mathsf{E}\left[\widehat{\mathbf{e}}_{T+1}\widehat{\mathbf{e}}_{T+1}'\right]\right]\right) \\ &= tr\left(\left(\boldsymbol{\delta}\boldsymbol{\delta}'-\mathsf{V}\left[\widehat{\psi}\right]\right)\mathsf{E}\left[\mathbf{X}_T'\boldsymbol{\Omega}^{-1}\mathbf{X}_T\right]\right) \\ &= T^{-1}tr\left[\left(T\boldsymbol{\delta}\boldsymbol{\delta}'-\boldsymbol{\Omega}\otimes\mathbf{Q}^{-1}\right)\left(\boldsymbol{\Omega}^{-1}\otimes\mathbf{Q}\right)\right] \\ &= T^{-1}\left[T\boldsymbol{\delta}'\mathbf{H}^{-1}\boldsymbol{\delta}-tr\left(\mathbf{I}_{n^2}\right)\right] = T^{-1}n^2\left(\Phi^2_{\boldsymbol{\delta}=\mathbf{0}}-1\right).\end{aligned} \tag{12.80}$$

Thus $\Phi^2_{\boldsymbol{\delta}=\mathbf{0}} > 1$ is necessary, but not sufficient, for estimation to dominate imposition of the value of $\boldsymbol{\Psi}$.

Turning to an h-step forecast where $\widehat{\mathbf{x}}_{T+h} = \widehat{\boldsymbol{\Psi}}^h\mathbf{x}_T$:

$$\widehat{\mathbf{e}}_{T+h} = \mathbf{x}_{T+h}-\widehat{\mathbf{x}}_{T+h} = \left(\boldsymbol{\Psi}^h-\widehat{\boldsymbol{\Psi}}^h\right)\mathbf{x}_T+\sum_{j=0}^{h-1}\boldsymbol{\Psi}^j\boldsymbol{\epsilon}_{T+h-j}, \tag{12.81}$$

and hence:

$$\mathsf{E}\left[\widehat{\mathbf{e}}_{T+h}\widehat{\mathbf{e}}_{T+h}'\right] = \mathbf{X}_T\mathsf{V}\left[\left(\boldsymbol{\Psi}^h\right)^v-\left(\widehat{\boldsymbol{\Psi}}^h\right)^v\right]\mathbf{X}_T'+\sum_{j=0}^{h-1}\boldsymbol{\Psi}^j\boldsymbol{\Omega}\boldsymbol{\Psi}^{j\prime}. \tag{12.82}$$

From the vector analogue of (12.69) where $\boldsymbol{\Upsilon} = (\widehat{\boldsymbol{\Psi}}-\boldsymbol{\Psi})$ and hence $\boldsymbol{\Upsilon}^v = (\widehat{\psi}-\psi)$:

$$\widehat{\boldsymbol{\Psi}}^h = \left(\boldsymbol{\Psi}+\boldsymbol{\Upsilon}\right)^h \simeq \boldsymbol{\Psi}^h+\sum_{j=0}^{h-1}\boldsymbol{\Psi}^j\boldsymbol{\Upsilon}\boldsymbol{\Psi}^{h-j-1\prime}, \tag{12.83}$$

for $h \geq 1$:

$$\left(\widehat{\boldsymbol{\Psi}}^h\right)^v \simeq \left(\boldsymbol{\Psi}^h\right)^v+\left(\sum_{j=0}^{h-1}\boldsymbol{\Psi}^j\otimes\boldsymbol{\Psi}^{h-j-1\prime}\right)\left(\widehat{\psi}-\psi\right) = \left(\boldsymbol{\Psi}^h\right)^v+\mathbf{D}_h\left(\widehat{\psi}-\psi\right), \tag{12.84}$$

where:

$$\mathbf{D}_h = \left(\sum_{j=0}^{h-1} \boldsymbol{\Psi}^j \otimes \boldsymbol{\Psi}^{h-j-1\prime} \right),$$

so that:

$$\mathsf{E}\left[\widehat{\mathbf{e}}_{T+h}\widehat{\mathbf{e}}'_{T+h}\right] = \mathbf{X}_T\mathbf{D}_h\mathsf{V}\left[\widehat{\boldsymbol{\psi}}\right]\mathbf{D}_h{}'\mathbf{X}'_T + \sum_{j=0}^{h-1}\boldsymbol{\Psi}^j\boldsymbol{\Omega}\boldsymbol{\Psi}^{j\prime}. \tag{12.85}$$

In comparison, when $\boldsymbol{\Psi}$ is fixed at $\boldsymbol{\Psi}^*$ and $\widetilde{\mathbf{x}}_{T+h} = \boldsymbol{\Psi}^{*h}\mathbf{x}_T$:

$$\left(\boldsymbol{\Psi}^h - \boldsymbol{\Psi}^{*h}\right)^v = h^{-1}\mathbf{D}_h\boldsymbol{\psi} - h^{-1}\mathbf{D}^*_h\boldsymbol{\psi}^* = h^{-1}\left(\mathbf{D}_h\boldsymbol{\delta} + \boldsymbol{\eta}\right), \tag{12.86}$$

where:

$$\boldsymbol{\eta} = \left(\mathbf{D}_h - \mathbf{D}^*_h\right)\boldsymbol{\psi}^*,$$

and:

$$\mathbf{D}^*_h = \left(\sum_{j=0}^{h-1} \boldsymbol{\Psi}^{*j} \otimes \boldsymbol{\Psi}^{*h-j-1\prime} \right).$$

Then for $\widetilde{\mathbf{e}}_{T+h} = \mathbf{x}_{T+h} - \widetilde{\mathbf{x}}_{T+h}$:

$$\begin{aligned} \widetilde{\mathbf{e}}_{T+h} &= \left(\boldsymbol{\Psi}^h - \boldsymbol{\Psi}^{*h}\right)\mathbf{x}_T + \sum_{j=0}^{h-1}\boldsymbol{\Psi}^j\boldsymbol{\epsilon}_{T+h-j} \\ &= h^{-1}\mathbf{X}_T\left(\mathbf{D}_h\boldsymbol{\delta} + \boldsymbol{\eta}\right) + \sum_{j=0}^{h-1}\boldsymbol{\Psi}^j\boldsymbol{\epsilon}_{T+h-j}, \end{aligned} \tag{12.87}$$

and hence:

$$\mathsf{E}\left[\widetilde{\mathbf{e}}_{T+h}\widetilde{\mathbf{e}}'_{T+h}\right] = h^{-2}\mathbf{X}_T\boldsymbol{\Lambda}\mathbf{X}'_T + \sum_{j=0}^{h-1}\boldsymbol{\Psi}^j\boldsymbol{\Omega}\boldsymbol{\Psi}^{j\prime}, \tag{12.88}$$

where:

$$\boldsymbol{\Lambda} = \left(\mathbf{D}_h\boldsymbol{\delta} + \boldsymbol{\eta}\right)\left(\mathbf{D}_h\boldsymbol{\delta} + \boldsymbol{\eta}\right)'.$$

Finally:

$$\mathsf{E}\left[\widetilde{\mathbf{e}}_{T+h}\widetilde{\mathbf{e}}'_{T+h}\right] - \mathsf{E}\left[\widehat{\mathbf{e}}_{T+h}\widehat{\mathbf{e}}'_{T+h}\right] = h^{-2}\mathbf{X}_T\left(\boldsymbol{\Lambda} - h^2T^{-1}\mathbf{D}_h\mathbf{H}\mathbf{D}'_h\right)\mathbf{X}'_T, \tag{12.89}$$

so that the impact of the variance matrix in the centre has increased by h^2. The precision of estimation must increase correspondingly to maintain an advantage over simply imposing the autoregressive matrix at a fixed value.

Again consider the trace L_h of the expected relative loss, in the special case that $\psi^* = \mathbf{0}$ (i.e., the unconditional mean predictor $\widetilde{\mathbf{x}}_{T+h} = \mathbf{0}$) so that $\boldsymbol{\eta} = \mathbf{0}$:

$$\begin{aligned} \mathsf{L}_h &= tr\left\{\boldsymbol{\Omega}^{-1}\mathsf{E}\left[\mathsf{E}\left[\widetilde{\mathbf{e}}_{T+h}\widetilde{\mathbf{e}}'_{T+h}\right] - \mathsf{E}\left[\widehat{\mathbf{e}}_{T+h}\widehat{\mathbf{e}}'_{T+h}\right]\right]\right\} \\ &= h^{-2}tr\left\{\left(\boldsymbol{\delta}\boldsymbol{\delta}' - h^2T^{-1}\mathbf{H}\right)\mathbf{D}'_h\left[\boldsymbol{\Omega}^{-1}\otimes\mathbf{Q}\right]\mathbf{D}_h\right\} \\ &= T^{-1}h^{-2}tr\left[\left(T\boldsymbol{\delta}\boldsymbol{\delta}' - h^2\mathbf{H}\right)\mathbf{P}\right] \\ &= T^{-1}h^{-2}\left[T\boldsymbol{\delta}'\mathbf{P}\boldsymbol{\delta} - h^2tr\left(\mathbf{HP}\right)\right], \end{aligned} \tag{12.90}$$

where:

$$\mathbf{P} = \left(\sum_{i=0}^{h-1}\sum_{j=0}^{h-1}\boldsymbol{\Psi}^{i\prime}\boldsymbol{\Omega}^{-1}\boldsymbol{\Psi}^{j}\otimes\boldsymbol{\Psi}^{h-i-1}\mathbf{Q}\boldsymbol{\Psi}^{h-j-1\prime}\right).$$

In general, $\boldsymbol{\eta} \neq \mathbf{0}$, so there will be extra elements in the first term and a more complicated expression will result. Nevertheless, as h increases, a negative sign must eventually occur, albeit with a small overall size due to the scale factor of $h^{-2}T^{-1}$. When $\boldsymbol{\Psi} \simeq \mathbf{I}_n$, then $\mathbf{P} \simeq \mathbf{H}^{-1}$ and (12.80) results.

The alternative predictor is the no-change forecast $\breve{\mathbf{x}}_{T+h} = \mathbf{x}_T$ so $\boldsymbol{\Psi}^* = \mathbf{I}_n$ and $\mathbf{D}_h^* = \mathbf{I}_{n^2}$:

$$\left(\boldsymbol{\Psi}^h - \mathbf{I}_n\right)^v = h^{-1}\mathbf{D}_h\psi - h^{-1}\psi^* = h^{-1}\left(\mathbf{D}_h\boldsymbol{\delta} + \boldsymbol{\eta}\right), \tag{12.91}$$

where

$$\boldsymbol{\eta} = \left(\mathbf{D}_h - \mathbf{I}_{n^2}\right)\psi^*,$$

and $\breve{\mathbf{e}}_{T+h} = \mathbf{x}_{T+h} - \breve{\mathbf{x}}_{T+h}$. No obvious simplification results in (12.89).

Finally, we note the benefits from knowing rather than forecasting one of the regressors, since greater accuracy should result with an intercept than a stochastic regressor. From (12.26):

$$y^*_{T+h} = \mu^*\left(1-\rho^h\right)\left(1-\rho\right)^{-1} + \rho^h y^*_T + \sum_{j=0}^{h-1}\rho^j\epsilon^*_{T+h-j}, \tag{12.92}$$

whereas if the system were a bivariate VAR, (12.74) shows the accumulation of two errors. Thus, the formula in (12.92) retains additional information for deterministic regressors. Estimation will enhance this effect as additional VAR parameters will be needed to model the stochastic regressor. To compare dynamic models with known versus predicted stochastic regressors, reconsider the form of equation in (12.33):

$$y_t = \gamma z_t + \alpha y_{t-1} + v_t,$$

but where the process generating z_t is:

$$z_t = \rho z_{t-1} + u_t, \tag{12.93}$$

and $\mathsf{E}[u_t v_s] = 0 \;\forall t, s$ when $-1 < \rho < 1$. Then:

$$y_t = \gamma \rho z_{t-1} + \alpha y_{t-1} + v_t + \gamma u_t.$$

When z_{T+1} is known:

$$\widehat{y}_{T+1} = \widehat{\gamma} z_{T+1} + \widehat{\alpha} y_T,$$

with a forecast error of $y_{T+1} - \widehat{y}_{T+1} = \widehat{v}_{T+1}$ so that for $\mathbf{x}_t' = (y_t, z_t)$ and $\mathbf{x}^*_{T+1} = (y_T, z_{T+1})'$:

$$\mathsf{E}\left[\widehat{v}^2_{T+1} \mid \mathbf{x}_{T+1}\right] = \sigma^2_v \left(1 + \mathbf{x}^{*\prime}_{T+1} (\mathbf{X}'\mathbf{X})^{-1} \mathbf{x}^*_{T+1}\right).$$

When z_{T+1} has to be predicted, the VAR form is required as in (12.73):

$$\mathbf{x}_t = \boldsymbol{\Psi} \mathbf{x}_{t-1} + \boldsymbol{\epsilon}_t,$$

where $\epsilon_{1t} = v_t + \gamma u_t$, so $\sigma^2_\epsilon = \sigma^2_v + \gamma^2 \sigma^2_u$. The 1-step ahead outcome is given by:

$$\mathbf{x}_{T+1} = \boldsymbol{\Psi} \mathbf{x}_T + \boldsymbol{\epsilon}_{T+1}.$$

Using $\widehat{\mathbf{x}}_{T+1} = \widehat{\boldsymbol{\Psi}} \mathbf{x}_T$ with $\widehat{e}_{T+1} = \mathbf{x}_{T+1} - \widehat{\mathbf{x}}_{T+1}$, then from (12.75):

$$\mathsf{E}\left[\widehat{\mathbf{e}}_{T+1} \widehat{\mathbf{e}}'_{T+1} \mid \mathbf{x}_T\right] = \boldsymbol{\Omega} \left(1 + \mathbf{x}'_T (\mathbf{X}'\mathbf{X})^{-1} \mathbf{x}_T\right). \tag{12.94}$$

Consequently, for the first element in $\mathsf{E}[\widehat{\mathbf{e}}_{T+1} \widehat{\mathbf{e}}'_{T+1} | \mathbf{x}_T]$, corresponding to predicting y_{T+1}, compared to $\mathsf{E}[\widehat{v}^2_{T+1} | \mathbf{x}_{T+1}]$ we find $\mathsf{E}[\widehat{e}^2_{1,T+1} | \mathbf{x}_T] - \mathsf{E}[\widehat{v}^2_{T+1} | \mathbf{x}_{T+1}]$ is equal to:

$$\begin{aligned} & \sigma^2_\epsilon \left(1 + \mathbf{x}'_T (\mathbf{X}'\mathbf{X})^{-1} \mathbf{x}_T\right) - \sigma^2_v \left(1 + \mathbf{x}^{*\prime}_{T+1} (\mathbf{X}'\mathbf{X})^{-1} \mathbf{x}^*_{T+1}\right) \\ = \;& \gamma^2 \sigma^2_u + tr\left\{ (\mathbf{X}'\mathbf{X})^{-1} \left[\gamma^2 \sigma^2_u \mathbf{x}_T \mathbf{x}'_T - \sigma^2_v \left(\mathbf{x}^*_{T+1} \mathbf{x}^{*\prime}_{T+1} - \mathbf{x}_T \mathbf{x}'_T\right)\right]\right\}, \end{aligned}$$

so that $\mathsf{E}[\mathsf{E}[\widehat{e}^2_{1,T+1} | \mathbf{x}_T] - \mathsf{E}[\widehat{v}^2_{T+1} | \mathbf{x}_{T+1}]]$ is approximately equal to:

$$\begin{aligned} & \gamma^2 \sigma^2_u + T^{-1} tr \left\{ \gamma^2 \sigma^2_u \mathbf{I}_2 - \sigma^2_v \boldsymbol{\Omega}^{-1} \mathsf{E} \left[\begin{array}{cc} 0 & y_T \Delta z_{T+1} \\ y_T \Delta z_{T+1} & z^2_{T+1} - z^2_T \end{array} \right] \right\} \\ = \;& \gamma^2 \sigma^2_u \left(1 + 2T^{-1}\right). \end{aligned}$$

Thus the loss is essentially that from not knowing z_{T+1}.

12.6 Collinearity in forecasting

In this section, we consider the role of parsimony when there is substantial 'collinearity' in the explanatory variables. Consider the static regression model :

$$y_t = \boldsymbol{\beta}' \mathbf{x}_t + \nu_t \;\text{ where }\; \nu_t \sim \mathsf{IN}\left[0, \sigma^2_v\right], \tag{12.95}$$

where $\mathbf{x}_t$ is a k-dimensional vector of explanatory variables, and further $\mathbf{x}_t \sim \mathsf{IN}_k[\mathbf{0}, \boldsymbol{\Omega}]$ independently of $\{\nu_t\}$. For large T:

$$\sqrt{T}\left(\widehat{\boldsymbol{\beta}} - \boldsymbol{\beta}\right) \sim \mathsf{N}_k\left[\mathbf{0}, \sigma_v^2 \boldsymbol{\Omega}^{-1}\right].$$

Then for k regressors with estimated coefficients and known future values of $\mathbf{x}$:

$$\widehat{y}_{T+1} = \widehat{\boldsymbol{\beta}}' \mathbf{x}_{T+1},$$

so that:

$$\mathsf{E}\left[\widehat{\nu}^2_{T+1} \mid \mathbf{x}_{T+1}\right] = \sigma_v^2 + \mathbf{x}'_{T+1} \mathsf{V}\left[\widehat{\boldsymbol{\beta}}\right] \mathbf{x}_{T+1} \simeq T^{-1} \sigma_v^2 \left(T + \mathbf{x}'_{T+1} \boldsymbol{\Omega}^{-1} \mathbf{x}_{T+1}\right). \tag{12.96}$$

Now, factorize $\boldsymbol{\Omega}$ as $\mathbf{H}'\boldsymbol{\Lambda}\mathbf{H}$, where $\boldsymbol{\Lambda}$ is diagonal and $\mathbf{H}'\mathbf{H} = \mathbf{I}_k$, and let $\mathbf{H}\mathbf{x}_t = \mathbf{z}_t$, so that $\mathbf{z}_t \sim \mathsf{IN}_k[\mathbf{0}, \boldsymbol{\Lambda}]$, then we can write (12.95) in terms of $\mathbf{z}_t$ as:

$$y_t = \boldsymbol{\gamma}' \mathbf{z}_t + \nu_t, \tag{12.97}$$

where $\boldsymbol{\gamma} = \mathbf{H}\boldsymbol{\beta}$ and the disturbance term is the same as in (12.95). Then:

$$\begin{aligned} \mathbf{x}'_{T+1} \boldsymbol{\Omega}^{-1} \mathbf{x}_{T+1} &= \mathbf{x}'_{T+1} \left(\mathbf{H}'\boldsymbol{\Lambda}\mathbf{H}\right)^{-1} \mathbf{x}_{T+1} \\ &= \mathbf{x}'_{T+1} \mathbf{H}' \boldsymbol{\Lambda}^{-1} \mathbf{H} \mathbf{x}_{T+1} \\ &= \mathbf{z}'_{T+1} \boldsymbol{\Lambda}^{-1} \mathbf{z}_{T+1} \\ &= \sum_{i=1}^{k} \frac{z^2_{i,T+1}}{\lambda_i}. \end{aligned} \tag{12.98}$$

On average, $\mathsf{E}[z^2_{i,T+1}] = \lambda_i$, and, therefore, $\mathsf{E}[\mathbf{x}'_{T+1} \boldsymbol{\Omega}^{-1} \mathbf{x}_{T+1}] = k$. This shows that any 'collinearity' in $\mathbf{x}_t$ is irrelevant for 1-step forecasting. This naturally follows from the model being invariant to linear, and therefore orthogonal, transformations (see section 3.5). Clearly the transformation from $\mathbf{x}_t$ to $\mathbf{z}_t$ is linear and non-singular.

However, when the marginal process ($\mathbf{x}_t$ or $\mathbf{z}_t$) is non-constant, then as we sketch out below, the case for parsimony (i.e., dropping some of the $\mathbf{x}_t$, or more generally, singular transformations of the explanatory variables) becomes persuasive.

To illustrate, suppose $\boldsymbol{\beta}$ stays constant, but $\boldsymbol{\Omega}$ changes to $\boldsymbol{\Omega}^*$, with $\boldsymbol{\Lambda}$ changing to $\boldsymbol{\Lambda}^*$ then:

$$\mathsf{E}\left[\sum_{i=1}^{k} \frac{z^2_{i,T+1}}{\lambda_i}\right] = \sum_{i=1}^{k} \frac{\lambda_i^*}{\lambda_i}. \tag{12.99}$$

The implication is that the least-well determined β_i, which corresponds to the smallest λ_i, will induce the biggest relative changes in $\mathsf{E}[\widehat{\nu}^2_{T+1} | \mathbf{x}_{T+1}]$ from (12.96) and (12.98). Thus simplification (omitting the least-well determined explanatory variables) might help.

In the remainder of this section we develop the algebra for the bivariate case $k = 2$, to illustrate the magnitude of the effects involved, and in section 12.7, we consider simplification in the much-studied empirical model of money demand.

For $k = 2$, the covariance matrix of the regressors is:

$$\mathbf{\Omega} = \begin{pmatrix} \sigma_{11}^2 & \rho\sigma_{11}\sigma_{22} \\ \rho\sigma_{11}\sigma_{22} & \sigma_{22}^2 \end{pmatrix},$$

with:

$$\mathbf{\Omega}^{-1} = \frac{1}{\sigma_{11}^2\sigma_{22}^2\left(1-\rho^2\right)} \begin{pmatrix} \sigma_{22}^2 & -\rho\sigma_{11}\sigma_{22} \\ -\rho\sigma_{11}\sigma_{22} & \sigma_{11}^2 \end{pmatrix}.$$

Let:

$$x_{1,t} = \alpha x_{2,t} + v_t \text{ where } \mathsf{E}\left[x_{2,t}v_t\right] = 0.$$

Then $\sigma_{11}^2 = \alpha^2\sigma_{22}^2 + \sigma_v^2$.and $\rho = \alpha\sigma_{22}/\sigma_{11}$. The eigenvalues of $\mathbf{\Omega}$ are:

$$\begin{aligned} \left|\lambda\mathbf{I}_2 - \mathbf{\Omega}\right| &= \begin{vmatrix} \lambda - \alpha^2\sigma_{22}^2 - \sigma_v^2 & -\alpha\sigma_{22}^2 \\ -\alpha\sigma_{22}^2 & \lambda - \sigma_{22}^2 \end{vmatrix} \\ &= \lambda^2 - \lambda\left(\left(\alpha^2+1\right)\sigma_{22}^2 + \sigma_v^2\right) + \sigma_{22}^2\sigma_v^2 = 0. \end{aligned}$$

The roots are:

$$\frac{1}{2}\left[\left(\left(\alpha^2+1\right)\sigma_{22}^2 + \sigma_v^2\right) \pm \sqrt{\left(\left(\alpha^2+1\right)\sigma_{22}^2 + \sigma_v^2\right)^2 - 4\sigma_{22}^2\sigma_v^2}\right].$$

Scaling $x_{1,t}$ such that $\sigma_v^2 = 1$ and x_{2t} so that $\sigma_{22}^2 = 1$:

$$\frac{1}{2}\left[\left(\alpha^2+2\right) \pm \alpha\sqrt{\alpha^2+4}\right]$$

$$\lambda_1 = 1 + \alpha\left[\frac{\alpha}{2} + \sqrt{1+\alpha^2/4}\right] \text{ and } \lambda_2 = 1 + \alpha\left[\frac{\alpha}{2} - \sqrt{1+\alpha^2/4}\right],$$

where λ_2 is the smaller root for $\alpha > 0$.

Assuming $\sigma_v^2 = 1$, $\sigma_{22}^2 = 1$ then $\rho = \alpha/\sqrt{(1+\alpha^2)}$ and thus:

$$\mathbf{\Omega} = \begin{pmatrix} 1+\alpha^2 & \alpha \\ \alpha & 1 \end{pmatrix} \text{ with } \mathbf{\Omega}^{-1} = \begin{pmatrix} 1 & -\alpha \\ -\alpha & 1+\alpha^2 \end{pmatrix}.$$

If the correlation between $x_{1,t}$ and $x_{2,t}$ changes from $\rho = 0.986$ (such that $\alpha = 6$), to $\rho^* = 0.89$ (so $\alpha^* = 2$), then:

$$\lambda_2 = 19 - 6\sqrt{10} = 0.0263,$$

whereas:

$$\lambda_2^* = 3 - 2\sqrt{2} = 0.1716.$$

Also:

$$\lambda_1 = 1 + \alpha \left[\frac{\alpha}{2} + \sqrt{1 + \alpha^2/4} \right] = 19 + 6\sqrt{10} = 37.9737$$

whereas:

$$\lambda_1^* = 3 + 2\sqrt{2} = 5.8284,$$

so:

$$\sum_{i=1}^{2} \frac{\lambda_i^*}{\lambda_i} = \frac{5.8284}{37.974} + \frac{0.1716}{0.0263} = 0.153 + 6.525 = 6.68 \qquad (12.100)$$

which is a 330 percent increase from that component. If $\rho = 0.999$, so $\alpha = 25$, then:

$$\lambda_2 = 1 + 25 \left[12.5 - \sqrt{157.25} \right] = 0.0016$$

so a fall in ρ to $\rho^* = 0.986$ would induce:

$$\frac{\lambda_2^*}{\lambda_2} = \frac{0.0263}{0.0016} = 16.4$$

as against unity when no change occurs; and the drop to $\rho^* = 0.89$ leads to an increase to 107. Thus, the magnitudes of this effect could be large: Hendry and Doornik (1997) suggest an empirical example in forecasting UK house prices.

12.7 Simplification in model selection

Consider the following simplified model of money demand where m, p, y and R respectively denote logs of nominal money, the price level, and aggregate income, and the level of the interest rate, expressed in restricted velocity form as:

$$\Delta m_t = \rho_0 - \rho_1 \Delta (m - p - y)_{t-1} - \rho_2 (m - p - y)_{t-2} - \rho_3 R_t + \epsilon_t. \qquad (12.101)$$

The model embodies unit long-run, but zero short-run, price and income homogeneity (see Hendry and Ericsson, 1991) and has four structural parameters: once such a formulation is known, it is trivial to estimate. However, the exact specification of the dynamic reactions is unlikely to be known, so we contrast (12.101) with an initial unrestricted equation of the form:

$$m_t = \gamma_0 + \sum_{i=0}^{2} \gamma_{1+i} p_{t-i} + \sum_{i=1}^{2} \gamma_{3+i} m_{t-i} + \sum_{i=0}^{2} \gamma_{6+i} y_{t-i} + \sum_{i=0}^{2} \gamma_{9+i} R_{t-i} + e_t. \quad (12.102)$$

Then:

$$\gamma_0 = \rho_0; \gamma_1 = 0; \gamma_2 = \rho_1; \gamma_3 = -\rho_1 + \rho_2; \gamma_4 = 1 - \rho_1; \gamma_5 = \rho_1 - \rho_2;$$
$$\gamma_6 = 0; \gamma_7 = \rho_1; \gamma_8 = -\rho_1 + \rho_2; \gamma_9 = -\rho_3; \gamma_{10} = 0; \gamma_{11} = 0.$$

It is hard to imagine the sample dependence of the coefficients in (12.102) not exceeding that of the parameters in (12.101) since the presence of many free regressors allows the general equation to capture accidental features of the sample. In such a case, simplification to (12.101) clearly reduces sample dependence. To illustrate the analysis empirically, consider the small monetary model in Hendry and Ericsson (1991), also studied by Boswijk (1995), Ericsson, Campos and Tran (1990), Ericsson, Hendry and Tran (1994), Hendry and Mizon (1993) and Johansen (1992b). Then $\mathbf{x}_t = ((m-p)_t, y_t, \Delta p_t, R_{nt})'$, where M, Y, P and R_n are nominal M_1, real total final expenditure (TFE) at 1985 prices, the TFE deflator, and the (learning adjusted) opportunity cost of holding money. The data are quarterly, seasonally adjusted over 1963(1)–1989(2).[1] The unrestricted estimates are shown in table 12.1, with the restricted solution from (12.101) in brackets.

Table 12.1 Money demand equation

	0	1	2	$\sum$
$m-p$	-1 —	0.63 [0.72] (0.10)	0.28 [0.19] (0.09)	−0.10 (0.015)
y	0.00 [0.0] (0.10)	0.20 [0.28] (0.13)	−0.10 [−0.19] (0.10)	0.10 (0.01)
Δp	−0.89 [−1.0] (0.19)	−0.00 [0.0] (0.22)	0.22 [0.0] (0.18)	−0.67 (0.15)
R_n	−0.46 [−0.56] (0.11)	0.27 [0.0] (0.17)	0.03 [0.0] (0.12)	−0.70 (0.095)
1	−0.06 [0.02] (0.13)	–	–	−0.06 (0.13)

The long-run solved equation from (12.102) was:

$$m - p = \underset{(1.4)}{-0.60} + \underset{(0.13)}{1.08}\, y - \underset{(1.9)}{7.0}\, \Delta p - \underset{(0.7)}{7.3}\, R_n,$$

which matches most of the theoretical postulates at the commencement of this section.

Simplification could also exacerbate sample dependence if the influences of accidental aspects were captured more 'significantly' by linear combinations of the variables effectively acting as dummies for chance coincidences of 'blips'. This difficulty

[1] Long-run price homogeneity was imposed to reduce the analysis from $\mathsf{I}(2)$. The resulting series are $\mathsf{I}(1)$ for most of the sample but degree of integration is not an inherent property: before 1984, R_n is an $\mathsf{I}(1)$ level, whereas after 1984, it is a stationary differential. While such 'regime shifts' affect some approaches more than others, an analysis which concludes with an $\mathsf{I}(0)$ congruent, invariant and encompassing explanation is not dependent on assuming a constant degree of integration.

may be offset by reference to a theory model, but anyway is a transient problem since an extended data sample will reveal the accidental nature of the earlier effects by their becoming less significant. A major focus of empirical modelling must be to mitigate the sample dependence of findings as well as linking evidence and theory.

Imposing the long-run solution in slightly modified form as a cointegration vector:

$$ci_t = m_t - p_t - y_t - 0.21 + 7\Delta p_t + 7R_{n,t},$$

then simplifying the table 12.1 equation, re-expressed in differences and the cointegration relation, over $T = 1963(3) - 1989(2)$ delivers:[2]

$$\begin{aligned}\Delta(m-p)_t &= -\underset{(0.06)}{0.17}\,\Delta(m-y-p)_{t-1} - \underset{(0.16)}{0.85}\,\Delta^2 p_t \\ &\quad - \underset{(0.10)}{0.51}\,\Delta R_{n,t} - \underset{(0.007)}{0.093}\,ci_{t-1} + \underset{(0.001)}{0.005} \qquad (12.103)\end{aligned}$$

$$\begin{aligned}\mathsf{R}^2 &= 0.76\ \hat{\sigma} = 1.29\%\ V = 0.24\ J = 0.84\ SC = -8.5 \\ \mathsf{F}_{\mathsf{ar}}(4,95) &= 2.2\ \mathsf{F}_{\mathsf{arch}}(4,91) = 0.59\ \chi^2_{\mathsf{nd}}(2) = 2.8\ \mathsf{F}_{\mathsf{het}}(8,90) = 0.60.\end{aligned}$$

In (12.103), $\hat{\sigma}$ is the standard deviation of the residuals (as a percentage of $(m-p)$), adjusted for degrees of freedom; and OLS standard errors are shown in parentheses. The diagnostic tests are of the form $\mathsf{F}_{\mathsf{j}}(k, T-l)$ which here denotes an F-test against the alternative hypothesis j for: 4th-order serial correlation (F_{ar}: see Godfrey, 1978), 4th-order autoregressive conditional heteroscedasticity ($\mathsf{F}_{\mathsf{arch}}$: see Engle, 1982), heteroscedasticity ($\mathsf{F}_{\mathsf{het}}$: see White, 1980); and a chi-square test for normality ($\chi^2_{\mathsf{nd}}(2)$: see Doornik and Hansen, 1994): * and ** denote significance at the 5 percent and 1 percent levels respectively. V and J are the variance-change and joint parameter-constancy tests from Hansen (1992). $\Delta x_t = x_t - x_{t-1}$ and $\Delta^2 x_t = \Delta x_t - \Delta x_{t-1}$.

Equation (12.103) satisfies all the reported diagnostic tests, with interpretable parameters in a parsimonious model, and coherently simplifies table 12.1 ($\mathsf{F}(7,92) = 0.51$). As figure 12.3 shows, the recursively estimated parameters are also constant. Reading from left to right, then top to bottom, the first five graphs show the parameter estimates recursively, with ± 2 standard errors on either side; then the recursive residuals with $0 \pm 2\hat{\sigma}_t$; and, finally, 1-step and break-point Chow (1960) statistics, scaled by their 5 percent significance levels (shown as a straight line at unity). Despite using one-off significance levels, none of the break-point tests exceeds its 5 percent critical value anywhere in the sample, and under 5 per cent of the 1-step tests do so.

Compared to the initial postulate, the short-run impact of inflation and interest rates is far from zero; and the rate of inflation also influences the long-run outcome. There is evidence of autonomous (unmodelled) growth in money demand relative to its determinants, at about the growth rate of the UK economy.

---

[2] The change in the intercept reflects the altered mean value from rounding the coefficients, so *ci* retains a mean of zero.

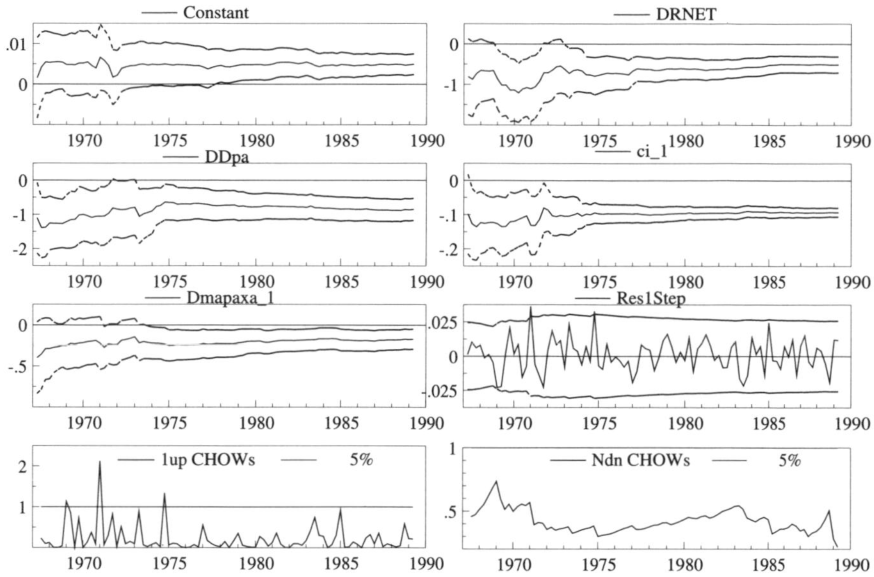

Figure 12.3 Recursive estimates and test statistics

There are no additional data on which to test the impact of the simplifications by *ex ante* forecasting, but we can simply go back 12 periods for estimation and compare the respective '1-step forecasts' of the table 12.1 equation, (12.103), a second-order autoregression in $\Delta(m-p)_t$, and an estimate of (12.101), denoted 'theoretical': figure 12.4 shows the outcomes for all four models, on a common scale, in terms of forecasting $\Delta(m-p)_t$.

The most obvious features are that all four predictors do well; the more 'parsimonious' models have tighter forecast confidence bands, but are not dramatically better; and that the addition of known future regressors does not greatly enhance performance (even when the equation is known to be constant).

To extend these results to multi-step forecasts requires modelling the system, and we follow the approach in Hendry and Doornik (1994). The VAR is their unrestricted system in I(1) space for m, p, y, R_n; FIML denotes full information maximum likelihood estimation of their I(0) representation in differences with two cointegration relations; the AR(2) uses a scalar AR(2) process for each of the endogenous variables in differences; and the 'theoretical' uses (12.101) in place of (12.103) for the money relation, retaining the Hendry and Doornik specification for the remaining variables. The outcome is shown in figure 12.5 on the same scale as figure 12.4 (the forecast confidence bands allow for parameter and error uncertainty: see Doornik and Hendry, 1997).

Again, there is little to choose between the forecasts; the AR(2) and 'theoretical' have somewhat wider confidence bands (suggesting possible dangers in forecasting

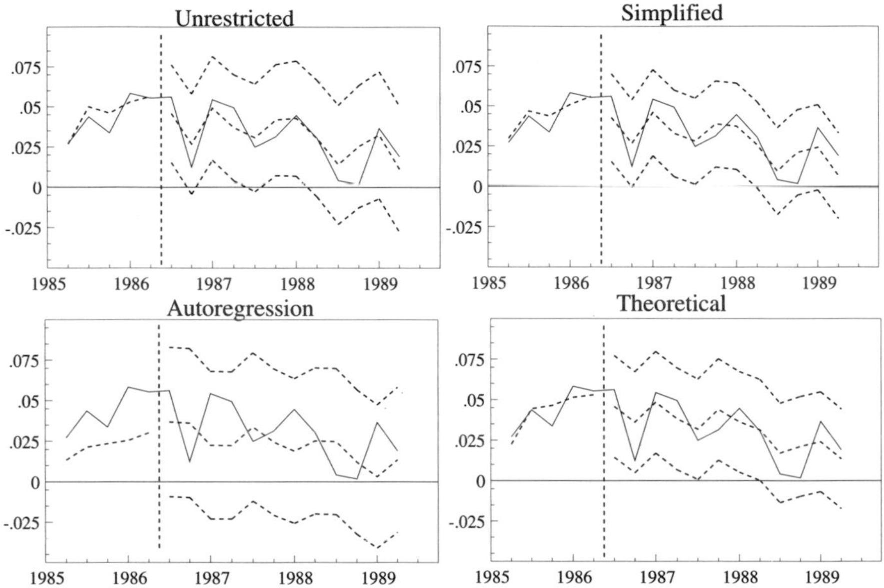

Figure 12.4 Relative 1-step forecast performance

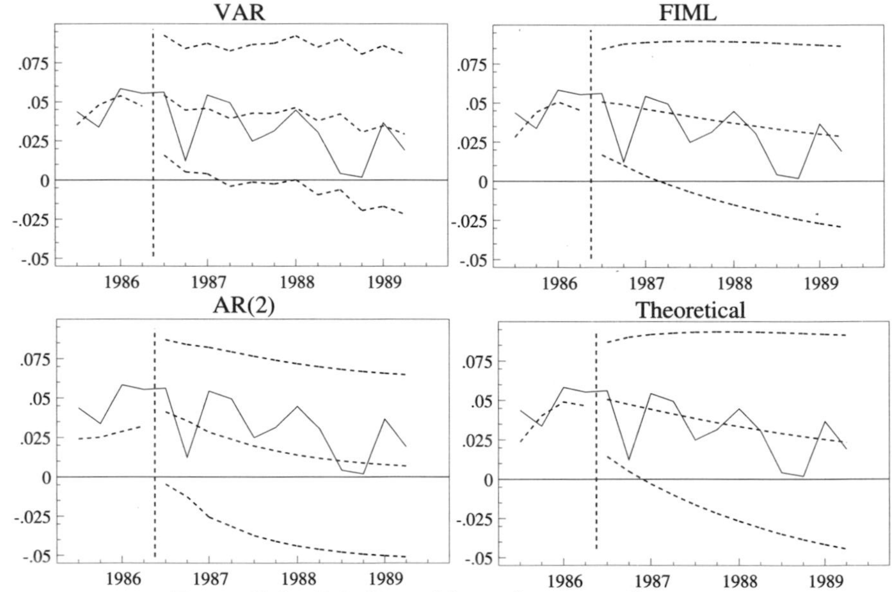

Figure 12.5 Relative multi-step forecast performance

from too little or too much 'theory dependence': see Hendry, 1995b); the VAR bands reflect the oscillations in its forecasts; and those for the preferred model are perhaps best, but all four steadily increase in the horizon as in chapter 1. Overall, on the dimensions considered here (from about 60 parameters in the VAR to 25 in the most restricted), parameter restrictions do not seem to deliver important gains in forecast accuracy.

12.8 Overview

The selection of models for forecasting in processes with unknown parameters is not a direct generalization of standard results for estimating models. Using a sequence of simple examples, we have shown that even simple members of the ARIMA class of predictors can beat the estimated DGP; that parsimony is more desirable for forecasting than for fit; that imposing restrictions on the intercepts and coefficients which implicitly satisfy the type of criterion that $\phi^2 < h$ may yield a MSFE gain; and thus imposing a unit root (i.e., differencing) for forecasting can be advantageous even for stationary processes (see figure 12.1, the panel for $\rho = 0.95$ and the line for $T = 25$); that the non-monotonicity of forecast confidence intervals can be explained; and that the best model at one horizon need not be best at all horizons.

In addition, restricted Box–Jenkins or BVAR methods might outperform econometric models in forecasting, even when the latter are the DGP within sample, by imposing differences so that unknown shifts in means become blips and robustness is achieved (see section 8.6, and Clements and Hendry, 1996b).

In the discussion of 'collinearity' in section 12.6, we also suggested that changing correlations between variables pointed toward an advantage from greater parsimony.

An obvious implication of these results is that *ex ante* forecast performance is not a reliable guide to model validity: the DGP would be rejected in many of the examples above if its poorer *ex ante* forecast errors were deemed decisive. However, the econometric model should encompass the time-series model. Such evidence could clarify the status of the rival predictors, and may ensure the future forecast dominance of the econometric model as corroborative evidence accrues, but cautions against drawing hasty conclusions from *ex ante* forecasting competitions between rival models.

Conversely, there is a 'forecasting *versus* policy' dilemma: the DGP clearly provides the better guide to policy, but may not forecast as well as an extrapolative predictor despite the former being correctly specified and more informative. However, sufficiently well determined (or fixed) parameter values could ensure the dominance of the former, and this offers a rather different role for economic theory-based hypotheses about parameter values. If conjectured parameter values are not data rejected in a congruent model, there may be a case for imposing such values when forecasting, subject to simulation analysis of data basing confirming the advantages of such choices.

Chapter 13

Testing forecast accuracy

Structural stability is often tested by checking whether the coefficients of a regression model are constant across different sub-samples. Such tests are commonly used as a general specification test, based on the belief that a correctly specified model should have constant parameters (or 'invariant' parameters if some aspect of the economic regime or policy stance has changed). A related set of testing procedures is the focus of this chapter, where we wish to test whether a model estimated over one period can provide adequate forecasts over a subsequent period. Such tests are known as tests of predictive failure. Finally, we consider the problems inherent in directly comparing two sets of rival forecasts of the same phenomena independently of the models from which they were produced.

13.1 Introduction

There is a large literature on testing for structural stability based on testing whether the coefficients of a regression model are constant across different sub-samples. Such tests are commonly used as a general specification test, based on the belief that a correctly specified model should have constant parameters (or 'invariant' parameters if some aspect of the economic regime or policy stance has changed). Constant parameters may characterize the economy at the 'deep' level of tastes and technologies, or more pragmatically, may be deemed a necessary pre-requisite in-sample if the model is to be used to predict out of sample. Tests of structural change in this tradition typically test the constancy of parameter estimates and error variances across two sub-samples, possibly each conditionally upon the constancy of the other. Pesaran, Smith and Yeo (1985) review the various hypotheses and associated test statistics that can be used in each case: also see Chow (1960), Christ (1966), Hendry (1979b) and Krämer (1989).

Whilst we have touched upon testing in previous chapters, such as forecast encompassing in section 10.3, our treatment has not been systematic. It is helpful to distinguish between two different strands to testing in the forecasting context. One is an extension of in-sample model evaluation techniques to post-sample model evaluation. Typically the investigator determines the separation between in- and post-sample by holding back some observations at the model design and estimation stage to enable 'forecasting tests' to be carried out. Efficiency dictates that whatever the outcome of the 'pre-tests', these observations will eventually influence the finally selected model. Giles and Giles (1993) survey the literature on pre-test estimation and testing in econometrics. Testing generally raises awkward issues of when 'tests' are design criteria and when they are genuine tests (sometimes confused with 'data mining'), and there is now a large literature on this subject. This puts a premium on evaluating models against information sets not available to their proprietors at the time of model construction: the obvious candidates in the forecasting context are observations which have only subsequently become available.[1] In section 13.2, we discuss tests of predictive failure: whether a model estimated over a particular sample period can account for subsequent realizations of the data generating process.

The second main strand is more closely related to the comparison of rival forecasts of the same phenomenon, as in chapter 3, but recognizes that comparing and testing are distinct. The appeal of testing in the forecasting context, as in any other, is persuasive: are apparent differences in forecast accuracy statistically significant? There are a number of problems that make formal testing difficult: these are discussed in section 13.3 along with some of the solutions that have been advanced.

13.2 Testing for predictive failure

We have commented on the practice of assessing forecast accuracy by comparing a model's forecast performance against how well it fared over the past (or estimation sample period). This idea underlies the formal tests of predictive failure which compare an estimate of the forecast-error variance obtained from the past residuals with the actual mean squared error of the forecast. Alternatively put, we are 'comparing a set of forecasts made at some point of possible change with actuality' (Box and Tiao, 1976, p.200). We also made the point that this will not provide an absolute measure of predictive accuracy, but only of how well the model performs in the future relative to the past. Nevertheless, such tests are commonly used and will be reviewed in this section.

The tests in the following sub-sections are Wald tests. Tests can also be derived using the likelihood ratio principle and the Lagrange multiplier approach (see Hylleberg, Mizon and O'Brien, 1993, for examples based on the former). We focus on Wald tests following the historical development of the subject. Our aim is not to provide in-depth coverage of the field, but to bring out some of the issues involved in testing in the forecasting context, and, in particular, the relationship between tests based on h-step and 1-step ahead errors, and the invariance of some tests to linear transforms of the variables. Of course, these tests are essentially impotent to detect model mis-specification

[1] An example of this in the aggregate time-series consumption literature is the work by Davidson, Hendry, Srba and Yeo (1978) and Hendry and von Ungern-Sternberg (1981) and the subsequent reappraisals by Davidson and Hendry (1981), Hendry (1983), Carruth and Henley (1990) and Hendry, Muellbauer and Murphy (1990).

in a stationary process. Provided the errors are IID, or the estimated parameter and error variances reflect the unmodelled residual autocorrelation or heteroscedasticity, then even badly mis-specified models will not be rejected when the forecast observations are indeed drawn from the same distribution as those used in sample. If consistently estimated variances are not used (see, e.g., White, 1980, and Andrews, 1991), then rejection merely reflects an incorrectly sized test, and although that happens to be a correct decision, it is an inefficient way of revealing the problems with the residuals.

13.2.1 Box–Tiao test: scalar case with multiple forecast periods

We base our discussion on the Box and Tiao (1976) test, which was proposed as a means of testing for parameter change at a particular point. Within this framework, it is straightforward to show how multi-step forecast tests can often be reduced to 1-step ahead forecast tests. We can also show why such tests are typically invariant to non-singular linear transforms of the type discussed in section 3.5.

Consider a scalar process given by the Wold representation:

$$y_t = \psi(L)\,\epsilon_t, \tag{13.1}$$

where $\epsilon_t \sim \mathsf{IN}[0, \sigma_\epsilon^2]$ and $\psi(L) = 1 + \psi_1 L + \psi_2 L^2 + \cdots$, assuming $\psi(L)$ is invertible:

$$\varphi(L)\,y_t = \epsilon_t, \quad \text{where } \varphi(L) = \psi(L)^{-1}. \tag{13.2}$$

The actual value of the process at $T + h$ is:

$$y_{T+h} = \sum_{j=0}^{h-1} \psi_j \epsilon_{T+h-j} + \sum_{j=h}^{\infty} \psi_j \epsilon_{T+h-j},$$

where $\psi_0 = 1$ and T is the forecast origin. Then the h-step MMSFE forecasts are:

$$\widetilde{y}_{T+h} = \sum_{j=h}^{\infty} \psi_j \epsilon_{T+h-j},$$

and so the forecast error for known parameters is:

$$e_{T+h} = y_{T+h} - \widetilde{y}_{T+h} = \sum_{j=0}^{h-1} \psi_j \epsilon_{T+h-j}. \tag{13.3}$$

The multi-period errors in forecasting $(y_{T+1}, \ldots, y_{T+h})$ conditional on period T are:

$$\mathbf{e}_h = \boldsymbol{\psi}\boldsymbol{\epsilon}_h, \tag{13.4}$$

where $\mathbf{e}_h = (e_{T+1}, \ldots, e_{T+h})'$, $\boldsymbol{\epsilon}_h = (\epsilon_{T+1}, \ldots, \epsilon_{T+h})'$, and:

$$\boldsymbol{\psi} = \begin{pmatrix} 1 & 0 & 0 & \cdots & 0 & 0 \\ \psi_1 & 1 & 0 & \cdots & 0 & 0 \\ \psi_2 & \psi_1 & 1 & \ddots & 0 & 0 \\ \vdots & \vdots & \ddots & \ddots & 0 & 0 \\ \psi_{h-2} & \psi_{h-3} & \cdots & \psi_1 & 1 & 0 \\ \psi_{h-1} & \psi_{h-2} & \cdots & \psi_2 & \psi_1 & 1 \end{pmatrix}.$$

Alternatively, we can also write:

$$\boldsymbol{\epsilon}_h = \boldsymbol{\varphi}\mathbf{e}_h \quad \text{where} \quad \boldsymbol{\varphi} = \boldsymbol{\psi}^{-1}, \tag{13.5}$$

when $\mathbf{e}_h$ is the stacked vector of forecast errors up to and including the h-step ahead error, where (13.4) and (13.5) give the relationship between the forecast errors and the vector of disturbance terms.

Then, in the notation of section 3.6:

$$\boldsymbol{\Phi}_h = \mathsf{E}\left[\mathbf{e}_h\mathbf{e}_h'\right] = \boldsymbol{\psi}\mathsf{E}\left[\boldsymbol{\epsilon}_h\boldsymbol{\epsilon}_h'\right]\boldsymbol{\psi}' = \sigma_\epsilon^2\boldsymbol{\psi}\boldsymbol{\psi}',$$

since $\mathsf{E}[\boldsymbol{\epsilon}_h\boldsymbol{\epsilon}_h'] = \sigma_\epsilon^2\mathbf{I}_h$. Thus, if the model appropriate over $[1, \ldots, T]$ remains so over the forecast horizon, then:

$$Q = \mathbf{e}_h'\boldsymbol{\Phi}_h^{-1}\mathbf{e}_h \sim \chi_h^2, \tag{13.6}$$

where $\boldsymbol{\Phi}_h^{-1} = \sigma_\epsilon^{-2}\boldsymbol{\psi}^{-1\prime}\boldsymbol{\psi}^{-1} = \sigma_\epsilon^{-2}\boldsymbol{\varphi}'\boldsymbol{\varphi}$. Under the null, $\mathbf{e}_h \sim \mathsf{N}_h[\mathbf{0}, \boldsymbol{\Phi}_h]$, the distribution of Q follows from that of a quadratic form in normally distributed variables (see, e.g., Lütkepohl, 1991, proposition B.3, p.481).

Again following Box and Tiao, it is straightforward to show that we can replace the stacked vector of forecast errors in (13.6) by sums of the 1-step ahead forecast errors made over the period $[T+1, \ldots, T+h]$, where the forecast origin is no longer assumed fixed at T, but moves through the forecast period. To see this, we use:

$$Q = \mathbf{e}_h'\boldsymbol{\Phi}_h^{-1}\mathbf{e}_h = \frac{\mathbf{e}_h'\boldsymbol{\varphi}'\boldsymbol{\varphi}\mathbf{e}_h}{\sigma_\epsilon^2} = \frac{\boldsymbol{\epsilon}_h'\boldsymbol{\epsilon}_h}{\sigma_\epsilon^2} = \sigma_\epsilon^{-2}\sum_{j=1}^{h}\epsilon_{T+j}^2. \tag{13.7}$$

From (13.3), the 1-step ahead forecast error made in forecasting y_{T+i} at period $T+i-1$ is simply ϵ_{T+i}, so that (13.6) is proportional to the sum of squares of the h successive 1-step ahead forecast errors. Because $\mathbf{e}_h$ and $\boldsymbol{\epsilon}_h$ are related by a non-singular transform ($|\boldsymbol{\psi}| = 1$), the same statistic results: this is also the test in Hendry (1974).

Since in practice we will require an estimate of σ_ϵ^2 to calculate Q, Box and Tiao suggest an approximate F-variant defined by:

$$\widehat{Q} = h^{-1}\widehat{\sigma}_\epsilon^{-2}\sum_{j=1}^{h}\epsilon_{T+j}^2 \sim \mathsf{F}_{T-p}^{h}(0), \tag{13.8}$$

where p denotes the number of parameters estimated in the model when obtaining $\widehat{\sigma}_{\epsilon}^2$, and h is the number of forecasts.

Two points are worth noting in the context of the above analysis. First, the test is for several forecast periods (all steps ahead up to and including h), and takes into account the correlation between the different step-ahead forecast errors. Secondly, in practice the e_{T+h} will not be known but will have to be calculated from estimates of the ψ_j parameters. This aspect is discussed in more detail in the vector generalizations of the test presented in the next two sub-sections.

The relation in (13.6) does not apply to singular transforms, so Chong and Hendry (1986) considered testing annual-average forecast errors from quarterly models, where a singular transform is involved. Since $\mathbf{e}_h = (e_{T+1}, \ldots, e_{T+h})'$, then for the notationally simplest case where $h = 4J$ for J years of forecasts from a quarterly model for $j = 1, \ldots, J$:

$$\overline{e}_{T+j} = \sum_{i=4(j-1)+1}^{4j} e_{T+i}$$

so, letting $\boldsymbol{\iota}_4' = (1\ 1\ 1\ 1)$:

$$\overline{\mathbf{e}}_J = \begin{pmatrix} \boldsymbol{\iota}_4' & \mathbf{0}' & \cdots & \mathbf{0}' \\ \mathbf{0}' & \boldsymbol{\iota}_4' & \ddots & \mathbf{0}' \\ \vdots & \ddots & \ddots & \vdots \\ \mathbf{0}' & \cdots & \mathbf{0}' & \boldsymbol{\iota}_4' \end{pmatrix} \mathbf{e}_h = \boldsymbol{\Lambda}\mathbf{e}_h,$$

where $\boldsymbol{\Lambda}$ is $p \times 4J$. Now, different test statistics result as:

$$\mathsf{E}\left[\overline{\mathbf{e}}_J\overline{\mathbf{e}}_J'\right] = \boldsymbol{\Lambda}\mathsf{E}\left[\mathbf{e}_h\mathbf{e}_h'\right]\boldsymbol{\Lambda}' = \sigma_\epsilon^2\boldsymbol{\Lambda}\boldsymbol{\psi}\boldsymbol{\psi}'\boldsymbol{\Lambda}' = \boldsymbol{\Xi}_J \tag{13.9}$$

which is $J \times J$ with:

$$Q = \overline{\mathbf{e}}_J'\boldsymbol{\Xi}_J^{-1}\overline{\mathbf{e}}_J \sim \chi_J^2. \tag{13.10}$$

We return to their finite-sample findings about such tests in section 13.2.3 below.

13.2.2 Box–Tiao test: a single horizon for a vector process

Extensions of the Box and Tiao test to vector processes pose no unusual problems, and are available in the literature (see, for example, Lütkepohl, 1991). We begin with a vector process and derive the appropriate test statistic for a single h-step ahead forecast. In the following sub-section, we generalize this to look at the range of step-ahead forecast errors up to the h-step ahead.

For an n-dimensional process, the forecast error defined by (13.3) is:

$$\mathbf{e}_{T+h} = \mathbf{x}_{T+h} - \widetilde{\mathbf{x}}_{T+h} = \sum_{j=0}^{h-1} \boldsymbol{\psi}_j\boldsymbol{\epsilon}_{T+h-j},$$

where ψ_j is $n \times n$ with $\psi_0 = \mathbf{I}_n$, and ϵ_{T+h-j} is $n \times 1$. Assuming that ϵ_t has a multivariate normal distribution, $\epsilon_t \sim \mathsf{IN}_n[\mathbf{0}, \mathbf{\Omega}]$, then:

$$\mathbf{e}_{T+h} \sim \mathsf{N}_n\left[\mathbf{0}, \mathbf{\Omega}_{e_h}\right],$$

where:

$$\mathbf{\Omega}_{e_h} = \mathsf{E}\left[\mathbf{e}_{T+h}\mathbf{e}'_{T+h}\right] = \sum_{j=0}^{h-1} \psi_j \mathbf{\Omega} \psi'_j.$$

Thus, analogously to (13.6) the test statistic for the h-step ahead forecast from the vector process:

$$\underline{Q} = \mathbf{e}'_{T+h}\mathbf{\Omega}_{e_h}^{-1}\mathbf{e}_{T+h},$$

which is χ^2_n under the null hypothesis that the process which generated $\mathbf{x}_{T+h}$ is the same as that which generated $(\mathbf{x}_1, \ldots, \mathbf{x}_T)$.

Lütkepohl (1991, pp.160–1) explicitly considers the complications that arise from parameter estimation uncertainty. By estimating the VAR representation of the process, we can obtain an estimate $\widehat{\mathbf{\Omega}}$ in the usual way, and from the VAR coefficient matrices we can derive estimates of the ψ_j, denoted $\widehat{\psi}_j$. We can then calculate $\widehat{\mathbf{e}}_{T+h}$ as $\widehat{\mathbf{e}}_{T+h} = \mathbf{x}_{T+h} - \widehat{\mathbf{x}}_{T+h}$, where a $\widehat{}$ indicates that the forecasts are generated from a model with estimated parameters. From $\widehat{\mathbf{\Omega}}$ and the $\widehat{\psi}_j$, we can obtain an estimate of $\mathbf{\Omega}_{e_h}$ as $\widehat{\mathbf{\Omega}}_{\widehat{e}_h}$. Given these estimates, we can then form a test statistic $\widehat{\underline{Q}}$, which has the same asymptotic distribution as $\underline{Q}$, assuming that the estimates of the relevant quantities are consistent. That is:

$$\widehat{\underline{Q}} = \widehat{\mathbf{e}}'_{T+h}\widehat{\mathbf{\Omega}}_{\widehat{e}_h}^{-1}\widehat{\mathbf{e}}_{T+h} \underset{a}{\sim} \chi^2_n,$$

where:

$$\widehat{\mathbf{\Omega}}_{\widehat{e}_h} = \sum_{j=0}^{h-1} \widehat{\psi}_j \widehat{\mathbf{\Omega}} \widehat{\psi}'_j.$$

Lütkepohl (1991), p.161, suggests an adjustment to $\widehat{\underline{Q}}$ to take account of parameter-estimation uncertainty, and also an F variant that makes a degrees-of-freedom adjustment for the number of estimated parameters (Lütkepohl, 1991, eq. 4.6.8, p.161).

13.2.3 Box–Tiao test: multiple horizons for a vector process

Again, in principle it is straightforward to generalize the test for several forecast periods (as given in section 13.2.1) to the vector case. We begin with (13.4) which becomes:

$$\underline{\mathbf{e}}_h = \underline{\psi}\underline{\epsilon}_h, \tag{13.11}$$

where $\underline{\mathbf{e}}_h = (\mathbf{e}'_{T+1}, \ldots, \mathbf{e}'_{T+h})'$, $\underline{\boldsymbol{\epsilon}}_h = (\boldsymbol{\epsilon}'_{T+1}, \ldots, \boldsymbol{\epsilon}'_{T+h})'$ and:

$$\underline{\boldsymbol{\psi}} = \begin{pmatrix} \mathbf{I}_n & \mathbf{0} & \mathbf{0} & \cdots & \mathbf{0} & \mathbf{0} \\ \boldsymbol{\psi}_1 & \mathbf{I}_n & \mathbf{0} & \cdots & \mathbf{0} & \mathbf{0} \\ \boldsymbol{\psi}_2 & \boldsymbol{\psi}_1 & \mathbf{I}_n & \ddots & \vdots & \vdots \\ \vdots & \vdots & \ddots & \ddots & \mathbf{0} & \mathbf{0} \\ \boldsymbol{\psi}_{h-2} & \boldsymbol{\psi}_{h-3} & \cdots & \boldsymbol{\psi}_1 & \mathbf{I}_n & \mathbf{0} \\ \boldsymbol{\psi}_{h-1} & \boldsymbol{\psi}_{h-2} & \cdots & \boldsymbol{\psi}_2 & \boldsymbol{\psi}_1 & \mathbf{I}_n \end{pmatrix}.$$

Now:

$$\boldsymbol{\Omega}_{\underline{\mathbf{e}}_h} = \mathsf{E}\left[\underline{\mathbf{e}}_h \underline{\mathbf{e}}'_h\right] = \mathsf{E}\left[\underline{\boldsymbol{\psi}}\underline{\boldsymbol{\epsilon}}_h \underline{\boldsymbol{\epsilon}}'_h \underline{\boldsymbol{\psi}}'\right] = \underline{\boldsymbol{\psi}}\left(\boldsymbol{\Omega} \otimes \mathbf{I}_h\right)\underline{\boldsymbol{\psi}}'$$

so that:

$$\underline{\mathbf{e}}_h \sim \mathsf{N}_{nh}\left[\mathbf{0}, \boldsymbol{\Omega}_{\underline{\mathbf{e}}_h}\right]$$

suggesting a test statistic of the form:

$$\underline{Q}_h = \underline{\mathbf{e}}'_h \boldsymbol{\Omega}^{-1}_{\underline{\mathbf{e}}_h} \underline{\mathbf{e}}_h \sim \chi^2_{hn}. \tag{13.12}$$

The null hypothesis for (13.12) is that the process generating $(\mathbf{x}_{T+1}, \ldots, \mathbf{x}_{T+h})$ is the same as that which generated $(\mathbf{x}_1, \ldots, \mathbf{x}_T)$.

By substituting for $\underline{\mathbf{e}}_h$ from (13.11) we obtain:

$$\begin{aligned} \underline{\mathbf{e}}'_h \boldsymbol{\Omega}^{-1}_{\underline{\mathbf{e}}_h} \underline{\mathbf{e}}_h &= \underline{\boldsymbol{\epsilon}}'_h \underline{\boldsymbol{\psi}}' \boldsymbol{\Omega}^{-1}_{\underline{\mathbf{e}}_h} \underline{\boldsymbol{\psi}} \underline{\boldsymbol{\epsilon}}_h \\ &= \underline{\boldsymbol{\epsilon}}'_h \left(\boldsymbol{\Omega}^{-1} \otimes \mathbf{I}_h\right) \underline{\boldsymbol{\epsilon}}_h \\ &= \sum_{i=1}^{h} \boldsymbol{\epsilon}'_{T+i} \boldsymbol{\Omega}^{-1} \boldsymbol{\epsilon}_{T+i}, \end{aligned} \tag{13.13}$$

where the middle line follows by substituting $\boldsymbol{\Omega}^{-1}_{\underline{\mathbf{e}}_h} = \underline{\boldsymbol{\psi}}'^{-1}(\boldsymbol{\Omega}^{-1} \otimes \mathbf{I}_h)\underline{\boldsymbol{\psi}}^{-1}$.

Equation (13.13) is the direct vector analogue to (13.7). Since we can interpret the $\boldsymbol{\epsilon}_{T+i}$ as the 1-step ahead forecast errors as we move through the forecast period, the test for h-step ahead forecast accuracy is equivalent to a weighted sum of squares of the h successive 1-step ahead forecast errors (as in the scalar case of section 13.2.1: see, e.g., Chong and Hendry, 1986). Lütkepohl (1991, pp.162–3) outlines various small-sample adjustments and an F variant that may be useful in practice when unknown quantities are replaced by estimates; Doornik and Hendry (1997) describe the implementation of χ^2 and F forms of this test statistic in PcFiml.

Chong and Hendry (1986) record the findings of a Monte Carlo simulation analysis of the finite-sample properties of tests based on 'quarterly' (equation (13.12)) and 'annual-average' (the multi-equation analogue of (13.10)) multi-step forecast errors for a first-order dynamic, simultaneous equations system with the VAR reduced form:

$$\mathbf{x}_t = \boldsymbol{\Gamma}\mathbf{x}_{t-1} + \boldsymbol{\epsilon}_t, \quad \text{where} \quad \boldsymbol{\epsilon}_t \sim \mathsf{IN}_n[\mathbf{0}, \boldsymbol{\Omega}]$$

when $n = 2$, for $h = 4$ and 8. Their tests allowed for both error-variance and parameter-variance uncertainties, the latter based on the simplification by Calzolari (1981) of the formulae in Schmidt (1974) and Baillie (1979b). Various values of T, $\mathbf{\Omega}$ and $\mathbf{\Gamma}$ were considered, involving a total of 256 'states of nature'.[2] To simulate model mis-specification in the face of changed data correlations, impulse $(1, 0, \ldots, 0)$, step $(1, 1, \ldots, 1)$ and trend $(1, 2, \ldots, h)$ shocks were added to the post-sample data, as well as the null case $(0, \ldots, 0)$.

The large-sample (asymptotic in T) properties of the tests were derived, and calculated numerically in each experiment. For completeness, we record the derivation and form of these formulae in appendix 13.5. Even for $T = 36$, the large-sample power formulae accounted for over 90 percent of the observed interexperiment variations in the test rejection frequencies (called 'power', although the test size was not recalibrated to 5 percent). Table 13.1 records the mean rejection frequencies across all the relevant experiments, and the corresponding asymptotic results for both the h-step test and the 'annual-average' test, for $h = 4, 8$ and $T = 36, 81$.

Table 13.1 Average forecast-test rejection frequencies

	h/T	36	81	36	81
		null		impulse	
h-step	4	0.08 (0.05)	0.05 (0.05)	0.15 (0.11)	0.12 (0.12)
	8	0.11 (0.05)	0.07 (0.05)	0.17 (0.09)	0.11 (0.09)
'annual'	4	0.06 (0.05)	0.05 (0.05)	0.09 (0.07)	0.09 (0.095)
	8	0.08 (0.05)	0.05 (0.05)	0.11 (0.07)	0.08 (0.08)
		step		trend	
h-step	4	0.31 (0.23)	0.29 (0.26)	0.25 (0.18)	0.26 (0.22)
	8	0.51 (0.37)	0.47 (0.42)	0.71 (0.54)	0.71 (0.65)
'annual'	4	0.39 (0.33)	0.41 (0.40)	0.27 (0.24)	0.28 (0.27)
	8	0.62 (0.55)	0.62 (0.61)	0.73 (0.63)	0.77 (0.73)

Notes: Asymptotic test powers in parentheses; standard errors <0.008.

The null rejection frequencies are somewhat in excess of 0.05 despite taking parameter variances into account, but are acceptable except for $T = 36$ when $h = 8$ (the Monte Carlo estimated standard errors are around 0.003 for the null). As expected, impulse changes are not easily detected: alternatively, the tests are robust to such a shock of the relative magnitude they considered. Otherwise 'power' is usually substantially higher for $h = 8$ than $h = 4$, with h-step being about 10 – 30 percent worse than the annual-average test. 'Power' is surprisingly little affected by T increasing from 36 to 81, perhaps because the actual size becomes more accurate for the nominal.

[2] Their study exploited the parallel computation facilities of a 64×64 ICL Distributed Array Processor at Queen Mary College, London, to obtain 4,096 replications simultaneously.

They also provided response surfaces characterizing the test powers, which confirmed the validity of the asymptotic calculations in explaining their finite-sample counterparts. Their regressions also revealed h/T to be the main determinant of the deviation of the finite-sample from the asymptotic outcomes, and confirmed a role for the eigenvalues of $\mathbf{\Gamma}$ in affecting test power.

Finally, while forecast comparisons based on MSFEs may depend on the chosen transformation of the variables (see section 3.5), we now show that the parameter constancy forecast tests are invariant to linear transforms. Suppose we consider the problem of forecasting $\mathbf{Mx}_t$ instead of $\mathbf{x}_t$. Then from (the vector generalization of (13.1)):

$$\mathbf{Mx}_t = \mathbf{M}\boldsymbol{\psi}(L)\,\boldsymbol{\epsilon}_t.$$

From (13.3):

$$\mathbf{e}^*_{T+h} = \mathbf{Me}_{T+h} = \mathbf{M}\left(\mathbf{x}_{T+h} - \widetilde{\mathbf{x}}_{T+h}\right) = \mathbf{M}\sum_{j=0}^{h-1}\boldsymbol{\psi}_j\boldsymbol{\epsilon}_{T+h-j} = \sum_{j=0}^{h-1}\boldsymbol{\psi}^*_j\boldsymbol{\epsilon}_{T+h-j}.$$

In terms of the notation of section 13.2.3:

$$\underline{\mathbf{e}}^*_h = (\mathbf{M}\otimes\mathbf{I}_h)\,\underline{\mathbf{e}}_h = (\mathbf{M}\otimes\mathbf{I}_h)\,\underline{\boldsymbol{\psi}}\underline{\boldsymbol{\epsilon}}_h = \underline{\boldsymbol{\psi}}^*\underline{\boldsymbol{\epsilon}}_h,$$

from (13.11), where $\underline{\boldsymbol{\psi}}^* = (\mathbf{M}\otimes\mathbf{I}_h)\underline{\boldsymbol{\psi}}$. Also:

$$\boldsymbol{\Omega}^*_{\underline{e}_h} = \mathsf{E}\left[\underline{\mathbf{e}}^*_h\underline{\mathbf{e}}^{*\prime}_h\right] = \mathsf{E}\left[\underline{\boldsymbol{\psi}}^*\underline{\boldsymbol{\epsilon}}_h\underline{\boldsymbol{\epsilon}}^{\prime}_h\underline{\boldsymbol{\psi}}^{*\prime}\right] = (\mathbf{M}\otimes\mathbf{I}_h)\,\boldsymbol{\Omega}_{\underline{e}_h}\,(\mathbf{M}\otimes\mathbf{I}_h)'.$$

Thus, the test statistic for the transformed model is:

$$\begin{aligned}\underline{\mathbf{e}}^{*\prime}_h\boldsymbol{\Omega}^*_{\underline{e}_h}\underline{\mathbf{e}}^*_h &= \underline{\boldsymbol{\epsilon}}^{\prime}_h\underline{\boldsymbol{\psi}}'\,(\mathbf{M}\otimes\mathbf{I}_h)'\,(\mathbf{M}\otimes\mathbf{I}_h)'^{-1}\,\boldsymbol{\Omega}^{-1}_{\underline{e}_h}\,(\mathbf{M}\otimes\mathbf{I}_h)^{-1}\,(\mathbf{M}\otimes\mathbf{I}_h)\,\underline{\boldsymbol{\psi}}\underline{\boldsymbol{\epsilon}}_h \\ &= \underline{\boldsymbol{\epsilon}}^{\prime}_h\underline{\boldsymbol{\psi}}'\boldsymbol{\Omega}^{-1}_{\underline{e}_h}\underline{\boldsymbol{\psi}}\underline{\boldsymbol{\epsilon}}_h = \underline{Q}_h\end{aligned} \tag{13.14}$$

so that the test is invariant to linear transformations of the model. This is a natural result for linear models, and it is the non-invariance of MSFE comparisons to linear transformations that is at first sight surprising. Intuitively, forecast tests are invariant because the covariance matrix 'undoes' the transformation of the variables, as is apparent from (13.14).

Tests of parameter constancy are also invariant to $\mathbf{P}$-transforms (see section 3.5). This result can be established formally, but follows immediately once we recall that h-step ahead tests reduce to functions of 1-step ahead errors as shown above. In section 3.5.4, we demonstrated MSFE invariance to $\mathbf{P}$-transforms for 1-step ahead (following from the conditional nature of the forecasts).

13.3 Tests of comparative forecast accuracy

Although there is a large literature on forecast accuracy comparisons, there are few formal comparisons of rival forecasts of the same phenomena (see, however, Andrews,

Minford and Riley, 1996). By formal, we mean comparisons which attempt to assess whether differences between rival forecasts can be attributed to sampling variability, or whether they are 'significant', in a sense to be defined below (see Hendry, 1986). Diebold and Mariano (1995) propose and evaluate tests of the null of no difference between two forecasts, building on Granger and Newbold (1977). Harvey, Leybourne and Newbold (1997) offer some refinements of the tests. The discussion in this section is based on these four papers.

The difficulties with formal testing are that the forecast errors may not be normally distributed, nor zero mean; multi-step forecasts are serially correlated and heteroscedastic; rival forecasts will tend to be contemporaneously correlated; and the 'economic loss' from forecast errors may not correspond to statistical notions such as MSFE.

13.3.1 Encompassing tests

We discussed the basis for forecast encompassing tests in section 10.3 in relation to pooling forecasts; here we focus on their role in testing. Chong and Hendry (1986) envisaged that the main application of forecast encompassing tests would be to small sets of forecasts from large systems estimated from under-sized samples (i.e., fewer observations than the total number of parameters), where formal methods of model evaluation were inapplicable. For large, or non-lincar, dynamic systems, it is essentially impossible to allow for the variances of all the model's parameter estimates, so any test will be approximate unless T is very large. Thus, we assume that the available forecasts are a sample of size h from $T+1$ to $T+h$, on 1-step forecasts, where data on outcomes are also available. We consider the scalar case – one variable of interest from the system – although vector generalizations are available. The first results we report are based on Hendry (1986).

Forecast-encompassing tests seek to evaluate one model, M_a, by testing whether another model M_b can explain the forecast errors made by M_a (and vice versa). By way of notation, denote the two rival forecasts of a scalar process y_t, by $\widehat{y}_t$ and $\widetilde{y}_t$, where $t \in [1, \ldots, h]$. If information is restricted to *ex-ante* forecasts only, the simplest test is to regress M_a's 1-step forecast errors ($e_{T+j} = y_{T+j} - \widehat{y}_{T+j}$) on the difference between M_a's and M_b's forecasts, ($\widetilde{y}_{T+j} - \widehat{y}_{T+j}$) and test for a non-null relationship. Hendry calculated the t-test for the regression coefficient, conditional on the values of both model's forecasts. If the null is rejected at a reasonable significance level, then M_a does not forecast encompass M_b and hence is not an adequate data description over the forecast horizon. The test statistics were described in section 10.3; that actually used for the Monte Carlo was the t-test on α in:

$$e_{T+j} = \alpha \widetilde{y}_{T+j} + \zeta_{T+j}, \tag{13.15}$$

although that form is inappropriate in general (see section 10.3). However, even in stationary stochastic processes, this class of forecast-based test can have power in assessing model specification. Moreover, large-sample power can be computed from a non-central t-distribution, where the non-centrality is a function of the degree of model mis-specification.

For the same dynamic process as in section 13.2.3, but at one population parameter point only, and with no non-stationary shocks, two alternative approximations to one of the underlying equations were tested. The model M_a omitted one important variable but included another correlated with it, whereas M_b mis-specified the lag structure but included the variable which M_a omitted.

Table 13.2 Rejection frequencies of the forecast encompassing test

	h	5	6	7	8	10	12	14
M_a vs M_b	$\widehat{\mathsf{p}}$	0.31	0.38	0.43	0.46	0.50	0.54	0.56
	p^*	0.41	0.49	0.57	0.64	0.76	0.85	0.91
M_b vs M_a	$\widehat{\mathsf{p}}$	0.56	0.63	0.69	0.73	0.80	0.85	0.89
	p^*	0.79	0.88	0.94	0.97	0.99	1.00	1.00

Table 13.2 records the rejection frequencies of the forecast-encompassing test to detect these mis-specifications, using from five to 14 outside-sample observations when $T = 25$. Despite the small sample of data, the small amounts of forecast information available, and the approximate nature of the test (shown by the divergence between the theoretical (p^*) and observed ($\widehat{\mathsf{p}}$) powers), reasonable power is manifest. For stationary processes, this form of forecast encompassing test can help evaluate models even though pure forecast tests cannot.

That conclusion has been questioned by Harvey *et al.* (1997), who show that this general form of forecast-encompassing test performs badly when there are large samples of forecast observations. Thus, it should not be used in that setting, and, as argued by Ericsson (1992), a preferable approach for large h would be to test forecast-model encompassing, or use the better-behaved test discussed in the next section. However, in the Monte Carlo reported by Harvey *et al.* (1997), the encompassing test continues to perform about as well as any test for small h (i.e., $h \leq 4$)

13.3.2 Variance-based tests

To begin with, in this sub-section, we assume that many of the difficulties discussed at the start of this section do not arise. Specifically:

1 forecasts are evaluated according to squared error loss (MSFE);

2 forecast errors are:

  2.1 zero mean;

  2.2 normally distributed; and

  2.3 serially uncorrelated.

As before, $\widehat{y}_{T+j}$ and $\widetilde{y}_{T+j}$ refer to the j-step forecasts made at period T. The forecast errors are $\widehat{e}_{T+j}$ and $\widetilde{e}_{T+j}$, and $\widehat{\mathbf{e}} = (\widehat{e}_{T+1}, \ldots, \widehat{e}_{T+h})'$ and $\widetilde{\mathbf{e}} = (\widetilde{e}_{T+1}, \ldots, \widetilde{e}_{T+h})'$.

2.1 assumes that the forecasts are unbiased, which is perhaps the least objectionable assumption. Since even optimal h-step forecasts are serially correlated of order $h-1$, assumption 2.3 requires $h = 1$, so that attention is restricted to 1-step ahead forecasts. Then the following test due to Granger and Newbold (1977) (and sometimes known as the Morgan–Granger–Newbold test in recognition of Morgan, 1940) is the uniformly most powerful unbiased. Under these assumptions, equality of MSFE of $\widehat{\mathbf{e}}$ and $\widetilde{\mathbf{e}}$ amounts to equality of variances (under unbiasedness). The test of equal variances can be implemented by the use of an orthogonalizing transformation (due to Morgan, 1940) to construct $u_{1,T+j} = \widehat{e}_{T+j} - \widetilde{e}_{T+j}$ and $u_{2,T+j} = \widehat{e}_{T+j} + \widetilde{e}_{T+j}$, and then test for zero correlation between $u_{1,T+j}$ and $u_{2,T+j}$. The test statistic is:

$$\frac{\mathsf{r}}{\sqrt{(h-1)^{-1}(1-\mathsf{r}^2)}} \sim \mathsf{t}_{h-1}(0), \qquad (13.16)$$

where:

$$\mathsf{r} = \frac{\mathbf{u}_1'\mathbf{u}_2}{\sqrt{\mathbf{u}_1'\mathbf{u}_1\mathbf{u}_2'\mathbf{u}_2}}$$

and $\mathbf{u}_i' = (u_{i,T+1}, \ldots u_{i,T+h})$, $i = 1, 2$. Diebold and Mariano (1995) discuss the degree to which some of the assumptions on which this statistic is based can be relaxed, and note that assumption 1 is fundamental.

Harvey *et al.* (1997) suggest a modification to (13.16) to counteract the tendency of the statistic to be seriously over-sized (reject the null too often when it is true) when the forecast errors come from a heavy tailed distribution, invalidating assumption 2.2 of normality.

If we are prepared to grant the above assumptions, and make the additional assumption that the errors are contemporaneously uncorrelated, then the ratio of the sample variances under the null hypothesis is:

$$\frac{h^{-1}\widehat{\mathbf{e}}'\widehat{\mathbf{e}}}{h^{-1}\widetilde{\mathbf{e}}'\widetilde{\mathbf{e}}} = \frac{\widehat{\mathbf{e}}'\widehat{\mathbf{e}}}{\widetilde{\mathbf{e}}'\widetilde{\mathbf{e}}} \sim \mathsf{F}_h^h(0)$$

that is, has a central F distribution with degrees of freedom h, h. However, in practice, forecast errors are likely to be highly correlated, rendering this statistic of little value.

Diebold and Mariano (1995) also discuss a test statistic due to Meese and Rogoff (1988) based on the covariance between $u_{1,T+j}$ and $u_{2,T+j}$ which relies on squared error loss, as well as normality and unbiasedness.

Finally, Diebold and Mariano (1995) introduce a test statistic that dispenses with assumptions 1 and 2.1–2.3. They allow an arbitrary loss function in place of squared error loss, which we can write as $g(y_t, f_{i,T+j})$, where $f_{i,T+j}$ is now a forecast using model/method i. Their discussion is based on the specialization $g(e_{i,T+j})$

($e_{i,T+j} \equiv y_{T+j} - f_{i,T+j}$), but this is only a notational convenience, and the argument applies to the more general function. Next, define the loss differential as $d_{T+j} \equiv [g(e_{i,T+j}) - g(e_{j,T+j})]$ for rival forecasts i and j, so that equal forecast accuracy entails the condition that $\mathsf{E}[d_{T+j}] = 0$. Given a covariance-stationary sample realization $\{d_t\}$, the asymptotic distribution of the sample mean loss differential $\overline{d}$ ($\overline{d} = h^{-1} \sum_{j=1}^{h} d_{T+j}$) is given by:

$$\sqrt{h}\left(\overline{d} - \mu\right) \xrightarrow{D} \mathsf{N}\left[0, 2\pi f_d\left(0\right)\right]$$

where:

$$f_d\left(0\right) = \frac{1}{2\pi} \sum_{\tau=-\infty}^{\infty} \gamma_d\left(\tau\right),$$

is the spectral density of the loss differential at frequency zero, and γ_d is the autocovariance function. Under the assumptions of serially uncorrelated and contemporaneously uncorrelated forecast errors, $\gamma_d(\tau) = 0$, $\tau \neq 0$, but the approach ensures the variance is estimated consistently when these assumptions fail to hold.

Thus the large-sample statistic that Diebold and Mariano (1995) propose for testing the null of equal forecast accuracy is:

$$\frac{\overline{d}}{\sqrt{h^{-1} 2\pi \widehat{f}_d\left(0\right)}} \underset{app}{\frown} \mathsf{N}\left[0, 1\right],$$

where $\widehat{f}_d(0)$ is a consistent estimate of $f_d(0)$, based on a weighted sum of the sample autocovariances. Diebold and Mariano (1995) discuss the choice of lag window and truncation lag. Harvey *et al.* (1997) propose a modified version of this test statistic that corrects for the tendency of the statistic to be over-sized, and present simulation evidence that attests to the usefulness of the modification.

13.4 Overview

In this chapter we have looked at tests of comparative forecast accuracy which are essentially tests of 'post-sample' model adequacy, noting that the separation between in- and post-sample is under the control of the investigator. The 'comparative' aspect relates to the model characterizing the post-sample observations as well as being predicted by the in-sample fit. We also noted that efficiency dictates that the observations held back at the 'testing' stage will eventually influence the chosen form of the empirical model, so that the distinction between 'genuine testing' and model design is far from clear cut, which puts a premium on evaluating models against information sets not available to their proprietors at the time of construction if 'quality-control' tests are desired.

Tests of predictive failure are essentially tests based on 1-step forecast errors, and as a consequence are invariant to linear transformations, in contrast to multi-period forecast accuracy comparisons based on MSFE-measures.

The second main strand of analysis is more closely related to the comparison of rival forecasts of the same phenomenon as in chapter 3, but seeks to establish a framework for determining whether apparent differences in forecast accuracy are statistically significant.

13.5 Appendix: Multi-step forecast-error variances

We assume that the n variables in the VAR are I(0), and write the system as the multivariate linear regression (see, e.g., Anderson, 1984, Spanos, 1986, Lütkepohl, 1991 and Ooms, 1994):

$$\mathbf{x}_t = \mathbf{\Pi}\mathbf{w}_t + \mathbf{v}_t \text{ where } \mathbf{v}_t \sim \mathsf{IN}_n [\mathbf{0}, \mathbf{\Omega}], \tag{13.17}$$

for $t = 1, \ldots, T$, when $\mathbf{w}$ contains m lags of $\mathbf{x}$:

$$\mathbf{w}_t' = \left(\mathbf{x}_{t-1}', \ldots, \mathbf{x}_{t-m}'\right).$$

Letting $\mathbf{X}' = (\mathbf{x}_1\ \mathbf{x}_2 \ldots \mathbf{x}_T)$, and defining $\mathbf{W}'$, $\mathbf{V}'$ correspondingly:

$$\mathbf{X}' = \mathbf{\Pi}\mathbf{W}' + \mathbf{V}', \tag{13.18}$$

in which $\mathbf{X}'$ is $(n \times T)$, $\mathbf{W}'$ is $(nm \times T)$ (assuming no data have been dropped in forming lags), and $\mathbf{\Pi}$ is $(n \times nm)$. In vectorized form (see section 7.3), let $\boldsymbol{\pi} = (\mathbf{\Pi})^{v}$, $\mathbf{x} = (\mathbf{X}')^{v}$ and $\mathbf{v} = (\mathbf{V}')^{v}$, then (13.18) is:

$$\mathbf{x} = (\mathbf{I}_n \otimes \mathbf{W})\boldsymbol{\pi} + \mathbf{v}, \tag{13.19}$$

so the OLS estimates of the coefficients and residual covariance are:

$$\widehat{\boldsymbol{\pi}} = \left([\mathbf{I}_n \otimes \mathbf{W}]' [\mathbf{I}_n \otimes \mathbf{W}]\right)^{-1} (\mathbf{I}_n \otimes \mathbf{W})' \mathbf{x} = \left(\mathbf{I}_n \otimes (\mathbf{W}'\mathbf{W})^{-1} \mathbf{W}'\right) \mathbf{x} \tag{13.20}$$

so that:

$$\widehat{\boldsymbol{\pi}} - \boldsymbol{\pi} = \left(\mathbf{I}_n \otimes (\mathbf{W}'\mathbf{W})^{-1} \mathbf{W}'\right) \mathbf{v}, \tag{13.21}$$

and:

$$\widehat{\mathbf{\Omega}} = (T-k)^{-1} \widehat{\mathbf{V}}'\widehat{\mathbf{V}}, \tag{13.22}$$

with residuals:

$$\widehat{\mathbf{V}} = \mathbf{X} - \mathbf{W}\widehat{\mathbf{\Pi}}', \tag{13.23}$$

where $\widehat{\mathbf{\Pi}}$ is the matrix version of $\widehat{\boldsymbol{\pi}}$. The finite-sample variance matrix of the estimated coefficients is:

$$\mathsf{V}[\widehat{\boldsymbol{\pi}}] = \mathsf{E}\left[(\widehat{\boldsymbol{\pi}} - \boldsymbol{\pi})(\widehat{\boldsymbol{\pi}} - \boldsymbol{\pi})'\right], \tag{13.24}$$

which is intractable in dynamic systems, so the following asymptotic approximation is used. Letting $\mathbf{M} = \text{plim}_{T\to\infty} T^{-1}\mathbf{W}'\mathbf{W}$:

$$\sqrt{T}\left(\widehat{\boldsymbol{\pi}} - \boldsymbol{\pi}\right) \xrightarrow{D} \mathsf{N}_{n^2m}\left[\mathbf{0}, \boldsymbol{\Omega} \otimes \mathbf{M}^{-1}\right], \tag{13.25}$$

so the estimated variance matrix of the coefficients is:

$$\mathsf{V}[\widehat{\widehat{\boldsymbol{\pi}}}] = \widehat{\boldsymbol{\Omega}} \otimes \left(\mathbf{W}'\mathbf{W}\right)^{-1}. \tag{13.26}$$

13.5.1 Variances of non-linear vector functions

The basic result we need for the variances of multi-step forecasts is that when $\boldsymbol{\Psi} = \mathbf{f}(\boldsymbol{\Pi})$, where $\boldsymbol{\Psi}$ is a $(q \times n)$ matrix, using a Taylor-series approximation (generalizing section 4.11):

$$\widehat{\boldsymbol{\Psi}}^v - \boldsymbol{\Psi}^v = \mathbf{f}\left(\widehat{\boldsymbol{\Pi}}\right)^v - \mathbf{f}\left(\boldsymbol{\Pi}\right)^v \simeq \mathbf{J}\widehat{\boldsymbol{\Pi}}^v - \mathbf{J}\boldsymbol{\Pi}^v = \mathbf{J}\left(\widehat{\boldsymbol{\pi}} - \boldsymbol{\pi}\right),$$

where $\mathbf{J}$ is the $nq \times n^2m$ Jacobian matrix of the transformation $\boldsymbol{\Psi} = \mathbf{f}(\boldsymbol{\Pi})$:

$$\mathbf{J} = \frac{\partial \boldsymbol{\Psi}^v}{\partial \left(\boldsymbol{\Pi}^v\right)'}. \tag{13.27}$$

Then, the variance matrix of $\widehat{\boldsymbol{\psi}} = \widehat{\boldsymbol{\Psi}}^v$ is:

$$\mathsf{V}\left[\widehat{\boldsymbol{\psi}}\right] \simeq \mathbf{J}'\mathsf{V}\left[\widehat{\boldsymbol{\pi}}\right]\mathbf{J}. \tag{13.28}$$

This approximation is asymptotically valid, in that from (13.25):

$$\sqrt{T}\left(\widehat{\boldsymbol{\psi}} - \boldsymbol{\psi}\right) \xrightarrow{D} \mathsf{N}_{nq}\left[\mathbf{0}, \mathbf{J}\left(\boldsymbol{\Omega} \otimes \mathbf{M}^{-1}\right)\mathbf{J}'\right].$$

Here, we are interested in cases where $\mathbf{f}(\cdot)$ is the power transform, $\boldsymbol{\Psi} = \boldsymbol{\Pi}^h$:

$$\mathbf{J} = \frac{\partial \boldsymbol{\Psi}^v}{\partial \left(\boldsymbol{\Pi}^v\right)'} = \frac{\partial \left(\boldsymbol{\Pi}^h\right)^v}{\partial \left(\boldsymbol{\Pi}^v\right)'}. \tag{13.29}$$

Let:

$$\widehat{\boldsymbol{\Pi}} = \boldsymbol{\Pi} + \boldsymbol{\delta}, \tag{13.30}$$

where $\boldsymbol{\delta}$ is $O(1/T)$ so that, ignoring higher-order terms in $\boldsymbol{\delta}$:

$$\begin{aligned} \widehat{\boldsymbol{\Pi}}^h &= \left(\boldsymbol{\Pi} + \boldsymbol{\delta}\right)^h \\ &\approx \boldsymbol{\Pi}^h + \sum_{i=0}^{h-1} \boldsymbol{\Pi}^i \boldsymbol{\delta} \boldsymbol{\Pi}^{h-1-i} \\ &= \boldsymbol{\Pi}^h + \sum_{i=0}^{h-1} \boldsymbol{\Pi}^i \left(\widehat{\boldsymbol{\Pi}} - \boldsymbol{\Pi}\right) \boldsymbol{\Pi}^{h-1-i} \end{aligned} \tag{13.31}$$

and hence:

$$\left(\widehat{\mathbf{\Pi}}^h - \mathbf{\Pi}^h\right)^v = \sum_{i=0}^{h-1}\left(\mathbf{\Pi}^i\boldsymbol{\delta}\mathbf{\Pi}^{h-1-i}\right)^v = \sum_{i=0}^{h-1}\left(\left(\mathbf{\Pi}'\right)^{h-1-i}\otimes\mathbf{\Pi}\right)\boldsymbol{\delta}^v.$$

Thus:

$$\mathbf{J} = \frac{\partial\left(\mathbf{\Pi}^h\right)^v}{\partial\left(\mathbf{\Pi}^v\right)'} = \sum_{i=0}^{h-1}\left(\mathbf{\Pi}'\right)^{h-1-i}\otimes\mathbf{\Pi}^i. \tag{13.32}$$

This result is used below.

13.5.2 1-step forecast-error variance formulae

Forecast-accuracy, or constancy, tests that allow for parameter uncertainty require the full variance matrix of all forecast errors, so we begin with the 1-step case. The notation distinguishes the step-ahead as:

$$\widehat{\mathbf{e}}_{T+i,1} = \mathbf{x}_{T+i} - \widehat{\mathbf{x}}_{T+i,1} = \left(\mathbf{I}_n\otimes\mathbf{w}'_{T+i}\right)\left(\widehat{\boldsymbol{\pi}}-\boldsymbol{\pi}\right) + \mathbf{v}_{T+i}. \tag{13.33}$$

To a first approximation, $\widehat{\mathbf{\Pi}}$ is an unbiased estimator of $\mathbf{\Pi}$ for forecasting purposes (see section 5.4), so $\mathsf{E}[\widehat{\mathbf{e}}_{T+i,1}] \simeq \mathbf{0}$ and:

$$\begin{aligned}\mathsf{V}\left[\widehat{\mathbf{e}}_{T+i,1}\right] &= \mathbf{\Omega} + \left(\mathbf{I}_n\otimes\mathbf{w}'_{T+i}\right)\mathsf{V}\left[\widehat{\boldsymbol{\pi}}\right]\left(\mathbf{I}_n\otimes\mathbf{w}_{T+i}\right) \\ &= \mathbf{\Omega}\left(1+\mathbf{w}'_{T+i}\left(\mathbf{W}'\mathbf{W}\right)^{-1}\mathbf{w}_{T+i}\right) = \mathbf{\Psi}_{T+i},\end{aligned} \tag{13.34}$$

so that:

$$\widehat{\mathbf{e}}_{T+i,1} \underset{app}{\widetilde{\ }} \mathsf{IN}_n\left[\mathbf{0},\mathbf{\Psi}_{T+i}\right], \tag{13.35}$$

where $\mathbf{\Psi}_{T+i}$ reflects both innovation and parameter uncertainty (see, e.g., Chong and Hendry, 1986). The parameter uncertainty is of order T^{-1} and tends to be small relative to $\mathbf{\Omega}$.

Stacking the h rows of (13.33) as:

$$\widehat{\mathbf{E}} = \mathbf{W}_h\left(\mathbf{\Pi}-\widehat{\mathbf{\Pi}}\right)' + \mathbf{V}_h, \tag{13.36}$$

then $\widehat{\mathbf{E}}$ is the $(h\times n)$ matrix of 1-step forecast errors, $\mathbf{W}_h$ is the $(h\times nm)$ matrix of data for the forecast period $T+1,\ldots,T+h$, so:

$$\widehat{\mathbf{e}} = \widehat{\mathbf{E}}^v = \left(\mathbf{I}_h\otimes\mathbf{W}_h\right)\left(\widehat{\boldsymbol{\pi}}-\boldsymbol{\pi}\right) + \left(\mathbf{V}_h\right)^v. \tag{13.37}$$

Thus:

$$\mathsf{E}[\widehat{\mathbf{e}}\widehat{\mathbf{e}}'] \simeq \mathbf{\Omega}\otimes\left(\mathbf{I}_h+\mathbf{W}_h\left(\mathbf{W}'\mathbf{W}\right)^{-1}\mathbf{W}'_h\right) = \mathbf{\Psi}. \tag{13.38}$$

Under the null of no parameter change, tests can be based on the approximate statistic:

$$\left(nh\right)^{-1}\widehat{\mathbf{e}}'\widehat{\mathbf{\Psi}}^{-1}\widehat{\mathbf{e}} \underset{app}{\widetilde{\ }} \mathsf{F}^{nh}_{T-nm}\left(0\right) \tag{13.39}$$

which reflects parameter-estimation uncertainty (see equation (1.12) above).

13.5.3 Multi-step forecast-error variance formulae

To derive the corresponding expressions for dynamic forecasts, we consider a VAR with just one lag, written as:

$$\mathbf{x}_t = \mathbf{\Pi}\mathbf{x}_{t-1} + \mathbf{v}_t \tag{13.40}$$

so:

$$\mathbf{x}_{T+h} = \mathbf{\Pi}^h\mathbf{x}_T + \sum_{j=0}^{h-1}\mathbf{\Pi}^j\mathbf{v}_{T+h-j}, \tag{13.41}$$

where the h-step ahead forecast from T is:

$$\widehat{\mathbf{x}}_{T+h,h} = \widehat{\mathbf{\Pi}}^h\mathbf{x}_T, \tag{13.42}$$

with forecast error:

$$\widehat{\mathbf{e}}_{T+h,h} = \mathbf{x}_{T+h} - \widehat{\mathbf{x}}_{T+h,h} = (\mathbf{\Pi}^h - \widehat{\mathbf{\Pi}}^h)\mathbf{x}_T + \sum_{j=0}^{h-1}\mathbf{\Pi}^j\mathbf{v}_{T+h-j} \tag{13.43}$$

(if there are m lags, use the companion form approach in (6.9) above).

Following Schmidt (1974), the parameter-uncertainty component of the forecast errors is:

$$\left(\mathbf{\Pi}^h - \widehat{\mathbf{\Pi}}^h\right)\mathbf{x}_T = \left(\mathbf{x}_T' \otimes \mathbf{I}_n\right)\left(\mathbf{\Pi}^h - \widehat{\mathbf{\Pi}}^h\right)^v, \tag{13.44}$$

so that

$$\widehat{\mathsf{V}\left[\left(\mathbf{\Pi}^h - \widehat{\mathbf{\Pi}}^h\right)\mathbf{x}_T\right]} \approx \left(\mathbf{x}_T' \otimes \mathbf{I}_n\right)\widehat{\mathbf{J}}\widehat{\mathsf{V}}\left[\widehat{\boldsymbol{\pi}}\right]\widehat{\mathbf{J}}'\left(\mathbf{x}_T \otimes \mathbf{I}_n\right), \tag{13.45}$$

where, from (13.32)

$$\mathbf{J} = \sum_{i=0}^{h-1}\left(\mathbf{\Pi}'\right)^{h-1-i} \otimes \mathbf{\Pi}^i.$$

Although the $\mathbf{J}$ matrix can be large (see Calzolari, 1987):

$$\left(\mathbf{x}_T' \otimes \mathbf{I}_n\right)\mathbf{J} = \sum_{i=0}^{h-1}\mathbf{x}_T'\left(\mathbf{\Pi}'\right)^{h-1-i} \otimes \mathbf{\Pi}^i, \tag{13.46}$$

so the results in Schmidt (1974) do not require storage of $\mathbf{J}$ (see Doornik and Hendry, 1997).

Chapter 14

Postscript

The book has discussed economic forecasting in processes that are reducible to stationarity after differencing or cointegration transforms. It explicitly allowed for the model being used to be a mis-specified representation of the data generation process, and for the evaluation of forecast accuracy by MSFEs to depend on which isomorphic form of the model was used. This chapter looks back at the results established, and forward to our other book which addresses processes that are subject to structural breaks. We showed that many results changed radically when parameter non-constancy was introduced: examples above included the role of causal variables in forecasting relative to non-causal; the value added that could follow from intercept corrections or differencing; and encompassing when models were differentially susceptible to structural breaks. These are the focus of the *Zeuthen Lectures*, where we will investigate economic forecasting in the face of structural breaks, delineate its main causes, and evaluate their importance by Monte Carlo experiments and empirical examples.

14.1 Summary

A theory of model-based macroeconomic forecasting that assumes that models are correctly specified for a constant, time invariant DGP is unlikely to explain either current forecasting practice or the difficulties experienced by applied forecasters. This book is a step towards bridging the gap between 'textbook' theory and empirical practice. We explicitly recognise that models are at best crude approximations to reality, and that the economy itself is evolving and subject to structural breaks and regime shifts. We hope that an econometric theory of forecasting that captures these features of the real world will deliver empirically relevant conclusions about particular approaches to forecasting.

We have covered a lot of ground, and some of the main findings are briefly reviewed below, but we believe much remains to be done, particularly on forecasting in the presence of deterministic non-stationarities, and we intend to publish the progress of currently on-going research in this area in a companion volume, *The Zeuthen Lectures on Economic Forecasting*. The present volume is concluded by looking forward to some of those issues.

We began by distinguishing a number of concepts that serve to bring to the fore the difficulties that face the forecaster. In particular, while predictability is a statistical concept that refers to the relationship between a random variable and an information set – whereby a variable is unpredictable if the conditional predictive distribution coincides with the unconditional distribution – forecastability requires knowledge of the form of the conditional density of the variable. This knowledge is akin to knowing the DGP, i.e., the model being correctly specified for the DGP. Only under this assumption of omniscience do the two notions of predictability and forecastability coincide. In practice, the predictive distribution is likely to change over time. When such shifts occur, the current accumulated stock of knowledge borne of careful investigation of the past relationships between the variables will be instantly devalued. Indeed, if the model is mis-specified and the DGP undergoes a structural break then it is impossible to establish that 'causal' variables are more relevant than 'non-causal' ones for forecasting.

Early on we noted the optimal predictor for squared-error loss functions is given by the conditional expectation, but that other loss functions may be minimized by other predictors, and that intuitively in certain circumstances the costs attached to under and over-predictions (of a similar amount) differ radically. Nevertheless, we argued that context-specific loss functions are rarely available to the macroeconomic forecaster, so we evaluated forecasts primarily on the basis of squared-error loss. It remains the case that the MSFE criterion could lead to ambiguities about the accuracy of rival models if, as may often be the case, there is no compelling reason to choose the MMSFE predictor of the levels, as opposed to, say, the MMSFE predictor of the rates of change of the variables. To help resolve this conundrum, we proposed a related measure that yields rankings which are invariant to linear transformations of the variables to be forecast, but noted that in empirical settings (as opposed to Monte Carlo) for multi-step forecast evaluation in systems, the number of forecasts required may be exacting.

Before attempting to describe the task faced by the applied forecaster, and in particular, all the sources of possible error that afflict model-based forecasts, we considered forecasting in simple univariate linear autoregressive models. By abstracting from most of the sources of error that arise in practice, we were able to put a bound on just how well the forecaster would be able to do in ideal circumstances. Although not attainable in practice (or even calculable as it requires a knowledge of the DGP), this showed the crucial dependence of the properties of forecasts and prediction intervals on the time-series properties of the variables.

We also analysed forecasting based on systems of integrated-cointegrated variables, again abstracting from many of the sources of error, to focus on this particular aspect, and to compare the implications for forecasting of the traditional time-series approach of Box and Jenkins (1976) with that which explicitly attempts to model the long-run relationships between variables (e.g., Sargan, 1964, Davidson, Hendry, Srba and Yeo, 1978 and some of the papers in Granger, 1990). We made extensive use of Monte Carlo techniques to explore the impact of parameter estimation uncertainty on forecast accuracy in cointegrated systems, and provided a separate chapter that can be read as an introduction to the use of simulation techniques in econometrics.

With the background material in place, we then developed a formal 'accounting' framework, or taxonomy, of forecast errors that attributes errors to a number of sources, such as parameter non-constancy, model mis-specification, sampling variability, variable mis-measurement and error uncertainty. This builds on the sampling and error uncertainty elements previously discussed, broadening the coverage to include the diverse errors that arise in large-scale macroeconomic model forecasting so all the sources of error could be explored within a unified framework. The taxonomy has prescriptive content, and, in particular, helps to explain the 'adjustments' (intercept corrections) often made to model-based forecasts en route to producing a final forecast.

Our argument that it is impossible to prove that causal information is superior to non-causal information, in the situation that typically confronts the forecaster (i.e., the model is mis-specified and the DGP is non-constant), would appear to give licence to all manner of models and techniques. Thus, we can not formally establish the primacy for forecasting of econometric models, that seek to capture behavioural relationships between variables, over either systems of leading indicators or over econometric models supplemented with LIs or CLIs. Nevertheless, a case can be made for the pre-eminence of causal information on the grounds that the likelihood of models based on causally relevant variables capturing persistent relationships between variables exceeds the likelihood of bivariate correlations between variables persisting.

We noted that leading indicator systems are altered sufficiently frequently to suggest they do not systematically lead for long, and argued that CLIs seem at best an adjunct to, and not a substitute for, econometric modelling. Indeed, in February 1997, the UK Office of National Statistics formally decided to stop preparing such indices.

There is a large literature on forecast combination supported by the empirical finding that often a combination may prove superior to any of the individual forecasts. However, if the aim of an econometric modelling exercise is to build forecasting models that can be reliably used to forecast on an on-going basis, then combination might be viewed as a convenient stop-gap measure. It is difficult to see how a *fixed* combination of forecasts could be expected to consistently do well if the models from which the individual forecasts are generated are mis-specified and incomplete. These shortcomings echo those we attribute to systems of LIs.

However, the technology of combination can be re-applied as a test for forecast encompassing, and leads naturally to a progressive research strategy, whereby models found wanting in certain areas (e.g., the inability to forecast certain states of nature as well as a rival) are re-cast to incorporate the superior features of rivals.

Finally, we assessed the case for tailoring the estimation criterion to the forecast horizon (minimizing in-sample h-step errors for forecasting h-periods ahead) and whether the dictates of parsimony weigh differently for forecasting as compared to data characterization or explanation. On the former, a case for multi-step estimation could be made in some circumstances. On the latter, we suspect that there may be a justification for parsimony in systems subject to structural breaks, more so than in stationary systems.

14.2 The way ahead

Despite the 'folklore' that parameter uncertainty plays a large role in forecast accuracy or precision, we found few cases where it alone was crucial: contrast figures 11.2 and 11.3 in chapter 11 for example. A possible explanation for this different perception is the non-existence of forecast-error variances from large models. As shown in Sargan (1964a), full information maximum likelihood (FIML) estimates of simultaneous systems have finite second-moments of reduced-form parameter estimates, whereas methods which directly estimate the 'structural' coefficients (e.g., three stage least squares: 3SLS) may not, with a consequential impact on forecast second moments. Hoque, Magnus and Pesaran (1988) show that high-order forecast-error moments need not exist in autoregressive processes, and Ericsson and Marquez (1996) explore this issue in a large practical forecasting system. This phenomenon suggests checking that the relevant moments exist, and using a modification like that suggested in Maasoumi (1978).

In our forthcoming volume we intend to concentrate on the impact of structural breaks on forecasting. The motivation is our contention that non-constancies are responsible for some of the major episodes of predictive failure, when model forecasts have systematically over- or under-predicted for substantial periods, and realized outcomes have been well outside any reasonable *ex ante* confidence interval computed from the uncertainties due to parameter estimation and lack of fit. We plan to explore more fully a number of techniques that can be used to counter the non-constancies that plague linear macroeconometric models. Some are discussed in this volume, such as differencing and intercept corrections, but we will also consider others, such as, for example, the roles of continual model re-specification and updating of parameter values, various non-linear models which model the structural break or regime shift as 'switching-regression' behaviour, and 'co-breaking'. Moreover, we will more precisely delineate what forms of break are most inimical to the forecasting enterprise, and re-analyse the roles of collinearity, parsimony and model mis-specification in the context of systems that are subject to structural change.

All these methods have strengths and weaknesses that need to be understood. The idea that it might be possible to model the structural change using a switching-regression model is naturally appealing, but with a few exceptions such methods have so far been confined to univariate models. However, by explicitly building in to the probabilistic structure of the model the possibility that regime changes may occur provides a more accurate picture of the uncertainty surrounding predictions than would result from the use of dummy variables to 'model' such events. Hamilton (1989) is an important paper in the tradition of Goldfeld and Quandt (1973) that suggests using a Markov chain to model the unobserved switch in regime, although as we saw in section 4.7, there are other possibilities. We also noted, however, that from a forecasting perspective there appears to be no clear consensus as to whether allowing for non-linearities of these types leads to a much improved forecast performance (see, for example, De Gooijer and Kumar, 1992, Clements and Krolzig, 1998 and Clements and Smith, 1998, 1997, on the forecast performance of SETAR models).

Alternatively, in some circumstances, rather than attempting to model the structural change it may prove fruitful to explore schemes that make a more judicious use of intercept corrections. Such schemes might involve intercept-correcting based on the outcome of sequential testing procedures, such as that of Chu, Stinchcombe and White (1996), which monitor for structural change as new observations accrue. That is, pre-testing may allow us to do better than the automatic application of such corrections as in section 8.6. In turn, intercept corrections clarify the conditions under which forecast combinations might prove beneficial.

Intercept correcting and modelling the structural change epitomise two quite different responses to the recognition that for a range of empirical phenomena, constant parameter linear models may not yield the best attainable forecasts, and these are illustrative of the range of alternatives that we will analyse further in future research.

Glossary

$\alpha(L)$	polynomial in the lag operator L
$\boldsymbol{\beta}$	$k \times 1$ parameter vector $(\beta_1 \ldots \beta_k)'$
$\boldsymbol{\gamma}'$	$1 \times n$ (row) vector of parameters $(\gamma_1 \ldots \gamma_n)$
$\Delta_n x_t$	n-period time difference of x_t, $x_t - x_{t-n}$
$\Delta^d z_t$	d^{th}-order time difference of z_t
$\boldsymbol{\epsilon}_t$	stochastic error (usually white noise)
λ_i	i^{th} eigenvalue
$\boldsymbol{\Lambda}$	diagonal matrix of eigenvalues
$\boldsymbol{\mu}$	parameter or intercept
ν_t	unpredictable, or innovation, error
$\boldsymbol{\theta} \in \Theta$	parameter vector $(\theta_1 \ldots \theta_n)'$, an element in a parameter space Θ
$\boldsymbol{\theta}_p$	population parameter vector
π	ratio of circumference to diameter in a circle
$\boldsymbol{\pi}$	cointegration matrix
$\boldsymbol{\Pi}$	system reduced-form matrix
σ_u^2	variance of $\{u_t\}$
σ	standard deviation or standard error
$\sigma(\mathbf{X}_{t-1})$	sigma field generated by $\mathbf{X}_{t-1}$
$\sum$	summation over implicit range (text)
$\sum_{t=1}^{T}$	summation over range shown
$\boldsymbol{\Sigma}$	error variance matrix with elements $\{\sigma_{ij}\}$
χ_n^2	chi-square distribution with n degrees of freedom
$\chi_n^2(\psi^2)$	$\chi^2(n)$ with non-centrality ψ^2
$\boldsymbol{\Omega}$	error variance matrix with elements (ω_{ij})
$\{\cdot\}$	stochastic process or sequence
$\forall t$	for all admissible values of t
$\in$	element of a set
$\notin$	not an element of the relevant set
$\subset$	strict subset of
$\subseteq$	subset of
$\times$	product of two spaces or numbers
$\otimes$	Kronecker product $\mathbf{A} \otimes \mathbf{B} = (b_{ij}\mathbf{A})$ $((m \cdot n) \times (r \cdot s)$ yielding an $mr \cdot ns$ matrix)
$(\cdot)^v$	vectoring operator, stacks columns of a matrix in a vector
$(\cdot)^\Upsilon$	lagged variable matrix
$\lvert \cdot \rvert$	absolute value
$\lvert \mathbf{A} \rvert$	determinant of a matrix (depending on context)
$'$	transpose of a matrix
$\int$	integral
$\int_0^1$	integral over range shown
$\simeq$	approximately equal to

$\approx$ equivalent order of magnitude or order in probability

$\succeq$ matrix difference is negative semi-definite

$\preceq$ matrix difference is positive semi-definite

$\rightarrow$ tends to

$\Rightarrow$ weak convergence in probability measure

$\Leftrightarrow$ one-to-one mapping

$\sim$ is distributed as

$\underset{a}{\sim}$ is asymptotically distributed as

$\underset{app}{\sim}$ is approximately distributed as

$\underset{h}{\sim}$ hypothesised distribution

$\widehat{\ }$ an estimator (usually ML) or forecast value

$\widetilde{\ }$ an estimator or alternative forecast

$\bar{\ }$ sample mean or average forecast

$\mathrm{argmax}_{\boldsymbol{\theta}\in\Theta} f(\boldsymbol{\theta})$
value of $\boldsymbol{\theta} \in \Theta$ which yields the highest value of $f(\boldsymbol{\theta})$

$\mathsf{C}[y, z]$ covariance of y with z

$\mathsf{D}_{\mathsf{X}}(\mathbf{X}; \boldsymbol{\theta})$
joint density or distribution function of $\mathbf{X}$ with parameter $\boldsymbol{\theta} \in \Theta$

$\mathsf{D}_{\mathsf{x}}(\mathbf{x}_t; \boldsymbol{\theta})$
distribution of $\mathbf{x}_t$ with parameter $\boldsymbol{\theta}$

$\mathsf{D}_{\mathsf{y|z}}(y_t|z_t, \cdot)$
conditional distribution of y_t given z_t

$\mathsf{D}_{\mathsf{x}}(\mathbf{x}_t|\mathcal{I}_{t-1}, \cdot)$
sequential distribution of $\mathbf{x}_t$ given $\mathcal{I}_{t-1}$

$\mathsf{E}[Y]$ expectation of the random variable Y

$\mathsf{E}[y_t|\mathbf{z}_t]$ conditional expectation of the random variable y_t given $\mathbf{z}_t$

$\mathsf{E}_{\mathsf{Z}}(\mathsf{E}[Y|Z])$
expected value over Z of the conditional cxpectation of Y given Z

$\mathbb{E}[\cdot]$ expectation with respect to the random variables in a Monte Carlo

$\mathsf{F}^n_m(\phi)$ non-central F-distribution with $n,\ m$ degrees of freedom and non-centrality ϕ

H number of observations in the forecast period

H_0 null hypothesis

$\mathbf{I}_k$ unit matrix of dimension k

$\mathsf{I}(d)$ integrated of order d

$\mathcal{I}_{t-1}$ previous information

$\mathsf{IID}[\mu, \sigma^2_\epsilon]$
independent, identically distributed with mean μ and variance σ^2_ϵ

$\mathsf{IN}[\mu, \sigma^2]$
independent normal distribution with mean μ and variance σ^2

$\mathsf{IN}_{\mathsf{k}}[\boldsymbol{\mu}, \boldsymbol{\Sigma}]$
k-dimensional multivariate independent normal distribution with mean $\boldsymbol{\mu}$ and variance matrix $\boldsymbol{\Sigma}$

L lag operator $L^k x_t = x_{t-k}$

$\lim_{T\rightarrow\infty}$
limit as T tends to infinity

log natural logarithm

$\max_{\boldsymbol{\theta}\in\Theta} f(\boldsymbol{\theta})$
highest value of a function $f(\cdot)$ with respect to its argument $\boldsymbol{\theta}$

R number of Monte Carlo replications

M	second-moment matrix
$\mathsf{N}[0,1]$	normal density function with zero mean and unit variance
$\mathcal{N}(\theta)$	neighbourhood of θ
$o(1)$	of smaller order than unity
$O(1)$	at most of order unity
p	probability, or test-rejection probability
$\text{plim}_{T\to\infty} Z_T$	probability limit of the random variable Z_T
$\text{rank}(\mathbf{A})$	rank of $\mathbf{A}$
R^2	the squared multiple correlation
$\mathbb{R}$	the real line
$\mathbb{R}^k$	k-dimensional real space
$\mathsf{t}_n(\psi)$	Student's t-distribution with n degrees of freedom and non-centrality parameter ψ
T	number of observations in a time series
$\text{tr}(\mathbf{A})$	trace of $\mathbf{A}$ (sum of the diagonal elements)
$\mathcal{T}$	the time sequence $\{\ldots,-2,-1,0,1,2,\ldots\}$
$\mathsf{V}[\mathbf{x}]$	variance (matrix) of X
$\mathcal{V}[\cdot]$	variance in a Monte Carlo
$W(j)$	continuous Wiener process for $j \in [0,1]$
$\bar{x}$	sample mean
$\mathbf{x}_t$	vector random variable (or realization thereof) $(x_{1t}\ldots x_{kt})'$
$\mathbf{X}$	sample observation matrix $(T \times k)$ $(\mathbf{x}_1 \ldots \mathbf{x}_k)$
$\mathbf{X}_{t-1}^1$	$(\mathbf{x}_1 \ldots \mathbf{x}_{t-1})$
$\mathbf{X}_{t-1}$	$(\mathbf{X}_0, \mathbf{x}_1, \ldots, \mathbf{x}_{t-2}, \mathbf{x}_{t-1}) = (\mathbf{X}_0, \mathbf{X}_{t-1}^1)$
$Y_T \overset{D}{\to} Y$	Y_T tends in distribution to Y

References

Aitchison, J. and Brown, J. A. C. (1957). *The Lognormal Distribution.* London: Cambridge University Press.

Akaike, H. (1985). Prediction and entropy. In Atkinson, A. C. and Fienberg, S. E. (eds.), *A Celebration of Statistics*, Ch. 1. New York: Springer-Verlag.

Al-Qassam, M. S. and Lane, J. A. (1989). Forecasting exponential autoregressive models of order 1. *Journal of Time Series Analysis*, **10**, 95–113.

Albert, J. and Chib, S. (1993). Bayes inference via Gibbs sampling of autoregressive time series subject to Markov mean and variance shifts. *Journal of Business and Economic Statistics*, **11**, 1–16.

Anderson, T. W. (1984). *An Introduction to Multivariate Statistical Analysis,* 2nd edn. New York: John Wiley & Sons.

Andrews, D. W. K. (1991). Heteroskedasticity and autocorrelation consistent covariance matrix estimation. *Econometrica*, **59**, 817–858.

(1993). Tests for parameter instability and structural change with unknown change point. *Econometrica*, **61**, 821–856.

Andrews, M. J., Minford, A. P. L. and Riley, J. (1996). On comparing macroeconomic forecasts using forecast encompassing tests. *Oxford Bulletin of Economics and Statistics*, **58**, 279–305.

Artis, M. J., Bladen-Hovell, R. C., Osborn, D. R., Smith, G. W. and Zhang, W. (1995). Turning point prediction in the UK using CSO leading indicators. *Oxford Economic Papers*, **47**, 397–417.

Artis, M. J., Moss, S. and Ormerod, P. (1992). A smart automated macroeconometric forecasting system. Unpublished paper, University of Manchester.

Ash, J. C. K. and Smyth, D. J. (1973). *Forecasting the United Kingdom Economy*. Farnborough, England, and Lexington Books, Lexington, MA: Saxon House.

Auerbach, A. J. (1982). The index of leading indicators: Measurement without theory thirty-five years later. *Review of Economics and Statistics*, **64**, 589–595.

Baillie, R. T. (1979a). The asymptotic mean squared error of multistep prediction from the regression model with autoregressive errors. *Journal of the American Statistical Association*, **74**, 175–184.

(1979b). Asymptotic prediction mean squared error for vector autoregressive models. *Biometrika*, **66**, 675–678.

(1993). Comment on 'On the limitations of comparing mean squared forecast errors', by M.P. Clements and D.F. Hendry. *Journal of Forecasting*, **12**, 639–641.

Baillie, R. T. and Bollerslev, T. (1992). Prediction in dynamic models with time-dependent conditional variances. *Journal of Econometrics*, **52**, 91–113.

Banerjee, A., Dolado, J. J., Galbraith, J. W. and Hendry, D. F. (1993). *Co-integration, Error Correction and the Econometric Analysis of Non-Stationary Data*. Oxford: Oxford University Press.

Banerjee, A., Dolado, J. J., Hendry, D. F. and Smith, G. W. (1986). Exploring equilibrium relationships in econometrics through static models: Some Monte Carlo evidence. *Oxford Bulletin of Economics and Statistics*, **48**, 253–277.

Banerjee, A. and Hendry, D. F. (1992). Testing integration and cointegration: An overview. *Oxford Bulletin of Economics and Statistics*, **54**, 225–255.

Banerjee, A., Hendry, D. F. and Mizon, G. E. (1996). The econometric analysis of economic policy. *Oxford Bulletin of Economics and Statistics*, **58**, 573–600.

Barnard, G. A. (1963). New methods of quality control. *Journal of the Royal Statistical Society A*, **126**, 255–259.

Bates, J. M. and Granger, C. W. J. (1969). The combination of forecasts. *Operations Research Quarterly*, **20**, 451–468.

Bera, A. K. and Higgins, M. L. (1993). ARCH models: Properties, estimation and testing. *Journal of Economic Surveys*, **7**, 305–366.

Bhansali, R. J. (1996). Asymptotically efficient autoregressive model selection for multistep prediction. *Annals of Institute of Statistical Mathematics*, **48**, 94–134.

Bianchi, C. and Calzolari, G. (1982). Evaluating forecast uncertainty due to errors in estimated coefficients: Empirical comparison of alternative methods. In Chow and Corsi (1982), Ch. 13.

Bjørnstad, J. F. (1990). Predictive likelihood: A review. *Statistical Science*, **5**, 242–265.

Bladen-Hovell, R. C. and Zhang, W. (1992). A BVAR model for the UK economy: A forecast comparison with LBS and NI models. Mimeo, Economics department, University of Manchester.

Bollerslev, T., Chou, R. S. and Kroner, K. F. (1992). ARCH modelling in finance – A review of the theory and empirical evidence. *Journal of Econometrics*, **52**, 5–59.

Bollerslev, T., Engle, R. F. and Nelson, D. B. (1994). ARCH models. In Engle, R. F. and McFadden, D. (eds.), *The Handbook of Econometrics, Volume IV*, pp. 2959–3038: North-Holland.

Boswijk, H. P. (1992). *Cointegration, Identification and Exogeneity*, Vol. 37 of *Tinbergen Institute Research Series*. Amsterdam: Thesis Publishers.

(1995). Efficient inference on cointegration parameters in structural error correction models. *Journal of Econometrics*, **69**, 133–158.

Bougerol, P. and Picard, N. (1992). Stationarity of GARCH processes and of some nonnegative time series. *Journal of Econometrics*, **52**, 115–127.

Box, G. E. P. and Jenkins, G. M. (1976). *Time Series Analysis, Forecasting and Control*. San Francisco: Holden-Day. First published, 1970.

Box, G. E. P. and Newbold, P. (1971). Some comments on a paper of Coen, Gomme and Kendall. *Journal of the Royal Statistical Society A*, **134**, 29–40.

Box, G. E. P. and Tiao, G. C. (1976). Comparison of forecast and actuality. *Applied Statistics*, **25**, 195–200.

Brandner, P. and Kunst, R. S. (1990). Forecasting vector autoregressions – The influence of cointegration. A Monte Carlo study. Research memorandum 265, Institute for Advanced Studies, Vienna.

Brown, B. W. and Maital, S. (1981). What do economists know? An empirical study of experts' expectations. *Econometrica*, **49**, 491–504.

Brown, B. Y. and Mariano, R. S. (1984). Residual based stochastic predictors and estimation in nonlinear models. *Econometrica*, **52**, 321–343.

(1989). Predictors in dynamic nonlinear models: Large sample behaviour. *Econometric Theory*, **5**, 430–452.

Brown, T. M. (1954). Standard errors of forecast of a complete econometric model. *Econometrica*, **22**, 178–192.

Burns, A. F. and Mitchell, W. C. (1946). *Measuring Business Cycles*. New York: NBER.

Burns, T. (1986). The interpretation and use of economic predictions. In *Proceedings of the Royal Society*, No. A407, pp. 103–125.

Calzolari, G. (1981). A note on the variance of ex post forecasts in econometric models. *Econometrica*, **49**, 1593–1596.

(1987). Forecast variance in dynamic simulation of simultaneous equations models. *Econometrica*, **55**, 1473–1476.

Campbell, J. Y. and Mankiw, N. G. (1987). Are output fluctuations transitory?. *Quarterly Journal of Economics*, **102**, 857–880.

Campos, J. (1992). Confidence intervals for linear combinations of foecasts from dynamic econometric models. *Journal of Policy Modeling*, **14**, 535–560.

Carruth, A. and Henley, A. (1990). Can existing consumption functions forecast consumer spending in the late 1980s?. *Oxford Bulletin of Economics and Statistics*, **52**, 211–222.

Central Statistical Office, UK (1975). Cyclical indicators for the United Kingdom economy. *Economic Trends*, **257**, 95–99.

(1983). Output measures: Calculation and interpretation of the cyclical indicators of the UK economy. Occasional Paper no.16 (revised), Central Statistical Office, London, UK.

Chambers, M. J. (1993). A note on forecasting in co-integrated systems. *Computers Math. Applic.*, **25**, 93–99.

Chatfield, C. (1993). Calculating interval forecasts. *Journal of Business and Economic Statistics*, **11**, 121–135.

Chong, Y. Y. and Hendry, D. F. (1986). Econometric evaluation of linear macro-economic models. *Review of Economic Studies*, **53**, 671–690. Reprinted in Granger, C. W. J. (ed.) (1990), *Modelling Economic Series*. Oxford: Clarendon Press.

Chow, G. C. (1960). Tests of equality between sets of coefficients in two linear regressions. *Econometrica*, **28**, 591–605.

Chow, G. C. and Corsi, P. (eds.)(1982). *Evaluating the Reliability of Macro-Economic Models*. New York: John Wiley.

Christ, C. F. (1966). *Econometric Models and Methods*. New York: John Wiley.

Christoffersen, P. F. and Diebold, F. X. (1996). Optimal prediction under asymmetric loss. Manuscript, Department of Economics, University of Pennsylvania. Revision of NBER Technical Working Paper No. 167, 1994.

Chu, C.-. S., Stinchcombe, M. and White, H. (1996). Monitoring structural change. *Econometrica*, **64**, 1045–1065.

Clemen, R. T. (1989). Combining forecasts: A review and annotated bibliography. *International Journal of Forecasting*, **5**, 559–583.

Clements, M. P. (1990). The mathematical structure of models that exhibit cointegration: A survey of recent approaches. Applied Economics Discussion Paper No. 85, Institute of Economics and Statistics, University of Oxford.

(1995). Rationality and the role of judgement in macroeconomic forecasting. *Economic Journal*, **105**, 410–420.

(1997). Evaluating the rationality of fixed-event forecasts. *Journal of Forecasting*, **16**, 225–239.

Clements, M. P. and Hendry, D. F. (1993a). On the limitations of comparing mean squared forecast errors. *Journal of Forecasting*, **12**, 617–637. (With discussion.)

(1993b). On the limitations of comparing mean squared forecast errors: A reply. *Journal of Forecasting*, **12**, 669–676.

(1994). Towards a theory of economic forecasting. In Hargreaves (1994), pp. 9–52.

(1995a). Forecasting in cointegrated systems. *Journal of Applied Econometrics*, **10**, 127–146.

(1995b). Macro-economic forecasting and modelling. *Economic Journal*, **105**, 1001–1013.

(1996a). Forecasting in macro-economics. In Cox, D. R., Hinkley, D. V. and Barndorff-Nielsen, O. E. (eds.), *Time Series Models: In Econometrics, Finance and Other Fields*. London: Chapman and Hall.

(1996b). Intercept corrections and structural change. *Journal of Applied Econometrics*, **11**, 475–494.

(1996c). Multi-step estimation for forecasting. *Oxford Bulletin of Economics and Statistics*, **58**, 657–684.

Clements, M. P. and Krolzig, H. M. (1998). A comparison of the forecast performance of markov-switching and threshold autoregressive models of US GNP. *The Econometrics Journal*, **1**, C47–C75.

Clements, M. P. and Mizon, G. E. (1991). Empirical analysis of macroeconomic time series: VAR and structural models. *European Economic Review*, **35**, 887–932.

Clements, M. P. and Smith, J. (1997). The performance of alternative forecasting methods for SETAR models. *International Journal of Forecasting*, **13**, 463–475.

(1998). A Monte Carlo study of the forecasting performance of empirical SETAR models. *Journal of Applied Econometrics*. Forthcoming.

Coen, P. G., Gomme, E. D. and Kendall, M. G. (1969). Lagged relationships in economic forecasting. *Journal of the Royal Statistical Society A*, **132**, 133–163.

Cook, S. (1995). Treasury economic forecasting. Mimeo, Institute of Economics and Statistics, University of Oxford.

Cook, S. and Hendry, D. F. (1993). The theory of reduction in econometrics. *Poznań Studies in the Philosophy of the Sciences and the Humanities*, **38**, 71–100.

Cooper, R. L. (1972). The predictive performance of quarterly econometric models of the United States. In Hickman, B. G. (ed.), *Econometric Models of Cyclical Behaviour*, No. 36 in National Bureau of Economic Research Studies in Income and Wealth, pp. 813–947. New York: Columbia University Press.

Coulson, N. F. and Robins, R. P. (1993). Forecast combination in a dynamic setting. *Journal of Forecasting*, **12**, 63–68.

Cox, D. R. (1961a). Prediction by exponentially weighted moving averages and related methods. *Journal of the Royal Statistical Society B*, **23**, 414–422.

(1961b). Tests of separate families of hypotheses. In *Proceedings of the Fourth Berkeley Symposium on Mathematical Statistics and Probability*, Vol. 1, pp. 105–123 Berkeley: University of California Press.

(1962). Further results on tests of separate families of hypotheses. *Journal of the Royal Statistical Society B*, **24**, 406–424.

Cox, D. R. and Miller, H. D. (1965). *The Theory of Stochastic Processes*: Chapman and Hall.

Davidson, J. E. H. (1988). The cointegration properties of VAR models. Mimeo, UCSD and London School of Economics.

Davidson, J. E. H. and Hendry, D. F. (1981). Interpreting econometric evidence: Consumers' expenditure in the UK. *European Economic Review*, **16**, 177–192. Reprinted in Hendry, D. F. (1993c), *Econometrics: Alchemy or Science?* Oxford: Blackwell Publishers.

Davidson, J. E. H., Hendry, D. F., Srba, F. and Yeo, J. S. (1978). Econometric modelling of the aggregate time-series relationship between consumers' expenditure and income in the United Kingdom. *Economic Journal*, **88**, 661–692. Reprinted in Hendry, D. F. (1993c).

Davidson, R. and MacKinnon, J. G. (1993). *Estimation and Inference in Econometrics*. Oxford: Oxford University Press.

De Gooijer, J. G. and De Bruin, P. (1997). On SETAR forecasting. *Statistics and Probability Letters*. Forthcoming.

De Gooijer, J. G. and Kumar, K. (1992). Some recent developments in non-linear time series modelling, testing and forecasting. *International Journal of Forecasting*, **8**, 135–156.

De Leeuw, F. (1991). Toward a theory of leading indicators. In Lahiri and Moore (1991), Ch. 2.

Dempster, A. P., Laird, N. M. and Rubin, D. B. (1977). Maximum likelihood estimation from incomplete data via the EM algorithm. *Journal of the Royal Statistical Society*, **B 39**, 1–38.

Department of Commerce, US (1977). *Handbook of Cyclical Indicators*. Washington: US Department of Commerce.

Dhrymes, P. J. (1984). *Mathematics for Econometrics*, 2nd edn. New York: Springer-Verlag.

Dhrymes, P. J. *et al.* (1972). Criteria for evaluation of econometric models. *Annals of Economic and Social Measurement*, **1**, 291–324.

Dickey, D. A. and Fuller, W. A. (1979). Distribution of the estimators for autoregressive time series with a unit root. *Journal of the American Statistical Association*, **74**, 427–431.

(1981). Likelihood ratio statistics for autoregressive time series with a unit root. *Econometrica*, **49**, 1057–1072.

Diebold, F. X. (1988). Serial correlation and the combination of forecasts. *Journal of Business and Economic Statistics*, **6**, 105–111.

(1989). Forecast combination and encompassing: Reconciling two divergent literatures. *International Journal of Forecasting*, **5**, 589–592.

Diebold, F. X., Lee, J. H. and Weinbach, G. C. (1994). Regime switching with time-varying transition probabilities. In Hargreaves (1994), pp. 283–302.

Diebold, F. X. and Mariano, R. S. (1995). Comparing predictive accuracy. *Journal of Business and Economic Statistics*, **13**, 253–263.

Diebold, F. X. and Rudebusch, G. D. (1989). Scoring the leading indicators. *Journal of Business*, **62**, 369–391.

(1991a). Forecasting output with the composite leading index: An ex ante analysis. *Journal of the American Statistical Association*, **86**, 603–610.

(1991b). Turning point prediction with the composite leading index: An ex ante analysis. In Lahiri and Moore (1991), pp. 231–256.

Diebold, F. X., Rudebusch, G. D. and Sichel, D. E. (1993). Further evidence on business cycle duration dependence. In Stock, J. and Watson, M. (eds.), *Business Cycles, Indicators, and Forecasting*, pp. 255–280: Chicago: University of Chicago Press and NBER.

Doan, T., Litterman, R. and Sims, C. A. (1984). Forecasting and conditional projection using realistic prior distributions. *Econometric Reviews*, **3**, 1–100.

Doornik, J. A. and Hansen, H. (1994). A practical test for univariate and multivariate normality. Discussion Paper, Nuffield College.

Doornik, J. A. and Hendry, D. F. (1996). *GiveWin: An Interactive Empirical Modelling Program*. London: Chapman and Hall.

(1997). *Modelling Dynamic Systems Using PcFiml 9 for Windows*. London: International Thomson Business Press.

Dufour, J.-M. (1985). Unbiasedness of predictions from estimated vector autoregressions. *Econometric Theory*, **1**, 387–402.

Durland, J. M. and McCurdy, T. H. (1994). Duration dependent transitions in a Markov model of US GNP growth. *Journal of Business and Economic Statistics*, **12**, 279–288.

Emerson, R. A. (1994). Two essays on Investment Trusts and one on leading indicators. Unpublished doctoral thesis, Oxford University.

Emerson, R. A. and Hendry, D. F. (1996). An evaluation of forecasting using leading indicators. *Journal of Forecasting*, **15**, 271–91.

Engle, R. F. (1982). Autoregressive conditional heteroscedasticity, with estimates of the variance of United Kingdom inflations. *Econometrica*, **50**, 987–1007.

Engle, R. F. (ed.)(1995). *ARCH*. Oxford: Oxford University Press.

Engle, R. F. and Bollerslev, T. (1987). Modelling the persistence of conditional variances. *Econometric Reviews*, **5**, 1–50.

Engle, R. F. and Granger, C. W. J. (1987). Cointegration and error correction: Representation, estimation and testing. *Econometrica*, **55**, 251–276.

Engle, R. F. and Hendry, D. F. (1993). Testing super exogeneity and invariance in regression models. *Journal of Econometrics*, **56**, 119–139.

Engle, R. F., Hendry, D. F. and Richard, J.-F. (1983). Exogeneity. *Econometrica*, **51**, 277–304. Reprinted in Hendry, D. F. (1993c).

Engle, R. F. and Yoo, B. S. (1987). Forecasting and testing in co-integrated systems. *Journal of Econometrics*, **35**, 143–159.

(1991). Cointegrated economic time series: An overview with new results. In Engle, R. F. and Granger, C. W. J. (eds.), *Long-Run Economic Relationships*, pp. 237–266. Oxford: Oxford University Press.

Ericsson, N. R. (1992). Parameter constancy, mean square forecast errors, and measuring forecast performance: An exposition, extensions, and illustration. *Journal of Policy Modeling*, **14**, 465–495.

(1993). Comment on 'On the limitations of comparing mean squared forecast errors', by M.P. Clements and D.F. Hendry. *Journal of Forecasting*, **12**, 644–651.

Ericsson, N. R., Campos, J. and Tran, H.-A. (1990). PC-GIVE and David Hendry's econometric methodology. *Revista De Econometria*, **10**, 7–117.

Ericsson, N. R., Hendry, D. F. and Tran, H.-A. (1994). Cointegration, seasonality, encompassing and the demand for money in the United Kingdom. In Hargreaves (1994), pp. 179–224.

Ericsson, N. R. and Irons, J. S. (1995). The Lucas critique in practice: Theory without measurement. In Hoover, K. D. (ed.), *Macroeconometrics: Developments, Tensions and Prospects*. Dordrecht: Kluwer Academic Press.

Ericsson, N. R. and Marquez, J. R. (1989). Exact and approximate multi-period mean-square forecast errors for dynamic econometric models. International Finance Discussion Paper 348, Federal Reserve Board.

(1996). A framework for simulated and analytical properties of economic forecasts. In Mariano, R., Weeks, M. and Schuermann, T. (eds.), *Simulation-based Inference in Econometrics: Methods and Applications*: Cambridge: Cambridge University Press. Forthcoming.

Fair, R. C. (1980). Estimating the expected predictive accuracy of econometric models. *International Economic Review*, **21**, 355–378.

(1982). The effects of misspecification on predictive accuracy. In Chow and Corsi (1982), Ch. 11.

(1986). Evaluating the predictive accuracy of models, 1981–95. In Griliches, Z. and Intriligator, M. D. (eds.), *Handbook of Econometrics*, Vol. 3. Amsterdam: North-Holland.

Favero, C. and Hendry, D. F. (1992). Testing the Lucas critique: A review. *Econometric Reviews*, **11**, 265–306.

Figlewski, S. and Wachtel, P. (1981). The formation of inflationary expectations. *Review of Economics and Statistics*, **63**, 1–10.

Filardo, A. J. (1994). Business–cycle phases and their transitional dynamics. *Journal of Business and Economic Statistics*, **12**, 299–308.

Fildes, R. and Makridakis, S. (1995). The impact of empirical accuracy studies on time series analysis and forecasting. *International Statistical Review*, **63**, 289–308.

Findley, D. F. (1983). On the use of multiple models for multi-period forecasting. *ASA Proc. Bus. Econ. Sec.*, 528–531.

Fisher, P. G. and Wallis, K. F. (1990). The historical tracking performance of UK macroeconometric models 1978-85. *Economic Modelling*, 179–197. April.

(1992). Seasonality in large-scale macroeconometric models. *Journal of Forecasting*, **11**, 255–270.

Florens, J.-P., Mouchart, M. and Rolin, J.-M. (1990). *Elements of Bayesian Statistics*. New York: Marcel Dekker.

Franses, P. H. (1996). *Periodicity and Stochastic Trends in Economic Time Series*. Oxford: Oxford University Press.

Friedman, M. (1940). Review of J. Tinbergen: Statistical testing of business-cycle theories, volume II: Business cycles in the United States of America 1919–1932. *American Economic Review*, **30**, 657–660.

Frisch, R. (1938). Statistical versus theoretical relations in economic macrodynamics. Mimeograph dated 17 July 1938, League of Nations Memorandum. Reproduced by University of Oslo in 1948 with Tinbergen's comments. Contained in Memorandum 'Autonomy of Economic Relations', 6 November 1948, Oslo, Universitets Økonomiske Institutt. Reprinted in Hendry D. F. and Morgan M. S. (1995).

Fuller, W. A. (1976). *Introduction to Statistical Time Series*. New York: John Wiley & Sons.

Fuller, W. A. and Hasza, D. P. (1980). Predictors for the first-order autoregressive process. *Journal of Econometrics*, **13**, 139–157.

Gallo, G. M. (1996). Forecast uncertainty reduction in nonlinear models. *Journal of Italian Statistical Society*, **5**, 73–98.

Geman, S. and Geman, D. (1984). Stochastic relaxation, Gibbs distributions and the Bayesian restoration of images. *IEEE Transactions on Pattern Analysis and Machine Intelligence*, **6**, 721–741.

Geweke, J. B. (1988a). Acceleration methods for Monte Carlo integration in Bayesian inference. In *Proceedings of the 20th Symposium on the Interface: Computing Science and Statistics*.

(1988b). Antithetic acceleration of Monte Carlo integration in Bayesian inference. *Journal of Econometrics*, **38**, 73–90.

Ghysels, E. (1994). On the periodic structure of the business cycle. *Journal of Business and Economic Statistics*, **12**, 289–298.

Gilbert, C. L. (1986). Professor Hendry's econometric methodology. *Oxford Bulletin of Economics and Statistics*, **48**, 283–307. Reprinted in Granger, C. W. J. (ed.) (1990).

Giles, J. and Giles, D. (1993). Pre-test estimation and testing in econometrics: Recent developments. *Journal of Economic Surveys*, **7**, 145–198.

Godfrey, L. G. (1978). Testing for higher order serial correlation in regression equations when the regressors include lagged dependent variables. *Econometrica*, **46**, 1303–1313.

Goldfeld, S. M. and Quandt, R. E. (1973). A Markov model for switching regressions. *Journal of Econometrics*, **1**, 3–16.

Goodwin, T. H. (1993). Business-cycle analysis with a Markov-switching model. *Journal of Business and Economic Statistics*, **11**, 331–339.

Granger, C. W. J. (1969). Investigating causal relations by econometric models and cross-spectral methods. *Econometrica*, **37**, 424–438.

(1986) Developments in the study of cointegrated economic variables. *Oxford Bulletin of Economics and Statistics*, **48**, 213–228.

(1993). Comment on 'On the limitations of comparing mean squared forecast errors', by M.P. Clements and D.F. Hendry. *Journal of Forecasting*, **12**, 651–652.

Granger, C. W. J. (ed.)(1990). *Modelling Economic Series*. Oxford: Clarendon Press.

Granger, C. W. J. and Deutsch, M. (1992). Comments on the evaluation of policy models. *Journal of Policy Modeling*, **14**, 497–516.

Granger, C. W. J. and Joyeux, R. (1980). An introduction to long memory time series models and fractional differencing. *Journal of Time Series Analysis*, **1**, 15–30.

Granger, C. W. J. and Newbold, P. (1973). Some comments on the evaluation of economic forecasts. *Applied Economics*, **5**, 35–47.

(1975). Economic forecasting: The atheist's viewpoint. In Renton, G. A. (ed.), *Modelling the Economy*. London: Heinemann Educational Books.

(1977). *Forecasting Economic Time Series*. New York: Academic Press.

(1986). *Forecasting Economic Time Series,* 2nd edn. New York: Academic Press.

Granger, C. W. J. and Pesaran, M. H. (1996). A decision theoretic approach to forecast evaluation. Mimeo, Trinity College, Cambridge.

Granger, C. W. J. and Ramanathan, R. (1984). Improved methods of combining forecasts. *Journal of Forecasting*, **3**, 197–204.

Granger, C. W. J. and Teräsvirta, T. (1993). *Modelling Nonlinear Economic Relationships*. Oxford: Oxford University Press.

Haache, G. and Townend, J. (1981). Exchange rates and monetary policy: modelling sterling's effective exchange rate, 1972–80. In Eltis, W. A. (ed.), *The Money Supply and the Exchange Rate, 201–47*. Oxford: Oxford University Press.

Haavelmo, T. (1944). The probability approach in econometrics. *Econometrica*, **12**, 1–118. Supplement.

Hajivassiliou, V. A. and Ruud, P. A. (1994). Classical estimation methods for LDV models using simulation. In Engle, R. F. and McFadden, D. L. (eds.), *Handbook of Econometrics, Volume IV*, pp. 2384–2441. Amsterdam: North-Holland.

Hall, A. (1989). Testing for a unit root in the presence of moving average errors. *Biometrika*, **76**, 49–56.

Hall, P. (1994). Methodology and theory for the bootstrap. In Engle, R. F. and McFadden, D. L. (eds.), *Handbook of Econometrics, Volume IV*, pp. 2341–2381. Amsterdam: North-Holland.

Hall, S. G. (1995). Macroeconomics and a bit more reality. *Economic Journal*, **105**, 974–988.

Hamilton, J. D. (1988). Rational-expectations econometric analysis of changes in regime. An investigation of the term structure of interest rates. *Journal of Economic Dynamics and Control*, **12**, 385–423.

(1989). A new approach to the economic analysis of nonstationary time series and the business cycle. *Econometrica*, **57**, 357–384.

(1990). Analysis of time series subject to changes in regime. *Journal of Econometrics*, **45**, 39–70.

(1994). *Time Series Analysis*. Princeton: Princeton University Press.

Hammersley, J. M. and Handscomb, D. C. (1964). *Monte Carlo Methods.* London: Chapman and Hall.

Hannan, E. J. and Quinn, B. G. (1979). The determination of the order of an autoregression. *Journal of the Royal Statistical Society*, 190–195.

Hansen, B. E. (1992). Testing for parameter instability in linear models. *Journal of Policy Modeling*, **14**, 517–533.

(1996). Inference when a nuisance parameter is not identified under the null hypothesis. *Econometrica*, **64**, 413–430.

Hansen, L. P. and Hodrick, R. J. (1980). Forward exchange rates as optimal predictors of future spot rates: An econometric analysis. *Journal of Political Economy*, **88**, 829–853.

Hargreaves, C. (ed.)(1994). *Non-stationary Time-series Analysis and Cointegration*. Oxford: Oxford University Press.

Harvey, A. C. (1981a). *The Econometric Analysis of Time Series*. Deddington: Philip Allan.

(1981b). The kalman filter and its applications in econometrics and time-series analysis. Invited paper, Symposium über Operations Research, Augsburg.

(1981c). *Time Series Models*. London: Philip Allan.

(1989). *Forecasting, Structural Time Series Models and the Kalman Filter*. Cambridge: Cambridge University Press.

(1992). *Forecasting, Structural Time Series Models and the Kalman Filter*. Cambridge: Cambridge University Press.

(1993). *Time Series Models* 2nd edn.(first edition 1981). Hemel Hempstead: Harvester Wheatsheaf.

Harvey, A. C. and Scott, A. (1994). Seasonality in dynamic regression models. *Economic Journal*, **104**, 1324–1345.

Harvey, A. C. and Shephard, N. (1992). Structural time series models. In Maddala, G. S., Rao, C. R. and Vinod, H. D. (eds.), *Handbook of Statistics*, Vol. XI. Amsterdam: North-Holland.

Harvey, D., Leybourne, S. and Newbold, P. (1997). Testing the equality of prediction mean squared errors. *International Journal of Forecasting*, **13**, 281–291.

Hendry, D. F. (1974). Stochastic specification in an aggregate demand model of the United Kingdom. *Econometrica*, **42**, 559–578. Reprinted in Hendry, D. F. (1993c).

(1979a). The behaviour of inconsistent instrumental variables estimators in dynamic systems with autocorrelated errors. *Journal of Econometrics*, **9**, 295–314.

(1979b). Predictive failure and econometric modelling in macro-economics: The transactions demand for money. In Ormerod (1979), pp. 217–242. Reprinted in Hendry, D. F. (1993c).

(1980). Econometrics: Alchemy or science?. *Economica*, **47**, 387–406. Reprinted in Hendry, D. F. (1993c).

(1983). Econometric modelling: The consumption function in retrospect. *Scottish Journal of Political Economy*, **30**, 193–220. Reprinted in Hendry, D. F. (1993c).

(1984). Monte Carlo experimentation in econometrics. In Griliches, Z. and Intriligator, M. D. (eds.), *Handbook of Econometrics*, Vols. II–III, Ch. 16. Amsterdam: North-Holland.

(1986). The role of prediction in evaluating econometric models. In *Proceedings of the Royal Society*, Vol. A407, pp. 25–33.

(1987). Econometric methodology: A personal perspective. In Bewley, T. F. (ed.), *Advances in Econometrics*, Ch. 10. Cambridge: Cambridge University Press.

(1990). Using PC-NAIVE in teaching econometrics. *Oxford Bulletin of Economics and Statistics*, **53**, 199–223.

(1993a). The role of econometrics in scientific economics. Unpublished paper, Institute of Economics and Statistics, Oxford.

(1993b). The roles of economic theory and econometrics in time-series economics. Invited address, European Econometric Society, Uppsala.

(1993c). *Econometrics: Alchemy or Science?*, Oxford: Blackwell Publishers.

(1994). HUS revisited. *Oxford Review of Economic Policy*, **10**, 86–106.

(1995a). *Dynamic Econometrics*. Oxford: Oxford University Press.

(1995b). Econometrics and business cycle empirics. *Economic Journal*, **105**, 1622–1636.

(1995c). A theory of co-breaking. Mimeo, Nuffield College, University of Oxford.

(1997). The econometrics of macro-economic forecasting. *Economic Journal*, **107**, 1330–1357.

Hendry, D. F. and Clements, M. P. (1993). On model selection when forecasting. Mimeo, Economics department, University of Oxford.

(1994a). Can econometrics improve economic forecasting? *Swiss Journal of Economics and Statistics*, **130**, 267–298.

(1994b). On a theory of intercept corrections in macro-economic forecasting. In Holly, S. (ed.), *Money, Inflation and Employment: Essays in Honour of James Ball*, pp. 160–182. Aldershot: Edward Elgar.

Hendry, D. F. and Doornik, J. A. (1994). Modelling linear dynamic econometric systems. *Scottish Journal of Political Economy*, **41**, 1–33.

(1996a). *Empirical Econometric Modelling Using PcGive 9 for Windows*. London: International Thomson Business Press.

(1996b). *Empirical Econometric Modelling Using PcGive for Windows*. London: International Thomson Business Press.

(1997). The implications for econometric modelling of forecast failure. *Scottish Journal of Political Economy*, **44**, 437–461.

Hendry, D. F. and Ericsson, N. R. (1991). Modeling the demand for narrow money in the United Kingdom and the United States. *European Economic Review*, **35**, 833–886.

Hendry, D. F. and Mizon, G. E. (1978). Serial correlation as a convenient simplification, not a nuisance: A comment on a study of the demand for money by the Bank of England. *Economic Journal*, **88**, 549–563. Reprinted in Hendry, D. F. (1993c).

(1990). Procrustean econometrics: or stretching and squeezing data. In Granger, C. W. J. (ed.), *Modelling Economic Series*, pp. 121–136. Oxford: Clarendon Press.

(1993). Evaluating dynamic econometric models by encompassing the VAR. In Phillips, P. C. B. (ed.), *Models, Methods and Applications of Econometrics*, pp. 272–300. Oxford: Basil Blackwell.

Hendry, D. F. and Morgan, M. S. (1995). *The Foundations of Econometric Analysis*. Cambridge: Cambridge University Press.

Hendry, D. F., Muellbauer, J. N. J. and Murphy, T. A. (1990). The econometrics of DHSY. In Hey, J. D. and Winch, D. (eds.), *A Century of Economics*, pp. 298–334. Oxford: Basil Blackwell.

Hendry, D. F., Neale, A. J. and Ericsson, N. R. (1991). *PC-NAIVE, An Interactive Program for Monte Carlo Experimentation in Econometrics. Version 6.0*. Oxford: Institute of Economics and Statistics, University of Oxford.

Hendry, D. F. and Richard, J.-F. (1982). On the formulation of empirical models in dynamic econometrics. *Journal of Econometrics*, **20**, 3–33. Reprinted in Granger, C. W. J. (ed.) (1990) and in Hendry D. F. (1993c).

(1983). The econometric analysis of economic time series (with discussion). *International Statistical Review*, **51**, 111–163. Reprinted in Hendry, D. F. (1993c).

(1989). Recent developments in the theory of encompassing. In Cornet, B. and Tulkens, H. (eds.), *Contributions to Operations Research and Economics. The XXth Anniversary of CORE*, pp. 393–440. Cambridge, MA: MIT Press.

(1991). Likelihood evaluation for dynamic latent variables models. In Amman, H. M., Belsley, D. A. and Pau, L. F. (eds.), *Computational Economics and Econometrics*, Ch. 1. Dordrecht: Kluwer.

Hendry, D. F. and Trivedi, P. K. (1972). Maximum likelihood estimation of difference equations with moving-average errors: A simulation study. *Review of Economic Studies*, **32**, 117–145.

Hendry, D. F. and von Ungern-Sternberg, T. (1981). Liquidity and inflation effects on consumers' expenditure. In Deaton, A. S. (ed.), *Essays in the Theory and Measurement of Consumers' Behaviour*, pp. 237–261. Cambridge: Cambridge University Press. Reprinted in Hendry, D. F. (1993c).

Hinkley, D. V. (1988). Bootstrap methods. *Journal of the Royal Statistical Society B*, **50**, 321–337.

Hoel, P. G. (1947). On the choice of forecasting formulas. *Journal of the American Statistical Association*, **42**, 605–611.

Holden, K. and Peel, D. A. (1990). On testing for unbiasedness and efficiency of forecasts. *Manchester School*, **58**, 120–127.

Holt, C. C. (1957). Forecasting seasonals and trends by exponentially weighted moving averages. Onr research memorandum 52, Carnegie Institute of Technology, Pittsburgh, Pennsylvania.

Hoque, A., Magnus, J. R. and Pesaran, B. (1988). The exact multi-period mean-square forecast error for the first-order autoregressive model. *Journal of Econometrics*, **39**, 327–346.

Hosking, J. R. M. (1981). Fractional differencing. *Biometrika*, **68**, 165–176.

Howrey, E. P. (1993). Comment on 'On the limitations of comparing mean squared forecast errors', by M.P. Clements and D.F. Hendry. *Journal of Forecasting*, **12**, 652–654.

Hylleberg, S. (ed.)(1992). *Modelling Seasonality*. Oxford: Oxford University Press.

(1994). Modelling seasonal variation. In Hargreaves (1994), pp. 153–178.

Hylleberg, S., Engle, R. F., Granger, C. W. J. and Yoo, B. S. (1990). Seasonal integration and cointegration. *Journal of Econometrics*, **44**, 215–238.

Hylleberg, S. and Mizon, G. E. (1989). Cointegration and error correction mechanisms. *Economic Journal*, **99**, 113–125. Supplement.

Hylleberg, S., Mizon, G. E. and O'Brien (1993). Testing for parameter constancy in systems of cointegrated variables. Mimeo, European University Institute, Florence.

Jarque, C. M. and Bera, A. K. (1980). Efficient tests for normality, homoscedasticity and serial independence of regression residuals. *Economics Letters*, **6**, 255–259.

Johansen, S. (1988a). Statistical analysis of cointegration vectors. *Journal of Economic Dynamics and Control*, **12**, 231–254.

(1988b). The mathematical structure of error-correction models. *Contemporary Mathematics*, **80**, 359–386.

(1991). Estimation and hypothesis testing of cointegration vectors in Gaussian vector autoregressive models. *Econometrica*, **59**, 1551–1580.

(1992a). A representation of vector autoregressive processes integrated of order 2. *Econometric Theory*, **8**, 188–202.

(1992b). Testing weak exogeneity and the order of cointegration in UK money demand. *Journal of Policy Modeling*, **14**, 313–334.

(1995). *Likelihood-based Inference in Cointegrated Vector Autoregressive Models*. Oxford: Oxford University Press.

Johansen, S. and Juselius, K. (1990). Maximum likelihood estimation and inference on cointegration – With application to the demand for money. *Oxford Bulletin of Economics and Statistics*, **52**, 169–210.

Johnson, N. L. and Kotz, S. (1970). *Distributions in Statistics*. New York: John Wiley.

Judge, G. G., Griffiths, W. E., Hill, R. C., Lütkepohl, H. and Lee, T.-C. (1985). *The Theory and Practice of Econometrics*, 2nd edn. New York: John Wiley.

Kähler, J. and Marnet, V. (1994). Markov-switching models for exchange rate dynamics and the pricing of foreign-currency options. In Kähler, J. and Kugler, P. (eds.), *Econometric Analysis of Financial Markets*: Heidelberg: Physica Verlag.

Kalman, R. E. (1960). A new approach to linear filtering and prediction problems. *Journal of Basic Engineering*, **82**, 35–45.

Keane, M. P. and Runkle, D. L. (1990). Testing the rationality of price forecasts: new evidence from panel data. *American Economic Review*, **80**, 714–735.

Kennedy, P. (1983). Logarithmic dependent variables and prediction bias. *Oxford Bulletin of Economics and Statistics*, **45**, 389–392.

Keynes, J. M. (1939). Professor Tinbergen's method. *Economic Journal*, **44**, 558–568.

Kim, C. J. (1994). Dynamic linear models with Markov-switching. *Journal of Econometrics*, **60**, 1–22.

Kiviet, J. F. (1986). On the rigor of some mis-specification tests for modelling dynamic relationships. *Review of Economic Studies*, **53**, 241–261.

Klein, L. R. (1950). *Economic Fluctuations in the United States, 1921–41*. No. 11 in Cowles Commission Monograph. New York: John Wiley.

(1971). *An Essay on the Theory of Economic Prediction*. Chicago: Markham Publishing Company.

Klein, L. R. (ed.)(1991). *Comparative Performance of US Econometric Models*: Oxford University Press.

Klein, L. R. and Burmeister, E. (eds.)(1976). *Econometric Model Performance*. Philadelphia: University of Pennsylvania Press.

Klein, L. R., Howrey, E. P. and MacCarthy, M. D. (1974). Notes on testing the predictive performance of econometric models. *International Economic Review*, **15**, 366–383.

Koch, P. and Rasche, R. H. (1988). An examination of the commerce department leading-indicator approach. *Journal of Business and Economic Statistics*, **6**, 167–187.

Koopmans, T. C. (1937). *Linear Regression Analysis of Economic Time Series*. Haarlem: Netherlands Economic Institute.

(1947). Measurement without theory. *Review of Economics and Statistics*, **29**, 161–179.

Krämer, W. (ed.)(1989). *Econometrics of Structural Change*. Heidelberg, Physica-Verlag: New York, Springer-Verlag.

Krolzig, H.-M. (1996). Markov switching vector autoregressions: Modeling, statistical inference and application to Business Cycle analysis. Doctoral thesis, Humboldt Universität, Berlin.

Krolzig, H.-M. and Lütkepohl, H. (1995). Konjunkturanalyse mit Markov–Regimewechselmodellen. In Oppenländer, K. H. (ed.), *Konjunkturindikatoren. Fakten, Analysen, Verwendung*, pp. 177–196: Oldenbourg: München Wien.

Krüger, L., Gigerenzer, G. and Morgan, M. S. (eds.)(1987). *The Probabilistic Revolution*, Vol. II: MIT Press.

Lahiri, K. and Moore, G. H. (eds.)(1991). *Leading Economic Indicators: New Approaches and Forecasting Records*. Cambridge: Cambridge University Press.

Lahiri, K. and Wang, J. G. (1994). Predicting cyclical turning points with leading index in a Markov switching model. *Journal of Forecasting*, **13**, 245–263.

Lam, P.-S. (1990). The Hamilton model with a general autoregressive component. Estimation and comparison with other models of economic time series. *Journal of Monetary Economics*, **26**, 409–432.

Layard, R., Nickell, S. J. and Jackman, R. (1991). *Unemployment Macroeconomic Performance and the Labour Market*. Oxford: Oxford University Press.

Lin, J.-L. and Tsay, R. S. (1996). Co-integration constraint and forecasting: An empirical examination. *Journal of Applied Econometrics*, **11**, 519–538.

Lu, M. and Mizon, G. E. (1991). Forecast encompassing and model evaluation. In Hackl, P. and Westlund, A. H. (eds.), *Economic Structural Change, Analysis and Forecasting*, pp. 123–138. Berlin: Springer-Verlag.

Lucas, R. E. (1973). Some international evidence on output-inflation trade-offs. *American Economic Review*, **63**, 326–334.

(1976). Econometric policy evaluation: A critique. In Brunner, K. and Meltzer, A. (eds.), *The Phillips Curve and Labor Markets*, Vol. 1 of *Carnegie-Rochester Conferences on Public Policy*, pp. 19–46. Amsterdam: North-Holland.

Lütkepohl, H. (1991). *Introduction to Multiple Time Series Analysis*. New York: Springer-Verlag.

Lütkepohl, H. and Claessen, H. (1993). Analysis of cointegrated VARMA processes. Mimeo, Institut für Statistik und Ökonometrie, Humboldt Universität, Berlin.

Maasoumi, E. (1978). A modified Stein-like estimator for the reduced form coefficients of simultaneous equations. *Econometrica*, **46**, 695–704.

Magnus, J. R. and Pesaran, B. (1991). The bias of forecasts from a first-order autoregression. *Econometric Theory*, **7**, 222–235.

Makridakis, S. et. al. (1982). The accuracy of extrapolation (time series) methods: Results of a forecasting competition. *Journal of Forecasting*, **1**, 111–153.

Malinvaud, E. (1970). *Statistical Methods of Econometrics*, 2nd edn. Amsterdam: North-Holland.

Marget, A. W. (1929). Morgenstern on the methodology of economic forecasting. *Journal of Political Economy*, **37**, 312–339.

Mariano, R. S. and Brown, B. W. (1983). Asymptotic behaviour of predictors in a nonlinear simultaneous system. *International Economic Review*, **24**, 523–536.

(1991). Stochastic-simulation tests of nonlinear econometric models. In Klein (1991), pp. 250–259.

Marris, R. L. (1954). The position of economics and economists in the Government Machine: a comparative critique of the United Kingdom and the Netherlands. *Economic Journal*, **64**, 759–783.

Marsland, J. and Weale, M. (1992). The leading indicator in a VAR model of the UK. Unpublished paper, Downing College and Clare College, University of Cambridge.

McCabe, B. and Tremayne, A. R. (1993). *Elements of Modern Asymptotic Theory with Statistical Applications*. Manchester: Manchester University Press.

McCulloch, R. E. and Tsay, R. S. (1994). Bayesian analysis of autoregressive time series via the Gibbs sampler. *Journal of Time Series Analysis*, **15**, 235–250.

McNees, S. K. (1991). Forecasting cyclical turning points: The record in the past three recessions. In Lahiri and Moore (1991), Ch. 9.

Meese, R. A. and Rogoff, K. (1988). Was it real? The exchange rate-interest differential relation over the modern floating-rate period. *Journal of Finance*, **43**, 933–948.

Mincer, J. and Zarnowitz, V. (1969). The evaluation of economic forecasts. In Mincer, J. (ed.), *Economic Forecasts and Expectations*. New York: National Bureau of Economic Research.

Mitchell, W. C. and Burns, A. F. (1938). *Statistical Indicators of Cyclical Revivals*: National Bureau of Economic Research.

Mizon, G. E. (1984). The encompassing approach in econometrics. In Hendry, D. F. and Wallis, K. F. (eds.), *Econometrics and Quantitative Economics*, pp. 135–172. Oxford: Basil Blackwell.

Mizon, G. E. and Richard, J.-F. (1986). The encompassing principle and its application to non-nested hypothesis tests. *Econometrica*, **54**, 657–678.

Molinas, C. (1986). A note on spurious regressions with integrated moving average errors. *Oxford Bulletin of Economics and Statistics*, **48**, 279–282.

Moore, B. (1993). A review of CSO cyclical indicators. *Economic Trends*, **477**, 99–107.

Moore, G. (ed.)(1961). *Business Cycle Indicators*: National Bureau of Economic Research. 2 vols.

Moore, G. and Shiskin, J. (1967). *Indicators of Business Expansions and Contractions*: National Bureau of Economic Research.

Morgan, M. S. (1990). *The History of Econometric Ideas*. Cambridge: Cambridge University Press.

Morgan, W. A. (1939-1940). A test for significance of the difference between the two variances in a sample form a normal bivariate population. *Biometrika*, **31**, 13–19.

Morgenstern, O. (1928). *Wirtschaftsprognose: eine Untersuchung ihrer Voraussetzungen und Möglichkeiten*. Vienna: Julius Springer.

Murphy, A. H. and Winkler, R. L. (1992). Diagnostic verification of probability forecasts. *International Journal of Forecasting*, **7**, 435–445.

Naylor, T. H., Seaks, T. G. and Wichern, D. W. (1972). Box-Jenkins methods: An alternative to econometric models. *International Statistical Review*, **40**, 123–137.

Neftci, S. N. (1979). Lead-lag relations, exogeneity and prediction of economic time series. *Econometrica*, **47**, 101–113.

Nelson, C. R. (1972). The prediction performance of the FRB-MIT-PENN model of the US economy. *American Economic Review*, **62**, 902–917.

Nelson, C. R. and Plosser, C. I. (1982). Trends and random walks in macroeconomic time series: some evidence and implications. *Journal of Monetary Economics*, **10**, 139–162.

Nelson, D. B. (1990). Stationarity and persistence in the GARCH(1,1) model. *Econometric Theory*, **6**, 318–334.

Nerlove, M. (1982). Discussion of 'model validation and forecast comparisons: Theoretical and practical considerations', by M. Salmon and K. F. Wallis. In Chow and Corsi (1982).

(1983). Expectations, plans, and realizations in theory and practice. *Econometrica*, **51**, 1251–1279.

Newbold, P. (1993). Comment on 'On the limitations of comparing mean squared forecast errors', by M.P. Clements and D.F. Hendry. *Journal of Forecasting*, **12**, 658–660.

Newbold, P. and Granger, C. W. J. (1974). Experience with forecasting univariate time series and the combination of forecasts. *Journal of the Royal Statistical Society A*, **137**, 131–146.

Nordhaus, W. D. (1987). Forecasting efficiency: Concepts and applications. *Review of Economics and Statistics*, **69**, 667–674.

Ooms, M. (1994). *Empirical Vector Autoregressive Modeling*. Berlin: Springer-Verlag.

Ord, J. K. (1988). Future developments in forecasting. The time series connexion. *International Journal of Forecasting*, **4**, 389–401.

Ormerod, P. (ed.)(1979). *Economic Modelling*. London: Heinemann.

Pagan, A. R. (1989). On the role of simulation in the statistical evaluation of econometric models. *Journal of Econometrics*, **40**, 125–139.

Pain, N. and Britton, A. (1992). The recent experience of economic forecasting in Britain: some lessons from National Institute forecasts. Discussion Paper (new series) 20, National Institute.

Pakes, A. and Pollard, D. (1989). Simulation and the asymptotics of optimization estimation. *Econometrica*, **57**, 1027–1058.

Parigi, G. and Schlitzer, G. (1995). Quarterly forecasts of the Italian business cycle by means of monthly economic indicators. *Journal of Forecasting*, **14**, 117–141.

Patterson, K. D. (1995). An integrated model of the data measurement and data generation processes with an application to consumers' expenditure. *Economic Journal*, **105**, 54–76.

Peña, D. (1994). Second-generation time series models: A comment on 'Some advances in non-linear and adaptive modelling in time-series', by Tiao and Tsay. *Journal of Forecasting*, **13**, 133–140.

Persons, W. M. (1924). *The Problem of Business Forecasting*. No. 6 in Pollak Foundation for Economic Research Publications. London: Pitman.

(1925). Statistics and economic theory. *Review of Economics and Statistics*, **7**, 179–197.

Pesaran, M. H. and Pesaran, B. (1993). A simulation approach to the problem of computing Cox's statistic for testing nonnested models. *Journal of Econometrics*, **57**, 377–392.

Pesaran, M. H., Smith, R. P. and Yeo, J. S. (1985). Testing for structural stability and predictive failure: A review. *Manchester School*, **3**, 280–295.

Phillips, K. (1991). A two-country model of stochastic output with changes in regime. *Journal of International Economics*, **31**, 121–142.

Phillips, P. C. B. (1987). Time series regression with a unit root. *Econometrica*, **55**, 277–301.

(1991). Optimal inference in cointegrated systems. *Econometrica*, **59**, 283–306.

(1994). Bayes models and forecasts of Australian macroeconomic time series. In Hargreaves (1994), pp. 53–86.

Phillips, P. C. B. and Durlauf, S. N. (1986). Multiple time series regression with integrated processes. *Review of Economic Studies*, **53**, 473–495.

Platt, R. B. (1971). Some measures of forecast accuracy. *Business Economics*, **6**, 30–39.

Potter, S. (1995). A nonlinear approach to US GNP. *Journal of Applied Econometrics*, **10**, 109–125.

Ramsey, J. B. (1969). Tests for specification errors in classical linear least squares regression analysis. *Journal of the Royal Statistical Society B*, **31**, 350–371.

Rao, C. R. (1965). *Linear Statistical Inference and its Applications*. New York: Wiley.

Reichlin, L. (1989). Structural change and unit root econometrics. *Economics Letters*, **31**, 231–233.

Reid, D. J. (1969). A comparative study of time series prediction techniques on economic data. Unpublished Ph.D. thesis, University of Nottingham, Dept. of Mathematics.

Richard, J.-F. and Zhang, W. (1996a). Accelerated importance sampling. Mimeo, University Of Pittsburg.

(1996b). Accelerated Monte Carlo integration: An application to dynamic latent variable models. In Mariano, R., Weeks, M. and Schuermann, T. (eds.), *Simulation Based Inference in Econometrics: Methods and Applications*. Cambridge: Cambridge University Press. Forthcoming.

Ripley, B. D. (1987). *Stochastic Simulation*. New York: John Wiley & Sons.

Robbins, L. (1932). *An Essay on the Nature and Significance of Economic Science*. London: Macmillan.

Salmon, M. and Wallis, K. F. (1982). Model validation and forecast comparisons: Theoretical and practical considerations. In Chow and Corsi (1982), Ch. 12.

Sampson, M. (1991). The effect of parameter uncertainty on forecast variances and confidence intervals for unit root and trend stationary time-series models. *Journal of Applied Econometrics*, **6**, 67–76.

Samuelson, P. A. (1987). Paradise lost and refound: The Harvard ABC barometers. *Journal of Portfolio Management*, **4**, 4–9.

Sargan, J. D. (1964). Wages and prices in the United Kingdom: A study in econometric methodology (with discussion). In Hart, P. E., Mills, G. and Whitaker, J. K. (eds.), *Econometric Analysis for National Economic Planning*, Vol. 16 of *Colston Papers*, pp. 25–63. London: Butterworth Co. Reprinted as pp. 275–314 in Hendry D. F. and Wallis K. F. (eds.) (1984). *Econometrics and Quantitative Economics*. Oxford: Basil Blackwell, and as pp. 124–169 in Sargan J. D. (1988), *Contributions to Econometrics*, Vol. I, Cambridge: Cambridge University Press.

(1964a). Three-stage least-squares and full maximum likelihood estimates. *Econometrica*, **32**, 77–81. Reprinted as pp. 118–123 in Sargan J. D. (1988), *Contributions to Econometrics*, Vol. I, Cambridge: Cambridge University Press.

(1982). On Monte Carlo estimates of moments that are infinite. In Basmann, R. L. and Rhodes, G. F. (eds.), *Advances in Econometrics: A Research Annual*, Vol. I, pp. 267–299. Greenwich, Connecticut: Jai Press Inc.

Schmidt, P. (1974). The asymptotic distribution of forecasts in the dynamic simulation of an econometric model. *Econometrica*, **42**, 303–309.

Schmidt, P. (1977). Some small sample evidence on the distribution of dynamic simulation forecasts. *Econometrica*, **45**, 97–105.

Schwartz, G. (1978). Estimating the dimension of a model. *Annals of Statistics*, **6**, 462–464.

Schweppe, F. (1965). Evaluation of likelihood functions for Gaussian signals. *IEEE Transactions on Information Theory*, **11**, 61–70.

Schwert, G. W. (1989). Tests for unit roots: A Monte Carlo investigation. *Journal of Business and Economic Statistics*, **7**, 147–159.

Sensier, M. (1996). Investigating Business Cycle Asymmetries in the UK. Ph.D. Thesis. University of Sheffield.

Shephard, N. (1996). Statistical aspects of ARCH and stochastic volatility. In Cox, D. R., Hinkley, D. V. and Barndorff-Nielsen, O. E. (eds.), *Time Series Models: In Econometrics, Finance and Other Fields*. London: Chapman and Hall.

Shiskin, J. and Moore, G. (1968). *Composite Indexes of Leading, Coinciding and Lagging Indicators, 1948–1967*. New York: National Bureau of Economic Research. Supplement to National Bureau Report 1.

Sims, C. A. (1980). Macroeconomics and reality. *Econometrica*, **48**, 1–48. Reprinted in Granger, C. W. J. (ed.) (1990).

Sims, C. A., Stock, J. H. and Watson, M. W. (1990). Inference in linear time series models with some unit roots. *Econometrica*, **58**, 113–144.

Sowell, F. (1992). Modeling long-run behaviour with the fractional ARIMA model. *Journal of Monetary Economics*, **29**, 277–302.

Spanos, A. (1986). *Statistical Foundations of Econometric Modelling*. Cambridge: Cambridge University Press.

(1989). Early empirical findings on the consumption, stylized facts or fiction: A retrospective view. *Oxford Economic Papers*, **41**, 150–169.

Spitzer, J. J. and Baillie, R. T. (1983). Small sample properties of predictions from the regression model with autoregressive errors. *Journal of the American Statistical Association*, **83**, 258–263.

Stekler, H. O. (1991). Turning point predictions, errors and forecasting procedures. In Lahiri and Moore (1991), Ch. 10.

Stock, J. H. (1988). A re-examination of Friedman's consumption puzzle. *Journal of Business and Economic Statistics*, **6**, 401–407.

Stock, J. H. and Watson, M. W. (1988). Testing for common trends. *Journal of the American Statistical Association*, **83**, 1097–1107.

(1989). New indexes of coincident and leading economic indicators. *NBER Macro-Economic Annual*, 351–409.

(1992). A procedure for predicting recessions with leading indicators: Econometric issues and recent experience. Working Paper 4014, NBER.

Stoica, P. and Nehorai, A. (1989). On multistep prediction error methods for time series models. *Journal of Forecasting*, **8**, 357–368.

Theil, H. (1961). *Economic Forecasts and Policy,* 2nd edn. Amsterdam: North-Holland.

(1966). *Applied Economic Forecasting*. Amsterdam: North-Holland.

Tiao, G. C. and Tsay, R. S. (1994). Some advances in non-linear and adaptive modelling in time-series. *Journal of Forecasting*, **13**, 109–131.

Tinbergen, J. (1939). *Statistical Testing of Business-Cycle Theories*. Geneva: League of Nations. Vol. I: *A Method and its application to Investment Activity*; Vol. II: *Business Cycles in the United States of America, 1919–1932*.

Todd, R. M. (1990). Improving economic forecasts with Bayesian vector autoregression. In Granger (1990), Ch. 10.

Tong, H. (1978). On a threshold model. In Chen, C. H. (ed.), *Pattern Recognition and Signal Processing*, pp. 101–141. Amsterdam: Sijhoff and Noordoff.

(1983). *Threshold Models in Non-Linear Time Series Analysis*. New York: Springer-Verlag.

(1995). *Non-linear Time Series. A Dynamical System Approach*. Oxford: Clarendon Press. First published 1990.

Tong, H. and Lim, K. S. (1980). Threshold autoregression, limit cycles and cyclical data. *Journal of The Royal Statistical Society*, **B 42**, 245–292.

Tsay, R. S. (1993). Comment: Adaptive forecasting. *Journal of Business and Economic Statistics*, **11**, 140–142.

Turner, D. S. (1990). The role of judgement in macroeconomic forecasting. *Journal of Forecasting*, **9**, 315–345.

Varian, H. R. (1975). A Bayesian approach to real estate assessment. In Fienberg, S. E. and Zellner, A. (eds.), *Studies in Bayesian Econometrics and Statistics in Honor of Leonard J. Savage*, pp. 195–208. Amsterdam: North-Holland.

Vining, R. (1949). Methodological issues in quantitative economics. *Review of Economics and Statistics*, **31**, 77–86.

Wallis, K. F. (1984). Comparing time-series and nonlinear model-based forecasts. *Oxford Bulletin of Economics and Statistics*, *46*(4), 383–389.

(1989). Macroeconomic forecasting: A survey. *Economic Journal*, **99**, 28–61.

Wallis, K. F., Andrews, M. J., Bell, D. N. F., Fisher, P. G. and Whitley, J. D. (1984). *Models of the UK Economy, A Review by the ESRC Macroeconomic Modelling Bureau.* Oxford: Oxford University Press.

(1985). *Models of the UK Economy, A Second Review by the ESRC Macroeconomic Modelling Bureau.* Oxford: Oxford University Press.

Wallis, K. F., Andrews, M. J., Fisher, P. G., Longbottom, J. and Whitley, J. D. (1986). *Models of the UK Economy: A Third Review by the ESRC Macroeconomic Modelling Bureau.* Oxford: Oxford University Press.

Wallis, K. F., Fisher, P. G., Longbottom, J., Turner, D. S. and Whitley, J. D. (1987). *Models of the UK Economy: A Fourth Review by the ESRC Macroeconomic Modelling Bureau.* Oxford: Oxford University Press.

Wallis, K. F. and Whitley, J. D. (1991). Sources of error in forecasts and expectations: UK economic models 1984–8. *Journal of Forecasting*, **10**, 231–253.

Weiss, A. A. (1991). Multi-step estimation and forecasting in dynamic models. *Journal of Econometrics*, **48**, 135–149.

(1996). Estimating time series models using the relevant cost function. *Journal of Applied Econometrics*, **11**, 539–560.

Weller, B. R. (1979). Usefulness of the newly revised composite index of leading indicators as a quantitative predictor. *Journal of Macroeconomics*, **1**, 141–147.

West, K. D. (1988). Asymptotic normality when regressors have a unit root. *Econometrica*, **56**, 1397–1417.

(1993). Comment on 'On the limitations of comparing mean squared forecast errors', by M.P. Clements and D.F. Hendry. *Journal of Forecasting*, **12**, 666–667.

White, H. (1980). A heteroskedastic-consistent covariance matrix estimator and a direct test for heteroskedasticity. *Econometrica*, **48**, 817–838.

White, J. (1961). Asymptotic expansions for the mean and variance of the serial correlation coefficient. *Biometrika*, **48**, 85–95.

Whittle, P. (1963). *Prediction and Regulation by Linear Least-Square Methods*. Princeton: D. Van Nostrand.

Wiener, N. (1949). *Extrapolation, Interpolation and Smoothing of Stationary Time Series*. New York: Wiley.

Williams, D. A. (1970). Discrimination between regression models to determine the pattern of enzyme synthesis in synchronous cultures. *Biometrics*, 23–32.

Williams, E. J. and Kloot, N. H. (1953). Interpolation in a series of correlated observations. *Australian Journal of Applied Science*, **4**, 1–17.

Winters, P. R. (1960). Forecasting sales by exponentially weighted moving averages. *Management Science*, **6**, 324–342.

Wold, H. O. A. (1938). *A Study in The Analysis of Stationary Time Series*. Stockholm: Almqvist and Wicksell.

Young, R. M. (1979). Forecasting the US economy with an econometric model. In Ormerod (1979).

Zarnowitz, V. (1985). Rational expectations and macroeconomic forecasts. *Journal of Business and Economic Statistics*, **3**, 293–311.

Zarnowitz, V. and Boschan, C. (1977a). Cyclical indicators: An evaluation and new leading indexes. In *Handbook of Cyclical Indicators* (1977), pp. 170–183.

(1977b). New composite indexes of coincident and lagging indicators. In *Handbook of Cyclical Indicators* (1977), pp. 185–198.

Zarnowitz, V. and Braun, P. (1992). Major macroeconomic variables and leading indicators: Some estimates of their interrelations, 1886–1982. Working paper 2812, National Bureau of Economic Research, New York.

Zellner, A. (1986). Biased predictors, rationality and the evaluation of forecasts. *Economics Letters*, **21**, 45–48.

Author index

Subject index